ALTHUSSER

Historical Materialism Book Series

More than ten years after the collapse of the Berlin Wall and the disappearance of Marxism as a (supposed) state ideology, a need for a serious and long-term Marxist book publishing program has risen. Subjected to the whims of fashion, most contemporary publishers have abandoned any of the systematic production of Marxist theoretical work that they may have indulged in during the 1970s and early 1980s. The Historical Materialism book series addresses this great gap with original monographs, translated texts and reprints of "classics."

Editorial board: Paul Blackledge, Leeds; Sebastian Budgen, London; Jim Kincaid, Leeds; Stathis Kouvelakis, Paris; Marcel van der Linden, Amsterdam; China Miéville, London; Paul Reynolds, Lancashire.

Haymarket Books is proud to be working with Brill Academic Publishers (http://www.brill.nl) and the journal *Historical Materialism* to republish the Historical Materialism book series in paperback editions. Current series titles include:

Alasdair MacIntyre's Engagement with Marxism: Selected Writings 1953–1974
Edited by Paul Blackledge and Neil Davidson

Althusser: The Detour of Theory, Gregory Elliott

Between Equal Rights: A Marxist Theory of International Law, China Miéville

The Capitalist Cycle, Pavel V. Maksakovsky, Translated with introduction and commentary by Richard B. Day

The Clash of Globalisations: Neo-Liberalism, the Third Way, and Anti-globalisation, Ray Kiely

Critical Companion to Contemporary Marxism, Edited by Jacques Bidet and Stathis Kouvelakis

Criticism of Heaven: On Marxism and Theology, Roland Boer

Exploring Marx's Capital: Philosophical, Economic, and Political Dimensions, Jacques Bidet

Following Marx: Method, Critique, and Crisis, Michael Lebowitz

The German Revolution: 1917–1923, Pierre Broué

Globalisation: A Systematic Marxian Account, Tony Smith

Impersonal Power: History and Theory of the Bourgeois State,
Heide Gerstenberger, translated by David Fernbach

Lenin Rediscovered: What Is to Be Done? *In Context*, Lars T. Lih

Making History: Agency, Structure, and Change in Social Theory, Alex Callinicos

Marxism and Ecological Economics: Toward a Red and Green Political Economy, Paul Burkett

A Marxist Philosophy of Language, Jean-Jacques Lecercle and Gregory Elliott

The Theory of Revolution in the Young Marx, Michael Löwy

Utopia Ltd.: Ideologies of Social Dreaming in England 1870–1900, Matthew Beaumont

Western Marxism and the Soviet Union: A Survey of Critical Theories and Debates Since 1917
Marcel van der Linden

ALTHUSSER
THE DETOUR OF THEORY

GREGORY ELLIOTT

Haymarket Books
Chicago, Illinois

First published in 2005 by Brill Academic Publishers, The Netherlands
© 2006 Koninklijke Brill NV, Leiden, The Netherlands

Published in paperback in 2009 by
Haymarket Books
P.O. Box 180165
Chicago, IL 60618
773-583-7884
www.haymarketbooks.org
ISBN: 978-1-608460-27-4

Trade distribution:
In the U.S., Consortium Book Sales, www.cbsd.com
In the UK, Turnaround Publisher Services, www.turnaround-psl.com
In Australia, Palgrave Macmillan, www.palgravemacmillan.com.au
In all other countries, Publishers Group Worldwide, www.pgw.com

Cover design by Ragina Johnson. Cover image by Liubov Popova, 1915.

This book was published with the generous support of Lannan Foundation and
the Wallace Global fund.

Printed in the United States.

10 9 8 7 6 5 4 3 2

Library of Congress Cataloging-in-Publication Data is available.

To Louis Althusser

Let us do him the duty, which is the duty of every historian, of taking him not at his word, but at his work.

Contents

Preface to the Second Edition

'Never apologise, never explain', runs a familiar adage. The appearance of a second edition of *Althusser: The Detour of Theory* close on two decades after it was originally published calls for a few words of explanation and apology alike.

Released by Verso in 1987 as the revised version of a doctoral thesis, and possibly aided by the impending twentieth anniversary of May '68, the book attracted a fair amount of generally positive attention. Of the twenty-five or so reviews that I am aware of, while most derived from the UK and the US, others hailed from as far afield as India and Australia. (As I only learnt ten or more years later, the text even received the – backhanded – compliment of a pirate translation in South Korea.) Notwithstanding the numerous local and general criticisms directed at it – to some of which I shall return – *The Detour of Theory* was not infrequently welcomed as the fullest account to date in English of Althusser's philosophico-political career in the 1960s and 1970s. For whatever reason, long after it became out of date (not to mention print), it would seem to retain that reputation, thus one hopes rendering republication of more than merely antiquarian interest.

Although gratified by initial reception and residual reputation, I have never been misled by them. On the one hand, they actually attest to the marked decline in interest in, and output on, Althusser's work from the turn of the 1970s, other than as a historical reference-point in some areas. On the other, in the 1987 Foreword, I had myself underscored the incompleteness and imperfections of my study, looking forward to remedial action by others. With the gradual emergence of a posthumous edition of Althusser's writings from 1992 onwards, which soon dwarfed in quantity if not quality what had been published in his lifetime, the need for a new synthesis, rendering these pages redundant, became increasingly apparent.

After 1987, I continued to work intermittently on Althusser, whether as editor, author, or translator; and, for some years, projected a comprehensive intellectual biography, taking the story back to the 1940s and up to the 1980s, which I began to read for in 1995–6. A combination of factors led me to desist. Of these, the most salient was a sense that the undertaking lay beyond my powers – that it was indeed, as anticipated in 1987, 'another story, for a different teller'. For a start, there was the sheer size of the task, which would have necessitated investigating the mass of unpublished material held at the Institut Mémoires de l'Édition Contemporaine, as well as mastering the new primary and secondary published literature (in all the main European languages – and others besides). As if this was not sufficient deterrent, it would have involved revisiting in depth and detail a whole range of topics – Hegelianism or Communism, Spinozism or (post)structuralism – on which (as I am acutely conscious and as readers will soon see for themselves) I all too often pronounced *en méconnaissance de cause*, with the misplaced confidence of youth. Finally, better qualified candidates for the endeavour were duly entering the lists, with a much surer grasp of intellectual terrain onto which I had ventured more or less ill-equipped.

As for *The Detour of Theory* itself, I readily concede the justice of some of the detailed charges levelled at it, whether they concern indulging in the leftist myth of May '68, inaccurate tracking of Althusser's attitude towards Eurocommunism, or levity in discussing Maoism.[1] Others I find less compelling – for example, cavilling at the attempt to periodise Althusser's thinking (which seems to me premised on a philosophical subtlety not obviously serviceable to an intellectual historian).[2] Above all, however, the underlying problem with the text below was identified at the time by at least two reviewers, Joseph McCarney and Peter Osborne.[3] Probing the category of 'anti-anti-Althusserianism' in which I had encapsulated my critical orientation, the latter suggested that '[It]is not . . . so easy to be "anti-anti-Althusserian" without being *for* Althusser'.[4] Quite: the problem of the appropriate historical evaluative criteria to employ was badly posed, and falsely solved, by counterposing the

---

[1] The first was pressed in a personal communication by Jean-Jacques Lecercle; the second, likewise in a personal communication, by Geoffrey Goshgarian; the third by McCarney 1989.
[2] See Matheron 2001, p. 382, n. 23.
[3] See McCarney 1989 and Osborne 1989.
[4] Osborne 1989, p. 44.

overarching emancipatory effects of Althusser's intervention to the various misdirections in his reconstruction of historical materialism. Implicit in this modus operandi was a certain – broadly Deutscherite – conception of Marxism, *index falsi* as it were, in the light of which I declared for and/or against Althusser on any particular point, from the sublime to the ridiculous (say: V.I. Lenin to B.-H. Lévy). Following the geopolitical earthquake of 1989–91, and in the utterly changed context of the present, what remained an unresolved issue twenty years ago constitutes a profound enigma to me today, revolving around not only *what* to be for and against in Althusser and *how*, but the *whys and wherefores* of the very operation.

My misreading of Althusser's political stance in the second half of the 1970s helps illustrate the wider dilemma. For while it would require me to rectify my exposition, I would now want to reverse my assessment, on the point at issue. In 1987 I construed Althusser as gravitating towards 'left Eurocommunism' in the debates in the French Communist Party over the dictatorship of the proletariat; and reproved this departure from Leninism. Were I rewriting the book today, while registering remaining ambiguities likely to have occasioned his immediate expulsion from the Comintern in Lenin's day, I would regret Althusser's failure to break out of a disabling orthodoxy. It may safely be left to others to judge whether this is tantamount to peremptory inconsistency.

Meanwhile, insofar as it has awakened me from a dogmatic anti-Hegelian slumber, recent acquaintance with the stimulating work of various Italian Marxists – in particular, Domenico Losurdo and Costanzo Preve – has only served to exacerbate the problem. In any event, varying Gramsci's dictum that 'to write the history of a party means nothing less than to write the general history of a country from a monographic viewpoint',[5] I now strongly incline to the view that to write the intellectual biography of Louis Althusser would almost mean nothing less than writing the general history not just of French Marxism, but of Marxism *tout court* (and, what is more, communism), from a monographic point of view. May who dares win.

Considerations such as these explain why I have not sought to revise, let alone recast, *The Detour of Theory*. Accordingly, this second edition, kindly

---

[5] Gramsci 1971, p. 151.

solicited by Sebastian Budgen and his fellow-editors of the *Historical Materialism* series at Brill, differs in only three respects from its predecessor. First, in retyping the original text to align it with house style, I have taken the opportunity to revise quotations and references where material unavailable in English in the 1980s has subsequently been translated, but, some emendation of punctuation and spelling aside, have resisted all temptation to alter the numerous stylistic and substantive points that caused me to blush or blanch as I re-read what I had written in 1985–7. Secondly, I have updated – and hence very significantly expanded – the bibliography of Althusser's published writings, happily consigning to Althusserian aficionados the pleasure of correcting and completing it. Lastly, and most importantly, I have added a long postscript, whose dedication speaks for itself, in which I seek to take stock of the posthumously published work, with side-glances at some of the contemporary secondary literature. Largely distilled from texts published at various times in the 1990s in *Economy and Society, Radical Philosophy, Rethinking Marxism*, the *Edinburgh Encyclopedia of Continental Philosophy*, and the Introduction to the English edition of Althusser's *Machiavelli and Us*, to all of whose editors I am grateful, the Postscript manifestly does less than justice to the rich complexity of its subject-matter and – if it has not already been – is doubtless set to be superseded at some point in the near future.

To close, as I began, with a – related – adage. Readers of his 'traumabiography' will know of Althusser's fondness for de Gaulle's dictum: *l'avenir dure longtemps*. As they prepare to turn the page, and therewith turn back the clock, they can rest assured of one thing: however long the future lasts, this will, for better or worse, be my final written word on the subject of Louis Althusser.

Edinburgh, November 2005

Foreword

In the international renaissance of Marxist theory in the 1960s and early 1970s, few projects generated as much excitement, or aroused such controversy, as the 'return to Marx' conducted by the French philosopher Louis Althusser. One of the most ambitious and influential enterprises in the postwar history of Marxism, Althusser's systematic reconstruction of 'dialectical and historical materialism' from within the French Communist Party (PCF) was heralded as a renewal of Marxism in some quarters, dismissed as a specimen of Stalinism in others.

Today, more than twenty years after the publication of his major works, *For Marx* and *Reading 'Capital'* (1965), and amid the profound contemporary crisis of Marxism, Althusser is the victim, rather than the beneficiary, of philosophical fashion and political circumstance – a symbol for many of an era of vain, or at any rate disappointed, hopes, to be interred alongside them. The contrast is arresting: nowadays it is as common disdainfully to eschew, as it was once *de rigueur* uncritically to espouse, the extraordinary re-theorisation of Marxism – and Leninism – known by the name of Althusserianism.

In his own country, scene of his *succès de scandale* two decades ago, Althusser is practically a 'dead dog'.[1] Althusserianism, to quote a recent critique of modern French philosophy, 'seems very dated and, like the Beatles' music or Godard's first films, inevitably evokes a recent but vanished past'.[2] Why? Briefly, it is to the settled anti-Marxist consensus among the majority of the French intelligentsia, to the indifference of an embattled PCF (whose 'official philosopher' Althusser never was),[3] and to the understandable demoralisation

---

[1] A point made by Alain Lipietz, protesting at this treatment, in Lipietz 1985, p. 159.

[2] Ferry and Renaut 1985, p. 200.

[3] This tenacious myth, which has bedevilled much interpretation, has most recently been given credence in Feather 1986, p. 32. If for no other reason, its implausibility

of the remaining Althusserian Marxists, that we must look for an explanation of the virtual collective amnesia surrounding his work, despite its wide diffusion. By the end of the 1970s, an anti-Marxist turn in France was complete, part and parcel of a recessive pattern in Southern Europe generally, whose matrix lay in contemporary political history: the discrediting of alternatives to Soviet 'real socialism' abroad (above all, in Maoist China) and the momentous defeat of the European workers' movement at home (in France and Italy, in Portugal, Greece and Spain). And it was not to be reversed thereafter, the debacle of Gallocommunism rapidly being compounded by the ignominy of French Eurosocialism. Since 1975, the whole intellectual landscape of France has undergone alteration. Under the impact of its own undoubted weaknesses, an inclement history, philosophical challenges, and a concerted ideological campaign, Marxism – a paradigm which had enjoyed enormous prestige since the Liberation – has been reduced to marginal status. There are signal exceptions to the rule of apostasy in these years (one thinks of Henri Lefebvre, Maurice Godelier, Étienne Balibar). Yet they prove it as, one after another, 1960s rebels have succumbed to disillusionment, bidding *adieu* to failed gods, *bonjour* to new ones. André Glucksmann, Bernard-Henri Lévy and Co., reinforced by that unlikely Cold-War troubadour Yves Montand, have won high marks of late for being neither red nor dead and defending the open society against its enemies – if necessary, at the cost of support for imperialist terror against Nicaragua. Such has been the depth of the transformation that, in his 1983 report on historical materialism since the mid-1970s, Perry Anderson could write: 'Paris today is the capital of European intellectual reaction.'[4] There, at any rate, Althusser is a non-person, his career only one instance – however blatant – of the intellectuals' baleful flirtation with political 'totalitarianism' and its philosophical concentrate, 'totalising' theory.

What of Althusser across the Channel? Here too, the 'anti-Althusser band-wagon'[5] has been rolling in the changed political conjuncture of the last

---

should be evident from the fact that the PCF imprint Éditions Sociales only ever issued one collection of essays by Althusser – and that in 1976. Following Roger Garaudy's departure for a higher calling, the status of official PCF philosopher was held (if by anyone) by Lucien Sève – a critic of Althusser and, unlike him, a member of the Party's Central Committee.

[4] Anderson 1983, p. 32.
[5] See the thoughtful review article under that title by Rée 1982.

decade. First introduced by *New Left Review* in 1967,[6] Althusser's reception in Britain following the appearance in translation of *For Marx* (1969) and *Reading 'Capital'* (1970), was initially quite favourable. Indeed, his work temporarily enjoyed something of a vogue, having a considerable impact on the sizeable Marxist intelligentsia thrown up by the contemporary radicalisation. Yet this, in turn, prompted a counter-reaction when the heady days of the late 1960s gave way to the doldrums, then the depression, of subsequent years.

The domestic controversy caused by Althusserian Marxism reached a peak in 1978, when E.P. Thompson, veteran of the first New Left and one of the foremost Marxist historians in the world, came to bury Althusser and his (franglophone) progeny in *The Poverty of Theory*. Memorably accentuating the indictments of the Frenchman's anti-humanism, anti-historicism and anti-empiricism drafted by continental critics of all persuasions,[7] Thompson excoriated Althusser's philosophy as an idealism, his social theory as bourgeois ideology, his politics as Stalinist. For him, Althusser was little more than a Kremlin amanuensis. 'Althusserianism,' he declared '*is* Stalinism reduced to the paradigm of Theory. It is Stalinism at last, theorised as ideology'. It is 'a manifestation of a general police action within ideology' launched to counteract the socialist-humanist rebellion against the Soviet intervention in Hungary in 1956 – part of an operation designed 'to reimpose the disciplinary controls of State and Party, to re-establish ideological orthodoxy – in effect, to reconstruct, within changed circumstances, Stalinism without Stalin'.[8]

---

[6] See *New Left Review* 1967, pp. 1–2, 11–14, for commendatory editorial comments prefacing the translation of 'Contradiction and Overdetermination'.

[7] A representative sample from the copious literature would be:
- from the ranks of independent Marxism: Goldmann 1970; Lefebvre 1975; and Schmidt 1981;
- from the ranks of Trotskyism: Fougeyrollas 1976; Löwy 1973; and Vincent et al. 1974;
- from the ranks of Maoism: Lisbonne 1981 and, above all, Rancière 1974;
- from the ranks of Communism: Garaudy 1969 and 1970; Schaff 1978; and Sève 1978.

[8] Thompson 1978, pp. 374, 332–3. (A similar line is pursued by Simon Clarke in his 1980.) At a *History Workshop* Conference the following year, Thompson repeated his strictures, in the face of all attempts at mediation: see Thompson 1981 and cf. Hall 1981 and Johnson 1981. For a powerful plea against Manichaeism from a historian strongly influenced by Althusser, see Stedman Jones 1979.

Thompson's is the most celebrated example in English of vehement repudiation of Althusser's Marxism; and it proved influential. In his assault, he passed (as he once remarked of an interlocutor) 'from irony to caricature: or to mere abuse'.[9] Though directed at the French philosopher, his animus was probably primarily provoked by the distinctive brand of English Althusserianism associated with the sociologists Barry Hindess and Paul Hirst. Their early work had represented an attempt to domesticate a version of Althusser's system, to the exclusion of almost everything else, as the apogee of scientificity. Via two journals, *Theoretical Practice* (1971–3) and *Economy and Society* (1972–4), Hindess, Hirst and their colleagues castigated the theoretical poverty of British Marxism and social science – a state of affairs they proposed to rectify by the importation of Althusser's 'problematic'. By 1975, however, they were criticising their philosopher-general for his attachment to the project of a 'science of history'. More Althusserian than Althusser, they confidently proceeded to an anti-historical reconstruction of Marxist theory, only to discover two years later that Marxism per se was vulgar and revolutionary socialism utopian.[10] Arguably, Thompson read Althusser's œuvre through the distorting lens of Hindess and Hirst's, overlooking the fact that their incessant admonitions against 'empiricism' and 'historicism' in *Pre-Capitalist Modes of Production* were often as not addressed to Althusser; and that they were in transit from hyper- to post-Althusserianism. In any event, 1978 saw the publication not only of Thompson's polemic, but of the second volume of *Marx's 'Capital' and Capitalism Today*, wherein the reformist political implications of the incineration of historical materialism (Althusserian or otherwise) conducted in the first were spelt out. Even as Thompson was excommunicating

---

Althusser was invited to respond to *The Poverty of Theory* in the pages of *New Left Review* in 1979. He declined, stating that although he had found it 'interesting' and was 'perfectly conscious of the very summary (and therefore unilateral) character of the few paragraphs devoted to "history" in the polemical context of *Reading Capital*', he lacked the requisite expertise in British Marxist historiography – and the time to remedy it. (See Anderson 1979a and 1979b and Althusser 1979a.) No response to Thompson by an Althusserian was ever forthcoming. One reason for the apparent (but mistaken) insouciance may have been that, however inimitably performed, his reproaches amounted to a largely familiar refrain.

[9] Thompson 1978, p. 130 (the interlocutor was Leszek Kolakowski).

[10] For this evolution, see Hindess and Hirst 1975 and 1977; and Cutler et al. 1977–8. Hirst's current (high) estimation of Althusser's contribution can be consulted in Chapter 1 of his 1985.

the French reprobate and his English familiars, the latter were announcing their reconciliation with the 'broad church'.

Thus, unlike the revolt of some of Althusser's French disciples in the later 1960s, the British equivalent of the second half of the 1970s was a right – not a left – critique of Althusserianism Marxism – a deconstructive initiative which coalesced with other efforts to plot a reformist course for Britain in a period marked by the retreat of social democracy and the rise of the New Right. Not surprisingly, especially given his express attachment to Leninism, Althusser's reputation has further declined with the ensuing anti- or 'post'-Marxist turn among left-wing intellectuals induced by the installation (not to mention persistence) of Thatcherism, and the perplexity of its socialist opponents. Albeit an extreme example, Ernesto Laclau and Chantal Mouffe's *Hegemony and Socialist Strategy* (1985) is representative in this regard.

If Althusserianism has found itself relegated politically, often in favour of a particular appropriation of the Gramscian legacy, simultaneously its academic lustre has been dimmed. First, by the paramountcy in progressive circles of various forms of poststructuralism – a non-Marxist constellation encompassing the work of Roland Barthes, Gilles Deleuze, Jacques Derrida, Michel Foucault, Jacques Lacan and others, descended from, and soon supplanting, the structuralism with which Althusser's system had some filiation. Secondly, by the initiation and consolidation of an Anglo-American Marxian paradigm – 'analytical Marxism' – whose founding document, G.A. Cohen's *Karl Marx's Theory of History: A Defence*, was likewise published in 1978. In a powerful challenge to the whole Western-Marxist tradition, Cohen propounded a reconstruction of historical materialism which, in its firm reinstatement of the explanatory primacy of the productive forces and centrality of human nature, was antithetical to Althusser's – and professed itself to be.[11] Nevertheless, the French theoretician's work remained a major, if largely implicit (and negative), point of reference for Cohen – as it had for the majority of British Marxists, whatever their evaluation of it, in the 1970s. Yet, having contributed to the revival of Marxism in Britain, and having stimulated a widespread discussion of historical materialism, Althusser is largely absent from current

---

[11] See Cohen 1978, p. x. Whilst criticising Althusser, Cohen paid tribute to *For Marx* for reasserting the priority of Marx's later works.

Marxist debate, the high ground of which is occupied by an analytical current that has declined critical engagement with him, and whose attitude to Marx's doctrine is very different from what it was ten years ago.[12] At its hands, Althusser (but not only him) is treated by simple preterition or with passing hauteur,[13] thus perpetuating a practice in which he and his followers all too often indulged at the expense of their peers – and whose termination is a necessary, if insufficient, condition of fruitful exchange and real progress in Marxism.

The back cover of *The Poverty of Theory* had invoked Marx's consignment of Proudhon to 'oblivion' in the 1847 polemic whose title Thompson's own echoed. It may be doubted whether Thompson is single-handedly responsible, but, in the intervening years, Althusser has indeed become something of a historical curiosity, his work consigned, whether by humanist, post-, or analytical Marxists, to what one historian of French Marxism calls 'the trough of oblivion which accommodates old news before it is resurrected as history'.[14] Unjust though it is, paradoxically this fate affords an opportunity: the resurrection of Althusser's intellectual and political career *as history*. In other words, one advantage of Althusser's disappearance from the scene is that it makes possible a reassessment which advances beyond the adulation (Althusserianism, meridian of Marxism), and anathemas (Althusserianism, apotheosis of Stalinism – or 'grand theory for little minds'),[15] characteristic of many responses to the philosopher's advent and ascendancy. A more equitable presentation and appraisal of an œuvre simultaneously, if differentially, affiliated to the Communist, Western-Marxist and Maoist traditions may not be without interest at a time when all three, to varying degrees, are in a critical state. A return to, and reconsideration of, Althusser may aid a fuller appreciation not only of his enterprise but, via an account of its rise and eclipse, of some of the background to the present acute crisis of Marxism.

---

[12] See, for example, the prefatory remarks by Jon Elster in his 1985, p. xiv and John Roemer's comments in his 1986, p. 2.

[13] For examples of the latter, see Wood 1981, pp. 245, n. 5 and 255, n. 2; and Elster 1986, p. 16. With these might be compared Cohen's own comments and the generous review of his book by a pupil of Althusser's: Lock 1988.

[14] Kelly 1982, p. 232.

[15] See Scruton 1984. Judgements of this order have by no means been restricted to right-wing critics.

'With hindsight, one can judge things better', Althusser once wrote in connection with his project.[16] The ambition of my historical retrospect, taking Althusser not at his word but at his work, is precisely that. It is not without precedent, of course. For if much ink (and some vitriol) has been spilt on Althusser, more balanced reactions than those cited earlier have not been wanting. In particular, judicious studies by Norman Geras, Alex Callinicos and, most recently, Ted Benton have defended his Marxism against many of the accusations levelled against it, without ignoring its many inadequacies.[17] My debt to them will be obvious. Yet none can be said to have pursued in detail the investigation counterposed to Thompson's requisitory by Anderson, in the course of his scrupulous sounding of the differences between the British historian and the French philosopher in *Arguments within English Marxism*. Rebutting Thompson's wilder allegations and misrepresentations, Anderson reminded him that 'any historian, Marxist or non-Marxist, should know that the political character of a body of thought can only be established by a responsible study of its *texts* and *context*'.[18] The intention of *Althusser: The Detour of Theory* is two-fold: first, to extend the commentaries of such authors as Geras, Callinicos and Benton and, in particular, to attend at greater length to the later, more directly political phase of Althusser's career; secondly, to elaborate the research programme signalled by Anderson – that is, respecting Althusser's own request,[19] to study his texts in their contexts as the prerequisite for an evaluation of them. (To these ends, I draw on writings unavailable to, or neglected by, other English commentators, and on information derived from interviews.) Hence, it is intended as an essay in the history of ideas. At the risk of what Althusser would call historicism (the reduction of a theoretical discourse to its historical conditions of production), the politics of theory will be my focus, the reconstruction, so far as is possible, of the contexts and sub-text of Althusser's work my aim. If emphasis on the non-theoretical conditions of existence of theory and analysis of it *sub specie temporis* are historicist, then this book willingly stands condemned. For although much of it is given over to textual exposition and criticism, it proceeds in accordance with the view

---

[16] Althusser 1976a, p. 36.
[17] See Geras 1986a; Callinicos 1976 and 1982, Chapter 3; and Benton 1984.
[18] Anderson 1980, p. 105.
[19] See Althusser 1969a, p. 9 and Althusser 1976a, pp. 78–9.

that a Marxism of Althusser's, as of any other Marxism, requires the kind of conjoint external and internal history whose protocols have been set out by Anderson.[20] A historical-critical account, it at least aims to avoid two common approaches: hierophantic theoreticism and virulent travesty.

So much for what this book is – or hopes to be. A word is also in order regarding what it is not. No reader already acquainted with the subject will fail to notice that it is a far from exhaustive survey. Aside from space constraints, its incompleteness can in part by explained by the simple fact that it is still too soon to write a definitive study of Althusser's career from 1945 to 1980. Too much information is lacking, too many texts remain unpublished, for such a project to be feasible. Yet even were it to be, I would not be qualified to execute it. For the imperfections of my study are also attributable to authorial failings – an inability to cover Spanish, Italian and German debates, for instance, which inevitably renders my account partial. Accordingly, *Althusser: The Detour of Theory* is offered for what is: a provisional work, an interim report on research in progress. It will have served its purpose if it makes Althusser accessible and interesting to new readers, and if it encourages others to return to him – and remedy its shortcomings.

Also falling outside its purview, appearing only the margins, is the private drama which accompanied – and affected – the intellectual and political endeavour analysed here, and which cannot be totally passed over in silence. I refer to that 'war without memoirs or memorials', evoked by him,[21] which Louis Althusser had been fighting for so long against the severe manic-depressive illness that tormented him with ever-greater frequency and intensity after May 1968, and which, in the autumn of 1980, issued in the desperate act that ended Hélène Althusser's life and terminated her husband's career. Reticence is dictated on several accounts – not least insufficient information and the danger of crude psychologising. Yet this is a lacuna. For that recurrent illness contributed, for example, to Althusser's failure to produce anything comparable to *For Marx* and *Reading 'Capital'* after 1965 (a failure which, in turn, exacerbated the illness) cannot be doubted. It is useless speculating on what he might have achieved over and above the essays, seminars, conference papers, interviews and notes that we possess, had his career been less fitful,

---

[20] See Anderson 1983, p. 14.
[21] See Althusser 1971, pp. 189–90.

had other things been equal: they never were. For Althusser, at least, it was scarcely 'simple to be a Marxist in philosophy'. The only wonder, perhaps, is that he should have managed for some thirty years. The austere theoretician who read *Capital* spoke of the workers' movement as 'our only hope and our destiny'.[22] Deprived of that hope, Louis Althusser's destiny was to be a tragic one. But that is another story, for a different teller.[23]

Before concluding, I will observe an Althusserian custom and lay my cards on the table – in the shape of some bald generalities. Although the present work is concerned less to press claims on Althusser's behalf than to situate his interventions historically, and to examine them theoretically and politically – to explain, not excuse, Althusser – its position is one that I would characterise as anti-anti-Althusser. Thus, whilst not an advocacy, it is an attempt at a redressment of the balance. My own view, akin to those of Callinicos and the French Marxist Robert Linhart,[24] is that Althusser is among the most significant Marxist thinkers this century; that his return to Marx has strong claims to be considered the most original enterprise in Communist, if not Marxist, philosophy since Lukács's *History and Class Consciousness* (and superior to it), and the most fruitful development of historical materialism since Gramsci's *Prison Notebooks* (though *not* superior to them); and that his work remains of relevance today. Nevertheless, there is no question of recommending a reversion to this Marxism *pur et dur*[25] for three reasons. First, because of its inherent inadequacy – the numerous intrinsic defects, considered in the pages that follow, which render it unsustainable. Secondly, because of its exclusivity vis-à-vis the rest of the Marxist tradition (with the exception of Marx, Lenin and Mao) – now being no time to indulge any of its representatives in an ultimately self-subversive certitude in the excusive superiority of their own optic and idiom. This is not to recommend indiscriminate, uncritical approbation or synthetic, superficial reconciliation, but a practice of discrimination and evaluation that

---

[22] Althusser and Balibar 1970, p. 13.

[23] Meanwhile, see Karol 1980 (an article unusual for recounting some of the career and qualities of Hélène Althusser); Johnson 1981; Macciocchi 1983, *passim*; and Roudinesco 1986, pp. 384–5, 389–90, 664. Roudinesco provides the most precise information yet on Althusser's illness and its treatment, refuting the legend that he was analysed by Jacques Lacan.

[24] See Callinicos 1982, pp. 2, 52, 71 and 1983, pp. 3, 7; interview with Robert Linhart, Paris, April 1986.

[25] The epithets of Henri Lefebvre in Lefebvre 1975, p. 202.

are conducive to a common socialist culture, rather than a set of competing intellectual sectarianisms. The third reason is Althusserian absolutism. The cause defended by Althusser some twenty years ago – the axiomatic scientificity of Marxism – cannot be championed today. My conviction is that Marxism can and should be defended against those detractors for whom it is a useless passion – or worse; that, to take the case of France, Goldmann is infinitely preferable to Gluckomann, Lefebvre to Lévy, Sartre to Sollers; and that we still have more to learn from Marxism, classical and post-classical, than from current *maîtres penseurs*. Yet the crisis of Marxism, and concomitant twilight of Western-Marxist idols, cannot be attributed solely to panic reactions among (fashion-conscious) intellectuals to the vicissitudes of contemporary history – as if its status was unaffected by them. For Marxism has precisely proven fallible in the face of the intractable questions and tests posed it by the twentieth century. Theory proposes, history disposes? Not exactly: historical materialism will only be superseded as a research programme when it has been improved upon; and it has not been thus improved upon. But if recent deconstructions of it have often been sheerly destructive, both politically – reinventing capitalism in the act of reconstructing socialism – and intellectually – mistaking a pseudo-radicalism for a defiance of Western metaphysics – Marxism *is* in need of renovation and substantial development if it is to aid the socialist project in the future. Pending their outcome, which cannot be predicted, Jean-Paul Sartre's sometime *marxisme faute de mieux*[26] is a more salutary maxim than the omnipotence of Marx's doctrine proclaimed contemporaneously by Louis Althusser.

The structure of this book is as follows. Chapter 1 is concerned to delineate the conjunctures in the international Communist movement, the French Communist Party, Marxist theory, and French philosophy in which Althusser conceived the project executed in *For Marx* and *Reading 'Capital'*, offering a preliminary definition of that project. In Chapters 2 and 3, the nature of the Marxism developed in these works is examined in detail, the former being devoted to Althusser's novel version of Marxist philosophy, the latter to his

---

[26] Sartre's gloss on some pertinent remarks by Merleau-Ponty: see Sartre 1964a, pp. 200–1.

re-reading of Marx and reconstruction of historical materialism. Althusser's subsequent evolution is charted in Chapter 4, which analyses the labour of auto-critique and rectification undertaken by him in relation to its external and internal logics. The philosopher's response to contemporary events – especially the Cultural Revolution in China and May '68 in France – (re)raises the question of his relation to the Stalinist legacy; and this will occupy us in Chapter 5, where the critique of Stalinism he sketched in 1972 will be employed as a springboard for a wider discussion. Chapter 6 highlights and investigates the changed political and theoretical direction of the last years of Althusser's career: the transition from quasi-Maoist to 'centrist' politics; the adoption of a more forthright anti-Stalinist position; and the conviction of a crisis of Marxism. Finally, in the Conclusion, a provisional balance-sheet of Althusser's contribution to Marxism will be attempted.

It only remains to acknowledge the enormous contribution made by others over the last five years – no mere formality this, since without it the book would likely as not never have been started, still less finished.

Doubtless 'bearing the scar of these circumstances', *Althusser: The Detour of Theory* began life as a doctoral thesis at Oxford. I am grateful to my various supervisors – Terry Eagleton, Tony Judt, and especially Steven Lukes and Alan Montefiore – for their encouragement and for guiding it to a conclusion; to Tony Dodd and Alex Callinicos for their invaluable support in the early stages; and to Professors G.A. Cohen and Douglas Johnson for the sympathy with which they examined it (and me). In the course of the research, I had the good fortune to meet and/or correspond with several participants in the history it treats: Étienne Balibar, Maurice Godelier, Jean-Jacques Lecercle, Robert Linhart, Grahame Lock, and Peter Schöttler. All of them gave generously of their time and expertise, patiently answering my many questions; and some made available source material difficult, if not impossible, to find elsewhere. Throughout I was able to call upon the great erudition and generosity of Perry Anderson – to my and, I hope, the text's benefit. A second draft completed, I was lucky to find in Norman Geras and particularly Michael Sprinker meticulous readers, whose kind advice has been of considerable assistance in revising the manuscript for publication. And I am also indebted to Paul Cammack, Bambina Carnwath, Rob Scrafton and especially Gyöngyi Vigh-Anderson for their respective translations of Spanish, Portuguese Italian, and Hungarian texts of Althusser's; to Patrick Camiller for making my own from the French more presentable; to the staff at Verso, past and present, for all their help; to Chris Bertram for his painstaking work on the proofs; to Neil Belton for last-minute editorial reassurance; and to Pierre Macherey for unwittingly supplying me with a sub-title. If, as is possible, I have inadvertently neglected to thank anyone, I apologise. One thing is certain: such demerits, errors, injustices, and so on as survive are solely my responsibility.

My final debt is difficult enough to calculate, impossible to repay: I hope Sarah Baxter will accept my heartfelt thanks instead. Last but not least of the things I owe her is that she will understand why this book is dedicated, in gratitude and solidarity, to a French Communist, partisan and artisan of Marxism, whom its author has never met.

Gregory Elliott
London, 1 June 1987

Chapter One
The Moment of Althusser

I would never have written anything were it not for the
Twentieth Congress and Khrushchev's critique of Stalinism
and the subsequent liberalisation. But I would never have
written these books if I had not seen this affair as a bungled
destalinisation, a right-wing destalinisation which instead
of analyses offered us only incantations; which instead
of Marxist concepts had available only the poverty of
bourgeois ideology. My target was therefore clear: these
humanist ravings, these feeble dissertations on liberty,
labour or alienation which were the effects of all this among
French Party intellectuals. And my aim was equally clear:
to make a start on the first *left-wing* critique of Stalinism,
a critique that would make it possible to reflect not only
on Khrushchev and Stalin but also on Prague and Lin Piao:
that would above all help put some substance back into
the revolutionary project here in the West.

Louis Althusser, 1975

'A philosophy does not make its appearance in
the world as Minerva appeared to the society of
Gods and men', Louis Althusser declared in 1975.[1]
This first chapter will be concerned with the
four inter-related areas which formed the context
and shaped the character of Althusser's original
intervention: the crisis in the international Communist

---

[1] Althusser 1976a, pp. 165–6.

movement after Stalin; the adjustment of the PCF to de-Stalinisation; the configuration of Marxist theory in the late 1950s and early 1960s; and the disposition of the French intellectual landscape when Althusser came to write. It will provide a summary account of Althusser's relation to the 'existing state of affairs' and his alternative to it, preliminary to a closer consideration of his reconstructions, their ramifications and rationale, in Chapters 2 and 3.

After Stalin, the deluge

However recondite their subject-matter, Althusser always insisted that his philosophical writings of 1960–5 were to be read and judged as complementary theoretical and political interventions in a particular conjuncture. On his own testimony, it was the Twentieth Congress of the Communist Party of the Soviet Union (CPSU) which 'obliged me to throw myself into the battle'. A decade after the publication of *For Marx* and *Reading 'Capital'*, he characterised their purpose thus:

> These texts . . . are explicit interventions in a definite conjuncture: political interventions in the existing world of Marxist philosophy, directed at one and the same time against dogmatism and the rightist critique of dogmatism; also philosophical interventions in politics, against economism and its humanist 'appendix'.[2]

The context of Althusser's intervention, then, was simultaneously theoretical and political. Politically, it was dominated by the two 'great events' signposted in the English introduction to *For Marx*: the Twentieth Congress and its aftermath (1956–) and the Sino-Soviet split in the international Communist movement (1960–).[3] Althusser's later statement to the effect that he 'would never have written anything were it not for the Twentieth Congress and Khrushchev's critique of Stalinism',[4] crucial as it is, can be deceptive. For the stress on the centrality of '1956 and all that' can obscure the equivalent significance of the breach between Moscow and Peking. It is essential to understand that Althusser intervened on some of the questions raised by

---

[2] Althusser 1976a, pp. 168–9. See also Althusser 1978b, pp. 7–8.
[3] See Althusser 1969a pp. 9–12; and cf. Althusser 1976a, pp. 78–9.
[4] Quoted in Anonymous 1975.

1956 in the light, and under the influence of, the debates and divisions of 1960–3. Accordingly, Anderson is quite right to argue that '[t]he founding moment of Althusser's work was *this* entirely different conflict. The Sino-Soviet dispute . . . is the real political background to the writing of *For Marx* and *Reading "Capital"*.[5] Failure to appreciate this point can lead to errors of interpretation. It is therefore necessary briefly to review some of the most important developments in the international Communist movement in these years.

The Twentieth Congress of the CPSU opened on 14 February 1956. Eleven days later, Khrushchev delivered what is known as his 'secret speech' ('On the Cult of Personality and its Consequences') to a closed session. 'Comrades!', he exhorted the delegates at its conclusion, 'We must abolish the cult of the individual decisively, once and for all; we must draw the proper conclusions concerning both ideological-theoretical and practical work.'[6] There ensued what Roy and Zhores Medvedev have described as an 'off-again on-again policy'[7] of de-Stalinisation which was criticised from two quarters: by those in the CPSU and the international movement opposed to the exposure, however limited, of the reality of Stalin's régime; and, conversely, by those for whom the anticipated process of revelation and renovation did not go far enough. It is these contrasting pressures, intensified by the volatile situation in Eastern Europe and internationally, which influenced Khrushchev's oscillations in the years that followed. The Soviet intervention in Hungary in the autumn of 1956 induced two reactions in the Communist world: a revolt in the non-East-European parties that remained minoritarian, but which ended with the exodus of many of the rebels; and support from every affiliate of the international movement and a rallying around the socialist mother country.

The Communist Party of China (CPC), ultimately one of the most strident supporters of the suppression of the Hungarian rebellion, had fired a warning shot to the Soviets when, on 5 April, it published a response to the initiatives of the Twentieth Congress – *On the Historical Experience of the Dictatorship of the Proletariat* – in which it signalled a certain fidelity to Stalin's memory.

---

[5] Anderson 1980, p. 106.
[6] Khrushchev 1984, pp. 270–1.
[7] Medvedev and Medvedev 1977, p. 71.

Nevertheless, for the time being, it toed the Russian line of controlled de-Stalinisation. Indeed, for a year or so, during the 'Hundred Flowers' campaign (summer 1956 – summer 1957), the CPC went further along the road of 'liberalisation' than the CPSU. The 'rectification campaign' foreshadowed in *On the Correct Handling of Contradictions among the People* (February 1957) led one contemporary observer, Isaac Deutscher, to deem Mao's text 'by far the most radical repudiation of Stalinism that has come out of any communist country so far'.[8] Yet, by the time it was published in June of the same year, a new 'anti-rightist' campaign had been undertaken. Soon, China was in the throes of the unsuccessful 'Great Leap Forward' and on a collision course with its socialist neighbour. Henceforth, Mao's face was to be set against any gesture of de-Stalinisation.

A tempestuous meeting in November 1957 of representatives of the Communist and workers' parties concluded with a final declaration which endorsed the positions proposed by the CPSU (rather than assenting to Mao's reflections on 'paper tigers'), although it included the Chinese thesis that 'revisionism' or 'right-wing opportunism' was the main danger facing international Communism. In December 1960, after a conference of 81 parties in Moscow, the Chinese delegation again signed a joint statement celebrating the 'unity of the socialist camp'. Yet both of these gatherings were largely exercises in papering over the cracks. On the ninetieth anniversary of Lenin's birth – April 1960 – the Chinese had published in *Hongqi* the broadside 'Long Live Leninism!' in defence of Marxist-Leninist orthodoxy against 'certain persons'. Explicitly rebuking Tito, but in reality dressing down Khrushchev, the article suggested that 'one may oppose dogmatism in the interests of Marxism-Leninism or one may actually oppose Marxism-Leninism in the name of opposing dogmatism'.[9] The Russians, aware that they were the real addressee and taking advantage of the fortuitous fortieth anniversary of the publication of Lenin's *'Left-Wing' Communism – An Infantile Disorder*, responded with fulsome extracts from that work. It was against the background of this public shadow-boxing that the results of the Twenty-Second Congress of the CPSU in October 1961 were to be condemned as 'revisionist' by the CPC. It

[8] Deutscher 1970, p. 104.
[9] Communist Party of China 1960, p. 16.

objected to two main aspects of the proceedings (which it considered to be related). First, Khrushchev's critique of Stalin was renewed. Secondly, the programme adopted by the CPSU confirmed the line of 'peaceful coexistence and competition' pursued by Khrushchev since he had assumed full control in the USSR. Khrushchev dubbed the Congress 'a congress of the builders of communism' and the party programme *a document of true communist humanism*. Referred to as 'The New Communist Manifesto', it set as the USSR's target the construction of communism within twenty years. The Soviet state was now declared to be a 'State of the Whole People' and the CPSU a 'Party of the Whole People'. 'Everything in the name of Man, for the benefit of Man' became the ideological watchword of Khrushchevism at home and abroad.[10]

Translated out of the Russian context, what these perspectives meant for the Communist parties and the 'socialist camp' was the prioritisation of the 'struggle for peace'. This had been the burden of the 'Peace Manifesto' agreed by them in 1957. The objective was for the USSR to outstrip the USA in industrial and technological prowess (hence the vaunting of the Sputnik launch in October 1957 and Gagarin's orbit of the Earth in April 1961), thereby demonstrating the inherent superiority of the rational, planned socialist system over the anarchic, 'historically outdated capitalist system'. Briefly put, the economic contest between the USSR and the USA was to be the 'main form of the class struggle'. The duty of the Communist parties was to fight to secure the kind of peaceful international environment in which the USSR, enjoying a period of respite, could implement its ambitious programme of communism in one country. This favoured the adoption by them of a gradualist, constitutional and national strategy for the transition to socialism, which would not disrupt the postwar division of 'spheres of influence'. Thus, once again, the strategy of the Communist parties – even in the absence of any international ruling body – was to be aligned with Soviet horizons as represented by Khrushchev's *détentisme* (and symbolised by his repeated invocation of the 'Camp David spirit'). An era of 'polycentrism' may, as Italian Communist Party leader Palmiro Togliatti later claimed, have dawned: it was characterised by a struggle for the 'preservation of the status quo'.

---

[10] See Communist Party of the Soviet Union 1961.

While the Russian line appealed to many Communist parties, anxious to return to the 'national road', the Chinese were simply not prepared to go along with it, because it was – so they believed – incompatible with their national interests and the construction of communism in their country. Still an outcast among (imperialist) nations, and locked in dispute with the USSR over economic aid, nuclear technology and the Sino-Indian conflict (as well as the Cuban Missile Crisis and the socialist merits of Yugoslavia and Albania), they had reached breaking-point. A meeting between delegations of the two parties scheduled for July 1963 was upstaged by the publication on 14 June of 'A Proposal Concerning the General Line of the International Communist Movement' from the Central Committee of the CPC, and of an equally fierce rejoinder from the CPSU one month later. The meeting got underway as planned, but, in this atmosphere of mutual recrimination, the talks made no progress and they were suspended on 20 July. (Five days later, to the fury of the Chinese, the Nuclear Test Ban Treaty was initialled in Moscow.) The first casualty was the unity of the international Communist movement.

Whatever one's retrospective judgement of the importance and sincerity of the ideological content of these and subsequent polemics, there can be no doubt of their significance for Communists at the time. Ultimately at issue for the Chinese was

> whether or not to accept the universal truth of Marxism-Leninism, whether or not to recognise the universal significance of the road of the October Revolution, whether or not to accept the fact that the people still living under the imperialist and capitalist system, who comprise two-thirds of the world's population, need to make revolution, and whether or not to accept the fact that people already on the socialist road, who comprise one-third of the world's population, need to carry their revolution forward to the end.[11]

Nine comments formed the reply to the Russian 'Open Letter' of 14 July. Castigating Khrushchev's 'phoney communism', they indicted the Soviets for collaboration with the Americans abroad and for abetting the restoration of capitalism at home. The famous *On the Question of Stalin*, by contrast, concluded

---

[11] Communist Party of China 1965, pp. 4–5.

that '[h]e was primarily correct, and his faults were secondary'; Stalin was 'a great Marxist-Leninist' and 'a great revolutionary'.[12] Two ideological disagreements recur in the Chinese polemics and were to be the doctrinal basis of the Eastern schism in the international Communist movement: the rejection of the Soviet conception of 'peaceful coexistence', considered to constitute an abandonment of anti-imperialism; and the repudiation of the perspective of a peaceful transition to socialism, perceived to be a line imposed by the exigencies of Soviet *raison d'état* rather than *raison de la révolution* – the reverse of a national strategy for socialism. The Russians stood accused of 'revisionism' – in a word, of anti-Leninism. Khrushchev's dismissal in the autumn of 1964 made no difference. As the new leadership of the CPSU set about de-Khrushchevisation, the Chinese began attacking 'Khrushchevism without Khrushchev'. The battle-lines in the Communist world were drawn up for the next decade or more.

Out of the ghetto?

Inevitably, Althusser will have seen much of this through the prism of the PCF, the second largest and most thoroughly 'Bolshevised' Communist party in Western Europe. 'Our epoch,' Sartre later remarked, 'obliged all men of letters to do a dissertation on French politics'.[13] In common with many other intellectuals of his generation, Althusser had been rallied to socialism by the ignominious collapse of the Third Republic, the subsequent Occupation, and the ensuing pattern of collaboration and resistance. The roles of the USSR and the PCF in the anti-fascist war had ensured that they emerged from the defeat of the Axis powers with enormous prestige. Boasting a membership of half a million in 1945, and commanding the loyalty of a quarter of the French electorate, the PCF was, as Sartre would recall, 'our only pole'[14] – the locus of effective action on the Left. Given this, two basic options were open – exemplified by the trajectories of Sartre and Merleau-Ponty on the one hand, Althusser on the other. The founders of *Les Temps Modernes* balked

[12] Communist Party of China 1965, pp. 120–1.
[13] Sartre 1964a, p. 217.
[14] Sartre 1964a, p. 228.

at the monolithic organisation, petrified doctrine and authoritarian practice of the PCF, opting for 'comprehension without adherence'[15] – 'anti-anti-communism'. The party's transformation was a precondition for the realisation of the aspirations borne by the Resistance. But the task of elaborating the *sui generis* Marxist philosophy which would aid this process could only be conducted outside its bureaucratised structures, albeit in 'fraternal dialogue' with it.

The existentialist-Marxist programme fared badly. For a start the PCF, unconditionally loyal to the USSR, rejected the very possibility of a 'third way' between American capitalism and Soviet Communism. And in any event, postwar political history delivered it its quietus, necessitating the stark choices which had earlier been refused in the name of a principled neutralism. Merleau-Ponty, persuaded by the Korean War of the imperialist nature of the Soviet Union and hence of the utopianism of Marxism, renounced it. For Sartre, by contrast, it was the 'end of idealism' and the beginning of 'realism'; in a Manichean political universe, he elected to persevere 'alongside' the PCF. Althusser's choice was similarly unequivocal. Before the war a militant in the Jeunesse Étudiante Chrétienne, he had been radicalised first by the Popular Front and then – decisively – by the experience of French defeat. Mobilised in September 1939, he was taken prisoner the following summer, spending the remainder of the War in a German camp. Similarly subjected to 'the terrible education of deeds',[16] unlike Sartre and Merleau-Ponty he was led by the turbulent post-Liberation years to join the PCF, his membership coinciding with deepening Cold War and intensifying class struggle. Althusser made his commitment in November 1948, just as a bitter, Communist-led miners' strike was being crushed by riot police at the behest of Socialist ministers.

Indeed, by this time the revolutionary hopes aroused by the Resistance had been conclusively dashed. The previous year, *le parti des fusillés*, having 'lowered the red flag before the tricolour'[17] and compromised with de Gaulle's *France Libre* at the War's close, had been ejected from Ramadier's government. The alliance between the USSR and the victorious capitalist powers was no more.

---

[15] Merleau-Ponty 1969, p. 148.
[16] Althusser 1969a, p. 21.
[17] Marx 1977, p. 46.

The Pax Americana had descended with its twin arms of Truman Doctrine and Marshall Plan, soon to be followed by the North Atlantic Treaty Organisation. The Cominform, established by Stalin in the autumn of 1947 to co-ordinate a unified Communist response, criticised the French and Italian parties for their erstwhile policy of national unity; decreed the existence of 'two camps' – the one socialist and wedded to peace, the other imperialist and bent on war; and dictated a 'left turn' by the Communist parties. With 'tripartism' over at home, the PCF switched to the offensive, mobilising its forces for the violent class struggles of the late 1940s. As French Socialists were converted to Atlanticism, the Communists reverted to a quasi-'third-period' rhetoric. Denounced as an arm of Russian totalitarianism, the PCF retreated into its Stalinist fortress, loyally executing Cominform demands as the Cold War worsened. Membership, which had risen from 545,000 in 1945 to 800,000 the following year, declined to little over 300,000 a decade later. Despite this, under the Fourth Republic, electoral support remained in the region of twenty-five per cent and the PCF retained its position as the premier working-class party.

Portraying opposition to American imperialism, and its Gaullist and Socialist allies, as the continuation of the Resistance; representing itself as the inheritor and defender of French revolutionary republicanism; and entrenching its position as the party of the working class, the embattled PCF remained a symbol of heroism for numerous intellectuals – the embodiment of indivisible socialist and national causes. Relations between the two were always strained, often tortured. Yet, if some were alienated in these years of 'Stalinist hard labour',[18] others – including Althusser – stayed the course. Sartre, an indefatigable polemicist throughout the Cold War, probably spoke for many when in 1952 he leapt to the PCF's defence, arguing that, in the current conjuncture, a defeat for Stalinism would, in reality, be a defeat of the working class. For, were the workers to abandon the sole unifying instance able to impart 'class-being' to them, 'the universe will be bourgeois': left-wing intellectuals' dystopia.[19] For his part, Sartre determined that 'un anti-

---

[18] Althusser 1978a, p. 35.
[19] See Sartre 1964 b, p. 252. Sartre's articles prompted the charge of 'ultrabolshevism' from Merleau-Ponty: see his 1973, Chapter 5.

communiste est un chien'[20] and adopted the role of *compagnon de route*, essaying a theorisation of the Party's political practice form outside its ranks.

For those inside, on the other hand, who likewise equated party and class, the Twentieth Congress came as an 'earthquake'.[21] The dismay of the PCF's leaders was initially even greater. Ever accommodating to Stalin's dictates and reversals of line, they at first found it difficult to accept Khrushchev's de-Stalinisation. General Secretary Maurice Thorez opposed the Congress's limited initiatives on Stalin (he always referred to the 'alleged Khrushchev report'), let alone speculations by Togliatti about systemic 'dégenerescence'; dissuaded Khrushchev from rehabilitating Bukharin and other victims of the Moscow trials; and, at the very least, was sympathetic to the 'anti-party plot' of Malenkov, Molotov and Kaganovich in June 1957 to oust the Soviet leader. Nevertheless, under his leadership, the PCF did adapt to the new line sponsored by the CPSU (until his death in 1964, Thorez avowed that 'proletarian internationalism is solidarity with the Soviet Union'). 'Peaceful coexistence' had been endorsed at the Party's Fourteenth Congress in July 1956. A Central Committee meeting in November 1961 affirmed the 'universal significance' of the CPSU's recent congress. 'From the historic decisions of the Twenty-Second Congress,' the resolution read, 'French Communists draw new reasons and strength for the struggle against the fascist threat and personal power, for peace in Algeria, for the restoration and renovation of democracy . . . for peaceful coexistence and general disarmament, for socialism.'[22] As regards the last, the Fifteenth and Sixteenth Congresses (1959 and 1961, respectively) marked the PCF's official orientation to 'peaceful transition'. By 1966, Thorez's successor, Waldeck Rochet, could announce on behalf of his colleagues that 'the position and desire of the PCF is clear; all its activity is directed to the goal of creating conditions favourable to a peaceful transition to socialism'.[23]

The PCF's adjustment to the Khrushchevite line arose not simply from fidelity to the bastion of world socialism, but because there was an underlying compatibility between the imperatives of 'internationalism' and domestic

---

[20] Sartre 1964a, p. 248.
[21] The recollection of leading PCF intellectual Jean-Toussaint Desanti, in Desanti 1985, p. 510.
[22] Quoted in Marcou 1979, p. 143.
[23] *Cahiers du Communisme* 1966, p. 316.

horizons. Regardless of its official doctrine, the PCF had, in a sense, been pursuing an analogous line, in impeccably French colours, ever since the Popular Front. The sharp turn of 1947 issued in campaigns centred on the 'struggle for peace', not plans for an insurrectionary *prise de pouvoir*. Defence of the USSR demanded the fostering of patriotic anti-Americanism with the aim of fomenting inter-imperialist contradictions. Paradoxically, intransigent internationalism took the form of a truculent nationalism (for example, in the drive against German rearmament), which claimed *la patrie* for its own against a perfidious bourgeoisie. As the international situation eased after the Korean War, the PCF once again looked to a 'united front' with the Socialists. Anxious to demonstrate its solicitude for *la France éternelle*, it was at best equivocal over the Algerian cause (as it had been over the Vietnamese) when the war of independence erupted in 1954; 'the Party must not be compromised', Thorez proclaimed. As proof of its respectability, it called for peace and a 'genuine union', voting 'special powers' to the Mollet administration in 1956 – only to discover two years later that salvation from the Algerian imbroglio was generally anticipated not from 'left unity', but from the return of de Gaulle. Evasive over French colonialism, the PCF was reduced to passivity as the Fourth Republic was buried beneath the Gaullist *treize mai* of 1958. That year, its vote fell to under twenty per cent for the first time since 1936. Thereafter, its sights were firmly fixed on the 'restoration and renovation of democracy' as an intermediary stage in any transition to socialism – an end whose means were an electoral alliance with the Socialists on a common 'democratic programme'. The consolidation of the Fifth Republic effected with the massive endorsement of *le pouvoir personnel* in the constitutional referendum of 1962 gave added impetus to the strategy of the 'outstretched hand'. Henceforth, the PCF was effectively in electoral alliance with the Socialists; the 'great schism' was over (even if the entente was not particularly cordial). In Althusser's *annus mirabilis* of 1965, the 'opening to the Right' extended to supporting François Mitterrand as the Left's sole presidential candidate.

The crisis provoked by the Russian intervention in Hungary in 1956 did not affect the PCF as badly as its Italian (or British) sister-parties. To be sure, the combination of pugnacious pro-Sovietism over Eastern Europe, timid nationalism over Algeria, and outright resistance to the least democratisation of the Party's internal régime led not only to Sartre's break – announced in *The Spectre of Stalin* – but to an active inner-party opposition. Disappointed by the political and theoretical fruits of de-Stalinisation, leading intellectuals like Henri Lefebvre and Jean-Toussaint Desanti collaborated on oppositional bulletins – and were expelled for their pains in 1958. The Sorbonne-Lettres cell was dissolved the same year for criticising the leadership's stand on Algeria.[24] Three years later, Marcel Servin and Laurent Casanova were brought to book for their premature Eurocommunism. In each case, order was restored.

Given the new crisis in the international Communist movement from 1960 onwards, however, the most urgent counter-reformation was one against 'left' – that is, Chinese – heresies. This the PCF excelled at. Mindful of the spread of the Maoist bacillus within its own cells, the Party vigorously supported the USSR in the Sino-Soviet controversies, provoking the riposte from Peking that its new course was 'out of keeping with [its] oath of dedication to communism'.[25] The critiques of 1956 inspired by the Stalinism-without-Stalin of that year were rapidly overtaken by this quite distinct development in the Communist world. By the early 1960s, with the CPSU taking the lead, the 'normalised' Communist parties had repackaged much of the critique formerly directed at them by dissidents as the basis for their own programmes. The Khrushchevites appropriated the arsenal of those who, 'through the smoke of Budapest',[26] had discerned the ghost of Stalin. The PCF's official intellectuals negotiated the passage from the ideological expediencies of Stalinism to those of Khrushchevism with relative facility. The Party's leading philosopher was Roger Garaudy, Politbureau member, editor of *Cahiers du communisme* and director of the Centre d'Études et de Recherches Marxistes. Formerly witch-finder general, now dispenser of extreme unction, in quick succession champion of Stalin and defender of the Khrushchevite faith, Garaudy led the way, becoming the symbol (to borrow one of his own titles) of the transition 'from anathema to dialogue'.

Thus were the co-ordinates of debate and division fundamentally restructured from 1960 onwards. Althusser, who remained in the PCF after Hungary,

---

[24] The loyalty of many party members was severely strained by official caution. Among those who seem to have taken a harder line was Althusser. According to a hostile commentator, together with his students he attended a militant demonstration over Algeria called by the student union UNEF in October 1960: see Lisbonne 1981, pp. 15–16, citing the testimony of Jean Daubier.
[25] Communist Party of China 1963, p. 155.
[26] The title of an article by E.P. Thompson in *The New Reasoner* in November 1956.

played no part in the ideological suppression of critics. Indeed, we have no contemporary statement from him on the events of 1956. By then, he had only a few brief articles on Marxist philosophy (published in an academic journal and not a party organ) to his name. What was their character? The first two – 'On Marxism' and 'Note on Dialectical Materialism' (1953) – formed a pair, being devoted to problems which would exercise Althusser throughout his career: the periodisation of Marx's œuvre and the nature of Marxism. Arguing that the importance attributed to the writings of the young Marx commanded the interpretation of Marxism, Althusser took his stand on Marx's own summary of his intellectual biography in the 1859 Preface to *A Contribution to the Critique of Political Economy*. Accordingly, Marx's texts prior to 1845 were informed by the problematic of German idealism; *The German Ideology* represented the critique of this 'philosophical consciousness'; *The Poverty of Philosophy* was the first entirely 'scientific text' from his pen. If conceived as attempts to impart substance to the philosophical themes of his youth – the end of alienation and the 'end of history' – Marx's later works (and those of his followers) were only worth as much as those themes: very little. For therewith Marxism was converted from a science into a philosophy.[27] Marxism comprised historical and dialectical materialism. The former was the science of history, designated historical *materialism* in order to differentiate it from all the idealist conceptions of history coeval with it. It had been founded not on men's self-consciousness or teleological utopian principles, but 'on the material dialectic of the forces of production and relations of production, the "motor" that determines historical development "in the final analysis"'.[28] And its 'most

---

[27] Althusser 1997, p. 244. '[I]n that case,' Althusser writes, 'Marxism sacrifices its scientific pretensions, to become, in some sort, the incarnation of an ideal, which, although certainly moving, is utopian, and, like any ideal, gets entangled in both theoretical contradictions and the "impurity" of concrete means the moment it seeks to bend reality to its demands. Conversely, if Marxism has nothing to do with any "philosophical" notion of this sort, if it is a science, it escapes the theoretical contradictions and practical tyranny of the ideal; the contradictions it runs up against are no longer those resulting from its philosophical pretensions, but simply the contradictions of reality itself, which it sets out to study scientifically and solve practically.'

[28] Althusser 1997, p. 245. Althusser refers readers to the 1859 Preface, further citing texts by Engels, Lenin and Stalin as instances of 'a profoundly scientific conception of history': Althusser 1997, p. 247. Such affidavits for Stalin were, of course, pro forma in the PCF in 1953.

profound characteristic' was that it 'not only inspires political action, but also seeks its verification in practice, developing and growing through political practice itself'.[29]

Passing in the second article to Marxist philosophy, Althusser commenced by noting that it had been developed by Engels, Lenin, and Stalin in particular.[30] Marx, Engels and their successors regarded the dialectic as 'the most advanced form of *scientific method*'. They had reproached the Hegelian dialectic for a '*schematism*' whereby violence is done to reality in order to mould it to the '*a priori* structure of the dialectic'. Transforming the instrument inherited from Hegel, they had

> retain[ed] its 'rational kernel', the general content of the dialectic (interaction, development, qualitative 'leaps', contradiction). . . . This puts us in a position to specify the meaning of the famous 'inversion'. It is neither reliance on a particular philosophical system, nor a sort of intrinsic virtue, an absolute 'logical' necessity, that makes the dialectic indispensable to Marx and Engels. *The dialectic is validated only by its concrete utilization, by its scientific fecundity.* This scientific use is the sole criterion of the dialectic. It alone makes it possible to speak of the dialectic as *method*.[31]

As Lenin had argued in *What the 'Friends of the People' Are and How They Fight the Social-Democrats*, Marx and Engels's dialectical method was simply the 'scientific method in sociology'.[32] Stalin had therefore been correct to excise the teleological 'negation of the negation' from the 'laws' of the dialectic, as had Mao to specify the concrete structure of its hitherto abstract notion of contradiction. The dialectic, Althusser proceeded, could only constitute a '*method of discovery*' if it expressed the '*structure of reality*'.[33] This did not amount to proof of the common charge of 'metaphysical materialism' entered against Marxism, however, since for dialectical materialism it 'is not for a metaphysics of nature to *deduce* the structure of reality; it is the role of the

---

[29] Althusser 1997, p. 246.
[30] Althusser 1997, p. 247. The bibliography provided by Althusser of 'the most important of the Marxist texts dealing with this subject' is standard for the period – with the interesting (and proleptic) exception of Mao's *On Contradiction*.
[31] Althusser 1997, pp. 248–9.
[32] Althusser 1997, p. 249. Cf. Lenin 1963, pp. 163–5.
[33] Althusser 1997, p. 249.

sciences to *discover* it'.[34] The object of Marxist materialism was not the object(s) of science(s). It was concerned with the fundamental epistemological question: primacy of matter or mind? Coming down firmly on the side of the former, it supported the 'spontaneous materialism' of the sciences, whose practice was the 'origin and criterion of all truth' – a conclusion that had nothing in common with mere 'pragmatism', but which did invalidate the epistemological question endemic in classical philosophy. Marxist philosophy, Althusser argued, 'articulate[s] and consciously draw[s] out the implications of the "spontaneous practice" of the sciences, straightforwardly affirming the *primacy of external reality*'.[35] Hence, the 'materialist theory of knowledge' was utterly distinct from its idealist antecedents, for it was not some Science of the sciences, de jure or de facto substituting itself for them. Nevertheless, it was 'verified' by them and had therefore rightly been adjudged a 'scientific philosophical theory'.[36] As such, materialism stood in 'a fundamental relation to the sciences: reminding them of their true nature, it ensures their survival and progress.' 'To safeguard the endless development of the sciences, . . . to preserve the sciences from all forms of dogmatism and idealism by reminding them of their fundamental reality – such is the aim of materialism', Althusser concluded.[37]

A third early text, 'On the Objectivity of History' (1955) – an open letter to Paul Ricoeur – also treated an issue which would preoccupy Althusser: the question of the foundation of a science of history. Reproving Raymond Aron for relativism, he argued that history possessed a similar 'rationality' to that of the natural sciences. Ricoeur was to be commended for demonstrating that:

the level of history is not that of immediate experience, that history as science is not – and cannot be – a resurrection of the past, that historical science is a *knowledge* of history. . . .

It is at this level that it is possible to discover in history a rationality 'of the same species' as that of the natural sciences. You clearly show that the moments of scientific practice in history – observation, abstraction,

[34] Althusser 1997, p. 250.
[35] Althusser 1997, pp. 251–2.
[36] Althusser 1997, p. 254. The last formula is Stalin's.
[37] Althusser 1997, pp. 255–6.

theory – correspond to the procedures of the experimental sciences (which are theoretical because experimental).[38]

Yet Ricoeur had attempted to found the objectivity of the discipline of history on the historian's 'intention to objectivity', whereas it could only be rooted in the conformity, however approximate, of a theory of the historical object to the historical reality of which it aimed to produce objective knowledge. History, too, could be verified (confirmed as scientific) or falsified (refuted as ideological) in the same manner as the other sciences. Ricoeur had neglected the crucial moment of experimentation. For Althusser, by contrast, *'history likewise can only be a science if it is experimental'* – subject, in its case, to the 'fundamental "critique"' of 'real history'.[39]

Likewise criticising arguments for a methodological distinction between the natural and the human sciences predicated upon philosophical humanism, Althusser observed that history was arraigned for 'threatening men with the loss of the charms or dramas of immediate existence, because it understands their necessity and their laws'. But this was quite mistaken, for:

> Just as knowledge of the laws of light has never prevented men from seeing . . . so knowledge of the laws that govern the development of societies does not prevent men from living, or take the place of labour, love and struggle. On the contrary: knowledge of the laws of light has produced the glasses which have transformed men's sight, just as knowledge of the laws of social development has given rise to endeavours which have transformed and enlarged the horizon of human existence.
>
> The antinomy of history-as-science and lived-history ends when we give up 'expecting' from science anything other than what it imparts. It ends when we conceptualise the *level* at which scientific truths are established; it ends when we conceive the *practical destination* of science, which starts out from immediacy and ascends to generality, to laws, only in order to return to the concrete – not as the duplicate of immediacy, but as an active understanding of it.[40]

---

[38] Althusser 1998, p. 20.
[39] Althusser 1998, p. 24.
[40] Althusser 1998, pp. 30–1.

Althusser's 'early works' seem to have attracted little attention at the time;[41] and have not done so since either. Yet they are of considerable interest insofar as they give some indication of his stance in the 1950s and allow us to measure the distance travelled by the time of *For Marx* and *Reading 'Capital'*. Thus, we shall see that the anti-Hegelianism, anti-historicism and anti-humanism already evident in them was to assume more substantial shape thereafter; that Althusser's later versions of the institutionalised duo of historical and dialectical materialism were to take a quite different, much more original form (less dependent on discredited authority for a start); that some positive aspects of these short texts disappeared (for example, insistence on the empirical moment in historical science), while others were to reappear (the conception of Marxist philosophy is, in certain respects, a striking anticipation of Althusser's second definition of it). In any event, they set out an agenda for the 'attentive and meticulous study' of Marxism invoked by Althusser.[42]

However, his first work of substance was a slender volume on Montesquieu in 1959.[43] It was followed in 1960 by an edition of Feuerbach's writings of 1839–45.[44] When Althusser's major writings began to appear in 1961, eight years after Stalin's death and five years after Khrushchev's 'secret speech', it was in what Anderson has called 'an altered historical landscape'.[45] For now the interpretation of Marxism criticised by him had been granted *droit de cité* by the Communist parties. His own 'philosophical manifestoes' were directed against the Russian line and the French replica of it, whilst intimating sympathy for the Chinese position. From Khrushchev's critique of Stalin, Althusser drew quite different conclusions from those of the Russian and French Parties 'concerning both ideological-theoretical and practical work'.

'De-Stalinization will de-Stalinize the de-Stalinizers', Sartre had confidently predicted in 1956.[46] It had not. What had happened, as Lucio Colletti put it

---

[41] The 'Note on Dialectical Materialism' was, however, treated to caustic criticism – for transforming Marxism into 'magic' – in a footnote in Merleau-Ponty 1973: see pp. 63–4 n.

[42] Althusser 1997, p. 256.

[43] *Montesquieu. La politique et l'histoire*, in Althusser 1972, pp. 9–109. This text seems to have been a by-product of a much larger (uncompleted) undertaking – the project for a *grande thèse* on classical French political philosophy proposed by Althusser in 1949–50: see Althusser 1976a, p. 165.

[44] See Feuerbach 1960.

[45] Anderson 1980, p. 106.

[46] Sartre 1969, p. 77 (translation modified).

ten years after his resignation from the PCI in 1964, was a 'process of renovation . . . in a patently rightward direction'.[47] Althusser, bound by party discipline, was not at liberty to express divergent political opinions. As he pointed out in the introduction to the English edition, the essays collected in *For Marx* treated the theoretical problems posed in/by the period – not the political issues.[48] Implicit in them, however, is the conclusion that Khrushchev's report, far from initiating a genuine de-Stalinisation, had been a right-wing critique which hastened a rightwards evolution in the Communist movement. The 'dogmatist night'[49] – Althusser's expression for the Stalin era – he considered to be primarily an abandonment of the revolutionary legacy of Marx and Lenin. Equidistant from Stalinism and Khrushchevism, he was for de-Stalinisation but against 'social-democratisation' (the regression of the Communist parties to the positions of the Second International) – or de-Stalinisation from the right. Unlike Colletti, Althusser still envisaged the possibility of return to revolutionary Marxism within the Communist parties in the 1960s. Althusser's project – his 'wager', as one of his ex-collaborators was later to describe it – was the *renovation of the political practice* of the PCF by a *restoration/renewal of Marxist theory*.[50] Khrushchev's liberalisation had opened up space for independent research after decades of stultifying orthodoxy: an opportunity. Simultaneously, it had stimulated revisionism and given the green light to reformism: a threat. (Like the CPC, Althusser believed that Marxism and Leninism were being opposed in the name of opposing dogmatism.) The requisite alternative was to return to the time before the Stalinist flood, to that original purity of Marxism which had been corrupted in the period which bears Stalin's name.

Ten years later, Althusser was to define the political direction of his work as 'mak[ing] a start on the first *left-wing* critique of Stalinism'.[51] Only ignorance of the work of Trotsky (among others) could allow Althusser to believe (in 1975) that, in the 1960s, he had embarked on the first such critique. But, from

---

[47] Colletti 1977, p. 319.
[48] Althusser 1969a, p. 10.
[49] Althusser 1969a, p. 31.
[50] See Rancière, pp. 58–9. Appropriately enough, then, Daniel Lindenberg has written that 'Althusser . . . wanted to be the Luther of French Marxism': Lindenberg 1975, p. 13.
[51] Quoted in Anonymous 1975, p. 44.

a Communist who had joined the PCF during the struggle against the 'Titoite-Trotskyists', such 'negligence' is less surprising. The fact is that Althusser's search for an alternative to the Khrushchevite status quo and the Stalinist status quo ante was circumscribed by the horizons of the international Communist movement to which he was loyal. And his *return to Marx* presaged, over and above any theoretical prescription, a complementary *turn to Peking*. For it was there that vehement dissent from the moderate politics of the CPSU and PCF post-Stalin was to be found. Given that the Chinese contrasted the revolutionary Stalin with the treacherous Khrushchev, the resultant critique of Stalin was likely to be ambiguous. But China, proclaiming 'uninterrupted revolution' and the 'victory of people's war', appeared to Althusser to offer the inspiration for the revolutionary project that was the raison d'être of the Communist parties. In the Communist movement too, the east wind was prevailing over the west.

Naturally, Althusser made no public statements in support of the CPC, to do which would have incurred his immediate expulsion from the PCF. Nevertheless, signs of his orientation are present in the essays collected in *For Marx*. It is confirmed by the testimony of Rancière and others.[52] Above all, perhaps, it can be detected from the patent divergence between the direction of Althusser's thought and the evolution of his party. Two examples will be given at this stage. With 'Contradiction and Overdetermination', the gulf between Althusser's coded sympathies and the PCF's visceral anti-Maoism became apparent, earning him the attentions of the Party's official philosophical spokesmen. Published in *La Pensée* in 1962, Althusser's essay offered an explicitly anti-Hegelian account of Marxist theory at a time when the PCF was broadcasting the virtues of the 'Hegelian legacy'. Not only did he reject the isomorphism of the Marxist and Hegelian dialectics; he did so by reference to Marxist political practice. And, if his novel theorisation of Lenin's theory and practice of revolution had a bizarre ring in comparison with the Politbureau's perspectives on Fifth Republic France, the acclaim accorded to Mao's *On Contradiction* bore a political import which was not lost on Althusser's superiors. Garaudy intervened to charge him with a perilous 'pluralism'

---

[52] See Rancière 1974, *passim*.

which impaired the 'monist' basis of Marxism.[53] Undeterred, Althusser renewed his attack and extended his research in an essay published the following August: 'On the Materialist Dialectic'.[54] Two months later, the PCF's Central Committee met at Ivry to ponder the Chinese threat. In the course of its deliberations, Lucien Sève rebuked any flirtation with Maoist categories by party intellectuals, singling out Althusser's writings on the dialectic for reprimand. The following month – November 1963 – Althusser was summoned before the editorial board of La Pensée to explain himself. Arraigned for leftism, he was obliged to affirm the correctness of the PCF's own line.[55]

Althusser's next major article, 'Marxism and Humanism', was written in October 1963. Published in June 1964, it followed hard on the PCF's Seventeenth Congress, where agreement with the Soviet Party had been registered on all the important issues. Opening laconically enough ('Today, Socialist "Humanism" is on the agenda'),[56] its echoes of the Chinese polemics are unmistakeable. In their assault on the CPSU's 'out-and-out revisionist programme' of 1961, the Chinese had laid the following charges against it:

> The Programme crudely revises the essence of Marxism-Leninism, namely,
> the teachings on proletarian revolution, on the dictatorship of the proletariat
> and on the party of the proletariat, declaring that the dictatorship of the

---

[53] See Garaudy 1963. The theoretical and political consequences of Althusser's rejection of the 'Hegelian legacy' were considered 'serious' by Garaudy: 'From the theoretical point of view, the introduction of this historical pluralism is effected to the detriment of materialist monism. Whatever the complexity of the mediations, human practice is one . . . its dialectic constitutes the motor of history. To blur it under the (real) multiplicity of "overdeterminations" is to obscure what is essential in Marx's Capital: the study of the major contradiction [between labour and capital], of the basic law of development of bourgeois society. How is it then possible to conceive the objective existence of a basic law of our age – the transition to socialism? From the practical point of view, it risks obscuring the fact that this contradiction defines the co-ordinates of our revolutionary action': Garaudy 1963, pp. 118–19. Other senior critics also fixed on Althusser's supposed 'pluralism': Besse 1963 was comparatively nuanced; Mury 1963, as the title of his article ('Matérialisme et hyperempirisme') suggests, very hostile.

[54] See Althusser 1969a, p. 163ff. for Althusser's repudiation of the charge of pluralism and counter-attack on his critics' invocation of monism. In an appendix to his text not reprinted in For Marx, Althusser suggested that Mury's critique demonstrated the inevitable consequences of conceiving Marx as Hegel 'inverted': 'serious theoretical distortions of Marx's thought'. See Althusser 1963.

[55] See Rancière 1974, p. 78 and Kessel 1972, pp. 64–6. We shall return to this episode in Chapter 4.

[56] Althusser 1969a, p. 221.

proletariat is no longer needed in the Soviet Union and that the nature of
the CPSU as the vanguard of the proletariat has changed, and advancing
fallacies of a 'state of the whole people' and a 'party of the whole people'.

It substitutes humanism for the Marxist-Leninist theory of class struggle
and substitutes the bourgeois slogan of Liberty, Equality, Fraternity for the
ideals of communism. It is a revisionist programme for the preservation and
restoration of capitalism.[57]

Whereas the Chinese directly attacked the abrogation of the dictatorship of
the proletariat, the promulgation of new slogans and so on, Althusser treated
the Russian – and French – positions sardonically, conveying his incredulity
sotto voce:

The dictatorship of the proletariat, rejected by the Social-Democrats in
the name of (bourgeois) personal 'humanism', and which bitterly opposed
them to the Communists, has been superseded in the USSR. Even better,
it is foreseeable that it might take peaceful and shortlived forms in the
West. From here we can see in outline a sort of meeting between two
personal 'humanisms', socialist humanism and Christian or bourgeois liberal
humanism. The 'liberalization' of the USSR reassures the latter. As for socialist
humanism, it can see itself not only as a critique of the contradictions of
bourgeois humanism, but also and above all as the consummation of its
'noblest' aspirations. Humanity's millenarian dreams, prefigured in the drafts
of past humanisms, Christian and bourgeois, will at last find realization in
it: in man and between men, the reign of Man will at last begin.[58]

Althusser proceeded to demonstrate to his own satisfaction that humanism
was an ideological concept, emphasising, however, that his purpose was 'not
to dispute the reality that the concept of socialist humanism is supposed to
designate, but to define the *theoretical* value of the concept'.[59] After an elliptical
and provocative run-through of Marx's theoretical development, he concluded
that one of the 'indissociable elements' of Marx's 'break' in 1845 was 'the
definition of humanism as an *ideology*'; and, moreover, that 'this rupture with

---

[57] Communist Party of China 1965, pp. 91–2. Cf. Communist Party of the Soviet
Union 1961, e.g., pp. 190–1, 261, 450.
[58] Althusser 1969a, p. 222.
[59] Althusser 1969a, p. 223.

every *philosophical* anthropology or humanism is no secondary detail; it is Marx's scientific discovery'. The logical conclusion was that the theoretical value of the concept was nil.[60] Socialist humanism, masquerading as Marxism, was no more than the 'practical ideology' of the USSR. It furnished a compelling ethical critique of the inhuman form taken by the dictatorship of the proletariat under Stalin, but was otherwise 'an imaginary treatment of real problems'[61] characteristic of ideology. Any critique cast in its terms remained ideological (the 'cult of personality' was said to be an 'unclassifiable concept in Marxist theory').[62] If Althusser, unlike the CPC, did not (publicly) doubt that the USSR, for all the deformations in its superstructure under Stalin, was a socialist country, he was effectively accusing the CPSU (and its supporters in the Communist movement) of abandoning Marxism in favour of bourgeois ideology.[63] In their 'recourse to ideology', the Soviets were circumventing a materialist explanation (and genuine rectification?) of 'what has not yet been completely superseded, in its effects or its misdeeds . . . terror, repression and dogmatism'.[64] The 'retreat' to humanism by the Soviets, their supporters and their critics would not yield the requisite scientific analysis of Stalinism and thus obstructed the provision of a political strategy for a non-Stalinist socialism.[65]

Althusser was not, then, an unregenerate Stalinist and his writings were not those of an apparatchik. He opposed socialist/Marxist humanism insofar as this labile theoretical current had become part of an apologetic orthodoxy which pointed to the USSR as the socialist utopia in demand. As he saw it, in conjunction with an economic evolutionism (the theory of 'state monopoly

---

[60] See Althusser 1969a, pp. 229–30. The same year as Althusser's anti-humanist article was written, Chou Yang was warning the Philosophy and Social Sciences Department of the Chinese Academy of Sciences that '[t]he modern revisionists and some bourgeois scholars try to describe Marxism as humanism and call Marx a humanist. Some people counterpose the young Marx to the mature proletarian revolutionary Marx. In particular they make use of certain views on "alienation" expressed by Marx in his *Economic and Philosophical Manuscripts* . . . to depict him as an exponent of the bourgeois theory of human nature. They do their best to preach so-called humanism by using the concept of alienation. This, of course, is futile': quoted by Soper in her valuable 1986, p. 87.

[61] Althusser 1969a, p. 247.

[62] Althusser 1969a, p. 240.

[63] See Althusser 1969a, pp. 240–1.

[64] Althusser 1969a, p. 237.

[65] See Benton 1984, p. 15.

capitalism'),[66] it was being employed pragmatically by the PCF as a theoretical garb for political opportunism. The distinct danger was that it would be used to license a social-democratisation of the Communist parties. The PCF, it appeared, had emerged from the ghetto at the price of a flight into 'democratic adventurism'. The alternative to Stalinism and social democracy alike was a revival of Leninism. Althusser's Leninism may have been neo-Maoist, but Marxist/socialist humanism was, in general, anti-Leninist. To adhere to its positions, Althusser believed, was to wrench political practice from its orientation towards the class struggle and consecrate in theory the practical abandonment of the revolutionary project. The real danger was political. But its *site* for Althusser was *theoretical*: was Marxism a humanism? In the theoretical conjuncture of Althusser's intervention, most answers to this question were in the affirmative. An apparently Marxological issue, it was far from trivial in its practical implications. It was precisely the political content and effects of this theoretical position within the Communist movement which determined the implacability of Althusser's opposition to it. In combating it theoretically, Althusser was contributing to a political cause.

The misadventures of Marxist theory

Althusser's first major essay on Marxist theory, 'On the Young Marx', was written in 1960 and published the following year. The opening shot in a concerted 'counter-attack',[67] its immediate target was a collection of essays, primarily by East-European Marxists, devoted to the relation between the young Marx and the 'mature' Marx.[68] Insisting that 'any discussion of Marx's Early Works' was a *'political discussion'*, Althusser noted that throughout Europe,

> Philosophers, ideologues, theologians have all launched into a gigantic enterprise of criticism and *conversion*: let Marx be restored to his source, and

---

[66] State monopoly capitalism ('stamocap') was theoretical orthodoxy for the international Communist movement: see Communist Party of the Soviet Union 1961, pp. 470–90 and the *Statement and Appeal of the World's Communist Parties* issued following the November 1960 conference in Moscow.

[67] Althusser 1976a, p. 168.

[68] See *Recherches internationales*, no. 19, 1960, containing articles by Hoeppner, Jahn, Lapine, Schaff and Togliatti, among others.

> let him admit at last that in him, the mature man is merely the young man
> in disguise. Or if he stubbornly insists on his age, let him admit the sins of
> his maturity, let him recognise that he sacrificed philosophy to economics,
> ethics to science, man to history. Let him consent to this or refuse it, his
> truth . . . is contained in [the] Early Works.[69]

Dissenting from the consensus he detected, Althusser retorted that Marx's youth pertained to Marxism only insofar as it was amenable to Marxist explanation.[70] (His article might well have been entitled 'Against the Young Marx'.) The following year, one of the early works under discussion – *The Economic and Philosophical Manuscripts* – appeared under the imprint of the PCF's publishing house, Éditions Sociales. Althusser greeted this 'theoretical event' with a short review in *La Pensée* (February 1963) in which he characterised the author of the Paris *Manuscripts* as 'the Marx *furthest from* Marx'.[71] As Althusser was well aware, his conclusions, consonant with the Chinese position, were something of a contemporary scandal. For the late 1950s and early 1960s were characterised throughout the continent by a return to the young Marx among Marxist intellectuals, both Communist and non-Communist.

If the Communist movement was in political peril, Marxist theory was ostensibly experiencing a renaissance. But it was a humanist revival. In France classics were rediscovered, new works produced. Georg Lukács's *History and Class Consciousness* (1923), condemned by the Comintern the year after its publication and hitherto known to a French audience largely through Merleau-Ponty's *Adventures of the Dialectic*, was at last translated into French in 1960. Karl Korsch's contemporaneous *Marxism and Philosophy* likewise emerged from oblivion courtesy of the *Arguments* series at Éditions de Minuit. Works by the Frankfurt-school thinker Herbert Marcuse began to appear in translation. Henri Lefebvre's *Dialectical Materialism* (1939), a product of the first encounter with the Paris *Manuscripts*, was reprinted in 1961 with a new foreword in

---

[69] Althusser 1969a, pp. 51–2. Althusser continues: 'So these good critics leave us with but a single choice: we must admit that *Capital* (and "mature Marxism" in general) is *either an expression of the Young Marx's philosophy, or its betrayal*. In either case, the established interpretation must be totally revised and we must return to the Young Marx, the Marx through whom spoke the Truth.' Althusser's reference to theologians was in earnest; see especially Calvez 1956.
[70] See Althusser 1969a, pp. 83–4.
[71] Althusser 1969a, p. 159.

which the author asserted that amid the dissolution of 'dogmatism' Marx's early writings became 'of the first importance'.[72] Of new works, Lucien Goldmann's *The Hidden God* had appeared in 1956; Sartre's *Search for a Method* and the monumental study it prefaced, *Critique of Dialectical Reason*, at the beginning of the decade. Not to be outdone by non- or ex-Communists, Garaudy contributed *Humanisme marxiste* in 1957 and *Perspectives de l'homme* two years later.

Rather than welcoming these developments, Althusser adduced them – or their analogues – as evidence of the deleterious effects of Khrushchev's critique. Flowers might be blooming and schools contending – but they were so many signs of the revisionist times. Surveying the field of Marxist theory in the early 1960s, Althusser delineated two main paradigms (though with many variations on the themes): what he called 'economism' and 'humanism/ historicism'. The former, he contended, represented a Marxist version of technological determinism, the latter a species of Hegelianism. Both derived in the final analysis from ideologies which Marx had transformed in order to produce the science of historical materialism – English political economy and German idealist philosophy – and both led, by however devious a route, to another (and this was the political rub): utopian socialism. Althusser's conviction was that, irrespective of their intentions, they were alike pseudo- and ultimately anti-Marxist. Neglecting the potentially critical effects of humanist Marxism on Stalinism, ignoring the humanist critique of those who left the Communist parties in 1956 but still remained Marxists, and attending to what he (and they)[73] regarded as the Stalinism with a human face of Garaudy et al., Althusser failed to engage in any depth with the humanist recasting of Marxism. Because the emperor's new clothes were socialist-humanist, Althusser perfunctorily consigned all such theoretical positions to the camp of the right-wing critique of Stalinism, regardless of their actual stance towards the Kremlin (or Place du Colonel Fabien). Whatever the danger of a turn to the right within socialist humanism after 1956, as opposed to an opening to the left – and the danger was not merely the figment of a Stalinist imagination[74] – such an eventuality was by no means inevitable.

---

[72] Lefebvre 1970, p. 19.
[73] Cf. Thompson 1978, p. 405.
[74] See Anderson 1980, pp. 108–9.

In his monitoring of Marxism, Athusser thus failed to relate to the conjuncture *en connaissance de cause*. Yet it must be reiterated that his political suspicion of, and consequent animosity towards, such doctrines emanated from their confiscation and instrumentalisation by the Communist parties. Having missed the moment of 1956, Althusser was confronted in the early 1960s by something approaching a transvaluation of values. Oblivious of the extent to which 'Marxism-Leninism' (talisman of CPC and CPSU alike) was itself part of Stalin's legacy to the Communist movement, he raised its banner, castigating the heresy he saw all around him – except in a Peking impervious to the blandishments of Marxist humanism. Socialist humanism was now being exploited by the Communist parties in their ideological struggle with 'barracks (i.e. Chinese) communism'. In the Manichean world of 'theoretical practice', there was science and there was ideology. Marxism was the former; socialist humanism, with its counter-position of the young Marx to Stalin and systematic neglect of Lenin, the latter. The pervasive siren song of *bien pensant* humanism was not for Althusser. It represented, on the contrary, the main contemporary enemy. For such 'revisionism' was the source of reformism and only 'orthodoxy' could effect a return to revolutionary rectitude.

According to Althusser's theoretical typology, humanism and historicism constituted a 'return to Hegel' by Marxist intellectuals when Marx had done hard theoretical labour to break with Hegel and the entire 'German ideology'. As paradigms, they negated what he called the 'epistemological break' which separated the science of history from any and every speculative philosophy of history. Humanism was precisely the specious theoretical formation with which Marx and Engels had decisively begun to part company in *The German Ideology* in 1845. Its modern protagonists were consequently engaged not simply in an inaccurate exercise in Marxology, but in an erasure of the distinction between Marxism-as-science and Marxism-as-ideology, between Marx himself and his own ideological past, between *Capital* (the Marx that mattered) and the early works (most seductive of all the mirages in the post-Stalin theoretical desert). Above and beyond their accuracy as scholarly theses, Althusser's perspectives had these implications: that the truth of Marxism was not to be attenuated by any kind of pragmatism; that to be 'for Marx' was to be for the pre-eminence and scientificity of his mature theory, historical materialism; that to deny or distort the scientific status of that theory was to oppose progress in Marxism – in theory and in politics. Althusser's 'essential thesis', the guiding principle of his whole intervention, was that Marx had 'founded a new science, the science of History'.[75]

Preparatory to any rearticulation of the scientificity of Marxism was a critique of the 57 varieties of alleged impostor now occupying centre-stage. One would expect at the minimum an extended discussion by Althusser of Sartre's attempt to rejuvenate Marxism as the 'philosophy of our time'.[76] As it is, one of the most salient features of his writing in this – and subsequent – periods is their lack of detailed attention to other contemporary versions of Marxism. Whilst this may be a structural trait of the Western-Marxist tradition,[77] it is particularly reprehensible in his case since he was conversant with (among others) Sartre, Lefebvre and Politzer on the national stage, and Lukács, Korsch, Gramsci, Della Volpe and Colletti on the international scene.[78] Also to be regretted, yet underscored, is the mode of Althusser's critique of these writers. Despite elements of a historical and comparative analysis, all too often he essayed a reading in which authors, despite the enormous differences between them, are distributed to common 'problematics' and for which the location of a putatively non-Marxist element is sufficient to disqualify their claims (sometimes even to be a Marxist). What, briefly, was the underlying logic of Althusser's Marxism of Marxism?

Both 'economism' and 'Hegelianism' had a long history. For the Second International, the ontological version of dialectical materialism extracted from Hegel's *Logic* by Engels, and of which historical materialism was in effect merely a sub-set, acted as a guarantor of the inevitability of socialist revolution. The auto-development of the economic base, motored by the contradiction between socialised forces of production and restrictive relations of production (private property), would terminate the crisis-ridden capitalist system. 'Natural necessity' and the 'guarantees of history' thus exonerated the reformist strategy of, for example, the German SPD. After the 'great betrayal' of 1914 and the

---

[75] Althusser 1976a, p. 151.
[76] Sartre 1968, p. 30.
[77] See Anderson 1976, pp. 69–70.
[78] In Althusser and Balibar 1970, p. 77, Althusser also cites the Austro–Marxists (whom he cursorily dismisses, however) and the Russian Marxists Rosenthal and Ilyenkov, alongside such classical figures as Lenin and Plekhanov. Elsewhere (Althusser and Balibar 1970, p. 13), even Trotsky gets a mention – in the company of Engels, Kautsky, Lenin, Luxemburg and Stalin – as a reader of *Capital*.

Russian Revolution of 1917 (that 'revolution against *Capital*' *à la* Kautsky and Plekhanov),[79] a new generation of Marxist philosophers (the founders of 'Western Marxism') had sought to rescue Marxist theory, compromised by its association with imperialist carnage, vindicated by revolution in a 'backward' country, by an anti-naturalist reaction against Second-International orthodoxy. In the case of Korsch and Lukács at least, this further involved rejection of the supposedly debilitating philosophical legacy of the late Engels. The redemption of Marxist theory – namely, its rediscovery of its revolutionary vocation – was to be achieved by reinterpreting Marxism as the 'supersession' of classical German philosophy. This amounted to converting Marxism into a close cousin of the Hegelianism of the young Hegelians, an anthropological version of Hegel's *Phenomenology*. For the 'poor man's Hegelianism'[80] – economic evolutionism – which was official Marxism, they substituted the richer fare of the young Marx. Lined up against the Hegel of the *Logic* and the Marx of *Capital* were the younger Hegel of Jena and the young Marx of Paris. The proletariat, Lukács avowed in 1919, 'is the sole legitimate heir to [classical German] philosophy and . . . *its true executor*'.[81]

In this perspective, theoretical Stalinism was, as Althusser later put it, a kind of '*posthumous revenge of the Second International*'.[82] Hostile to Marx's early works, it liquidated the overtly Hegelian heritage from Marxism and reimposed a mechanical materialism of the productive forces as unquestionable orthodoxy within the international Communist movement. From 1938 onwards, this version of Marxism was enshrined in Stalin's *Dialectical and Historical Materialism*, which was to serve as a catechism for all Communists. Therewith, Sartre reflected twenty years later, Marxism 'had come to a stop'.[83]

If this spurious and sclerotic doctrine was what counted as Marxist theory, it seemed an obvious and beneficial move to many Marxist intellectuals after Stalin's death to go back to the beginning, to the young Marx, to pose once more the question of Marx's relation to Hegel in the light of the newly available early works, to search for a Marxism shorn of its Cold-War rigidities. The

---

[79] See Gramsci's December 1917 article of that title in Gramsci 1977, pp. 34–7.
[80] Althusser 1971, p. 89.
[81] Lukács 1972, p. 17.
[82] Althusser 1976a, p. 89.
[83] Sartre 1968, p. 21.

renewal of Marxism after a quarter of a century's virtual stagnation demanded drastic surgery. Redemption from Stalinised Marxism seemed to require one or all of: revocation of any 'scientistic' pretensions to scientificity; positive re-evaluation of the young Marx; recasting of the whole of Marx's œuvre along the lines of the early works, or, alternatively, demotion of almost everything after the *Communist Manifesto*. At the very least, Engels had to go. In general, one can say that, where the 1859 Preface had been, there the 1844 *Manuscripts* would be. Where once the centre-piece of Marxism had been the productive forces, now it was to be alienation, reification and cognate themes. This philosophical strategy was accelerated by Khrushchev's critique of Stalinism's inhumanity and the subsequent cultural thaw. 'The thaw of the ice-cap,' writes Eric Hobsbawm, 'watered the numerous plants of heterodoxy, schism or mere unofficial growth which had survived on the margin of, or under, the giant glacier.'[84] By the early 1960s, the disposition of forces was clear: the young Marx against Stalin.

The irony of theoretical history, according to Althusser, was that the Kautskyist-Stalinist rendition of Marxism and its intended rectification – the Hegelian – were, in their conceptual structures at least, mirror images.[85] Briefly put, Althusser argued that, in the Hegelian scheme of things, history is a process with a subject – Man or the Working Class – and an end – communism. History is the journey of this subject (and its *praxis*) through the triadic, teleological structures of the Hegelian dialectic (or *marxisant* variation thereon), from original unity via self-estrangement to the eventual reappropriation of, and reconciliation with, the alienated human essence. Human liberation is the realisation of a potential present at the origin. Economic evolutionism exhibits an analogous teleological structure, but with the productive forces occupying the central position and the 'negation of the negation' and/or the 'transformation of quantity into quality' securing the transition from one mode of production to another, superior mode via the intermediary of the class struggle. In this schema, history is no longer the odyssey of humanity, but an epic of the productive forces – the linear progression in strict order of modes of production, wherein the potential of the productive forces developed

---

[84] Hobsbawm 1982, p. 142.
[85] See, for example, Althusser 1969a, pp. 107–8 and Althusser and Balibar 1970, pp. 138–9.

by humanity is realised in the course of historical time within the integument of corresponding social forms. Communism is the appointed destination of history – the realm of material abundance and collective appropriation vouchsafed Man by the forward march of the productive forces, from primitive communism via class society to communism.

It was the isomorphism of these otherwise quite distinct conceptions of historical materialism that supposedly facilitated their amalgamation. Each paradigm had had two moments. A crude economism and evolutionism were common to Kautskyism (the Second International before the First World War) and Stalinism (the Third International after Lenin) alike. The second current – the reversion to 'Hegelianism' – had been the route out of 'positivism' for the Western-Marxist tradition and from Stalinist dogmatism for the class of 1956. There is, however, an important nuance to Althusser's position. Whereas the Hegelian Marxism of those whom he categorised as 'theoretical leftists' (Lukács, Korsch, Gramsci) had erred in a commendable *political* direction, its resurrection under any guise was retrograde – a 'rightist' phenomenon.[86] Whatever, neither schema – economism or historicism/humanism – offered a viable basis for scrupulous scientific analysis of the real world, for an investigation and explanation of the complexities of concrete socio-historical processes – a theoretical demerit with practical, political implications.

Althusser's typology borders on travesty, assimilating as it does disparate figures in Western Marxism – Lukács, Korsch and Gramsci, Sartre and Goldmann, Della Volpe and Colletti – to a single problematic of historicism, derived from Hegel, reworked by Feuerbach and the young Marx, superseded in *Capital*, wherein Marx had criticised those errors of his youth to which his posterity had reverted. Indeed, Althusser's panorama of the contemporary scene bears a strong resemblance to the 'expressive totality' he reprehended in the leading representatives of West-European Marxism. Since one result of this is to obscure the novelty – and merits – of his own Marxism in relation to theirs, a few observations – inevitably cursory and simplistic – on the balance-sheet of the great Western-Marxist tradition at the point of Althusser's intervention are called for.

---

[86] See Althusser and Balibar 1970, pp. 119–20 and cf. Hobsbawm 1982, p. 145. See also Dollé 1966.

Western Marxism originated in, and was reproduced by, a 'basic historical impasse'[87] consequent upon the uniform pattern of revolutionary politics in Central and Western Europe after the First World War: defeat. Very schematically, in this complex history four main moments can be identified. The first is the initiation of the tradition by Lukács, Korsch and Gramsci in the 1920s. Here, it is perhaps legitimate to speak of an 'Hegelian Marxism' (and not solely because all three attested to Hegel's centrality). In any event, contesting the Engelsian legacy, their enterprises shared two basic features: (i) in opposition to positivism, a historicism whereby Marxism was conceived not as an (analytical) science on the naturalist model, but rather as a revolutionary (dialectical) ideology expressive of the proletariat's *Weltanschauung*; and (ii) in opposition to 'objectivism', a humanism wherein humanity's creative role in the practical constitution and transformation of the world was enhanced at the expense of economic determinism. The achievements of the founders were not of the same magnitude. Lukács's conjugation, in *History and Class Consciousness*, of Hegelianism and neo-Kantianism with the young Marx's problematic reinstated aspects of Marx's thought repressed in official doctrine – above all, the theories of commodity fetishism and alienation. Yet, for all that it was a brilliant anticipation of the as yet unpublished *Economic and Philosophical Manuscripts*, it ultimately summed up to a romantic anti-capitalism and anti-scientism, as politically voluntarist as it was philosophically speculative. By contrast, Gramsci's disdain for the 'imbecile complacency' of economic evolutionism and reconceptualisation of Marxism as the 'philosophy of *praxis*', although informed by Crocean idealism, did not inhibit either highly significant, empirically substantiated conceptual departures (especially the theory of hegemony) or enormously suggestive concrete analyses of both past and present.[88]

---

[87] Anderson 1976, p. 80. For scholarly work on the subject of Western Marxism, readers are referred to Anderson 1976; Jameson 1974; Jay 1984; and *New Left Review* (ed.) 1977.

[88] It is worth remarking here that prior to his discussion of Gramsci in *Reading 'Capital'*, Althusser, describing the Italian Communist's œuvre as 'this enormously delicate and subtle work of genius', expressed his fear that 'the reader may be drawn against my will to extend to Gramsci's fruitful discoveries in the field of *historical materialism*, the theoretical reservations I want to formulate with respect only to his interpretation of *dialectical materialism*': Althusser and Balibar 1970, p. 126.

Called to order by the Comintern, Lukács disavowed his work, mainly concentrating on the development of a Marxist theory of literature for the duration of the Stalinist freeze. Gramsci, meanwhile, fell victim not to the degeneration of the revolution in the East, but to fascist counterrevolution in the West. The second major episode in Western Marxism – not so much as alluded to by Althusser – bears the impress of this dark historical moment: the consolidation of Stalinism and the triumph of Nazism. Convinced that orthodox Marxism was incapable of explaining these disasters, the key figures of the Frankfurt school – Adorno, Horkheimer and Marcuse – elaborated what can be loosely referred to as 'critical theory'. Capitalism having undergone fundamental alteration in the intervening years, Marx's nineteenth-century doctrine was no longer adequate for the analysis of modern history. A critique of advanced capitalist society geared to the prospect of human emancipation had, perforce, to draw on other theoretical traditions, whether philosophical (such as Kant and Hegel), sociological (for example, Weber), or psychoanalytical (Freud). And its main focus was to shift from political economy to what, for classical Marxism, were 'superstructural' phenomena – in particular, cultural forms and the ideologies underpinning and legitimating oppressive social relations. Among the positive aspects of this mutation in Marxism up to the early 1960s was an unparalleled flowering of aesthetics. Its negative features were also pronounced, however. If anything accentuating Lukácsian antipathies, the Frankfurt school tended to a quietism and/or pessimism in the face of a totalitarian capitalism pervaded by the 'instrumental rationality' characteristic of the natural sciences and the 'mass deception' practised (successfully) by the 'culture industry'. For what Adorno and his colleagues precisely lacked, of course, was their Hungarian predecessor's confidence in the proletariat as a potential agent of revolutionary redemption. Perceiving no substitute for it, critical theory did indeed 'remain negative', persisting with the 'Great Refusal' from a philosophical standpoint of whose practical realisation it despaired.[89]

---

[89] See the conclusion to Marcuse 1964, p. 257. Adorno's philosophical masterpiece, *Negative Dialectics*, was published in 1966. The ambitious reconstruction of Frankfurt Marxism undertaken by Jürgen Habermas likewise largely postdates Althusser's principal work.

Exile in America and residence in the Federal Republic of Germany were perhaps hardly conducive to anything other than such pessimism of the intelligence and will. In France, on the other hand, a strong Communist tradition had survived the War unbroken, thereafter buttressing a politically engaged independent Marxism critical of it. It was here that the next chapter in Western-Marxist history was written: the attempted synthesis of Marxism and existentialism primarily associated with Sartre. Prior to the War, Communists such as Henri Lefebvre and Auguste Cornu had begun to remedy the shallowness of Gallic Marxist culture. Lefebvre's initiative, however, issued in a humanist recasting of Marxism which was already suspect in the PCF in the 1930s. With Nizan dead at Dunkirk, Politzer murdered by the Nazis, Lefebvre effectively neutralised, and Zhdanovism domesticated, creative Marxist work in the postwar years migrated to the existentialist milieu operating on the PCF's left flank. Philosophically of Heideggerian and Husserlian formation, Sartre and his colleagues' transition to Marxism was mediated by Kojève's influential interpretation of Hegel. For them, *Capital* was not only the culmination of the Paris *Manuscripts*, but 'a concrete *Phenomenology of Mind* . . . inseparably concerned with the working of the economy and the realization of man'.[90]

The eventual landmark of the projected Marxist-existentialist synthesis was to be Sartre's *Critique of Dialectical Reason*, an implicit response to the Merleau-Pontyan challenge in which he sought to furnish the '*living Marxism*' he had earlier invoked against Communist doctrine.[91] A product of the history it sought to render intelligible, Marxism was the 'untranscendable philosophy of our time' and dialectical reason the 'ideology of the rising class'.[92] Under Stalinism, however, theory and practice had been sundered, the latter degenerating into pragmatism, the former into dogmatism.[93] Thus, there was a link between the fate of the Russian Revolution, the current impasse of the Western Communist parties, and the sclerosis of Marxist theory. Theoretical Stalinism was condemned on two main scores: for its economic-determinist account of the historical process, which negated the specificity of human

---

[90] Merleau-Ponty 1969, p. 101.
[91] Sartre 1965, pp. 117–18.
[92] Sartre 1976, pp. 25, 882.
[93] See Sartre 1968, pp. 21–2.

history, suppressing its complexity and the role of creative human agency therein; and for its conception of Marxism as a natural science, which betrayed its dialectical particularity, severing theory from lived experience. If Stalin had carried this to the point of paroxysm, Engels's dialectic of nature, projected onto history, was the source of the theoretical debacle. Therefore it was not simply a matter of clearing away the Stalinist detritus in order to recover pure Marxism. Since there was ample warrant for such constructions, Marxism had to be reconstructed as a theory of human self-emancipation in which its 'first truth' – that 'men make history' – was restored to it.[94]

The details of this remarkable endeavour cannot detain us here. But the outcome of Sartre's intricate analysis of the 'elementary formal structures' of any possible history – the transhistorical mechanisms underlying the formation and transformation of 'practical ensembles' (human groups) – might roughly be summarised thus. The *Critique*'s problematic of the dialectic of *praxis* and scarcity establishes the open-endedness of the historical process, denying the ineluctability of socialism, and provides a fertile set of categories for the investigation of state, class and party – hence of the history made in Marxism's name. Yet, despite the historicisation of the concepts of *Being and Nothingness* it essays, the *Critique* remains imprisoned in an ontology of mind and matter, self and other, history and nature, whereby alienation is effectively equated with social structure, Marxism subsumed into existentialism, communism precluded by the inexorable logic of scarcity. Accordingly, it is the less surprising that the promised second volume, which was to ascend from the abstract to the concrete, was abandoned. For the Sartrean attempt to found the 'intelligibility of history' on individual *praxis* had precisely the opposite effect, rendering it unintelligible – unless, that is, resort was made to an illegitimate device: totalisation with a totaliser.[95]

Sartre's work was written against the backdrop of sanguinary counter-insurgency in Algeria and the rise of the Right at home – a conjuncture of political emergency in which his dismay at the PCF's ghettoisation found powerful expression. Like other French Marxist intellectuals, he would contrast with its stasis the relative dynamism of an Italian Communism now

---

[94] Sartre 1985, p. 316.
[95] See Anderson 1980, pp. 51–3.

appropriating the Gramscian legacy in support of its strategy for a national road to socialism. The fourth main current in Western Marxism – the Della Volpean school inside the PCI – went against the grain of its party's orthodoxy. Galvano Della Volpe and his disciples (in the front rank, Colletti and Pietranera) were uncompromisingly anti-Hegelian, emphatically reasserting the complete rupture between Marx's œuvre and Hegelian philosophy, the scientificity of Marxism, the paramountcy of *Capital*. Moreover, they made no secret of their sympathy for Lenin's political positions and philosophical thought. In the charter of this vindication of the classical tradition – *Logic as a Positive Science* (1950) – Della Volpe sought to cast historical materialism as a '*moral Galileanism*', a scientific materialist sociology based upon the young Marx's critique of Hegel's '*delirium logicum*' and graduation from 'hypostasis to hypothesis, from *a priori* assertions to experimental forecasts'.[96] Whatever its author's temperament, at the hands of his followers Della Volpe's epistemological meditation was not lacking in political implications inconsistent with the PCI's cautious perspectives on Italian state and society – as the controversies of the late 1950s and early 1960s were to demonstrate.[97] But, to restrict ourselves to the theoretical level, three conclusions on the record of this professedly scientific Marxism by the mid-1960s (namely, prior to Colletti's major work) suggest themselves. Meticulous readers of the Marxist canon, the Della Volpeans offered no major additions to, or modifications of, the corpus – satisfied, in the first instance, to reclaim it from contemporary distortion or revision. Next, the account of the hypothetico-deductive modality of social science, however sophisticated compared with 'Communist orthodoxy and commendable in a hitherto tenaciously anti-scientific Western tradition, was naturalist in the extreme. Finally, an undifferentiated concept of science was complemented by a continuist conception of its history, yielding, for example, an undiscriminating view of Marx's thought as a linear progression from the early works to *Capital*.

Althusser was to refer to Della Volpe as having 'set out on the same path' as him and in 1965 noted the similarities and differences between their respective enterprises.[98] Althusserian and Della Volpean Marxism both

[96] Della Volpe 1980, pp. 127, 198.
[97] See Anderson 1976, pp. 41–2.
[98] See Althusser 1976a, p. 173; Althusser 1969a, pp. 37–8, 165 n. 4; and Althusser

represented *counter-idealist* trends in Western Marxism, at once irreconcilably hostile to Hegelianism and vehemently affirmative of Marxism's scientific status. Yet they were nevertheless distinct. Locating Marx's rupture with Hegel virtually at the outset of his career (in the Introduction to the *Contribution to the Critique of Hegel's Philosophy of Right* [1843]), Della Volpe et al. accepted the Marxist credentials of the early works – with serious historicist consequences, so Althusser suggested, for their interpretation of Marx's science and philosophy.[99]

What, then, was the *differentia specifica* of Althusser's project within Western Marxism? Over and above his repudiation of Hegel and the young Marx and endorsement, in their place, of the mature Marx, Lenin and Mao, it might approximately be defined as follows. According to Althusser, with the exception of the Della Volpeans, the various schools of Western Marxism negated 'what is specific to the sciences: the production of objective knowledge'.[100] They did so in their different ways: either by treating the natural sciences as bourgeois, and Marxism as proletarian, science; or by sharply distinguishing the natural from the human and social sciences. In each case, however, the result was the same: relativism and hence a 'relativisation' of historical materialism and consequent attenuation of its scientificity. *Contra* the anti-naturalist currents, the natural sciences were cognitively autonomous sciences independent of class subjects and there existed no distinction between them and social science (Marxism for Althusser) in terms of the relative dignity of their results: objective knowledge of their respective objects. Thus, historical materialism, the science of social formations and their transformation, was a science 'among others'. But *contra* the Della Volpean current, the 'unity of scientificity'[101] was of an epistemological – not a methodological – character. So, if Althusserianism was not unique in campaigning against the misconception of science majoritarian in Western Marxism, it was distinguished by its particular anti-

---

and Balibar 1970, pp. 47, 77, 86, 115–16, 135–6, 137 n., and 139. It should be said that neither Della Volpe nor Colletti reciprocated Althusser's high estimation: see, for example, Colletti 1977, pp. 332–4.

[99] In Althusser and Balibar 1970, p. 135, Althusser even conflates Colletti with Gramsci as an exponent of 'absolute historicism' – a confusion which he later confessed to be such (see Althusser 1968a).

[100] See Althusser 1968a.

[101] Althusser 1964c, p. 29.

empiricist conception of the sciences – as opposed to the notion of general scientific method to which, in the Della Volpean set-up, the sciences must conform to merit the stamp of scientificity. In other words, whilst the anti-naturalists compromised the scientificity of Marxism in the act of vindicating its autonomy, the Italian naturalists compromised its autonomy in the act of vindicating its scientificity – rendering it conformable to a misconceived, neo-positivist model of the natural sciences.[102] For Althusser, by contrast, historical materialism was both scientific and autonomous, governed, like the natural sciences, solely by the exigencies of the pursuit of objective knowledge, yet possessing its own theory, method and object. Western Marxism had originated in an impasse: Althusser's singularity within it was that he sought to break the impasse – to put substance back into the revolutionary project in the West – via a revindication of scientific Marxism from its positivist parody or misrepresentation by both orthodoxy and heterodoxy. Kautskyism or Stalinism were not the inevitable price to be paid for historical materialism being genuinely scientific. Althusser concurred with Sartre's judgement that 'the Marxist universe [was] full of deserts and unexplored lands',[103] but differed on the means of remedying this situation. Theoretical de-Stalinisation must not surrender the critical instrument potentially capable of reanimating revolutionary politics to its Stalinisation, but, on the contrary, reclaim and develop it.

Part, nonetheless, of the tradition he criticised, Althusser, as we shall see, also compromised historical materialism. He did so as a result of his assimilation into Marxism of the two intellectual traditions to which, by his own admission, he turned in an attempt to force an exit from the crisis of Marxism. The first of these was what he later described as 'a certain French materialist tradition of rationalism (that of Bachelard – Canguilhem . . .)'[104] – a tradition whose conventionalism and 'historical epistemology', it has been suggested, must ultimately be traced back to Auguste Comte.[105] And the second, in significant

---

[102] See the excellent discussion, on which I draw here, in Stedman Jones 1977, pp. 58–60.
[103] Sartre 1965, p. 112.
[104] Althusser 1978b, p. 10. Interestingly, Althusser specifies: 'above all, Canguilhem'.
[105] See Dews's outstanding 1994, p. 19. Althusser's references to Comte, though few and far between, are uniformly laudatory. Thus, in Althusser 1969a p. 25, he is described as 'the only mind worthy of interest' in French philosophy from the 1789 Revolution

respects compatible with a French epistemological tradition characterised by its prioritisation of theory over experience, was the rationalist philosophy of Spinoza, with its total differentiation between rational knowledge and 'opinion' or 'imagination' derived from random sense experience.[106] 'People always situate themselves in relation to someone,' Althusser confided to the Société française de philosophie in 1968, 'but my reference point would be neither Kant nor Hegel; it would be Spinoza.... I'm a Spinozist.'[107] The details of Althusser's affiliations, and their consequences for both his construction of a Marxist epistemology and his reconstruction of historical materialism, will occupy us later. But, for better or worse, it is they that determined the distinctive shape assumed by epistemological anti-empiricism and social-scientific anti-historicism, anti-humanism and anti-economism – which determined, in short, the specificity of Althusserian Marxism.

However unsatisfactory Althusser's treatment of his peers remains, we can now at least see something of its logic and thus understand why, for him, the end of dogmatism had not issued in the restoration of Marxism: the contemporary rediscovery and repetition of pre-Stalinist initiatives was a false trail. The current theoretical poverty of the PCF was, moreover, held to be compounded by a specifically '"French misery"': the stubborn, profound absence of any real *theoretical* culture in the history of the French workers' movement'.[108] Founded at a time when the influence of pre-Marxist ideologies on the French labour movement was still strong, the PCF had further suffered

---

down to the 1920s and in Althusser 1971, p. 34, as a 'great mind'; while in Althusser and Balibar 1970, he is credited with having 'often c[o]me very close' to the concept of scientific problematic. See also the remarks by Étienne Balibar in Althusser and Balibar 1970, pp. 205–6 n.; Althusser 1998b, pp. 163–4; and Lecourt 1975, p. 126. In Althusser 1968a, p. 24, Althusser accepted that his 'emphasis on the sciences' owed something to 'the "French cultural tradition": to its "Enlightenment"'. The precise Comtean connection here would make an interesting subject for further research.

[106] Althusser's discussion of his 'detour via Spinoza', intimated in *For Marx* and *Reading 'Capital'*, can be found in Althusser 1976a, pp. 132–41, 187–93. For documentation, see Anderson 1976, pp. 64–5.

[107] Althusser 1968b, p. 164.

[108] See Althusser 1969a, p. 23ff. Of course, Althusser's sweeping judgement does less than justice not only to Lefebvre, for example, but also to Desanti – neither of them philosophical nullities. And we might also note that independently of him other Communist intellectuals were taking advantage of the 'thaw' to explore *terra incognita* – for example, Maurice Godelier, whose work was cited respectfully in Althusser and Balibar 1970, p. 160 n. 36.

from 'the burden of a long century of official philosophical stupidity' in the national, 'provincialist' culture.[109] Born into a 'theoretical vacuum', the Party had produced no philosophical 'masters'.[110] Before it could, the 'dogmatist night' had descended. Indoctrination, not research, became the order of the day. Independent spirits were either marginalised (Lefebvre) or put to work in party schools (Politzer). With Zhdanovism, the *primacy of politics* that had always characterised the French Communist tradition – to the detriment of theory – reappeared in particularly aberrant form. Althusser's adherence to the PCF coincided with the pronouncement of the ultra-leftist line of the 'two sciences' which ushered in an era of 'theoretical monstrosity' – when psychoanalysis was a 'cosmopolitan', 'reactionary ideology', relativity theory relativist, 'epigones of bourgeois music' dangerous elements; and when Stalin, 'Great Father of the Peoples', doubled up as 'the highest scientific authority in the world'. In circumstances as inclement as these, a Marxist who was also trying to be a Marxist in philosophy could not even invoke the precedent of Marx and Engels in *The German Ideology* and abandon philosophy's abstract speculation for the concrete knowledge promised by the empirical science of history. Nor could he attempt to work out a version of the 'Logic' Marx had never written. During the 'long night of theory',[111] the only possible course for a Communist philosopher was to work within the parameters of 'diamat' as inflected by Stalin – while looking over his shoulder at the Control Commission. It was a time for automatic loyalty to the (oscillating) party line; the alternative was expulsion and denunciation. The PCF was second to none in the vigour with which it prosecuted the ideological Cold War – inside as well as outside the Party. (Thirty years later, Althusser recalled that there had been 'real "Moscow trials" right here in France'.[112])

---

[109] As we have seen, only Comte was exempted from Althusser's censure. In Althusser 1971, Durkheim was added to what can scarcely be called a list.

[110] In Althusser 1969a, p. 27, Althusser adjudges the great Germanist and historian of Marxism, Auguste Cornu, 'the only name fit for display beyond our frontiers'. Cornu's *magnum opus*, *Karl Marx et Friedrich Engels*, was unfinished at his death (see Cornu 1955–70).

[111] Anderson 1965, p. 222. It should be noted that in addition to loyally promoting Soviet fashions (Zhdanovism, Lysenkosim, etc.), the PCF's leadership was responsible in this era for some theoretical aberrations of its own – for example, Thorez's thesis of the 'absolute pauperization' of the proletariat in postwar France.

[112] Althusser 1978a, p. 39. See Claudin 1975, pp. 543–4 for some details and testimony. A minor example of the genre, never mentioned by him, apparently concerned Althusser

Althusser had to endure Stalin's 'implacable rule' over the PCF for only five years. That they, and this whole tempestuous period, left their mark is obvious to anyone who reads the 'autobiographical' pages with which *For Marx* opens. As the moving introduction, 'Today', indicates, 'Stalinist dogmatism' for Althusser meant above all this: the degeneration of Marxism into a set of 'Famous Quotations',[113] which party intellectuals were obliged, on pain of inquisition, to reproduce. 'What then counted as philosophy,' he wrote, 'could only choose between commentary and silence, between conviction, whether inspired or forced, and dumb embarrassment.'[114] Silence would appear to have been Althusser's course. When he broke it in the early 1960s, it was scarcely to perform the functions traditionally expected of its intellectuals by the PCF: justification of the Party's political line; illustration of the 'Marxist method' in their specialist domains; bestowal of prestige on the Party by their allegiance.[115] Althusser challenged the very definition of 'method'; he did not propagandise on behalf of 'the line'; he lent such prestige as he had to independent theoretical research. As Rancière points out, the very idea of a 'return to Marx' was suspect to his seniors, implying as it did a source of authority outside the Party (or rather its leadership).[116] And indeed, such a project signified not only a re-reading of Marx's œuvre, but a suspension of belief in the authorities (and patented intellectuals) who guarded the tablets on which successive orthodoxies were inscribed.

Extraordinary as it may seem, there is little doubt that Althusser traced many of the vicissitudes of Communism after Lenin to lacunae in, and infidelities to, Marxist theory.[117] (Absence of – or wrong – theory was the root

---

himself. In his memoirs the historian and former Communist, Emmanuel Le Roy Ladurie, relates that, during this period, he and others were ordered by high-ranking party officials to instruct Althusser to sever relations with his companion Hélène Rytman (who had already been expelled from the PCF under suspicion of Trotskyist sympathies). See Le Roy Ladurie 1982, pp. 76–7, where Althusser's 'great dignity' amidst 'intolerable ideological and moral pressure' is recalled.

[113] Althusser 1969a, p. 27.

[114] Althusser 1969a, p. 22. Althusser traces the pliancy of many Communist intellectuals (like himself) to the fact that 'the intellectuals of petty bourgeois origin who came to the Party at that time felt that they had to pay in pure activity, if not in political activism, the imaginary Debt they thought they had contracted *by not being proletarian*': Althusser 1969a, p. 27. Cf. Thompson 1978, pp. 405–6.

[115] See Rancière 1974, p. 74.

[116] Rancière 1974, p. 73.

[117] See, for instance, Althusser 1969a, pp. 168–9.

of evils.) Against humanist Marxism, Althusser insisted that Marx and Engels's worthy ambition had been to found a *scientific socialism* – one that superseded its utopian predecessors or contemporaries by its attention to preconditions, means, and goals. 'Marxists know,' he concluded 'Marxism and Humanism', 'that there can be no tactics that do not depend on a strategy – and no strategy that does not depend on theory.'[118] Addressing 'burning questions of our movement' in 1902, Lenin had asserted that '[w]ithout revolutionary theory there can be no revolutionary movement'. Citing Lenin approvingly, Althusser added that the theory in question was historical materialism, 'the Marxist science of the development of social formations'.[119] In principle, possession of it distinguished the Communist parties, vanguards of their respective proletariats, from their social-democratic rivals. The problem, sixty years on from Lenin's injunction, was that Marxist theory had scarcely developed since him, largely owing to:

> the conditions in which the international working-class movement was enmeshed by the politics of the 'cult' [of personality], by its countless victims in the ranks of very valuable militants, intellectuals and scientists, by the ravages inflicted by dogmatism on the intellect. . . . [F]or many years, [it] literally sacrifice[d] and block[ed] all development of Marxist-Leninist theory. . . .[120]

The great opportunity afforded by Khrushchev's 'liberalisation' was that it had introduced 'a real freedom of investigation' which must not be squandered. It was being squandered. But if the new era had not 'restored Marxist philosophy to us in its integrity', there was an additional reason:

> The end of dogmatism puts us face to face with this reality: that Marxist philosophy . . . has still largely to be constituted . . . ; that the theoretical difficulties we debated in the dogmatist night were not completely artificial – rather they were largely the result of a meagrely elaborated Marxist philosophy; or better, that in the rigid caricatural forms we suffered or maintained, including the theoretical monstrosity of the two sciences,

---

[118] Althusser 1969a, p. 241.
[119] See Lenin 1961a, p. 369 and Althusser 1969a, p. 168. See also Althusser 1990, p. 4.
[120] Althusser 1990, p. 21.

> something of an unsettled problem was really present in grotesque and
> blind forms . . .; and finally, that our lot and our duty today is quite simply
> to pose and confront these problems in the light of day, if Marxist philosophy
> is to acquire some real existence or achieve a little theoretical consistency.[121]

Reminiscence of Marx's philosophy was impossible, since he had never
elaborated the Marxist philosophy or epistemology initiated with the foundation
of historical materialism, and which rendered apodictic the veridical nature
of that theoretical discourse. He had not produced the 'Logic'[122] which has
preoccupied Marxist philosophers ever since. His reflections in the Postface
to the second edition of *Capital* were problematic and Engels's late works no
substitute. If Leninism had to be extricated from Stalinism, Marx had to be
retrieved from (some of) Engels. So Althusser could not simply lay hold of
the authentic Marxist 'Discourse on Method', employ it as a touchstone, and
condemn other Marxists for infidelity to its principles. Eighty years after the
death of Marx, his followers were confronted by '*the* essential *question*,
irresistibly drawn from us even by our trials, failures and impotence: What
is Marxist philosophy? Has it any theoretical right to existence? And if it does exist
in principle, how can its specificity be defined?'[123] What was to be done?

Althusser's programme in *For Marx* and *Reading 'Capital'* was two-fold: to
construct an authentically – non-empiricist – Marxist philosophy (in accordance
with tradition, 'dialectical materialism') and to reconstruct Marxist science
('historical materialism') in non-economistic, non-humanist and non-historicist
form. The provision of a philosophy was the prime desideratum, because it
could prevent a repetition of the Zhdanovist delirium; it would act as a
bulwark against other kinds of theoretical pragmatism; and it would provide
an epistemological foundation and guarantee for historical materialism, thus
defending it against the enemy within and without the gates. If there were
difficulties in the path of this programme, there were also resources. For, as
Lenin had discovered, Marx had bequeathed the 'logic of *Capital*'.[124] Marxist
philosophy, the underwriter of Marxist science and its development, was
present in the 'practical state' in Marx's great scientific work (his science was,

---

[121] Althusser 1969a, pp. 30–1.
[122] See Marx's letter to Engels of 14 January 1858, in Marx and Engels 1975, p. 93.
[123] Althusser 1969a, p. 31.
[124] Lenin 1961b, p. 319.

as it were, epistemology in action). But it had to be extracted and cast in rigorous theoretical form, rendered explicit so that the development of historical materialism proceeded along the right lines. Mission accomplished, dialectical materialism would verify the scientificity of historical materialism, superintend extensions of it, and represent it thereafter in the theoretical *Kampfplatz*. The available theoretical resources were to be supplemented by the 'practical works' of Marxism – for example, the Russian and Chinese Revolutions – which also contained latent theoretical elements available for extraction. Since Marxist political practice was potentially in advance of theory, this operation was an urgent task.[125] Marxist science and politics alike represented 'a theoretical revolution in action';[126] for the sake of that science and those politics, Marxist philosophy must become contemporary with them.

The French ideology

Althusser's 'return to Marx', he reflected a decade later,

> did have something original about it . . . in the fact that it criticized dogmatism not from the right-wing positions of humanist ideology, but from the left-wing positions of theoretical anti-humanism, anti-empiricism and anti-economism. . . . We were attempting to give back to Marxist theory, which had been treated by dogmatism and by Marxist humanism as the first available ideology, something of its status as a theory, a revolutionary theory.[127]

Althusser's theoretical predilections may have gone against the grain of contemporary French Marxism, but they were in conformity with the national philosophical culture. For, in France at the turn of the 1950s, the sun of Hegelian Marxism was no sooner rising than it was setting. Althusser was only one of a generation of intellectuals in that epoch 'trying to escape

---

[125] See Althusser 1969a, pp. 161–218. For a summary of the 'difficulties and resources' of contemporary Marxist theoretical work, see Althusser 1990, pp. 43–67. In Althusser and Balibar 1970, p. 34 n. 14, Althusser refers to 'the "reading" of those new works of Marxism which . . . contain in them something essential to the future of Marxism: what Marxism is producing in the vanguard countries of the "third world" which is struggling for its freedom, from the guerrillas of Vietnam to Cuba.'

[126] Althusser 1969a, p. 173.

[127] Ibid.

Hegel'[128] – in his case, paradoxically, via Marx. At the very moment when Marxists were rediscovering the young Marx and re-evaluating his Hegelian roots, a major transition in French philosophy was in progress: the passage from 'phenomenology' to 'structuralism' – more broadly, from the legacy of the 'three H's' (Hegel, Husserl, Heidegger) to that of the three 'masters of suspicion' (Marx, Nietzsche, Freud).[129]

The astonishing rise to paramountcy of structuralism can be dated from the second half of the 1950s. In 1957, Roland Barthes's virtuoso *Mythologies* appeared, annexing everything from soap-powder to steak and chips, from Garbo's face to Einstein's brain, to the domain of semiology. More important philosophically was the publication the following year of Claude Lévi-Strauss's collection of essays, *Structural Anthropology*. In it, taking his cue from a remark of Saussure's, he conjectured that all social practices were symbolic and hence susceptible to semiotic treatment.[130] If remodelled along the lines of Saussure and Troubetzkoy's revolutions in linguistics, the social and human sciences could cross the threshold of scientificity. What Lévi-Strauss did for anthropology and the study of myths, others attempted for literature (Barthes), cinema (Christian Metz), fashion (Barthes again), and so on. In his *Elements of Semiology* (1964), Barthes noted 'a kind of demand'[131] for the new doctrine: he and his colleagues sought to assuage it. The philosopher's stone of the human sciences – long in quest of scientific status – had apparently been discovered. In reality, the French ideology had been born.

The challenge to pre- or post-Stalinist constructions of historical materialism implicit in the new paradigm became explicit with Lévi-Strauss's *The Savage Mind*. Its final chapter, 'History and Dialectic', launched a frontal attack on Sartre's *Critique of Dialectical Reason* and its proposal for a 'concrete anthropology'. 'Marxism ought to study real men in depth, not dissolve them in a bath of sulphuric acid', Sartre had written in *Search for a Method*.[132] 'I believe the ultimate goal of the human sciences to be not to constitute, but to dissolve man', retorted Lévi-Strauss (who nevertheless described Marxism

---

[128] Foucault 1971, p. 74.
[129] Descombes 1981, p. 3. The phrase 'masters of suspicion' is likewise Foucault's and dates from 1964.
[130] See Lévi-Strauss 1977, e.g. pp. 58–9 and Saussure 1981, p. 16.
[131] Barthes 1978, p. 9.
[132] Sartre 1968, pp. 43–4.

as his 'point of departure').[133] Sartre, he argued, had remained a Cartesian, commencing with, and for ever after being ensnared by, the actor's conscious project. He had eluded cultural and historical relativism only by illegitimately interpreting past forms from the standpoint of the Western present, thus erasing real historical discontinuity in a spurious continuity. Sartre's anthropocentric history and subjectivist epistemology were alike ideological – the former a modern myth, the latter a perennial illusion. Ethnocentric dialectical reason and contingent historical diachrony were inimical to scientificity. Thus, Sartre had discovered in historicity 'the last refuge of a transcendental humanism'.[134] The problem of the relations between structure(s) and subject(s), which had preoccupied (and divided) Sartre and Merleau-Ponty, demanded a scientific not a philosophical answer. Structural anthropology, considered by Lévi-Strauss at least to be a 'hard' science, was the requisite research programme ('structural thought now defends the cause of materialism', he would claim two years later in the 'Overture' to his masterpiece *Mythologiques*).[135] History, all too dependent on human subjectivity and vitiated by (Eurocentric) evolutionism, was its epistemological antithesis.

While Lévi-Strauss sought to 'escape Hegel' via Saussure, the same year, in a portent of the future, Gilles Deleuze made the identical bid via Nietzsche. His *Nietzsche and Philosophy* impugned dialectical thought of any Hegelian inspiration or affiliation. The hero of Michel Foucault's 'structuralist' *The Order of Things*, written contemporaneously with *Reading 'Capital'* but published the following year, was likewise Nietzsche. He it was who 'burned for us, even before we were born, the intermingled promises of the dialectic and anthropology', offering – 'as both promise and task' – 'the death of man', Foucault announced in the course of a critique of the historicist 'episteme' to which he allocated Marxism.[136]

'Humanism' and 'historicism' were thus under attack from many sides. Whether in the name of the Swiss linguist or the German philosopher, they were being invited to vacate the privileged position they had allegedly hitherto occupied in Western thought. Historical materialism, identified with them

---

[133] Lévi-Strauss 1982, pp. 246–7.
[134] Lévi-Strauss 1982, p. 262.
[135] Lévi-Strauss 1986, p. 27.
[136] See Foucault 1977, pp. 262–3, 342.

and deemed similarly archaic, was in the dock. In the hectic world of Parisian philosophical fashion, Marxism *à la* Sartre, Lefebvre or Goldmann (let alone Garaudy), with its 'subject-centred history and subject-constituted knowledge',[137] was rapidly eclipsed. Man's end was anticipated, history was a myth, Sartrean Marxism its highest stage.[138] The audacity – and perilousness – of Althusser's initiative can now perhaps be better appreciated. In order to escape Hegel and rescue Marxism from the discredit into which it was apparently falling by association with him, Althusser carried out an adroit reversal of alliances. Perceiving a convergence between the astringent anti-humanism of structuralism and his own Marxist positions, Althusser informed the Italian Communist newspaper *Rinascita* in 1964 that Lévi-Strauss was more of an immediate ally of historical materialism than Sartre.[139] Quite the reverse of the mere ' "flirt" with structuralist terminology' to which he reduced this episode in his later auto-critique, Althusser's *Theoriepolitik* dictated something approaching what Nicos Poulantzas would describe as an alliance with

---

[137] Benton 1984, p. 10.

[138] Sartre offered no considered response to the ascendant paradigm, displaying instead sheer exasperation: see, e.g., Sartre 1966, especially pp. 87–8, for a violent attack on Foucault. His comments on Althusser, by contrast, are surprisingly moderate: see Sartre 1966, pp. 93–4 and Sartre 1983, p. 134.

[139] See Althusser 1964b and 1964c. It should be noted, however, that Althusser was far from uncritical of structuralism in these texts. If it was valid in linguistics and partially so in anthropology, it was invalid outside these domains – ideological, and hence incapable of furnishing a scientific interpretation of the world. Only Marxism could offer this. Umberto Eco's particular appropriation of it for historical materialism led not to the renewal of Marxism, but to its 'theoretical liquidation'. In a text published the previous summer, 'Philosophy and the Human Sciences', questioning whether 'the disciplines which present themselves under the label of "Human Sciences" are not only genuinely human, but also, and above all, truly sciences', Althusser had signalled his opposition both to a retreating humanism and to an advancing technocratism. Among those criticised were 'philosophers like Lévi-Strauss (I am not referring to his admirable concrete analyses, but to the *"philosophy"* attached to them), who have discovered the means – the dream of every *bricoleur* – of holding together, in the ontology of binarism, avant–garde linguistics, information theory, mathematics and physics, Marx, Freud, Goldstein, Comte, the exchange of words, women and goods, von Neumann, the shamans and Lacan, Rousseau and the ethnologist himself . . .: all these "philosophers" . . . produce what they consider . . . to be a philosophy – but which is a philosophy-fiction, which is merely the *point d'honneur* of technocratic thinking'. An accompanying footnote was even more damning of 'vulgarized structuralism': 'An appropriate manipulation of metonymy and metaphor, for example, of paradigm and syntagm, etc., provides . . . rapid and astonishing results. Some have already been published; others will soon follow. A huge expansion of structuralist output is already foreseeable; it panders . . . to the taste for rapid results': Althusser 1998a, pp. 52, 56 and n. 20.

'structuralism against historicism, Lévi-Strauss against Sartre'.[140] Thus, if Althusser simultaneously opposed phenomenological anti-naturalism and vindicated, *contra* Lévi-Strauss, the project of a science of history, in 'Marxism and Humanism', without referring to *The Savage Mind*, he gave his imprimatur to the new theme of the 'end of man' and explained the reasons for his acquiescence:

> Strictly in respect to theory . . . one can and must speak openly of *Marx's theoretical anti-humanism*, and see in this *theoretical anti-humanism* the absolute (negative) precondition of the (positive) knowledge of the human world itself, and of its practical transformation. It is impossible to *know* anything about men except on the absolute precondition that the philosophical (theoretical) myth of man is reduced to ashes. So any thought that appeals to Marx for any kind of restoration of a theoretical anthropology or humanism is no more than ashes, theoretically. But in practice it could pile up a monument of pre-Marxist ideology that would weigh down on real history and threaten to lead it into blind alleys.[141]

For Althusser, Sartre was of the devil's party without knowing it. Both Merleau-Ponty and Lévi-Strauss had identified his Cartesianism as what separated him from Marxism and/or materialism. This appears to have been the burden of Althusser's intervention following a lecture by Sartre at the École Normale Supérieure shortly after the publication of the *Critique of Dialectical Reason*.[142] Reportedly finding the accusation of having resurrected the *cogito* in the shape of a philosophy of *praxis* incomprehensible, Sartre failed to counter it. His consternation possibly decided the philosophical allegiances of a generation of French Marxist intellectuals. At any rate, thereafter Althusser pursued this line of attack, contending that Sartre's epistemological starting-point in individual human agency led only to a regression to infinity which left him quite incapable of explaining history.[143] Men were not the constitutive subjects *of* history, but constituted subjects *in* history – agents subsumed under, and

---

[140] Poulantzas 1980, pp. 22–3. Cf. Althusser 1976a, pp. 126–31. The comments quoted in n. 139 above qualify, without contradicting, Poulantzas's description.

[141] Althusser 1969a, pp. 229–30.

[142] See Debray 1975, p. 83 and Cohen-Solal, p. 576. According to Debray, the debate took place in March 1961.

[143] See Althusser 1969a, pp. 111–27.

allotted their places/functions by, a set of social structures (economic, political and ideological) anterior and exterior to them, governed by their own peculiar laws.[144] History was a 'process without a subject', which only a science disjunct from the consciousness and illusions of human subjects could illuminate, thereby enabling its transformation and their liberation. *Reading 'Capital'*, it has justly been said, is an 'anti-*Critique of Dialectical Reason*'.[145]

Althusser, then, believed that the cause of Marxist materialism could best be defended in the early 1960s in conjunction with aspects of structuralism. That he turned to contemporary French philosophy, as well as to the Marxist classics, for aid in the construction of a post-Stalinist Marxism, is readily apparent from the affiliations he announced to Lacan's anti-humanist re-reading of Freud and especially to Bachelardian 'historical epistemology'. While Althusser was proposing a return to Marx, Lacan was conducting a return to Freud. In an essay dating from 1964 – 'Freud and Lacan' – which reopened the dialogue between Marxism and psychoanalysis proscribed by Zhdanovism, Althusser endorsed both Lacan's construction of Freud and his representation of it as a rejoinder to revisionism. Repeating an analogy already drawn by Freud and his French disciple, he concluded by making the same bid for Marxism:

> Not in vain did Freud sometimes compare the critical reception of his discovery with the upheavals of the Copernican Revolution. Since Copernicus, we have known that the earth is not the 'centre' of the universe. Since Marx, we have known that the human subject, the economic, political or philosophical ego is not the 'centre' of history – and even, in opposition to the Philosophers of the Enlightenment and to Hegel, that history has no 'centre' but possesses a structure which has no necessary 'centre' except in ideological misrecognition. In turn, Freud has discovered for us that the real subject, the individual in his unique essence, has not the form of an ego, centred on the 'ego', on 'consciousness' or on 'existence' . . . that the human subject is de-centred, constituted by a structure which has no 'centre' either, except in the imaginary misrecognition of the 'ego', i.e. in the ideological formations in which it 'recognizes' itself.[146]

---

[144] See, e.g., Althusser and Balibar 1970, pp. 119–44, 174–5, 270–1.
[145] Cotten 1979, p. 71 n. 33.
[146] Althusser 1971, pp. 200–1. Cf. Lacan 1982, p. 114. Althusser's article, originally

Althusser had already utilised Lacanian psychoanalysis for the theory of ideology proposed in 'Marxism and Humanism' and, as we shall see, would have further recourse to it. He evidently believed Lacan's project vis-à-vis Freud to coalesce with his own. As Michel Pêcheux once remarked, something approaching a 'Triple Alliance' was hereafter concluded between Althusserian Marxism, Lacanian psychoanalysis and Saussurean linguistics.[147] At all events, the two non-Marxist discourses made the Althusserian grade. They did so according to the norms of an epistemology derived in large part from the French philosopher of science, Gaston Bachelard. Whilst Althusser entered into an alliance of convenience with Lévi-Strauss and one of principle with Lacan, his rapprochement with Bachelardian epistemology and historiography was central to his enterprise. For his aspiration was to demonstrate that Marxism, in reality as well as principle, was the science of history and a science 'like the others' (on an epistemological par with its 'royal' *confrères*). And he aimed to do that by the simultaneous construction/application of Marxist philosophy. Althusser's version of the latter was in fact to be a transformed, *marxisant* Bachelardian epistemology combined with certain Spinozist and structuralist theses, and with elements of Marx's own reflections. (The latter were drawn from the 1857 Introduction, which supplied a canonical blessing for the union of the classical and the contemporary.) It would be an anti-empiricist epistemology, a 'theory of the production of knowledges' – one whose 'central thesis would be the opposition of consciousness and concept'.[148] Bachelard's 'rational materialism' had been forged to represent and defend the revolutionary novelty of modern physics and chemistry. If

---

published in *La Nouvelle Critique* in 1964, came fifteen years after the appearance of 'La psychanalyse, une idéologie réactionnaire' in the same journal. Reprinting it in 1976, he noted that in 1964 psychoanalysis was still not 'in good odour' among Communists (Althusser 1976b, p. 7). The part played by Althusser in the enhancement of psychoanalysis in France, whether via his invitation to Lacan to conduct his seminar at the École normale or his pioneering essay, is justly highlighted by Roudinesco in her 1986. Unlike Lévi-Strauss, who is reported not to have read *For Marx* or *Reading 'Capital'* (see Aron 1983, p. 579), on one occasion at least, Lacan reciprocated the interest shown by Althusser in his work. In *Figaro littéraire*, 29 December 1966, Lacan stated his conviction that Althusser's 'division [of] Marx's thought may be taken as definitive' (quoted in Roudinesco 1986, p. 424).

[147] Pêcheux 1982, p. 211.

[148] Descombes 1981, p. 119. The classical expression of this antithesis for Althusser would have been Cavaillès 1960, especially p. 78.

historical materialism was submitted to a rigorous Bachelardian reading by the deployment of two sets of concepts – science/ideology (Marxist) and problematic/epistemological break (Bachelardian) – and passed the audition, it would simultaneously be rendered proof against philosophical threats and elevated to the promised land of plain science.

Althusser put the encounter between Bachelardian epistemology and his own effort to elaborate a Marxist philosophy in the forefront of the programme of the *Théorie* series he edited,[149] perhaps implicitly signalling a desire to heal the breach between French Communist Marxism and the scientific community caused by the Lysenko affair. And he acknowledged his debts to his 'masters in reading learned works' – Bachelard, Jean Cavaillès, Georges Canguilhem, and Michel Foucault – in *Reading 'Capital'*.[150] Although he attempted to cover himself against the charge of importing non-Marxist elements into Marxism by representing Marx and Engels as Bachelardians *avant la lettre*,[151] in his resort to Bachelard, as in his alliance with structuralism, Althusser was in fact engaged in an habitual strategy of Western Marxism – namely, a synthesis of Marxism and 'bourgeois' philosophy. And if Althusser's 'road to Marx' bypassed the Marxism of his peers in favour of contemporary non-Marxist discourses, it simultaneously took a 'detour' via a classical philosophical system: Spinoza's. Epistemologically at least, Spinoza – and not Hegel – was Marx's 'historical predecessor'. His rationalist and determinist philosophy was extolled for having 'introduced an unprecedented theoretical revolution in the history of philosophy, probably the greatest philosophical revolution of all time'[152] – some of whose key principles Althusser would seek to naturalise in Marxism.

---

[149] See the back cover of the first edition of *Lire 'le Capital'* (Althusser et al. 1965) and the first and subsequent editions of *Pour Marx* (Althusser 1965).

[150] See Althusser and Balibar 1970, pp. 16 n. 1, 44 n. 20, for laudatory comments on these figures as well as on Lacan. In Althusser 1971, pp. 163–4 and Althusser 1972, p. 34 n. 2, Althusser also paid tribute to the master of Hegel studies in France, Jean Hyppolite – one of whose last texts was a respectful discussion of his work (see Hyppolite 1971). In the foreword to his 1981, p. 9, Canguilhem acknowledged Althusser's 'original contribution'; while the introduction to Foucault's 1974, pp. 3–17 testifies to the temporary impact of the Althusserian re-reading of Marx on him.

[151] See, e.g., Althusser 1969a, p. 32 and Althusser and Balibar 1970, p. 145ff.

[152] Althusser and Balibar 1970, p. 102; see also Althusser 1969a, p. 78 n. 40. In Althusser 1972, p. 50, Althusser had credited Montesquieu with anticipating Marx with a dynamic but non-teleological theory of history. Three years later, however, he was arguing that the illicit Hegelian notion of totality derived from the Frenchman

Althusser's devaluation of French Marxism in favour of other currents in the national culture, and of Hegel in favour of Spinoza, resulted in an ironic situation. He was not a Stalinist in structuralist clothing, harking back to the days of 'diabolical and hysterical mysterialism'[153] and hankering after a re-edition of them. On the contrary, fearing that Marxist theory, so recently freed from the grip of Stalinism, was now in the vice of alien theoretical ideologies, and convinced that certain non-Marxist discourses could play a crucial role in releasing it, Althusser engaged in a complex theoretical 'war of position'. Yet the fact is that the philosopher who ceaselessly invoked the rigours of orthodoxy against the lax eclecticism of his contemporaries, counterposing the mature to the young Marx (and Stalin), was also 'the most promiscuous [of Western Marxists] in allowing non-Marxist influences to affect his ideas'.[154] Whether, in consequence, Althusser escaped the German ideology only to succumb to the French is a question that will detain us later.

For Marx, read *Capital*

The titles of Althusser's books were slogans. The ambition motivating his 'return to Marx' was the renewal of Marxist theory. His endeavour had to comprise three inter-related components: critique, reconstruction and defence – a programme of enormous scope. All three tasks were to be executed with the aid of theses which many Marxists considered (and still do) detrimental to Marxism and with a polemical cutting edge that enraged the partisans of Althusser's targets. His first – and overriding – concern was to demarcate a space for independent research within the PCF. His epistemology was constructed, he related in 1975,

> in *opposition to all forms of pragmatism*, to justify the thesis of the relative autonomy of theory and thus the right of Marxist theory not to be treated as a slave to tactical political decisions, but to be allowed to develop, in alliance with political and other practices, without betraying its own needs.[155]

(see Althusser 1969a, p. 103). It is worth noting that that other contemporary Parisian hero, Nietzsche, occasionally joined the select company of Marx and Freud as artisans of 'sciences or of criticism': see Althusser 1971, pp. 181–2 and Althusser and Balibar 1970, pp. 15–16.

[153] Thompson's memorable phrase, in another connection: see his 1978, p. 111.

[154] Jay 1984, p. 391.

[155] Althusser 1976a, p. 169.

In the event, this took the form of justifying within Marxism a unity of theory and practice *internal* to theory – in other words, an *autonomy* of theory. The severance between the two characteristic of Western Marxism was endowed with Marxist credentials. Such 'idealism' was part of the logic of remaining a member of the PCF. To Althusser, the Party was the party of the French working class. It (potentially) posed the only real threat to the order of capital in France; membership of it was thus a precondition of any kind of organic link with the class struggle. But the price to be paid for a party card and for theory's immunity was high: assent – or silence – on political issues. On the other hand, if, at a stroke, Althusser abolished the problem of the union of theory and practice, it was in the name of *future political practice*. The Marxist workers' movement needed scientific theory in order to 'change the world'.[156] Protected from the ravages of official pragmatism and opportunism, a detour via theory – at this time and in this place – was no diversion from the struggle, but the long-term, practically motivated continuation of politics by other means. (At least, this was how Althusser understood the theoretical labours of Marx and Lenin.[157]) Audacity in theory was to be accompanied politically by tactical moderation in the interests of strategic extremism. An open clash with the party leadership was to be avoided. The PCF's political practice was to be transformed by a theoretical labour insulated from the commotion and caprices of quotidian politics and the exigencies of practical verification, in a France whose polity had been stabilised after 1962 under Gaullist intendancy and whose economy was rapidly being modernised under technocratic supervision. After all, Lenin, no less, had said that Marxism was omnipotent because it was true and not vice versa.[158]

---

[156] Marx's eleventh thesis on Feuerbach – see Marx 1975, p. 423 – was pinned to the wall of Althusser's study, according to Macciocchi 1983, p. 382.

[157] See Althusser's letter of 7 March 1967 to Régis Debray (Althusser 1977a, p. 267): 'The struggle poses urgent demands. But it is sometimes ... *politically urgent* to withdraw for a while, and take stock; everything depends on the theoretical work done at that time. Marx and Lenin gave us our first examples of this. ... Time thus taken away from the struggle may ultimately be a saving of time – even for the struggle itself. ... I see this as being the duty of all working-class and revolutionary intellectuals. They are entrusted by the people in arms with the guardianship and extension of scientific knowledge. They must fulfil this mission with the utmost care, following in the footsteps of Marx himself, who was convinced that nothing was more important for the struggles of the workers' movement and those waging those struggles than the most profound and accurate knowledge.'

[158] Lenin 1968, p. 23. Cf., e.g., Althusser and Balibar 1970, p. 59.

For Althusser, it was a time for Marxist theory. 'Today' was different. Bypassing the PCF imprint Éditions Sociales, he opened a new series with the leftist publisher François Maspero, entitled simply *Théorie*. In quick succession, *Pour Marx* and the two-volume *Lire 'le Capital'* appeared in autumn 1965. 'For the first time,' writes Anderson, 'a major theoretical *system* was articulated within the organizational framework of French Communism, whose power and originality were conceded even by its most determined opponents.'[159] If Althusser's version of dialectical materialism was, at first sight, entirely novel, historical materialism *à la* Althusser bore little resemblance to what had previously passed for the science of history in the international Communist movement. Althusser's open return to Marx was greeted with distinct coolness by the PCF leadership, fearful of its practical implications. (The same year, the CPC published *The Polemic on the General Line of the International Communist Movement*, inviting a realignment from Moscow to Peking.) The PCF would learn to live with Althusser, if not to love him. Marxist theory had known few projects of such ambition and militancy and would not be quite the same again.

---

[159] Anderson 1976, p. 38.

Chapter Two

A Recommencement of Dialectical Materialism

> ... we are absolutely committed to a theoretical destiny:
> we cannot *read* Marx's scientific discourse without at the
> same time writing at his dictation the text of another
> discourse, inseparable from the first one but distinct from
> it: the discourse of Marx's *philosophy*.
>
> Louis Althusser, *Reading 'Capital'*

In Chapter 1, it was argued that Althusser considered
a transformation of the PCF's political practice to be
dependent upon a restoration of Marxist theory –
more specifically, a renewal of historical materialism.
But this, in turn, had three *theoretical* preconditions:
(i) a critique of the dominant accounts of historical
materialism, which supposedly departed from Marx,
thereby vitiating development of his theory; (ii) the
displacement of these versions and their eventual
replacement by the genuine article (in the event,
Althusser's own reconstruction); and (iii) the
elaboration of the veritable Marxist philosophy
which could underwrite the scientificity of historical
materialism and guide and guarantee the necessary
extensions of it. It should now be apparent why the
final component of the Althusserian programme was
in fact – for Althusser – of paramount importance:
'the *investigation* of Marx's *philosophical* thought
[was] indispensable if we were to escape from the ...

impasse in which history had put us'.[1] What was needed was a philosophical, that is, 'epistemological and historical',[2] reading of Marx's œuvre which barred the route – opened by Marx himself – pursued by Marxist intellectuals in reaction against the vulgarisation and Stalinisation of Marxism. The constitution of Marxist philosophy was a *sine qua non* of epistemological critique and scientific reconstruction. As Althusser put it in *Reading 'Capital'*, 'the theoretical future of historical materialism depends today on deepening dialectical materialism.'[3] The hour of the missing Marxist 'dialectics' had arrived.

Of course, Althusser was not the first to feel the need for an archaeological and methodological operation of this order. Marxist philosophers since Engels had attempted to remedy the absence of a 'Logic'. According to Althusser, however, complementary to the deformation of historical materialism after Marx was the proliferation of illegitimate versions of Marxist philosophy. For reasons that were both 'historico-political' and 'theoretical',[4] the requisite historical epistemology had not materialised within Marxism. Instead, Marxist philosophy had taken the form of a succession of 'philosophical ideologies' which posited an illicit relationship between themselves and historical materialism. The dogmatist night, moreover, had not given way to the Marxist dawn.

A Stalinist de-Stalinisation

The PCF had conducted its own inquiry into Stalinist philosophical dogmatism in June 1962. Presided over by Thorez and presented by Garaudy, it was published under the title of 'The Tasks of Communist Philosophers and the Critique of Stalin's Errors' in *Cahiers du Communisme*, the 'theoretical and political review' of the Central Committee. In his report to the Twentieth Congress, Khrushchev, notwithstanding his concluding injunction, was silent on the subject of Marxist theory. Following the amplification of his critique of Stalin at the Twenty-Second Congress, however, Soviet philosophers set to work on defining the 'tasks of Marxist-Leninist philosophy' on the 'road

---

[1] Althusser 1969a, p. 21.
[2] Althusser 1969a, p. 39.
[3] Althusser and Balibar 1970, p. 77.
[4] Althusser 1969a, p. 14.

to communism'. None other than Stalin's biographer M.B. Mitin, editor-in-chief of *Voprossy Filosofi* and vice-president of the Academy of Sciences, now criticised his former patron for schematism and underestimation of the Hegelian heritage. The abrogation of the 'negation of the negation', in particular, had been a serious mistake, he argued in an article published in *Recherches Internationales*.[5] At an assembly of French Communist philosophers in January 1962, Waldeck Rochet, speaking on behalf of the Politbureau, had defined Marxist philosophy as 'a scientific world-outlook' and had ended his address by expressing confidence that 'philosopher members of the party will take account of the important lessons on the ideological level issuing from the Twenty-Second Congress [of the CPSU], which has deepened the work of the Twentieth Congress in all domains'.[6] To Garaudy fell the lot later in the year of deducing the appropriate conclusions. He impugned Stalin's *Dialectical and Historical Materialism* on three main counts: (i) it had assimilated Marx's materialism to 'pre-Marxist dogmatic materialism', thus attenuating its revolutionary novelty; (ii) it had sundered the dialectic from contemporary science, thereby facilitating 'positivism' and 'scientism'; and (iii) it had amputated the 'philosophical heritage' from dialectical materialism, therewith impoverishing the latter.[7] Rectification of Stalin's original sin – 'underestimation of the Hegelian legacy' – consisted in a positive estimation of that heritage and restitution of the category of the negation of the negation. The root of Stalin's dogmatist 'errors', it was concluded, lay in his expunction of an integral 'source and component part' of Marxism from it. Unlike Bukharin or Trotsky, Hegel was to be officially rehabilitated.

Garaudy's preliminary admonition against rejecting Stalin's heritage in bloc speaks volumes.[8] Theoretical de-Stalinisation in the Soviet and French Communist Parties was effectively limited to 'disappearing' Stalin's writings. The theoretical bases of Stalinism were left largely untouched. Marxism-Leninism, a 'scientific world-outlook', remained official doctrine. It had three components: (i) Marxist philosophy; (ii) Marxist political economy; and (iii) the theory of scientific communism. Marxist philosophy was dialectical

[5] See Labica 1984, pp. 95–6.
[6] Waldeck Rochet, pp. 99, 125. Cf. Labica 1984, pp. 98–9.
[7] See Garaudy 1962, p. 91.
[8] Garaudy 1962, p. 88. Cf. Labica 1984, pp. 99–100.

materialism, the science of the laws of nature and thought. Applied to society, it became historical materialism, the science of the laws of social development. Two adjustments were made: the negation of the negation was restored to the corpus of dialectical materialism; the Asiatic mode of production to that of historical materialism.[9]

Althusser's 'Contradiction and Overdetermination', written at the same time as the PCF was holding its inquest, was in outright theoretical opposition to its findings. Suggesting that priority be assigned to *'a rigorous conception of Marxist concepts . . . and . . . what distinguishes them once and for all from their phantoms'*, Althusser's judgement on Hegel was categorical:

> One phantom is more especially crucial than any other today: the shade of Hegel. To drive this phantom back into the night we need *a little more light on Marx*, or what is the same thing, *a little more Marxist light on Hegel himself*. We can then escape from the ambiguities and confusions of the 'inversion'.[10]

'On the Materialist Dialectic', the following year, offered a full-scale alternative to Garaudy et al.'s conclusions. It was an ambitious attempt to clarify, *inter alia*, the Marx-Hegel relationship and to elaborate the Marxist philosophy which would superintend reconstruction of the Marxist architectonic. Althusser's aim, in other words, was to settle some of the accounts left open by Marx, incompletely settled by Engels and Lenin, and defaulted on by their successors. His viewpoint was diametrically opposed to the PCF's critique and rectification of Stalin's errors – something he made clear by his reference to it in a note added in 1965:

> Today it is official convention to reproach Stalin with having suppressed the 'laws of the dialectic', and more generally with having turned away from Hegel, the better to establish his dogmatism. At the same time, it is willingly proposed that a certain return to Hegel would be salutary. One day perhaps these declarations will become the object of some proof. In the meantime, it seems to me that it would be simpler to recognize that the expulsion of the 'negation of the negation' from the domain of the Marxist dialectic might be evidence of the real theoretical perspicacity of its author.[11]

---

[9] See Labica 1984, pp. 12–13, 105–6.
[10] Althusser 1969a, p. 116.
[11] Althusser 1969a, p. 200 n. 41.

Insisting on the total discontinuity between Marx and Hegel, Althusser enjoined a 'return to this simple fact: in the only Marxist practices that have really been constituted, the categories in use or in action are not Hegelian; in action in Marxist practice there are different categories, the categories of the Marxist dialectic'.[12] Contrary to Stalinist certitude, first among the *un*constituted Marxist practices was Marxist philosophy.

In two précis of *For Marx* and *Reading 'Capital'* – 'Theory, Theoretical Practice and Theoretical Formation. Ideology and Ideological Struggle' (1965) and 'Historical Materialism and Dialectical Materialism' (1966) – Althusser surveyed the fate of Marxist philosophy since Marx's eleventh thesis on Feuerbach. Marx was responsible for a 'double theoretical revolution'.[13] In the very act of founding the science of history, he had instituted 'another scientific discipline': Marxist philosophy. Yet he had only been able to lay the basis of it, in polemical works such as *The German Ideology* (1845–6) and *The Poverty of Philosophy* (1846–7); in an unpublished, compressed methodological text – the 1857 Introduction; and in a few passages in *Capital* (particularly the 1873 Postface to the second German edition of Volume One). Engels's *Anti-Dühring* (1878) and *Ludwig Feuerbach and the End of Classical German Philosophy* (1888) were also essentially polemical, interventions in the ideological struggle of the period. Lenin's *Materialism and Empirio-Criticism* (1908), however commendable a defence of science, was likewise the work of a 'partisan in philosophy', his (unpublished) *Philosophical Notebooks* (1895–1916) marginal notes. Still partially ideological, none of these texts, Althusser maintained, displayed 'a degree of elaboration and systematicity – and hence scientificity – comparable to the degree of elaboration of historical materialism that we possess in *Capital*'. What they did do, on the other hand, was indicate that the object of Marxist philosophy was 'the history of the production of knowledges – or . . . the historical difference between ideology and science, or the specific difference of scientificity'. In other words, in principle dialectical materialism was 'a *theory of the history of knowledge* – that is, of the real conditions . . . of the *process of production of knowledge*'.[14]

---

[12] Althusser 1969a, p. 200.
[13] Althusser 1966a, p. 90. See also Althusser 1969a, p. 33.
[14] Althusser 1990, p. 8.

In principle, but not in practice. For what Althusser called 'the secular form of religion'[15] – dogmatism – had supervened to pronounce Marx's theory complete and proscribe unlicensed investigations and developments. The underdevelopment of Marxist philosophy by Marx, Engels and Lenin on the one hand, and the ascendancy of Stalin on the other, meant that the project of a Marxist philosophy was unrealised. Indeed, it had not really progressed since *Materialism and Empirio-Criticism*.[16] The discovery and rediscovery of Marx's early writings had issued in interpretations which, rather than making good the deficiency, had subverted the very project. With the Garaudy report of 1962, the subversion had been made official. A return to Hegel was, theoretically, just as deleterious as the descent into a dogmatism no less dependent, beneath its 'materialist' carapace, on Hegel. So, eighty years after Marx's death and one hundred and twenty after the *Theses on Feuerbach*, the question of Marxist philosophy was back on the agenda. It had never been off it.

The adventures of the dialectic

Althusser alluded to 'historico-political' and 'theoretical' reasons for 'the remarkable history of Marxist philosophy, from its origins to the present day',[17] without undertaking a systematic analysis of them. Instead, he amalgamated very different philosophical systems into broad tendencies. Whilst he provided the outline of an explanation for the return to Hegel after the collapse of the Second International, he was far less forthcoming on the career of diamat. Despite pointing to the need for a Marxism of Marxism, Althusser signally failed to supply one. In order to comprehend the rationale for his own epistemology, and situate it, a few basic landmarks in the history of Marxist philosophy must be recalled.

The mandatory starting-point is the systematisation (indeed, construction) of Marxism post-Marx, its dissemination within the Second International, and the far-reaching consequences of the form these took. It is important to remember that some of Marx's most important texts were not merely unpublished at his death, but remained so for decades thereafter: the *Critique*

---

[15] Althusser 1966a, p. 122.
[16] See Althusser 1990, p. 18.
[17] Althusser 1969a, p. 34.

of Hegel's Doctrine of the State (only published in 1927); the *Economic and Philosophical Manuscripts* (1932); *The German Ideology* (1932); and the *Grundrisse* (1939–41). In the absence of these writings, leading figures in the Second International relied on two main sources for their conception of Marx's doctrine and the course of its constitution. First, Marx's 1859 Preface to *A Contribution to the Critique of Political Economy* could be considered to provide both the official autobiographical account of Marx and Engels's development and a summary of the 'materialist conception of history' to which it led. In addition, there were Marx's sporadic *obiter dicta* on his relationship to Hegel. Secondly, Engels's late works were available. Predictably, they were decisive for the young generation on the character of Marxism. *Anti-Dühring* (written while Marx was still alive and containing a chapter by him) was apprehended as the *summa* of the new 'world outlook'; *Ludwig Feuerbach* as the definitive account of Marx and Engels's engagement with post-Kantian German philosophy.

For Althusser, Engels's obligation to follow Dühring wherever he went led him onto the ideological *Kampfplatz*. For Engels, in contrast, '[a]s a result, my negative criticism became positive; polemic was transformed into a more or less connected exposition of the dialectical method and of the communist world outlook championed by Marx and myself'.[18] The first and longest part of *Anti-Dühring* is entitled 'Philosophy'. The question of a *sui generis* Marxist philosophy has always revolved around the problem of Marx's relation to Hegel. In his own reflections on the affinity between his dialectic and Hegel's in the 1873 Postface, Marx encapsulated the difference between them via the metaphor of 'inversion'. Distinguishing between two aspects of the dialectic, Marx referred to a process of inversion followed by extraction (of the 'rational kernel' from the 'mystical shell'), whose felicitous result was that his own 'dialectical method' was 'exactly opposite' to Hegel's. Through this operation, the dialectic was transformed from an idealist construct 'transfigur[ing] and glorify[ing] what exists' into a materialist dialectic which was 'in its very essence critical and revolutionary'.[19] The concordance between this account and the mode of critique employed thirty years earlier (in the *Critique of Hegel's Doctrine of the State*) is evident – and was intimated by Marx. Derived

---

[18] Engels 1977, p. 13.
[19] See Marx 1976a, pp. 102–3.

from Feuerbach, it posits the need for a (materialist) reversal of Hegel's (idealist) inversion of subject and predicate, reality and thought.[20]

When, after Marx's death, Engels came to reconsider the German ideology in *Ludwig Feuerbach*, he too reverted to the intellectual framework of his youth. In a reprise of the young Hegelians' distinction between 'system' and 'method', Engels sought to illuminate the German connection by locating a contradiction in Hegel's philosophy between an incipiently materialist (revolutionary) dialectical method and an irredeemably idealist (conservative) system.[21] This contradiction had been 'pulverised' by Feuerbach's *Essence of Christianity* (1841), which had 'placed materialism on the throne again'.[22] The 'ideological perversion' of Hegel's idealism having been disposed of,

> dialectics reduced itself to the science of the general laws of motion, both of the external world and of human thought ... the dialectic of concepts itself became merely the conscious reflex of the dialectical motion of the real world and thus the dialectic of Hegel was placed upon its head, or rather turned off its head, on which it was standing, and placed upon its feet.[23]

In 'Contradiction and Overdetermination', Althusser queried the rigour of Marx's inversion metaphor and Engels's system/method dichotomy. In a direct challenge to virtually ninety years of Marxist philosophy, he argued that, correctly interpreted, Marx's Postface did not license any *Aufhebung* of the Hegelian dialectic:

> in its approximation, this metaphorical expression ['inversion'] ... does not pose the problem of *the nature of the objects* to which a *single method* should be applied (the world of the Idea for Hegel – the real world for Marx), but rather the problem of the *nature of the dialectic* considered itself, that is, the problem of its *specific structures*; not the problem of the inversion of the 'sense' of the dialectic, but that of the *transformation of its structures*. . . .
>
> . . . [I]f the Marxist dialectic is 'in principle' the opposite of the Hegelian dialectic, if it is rational and not mystical-mystified-mystificatory, this radical

---

[20] See Marx 1976a and cf. Marx 1975, e.g., pp. 61, 65.
[21] See Marx and Engels 1977, p. 340.
[22] Marx and Engels 1977, p. 344. (A French translation of Feuerbach's work by Jean-Pierre Osier appeared in the *Théorie* series in 1968.)
[23] Marx and Engels 1977, p. 362.

distinction must be manifest in its essence, that is, in its *characteristic determinations and structures* . . . this means that *basic structures of the Hegelian dialectic* . . . *have for Marx (insofar as he takes them over, and he takes over by no means all of them) a structure different from the structure they have for Hegel.*[24]

'In principle', perhaps, but not in actuality. For, on the basis of his own interpretation, Engels appropriated Hegel's method and structures for Marxism. With Hegel, he avowed, philosophy came to an end in that, despite himself, Hegel 'showed us the way out of the labyrinth of systems to real positive knowledge of the world'.[25] Engels thus remained an unwitting captive of the Hegelian system. In *Anti-Dühring*, historical materialism was construed as a scientific 'political economy' (title of Part II) and Marxist philosophy expanded into a scientific meta-philosophy. The universality of the laws of the dialectic – their uniform application to nature, human history, and thought – resolved the epistemological problem; in Engels's 'reflection theory', epistemological correspondence was guaranteed by ontology.[26] The 'general laws' of the dialectic were taken from Hegel's *Logic* and held by Engels to be verified by contemporary scientific developments (most portentously, Darwin's theory of evolution).[27] There were three of them: the transformation of quantity into quality; the interpenetration of opposites; and the negation of the negation.[28] Via an article written by Plekhanov in 1891 (and endorsed by Engels) to commemorate the sixtieth anniversary of Hegel's death, the use of the expression 'dialectical materialism' to designate this philosophical system passed into the currency of the Second and Third Internationals. Simultaneously an ontology and an epistemology, dialectical materialism was conceived by Engels as a scientific philosophy which 'summed up', and was corroborated by, the results of the natural sciences. In turn, it verified historical materialism, which it now subsumed. The 'supersession' of Hegel's philosophical system, it consummated the break Marx and Engels had made in 1845–6, effecting an irrevocable parting of the ways with the German and all other ideologies.

---

[24] Althusser 1969a, pp. 93–4.
[25] Marx and Engels 1977, p. 342.
[26] See Engels 1976, pp. 266–7.
[27] See, e.g., Marx and Engels 1977, p. 364.
[28] Engels 1976, p. 62.

Thus it came about that the Second International could believe it had escaped the realm of 'philosophical rubbish',[29] and attained the realm of science, precisely when its doctrine remained fatally dependent on a 'poor man's Hegelianism'.[30] The German working-class movement did indeed inherit classical German philosophy.[31] On the credit of Engels's presentation, such teleological moments in Marx as Chapter 32 of *Capital*, Volume One ('The Historical Tendency of Capitalist Accumulation'), and the prestige of such doctrines in their own cultures, Marxism was pressed by Kautsky and Plekhanov, doyens of their respective national Marxisms, into a positivist and evolutionist mould. In 1877, Marx had remonstrated with one of his critics (Mikhailovsky) for 'transforming my historical sketch of the genesis of capitalism in Western Europe into a historico-philosophical theory of the general path prescribed by fate to all nations, whatever the circumstances in which they find themselves'; and gone on to reject 'using as one's master key a general historico-philosophical theory, the supreme virtue of which consists in being supra-historical'.[32] The problem was that the *passe-partout* had been partially cut by the founders of Marxism.

The crisis of Marxism provoked by the outbreak of World War One and the capitulation of the Second International stimulated a return to first principles on the Left of the revolutionary movement. Even after the Russian Revolution, the Second International was regarded by Bolshevik leaders as having been a revolutionary organisation until the eve of war, its major theoreticians bona fide Marxists until their apostasy in August 1914. Lenin's own return to Hegel towards the end of 1914 (recorded in his 'Conspectus' of the *Science of Logic*) issued in the revelation that it was 'impossible' to comprehend Marx's *Capital* without mastering Hegel's *Logic*: 'Consequently, half a century later none of the Marxists understood Marx!!'.[33] Lenin's inference may be true – but it does not follow from his premises. For, as we have seen, if the Second International could dispense with reading Hegel (as had Lenin in his anti-Hegelian *What the 'Friends of the People' Are and How They Fight the Social-Democrats* [1894]), it was because it had let Engels do its reading for it. Lenin's attempt to read

---

[29] Engels 1976, p. 210.
[30] Althusser 1971, p. 92.
[31] See Marx and Engels 1977, p. 376.
[32] See Marx and Engels 1975, pp. 293–4.
[33] Lenin 1961b, p. 180.

Hegel 'materialistically', by simply 'cast[ing] aside for the most part God, the Absolute, the Pure Idea, etc.', started from the same postulate as Engels's: that Hegel was 'materialism which has been stood on its head'.[34] Its outcome was similar to the initiatives of Engels and Plekhanov: 'dialectical materialism'. When Lenin thought he was breaking with Second-International theoretical orthodoxy, he was, in fact, miming it – on this issue, at any rate. The '*logic of Capital*' which remedied the absence of a Marxist 'Logic' was, on Lenin's reading, decidedly more Hegelian than Althusser was prepared to admit.[35] For Althusser, Lenin alone had somehow avoided both the economism of the Second International and the Hegelianism that emerged after 1917 on the (ultra) Left of the Third.

Althusser did not investigate the orthodoxy of the Second International in any depth. Nor did he explicitly indict Engels's contribution to it. Moreover, he exempted Marx and Lenin from any responsibility for the 'disastrously opportunist interpretations of the Second International'. Instead, while noting that neither these nor 'Stalinist dogmatism' had 'as yet been buried by History',[36] he focused on the return to Hegel associated with Lukács, Korsch and, to a lesser extent, Gramsci – the strategy whose reinvigoration post-Stalin was the main butt of his critique. Callinicos has argued that, philosophically, Hegel was less significant for these figures than 'the anti-naturalist revolt at the turn of the nineteenth century'.[37] Nevertheless, as he and others have amply documented, an alternative conception of the Marx-Hegel filiation to that entertained by Kautsky and his colleagues was an important component in their undertaking. In a philosophical break with orthodoxy which they believed complementary to the Bolsheviks' political challenge, the protagonists of the Hegelian-Marxist episode rebelled, as we have seen, against what Korsch called '*an anti-philosophical scientifico-positivist conception of Marxism*'.[38] In their contestation of it, they ratified their positivist adversaries' account (and misrepresentation) of science, seeking to deliver Marxism from its supposedly 'reified' mode of understanding. In opposition to the objectivism and 'reflection

---

[34] Lenin 1961b, p. 104. Cf. Marx and Engels 1977, p. 348.
[35] As Lenin's statement of 1915 intimates: see 1961b, p. 319.
[36] Althusser 1969a, p. 240.
[37] Callinicos 1983, p. 71.
[38] Korsch 1970, p. 118. Cf. Gramsci 1977, p. 34.

theory' of the Engelsian heritage, they concurred in regarding Marxism as 'the theoretical expression of the revolutionary movement of the proletariat'. According to this historicism, just as scientific socialism was the theoretical expression of a class subject, so the natural sciences were bourgeois ideology – *bourgeois* sciences which would be abolished together with the capitalist mode of production.[39] Contrariwise, as the theoretical expression of the 'universal' class of capitalist society – the proletariat – Marxism could attain to a genuine understanding of the social totality, which, according to these philosophies of *praxis*, was the creation and expression of humanity (of whose alienation and disalienation history was the unfolding drama). Thus, for Lukács, Marxism was the self-consciousness of the proletariat, itself the subject-object of history which would redeem all humanity in the act of emancipating itself. And 'orthodoxy' 'refer[red] exclusively to *method*' – the dialectical method inherited from Hegel and now restricted, *contra* Engels, to 'the realms of history and society'.[40] A 'proletarian science', historical materialism 'completed the programme of Hegel's philosophy of history, even though at the cost of the destruction of his system'.[41]

Althusser recognised the 'real historical merits' of this current. Its idealism, relativism and voluntarism had, he conceded, constituted a revolutionary protest against the fatalistic doctrine of the Second International.[42] Its essential demerits, on the other hand, were two-fold. It had, as it were, inverted the Second International's inversion of Hegel's philosophy of history, retaining its expressive totality – even if it substituted other principles for the dialectic between forces and relations of production. And, consequent upon this, it had assimilated the sciences into the superstructure and placed them in an expressive relationship with class subjects. The upshot was that Marxism was converted into a proletarian science – less the knowledge of an object than the expression of a subject – and thereby denuded of substantive epistemological justification, being conceived as the (self-)consciousness of a historical moment and/or its creator. In short, the return to Hegel *was* a 'revolution against *Capital*' – a fact confirmed by Lukács's valorisation of Marx's early writings.

---

[39] See Korsch 1970, pp. 45, 69.
[40] Lukács 1971, pp. 1, 24, n. 6.
[41] Lukács 1971, pp. 11, 18.
[42] Althusser and Balibar 1970, p. 119. For Althusser's critique, see Althusser and Balibar 1970, pp. 140–1.

Lukács and Korsch were rewarded for their labours with condemnation by Zinoviev for 'theoretical revisionism' at the Fifth Congress of the Comintern, and belaboured in the Soviet Union by leading party philosopher Abram Deborin. The failure of revolution in the West was soon followed by its bureaucratisation in the East. The philosophical controversy in the USSR between the 'dialecticians' (Deborin et al.) and the 'mechanists' (Stepanov, Bukharin, et al.) was decided in 1929 in favour of the former. The following year, however, 'Bolshevisation of Marxist philosophy' – that is, the theoretical consecration of Stalin's new course – began in earnest. Mitin and Yudin made their debut to assail the 'Menshevising idealism' of Deborin as the philosophical arm of Trotskyism, just as Deborin had indicted 'mechanical materialism' as the philosophical detachment of Bukharinism. On 25 January 1931, a resolution of the Central Committee condemned the Deborinites' journal *Under the Banner of Marxism*.[43] Thereafter, Marxist theory in the USSR and the international Communist movement was whatever Stalin (or his functionaries) decreed it to be. The adventures of the dialectic henceforth tracked the misadventures of 'socialism in one country'.

The Cold War in theory

In his 1961 foreword to *Dialectical Materialism*, Lefebvre recalled that, just at the point when Marx's intellectual youth was being excavated, 'the dogmatists were moving in the opposite direction'.[44] That the contrivance and consolidation of theoretical Stalinism – the ossification of dialectical materialism into 'a scientific philosophy of nature'[45] – involved a dogmatic dismissal of Hegel and the young Marx is undeniable. Stalin, 'associate of Lenin and continuator of Marxism', repudiated the Hegelian heritage in Marxism. He expelled the early works from the canon, the negation of the negation from the corpus. Lenin's *Philosophical Notebooks*, first published in 1929, fell under suspicion of taint of Hegelianism and were excluded from the fourth edition of the *Collected Works*. Coming from the 'scholar of genius' in the 1930s, such expediencies had the force of law. With *Dialectical and Historical Materialism*

---

[43] See Labica 1984, pp. 26–49.
[44] Lefebvre 1970, p. 14.
[45] Lefebvre 1970, p. 16.

(1938) – a section of the *History of the Communist Party of the Soviet Union (Bolsheviks)* – theoretical Stalinism assumed its definitive form. The dialectic, supposedly 'in its very essence critical and revolutionary', was transformed into a state ideology 'transfiguring and glorifying what exists': the scientific verification of everything from Lysenko to Beria.[46]

Paradoxically, however, minus the negation of the negation, 'Hegel' – albeit the Hegelianism of Engels and the Second International – was alive and well in Stalinist orthodoxy. Stalin had, as it were, rooted out the dragon-seed of Hegelianism from Marxism-Leninism, only to secrete an even more banalised yet obstinate version of it at the heart of his own system. He had ejected the German ideology from Marx's genealogy in favour of a Marxist *Naturphilosophie* whose precursor was G.W.F. Hegel. *Dialectical and Historical Materialism* commenced with the reminder that 'Marx and Engels took from the Hegelian dialectic only its "rational kernel", casting aside its idealistic shell, and developed it further so as to lend it a modern scientific form'.[47] In accordance with Engels's late works (including the *Dialectics of Nature*, published in 1925), dialectical materialism ('the world outlook of the Marxist-Leninist party') was construed as the general science of nature, history and thought. Its 'dialectical method' was the prescribed Marxist-Leninist methodology for any and every subject: the 'Marxist' realisation of the positivist dream of the methodological unity of the nature and social sciences. Historical materialism, bowdlerised into an evolutionism and economism ('histomat'), was the 'application' of diamat to 'social life, to the history of society':[48] a natural science on the positivist model. This was what counted as Marxist philosophy and science for the whole Communist movement during the Stalin period – and beyond.

In France, the translator of the *Short Course*, Georges Cogniot, described it as 'the compass of communism'.[49] Armed with its compass, the PCF negotiated the rapids of 1939, 1941 and 1947. In the latter year the most virulent phase of what Georges Labica has called 'the reign of diamat'[50] commenced: that associated with the dictatorships of A.A. Zhdanov over Soviet culture and T.D. Lysenko over Soviet science. The 'two camps' that divided the world

---

[46] As Althusser would later argue in his 1977b.
[47] Stalin 1973, p. 300.
[48] Stalin 1973, p. 333.
[49] Quoted in Spriano 1985, p. 87.
[50] The title of part two of Labica 1984.

politically were pronounced to exist in culture and science as well. Zhdanov's 'On Philosophy' (1947), recalling 'the Party character of philosophy, inherent in Marxism-Leninism',[51] set the tone and style of the Cold War in theory. Soviet philosophers were excoriated for their complacency about 'servility and fawning before bourgeois philosophy' and summoned to the class struggle on the 'philosophical front'.[52] (It was further made plain in this *ex cathedra* pronouncement that one subject was definitely not on the agenda: 'The question of Hegel was settled long ago.'[53]) The following year, Lysenko and his followers saw the triumph of their 'proletarian science' over the reactionary 'Mendelist-Morganists'. The PCF loyally promoted both Lysenkoism and Zhdanovism. In an editorial in *La Nouvelle Critique* ('Revue du marxisme militant') in 1950, Desanti argued that, as a 'social product', science was 'a historically relative ideology'; and that 'taking a proletarian stance in science and adopting the criteria of proletarian science' were 'preconditions for objectivity in scientific debate'.[54] Science, stripped of any cognitive autonomy, became a site of class struggle. Francis Cohen, asserting the congruence of Lysenko's biology with the *scientia scientiarum* imparted by 'the greatest scientist of our time' (Comrade Stalin), reminded faint hearts (such as the distinguished biologist Marcel Prenant) that '[t]here can no more be compromises in scientific matters than there can be compromises in the trade union struggle or in the struggle for peace. The struggle of the working class goes on in laboratories too'.[55] Laurent Casanova donned Zhdanov's mantle and, in a speech of 1949 entitled 'The Responsibilities of Communist Intellectuals', exhorted PCF intellectuals to 'defend in all circumstances and with the utmost resolution all the positions of the Party'.[56] Cogniot informed them that '[t]here is also a Marshall plan of the mind',[57] and urged the protection of French culture from bourgeois cosmopolitanism. Ultimate proof of *esprit de parti* consisted in readiness to abjure real or imaginary deviations: Garaudy obliged for this overestimation of the French heritage in scientific socialism; Lefebvre for his of the Hegelian.

---

[51] Zhdanov 1950, p. 87.
[52] Zhdanov 1950, pp. 103–4. For Zhdanov's lurid characterisation of the 'hostile ideology' to be repulsed, see pp. 108–9.
[53] Zhdanov 1950, p. 102.
[54] Quoted in Löwy 1984, p. 175.
[55] Quoted in Löwy 1984, p. 177.
[56] Quoted in Caute 1964, p. 55.
[57] Quoted in Caute 1964, p. 214.

This was the era evoked by Althusser in the introduction to *For Marx*:

> The War was just over. We were brutally cast into the Party's great political and ideological battles: we had to measure up to our choice and take the consequences.
>
> In our political memory this period remains the time of huge strikes and demonstrations, of the Stockholm Appeal and the Peace Movement.... In our philosophical memory it remains the period of intellectuals in arms, hunting out error from all its hiding-places; of the philosophers we were, without writings of our own, but making politics out of all writing, and slicing up the world with a single blade, arts, literatures, philosophies, sciences with the pitiless demarcation of class – the period summed up in caricature by a single phrase, a banner flapping in the void: 'bourgeois science, proletarian science'.[58]

Zhdanovism and Lysenkoism were the apotheosis of the philosophical 'subjectivism' and 'voluntarism' against which Althusser's own intervention was directed. That 'Stalinist dogmatism' was marked by such characteristics is a paradox noted not only by him.[59] That this postwar 'theoretical leftism' reproduced *certain* aspects of the Hegelians' leftism in the aftermath of the First World War has been remarked by Hobsbawm.[60] That there remains the world of difference between their initiative and the Stalinist instrumentalisation/ politicisation of theory in the interests of *raison d'état* appears to have escaped Althusser – or at least was not registered by him. Moreover,

> Paradoxically, it was none other than Stalin, whose contagious and implacable system of government and thought had induced this delirium, who reduced the madness to a little more reason. Reading between the lines of the few simple pages in which he reproved the zeal of those who were making strenuous efforts to prove language a superstructure, we could see that there were limits to the use of the class criterion and that we had been made to treat science, a status claimed by every page of Marx, as merely the first-

---

[58] Althusser 1969a, pp. 21–2. *Science bourgeoise et science prolétarienne* was the title of a collection of articles by Cohen, Desanti et al. published by the PCF in 1950. For Garaudy's retrospect on the period, see his 1970, p. 14. Cf. Hobsbawm 1982, p. 112.

[59] For just one example, see Timpanaro 1980, p. 33.

[60] See Hobsbawm 1982, p. 144. Cf. Althusser 1969a, p. 23 and Althusser and Balibar 1970, pp. 140–1.

comer amongst ideologies. We had to retreat, and, in semi-disarray, return to first principles.[61]

As we shall see in Chapter 5, such an affidavit for Stalin's intervention against one of his own malign proletarian-scientific creations (N.Y. Marr) in *Marxism and Linguistics* (1950) is at best inappropriate. However, neither it, nor Althusser's tribute to Stalin's 'theoretical perspicacity' regarding the negation of the negation, should be taken as proof positive of Stalinism. Althusser was in agreement with Stalin over the Hegelian category insofar as he identified it as the 'motor principle' of the Hegelian dialectic.[62] He was likewise in accord to the extent that Stalin *had*, albeit for reasons of his own, terminated the zenith of the Zhdanovist delirium. He was decidedly dissentient when it came to what Marxist philosophy should look like thereafter. Employing Zhdanovism as the negative lens through which the rest of Marxist philosophy was to be view and categorised – the yardstick against which it was to be measured for its proximity to 'subjectivism' – Althusser attempted a construction at its antipodes.

From *Capital* to Marx's philosophy

Althusser's 'return to first principles' was not exactly that, since it started out from a distinction between historical and dialectical materialism 'affirmed by the Marxist tradition, from Marx and Engels to Lenin and Stalin'.[63] It Althusser denied that Marxist philosophy existed in *theoretical* form, he asserted its presence in the 'practical' state in *Capital*. It was to be 'read' not in Engels's, Lenin's or Stalin's philosophical works, but in Marx. The requisite epistemology for a scientific investigation of Marx's work happened to be Marx's own. The road to it would be a difficult one. Fortunately, it was a ring-road. The itinerary, as the title of Althusser's introductory paper in *Reading 'Capital'* put it, would be 'from *Capital* to Marx's philosophy':

---

[61] Althusser 1969a, p. 22 (a plaudit repeated in Althusser and Balibar 1970, p. 133).
[62] Althusser 1969a, p. 214. It should be noted that Althusser's anti-Hegelianism was based upon close acquaintance with the œuvre both of Hegel and of the young Hegelians. In 1948 he had written a master's thesis *On Content in the Thought of G.W.F. Hegel* under the supervision of Bachelard, and in 1960 (as we have seen) edited and translated a selection of Feuerbach's writings, published in the prestigious *Épiméthée* series at Presses Universitaires de France directed by Jean Hyppolite.
[63] Althusser 1966a, p. 90.

> [A] philosophical reading of *Capital* is only possible as the application of
> that which is the very object of our investigation, Marxist philosophy. This
> circle is only epistemologically possible because of the existence of
> Marx's philosophy in the works of Marxism. It is therefore a question of
> producing . . . something which in a sense *already exists*.[64]

The 'circle' involved was further described in the introduction to *For Marx*:

> [T]he precondition of a reading of Marx is a Marxist theory of the differential
> nature of theoretical formations and their history, that is, a theory of
> epistemological history, which is Marxist philosophy itself; . . . this operation
> in itself constitutes an indispensable circle in which the application of Marxist
> theory to Marx himself appears to be the absolute precondition of an
> understanding of Marx and at the same time as the precondition even of
> the constitution and development of Marxist philosophy. . . . That Marxism
> can and must itself be the object of the epistemological question, that this
> question can only be asked as a function of the Marxist theoretical problematic,
> that is necessity itself for a theory which defines itself dialectically,
> not merely as a science of history (historical materialism) but also and
> simultaneously as a philosophy, a philosophy that is capable of accounting
> for the nature of theoretical formations and their history, and therefore *capable
> of accounting for itself*, by taking itself as its own object. Marxism is the only
> philosophy that theoretically faces up to this test.[65]

Granted for the time being that Marx's epistemology is at work – immanent
– in *Capital* and so on; and granted that Althusser's intention is to extract
and systematise it that it might be known to be Marx's philosophy, an
apparently insuperable barrier remains. If Althusser must construct the
appropriate epistemology with which to make (and justify) discriminations
within Marx's œuvre, he must first of all supply the reading protocols which
can facilitate its extraction and prove that it is both the *sui generis* Marxist
philosophy *and Marx's*. Otherwise, he would be vulnerable to the same
accusations of infidelity he levelled at his colleagues. This is, of course, to
bracket a powerful objection to Althusser's whole strategy – namely, that
there is something inherently dogmatic and viciously circular in employing

---

Marxist philosophy to guarantee the status of Marxist science. Althusser circumvents this objection and the preceding problem by having it both ways and playing both ends against his middle. On the one hand, by appealing to Marx's 1857 Introduction as the rough draft of the Marxist 'Discourse on Method',[66] he seeks to placate potential Marxist critics. On the other hand, by drawing on the prestigious Bachelardian tradition he aims to pre-empt the (Marxist or non-Marxist) accusation of dogmatism. The appropriation of Bachelardian theses allows Althusser to get his excursion underway. *En route*, he evidently believed, the scientificity of his version of dialectical materialism, pronounced to accord with Marx's own methodological reflections, would be demonstrated. Althusser's aim was not simply to plug a gap in the canon of Marxism, but to erect a scientific philosophy which respected the scientificity of the natural sciences and which, in turn, demanded recognition of the scientific status of historical materialism.

In order to justify his proposal for a *sui generis* Marxist philosophy, Althusser invoked historical precedent, maintaining that philosophical revolutions were attendant upon – 'induced by' – scientific revolutions. Thus, just as Greek mathematics had given rise to Platonic, and Galilean physics to Cartesian, philosophy, so historical had 'induced' dialectical materialism. Its advent *post festum* conformed to the pattern set by its predecessors.[67] Involved in all of them was 'the "reprise" of a basic scientific discovery in philosophical reflection and the production by philosophy of a *new form of rationality*'.[68] Marxist philosophy was, however, *primus inter pares*. The novelty of dialectical materialism was that with its arrival philosophy had passed 'from the condition of an *ideology* [to] a *scientific discipline*' – one capable of rendering a scientific account of its object: the history of the production of knowledge.[69] By virtue of his 'double theoretical revolution', Marx occupied an 'exceptional position . . . in the history of human knowledge'.[70] As a scientific philosophy, dialectical materialism could function as a 'guide' not only for the science of history, imperilled as it was by *garaudysme* and so on, but, if needs be, for all the

---

[66] See Althusser 1969a, pp. 182–3, 185, 190 and Althusser and Balibar 1970, pp. 40–2, 54, 86–7.
[67] See Althusser 1969a, pp. 14, 174.
[68] Althusser and Balibar 1970, p. 185.
[69] Althusser 1990, p. 10.
[70] Althusser 1966a, p. 97.

other sciences – natural and social alike – as well.[71] On this basis, Althusser criticised a common tendency in the history of Marxism: *'the negation of philosophy'*.[72] The recurrent temptation of the 'end of philosophy' had taken three major forms: (i) an 'ethical' form (inspired by Marx's early writings), in which philosophy, abstract discourse of the truth, would disappear upon its concrete 'realisation'; (ii) a 'historicist' form, in which philosophy passes away with the transient historical moment of which it is the transitory 'expression'; and (iii) a 'positivist' form (nourished by *The German Ideology* and *Ludwig Feuerbach*), in which (speculative) philosophy cedes to (empirical) science.[73] Against these was to be set the properly Marxist conception of philosophy. Marxist philosophy was not, as Sartre supposed, 'the philosophy of our time', unsurpassable, like its classical bourgeois antecedents, until 'man has gone beyond the historical moment which they express'.[74] It was a scientific discipline with its own object, theory and method, destined to outlive the moment of its birth and autonomous of any historical consciousness.

What is the cogency of Althusser's 'indispensable circle'? According to him, Marxist philosophy existed de jure and was active de facto. Its *practical content* now had to be given *theoretical form*. In other words, it remained to be constituted. For a non-Althusserian, however, why this philosophy remained to be constituted remains to be explained. If Althusser's schema is right, why is not the dialectical materialism of Engels, Lenin or Stalin the 'induced' philosophy? Why is it Althusser who, although he makes no such claim, must play the role of Descartes to Marx's Galileo? But is Althusser's schema right? Did Marx's new theory of history necessarily provoke a philosophical revolution? Was it a 'double theoretical revolution'? Or is Althusser's contentious initiative, seeking in an unsubstantiated analogy with the history of philosophy and in the unavailing labours of Engels and others its own justification, the product of, and (as he hoped) the deliverance from, a 'theoretical impasse' closer to home? This last question can be answered in the affirmative. Althusser needed Marxist philosophy for his own purposes – as was made abundantly clear in *Reading 'Capital'*:

---

[71] See, e.g., Althusser 1990, p. 13.

[72] Althusser 1966a, p. 99.

[73] See Althusser 1966a, pp. 99–102; Althusser 1969a, pp. 28–30; and Althusser and Balibar 1970, pp. 136–7.

[74] Sartre 1968, pp. 30, 7. Sartre's formula is criticised in Althusser and Balibar 1970, pp. 135–6.

In order to understand Marx we must treat him as one scientist among others and apply to his scientific work the same epistemological and historical concepts we would apply to others. . . . Marx thus appears as the founder of a science, comparable with Galileo or Lavoisier. . . . An understanding of Marx . . . leads us . . . to the concepts of a general theory of the history of the sciences. . . . It is one thing whether this general theory as yet only exists as a project or whether it has already partially materialized; it is another that it is *absolutely indispensable to a study of Marx*. The path Engels designates for us . . . is a path we must take at all costs: it is none other than the path of the philosophy founded by Marx in the act of founding the science of history.[75]

If Althusser's justification of *why* the philosophy remained to be constituted is, in intra-Marxist terms, exiguous, his conception of *how* it was to be constructed is controversial in the extreme – raising once again the question of the models (non-Marxist and Marxist) from which it departed.

The theory of theoretical practice

The presentation of the *Théorie* series defined the Althusserian project in philosophy. Marxist philosophy was to be a 'theory of the production of knowledges', a theory which broke with all forms of idealism. It comprised: (i) a theory of scientific and ideological discourse: theoretical practice – and what distinguished this practice from other practices; (ii) a theory of the history of the sciences – as distinct from other forms of history; and (iii) a theory of the structure and history of the other – non-theoretical – social practices with which theoretical practice is 'articulated'. 'Contained' in Marx's writings, this project coincided with the Bachelardian research programme. In the event, the philosophy Althusser supposedly wrote at Marx's dictation had non-Marxist dictators as well and hence, to change the metaphor, was more of an improvisation than a recitation.

First, there was the œuvre of Bachelard. Contemporary with the nadir of theoretical Stalinism in the USSR and the international Communist movement was the publication of Bachelard's second trio of major works (*Le Rationalisme*

---

[75] Althusser and Balibar 1970, p. 153. For the key passage of Engels's Preface to Volume Two of *Capital*, to which Althusser is referring, see Marx 1978, pp. 97–100.

appliqué [1949], *L'activité rationaliste de la physique contemporaine* [1951], and *Le Matérialisme rationnel* [1953]). Before all else, perhaps, Bachelard was himself one of the 'Anabaptist philosophers' he summoned to the defence of the contemporary natural sciences in 1951: a partisan of scientific knowledge and polemicist against its detractors.[76] Bachelard's ambition throughout his career was to construct 'a philosophy . . . genuinely adequate to constantly evolving scientific thought'.[77] This involved him in continual confrontation with other epistemologies and philosophies (empiricism, realism, phenomenology, and so on). Briefly put, Bachelard argued that there was a total disjunction between scientific knowledge and what he termed *connaissance commune*. For Bachelard, the latter is a-conceptual, but imbued with (unconscious) 'epistemological obstacles' – impediments to the development of scientific knowledge. Scientific knowledge, in contrast, is irreducibly conceptual, initiated by an 'epistemological break' which separates it from commonsense knowledge. An index of the difference between the scientific and non-scientific is to be found in the difference between their respective objects. Whereas the object of commonsense knowledge is 'given' by everyday experience, the object of a science is 'constructed' by/in its conceptual system. The concept of *rupture épistémologique* signifies the discontinuity between *episteme* and *doxa* in general and discontinuities in the history of already established sciences in particular. Given that the latter continue to exhibit epistemological discontinuities, an adequate epistemology could only be a historical one, focusing on the process of (trans)formation of concepts. The history of the sciences was conceived as being 'guided by a kind of autonomous necessity':[78] the progressive emergence (discontinuous but continual) of 'rational values' which devalued, and demarcated themselves from, the non-scientific.

As Peter Dews has noted,[79] if Bachelard assigns theory primacy over experience, and considers scientific progress to reside in increasing conceptual coherence and progressive mathematisation, he does not adopt a purely rationalist position; rectification of a theory on the basis of new evidence is envisaged. The second ancestor of Althusser's epistemology, on the other

---

[76] See Bachelard 1951, p. 106. For Althusserian discussion of Bachelard, see Lecourt 1974 and 1975.
[77] Bachelard 1975, p. 7.
[78] Quoted in Lecourt 1975, pp. 11–12.
[79] Dews 1994, pp. 123–4.

hand, adopted precisely such a position. In *Reading 'Capital'* Spinoza was credited with having been 'the first man in the world to have proposed both a theory of history and a philosophy of the opacity of the immediate'.[80] The latter, as Althusser concedes, is no novelty of Spinoza's or Bachelard's:

> An object cannot be defined by its immediately visible or sensuous appearance, it is necessary to make a detour via its concept in order to grasp it . . . : these theses have a familiar ring to them – at least they are the lesson of the whole history of modern science, more or less reflected in classical philosophy, even if this reflection took place in the element of an empiricism. . . .[81]

Spinoza's revolutionary singularity in the classical philosophical tradition consisted in the fact that he had contrived to avoid the myriad lures of 'empiricism'. He had made a categorical distinction between the 'true idea' (such as the idea of a circle) and its 'ideate' (the circle): a distinction mapped by Althusser onto the 1857 Introduction and rendered as the irreducible difference between the theoretical object (the 'object of knowledge') and the 'real object'.[82] Moreover, Spinoza had distinguished between 'three kinds of knowledge'. The first – 'opinion, or imagination' (whose source is random sense experience: *experientia vaga*) – was said to be 'the only source of falsity'. The other two – 'reason' and 'intuition' – supposedly yielded knowledge which was 'necessarily true'. What Althusser called Spinoza's 'theory of the difference between the imaginary and the true' was employed by him to think the Marxist opposition between science and ideology.[83] 'Truth is the standard both of itself and of falsity', wrote the author of the *Ethics* – an axiom upon which Althusser was later to confess his reliance.[84] Scientific knowledge – that is, the system of adequate ideas that are the concepts of their objects – is a criterion not only of itself, but of the non-scientific or ideological (or,

---

[80] Althusser and Balibar 1970, p. 16. Of course, Plekhanov, for whom Marxism was a materialist 'monism', had deemed Spinoza a 'precursor' of Marx in his time: see, e.g., Plekhanov 1908, pp. 19–20 and cf. Althusser's critical remarks in Althusser 1969a, pp. 201–2 n. 42.
[81] Althusser and Balibar 1970, p. 184.
[82] See Spinoza 1955, p. 12 and cf. Althusser and Balibar 1970, pp. 40–1, 105.
[83] Althusser and Balibar, p. 17. See Spinoza 1955, pp. 113–14 and cf. Althusser 1969a, p. 78 n. 40 and Althusser and Balibar 1970, pp. 16–17, 159.
[84] See Spinoza 1955, p. 115 and cf. Althusser 1976a, pp. 112, 137–8, 187–8.

inadequate ideas) as well.[85] Thus Spinoza rejected the traditional 'correspondence' conception of knowledge [*adaequatio rei et intellectus*]. Reversing this definition, he held that true ideas were not adequate to their objects because of their extrinsic correspondence to them; on the contrary, they corresponded to their objects because of their intrinsic adequacy.[86] Conjugating Spinoza and Marx, Althusser opted for the Dutchman's epistemological rationalism over the German's scientific realism.

In 'Theory, Theoretical Practice and Theoretical Formation', Althusser warned of the dangers of apprehending Marxist science in empiricist or dogmatist fashion. In the latter case, it was treated as 'an absolute, finished knowledge, which poses no problem of development or research'; in the former, as the 'direct', 'natural' reflection of the real – fruit of Marx's unclouded vision. '*The idea we have of science,*' Althusser wrote, '*is decisive for Marxist science itself.*' The first principle of a correct idea of science was the Spinozist-Bachelardian one that, 'far from reflecting the immediate givens of everyday experience and practice, [a science] is constituted only on the condition of calling them into question, and breaking with them'.[87] Scientific knowledge can be obtained only through a detour via the concept of an object. But before that, the concept must be produced.

In *On the Improvement of the Understanding* – a 'Discourse against Method'[88] – Spinoza had rejected the Cartesian search for a priori guarantees of the possibility of knowledge as both unavailing (for condemned to an infinite regress) and unnecessary ('for we have a true idea': *habemus enim ideam veram*).[89] Questions about the validity of knowledge must commence from the prior recognition of its facticity. And it was the possession of knowledge, criterion of itself and its other, which permitted the provision of further knowledge – a process illustrated by analogy with the 'making of tools'.[90] Indeed, the knowledge process could be viewed as a process of production of 'intellectual instruments'. Developing this conception of knowledge as production,[91] and

[85] See the helpful discussion in Patton 1978.
[86] See Macherey 1979, pp. 75–94.
[87] Althusser 1990, pp. 14–15.
[88] Macherey 1979, p. 57.
[89] Spinoza 1955, p. 12.
[90] Spinoza 1955, pp. 11–12.
[91] See the discussion in Althusser 1976a, pp. 137–8, 187–9.

associating Marx with it, Althusser argued that the production of knowledge of real objects by the production of their adequate concepts was the result of a specific practice: theoretical practice. Althusser's first move was to insist that theory was not the (abstract/spiritual) obverse of (concrete/material) practice, but itself exactly such a practice. Strictly speaking, there was no such thing as 'practice in general', only *distinct practices*.[92] To deny the specificity of theoretical practice was to nullify 'the reality of scientific practice'.[93] The effects of this traditional (and deep-rooted) denegation were not restricted to an inadequate comprehension of science in general. The theory/practice dichotomy could be brandished to embarrass Marxist intellectuals over their sojourn, *au-dessus de la mêlée*, in a conceptual limbo. Whether done out of benign or malignant motives, this underestimated the crucial role apportioned theory – scientific knowledge – by Marx, Engels and Lenin, and played by it in revolutionary politics. After the depredations of Zhdanovism, theory had to secure recognition of its justified claims to relative autonomy – precisely in order to fulfil its proper function as a 'guide' for practice.

Drawing on Marx's analysis of the labour process in *Capital*, Althusser dissected 'society' into four main practices: economic, political, ideological and theoretical, the ensemble of which constituted the 'complex unity of "social practice"'. Each practice was said to have three 'moments' – raw material, means of production and product:

> By *practice* in general I shall mean any process of *transformation* of a determinate given raw material into a determinate product, a transformation effected by a determinate human labour, using a determinate means (of 'production'). In any practice thus conceived, the *determinant* moment (or element) is neither the raw material nor the product, but the practice in the narrow sense: the moment of the *labour of transformation* itself, which sets to work, in a specific structure, men, means and a technical method of utilizing the means.

Althusser proceed to sketch outlines of economic, political and ideological practice – definitions to which we shall return in Chapter 3. Offering these as 'essential preliminary hypotheses', he made no attempt to substantiate the

---

[92] Althusser and Balibar 1970, p. 58.
[93] Althusser 1969a, p. 187.

case for his a priori characterisation of the contents of the social. Instead, he turned to a discussion of theoretical practice, defining it as follows:

> By theory . . . I shall mean a *specific form of practice*, itself belonging to the complex unity of the 'social practice' of a determinate human society. Theoretical practice falls within the general definition of practice. It works on a raw material (representations, concepts, facts) which it is given by other practices, whether 'empirical', 'technical' or 'ideological'. In its most general form theoretical practice does not only include *scientific* theoretical practice, but also pre-scientific theoretical practice, that is, 'ideological' theoretical practice. . . .[94]

Theoretical production, it was argued, shares the structure of the other practices. Its raw material (labelled 'Generality I') is itself theoretical (composed of 'representations, concepts, facts'), whether scientific or not. Its means of production (labelled 'Generality II') is its 'problematic' – the theoretical matrix in which the concepts of a discourse are ordered / unified and on the basis of which questions are asked and answered, problems posed and resolved (or not). Its products ('Generalities III') are knowledge(s). The determinant moment of theoretical practice is the second – namely, the 'labour of transformation': 'theoretical practice produces Generalities III by the work of Generality II on Generality I'.[95] An adequate account of this practice involved analysis not only of its labour process, but of its social relations of production as well – in other words, consideration and specification of its relations with the wider social structure:

> . . . thought is the historically constituted system of an *apparatus of thought*, founded on and articulated to natural and social reality. It is defined by the system of real conditions which make it . . . a determinate *mode of production* of knowledges. As such, it constituted by a structure which combines . . . the type of object (raw material) on which it labours, the theoretical means of production available (its theory, its method and its technique, experimental or otherwise) and the historical relations (both theoretical, ideological and social) in which it produces.[96]

Cognitively autonomous, socially, theory is relatively autonomous.

---

[94] Althusser 1969a, pp. 166–7. For Marx's analysis of the labour process – Althusser's 'authority' here – see Marx 1976a, pp. 283–92.
[95] See Althusser 1969a, pp. 183–5.
[96] Althusser and Balibar 1970, p. 41.

The prime enemy of this epistemology – the theory of theoretical practice – was dubbed 'the empiricist conception of knowledge'. As portrayed by Althusser, it embraced much more than, perhaps even the opposite of, empiricism as normally understood. To this paradigm he assimilated any theory of the cognitive process which represented it as the confrontation between (knowing) subject and object (to be known), and which conceived knowledge as abstraction by the subject of the essence of the object.[97] According to Althusser, this conception was the 'secular transcription' of a 'religious myth of *reading*'.[98] Knowledge was not *vision* but *production*, not *abstraction* (or purification) but *appropriation*. The putative Marxist authority for Althusser's representation of the cognitive process as a productive one wholly internal to thought was Marx's 1857 Introduction. It was the text that 'allows us to distinguish Marxist philosophy from every speculative or empiricist philosophy', for in it the 'order of thought' and the 'order of the real' were unequivocally differentiated. Marx had proposed two 'materialist' theses: 'the primacy of the real over thought about the real' and 'the specificity of thought and of the thought process'. Thus, the *'real object'* (Spinoza's circle or the cat which can miaow) is neither directly involved in, nor affected by, the process of theoretical production. The starting point (raw material) *and* result (product) of that practice is the *'object of knowledge'* (Spinoza's idea of the circle/the concept of cat which cannot miaow), via which theoretical object knowledge of the real object is 'appropriated'. The novelty and superiority of Althusser's epistemology – or so he believed – consisted in its acceptance (contrary to all forms of empiricism, which provoked the perennial 'problem of knowledge') that knowledge was an *intra-theoretical* process of production, without ceasing to be objective knowledge. Knowledge (the 'concrete-in-thought'), whilst utterly distinct from the real (the 'real-concrete'), was knowledge of a reality itself wholly independent of thought or discourse. In principle, Althusser's epistemology was simultaneously 'anti-empiricist' and 'materialist'.[99]

To the distinction between theoretical practice on the one hand, and economic, political and ideological practice on the other, was added a distinction internal

---

[97] See Althusser and Balibar 1970, pp. 35–9.
[98] Althusser and Balibar, pp. 17, 35.
[99] See Althusser and Balibar 1970, pp. 40–1, 86–7 and Althusser 1969a, pp. 185–6. Cf. Marx 1973, pp. 101–2.

to theoretical practice. In accordance with the classical-Marxist opposition between science and ideology, Althusser distinguished between scientific theoretical practice and pre-scientific or ideological theoretical practice. Some theoretical practices are scientific, that is, produce scientific knowledge, while others (the majority) are ideological, that is, produce ideological 'knowledge'. Althusser categorised the latter as 'the forms of "knowledge" that make up the pre-history of a science and their "philosophies"'.[100] To theorise the distinction between knowledge and 'knowledge', Althusser adopted two Bachelardian concepts: epistemological break and problematic. Following Bachelard, he posited a '"qualitative" theoretical and historical discontinuity' between science and theoretical ideology.[101] Since the discontinuity arises at a particular moment in theoretical history, it can only be located by an epistemological-historical – an epistemologically informed – genealogy of a science. The index of scientificity in the Althusserian, as in the Bachelardian, scheme of things is a 'rupture' between the scientific and the non-scientific within a particular theoretical region. With this 'break', a discourse crosses the threshold of scientificity and attains cognitive autonomy. Thereafter, the theoretical practice of a science is its own criterion. Its products require no prior guarantees or external confirmation. Verification is internal to the theory. As for Spinoza, truth is its own standard. In genuine sciences (including historical materialism), there is a 'radical inwardness of the criterion of practice':

> To speak of the criterion of practice where theory is concerned . . . receives its full sense: for *theoretical practice* is indeed its own criterion, and contains in itself definite protocols with which to *validate* the quality of its product, i.e., the criteria of the scientificity of the products of scientific practice. This is exactly what happens in the real practice of the sciences: once they are truly constituted and developed they have no need for verification from *external* practices to declare the knowledges they produce to be 'true', i.e., to be *knowledges*. . . . We should say the same of the science which concerns us most particularly: historical materialism. It has been possible to apply Marx's theory with success because it is 'true'; it is not true because it has been applied with success.[102]

---

[100] Althusser 1969a, p. 167.
[101] Althusser 1969a, pp. 167–8.
[102] Althusser and Balibar 1970, pp. 59–60.

Sparing the intrusions of the extra-theoretical in the shape of a Cardinal Bellarmine or Comrade Zhdavov, scientific theoretical practice serves neither God nor Mammon. Ideological practice, in contrast, is 'governed by "interests" beyond the necessity of knowledge alone'.[103] Following Spinoza, Althusser conceived theoretical ideology as a 'kind' of knowledge, but as an inferior species – one that 'designates ... existents, but ... does not give us their essences'.[104] 'Source of falsity', it was not falsity per se. Althusser defined ideology in general as an omni-historical phenomenon: 'the "lived" relation between men and the world'.[105] As a representation of this 'imaginary' relation, ideology is not mere error or illusion; it is an objective reality, a material practice whose theoretical relays can be confuted, but which cannot itself be dissipated, by science.[106] Theoretical ideology is a knowledge – but in the form of *recognition*, not *cognition*. This is so because it is governed by adventitious factors extraneous to science – what Althusser calls the 'practico-social function' as opposed to the 'theoretical function':

> In the theoretical mode of production of ideology ... the formulation of a *problem* is merely the theoretical expression of the conditions which allow a *solution* already produced outside the process of knowledge because imposed by extra-theoretical instances and exigencies ... to *recognize itself* in an artificial problem manufactured to serve it both as a theoretical mirror and as a practical justification.[107]

The result, in the words of Alan Badiou, is that whereas 'science is a process of *transformation*, ideology ... is a process of *repetition*'.[108]

The 'qualitative leap' or mutation marking the difference between a science and a theoretical ideology was situated by Althusser in the discourse's problematic. Although rarely employed by Bachelard, this concept was implicit in his work. 'The sense of the problem is characteristic of the scientific mind', he wrote in *La Formation de l'esprit scientifique* in a passage which anticipated Althusser's thesis on the modality of the formulation of problems in theoretical

---

[103] Althusser and Balibar 1970, p. 141.
[104] Althusser 1969a, p. 223.
[105] Althusser 1969a, p. 233.
[106] See, e.g., Althusser 1969a, pp. 230, 233.
[107] Althusser 1969a, p. 231; Althusser and Balibar 1970, p. 52.
[108] Badiou 1967, p. 449.

ideology.[109] As adapted by Althusser, the concept denoted 'the *typical systematic structure* unifying all the elements of the thought' and referred to a 'fact peculiar to the very existence of science':

> it can only pose problems on the terrain and within the horizon of a definite theoretical structure, its problematic, which constitutes its absolute and definite condition of possibility, and hence the absolute determination of *the forms in which all problems must be posed*, at any given moment in the science.[110]

A non-scientific problematic is characterised by its 'closure' – its repetitive revolution in an ideological circle; a scientific problematic by its 'openness' to pertinent problems and their rigorous solution, its capacity for (self-) rectification and development.[111] Because a problematic is both present and absent (in Althusser's structuralist terminology, 'diachronic' and 'synchronic') in any particular segment of theoretical discourse, a special kind of reading is required in order to reconstruct it: the 'symptomatic reading' which, like the Freudian analyst's technique, proceeds from the surface discourse to its latent system (or 'unconscious').[112] At stake is more than 'openness and closure in general'. For any adequate epistemology must concern itself with '*the typical, historically determined structures of this openness and closure*'.[113] Specific ruptures and transitions can be identified only by working from within the problematic of the already constituted science, since the *general* concept of the break (between the scientific and the ideological *tout court*) cannot specify the conditions of a *particular* break (for example, Marx's with classical political economy). The problematic with which a science breaks at the moment of its constitution (its 'point of no return') or its 'recasting' is a necessary, but insufficient, condition of the new problematic. In the case of historical materialism, for example, there would have been no such theory but for what preceded it (it was not created *ex nihilo* by Marx). At the same time, however,

---

[109] Bachelard 1980, p. 44.
[110] Althusser 1969a, p. 67; Althusser and Balibar 1970, p. 25. In Althusser 1969a, p. 25, Jacques Martin (a friend to whom *For Marx* is dedicated) is credited with the concept of problematic.
[111] See Althusser and Balibar 1970, pp. 53, 55, 69.
[112] See Althusser and Balibar 1970, pp. 28, 32–3, 69.
[113] Althusser and Balibar 1970, p. 90 n. 5.

it was not vouchsafed by the synthesis of pre-existing discourses/problematics (German philosophy, English political economy, French utopian socialism). The pre-scientific problematic forms part of the real history – the pre-history – of the science. So although a science is inaugurated 'by detaching it from the ideology of its past and by revealing this past as ideological'; and although, after its constitution, the science amounts, Spinoza-style, to a 'science of the ideology',[114] the science-ideology distinction must not be treated in Enlightenment fashion as the rationalist partition between truth and error, but *historically*. The strange 'Gods of Origins and Goals' are to be deposed in favour of 'the necessity of contingency'.[115] *Qua* historical epistemology, the theory of theoretical practice – 'the theory of science and of the history of science'[116] – joined with the Bachelardians in opening the path to

> a revolution in the traditional concept of the history of the sciences. . . . We are beginning to conceive this history as a history punctuated by radical discontinuities . . . profound reorganisations which, if they respect the continuity of the existence of regions of knowledge (and even this is not always the case), nevertheless inaugurate with their rupture the reign of a new logic, which, far from being a mere development . . . of the old one, *literally* takes its place.[117]

As Althusser was well aware, his (negative) demarcation of theoretical ideology from science is not a (positive) specification of the scientificity of science. This, in conjunction with his insistence on the autonomy of theory, prompts the traditional epistemological question. In Althusser's case and terms, it takes the following form: how do we know that the result or products of scientific theoretical practices are knowledges? Althusser straightaway rejects the problematic of the 'theory of knowledge' derived from the 'closed circle' of classical philosophy, reproving its variants as variations on a juridical practice of philosophy which 'makes laws for the science[s] in the name of

---

[114] Althusser 1969a, p. 168; Althusser and Balibar 1970, p. 46.

[115] Althusser 1969a, p. 71; Althusser and Balibar 1970, p. 45.

[116] Althusser's definition of philosophy in Althusser and Balibar 1970, p. 145. See also Macherey 1965, p. 216.

[117] Althusser and Balibar 1970, p. 44. Althusser cites the work of Bachelard, Cavaillès, Canguilhem, Foucault and Alexandre Koyré as 'remarkable' exceptions to the dominant teleological and continuist historiography. See also Althusser 1998b.

a right it arrogates to itself'.[118] The search for de jure or de facto guarantees must be renounced as an impermissible – ideological – project leading, at best, to an infinite regress. In the Althusserian 'theory of the history of the production of knowledges', it is accepted that the theoretical object of a theoretical practice is the 'appropriation of the *real* object, the real world'.[119] But is it? As has been noted, the motivation of Althusser's project was the definition and defence of the scientificity of historical materialism. The distinctiveness of his approach to the issue lay in his effort to erase any epistemological distinction between Marx's theory of history and the natural sciences, *without* lapsing into a discreditable positivism; Marxism was a science 'among others', at once autonomous *and* scientific. Althusser was fundamentally at variance with the existing Marxist tradition in spurning both the 'correspondence' theory of truth of classical Marxism and the pragmatist conception of truth of Stalinism, and replacing them by the self-sufficiency of the modes of proof of the established sciences. The inadequacy and circularity of such a criterion for the contemporary natural sciences is one thing; few would challenge their scientific status. With historical materialism, things stand rather differently – as a roll-call of Karl Popper, Thomas Kuhn and Imre Lakatos is sufficient to remind us. Without positive, compelling criteria of scientificity, Althusser's bid for historical materialism is imperilled and the theory of theoretical practice – considered by him 'the theory . . . of what constitutes the scientificity of the sciences'[120] – itself founders as a satisfactory account of science.

Althusser did have an answer to the epistemological problem – or rather, a question. In 'On the Materialist Dialectic', the pertinent response to the 'problem of knowledge' had been its dissolution; the 'non-problematicity of the relation between an object and the knowledge of it' was straightforwardly asserted.[121] The ingenuousness of this 'solution' presumably being apparent, in *Reading 'Capital'* Althusser took another tack. For epistemological guarantees the theory of theoretical practice substituted the question of the '*mechanism*' of the cognitive appropriation of the real. Therewith, Althusser believed,

---

[118] Althusser and Balibar 1970, p. 56 (see p. 52ff.)
[119] Althusser and Balibar 1970, pp. 56, 54.
[120] Althusser 1966a, p. 122.
[121] Althusser 1969a, p. 186.

philosophy made the transition from ideology to scientificity. The key question became:

> ... by what mechanism does the process of knowledge, which takes place entirely in thought, produce the cognitive appropriation of its real object, which exists outside thought in the real world? Or again, by what mechanism does the production of the object of knowledge produce the cognitive appropriation of the real object, which exists outside thought in the real world?[122]

Notoriously, this question received no real answer – an aporia all the more obvious for the lucidity of Althusser's posing of it. The 'knowledge effect' which is 'the peculiarity of those special products which are knowledges' remains unilluminated beyond cryptic, and in any case circular, allusions to the significance of the internal organisation and disposition of concepts – 'the systematicity of the system'.[123] Since it pertains to science and ideological theoretical practice alike, however, its elucidation would not answer our question. The reader may know how Part I of Reading 'Capital' ends. A subject: the knowledge mechanism. Ten pages of intricate questions; then silence.

If, as Althusser maintained, there are no innocent readings, by the same token, there are guilty silences. Arguably, Althusser's was one. For there is a solution to the problem of the correspondence between thought and the real in his work, only it is unavowed as such. To make it explicit is to reveal the contradictory character of Althusser's philosophical project.

According to the standard Soviet account of dialectical materialism, it is 'the science of the more general laws governing the development of nature, society and thought', of which historical materialism is a sub-set – 'a philosophical science concerned with the specific laws of social development as distinct from the universal laws of being'.[124] Mutatis mutandis, it can be said that these definitions have remained unchanged since Stalin's times. Both were certainly orthodoxy

---

[122] Althusser and Balibar 1970, p. 56.

[123] Althusser and Balibar 1970, pp. 67–8.

[124] Boguslavsky et al. 1976, pp. 38, 246. It is worth noting here that the only commentator (to my knowledge) to have undertaken a systematic comparison between Althusserian and orthodox Soviet conceptions of Marxism concludes: 'The differences between the Soviets and the Althusserians ... involve basic disagreements concerning principles. From the Soviet perspective Althusser and his followers seek to shed vast areas of Marxism' (Nemeth 1980, p. 381).

in the international Communist movement and the PCF at the beginning of
the 1960s. Althusser's schema was, in principle, quite different. Marx's
theoretical revolution comprised a 'double foundation in a single break':[125]
the birth of two new sciences. Marx founded Marxism. Marxism comprised
two autonomous disciplines, a science and a scientific philosophy. Historical
materialism was the science of the history of social formations, complete with
its theory (its conceptual corpus) and object (social formations and their
transformation). Dialectical materialism was the science of theoretical practice,
with its own concepts (science / ideology, problematic, epistemological break,
etc.) and object (theoretical discourse). As an epistemology, it broke with
anterior and contemporary 'philosophical ideologies'. It was a – the – scientific
philosophy. All this Althusser proclaimed, implying a simultaneous break
with orthodox conceptions of dialectical materialism as an ontology of matter
(in movement).

Inscribed in Althusser's enterprise from the outset, however, was the very
pitfall he was seeking to avoid. Regardless of the sophistication of the
Althusserian variant, Marxist philosophy was once again accorded the status
of that *contradictio in adjecto*, a scientific philosophy. As the Theory of theory
and Science of science, the theory of theoretical practice is a reprise of the
diamat tradition. Via its (weak) demarcation criteria, it is the theory capable
of adjudicating the scientificity of both historical materialism and its
competitors, the social and human sciences.[126] Whether it is appropriate for
Marxist philosophy to arrogate itself a right Althusser had forbidden classical
philosophy is one question; whether it is capable of making the adjudication
is another. At any rate, diamat, having been shown the front door, climbed
back in through an open window. In order to establish the specificity of
theoretical practice, Althusser differentiated it from the other practices. As is
made apparent in the presentation of the *Théorie* series, dialectical materialism
was at one and the same time a theory of theory and a theory of non-theory –
a 'Theory of practice in general'.[127] Althusser's epistemology was thus
supplemented – indeed, underpinned – by what Callinicos, following André
Glucksmann, terms an 'ontology of practices'.[128] Infinitely more original than

---

[125] Althusser 1969a, p. 33.
[126] See Althusser 1969a, pp. 171–2.
[127] Althusser 1969a, p. 168.
[128] See Callinicos 1976, p. 72 and Glucksmann 1977, p. 282ff.

the Soviet version it may be, but a diluted diamat it nonetheless is. Nowhere is this better attested than in the (unmarked) exit Althusser's *ontology* provided from his *epistemological* impasse. Dialectical materialism is:

> the general Theory (the dialectic) in which is theoretically expressed the essence of theoretical practice in general, through it the essence of practice in general, and through it the essence of the transformations, of the 'development' of things in general.[129]

Thus, the cognitive appropriation of the real object in and by theoretical practice is made possible by the homology of thought and the real, both of which are practices.

As Callinicos points out, the proximity of this (covert) solution to Engels's standpoint on the 'concordance of thought and being' in the *Dialectics of Nature* is striking.[130] The '*differential* nature of *scientific discourse*'[131] is assured by its identity with the structure of reality, the 'non-problematicity of the relation between an object and the knowledge of it' guaranteed by ontology. The very 'empiricism' disowned by Althusser secures the theory of theoretical practice against relativism. His epistemology can only perform the task of demarcation allotted it on this basis: an uncompelling one, in any case expressly precluded.

Now, it was suggested earlier that Althusser's definition of empiricism was of unusual breadth. Insofar as it encompassed epistemologies which posit an identity between knowledge and the object of which it is knowledge, it would therefore not only include Althusser's own, but also – and crucially – Spinoza's. For, if Althusserian insouciance about the objectivity of knowledge had Engelsian precedent, its direct ancestry was Spinozist – traceable to Spinoza's proposition that '*the order and connection of ideas is the same as the order and connection of things*'.[132] Just as, for Spinoza, the system of intrinsically true 'adequate ideas' reproduced in thought the order and connection of things, so, for Althusser, objects of knowledge were the concepts of their objects, the

---

[129] Althusser 1969a, p. 169. Althusser at once proceeds to criticise any 'application of the "laws" of the dialectic' to the established sciences: 'it makes not one iota of difference to [their] structure or development . . .; worse, it may turn into an ideological fetter' (p. 170).
[130] See Callinicos 1976, p. 76 and cf. Engels 1976, pp. 266–7.
[131] Althusser and Balibar 1970, p. 69.
[132] Spinoza 1955, p. 86. See Anderson 1976, p. 64.

order of theoretical practice (thought) 'expressing' the order of 'practice in general' and its development (the real) as a consequence of their prior identity.[133] Thus, the theory of theoretical practice's combination, via the category of 'production', of 'the theory of science and of the history of science' was facilitated by what Paul Patton calls Althusser's 'Spinozist absolutism'. A rationalist theory of knowledge allowed historical epistemology to dispense with the problematic of the theory of knowledge and assert the 'non-problematicity' of theory's accordance with reality.

'Le (Re)commencement du matéralisme dialectique', Badiou entitled his commendatory review of *For Marx* and *Reading 'Capital'* in 1967. The theory of theoretical practice was indeed conceived by Althusser as the commencement of Marxist philosophy and did terminate in a resumption of dialectical materialism in its pretension to be a 'Theory of practice in general'. Yet if, to this extent, it constituted a return of the repressed, it was one of indubitable ingenuity. And if, in search of what Labica has called 'l'introuvable philosophie marxiste',[134] Althusser assimilated Spinozist and Bachelardian theses, the result was an epistemology whose singularity – even brilliance – within the Marxist tradition was closely bound up with its shortcomings.

Althusser proposed an ontology of practices of which he vouchsafed little or no justification. Yet however aprioristic his construction, it would in turn be remiss not to recognise and applaud its distance from the dialectical materialism obtained by inversion of Hegel's dialectic. Althusser criticised Lenin and Mao for assuming a 'simple original unity' split into contradictory parts, manifest in the most apparently complex of contradictions that develop thereafter, and restored, albeit enriched, as the end of the process. In the place of such Hegelianism, Althusser argued that:

> Marxism establishes in principle the recognition of the givenness of the complex structure of any concrete 'object', a structure which governs both the development of the object and the development of the theoretical practice which produces the knowledge of it. There is no longer any original essence, only an ever-pre-givenness, however far knowledge delves into its past. There is no longer any simple unity, only a structured, complex unity. There

---

[133] See Patton 1978, pp. 17–18.
[134] Labica 1984, p. 116.

is no longer an original simple unity (in any form whatsoever), but instead,
the ever-pre-givenness of a structured complex unity.[135]

With Althusser's ontological anti-idealism (pre-givenness), anti-empiricism
(structured unity), and anti-historicism (complex unity), as Callinicos has
suggested, 'the concept of difference, of the irreducible heterogeneity of the
material world, is domesticated within Marxism'.[136] Althusser's 'complex
unity' was a unity of distinct yet imbricated and articulated practices, irreducible
one to another, and not appearances of the essence – whether spiritual (such
as Absolute Spirit) or 'material' (such as Humanity, the Proletariat, the
Economy). The fact that the ontological structure of social reality took this
form rendered it opaque and theory – one of the practices – necessary. The
theory that proposed this ontology, the 'Theory of practice in general', was
'the materialist *dialectic* which is none other than dialectical materialism'.[137]
Simultaneously, it was an epistemology – the theory of theoretical practice.

Like Althusserian ontology, Althusser's epistemology had great virtues.
Two were of particular conjunctural significance for Marxism. First, and above
all, it insisted, *contra* Zhdanov and his spectres, on the autonomy of the
veridical from State, Class, Party, or any other extra-scientific interest. Next,
it emphasised both the normality and the importance for the sciences –
including historical materialism – of continual development; openness to
rectification and the incessant production of new knowledge became criteria
of scientificity. 'A science that repeats itself, without discovering anything
new, is a dead science – no longer a science, but a fixed dogma. A science
only lives in its development – that is, from its discoveries'.[138] Thus, the basic
thrust of Althusser's philosophical intervention within Marxism was to
highlight its *incompleteness* – what remained to be done. Only the foundations
of historical and dialectical materialism had been laid and the Marxist theoretical
practice of the histories of science, ideology, philosophy, and art (among
others) had not been exhausted – indeed, largely remained to be constituted.[139]

The theory of theoretical practice possessed other positive features, of wider
relevance. It amounted to an attempt to incorporate the lessons of modern,

---

[135] Althusser 1969a, pp. 198–9; see p. 193ff.
[136] Callinicos 1983, p. 95.
[137] Althusser 1969a, p. 168.
[138] Althusser 1990, p. 16.
[139] See Althusser 1969a, p. 169.

non-Marxist philosophy of science into Marxism – more specifically, to integrate the compelling aspects of the conventionalist critique of empiricism and positivism into a 'materialist' epistemology.[140] Accordingly, Althusser sought to reconcile the conventionalist insistence on the historical, social and theoretical character of scientific practice with the realist insistence on the existence of an independent reality irreducible to theory (if knowable via it), to which theory refers and is obliged, indeed, to conform in order to count as scientific knowledge. In other words, Althusser sought to integrate historicity, sociality and scientificity, facticity and validity – in short, to capture the specificity of science. Thus, the distinction between the object of knowledge and the real object betokened the conjoint commitment to the reality of science – the production and transformation of intra-scientific conceptual objects – and to the reality of its referent – the real, extra-scientific world. The notion of epistemological break registered the *sui generis* nature of science as a counter-intuitive cognitive process irreducible to other forms of knowledge. The concept of problematic respected the uniqueness of individual theories as a function of their different conceptual systems, and hence the complexity characteristic of the actual history of the sciences, without sacrificing the possibility of scientific progress to mere scientific change – in principle, at least.

In principle. For the problem was, of course, that this marriage of conventionalism and materialism to form Althusserian anti-empiricism proved an unequal one – the former assuming dominance and maintaining, moreover, a liaison with rationalism equally injurious to the claims of the latter. In the process of securing the cognitive autonomy of Marxist theory, thereby creating space for its development, the theory of theoretical practice compromised its virtues in a set of serious vices. The 'relative autonomy' of science ultimately took the form of outright independence of the social formation and its history. Specificity became transcendence, as the epistemological break which initiated science sequestered it in the autonomous domain of theoretical practice where it 'escaped' the 'vicissitudes' of non-scientific history.[141] Notwithstanding references to the articulation of theoretical practice with the other social

---

[140] For an excellent concise discussion of empiricism, conventionalism and realism, see Lovell 1980, Chapter 1, whose own standpoint is greatly indebted to Bhaskar 1978.
[141] See Althusser and Balibar 1970, pp. 192–3 and compare the French original in Althusser et al. 1965, Volume One, p. 93.

practices, the 'sui generis'[142] history of the sciences was disarticulated from them and treated, instead, as a purely internal, epistemological affair of conceptual historicity. Among the costs of this conception, as we shall see, was to be an account of Marxism which quite implausibly severed it, in its foundation and development, from any socio-historical connections.

If science was separated from the social, it was similarly sundered from the empirical. Rationalism and conventionalism converged here to exclude the latter from scientific practice. Conflating the empirical and the empiricist, Althusser furthermore equated the experiential with the ideological – realm of the imaginary and 'false conceptions', antithesis of conceptual science and objective knowledge.[143] These collapses not only debarred any genuine input on the part of empirical evidence into theoretical practice; they ruled out any reference of theoretical constructs back to it for the purposes of evidential control. Falsification, in any real sense, was precluded, rectification rendered the merest concession to fallibilism. Indeed, the plenipotentiary powers granted Generality II – the problematic or means of theoretical production – over Generality I – its raw material – were such that the status of its products – Generalities III (knowledges) – was questionable. Not content with the determination of its own facts and the elaboration of its own theory and object, theoretical practice also supplied its own verification, validating its own results. Althusser introduced his propositions on the 'radical inwardness of the criterion of practice' in the sciences with the example of mathematical protocols of proof: a symptomatic presence.[144] Mathematics had provided Spinoza's model of science – a 'standard of verity' in the natural and human sciences alike.[145] If Althusser did not seek, in positivist fashion, to 'naturalise' the social sciences – by compelling their conformity to the procedures of the natural sciences – he did, so to speak, 'mathematise', in rationalist fashion, both the natural and the social sciences – projecting onto them the intrinsic method of proof characteristic of an a priori paradigm.

The distinction between science and ideology was the 'cardinal principle' of Althusser's epistemology.[146] The upshot for historical materialism – a science

---

[142] Althusser 1968a.
[143] See, e.g., Althusser 1990, pp. 22–31.
[144] See Althusser and Balibar 1970, p. 59.
[145] See Spinoza 1955, p. 77.
[146] Althusser 1990, p. 42.

among others – of his account of science as a 'detour of theory' whose itinerary was this detour,[147] was the compromising of both its autonomy and its claims to scientific status. That is, the often remarked, unintended consequence of the theory of theoretical practice was an attenuation of scientificity. For it fell short of realism and into conventionalism – a fate from which the rationalist assertion of the adequacy of the theoretical to the real object did not rescue it, only serving, on the contrary, to subvert the non-dogmatic conception of science essayed by Althusser. The Althusserian demarcation of science from ideology, on the basis of their respective counter-intuitive/intuitive, open/closed, theoretical/practico-social characteristics, however suggestive, fails – neither counter-intuitiveness nor openness being peculiar to science, for example.[148] The obvious 'materialist' (more properly, realist) criterion – (non)correspondence between theoretical constructions and their real objects – was eschewed as empiricist. Although Althusser was, in Terry Lovell's words, 'a realist by fiat',[149] the real was accorded purely honorific status by him, posited, in contradistinction to thought about it, but thereafter neutralised by being bracketed. No explanation of the appropriation of the non-theoretical real object by the conceptually constructed object of knowledge was offered, effectively divorcing theory from any extra-theoretical reference, thereby undermining the proposition that concept construction was the royal road to science. The failure to establish a plausible relation between theory and (the rest of) reality means that conceptual elaboration is the *via regia* only to more of the same. Theory-dependent knowledge of the real world is transmuted into reality-independent theory. The result? Since alchemy, for example, is a theoretical practice second to one in its possession of 'definite protocols with which to validate the quality of its product' (or to rationalise its absence – cf. Chaucer's *Canon's Yeoman's Tale*), how can we adjudge it a pseudo-science? How can we tell the difference between a chatterbox and a scientist?[150]

Althusser's severance of theory from any real referent, reflected in a conception of the history of science as one punctuated by radical discontinuities, provoked an acute form of the problem of commensurability, leaving him ill-

---

147 Macherey 1978, p. 120.
148 See Lovell 1980, pp. 34–6.
149 Lovell 1980, p. 17.
150 See Althusser 1990, p. 67.

placed to reconcile theoretical revolutions and scientific progress. For, despite occasional hints at a realist historical perspective, wherein a new problematic referred to the same real object as the problematic which it had superseded, the 'reign of new logics' was the primary Althusserian emphasis in opposition to teleological historiography.[151] Yet how can we even classify, say, historical materialism and classical political economy as competitors – let alone compare their respective (de)merits – if their objects are internal and their problematics peculiar to them – and there is no arbitration to be had outside these disparate conceptual systems?

To conclude, it can be seen that there was a contradiction between Althusser's epistemological project – the provision of a philosophy *for* science, one 'genuinely adequate to constantly developing scientific thought' – and the means by which he attempted to realise it. The effect of his particular assimilation of Spinoza and Bachelard was an unresolved tension between the realism to which he was committed as a Marxist and the relativism or rationalism to which their philosophies led. Oversimplifying, we might say that, having turned to conventionalism to escape the verities of diamat, Althusser depended upon rationalism to conjure away relativism, therewith partially returning to diamat. He considered Marxism omnipotent because it was true; on his own epistemology, it is impossible to say anything more than that it is true because it is true. If, then, Althusser broke with the vulgar materialism typical of orthodox Communist Marxism, he did so at the cost of the sophisticated idealism typical of heterodox Western Marxism – albeit that his variant is a quite distinct and superior form of it. He is not to be criticised for failing to resolve intractable problems in the philosophy of science, but for claiming to have solved them via a scientific philosophy when, in truth, he had either offered unsatisfactory answers or dissolved the very questions. At the same time, all credit is owed to him for a pioneering initiative in epistemology from within Marxism. Althusser is to be praised for having tabled – and with such determination – problems which Communist orthodoxy

---

[151] See Althusser 1969a, p. 185 and Althusser and Balibar 1970, pp. 156–7 and cf., e.g., Althusser and Balibar 1970, p. 40. In Althusser and Balibar 1970, pp. 156–7, Althusser alludes to Lenin's conception of the history of knowledge as a process of asymptotic correspondence to reality, translating it as '*the incessant deepening of the knowledge of a real object by incessantly reorganizing the object of knowledge*'. See also Althusser 1976a, p. 193.

did not even recognise. His efforts to theorise the specificity of theory yielded an account which, in its novelty and sophistication, its endeavour to avoid positivism without lapsing into a facile 'anti-scientism', superseded anything produced hitherto within the orbit of international Communism, simultaneously reconnecting Marxist with non-Marxist philosophy of science. To have elaborated the 'modernist' epistemology he did within the PCF, West-European cheer-leader of Lysenkoism, thus helping to liquidate the Cold-War heritage, was a major achievement, once whose audacity should not be forgotten.

A decade after the publication of *For Marx* and *Reading 'Capital'*, Althusser meditated on the significance of the distinction between the object of knowledge and the real object. It had been motivated by the wish to dramatise the enormous theoretical labour involved in Marx's foundation of historical materialism, to highlight the break with bourgeois common sense indispensable to a scientific theory of history, and to turn Marx's 'truth into a living and active truth for us'.[152] However worthy the ambition, the question must be posed: did Althusser's epistemological theses facilitate a restoration of, or in their turn deform, Marx's 'unprecedented break' and the theory that resulted? For the second 'cardinal principle' from which Althusser started – one derivative from his division of the world into the realms of the imaginary and the true – was that, left to its own devices, the proletariat was incapable of generating 'the *science* of society, and hence the science of [its] own practice, but . . . only . . . utopian or reformist ideologies of society'.[153] Marxism had been produced and developed outside the working class by the counter-intuitive theoretical practice of intellectuals (Marx, Engels and Lenin) and then '*imported*' into it. In line with this venerable Kautskyist and Leninist thesis,[154] Althusser argued that the relationship of Marxist theory to the proletariat and its practice was one of *exteriority*. Without Marxist philosophy, there could be no Marxist science; without Marxist science, no scientific socialism. Whether, in his

---

[152] See Althusser 1976a, pp. 193–4, where Althusser took the opportunity to note that the thesis could be insured against idealism (and had been by Marx) by its subordination to another: 'the *primacy of the real object over the object of knowledge*'.

[153] Althusser 1990, p. 16. See also Althusser 1969a, p. 24 and Althusser and Balibar 1970, p. 141.

[154] See Lenin 1961a, p. 373ff.

unilateral emphasis on Lenin's dictum of 1902 to the exclusion of an equally pertinent axiom from 1920,[155] Althusser compromised the novelty of historical materialism even as he strove to rearticulate it, is one of the questions to which we must now turn.

---

[155] *Viz.*: 'correct revolutionary theory . . . assumes final shape only in close connection with the practical activity of a truly mass and truly revolutionary movement' (Lenin 1966a, p. 25).

Chapter Three
Returning to Marx? A Reconstruction of Historical Materialism

> ... there is no such thing as an innocent reading.
>
> Louis Althusser, *Reading 'Capital'*

> If we were never structuralists, we can now explain why. . . . We were guilty of an equally powerful and compromising passion: *we were Spinozists*.
>
> Louis Althusser, *Elements of Self-Criticism*

Althusser's edition of Marxist philosophy, it has been argued, ultimately constitutes an *aggiornamento* of dialectical materialism. It would, however, be a characteristically Althusserian – and inadmissible – gesture to proceed in one move from the critique of an epistemology to the dismissal of the reading and reconstruction of Marxism based upon it. Althusser's (re)periodisation and reconceptualisation of Marxism do not necessarily fall with his revision of Marxist philosophy – even if the latter is untenable *and* incapable of establishing the scientificity of the former. On the other hand, both operations are conducted under the strict guidance of Althusser's epistemology – the theory of theoretical practice proffered as the theory of theory in general and the theory of Marx's theoretical practice (its philosophy and methodology) in particular. We should therefore not be surprised to find it taking its toll in both the canon and the corpus of historical materialism as understood by its founders. The costs and benefits of Althusser's recasting will be calculated as we go. What can be refused at the outset is the self-representation of the Althusserian version of historical materialism as Marxist orthodoxy. Althusser is no more orthodox than many of his opponents (and perhaps considerably less so than some). Whether his own rendition of Marxism is superior to Marx's, and his own revisions preferable to those of his contemporaries, is another matter.

Reading Marx: theoretical revolution or palace coup?

In the Introduction to *For Marx*, Althusser suggested that only the Marxist philosophy he hoped to endow with explicit theoretical form could yield 'an authentic [epistemological and historical] reading of Marx's writings'.[1] His commendable ambition was a rigorous analysis which defined 'the irreducible specificity of Marxist theory'.[2] Only a systematic reading employing the concept of problematic could provide that definition since, contrary to any analytical eclecticism, it treated theoretical texts and paradigms as unities, thus prohibiting arbitrary extraction of elements from their context; and it foreswore any teleological approach, whether anticipatory or retrospective.[3] In the case of Marx, it forbade any historiography 'in the "*future anterior*" ',[4] be it humanist or anti-humanist, idealist or materialist, ethical or scientific. Either way, *Capital* is assumed to be the culmination of the Paris *Manuscripts*, Marx's early work the anticipation of his *chef d'œuvre*. Whichever, the issue is prejudged, continuity presumed. Marx's signature, Althusser intimated, proved nothing.

Althusser's own reading was not innocent. He employed it (i) to attempt to demonstrate a simultaneously conceptual and epistemological discontinuity within Marx's œuvre between the supposedly non-Marxist early works of 1840–4 and the (unevenly) Marxist works of 1845–83; (ii) to recast historical materialism, in the light of this discontinuity, in non-economistic, non-humanist and non-historicist form. Historical materialism, as its founders had insisted,

---

[1] Althusser 1969a, p. 39.
[2] Althusser 1969a, p. 38.
[3] See Althusser 1969a, pp. 56–7.
[4] Althusser 1969a, p. 54.

was a science. But no discourse in social theory which was economistic, humanist or historicist could be scientific; by definition, it was ideological. So, any reading of Marx which construed his theory as one or all of these was doing violence to Marxism's titles to scientificity. To borrow Althusser's own epistemological schema, we could say that his work – 'a discourse with scientific pretensions'[5] – was conceived as an intra-scientific break accomplished by setting the Marxist problematic to work on the raw material of the Marx-Hegel/Marx-young Marx relationships, thus consummating Marx's own rupture with ideology, thereby marking it as a de jure, if not de facto, point of no return to ideology.

Because the Marxist-humanist 'revisionists' *could* appeal to the textual authority of Marx himself, amassing quotations against them was not only an illegitimate strategy based on a superficial mode of reading; it was futile. The early works, *fons et origo* of their constructions, had to be epistemologically differentiated from authentic Marxism at the level of their respective problematics and thus quarantined. Their partisans would thereby be proved to be revisionists – unwittingly or otherwise – not of theoretical Stalinism, but of Marxism. Althusser's return to Marx, like Lacan's return to Freud, was 'a return to his maturity'.[6] He sought to prove in three successive and, for him, indissolubly linked moves: (i) that historical materialism and theoretical humanism were conceptually incompatible; (ii) that historical materialism had come into existence through a rupture with theoretical humanism; and (iii) that this mutation in problematics amounted to an epistemological break which separated a science and its companion philosophy from all theoretical and philosophical ideologies, therewith indicating the ideological nature of Marx's pre-1845 problematic and the scientificity of his post-1845 problematic. In short, only after 1845 was Marx a Marxist; only after 1845 did Marxism become a science. Its constitution had involved nothing less than an 'immense theoretical revolution'.[7] An epistemological history of Marxist would simultaneously reflect that fact and confute its denegation. That Althusser and his colleagues' philosophical reading of Marx's reading was indeed guilty can be gleaned from the (loaded) questions which framed it:

---

[5] Althusser and Balibar 1970, p. 26, n. 8.
[6] Althusser 1971, p. 185.
[7] The title of Chapter 9 of Althusser's second paper in Althusser and Balibar 1970, 'The Object of *Capital*'.

Only this reading can determine the answer to a question that concerns the place *Capital* occupies in the history of knowledge. This question can be crystallized as follows: is *Capital* merely one ideological product among others, classical economics given a Hegelian form, the imposition of anthropological categories defined in the philosophical Early Works on the domain of economic reality; the 'realization' of the idealist aspirations of the *Jewish Question* and the *1844 Manuscripts*? Is *Capital* merely a continuation of classical political economy, from which Marx inherited both object and concepts? And is *Capital* distinguished from classical economics not by its object, but only by its method, the dialectic he borrowed from Hegel? Or, on the contrary, does *Capital* constitute a real epistemological mutation of its object, theory and method? Does *Capital* represent the founding moment of a new discipline, the founding moment of a science – and hence a real event, a theoretical revolution, simultaneously rejecting the classical political economy and the Hegelian and Feuerbachian ideologies of its prehistory – the absolute beginning of the history of a science?[8]

As the autonomous science of a precisely delimited terrain, the 'continent of history',[9] historical materialism was a science 'among others' – identical to the natural sciences in being governed solely by what Canguilhem has termed 'an axiological activity, the search for truth'; different in that it was confronted by the extra-scientific obstacles thrown up by its unbearable truth in class society.[10] The theoretical culpability of revisionisms consisted in their dissolution or distortion of this scientificity – their reversal of the trajectory of Marx's theoretical 'Long March'.[11] Historical materialism should, as Engels had boasted, have 'put an end to philosophy in the realm of history'.[12] It had not. It had not even put an end to philosophy within itself.

Why was the business unfinished? Intra-theoretically, it came down to this: Marx had not fully or correctly defined the theoretical revolution which

---

[8] Althusser and Balibar 1970, p. 15; see also pp. 73–8.
[9] See Althusser 1969a, pp. 13–14.
[10] See Canguilhem 1979, p. 19; Althusser 1972, p. 18; Althusser 1969a, p. 122; and Althusser and Balibar 1970, p. 185. On each occasion, Althusser refers to Hobbes's observation in *Leviathan* that 'such Truth, as opposeth no man's profit, nor pleasure, is to all men welcome'. Cf. Marx 1976a p. 92.
[11] Althusser 1969a, p. 84.
[12] Marx and Engels 1977, p. 375.

divided historical materialism from its 'sources', thereby forestalling any recrudescence of the ideological in Marxism. The break was indisputably there. But it was theoretically unreflected and hence vulnerable. Marx had 'produce[d] . . . the distinction between himself and his predecessors', but – like other path-breaking scientists (such as Freud) – had been unable to theorise it rigorously, often reverting to Hegelian concepts to expound it. The prevalence of such pre-Marxist theoretical motifs explained the misleading interpretations of his work made by followers who, with some justice, proclaimed their fidelity to its letter.[13] (If Althusser could never have assented to the proposition that 'the letter killeth while the spirit giveth life', he obviously concurred with Spinoza that there was no 'heretic without a text'.) Indeed, the total novelty of Marx's theory had partially blinded its author to his real achievement. He therefore had to be rescued not only from Engels's compromising defences of him, but from his own recidivism. The theory of the symptomatic reading enabled Althusser to claim that 'in the brief moment of [Marx's] . . . silence we are simply returning to him the speech that is his own'.[14] In actuality, and spurred on by the conviction that a theoretical revolution was just as threatened by the possibility of regression as a political revolution,[15] Althusser was attempting to complete Marx's revolution by specifying the 'concept' and 'theoretical implications' of his 'theoretically revolutionary step'. He was seeking, in other words, to establish what historical materialism would have to look like *if it were* to represent an unambiguous break with everything predating it *and that it did indeed* constitute such a rupture. In sum, he was attempting to out-Marx Marx.

It has been a commonplace among Marxists that Marxism somehow derived from three sources (Hegelian philosophy, political economy, utopian socialism), two revolutions (the French political and English industrial revolutions), and an intellectual movement (the Enlightenment and its romantic aftermath). The major interpretative battle-lines have been drawn up over the precise fashion in which this emergence should be understood and what significance to assign to it. A classic account by Lenin – 'The Three Sources and Three

---

[13] See Althusser and Balibar 1970, pp. 120–1. See also, e.g., Althusser and Balibar 1970, pp. 50–1, 189–92; Rancière 1965, pp. 143, 196–8; and Establet 1965, pp. 400–1.

[14] Althusser and Balibar 1970, p. 144.

[15] See, e.g., Althusser 1990, p. 56.

Component Parts of Marxism' (1913) – maintained that Marx's 'doctrine emerged as the direct and immediate *continuation* of the greatest representatives of philosophy, political economy and socialism'.[16] On Althusser's genealogy, the manifest continuity of Marx's development masked a latent, fundamental discontinuity. The sources were theoretical ideologies, raw materials (Generality I) wholly transformed into a scientific body of knowledge (Generalities III): Marx's doctrine. The closest Althusser approximated to Lenin's position was in conceiving of an utterly and previously transformed dialectic functioning as Generality II – the problematic which performed the productive work on the ideological raw material.[17] Althusser's central claim was that there was a discontinuity in Marx's development; that it occurred where Marx himself had located it in the 1859 Preface: *The German Ideology*; and that it was the site of an epistemological break.[18] He proposed the following periodisation of Marx's œuvre:

1. 1840–4: the *'Early Works'* (everything up to and including *The Holy Family*), subdivided into:
    (a) 1840–2: 'the liberal-rationalist moment' governed by a Kantian-Fichtean problematic;
    (b) 1842–4: 'the communist-rationalist moment' dominated by Feuerbach's anthropological problematic;
2. 1845: the *'Works of the Break'* (*Theses on Feuerbach, The German Ideology*), introducing Marx's new problematic;
3. 1845–57: the *'Transitional Works'* (from *The Poverty of Philosophy* to the *Grundrisse*);
4. 1857–83: 'the *Mature Works*' (above all, *Capital*).[19]

There are five preliminary points to be made about this chronology.

First, Althusser's graph of Marx's career was in conformity with Communist orthodoxy to the extent that the latter also looked to *The German Ideology* for

---

[16] Lenin 1968, p. 23.

[17] See Althusser 1972, pp. 170–1, where the ambitions of *Reading 'Capital'* are displayed in diagrammatic form.

[18] See Althusser 1969a, p. 32. For Marx's comments, see Marx 1975, p. 427. Citing them, Althusser was at pains to point out that Marx's declaration did not constitute proof of the existence of the break. His intention at least was to approach Marx as he had Montesquieu, trusting the tale, not the teller: see Althusser 1972, p. 15.

[19] See Althusser 1969a, pp. 34–5.

the initial formulation of historical materialism. This only serves to highlight the differences between their respective characterisations of it, however.

Secondly – as we have seen in Chapter 2 – according to Althusser, Marx's revolution consisted in a 'double foundation in a single break':[20] the birth of a new science and a new (scientific) philosophy. Although quite distinct, historical and dialectical materialism had three things in common: (i) their rupture with their bourgeois competitors; (ii) their scientificity; and (iii) their combined and uneven development by Karl Marx.

Thirdly, in this account, Marx became a communist before he became a Marxist; his practical, political break with the young Hegelians preceded his theoretical break with Feuerbach, but was in turn deepened by it. To confound the two was to confuse the issue.[21]

Fourthly – as can be inferred from the above schema and corroborated by consultation of his discussion – Althusser's location of a major caesura in Marx's progress did not ipso facto preclude sophisticated discriminations within his massive, heterogeneous output before and after 1845. More simply, Althusser was not claiming that everything which predated the break was excrescential, everything that postdated it sacrosanct.

Fifthly – and crucially – in common with the Della Volpean school, Althusser's periodisation focused attention predominantly on *Capital*, reinstating it in pride of place in the canon as the *locus classicus* of historical and dialectical materialism alike, therewith contesting what he (rightly) perceived as its contemporary devaluation.

In the opening paragraph of *Reading 'Capital'*, Althusser characterised his and his colleagues' analyses (running to 650 pages) as 'the mere beginnings of a reading'. Space, let alone intellectual qualification, certainly forbids more than that here.[22] All that is practicable is to set out the conclusions reached by Althusser and pinpoint some of their more obvious weaknesses, before reverting to the question posed at the outset (theoretical revolution or palace coup?), and interrogating it in turn.

---

[20] Althusser 1969a, p. 33.
[21] See Althusser 1969a, pp. 159–60.
[22] Among accounts of Marx's development, readers are referred to Balibar 1974, Chapter 1; Callinicos 1983, Chapter 2; Cornu 1955–70; Labica 1976; Therborn 1976, Chapter 6; and Stedman Jones 1988.

Immersion in the ideas of the age

The lion in the gate of Althusser's insistence on the utter theoretical novelty of historical materialism was, of course, Hegel(ianism). Consequently, Althusser himself inverted Marx's trajectory, attending to his relation to the German ideology to the virtual exclusion of the other two 'sources'.[23] As he noted in 'On the Young Marx',[24] the Hegel with whom Marx had to settle accounts was the Hegel of the young-Hegelian movement of the early 1840s, arguably a significantly different figure from the author of the *Phenomenology* and the *Science of Logic*. This Janus-faced Hegel had been inverted by Feuerbach, philosopher of the concrete, producing a 'materialist' philosophical anthropology – a humanist historicism – which represented history as a process with a subject – Man, pinnacle of nature – and an end – disalienation and self-realisation.[25] According to Althusser, Marx subscribed to it until 1845 – and this despite his encounters with 'material interests', the nascent industrial proletariat and its struggles, and political economy.

For Althusser, the climax of Marx's sojourn in the anthropological problematic was the *Economic and Philosophical Manuscripts*, written in Paris between April and August 1844. The site of an 'encounter of *philosophy* with Political Economy',[26] this was Marx's most Hegelian work, a 'genial synthesis of Feuerbach and Hegel'.[27] In his *Critique of Hegel's Doctrine of the State* (1843), Marx had assailed Hegel for what he described as his 'logical, pantheistic mysticism'[28] – the hypostatisation whereby predicates are separated from their true subject, transfigured into the subject, and then empirically incarnated. This dissection of the mechanism of Hegel's speculative philosophy was indebted to Feuerbach. As was the alternative to it and the whole 'German misery' proposed by Marx in the politically far more radical *Contribution to the Critique of Hegel's Philosophy of Right. Introduction* (1843–4). Feuerbach had completed the '*criticism of religion*',[29] laying bare the inversion of subject and

---

[23] For Althusser's retrospective delineation of his 'double intervention', see Althusser 1969a, pp. 12–13.
[24] Althusser 1969a, p. 65.
[25] For Althusser's insistence that it was Feuerbach – and not Marx – who had inverted Hegel, see, e.g., Althusser 1969a, pp. 48, 72 n. 36, 73, and 89.
[26] Althusser 1969a, p. 157.
[27] Althusser 1969a, pp. 35–6; see also p. 198, n. 40.
[28] Marx 1975, p. 61.
[29] Marx 1975, p. 243.

predicate, the estrangement of man's essence in an imaginary being, constitutive of it ('the secret of theology is anthropology'). The *immediate task of philosophy* was now to serve history by 'establish[ing] the *truth of this world*', by performing the same critical operation in the profane spheres of human existence.[30] Such criticism was rooted in the conviction that *'for man the supreme being is man'* and animated by 'the *categorical imperative to overthrow all conditions* in which man is a debased, enslaved . . . being'.[31] German emancipation demanded an alliance between reformed philosophy and the 'universal class' – the proletariat – whose revolutionary *praxis* would redeem both it and the rest of humanity from the hell of civil society and the artificial heaven of the state, therewith realising the humanist philosophy which, in the interim, provided the proletarian heart with a theoretical head.[32]

In the preface to the *Economic and Philosophical Manuscripts*, Marx credited Feuerbach with 'a real theoretical revolution' since only with him had *'positive humanistic and naturalistic criticism'* begun.[33] Feuerbach had already identified Man as the true subject of history. Marx was to take him one stage further by revealing the essential contradiction underlying the particular contradictions by which every sphere of human activity was rent. Marx's critique of political economy accepted the laws it propounded, but challenged its comprehension of what it had discovered, aspiring to decipher its human meaning. Under capitalism, he argued, man's 'life-activity' – the labour through which he realises himself – is estranged in an object – private property – to which the subject is subordinated. The human essence is alienated even as it is expressed. Man's own creations, appropriated by other men, dominate him. The capitalist class, material beneficiary of this state of affairs, is condemned to inhumanity; the proletariat, its impoverished victim, to non-humanity. 'Alienated labour', the scission of the human essence from the human subject, is the basic contradiction of contemporary existence, with whose advent, however, a potential restoration of the original unity of subject and object can be divined. For the estrangement of man in private property is a necessary historical process – the social and material precondition for the realisation of communism,

---

[30] Marx 1975, pp. 244–5.
[31] Marx 1975, p. 251.
[32] See Marx 1975, pp. 256–7.
[33] Marx 1975, pp. 280–1.

the prelude to the dawn of the genuinely human community to which the 'entire movement of history' has been leading. Communism, writes Marx,

> is the complete restoration of man to himself as a *social*, i.e. human, being . . . the *genuine* resolution of the conflict between man and nature, and between man and man. . . . It is the solution to the riddle of history and knows itself to be the solution.[34]

Marx's characterisation of communism occurs in the third manuscript. At the end of this text, he essayed a critique of Hegel's system. Some of its ostensible young Hegelian critics, he suggested, were still 'imprisoned within Hegelian logic'.[35] Feuerbach, on the other hand, had 'destroyed the foundations of the old dialectic and philosophy' and 'founded *true materialism* and *real science* by making the social relation of "man to man" the basic principle of his theory'.[36] Althusser's main objection to Marx's writings of 1843–4 can now be formulated. They were inspired by Feuerbach's theoretical revolution. Yet this revolution was no revolution. The basic principle of Feuerbach's problematic militated against materialism and science. Feuerbach, too, had remained 'imprisoned within Hegelian logic', inverting Hegel to yield a philosophical anthropology centred on Man. Marx had preserved Feuerbach's problematic, historicising his conception of economy and society, rendering humanity the subject of history, the development of the human essence via alienation its motor, self-realisation in communism its predetermined end. The Marx of 1844, Althusser insisted, was not the author of a new theory of economy and society, but 'an *avant-garde* Feuerbachian applying *an ethical problematic to the understanding of human history*'.[37] From the standpoint of historical materialism, the young Marx was consequently an *arrière-garde*, ultra-left Hegelian, partaking in a normative and messianic philosophy of history dependent on the teleological structures of the Hegelian dialectic. A teleological reading of Marx's career was, moreover, the mirror image of the young Marx's teleological 'reading' of history. The complexity of a concrete historical process – Marx's intellectual development – is erased by the

---

[34] Marx 1975, p. 348.
[35] Marx 1975, p. 380.
[36] Marx 1975, pp. 380–1.
[37] Althusser 1969a, p. 46.

imposition of an evolutionary schema in which the goal is present in germ at the origin. Thus, the Paris *Manuscripts* are read through the grid of their purported realisation – *Capital* – or vice versa; a 'singular present' is reduced to a teleological moment.[38]

The allegedly grave misinterpretation of Marx censured by Althusser had powerful support in France. Lefebvre's *Dialectical Materialism*, recently reprinted, had been the first work by a French Communist philosopher to represent the *Economic and Philosophical Manuscripts* as historical materialism *in statu nascendi*, depicting history as the drama of the 'total man' who is its 'living subject-object'.[39] After the War, in *Humanism and Terror* (1947), Merleau-Ponty had endorsed a view of *Capital* as 'inseparably concerned with the working of the economy and the realization of man' – Marx being 'the "realization" of Hegel'.[40] Goldmann's *The Human Sciences and Philosophy* (1952) – a new edition of which appeared in 1966 – extolled Lukács's *History and Class Consciousness* and also accredited Korsch and Lefebvre artisans of the 'dialectical thought' sponsored by the young Marx.[41] For his part, Garaudy was now according the themes of the independent Marxists their *lettres de noblesse*, proposing 'an authentically universal humanism', citing a famous declaration by Marx from the 1843–4 Introduction as 'the fundamental inspiration of Marxism', declaring Marxism to be *'a philosophy of act'*, characterising communism as 'the project of and a demand for a total disalienation, the project of total man'.[42] And Garaudy was not alone. In 1966 – as we shall see in Chapter 4 – the Central Committee of the PCF adopted a resolution stating that 'there is a Marxist humanism, the humanism of our time'.

Althusser's perception of the contemporary situation of psychoanalysis in 'Freud and Lacan' equally applies to historical materialism.[43] Marxists were 'coming round to the world's positions', signing a pact of peaceful coexistence

---

[38] See Althusser 1969a, p. 156. Rancière's brilliant, if highly controversial, contribution to *Lire 'le Capital'* was devoted to the difference between Marx's critiques of political economy in the Paris *Manuscripts* and *Capital*: see Rancière 1965.

[39] See Lefebvre 1970, p. 148ff.

[40] Merleau-Ponty 1969, pp. 101–2.

[41] See Goldmann 1969, pp. 80–1; 149, n. 50.

[42] Garaudy 1970, pp. 36, 76, 84, 102. Marx's declaration – 'To be radical is to grasp things by the root. But for man the root is man himself' (Marx 1975, p. 251) – had furnished the epigraph to Lukács's 'Reification and the Consciousness of the Proletariat'.

[43] See Althusser 1971, p. 186.

with the reigning ideology to the detriment of Marxism. Historical materialism was neither Hegel inverted nor Feuerbach transcended – nor any other variation on a misleading theme. It was not the ideological offspring of the nineteenth century. Its foundation had involved a thorough-going labour of transformation which amounted to a change of terrain: from the quick sands of speculative ideology to the *terra firma* of conceptual science.[44]

Settling accounts

In 1845, with the *Theses on Feuerbach* and *The German Ideology*, a 'total theoretical revolution' commenced:

> In 1845, Marx broke radically with every theory that based history and politics on an essence of man. This unique rupture contained three indissociable elements.
>
> (1) The formation of a new theory of history and politics based on radically new concepts: the concepts of social formation, productive forces, relations of production, superstructure, ideologies, determination in the last instance by the economy, specific determination of other levels, etc.
>
> (2) A radical critique of the *theoretical* pretensions of every philosophical humanism.
>
> (3) The definition of humanism as an *ideology*.
>
> . . . This rupture with every philosophical anthropology or humanism is no secondary detail: it is Marx's scientific discovery.
>
> It means that Marx rejected the problematic of the earlier philosophy and adopted a new problematic in the one and the same act.[45]

The fundamental problem with this provocative thesis – as Althusser goes some way towards confessing – is that if something changed, not everything did.[46] In 1967, he noted that he and his colleagues had developed distinctions within Marx's œuvre inherited from the Marxist tradition.[47] That between *The German Ideology* and the early works is one of them. And it is not hard to see

---

[44] See, e.g., Althusser and Balibar 1970, p. 153.
[45] Althusser 1969a, p. 227.
[46] See Althusser 1969a, pp. 36–7.
[47] See Althusser 1990, p. 58, n. 10.

why. For it did mark a new stage in Marx's development, a qualitative (and quantitative) departure. In addition to renouncing philosophy (identified with ideology plain and simple) in favour of empirical science – a renunciation which found no favour with Althusser, of course[48] – Marx and Engels subjected Feuerbach to an acute critique over the thesis which had previously been taken to sum up his 'theoretical revolution': for 'posit[ing] "Man" instead of "real historical man"' and thus remaining within the confines of philosophical abstraction. 'As far as Feuerbach is a materialist,' they wrote, 'he does not deal with history, and as far as he considers history he is not a materialist'.[49] The utopian German socialisms generated by his and other idealist philosophies of history were derided in the second volume, as Marx and Engels sought to ground communism in the material-social conditions of capitalism. In the course of their complementary critiques, central elements of the very theoretical paradigm which had structured Marx's early works were harpooned and the 'premises' of their new conception set forth.[50] In a passage chosen by Althusser as the epigraph to 'On the Young Marx', Marx and Engels asserted that 'German criticism' had never freed itself from philosophy in general, Hegel's in particular. As a result, 'not only in its answers, even in its questions, there was a mystification'.[51]

The German Ideology instituted a research programme which Marx and Engels were to pursue for the remainder of their lives: historical materialism. But it only initiated it. The adumbration of historical materialism offered in this (unpublished) manuscript lacked some of the theory's most important later components (to name but two, the concept of relations of production and the theory of surplus-value). According to Althusser, the 'works of the break' had introduced the new problematic but in 'a partially negative and sharply polemical and critical form'.[52] Ambiguities persisted – among them, apparently, Marx's lapses into 'an individualist-humanist conception' of society, of which the critique of Feuerbach for abstraction per se was symptomatic.[53]

---

[48] See Marx and Engels 1976, pp. 37, 236 and cf. Althusser 1969a, pp. 28–30; 187, n. 23. On both occasions, Althusser expresses contrition for partially succumbing to the temptation of an 'end of philosophy' in 'On the Young Marx'.

[49] Marx and Engels 1976, pp. 39, 41.

[50] See Marx and Engels 1976, pp. 27–93.

[51] Marx and Engels 1976, p. 28.

[52] Althusser 1969a, p. 34.

[53] Althusser 1969a, p. 36. See also Althusser and Balibar 1970, p. 140.

We are thus confronted with the following paradox: on the one hand, Marx broke with philosophical anthropology; on the other, he did not. The paradox is of Althusser's own making, attributable as it is to his insistence that the foundation of historical materialism necessitated a break with *any* humanism, abstract or concrete, any theory of human nature – not just with those of classical political philosophy, Marx's German contemporaries, and the great utopian socialists. The sixth thesis on Feuerbach, he believed, pronounced precisely such a rupture with what had hitherto been the lynchpin of projects for a natural science of society.[54] Therewith Marx had adopted the position of theoretical anti-humanism and founded that science. Marx's statement in his 'Marginal Notes on Wagner' (1879–80) to the effect that 'my analytic method . . . does not start from *Man* but from the economically given period of society' was selected by Althusser as the epigraph to 'Marxism and Humanism', to crown its propositions with the old Marx's authority.[55] But do the sixth thesis and ensuing writings repudiate the category of human nature? Or do they reject abstract and eternalist conceptions of 'the essence of man' and foreground the historically mutable 'ensemble[s] of social relations' – the 'economically given period[s] of society' – which condition human nature? Norman Geras has criticised both Althusser's construction of Marx's thesis and his belief that the notion of a common human nature is incompatible with historical materialism as a social-scientific discourse.[56] Challenging, along with others, such sociologism, he has illustrated the extent to which Marx continued to employ the idea of a human nature as a normative concept and has maintained that it is also assigned an explanatory role in historical materialism.[57]

In a codicil to his main study (the 'Complementary Note on "Real Humanism"' of 1965), Althusser suggested that the sixth thesis presaged 'a

---

[54] See Marx 1975, p. 423 and cf. Althusser 1969a, pp. 227–9, where Althusser defines the 'invariant type-structure' of the humanist problematic pervading pre-Marxist political philosophy, political economy, history, ethics and philosophy: '*an empiricism of the subject always corresponds to an idealism of the essence (or an empiricism of the essence to an idealism of the subject).*'

[55] Marx 1972, p. 52. The later Althusser was also to invoke Marx's comment in the *Grundrisse* (Marx 1973, p. 265) that '[s]ociety does not consist of individuals' – declining, however, to complete the quotation: 'but expresses the sum of interrelations, the relations within which these individuals stand'. See Althusser 1976a, pp. 52–3, 201.

[56] See Geras 1983.

[57] Geras 1983, pp. 74, 83–4, 107–8.

displacement to be put into effect': 'to find the reality alluded to by seeking abstract man no longer but real man instead, it is necessary *to turn to society and to undertake an analysis of the ensemble of the social relations'.*[58] For such an analysis to be scientific, however, it would have to dispense with the services of the concept of man. In *The German Ideology,* 'that most precious of all the things Marx gave us – the possibility of scientific knowledge'[59] had commenced. With its acquisition, history could be scientifically understood, hence 'mastered'.[60] The world no longer had to be endured and/or bemoaned by its formerly benighted victims: they could change it. Whilst Marx and Engels would almost certainly have subscribed to Althusser's representation of historical materialism as the instrument for knowledge and transformation of social reality, there is little evidence to suggest they believed it entailed elimination of the notion of a human nature. Moreover, they entertained important ideas on the relation of their doctrine to the contemporary workers' movement which Althusser, intent on the deflation of the pretensions of theoretical humanism, passed over in silence. To these we shall return, content for the moment to note that if the developments in Marx's thought c. 1845 did indeed set him on the road which led to *Capital,* they did not amount to a break as conceived by Althusser: one involving the repudiation – and interdiction – of everything that preceded them.

The road to *Capital*

If Althusser's treatment of the 'works of the break' is unsustainable, his reading of the so-called 'transitional works' is, in all conscience, at best tendentious. For the actual content of this phase – stretching from 1845–57, and encompassing everything from *The Poverty of Philosophy* (1846–7) to the *Grundrisse* (1857–8) – belies his characterisation of them.[61]

To take *The Poverty of Philosophy* first. The campaign of theoretical and political iconoclasm waged by Marx against the German ideology was now transferred to the leading philosophical representative of French socialism,

---

[58] Althusser 1969a, p. 243.
[59] Althusser 1969a, p. 241.
[60] Althusser 1969a, p. 246.
[61] See Althusser 1969a, p. 34.

Proudhon. The poverty of his philosophy – its collapse into metaphysics – was related to his 'intrepidity in the matter of Hegelianism'.[62] The target of Marx's critique, however, was not simply the ersatz Hegelianism of the Frenchman. *En route*, 'bourgeois' political economy was criticised for its naturalisation and eternalisation of capitalism. Althusser accurately reflected that the basic criticism of political economy made by Marx from 1846 onwards was that it possessed 'an ahistorical, eternal, fixed and abstract conception of the categories of capitalism'. According to him, however, this was not Marx's '*real* critique'. It was 'superficial and ambiguous, whereas his real critique is infinitely more profound'.[63] Althusser's objection to an *idée reçue* of Marxist interpretation – that Marx's standard critique of political economy is a/the real critique (and a profound one at that) – stems from his conviction that it erases the novelty of Marx's problematic and construes Marxism as a historicism. It supposedly negates Marx's theoretical revolution by restoring a continuity of object between Marx and Ricardo and positing only a difference of method – the dialectical method, bequeathed by Hegel, with which Ricardian economics was historicised.[64] On this issue there can, of course, legitimately be discussion and debate. (Many interpreters have not thought it necessary to posit a *total* discontinuity of object for Marxism to be accorded revolutionary theoretical status vis-à-vis classical political economy – quite the reverse.) The important point to register here is that just as Althusser had to discard or discount contrary evidence in order to maintain his interpretation of the break with theoretical humanism, so too he claims Marx's implicit support – in contravention of the repetitive letter of his texts – for his own preferred alternative as regards the rupture with political economy: the initiation of a quite different, synchronic, structural analysis of capitalism, which has epistemological priority over questions of historical genesis and development.[65] Curiously enough, what gets overlooked in Althusser's references to *The*

---

[62] See Marx 1976b, pp. 161–5.
[63] Althusser and Balibar 1970, pp. 91–2. Cf., e.g., Marx 1976b, pp. 162, 165–6, 174; Marx 1973, p. 87; and Marx 1976a, p. 96.
[64] See Althusser and Balibar 1970, pp. 92–3 and also pp. 85–6. Gramsci is criticised on this score.
[65] See Althusser and Balibar 1970, pp. 97–8: pages whose own arbitrary extractions understandably provoke the ire of Thompson in his 1978, pp. 309–13. The passage cited by Althusser in support of his position occurs in Marx 1976b, p. 167.

Poverty of Philosophy is a crucial innovation: the introduction of the central concept of social relations of production. Considered by Lenin to be 'the basic idea of [Marx's] entire "system" ', it had been cited by Althusser as one of the 'radically new concepts' involved in Marx's revolution, yet was absent from *The German Ideology*.[66]

What of the *Grundrisse*? Here, we are faced by an astonishing lacuna. Aside from the separate 1857 Introduction and the section published in English as *Pre-Capitalist Economic Formations*, Althusser did not so much as refer to this manuscript. The 1857 Introduction was a primary source for Althusser's epistemology, *Pre-Capitalist Economic Formations* for Balibar's theory of modes of production. On the remaining 750 pages, not a word. It may be idle to speculate on the reasons for this. But it is plausible to regard it as symptomatic. For the *Grundrisse* is a protracted challenge to Althusser's periodisation of historical materialism, within whose logic it is quite anomalous. Terminologically and methodologically the most Hegelian of Marx's later writings, it displays a Marx in transit to something rather different from the Althusserian vision of *Capital*. For better, worse, or whatever, the *Grundrisse* witnesses to a reappearance of what – on Althusser's account – Marx had exorcised: the spectre of Hegel.[67] A work in which Marx was supposed to be developing 'a conceptual terminology and systematics that were adequate to his revolutionary theoretical project'[68] found him engaged in rather more than a flirtation with the redoubtable chief German ideologist. However this is interpreted, it is at least apparent that the famous settling of accounts was not an Althusserian one. Endorsement and repudiation of Marx's refractory manuscripts being equally impossible, silence served as a temporary substitute.

The continent of history

In his preface to the first edition of *Capital*, Volume One (1867), Marx specified as his object the capitalist mode of production. Through the 'power of

---

[66] Lenin 1961b, p. 30; Althusser 1969a, p. 227. See Therborn 1976, p. 365ff. and Callinicos 1983, pp. 49–52 for discussions of the significance of the concept in historical materialism.

[67] See Marx's letter of 14 January 1858 to Engels, informing his colleague of his methodological return to Hegel: Marx and Engels 1975, p. 93.

[68] See Althusser 1969a, p. 34.

abstraction', he aimed to uncover and propound 'the economic law of motion of modern society', thereby founding a (natural) science of society.[69] Starting from this explicit programme, Althusser argued that in his (unfinished) masterpiece Marx had laid the corner-stones of historical materialism by: (i) theorising the *economic level* of the *capitalist mode of production*; and (ii) providing precious indications and guide-lines for the theorisation of (a) the *superstructural levels* of the *capitalist* mode of production; (b) *non-capitalist modes of production* (their infrastructures and superstructures); and (c) the forms of *transition* from one mode of production to another. In other words, in *Capital* Marx had founded a theory of history understood as a *general theory of modes of production and social formations.*[70] Althusser was not – it must be underscored – asserting that Marx had completed the research programme of historical materialism, so that any attempt to develop it would be a superfluous addition to, or an unwarrantable interference with, an inviolable totality. Quite the contrary, the purpose of the balance-sheet he drew up was to counter what he regarded as *revisionism* – retrogression – whilst (re)opening space for genuine *development* – progress.[71] If Marx had founded a *general* theory, he had not expounded a whole series of *regional* theories. 'We must recognise,' Althusser wrote, 'what Marx actually gave us and what he enabled us to obtain for ourselves, although he could not give it to us.'[72] What remained to be done was immense and urgent. History had put a multitude of new tasks and problems on the agenda since Lenin's death.[73] The theory of transition was top priority, relevant as it was both to the problems encountered by the 'socialist' states and the Third World and to the strategy of Communist parties in the imperialist countries. (The issue of the 'cult of personality' and the national road / peaceful transition to socialism both fell within its remit.) Equipped with the requisite theory, it would be possible 'to anticipate the future and theorize not only that future, but also and above all the roads and means that will secure us its reality'. In the absence of it, 'mankind . . . will

---

[69] See Marx 1976a, pp. 90–2.
[70] See, in addition to Althusser and Balibar 1970, Althusser 1990, pp. 6–7 and Althusser 1966a, pp. 91–4.
[71] See, e.g., Althusser 1990, p. 18. On his behalf, Althusser quotes Lenin 1960, pp. 210–12.
[72] Althusser and Balibar 1970, p. 197.
[73] See Althusser 1990, p. 20.

risk, as it has already discovered in the silences of the terror – and may do so again in the velleities of humanism – . . . entering a future still charged with dangers and shades, with a virgin conscience.'[74]

It can now be seen why Althusser considered the conception of *Capital* entertained by Marxists to be of such paramount importance. Their opinion of what *Capital* did or did not contain – in practice and in principle – was crucial in determining their representation of historical materialism, hence of scientific socialism. If it was construed as merely providing scientific knowledge of nineteenth-century capitalism or of capitalism in general, the validity of historical materialism was restricted to the present, contested for the more distant past or future.[75] For Althusser, in contrast, the concepts of historical materialism not only provided knowledge of the present – of social formations dominated by the capitalist mode of production (say, France in 1965). If properly understood and developed, they were valid for – that is, provided conceptual means of knowledge of – the past (such as the transition from feudalism to capitalism in Britain) and the future (for example, transitions from capitalism to socialism, from socialism to communism). Historical materialism was the *science of the history of social formations* with whose general theory (system of basic concepts) and specific concepts (already produced or still to be produced) the past could be understood, the present analysed and transformed, the future illuminated and dominated. With the advent of Marxism, socialism too had made the transition from utopianism to scientificity: the world could be changed because it could now be *scientifically* interpreted.[76]

Althusser and his colleagues' reading of *Capital* aimed to delineate both its explicit/implicit content and, as a function of this, historical materialism's terms of reference. This involved a series of prohibitions and prescriptions – many addressed to other Marxists (Lukács, Korsch, Gramsci, Della Volpe et al.), some to one or both of Marx and Engels. Historical materialism was neither an economism, nor a humanism. More fundamentally still, it was not a historicism.[77] The structure of Marx's work was radically anti-Hegelian, its

---

[74] Althusser and Balibar 1970, p. 198.

[75] See Althusser 1966a, p. 95 for the most explicit statement of this.

[76] See, in addition to Althusser 1969a, p. 246, Althusser 1990, pp. 3–7.

[77] See Althusser and Balibar 1970, p. 119ff. The title of Chapter 5 of 'The Object of *Capital*' is 'Marxism Is Not a Historicism'. For polemical purposes, Althusser used the negative formula *anti-*, rather than the privative, *a-*historicist, etc.

method no more inverted-Hegelian than it was Hegelian.[78] As a theory of history, historical materialism included a theory of the economic level of modes of production (the 'theoretical object' of *Capital* was the capitalist mode of production), but it was not simply a scientific political economy; the economic theory was dependent upon the theory of history.[79] *Capital* effected a critique of political economy at the level of its method *and* object. Marx's object was incommensurable with that of classical (and post-classical) economics:

> Here both the mirage of a theoretical anthropology and the mirage of a homogeneous space of *given* economic phenomena dissolve simultaneously. Not only is the economic a structured region occupying its peculiar place in the global structure of the social whole, but even in its own site, in its (relative) regional autonomy, it functions as a regional *structure* and as such determines its elements.[80]

In short, the object and problematic of *Capital* were wholly novel, irreducible to the 'sources and component parts'.

This set of conclusions was counterposed to Marx's own tendency to conceive his work as an intra-scientific break within the tradition of classical, as opposed to vulgar, political economy. A more immediate and formidable obstacle to it, perhaps, is the presence of Hegelian elements in *Capital*. In 'On the Materialist Dialectic', Althusser was confident (or rash) enough to assert their absence with the exception of '*two sole sentences*'.[81] In *Reading 'Capital'*, he conceded their presence, but treated them either as terminological residues or coquetry whose significance had been overestimated; or as the inadequate terminology in which Marx had couched what were in reality bona fide Marxist concepts (such as the exposition of the theory of fetishism).[82] Marx had relapsed because

---

[78] See Althusser and Balibar 1970, especially pp. 125–6; Rancière 1965, p. 152; Macherey 1965, pp. 247, 256; Balibar in Althusser and Balibar 1970, p. 274; and Establet 1965, pp. 358, 400–1.

[79] See Althusser and Balibar 1970, pp. 109, 117–18, 183.

[80] Althusser and Balibar 1970, p. 180. On the object of political economy, see Althusser and Balibar 1970, p. 160ff. Althusser's cursory discussion of it (a mere seven pages) is centred on the definition given in Lalande's *Dictionnaire philosophique*, whilst readers interested in contemporary economic theory are referred by him to Maurice Godelier's 'remarkable article', 'The Object and Method of Economic Anthropology' (1965), reprinted in Godelier 1966.

[81] Althusser 1969a, p. 200 and n 41.

[82] Rancière's paper was concerned to distinguish between the young Marx's theory

he lacked the requisite philosophical concept with which to articulate and consummate his theoretical revolution – and thus demarcate himself unequivocally from his predecessors. It was this concept that Althusser aimed to produce. A simple question summed up Marx's extraordinary scientific discovery: *'how is it possible to define the concept of a structural causality?'*[83] Marx had indicated the concept in that of *Darstellung*, but had not theorised it adequately.[84] Classical theories of causality had filled the vacuum in his work and that of his followers, erasing the novelty of the Marxist conception of the social whole. 'Alone, Marx looked around him for allies and supporters; who can reproach him for allowing himself to lean on Hegel?'.[85] Who indeed? But the real question lies elsewhere.

Althusser treated Hegel as a prop for the mature Marx, a known but exceeded quantity to whom he resorted in order to express a scientific discovery whose specificity he could not himself crystallise. Similarly, according to Althusser, Marx had over-rated his proximity to Ricardo – a thinker whom he had not merely surpassed but left floundering in theoretical anthropology. Althusser made two distinct and, on the face of it, mutually exclusive claims. First, Marx had simultaneously abandoned the ideological problematic of his youth and adopted a new (non-Hegelian, then non-Ricardian) scientific problematic. Secondly, in the work which consummated this rupture, he had frequently reverted to the German ideology and signalled a certain continuity with classical political economy. The proposition which rendered these two statements consistent was the thesis that Marx had indeed broken with these sources, but had intermittently expressed himself in the manner of Hegel (or Ricardo). Where necessary, Althusser took Marx neither at his word nor his work, seeking himself to complete the unfinished business of Marx's theoretical revolution. *Plus royaliste que le roi*, in his ascription of his own innovations to Marx he was guilty of *lèse-majesté*. For, in the event, his consummation of that revolution was the logical development of a dubious premise – namely, the

---

of alienation (ideological) and the mature Marx's theory of fetishism (scientific). In Althusser 1969a, p. 230, n. 7, Althusser had suggested that the then fashionable theory of reification resulted from the illicit projection of the former onto the latter.

[83] Althusser and Balibar 1970, p. 186.
[84] See Althusser and Balibar 1970, pp. 29–30, 188–93. On the proximity of the theory of fetishism and the concept of *Darstellung* to the Hegelian Doctrine of Essence, see Callinicos 1982, p. 122.
[85] Althusser and Balibar 1970, p. 193.

particular 'total theoretical revolution' he delineated. For Althusser, either historical materialism was such a revolution or it was a mere palace coup in the imperious domain of historicism: no alternative to abrupt discontinuity or seamless continuity was conceivable. The truth is almost certainly stranger than these polar fictions. There are surely a whole series of plausible intermediary positions between this dichotomy; and different conceptions of the terms of the dichotomy itself. Moreover, the thesis of continuity in Marx's œuvre is subject to positive and negative evaluations in the same way that the thesis of discontinuity is. The viewpoints of the early Lukács (for whom Marx's glory was to have 'completed' Hegel) and the later Colletti (for whom Marx's shame was to have remained Hegelian), on the one hand, and of Althusser and Thompson (for whom Marx backed into the cul-de-sac of 'anti-political economy' after 1848), on the other, bring home this point and the diversity of the ways in which continuity/discontinuity themselves can be understood.[86] One hundred years after Marx's death, and one hundred and forty years after the *Theses on Feuerbach*, the debate continues, enhanced but unchecked by Althusserian unilateralism of twenty years ago. Only one thing appears agreed upon: the road to *Capital* was not like the Nevsky Prospekt.

Althusser's contentious stand on this, as on other issues, is not the only problem with his discussion of Marx's development. In his determination to disqualify the early works as pre-scientific, Althusser made little or no attempt to substantiate his case for the scientificity of historical materialism. In other words, he conflated the (negative) operation of demarcation with the (positive) task of vindication.[87] The result is that his epistemological differentiation between the early and mature work is uncorroborated. Enlisting the support of Marx's 1859 Preface, Althusser conceived the 'settling of accounts with our former philosophical conscience' as a conceptual and epistemological break such that Marxism conformed to the criteria of Bachelardian epistemology. The problem with this was that it elided three quite distinct claims: (i) a *conceptual* claim for the incompatibility of historical materialism and theoretical humanism-historicism; (ii) a *historical-textual claim* for the existence of a rupture

---

[86] For the anti-Marxist Colletti, see his 1984 and for Thompson's novel periodisation of historical materialism, see his 1978, p. 251ff.

[87] See the illuminating discussion in Levine 1981.

between the two in Marx's œuvre; and (iii) an *epistemological* claim for the scientificity of historical materialism. Logically, it is possible to accept any one of these positions without thereby being enjoined to affirm both the others. Let us provisionally assent to (i), the thesis of incompatibility. Endorsement of it by means entails either (ii) that Marx unambiguously broke with philosophical anthropology or (iii) that historical materialism is ipso facto a science. Likewise, assent to (i) and (ii) in no way compels adherence to (iii). In other words, historical and conceptual discontinuity do not prove epistemological discontinuity. Yet this is precisely what Althusser seeks to elicit (because it breaks with philosophical anthropology, historical materialism is a science). Even if Althusser's reading had proved the conceptual incompatibility and the existence of a break, we have no grounds, given his internalist epistemology, for automatically dubbing historical materialism a science (it too might be a theoretical ideology). And, if the epistemological differentiation between the young Marx and Marx does not work in its Althusserian version, a fortiori the differentiation of Marxisms – humanist to the right, scientific to the left – falls with it.

Althusser took the scientificity of Marxism for granted – it was a *donné* of his whole enterprise. He elaborated an indigenous Marxist epistemology which he employed to exclude the early works from the canon and to purge historical materialism of any remaining ideological elements. Suitably rectified, historical materialism was submitted to the scrutiny of the epistemology, which proceeded triumphantly to uphold its claims to scientific status by virtue of its a-humanism and a-historicism: another circle of circles. What was never in doubt was the scientificity of Marxism: the raison d'être of Althusser's intervention was to defend that status. What is never essayed is a positive vindication of it: the fulcrum of Althusser's discussion is the inadequacy of the young Marx's problematic as a theoretical basis for historical materialism. Althusser's bias is not hard to explain. As he saw it, constructions of Marxism founded on the early works substituted humanist philosophy for scientific investigation, ethical evaluation for materialist explanation, reducing it to an ideological doctrine when what was needed was development of it as social science. This was a theoretical dereliction with practical repercussions. Unconducive to the 'concrete analysis of concrete situations' whose political indispensability was a leitmotif of Lenin and Mao's work, humanist Marxism was politically a-strategic. Moreover, by virtue of its universalist emphases it supposedly denied the centrality of the class struggle – thus constituting a political as well as an epistemological obstacle. In short, for Althusser, such Marxisms were anti-Leninist. In tandem with his epistemological periodisation of Marx's œuvre, Althusser was engaged in the political project of defending and renovating what he regarded as the theoretical bases of Leninism.[88] Thus, by an additional twist to the Althusserian conjuring-trick, 'Leninism' and 'Marxism-Leninism' were identified with plain Marxism and vindicated by its reflected epistemological lustre. Arguably, Althusser's reading was theoretically because politically culpable.

Althusser's co-option of Bachelardian epistemology misfired, precluding attainment of his goal – validation of a scientific theoretical revolution. He could sustain the postulate only through the licence offered by the concept of a problematic, which he tellingly defined on one occasion as an author's *'potential thoughts'*,[89] and which authorised categorisation of an inauspicious concept as a word, an auspicious word as a concept. The near silence on the 'transitional works' is a pregnant one. Hypothetically, in the transitional period, two or more modes of theoretical production coexisted until one – the scientific – became dominant in the theoretical formation, resulting in *Capital*. Yet this was textually indefensible. The Althusserian reading was in fact jammed by its key concept – problematic – which made it impossible to think: (i) the coexistence of, and relations between, elements from different paradigms in one theoretical ensemble; (ii) the decisive heuristic contribution of the eventually surpassed theoretical discourse(s) to the scientific discourse; and (iii) the relationship between the intrinsic and extrinsic (non-discursive) determinants of the discourse. Althusser's epistemology was not an adequate approach to the commencement and development of scientific research programmes in general. A theoretical revolution thought according to its dictates must supervene with such rapidity (cf. Kuhn's 'paradigm' and Foucault's 'episteme') in the autonomous domain of theory as to render it unintelligible. Given that a novel 'object of knowledge' accompanies the installation of a new conceptual system,[90] the whole construction becomes doubly vulnerable.

---

[88] For retrospective confirmation, see Althusser 1976a, pp. 114–15.
[89] Althusser 1969a, p. 66.
[90] See Althusser and Balibar 1970, pp. 156–7.

'Unfortunately it is customary in Germany to write the history of the sciences as if they had fallen from the skies', Engels once remarked to a correspondent.[91] What is unfortunate in the historiography of the sciences is that much more disquieting where Marxism – precisely *not* a science 'among others' – is concerned. Althusser wrote its history as if it had fallen from the sky, converting it into a purely intellectual history untrammelled by the extra-discursive and non-rational. He failed on his own terms, being unable to identify any determinant and beneficent role for the German source of Marxism other than that it had provided Marx with '*a formation for theory*',[92] an apprenticeship in theoretical abstraction. The emergence and development of historical materialism is inexplicable – or at least unexplained.

Althusser's own terms cannot, however, be accepted. For, in his concern to protect historical materialism from the relativism which was, he believed, the normal correlate of historicism, Althusser severed the process of its formation from the wider historical process. At best, the extra-theoretical was denied any status as an independent variable; at worst, it was considered an obstacle to Marx's theoretical revolution.[93]

In 'On the Young Marx', Althusser had adopted a position which, although not without problems, was at once more plausible, fruitful, and proximate to *The German Ideology*. For there he had conceived the break with philosophical abstraction and mystification as in some sense a '*return to real history*',[94] Marx's theoretical revolution as intimately bound up with contemporary history – and not as the product of an autonomous, logical history of ideas. Marx's 'retreat from ideology towards reality', he argued,

> came to coincide with the discovery *of a radically new reality* of which Marx and Engels could find *no echo in the writings of 'German philosophy'*. In France, Marx *discovered* the organised *working class*, in England, Engels discovered *developed capitalism* and *a class struggle obeying its own laws and ignoring philosophy and philosophers*.
>
> This double discovery played a decisive part in the Young Marx's intellectual evolution: the discovery beneath the ideology which had deformed

---

[91] Marx and Engels 1975, p. 441.
[92] Althusser 1969a, p. 85.
[93] See, e.g., Althusser and Balibar 1970, p. 60.
[94] Althusser 1969a, p. 76.

it of *the reality* [of 1840s Germany – GE] *it referred to* – and the discovery beyond contemporary ideology, *which knew it not*, of a *new reality*. Marx became himself by thinking this double reality in a rigorous theory, by changing elements – and by thinking the unity and reality of this new element.

... [I]f we are truly to be able to think this dramatic genesis of Marx's thought, it is essential ... to adopt ... *a logic of actual experience and real emergence*, one that would put an end to the illusions of *ideological immanence*; in short, to adopt a logic of *the irruption of real history in ideology itself*. . . .[95]

After 1961, such propositions were eschewed as empiricist and positivist, ideological postulates derived from the Feuerbachian vestiges in the 'works of the break'. Any connection between science and society, and science and class, was denied except in the negative form of epistemological obstacles. The working class – its struggles and organisations – disappeared, with all historico-political conditions and determinants, from the transcendent conceptual universe in which Marx had practised theoretically. The part of proletarian politics in his theoretical rupture was effaced, the role played by the practical affiliations of historical materialism in its subsequent development repressed. The terminus of this rationalism was precisely the unintelligibility of Marx's evolution foreseen – and deprecated – by Althusser in 'On the Young Marx'. The cognitive autonomy of Marx's science was secured at the cost of an explanation of its genesis, its epistemological dignity at the price of what Althusser once referred to as 'an aristocratism of theory and of its "thinkers" '.[96]

Althusser's reading of Marx, we can conclude, had the merit of foregrounding the emergence of the theory of history as the most decisive development in his thought, the demerit of obscuring its conditions of production and its affiliations. What, now, of his reconstruction of that theory once cured of its nostalgia for its youth?

---

[95] Althusser 1969a, pp. 81–2. The reader is directed by Althusser to the 'real history' of the young Marx by Cornu, to whom Althusser's essay is dedicated.
[96] Althusser and Balibar 1970, p. 129.

The algebra of revolution

In 1975, Althusser reflected that the theses on historical materialism proposed in *For Marx* and *Reading 'Capital'* had important political aims

> bearing on the temptations faced by the Labour Movement: the temptation
> of a messianic or critical idealism of the dialectic . . .; the temptation of . . . the
> poor man's Hegelianism, the evolutionism which has . . . taken the form of
> economism. In both cases, the dialectic functions in the old manner of pre-
> Marxist philosophy as a philosophical guarantee of the coming of revolution
> and of socialism. In both cases, materialism is either juggled away (in the
> case of the first hypothesis) or else reduced to the mechanical and abstract
> materiality of the productive forces (in the case of the second hypothesis).
> In all cases the practice of this dialectic runs up against the implacable test
> of the facts: the revolution did not take place in nineteenth-century Britain
> or in early twentieth-century Germany; it did not take place in the advanced
> countries at all, but elsewhere, in Russia, then later in China and Cuba, etc.[97]

Putting 'politics in command' as it were, Althusser sought to reconstruct historical materialism in such a way that it provided a viable basis for the investigation and illumination of the complexities of real history and concrete societies, thereby furnishing guidance to revolutionary politics. The obstacles to its scientific vocation were to be found not only outside but inside it. In the final analysis, these could be tracked down to a single culprit: Hegelianism. Althusser sought to secure the total novelty of Marx's theory by attempting to demonstrate: (i) the irreducibility of the Marxist dialectic to the Hegelian; (ii) the irreducibility of the Marxist conception of the social whole (and the causality governing it) to the Hegelian; and, as a consequence, (iii) the difference between the Marxist science of history and every philosophy of history (Hegel's being the most rigorous of the genre).

In Chapter 2, we saw that Althusser asserted the specificity of the Marxist dialectic, rejecting standard interpretations of Marx's relation to Hegel and arguing that the dialectic Marx had produced was distinct in its *'characteristic determinations and structures'*. Moreover,

> *these structural differences* can be demonstrated, described, determined and
> thought. And if this is possible, it is therefore *necessary*, I would go so far

---

[97] Althusser 1976a, p. 186.

> as to say *vital*, for Marxism . . . I say *vital*, for I am convinced that *the philosophical development of Marxism currently depends on this task*.[98]

Althusser dedicated himself to it in the belief that past and present experience attested to its urgency.[99] His adversaries were not confined to the minoritarian (if resurgent) tradition of Western Marxism. De-Stalinisation had, as we have seen, licensed a return to Hegel among Communist intellectuals. At the same time, the revision of histomat then underway preserved much of its theoretical basis. It has already been suggested that the Marxist-Leninist version of historical materialism secreted a Hegelianism – the 'rich man's evolutionism'[100] – that dared not speak its name: economism. Behind Stalin, paradoxically, stood Hegel. So any critique of Hegelianism and Second-International orthodoxy was simultaneously – albeit cautiously – directed against theoretical Stalinism and its spectres.[101] Althusser was going against official and underground currents – against 'right' and 'left' Hegelianism, past and present, alike.

In a short piece on Marx written in 1877, Engels credited him with two main scientific discoveries: the materialist conception of history and the theory of surplus-value.[102] The latter is the corner-stone of *Capital*; Marx never wrote a separate treatise on the former. His most compact definition of it is to be found in the Preface to *A Contribution to the Critique of Political Economy* (1859).[103] Introduced as the 'general conclusion' he had arrived at c. 1845, and which had thereafter served as the 'guiding principle' of his research, this summary has been enormously influential. As presented there, historical materialism is a technological determinism. The relations of production which constitute the economic structure/foundation of society, and which condition the superstructure and corresponding forms of social consciousness, are transformed when they impede, rather than facilitate, the growth of the productive forces. The 'era of social revolution' provoked by this 'fettering' ends with the installation of superior relations of production and – sooner or later – the transformation of the superstructure. The growth of the productive forces characterises and explains the general course of human history.

---

[98] Althusser 1969a, p. 94.
[99] See Althusser 1990, p. 111.
[100] Althusser 1990, p. 56.
[101] A point well made by Jameson in his 1981, pp. 27, n. 12; 37.
[102] See Marx and Engels 1877, pp. 77–87.
[103] See Marx 1975, pp. 425–6.

Capitalism is the last 'antagonistic' socio-economic formation. Its productive forces 'create . . . the material conditions for a solution of this antagonism' – a solution which will bring the 'prehistory of human society' to an end. History has a progressive trajectory. Historical development is explained by the intermittent non-correspondence – the recurrent structural incompatibility – between relations and forces of production. Within this pair, the productive forces have causal and explanatory primacy. Marx's conception of historical materialism will not be discussed in any more detail at this stage. For the time being, it is necessary to note two things. First, as interpreted by the ideologues of the Second International and by Stalin, Marx's conception amounted to a meta-theory of history, the *passe-partout* denounced by him as 'supra-historical' in 1877. Secondly, as it stands, this 'materialist conception of history' was anathema to Althusser – the speculative and evolutionist philosophy of history, all too often substituted for concrete socio-historical analysis, which he termed economism.

The nadir of the economistic interpretation of the 1859 Preface, and therewith of historical materialism, is Stalin's opuscule *Dialectical and Historical Materialism*.[104] Stalin's subsumption of historical materialism under diamat produced histomat – 'the extension of the principles of dialectical materialism to the study of social life, [their] application . . . to the phenomena of the life of society, to the study of society and its history'.[105] This extension led to a unilinear vision of history as the evolution in fixed sequence of progressive modes of production (and corresponding superstructures) – 'primitive communal, slave, feudal, capitalist, and Socialist' – according to the laws of a crypto-Hegelian dialectic.[106] For Stalin, the 'determining element' of economic development, and hence of the transition from one to another, higher mode of production, is the productive forces, whose quantitative progress induces qualitative change (revolution). In defence of his thesis of the primacy of the productive forces and, in particular, of 'the development of the instruments of production', he quotes a celebrated remark from *The Poverty of Philosophy*: 'The hand-mill gives you society with the feudal lord; the steam-mill, society

---

[104] Stalin describes the Preface as 'the most brilliant formulation of the essence of historical materialism', quoting its central passage at the end of his essay: see Stalin 1973, p. 331.

[105] Stalin 1973, p. 300.

[106] Stalin 1973, p. 323; see p. 323ff.

with the industrial capitalist.' Moreover, Stalin asserts that '[w]hatever is the mode of production of a society, such in the main is the society itself, its ideas and theories, its political views and institutions'.[107] Accordingly, the 'prime task' of the 'historical science' outlined by him is 'to study ... the laws of economic development of society'.[108] Historical materialism had, in effect, been reduced to a Marxist political economy whose laws are guaranteed by their consonance with those enunciated by diamat.

For obvious reasons, Stalin's productivist version of Marxism – a 'technological humanism'[109] – commanded the public loyalty at least of millions of Communists. It is impossible to overestimate its significance – and longevity. Minus some blatant crudities, it survived de-Stalinisation. *Analogous* constructions of historical materialism have been plentiful in the one hundred years since Marx's death. In *Fundamental Problems of Marxism* (1908), for example, Plekhanov also took his stand on the 1859 Preface, a text described by him as 'a genuine "algebra" – and purely materialist at that – of social development'.[110] Plekhanov's 'materialist monism' is operative in his attempt to specify the conception of the relationship between base and superstructure entertained by the founders of historical materialism, yielding a list of the components of the social formation in their invariant order of importance, from the productive forces via politics to ideologies.[111] On the authority of his 'algebra', Plekhanov would oppose the October Revolution as premature – a voluntarist attempt to terminate the bourgeois-democratic stage before its tasks had been executed and history could pursue its preordained socialist course.

Plekhanov was a doyen of the Second International and Menshevism – a reprobate in Bolshevik eyes. But the latter during Lenin's lifetime was not free of cognate schematism. Bukharin's *Historical Materialism* (1921), issued by the Comintern as a manual for Communist militants, sought to codify the theoretical orthodoxy inherited by them. Saluting Marx's 'magnificent formulation' in the 1859 Preface, Bukharin construed what he nominated

---

[107] Stalin 1973, pp. 319–20, 327–8. For Marx's maxim, see Marx 1978b, p. 166.
[108] Stalin 1973, p. 320.
[109] Raphael Samuel's coinage in his marvellous 1980, p. 83.
[110] Plekhanov 1908, p. 52.
[111] See Plekhanov 1908, p. 70.

'proletarian sociology' as an extreme technological determinism.[112] The 'historic mode of production, i.e., the form of society,' he wrote, 'is determined by the development of the productive forces, i.e., the development of technology'.[113] The relations of production were merely the 'envelope' in which the dynamic productive forces could flourish until such time as the contradiction between form and content – the progressive inadequacy of the relations to the forces of production – became insurmountable. Therewith 'social equilibrium' was disrupted and restored – at a higher level – only with the provision of a new (adequate) envelope.[114] In his Preface, Marx had furnished a 'general description of the process of social evolution': its end-state was communism, a metamorphosis of capitalism and the 'supersession' of previous modes of production.[115] Bukharin's postponement of any discussion of 'classes and class struggle' to the final chapter of his book is no accident; they appear as 'instrument[s] of social transformation', vehicles of natural necessity.[116]

As employed by Althusser, the category of economism had a somewhat wider theoretical significance than Lenin's use of it (for example in *What Is to Be Done?*) to criticise a tendency within Russian Marxism which, in the belief that capitalist economic development would engender its own gravediggers, discounted the importance of the political intervention of a revolutionary party, concentrating instead on economic struggle. Nevertheless, they were closely related. Althusser identified the economistic problematic as the root of the economistic deviation in politics – as the root, that is, of the reformist fatalism which relies on 'the inexorability of a natural process'[117] to destroy capitalism, evolution to perform the task of revolution. Abstract, reductionist and teleological, economism is a schema in which the economy (and its contradictions) is the pantheistic demiurge of history and individual societies are only variations ('backward' or 'advanced') on a universal model. For Althusser, its political fatalism is the reverse side of the same coin as the voluntarism of Hegelian Marxism, its denial of any autonomy and effectivity to the superstructures the hallmark of their common theoretical leftism. At

---

[112] Bukharin 1969, pp. 14, 207.
[113] Bukharin 1969, p. 124.
[114] Bukharin 1969, p. 242ff.
[115] See Bukharin 1969, pp. 243, 311.
[116] See Bukharin 1969, p. 272ff.
[117] Marx 1976a, p. 929.

best it is analytically jejune and politically impotent, legislating to concrete historical processes which decline to conform to it, discomfited by the 'implacable test of the facts', and therefore constantly surprised by real history – as in Russia in 1917. History's 'exceptions', Althusser insisted, prove the rule of exceptionalism, being aberrant only with respect to 'the *abstract*, but comforting and reassuring idea of a pure, simple "dialectical" schema'.[118]

In order to analyse social formations, a new conception of contradiction was required. In 'Contradiction and Overdetermination', Althusser attempted to furnish it. Taking Lenin's reflections on the Russian Revolution as his raw material, Althusser drew the following conclusion from them:

> if the general contradiction [between forces and relations of production] is sufficient to define the situation when revolution is the 'task of the day', it cannot of its own simple, direct power induce a 'revolutionary situation', nor *a fortiori* a situation of revolutionary rupture and the triumph of the revolution. If this contradiction is to become *'active'* in the strongest sense, to become a ruptural principle, there must be an accumulation of 'circumstances' and 'currents' so that whatever their origin and sense . . ., they *'fuse'* into a ruptural unity. . . .[119]

Both Lenin and Mao had displayed exemplary sensitivity to the complexity and specificity of 'concrete situations', meticulously analysing their multiple 'currents' and 'circumstances' in the recognition that any politics which aspired to transform them must take account of such realities. Lenin's analyses of February and October had highlighted *'the accumulation and exacerbation of historical contradictions'*[120] within the Russian social formation on the eve of absolutism's demise. The snapping of imperialism's 'weakest link' was a synthesis of many determinations, none of them reducible to 'the "beautiful" contradiction between Capital and Labour'.[121] What the Russian experience confirmed, *inter alia*, was that economic contradiction is invariably

> inseparable from the total structure of the social body in which it is found, inseparable from its formal *conditions* of existence, and even from the *instances* it governs; it is radically *affected by them*, determining and determined by

---

[118] Althusser 1969a, p. 104.
[119] Althusser 1969a, p. 99.
[120] Althusser 1969a, p. 97.
[121] Althusser 1969a, p. 104.

the various *levels* and *instances* of the social formation it animates; it might
be called *overdetermined in its principle*.[122]

In the Marxist dialectic, Althusser suggested, every contradiction is complex,
is an *overdetermined contradiction* – i.e. is 'complexly-structurally-unevenly-
determined'.[123] For Hegel, by contrast, contradiction is 'simple'. His dialectical
'method' cannot – as Engels thought – be detached from the content of his
philosophical system for the straightforward reason that it is not an optional
extra to it. Hegel's idealism is reflected *'in the very structures of his dialectic,*
particularly in the *"contradiction"* whose task is the magical movement of the
concrete contents of a historical epoch towards their ideological Goal'.[124] The
logic of the Hegelian dialectic (a 'circle of circles') is inexorable, teleological
and theological – a 'theoretical concentrate' of its author's conception of
history as the 'process of development and realization of Spirit'.[125] If historical
materialism was to be something more than an economic version of this
'theodicy', it must dispense with the services of a method which possessed
a mystical kernel and shell. In practice, Lenin and Mao had, acknowledging
the complexity constitutive of the Marxist concept of contradiction. Mao's
On Contradiction (1937), in particular, had developed a series of distinctions –
between principal and secondary contradictions, between the principal and
secondary aspects of contradictions, between antagonistic and non-antagonistic
contradictions – quite foreign to Hegelianism.[126] The leaders' 'practical break'
was to be theoretically consolidated and reflected by the importation of Freud's
concept of 'overdetermination' and the Lacanian version of his categories of
'condensation' and 'displacement'. The medley of endogenous contradictions
informing a social formation are not manifestations of some immanent, essential
contradiction (between the forces and relations of production). Although
organised into a hierarchy of dominance and subordination in any particular
conjuncture, a multiplicity of real and effective contradictions (co-)exists
throughout the regions of the social formation, permeating it. They are
simultaneously determinant and determined, 'overdetermining' each other –

---

[122] Althusser 1969a, p. 101; see also p. 106.
[123] Althusser 1969a, pp. 107, 209.
[124] Althusser 1969a, p. 104.
[125] Althusser 1969a, p. 197; Althusser and Balibar 1970, p. 112; Hegel 1956, p. 457.
[126] See Althusser 1969a, pp. 94, n. 6; 210–11.

a process which can result in their 'condensation' or 'fusion' in the 'ruptural unity' which is a revolutionary rupture.[127]

With his concept of overdetermined contradiction and stipulation of its universality, Althusser believed he had 'reached *the Marxist dialectic* itself'.[128] He habitually conducted his attack on the economism and technologism issuing from other, 'essentialist' versions of the dialectic at a historical remove. On at least one occasion, however, he struck rather closer to home. If Marx's comments on the hand-mill and steam-mill were taken literally,

> The logical destination . . . is the *exact mirror image of the Hegelian dialectic* – the only difference being that it is no longer a question of deriving the successive moments from the Idea, but from the Economy, by virtue of the same internal contradiction. This . . . results in the radical reduction of the dialectic of history to the dialectic generating the successive *modes of production*, that is, in the last analysis, the different production *techniques*.[129]

Whilst it might also fit others, this particular cap was made to measure for Stalin. And, if Stalin had misrepresented the structure of the Marxist dialectic, he had simultaneously and relatedly misconceived the nature of the (social) totality in which it is operative.

What is a society?

When in 1923 Korsch complained that, for 'vulgar Marxism', there are 'three degrees of reality' (economy, state/law and ideology in descending order), he voiced a sentiment that was to become an *idée fixe* of Western Marxism.[130] Althusser is no exception to this particular rule. In his case, however, Western Marxism – Gramsci as well as Korsch and Lukács, Della Volpe and Colletti as well as Sartre – equally finds itself in the dock for an erroneous conception of the nature and structure of society. By different routes, both traditions in historical materialism suppressed the '*specific effectivity of the superstructures*'.

---

[127] See Althusser 1969a, pp. 99–100, 215–16.
[128] Althusser 1969a, p. 217.
[129] Althusser 1969a, p. 108.
[130] Korsch 1970, p. 82. Thus, we might note, for example, that Bukharin's *Historical Materialism* had provoked highly critical responses from both Lukács 1972, pp. 134–42 and Gramsci 1971, pp. 419–72.

Marxism in fact lacked a theory of the latter and their relations to the economic base. It too was in need of construction.[131]

It was to this problem that Engels was obliged to devote some attention in his last years. In a series of admonitory letters, he sought to restate the basic thesis of historical materialism. Writing to Conrad Schmidt in August 1890, he reflected that 'the materialist conception of history has a lot of dangerous friends nowadays', people who were utilising it not as intended – 'a guide to study' – but as 'a lever for construction after the Hegelian manner'.[132] A little over a month later, he impressed on another correspondent (Joseph Bloch) that, according to historical materialism, the 'economic factor' was 'the *ultimately* determining factor in history'; to take it for the 'only' such factor was to reduce the main thesis of Marxism to 'a meaningless, abstract, absurd phrase'.[133] Conceding that he and Marx must shoulder some of the blame for unilateral emphasis on the determinacy of the economic, Engels referred to Marx's concrete analyses as genuine examples of the theory's application;[134] and attempted to amend matters by assignation of a reciprocal determinant role to the superstructures, postulating an interaction of superstructure and base.

Althusser rejected Engels's theoretical solution to the problem of the relationship between 'determination in the last instance' (by the economic) and the 'effectivity' of the superstructures as maladroit.[135] But he made Engels's starting-point his own. The complexity characteristic of the Marxist conception of 'society' dictated the suppression of this quotidian category in favour of a specifically Marxist concept employed by Marx in the 1859 Preface: social formation. Its utilisation signified Marx's distance from a whole tradition of political philosophy and economy culminating in Hegel, which employed the 'state/civil society' couplet. Without attributing it to Engels, Althusser demurred at a thesis he had advanced in *Ludwig Feuerbach*. Marx had not merely inverted the Hegelian model of society, filling the terms of the inherited couplet with new content and elevating civil society to prepotency, relegating

---

[131] Althusser 1969a, p. 113. Only Gramsci is credited with having built upon what Marx left; see Althusser 1969a, p. 114 and n 29.
[132] Marx and Engels 1975, p. 393.
[133] Marx and Engels 1975, p. 394.
[134] Marx and Engels 1975, p. 396.
[135] See Althusser 1969a, pp. 117–28 and cf. Marx and Engels 1975, pp. 395–6.

the state to a subaltern status. In other words, Marx had not written the equations: civil society = economy = infrastructure = (active) essence (cause); state = politics/law = superstructure = (passive) phenomena/appearances (effects). Terms and content *had* changed: mode of production supplanted civil society, for example; Hegel's conception of the state as 'the actuality of the ethical idea' was replaced by Marx's of it as an *'instrument'* of class domination. Yet of equal, indeed greater significance was the fact that the 'relations' between the terms underwent transformation. Marx had produced a novel conception of the relations between the regions of the social formation.[136] Unsuccessful in formulating it rigorously, he and Engels had nevertheless indicated its main constituents: *'determination in the last instance by the (economic) mode of production'* and *'the relative autonomy of the superstructures and their specific effectivity'*. How was this ultimate determination and relative autonomy conceived?

Without defending his thesis textually, Althusser argued that the Marxist topography divided the social formation into (i) the infrastructure – the economic level or instance, conceived as the unity of the relations and forces of production under the dominance of the former; and (ii) the superstructure – in class societies, the juridico-political and ideological levels or instances. Against the 'three degrees' of vulgar Marxism, Althusser reconceptualised these regions as constituted by distinct practices: economic, political, ideological and theoretical. 'Social practice' comprised the 'complex unity of the practices existing in a determinate society'.[137] Each of these practices was unique as regards its content (its particular object, means of production, product), if not its structure (as practices they were isomorphic). Each was articulated with, but relatively autonomous of, the other practices combined in the unity. The ensemble was precisely *complex*, but so structured that ultimately economic practice was the determinant one. Theoretical practice has already been considered; Althusser's definition of economic practice is uncontroversial; political practice is defined as that which 'transforms . . . social relations

---

[136] Althusser 1969a, p. 111; see pp. 108–11 and cf. Marx and Engels 1977, p. 369. In Althusser 1969a, pp. 203–4, n. 43, Althusser distinguishes between the Engelsian/Marxian reading of Hegel as the 'inverse' of Marx and an accurate reading of him, which reveals his political philosophy unsusceptible to any such interpretation. On the concept of 'civil society', see also Althusser and Balibar 1970, p. 162, n. 37.

[137] Althusser 1969a, p. 167. See also Althusser and Balibar 1970, p. 58.

into . . . new social relations'; ideological as that which 'transforms its object: men's "consciousness"'.[138] In 'Marxism and Humanism', Althusser attributed this 'historico-dialectical materialism of *praxis*' to Marx.[139]

In Chapter 2, it was noted, first, that Althusser's ontology of practices enabled him to affirm the 'primacy of practice' within his own epistemology and, secondly, that it was intended to counter Hegelian Marxism. The first move is unacceptable, the second (subject to certain qualifications) laudable. Reality, Althusser argued, is (and always has been) complex, multiform and heterogeneous – that is, overdetermined. Similarly, for Marxism, the social totality is 'a pre-given complex structured whole'.[140] It is – always was and always will be – irreducible to a 'substance', an 'essence' or an 'act' as the 'twin confusions of "mechanistic" materialism and the idealism of consciousness' would have it. To think otherwise is to revert to Hegel (or Haeckel).[141] The lineaments of the Marxist totality are quite other than those of the Hegelian. The latter is only complex at first sight. In actuality, like the Hegelian contradiction, it is 'simple' since its 'concrete differences' are no sooner posited than negated by the totality's internal principle, of which they are merely so many 'moments'.[142] The Hegelian totality is characterised by Althusser as an 'expressive totality' – one whose parts express each other and the totality's simple essence.[143] The diversity of the real and the social – 'difference' (a recurrent theme in *For Marx* and *Reading 'Capital'*) – is alien to it.[144] The Marxist totality, in contrast, conceals no essence to be expressed, no centre to be reflected. It is a 'structure of structures' comprising a '*plurality* of instances' (composed of a multiplicity of distinct practices) which are relatively autonomous of one another, endowed with their own 'specific effectivity', and possess a 'peculiar time and history'.[145] The superstructural

---

[138] Althusser 1969a, p. 167.

[139] Althusser 1969a, p. 229.

[140] Althusser 1969a, p. 193.

[141] Althusser 1969a, p. 202.

[142] Althusser 1969a, p. 203; see also p. 103.

[143] Althusser and Balibar 1970, p. 94; see also Althusser 1969a, pp. 203–4, n. 43.

[144] The appropriateness of Callinicos's highlighting of the notion of 'difference' in Althusser (see Callinicos 1982, pp. 62–5 and Callinicos 1983, pp. 90–1, 95) receives interesting confirmation from Macciocchi 1973a, p. 481. Assuming what she relates to be accurate, in an unpublished text dating from c. 1970 Althusser suggested that the two (commendable) concepts dominating Mao's writings are '*difference*' and '*unevenness*' (translation modified).

[145] Althusser and Balibar 1970, pp. 17, 99, 207.

levels are not the ruses of Economic Reason – second-order realities in relation to a primordial or superordinate material structure, the economic base. A social formation is a global structure, subsuming three regional structures with their own ineradicable reality. The economic instance is one such regional structure. The political and ideological instances are neither the punctual effects of a basic cause, nor the superstructural phenomena of an infrastructural essence. They are determinant as well as determined, 'conditions of existence' of the economic as much as it is theirs. Overdetermination is 'universal'. In short, Marxism is not an economism:

> the economic dialectic is never active *in the pure state*; in History, these instances, the superstructures, etc. – are never seen to step respectfully aside when their work is done or, when the Time comes, as his pure phenomena, to scatter before His Majesty the Economy as he strides along the royal road of the Dialectic. From the first moment to the last, the lonely hour of the last instance never comes.[146]

Althusser's preservation of the classical base/superstructure topography (determination in the last instance by the *economic*) is thus conjoined with a reconceptualisation of the conformation of social formations: the political and ideological levels enjoy relative autonomy, but not independence (determination in the *last instance*). At the same time, the 'last instance' never graces the social formation with its presence. What therefore remains of the classical-Marxist thesis of ultimate economic determination – the thesis with which Marx demarcated his theory of history from idealist philosophies of history? And, if the regions of the decentred, non-homogeneous social totality are composed of distinct practices, irreducible – spatially and temporally – to one another, is this totality a bona fide totality or a congeries of discrete interacting elements? Has pluralism, so to speak, been substituted for historical materialism? Althusser insisted that his concept of the social whole was Marxist and was a totality – albeit one that is simultaneously complex and unified, decentred and determined, heterogeneous and hierarchical. Complexity is constitutive of it; this distinguishes it form the Hegelian-Marxist model, which erases the 'real differences separating the levels'.[147] It is a 'structure in dominance'; this

---

[146] Althusser 1969a, p. 113.
[147] Althusser and Balibar 1970, p. 132.

rebuts the charge of pluralism, which effaces the totality subsuming these levels. For,

> to claim that this unity is not and cannot be the unity of a simple, original and universal essence is not . . . to sacrifice unity at the altar of 'pluralism' – it is to claim something quite different: that the unity discussed by Marxism is *the unity of complexity itself,* that the mode of organization and articulation of the complexity is precisely what constitutes its unity. It is to claim that *the complex whole has the unity of a structure articulated in dominance.*[148]

Every social formation is a 'structure in dominance', insofar as each contains a dominant element which organises the hierarchy and inter-relations of the various social practices. This dominant element, however, does not override the causal primacy of the economic. The economic is not always *dominant,* but it is always *determinant* in the last instance, responsible for the co-ordination of the instances, allotting the dominant role within the totality to one of them and subordinate roles to the others, fixing their degree of relative autonomy and efficacy. In capitalist social formations, it determines its own dominance. In other social formations, the allocation can vary: one of the non-economic instances can occupy the dominant position – and in feudalism, for example, it does. Any particular social formation is thus *'a variation of the – "invariant" – structure in dominance of the totality'.*[149] All this Althusser regarded as pertaining to 'the true Marxist tradition'. Only economism cast the economic level in the lead role in perpetuity, assigning the other levels bit- or walk-on parts. In 'real history' – the history Marxists were obliged to explain and act in/on – ultimate economic determination operates through the permutation of dominance between the different instances.[150]

This last point returns us to Lenin and Mao. Althusser's revision of the classical topography was not an aesthetic operation. He considered his theses of crucial importance to Marxist politics. Whereas economism does violence to historical reality, forcing it into a schema in which all contradictions are

---

[148] Althusser 1969a, pp. 201–2. See also Althusser and Balibar 1970, pp. 97–9.

[149] Althusser 1969a, p. 209.

[150] Althusser 1969a, p. 213. See also Balibar's comments in Althusser and Balibar 1970, p. 224. Somewhat confusingly, Balibar employs 'determinant' for 'dominant'. An amendment by Althusser to the useful glossaries appended to *For Marx* and *Reading 'Capital'* by their translator, Ben Brewster, clears up the ambiguity. See, e.g., Althusser 1969a, p. 255.

manifestations of the productive forces, the model constructed by Althusser was intended by him only as an 'abstract' but indispensable preliminary. For revolutionary practice, ascertainment of the *precise variations* of the invariant is what matters – not the knowledge that social formations are invariably structured in dominance. In other words, Althusser's recomposition of the Marxist topography was designed to permit – not substitute itself for – what Lenin had called 'the living soul of Marxism': 'a concrete analysis of a concrete situation'.[151] Lenin's analysis of the Russian 'conjuncture' in 1917 exemplified the latter, focusing on the specific relations then obtaining between the various levels of the social formation, the exact configuration of each level, the particular constellation of contradictions active within them, the correlation of forces confronting revolutionary political action.[152] The (strategic) concept of *conjuncture*, designating 'the structure of the real historical present',[153] was indispensable both to the Marxist theory of history and, a fortiori, to the Marxist science of politics. Concrete analysis of it formed the juncture between science and politics, facilitating an answer to the quintessential revolutionary question: what is to be done?

The law of overdetermination and its Maoist pair, the 'law of uneven development',[154] prevailed not only in pre- or non-revolutionary states, but post-revolutionary ones as well. And, with this point, we rejoin Stalin. For it provided Althusser with a theoretical framework for explaining Stalinism, since overdetermination entailed:

(i) that a revolution in the [economic] structure does not *ipso facto* modify the existing superstructures and particularly the *ideologies* at one blow (as it would if the economic was the *sole determinant factor*). . . .

(ii) that the new society produced by the revolution may itself *ensure the survival, that is, the reactivation, of older elements* (through both the forms of its new superstructures and specific (national and international) 'circumstances'.[155]

---

[151] Lenin 1966a, p. 166 (quoted in Althusser 1969a, p. 206). See also Lenin 1964, p. 43.

[152] See Althusser 1969a, pp. 178–9, 206–7.

[153] See Althusser and Balibar 1970, pp. 106–7.

[154] See, e.g., Althusser 1969a, pp. 200–1.

[155] Althusser 1969a, pp. 115–16. Althusser conjectures that, in the absence of such an analytical framework, it is impossible to account for the Stalin era and asserts the

At stake here was the distinction not only between Hegelian and Marxist concepts of the social totality, but also between the Hegelian conception of history/historical time and the Marxist – a distinction which again turns on the issue of simplicity/complexity and which was crystallised in a notion unveiled in *Reading 'Capital'*: differential temporality.

From the irreducibility of the complex social whole to any underlying essence or principle which could confer unity on it, Althusser derived the irreducibility of the individual histories of the levels (and their practices) to a common history. He argued that Hegel's concept of historical time was tributary to his expressivist concept of totality. It had two main features: 'homogeneous continuity' and 'contemporaneity'.[156] For Hegel, it is suggested, history is a continuum – a succession of expressive totalities instantiating the various phases of Absolute Spirit's 'development'. The elements of each totality, as appearances of the immanent-transcendent essence, are co-present in an identical time. Accordingly, Hegelian historical time is of a piece with empiricist conceptions of time. The complexity of the Marxist totality necessitated a rupture with these postulates. 'It is no longer possible,' Althusser wrote,

> to think the process of the development of the different levels of the whole *in the same historical time*. Each of these different 'levels' does not have the same type of historical existence. On the contrary, we have to assign to each level a *peculiar time*, relatively autonomous and hence relatively independent, even in its dependence, of the 'times' of the other levels.[157]

The economic mode of production, politics, literature, ideology, science, and so on all have their own 'time and history', their own peculiar rhythms, forms of development, kinds of continuity and discontinuity. These differential historical times do not exist in, and cannot be measured against, 'a simple ideological base time' – namely, a linear chronological time.[158] Yet this, in turn,

---

need for more theoretical and historical research. His own perspective at this stage was indicated in 'Marxism and Humanism', where it is claimed in passing that the relative autonomy of the superstructures 'explains very simply, in theory, how the socialist *infrastructure* (in the USSR) has been able to develop without essential damage during this period of errors affecting the superstructure': Althusser 1969a, p. 240.

[156] See Althusser and Balibar 1970, pp. 94–6.
[157] Althusser and Balibar 1970, p. 99.
[158] See Althusser and Balibar 1970, pp. 104–5.

does not mean that the 'different historical temporalities' are wholly independent of the social totality, hence of one another. The 'mode and degree of *independence*' of each is dependent upon the mode and degree of relative autonomy in the social whole enjoyed by the level whose time it is.[159] The 'complex combination of the different temporalities produced by the different levels of the structure ... constitutes the peculiar time' of the social formation's development.[160]

Althusser's theses on the indirect, two-stage determinacy of the economic, the overdetermination of any social formation, and the differential temporality that implies, involved the proposition of a new order of causality: structural causality. With this concept (deployed for the first time in *Reading 'Capital'*), Althusser sought to encapsulate the ultimate difference between Marxism and its economistic and historicist distortions. Said to be present in the 'practical state' in Marx's theoretical revolution, it had been anticipated by Spinoza and was now to be elaborated by Althusser. Marx had implicitly – but by no means explicitly – discarded two traditional models of causality. The first – of Cartesian patrimony – was 'transitive' (mechanical causality). The second – of Leibizian patrimony and Hegelian renown – was 'expressive'. Proper to Marx and Marxism, structural causality was intended to conceptualise '*the determination of the elements of a structure, and the structural relations between those elements, and all the effects of those relations by the effectivity of that structure*'.[161] In other words, as we saw earlier, it was designed to characterise the causal relationship obtaining between the global structure (the social totality) and its regional structures (economic, political, ideological) and between the regional structures and their elements (such as the economic structure and its elements – the forces and relations of production). Unlike transitive causality, it describes the effectivity of a whole on its parts; unlike expressive causality, it does not 'essentialise' the whole and is not reductive of the parts. In Spinozist fashion, *qua* cause the structure is 'immanent in its effects' and not external

---

[159] See Althusser and Balibar 1970, p. 99.

[160] Althusser and Balibar 1970, p. 104.

[161] Althusser and Balibar 1970, p. 186. Spinoza is credited with being the only philosopher prior to Marx 'to pose this problem and outline a first solution to it' (p. 187). The Spinozist notion of immanent causality – '*God is the immanent and not the transient cause of all things*' (Spinoza 1955, p. 62; translation modified) – provides the model for Althusser's structural causality: see Althusser and Balibar 1970, p. 189.

to them. Indeed, *'the whole existence of the structure consists of its effects'*.[162] The cause is *'absent'*, present only in and as its effects – and not wholly present ('in person') in any of them.[163]

All the foregoing – the multiplicity and irreducibility of practices and their different moments, the plurality of regional structures in a global structure and their different time, 'structural causality' – was the basis of Althusser's claim that Marxism is a theoretical a-/anti-humanism. For Althusser, history is a 'process without a subject'.[164] History and society are not the creations of a human subject, singular or collective. Men are not the subjects of social and historical processes; they are their 'supports':

> the structure of the relations of production determines the *places* and *functions* occupied and adopted by the agents of production, who are never anything more than the occupants of these places, insofar as they are the 'supports' (*Träger*) of these functions. The true 'subjects' (in the sense of constitutive subjects of the process) are therefore not these occupants or functionaries, are not 'concrete individuals', 'real men' – but *the definition and distribution of these places and functions. The true 'subjects' are these definers and distributors: the relations of production* (and political and ideological social relations). But since these are 'relations', they cannot be thought within the category *subject*.[165]

For Marx, Althusser argued, the relations of production involve the distribution of the means of production as well as the relations between 'men' (social agents) distributed to antagonistic social classes. To interpret them solely as inter-subjective human relations (as does Hegelian Marxism) is to indulge a 'remarkable presupposition: that the "actors" of history are the authors of its text, the subjects of its production'.[166] From first to last in Althusser's objectivist Marxism, the hour of the primacy of structure never ceased to strike. Foremost among these structures was the *mode of production* – the basic concept of historical materialism.[167] With it a science of economy, society and history

---

[162] Althusser and Balibar 1970, p. 189.
[163] Althusser and Balibar 1970, p. 188. For a retrospective, see Althusser 1976a, pp. 126–7, n. 20.
[164] Balibar in Althusser and Balibar 1970, p. 271.
[165] Althusser and Balibar 1970, p. 180. In Althusser 1969a p. 231, Althusser had suggested that '[t]he "subjects" of history are given human societies'.
[166] Althusser and Balibar 1970, p. 139; see pp. 139–40, 174–5, and 270–1. The presupposition is indulged in Marx 1976b, p. 170.
[167] Althusser and Balibar 1970, p. 167.

was initiated, since modes of production were 'the basic forms of unity of historical existence'.[168]

The forward march of the productive forces halted

The construction of an Althusserian theory of modes of production was largely delegated to Étienne Balibar in his impressive contribution to *Reading 'Capital'*, 'On the Basic Concepts of Historical Materialism' (the only paper besides Althusser's retained in the second, 1968 edition of *Lire 'le Capital'* from which the English translation was made). Althusser set out its protocols, however, in the last two chapters of 'The Object of *Capital'*.

The bulk of Marx's attention was of course focused on the capitalist mode of production and he devoted no full-scale work to 'precapitalist economic formations'. These, such as he conceived them, are listed in the 1859 Preface, discussed in an excursus in the *Grundrisse* (the *Formen*), and referred to throughout *Capital* – usually for comparative purposes. In Volume One of *Capital*, Marx proposed that 'economic formations' (hereafter modes of production) were distinguished from one another by their peculiar relations of production – the mode of exploitation of the direct producers by the possessors of the means of production. In a celebrated passage of Volume Three, he argued that these relations contained 'the innermost secret, the hidden basis of the entire social edifice', including the 'specific form' of the state. Relations of production thus have explanatory primacy over social formations. In turn, they 'always [correspond] to a certain level of the development of the type and manner of labour, and hence to its social productive power'. In other words, they correspond to the productive forces (means of production and labour-power).[169]

Citing this and other passages, Althusser conjectured that, via the 'combination' of the various elements enumerated by Marx – direct producers, owners of the means of production, instruments and objects of production, and so on – it was possible to 'reach a definition of the different *modes of production* which have existed and can exist in human history'.[170] Moreover,

---

[168] Althusser and Balibar 1970, pp. 195–6.
[169] See Marx 1976a, p. 325 and Marx 1981, p. 927.
[170] Althusser and Balibar 1970, p. 176.

since modes of production (in the restricted economic sense) require certain specific superstructural 'conditions of existence' – politico-legal and/or ideological forms functional for the relations of production – 'the whole superstructure of the society considered is . . . implicit and present in a specific way in the relations of production'.[171] In this, the expanded definition, the economic level was a regional structure (productive forces and relations of production) within a global structure – the mode of production – and could only be defined via the latter.[172]

Balibar's text opens by taking it as read that Marx's œuvre contained 'a general scientific theory of history'.[173] In the title given this general theory, the noun signified science: historical materialism thus meant no more and no less than 'science of history'.[174] The transformation of the theory of history into a science revolved around two principles: historical periodisation and the (asymmetrical) disposition and inter-relations of the regions of the social totality. This much the 1859 Preface made clear. Balibar's task was to work up its supposedly 'practical concepts' into a general theory of modes of production – their structure, their constitution, and the forms of transition from one to another – which would be a science of history as a 'discontinuous succession of modes of production'.[175]

On the basis of Marx's topography in the Preface, Balibar asserted that a 'plurality of instances must be an essential property of every social structure . . .; the problem of the science of society must be precisely the problem of the forms of variation of their articulation'.[176] What was true of the (structural-causal) relations between the regional structures of the global structure equally applied to the constituent elements of every (economic) mode of production, the regional structure which was the starting-point for an analysis of the global. Since Marx had constructed a scientific concept of the capitalist mode of production in Capital, Balibar considered that this should supply the key to the construction of the general theory of modes of production, thence to the construction of the concepts of non-capitalist modes of production.

---

171 Althusser and Balibar 1970, pp. 177–8.
172 See Althusser and Balibar 1970, pp. 182–3.
173 Althusser and Balibar 1970, p. 201.
174 Althusser and Balibar 1970, p. 202.
175 Althusser and Balibar 1970, p. 204; see pp. 203–8.
176 Althusser and Balibar 1970, p. 207.

Marshalling selected passages from *Capital*, Balibar analysed modes of production as being differentiated or individuated by a 'variation of the connexion between a small number of elements which are always the same'.[177] These comprise two 'connexions' between three 'elements':

- (1) labourer;
- (2) means of production;
    - (i) object of labour;
    - (ii) means of labour;
- (3) non-labourer;
- (A) property connexion;
- (B) real or material appropriation connexion.[178]

The economic mode of production, it is argued, is an articulated unity of the forces and relations of production. The 'property connexion' – the relations of production – and 'real appropriation connexion' – the productive forces – are in a state of correspondence with one another, except during transition periods – when the relations of production are the dominant term, enjoying explanatory primacy over the forces.

Balibar had earlier ventured that the theory of modes of production furnished a theoretical foundation for the opening lines of the *Communist Manifesto*. In other words, despite the apparent esotericism of his analysis, the following question underlay it: '*on what conditions can the claim that history is the history of class struggles be a scientific utterance?*'.[179] Now (and more contentiously in Marxist terms) he is signalling an attempt to theorise the ultimate primacy of the relations of production not only over the relations of distribution and so on, but also over the productive forces: a quasi-Maoist thesis. Thus, the technological determinism consequent upon Plekhanov et al.'s exclusion of labour-power from the productive forces, and the reduction of the latter to 'things', provoked a powerful – and novel – reaction on the part of the Althusserians. While mode of production was emphatically retained as the basic concept of historical materialism, it was drastically recast. The productive forces were deprived of their status as an independent variable and themselves

---

[177] Althusser and Balibar 1970, p. 225. See Marx 1978, p. 120.
[178] Althusser and Balibar 1970, p. 215.
[179] Althusser and Balibar 1970, p. 205.

conceived as a variety – or sub-set – of the relations of production: '"technical" social relations of production'.[180] The result, as we shall see, was that the contradictory dialectic of the forces and relations of production, which provided the principal dynamic of history on Marx's reading of it, disappeared – the capitalist mode of production, for example, as an articulated combination of forces and relations, containing no inherent tendencies to its own dissolution.

Following Althusser, Balibar argued that:

> By varying the combination of these elements according to the two connexions which are part of the structure of every mode of production ... we can reconstitute the various modes of production, i.e. we can set out the 'presuppositions' for the theoretical knowledge of them which are quite simply the concepts of the conditions of their historical existence. ... The final result would be a *comparative table of the forms* of different modes of production which all combine the same 'factors'.[181]

Moreover, with the tabulation of the invariants, Balibar claimed that it was possible to explain the precise modality of the economy's causal primacy in the various modes of production. Uniquely, in the capitalist mode of production the labour and surplus-labour processes coincide in time and space. Surplus labour is extracted from the producers (labourers doubly separated from the means of production) in the form of surplus-value by capitalists (non-labouring 'owners' of the means of production to whom workers sell their commodified labour-power) in the production process itself. Contrariwise, in the feudal mode of production, since the producers are not separated from the means of production, necessary and surplus labour do not coincide and extra-economic coercion is required for the performance of the latter (and hence the extraction of a surplus). The (non-)coincidence of the processes explains the two-stage determination exercised by the economic instance in any social formation; its exploitative modus operandi determines which of the instances is dominant. As a function of their homology in the capitalist mode, the economy is both determinant and dominant; as a function of their disjunction in the feudal mode, the economic instance determines the dominance of the (coercive) political instance (the state). The post of the 'last instance' is always

---

[180] See Althusser and Balibar 1970, pp. 233–5, 247.
[181] Althusser and Balibar 1970, p. 216.

occupied by the economic, but the position of dominance is permuted among the instances of the social totality according to exigencies of the appropriation of a surplus.[182]

The major problem with Balibar's proposed comparative analysis, as Glucksmann pointed out in a trenchant critique of Reading 'Capital' two years after its publication, is that it ultimately amounts to a theory solely of the uniqueness of capitalism.[183] What Glucksmann calls Balibar's 'indeterminable comparativism' can distinguish between the capitalist mode of production, on the one hand, and precapitalist modes of production on the other. (In the former, the direct producer is separated from the means of production and the economy, accordingly, is dominant; in the latter, the direct producer is not thus separated and hence the dominance of a non-economic instance is determined.) However, it cannot discriminate among precapitalist modes of production themselves (of which Balibar cites only the Asiatic and the feudal). Arguably, this outcome was inherent in Balibar's starting-point. For his procedure is based upon at least two unquestioned but questionable premises: (i) that Marx's inchoate reflections on precapitalist modes of production can serve, unsupplemented and unreconstructed, as the raw material for his own theoretical practice; and (ii) that 'Marx's method . . . completely abolishes the problem of "reference", of the empirical designation of the object of a theoretical knowledge' and that historical research, Marxist and non-Marxist alike, is therefore superfluous to the construction (and substantiation) of a typology of modes of production.[184]

Balibar strenuously denied that his was a structuralist project of 'an a priori science of modes of production', like Althusser asserting a categorical distinction between the structuralist 'combinatory' and (his own interpretation of) Marx's 'combination'.[185] Yet his account of the reproduction of modes of production

[182] See Althusser and Balibar 1970, pp. 216–24. Among other passages, Balibar quotes in his support Marx 1976a, p. 176, n. 25 and Marx 1981, pp. 926–7.

[183] See Glucksmann 1977, p. 299.

[184] See Althusser and Balibar 1970, p. 249 and cf. the critical remarks in the NLR introduction to Glucksmann 1977, p. 276 and n.

[185] Althusser and Balibar, p. 226; see also pp. 216, 241 and Althusser's comments on p. 176. Compare, however, Balibar in Althusser et al. 1965, Volume Two, p. 205. The original title of Chapter 1 of Balibar's paper was 'La Périodisation et sa combinatoire' – changed in the second edition to 'From Periodisation to Modes of Production'.

and the transition from one to another apparently brought him within the orbit of the French ideology he disavowed.

The characterisation of modes of production as variably articulated combinations of invariant elements conveyed the 'radically *anti-evolutionist* character of Marxist theory'.[186] They were not to be conceived, in the manner of Stalin, as self-subversive historical forms, whose quasi-Hegelian supersession – via the mechanism of inexorable laws of motion – was a matter of predetermined necessity. Quite the reverse, a mode of production was an 'eternity' – a 'theoretical object' with no empirical or historical existence. For his part, Althusser had criticised the structuralist couplet of synchrony (static structure) and diachrony (temporal development) for its alleged proximity to the Hegelian conception of historical time, nevertheless proposing to retain it to designate an intra-epistemological distinction. Therein the synchronic was *'eternity in Spinoza's sense*, or the adequate knowledge of a complex object by the knowledge of its complexity'; the diachronic, 'merely the false name for . . . *the development of forms*' in conceptual discourse.[187] Referring in a footnote to Balibar's employment of diachrony to designate the theory of historical transition, Althusser specified that 'the concept and the "development of its forms"' were involved here as well.[188] As a conceptual object, a mode of production was conceived by Balibar as a self-reproducing totality which reproduced both the forces and relations of production and their non-economic conditions of existence – that is, the requisite configuration of the other instances. The process of production involved economic, political and ideological reproduction.[189] What Balibar called the 'dynamics' of a mode of production were themselves to be understood synchronically as part of the 'eternal' reproduction of, for example, capitalist social relations. Accordingly, transition could not 'consist of the transformation of the structure by its functioning itself'.[190] In effect, the mode of production (in both its global and restricted senses) is a *perpetuum mobile*. (As Hindess and Hirst pointed out, if according to Althusser it was possible to describe Hegel as 'Spinoza set in

---

[186] Althusser and Balibar 1970, p. 225.
[187] Althusser and Balibar 1970, pp. 107–8.
[188] See Althusser and Balibar 1970, p. 108, n. 9 and Balibar's comments on pp. 297–8.
[189] See Althusser and Balibar 1970, p. 254ff.
[190] Althusser and Balibar 1970, p. 274. Balibar therefore rules out the 'transformation of quantity into quality' as an *explanans*.

motion', then 'Althusser comes very close to being Spinoza once again at rest.'[191])

Given this, how can the transition from one of mode of production to another be accounted for? Has teleology been discarded in favour of stasis? Or has evolutionism been eluded at the cost of indeterminacy? Are transition periods merely chaotic interludes, recalcitrant to theorisation, in which the structures are suddenly destructured preliminary to their equally instantaneous restructuration? Balibar's proposed solution to the problem was a general theory of transition centred on the postulate of transitional modes of production.[192] In the case of such a mode, it is argued, there is a non-correspondence between the forces and relations of production. The relations – the dominant term of the pair – so transform the forces that they are (re)adjusted to the relations. Correspondence is thereby re-established and, with it, a new (non-transitional) mode of production. Balibar takes the example of the transition from feudalism to capitalism discussed in Volume One of *Capital*. According to him, Marx's analysis in part eight concerns the '*pre-history*' of the 'elements' constitutive of the capitalist mode of production (in particular, the doubly 'free' labourer, separated from both feudal ties and the means of production, and capital).[193] The 'outline definitions' it contains must be

> related to a different analysis which is not an analysis of the *origins* but one
> of the *beginnings* of the capitalist mode of production, and which does not
> proceed element by element, but from the point of view of the whole structure.
> In the study of *manufacture* we have a notable example of this analysis of
> the beginnings.[194]

Manufacture is '*a form of transition*' from feudalism to capitalism characterised by a 'dislocation' between the forces and relations of production, in that labour is only 'formally subsumed' under capital. In the capitalist mode of production proper ('machinofacture'), there is a 'real subsumption' of labour to capital

---

[191] Hindess and Hirst 1975, p. 316. Althusser's remark occurs in Althusser and Balibar 1970, p. 92.

[192] See Althusser and Balibar 1970, pp. 273, 302.

[193] Althusser and Balibar 1970, pp. 277–80. From Marx's analysis, Balibar infers 'the relative independence of the formation of the different elements of the capitalist structure, and the *diversity of the historical roads to this formation*' (p. 280).

[194] Althusser and Balibar 1970, p. 302.

and thus a homology of the two connections (the labour and the surplus-labour processes).[195] From this, a general conclusion is deduced:

> the form of 'complexity' of the modes of production may be *either the correspondence or the non-correspondence* of the two connexions, of the productive forces and the relations of production. In the form of non-correspondence, which is that of phases of transition such as manufacture, the relationship no longer takes the form of a reciprocal limitation, but becomes *the transformation of the one by the effect of the other*: this is shown by the whole analysis of manufacture and the industrial revolution, in which the capitalist nature of the relations of production (the necessity of creating surplus-value in the form of relative surplus-value) determines and governs the transition of the productive forces to their specifically capitalist form. . . .[196]

The unsatisfactoriness of this solution, betrayed by the catch-all 'law of necessary correspondence or non-correspondence' which it yields,[197] has frequently been remarked. The concept of transitional mode of production cannot discharge the duties vested in it. In the words of Jean-Marie Vincent, it amounts to a 'squaring of the circle'.[198] For the general theory of transition propounded by Balibar (i) requires the distinction between the theoretical-abstract (synchronic) and the historical-concrete (diachronic) ruled out of epistemological order by Althusser; (ii) leads to the insoluble enigma of how to theorise the transition from a mode of production to a transitional mode of production (then to another mode of production); and (iii) surreptitiously restores the very teleological representation of history, prohibited in Althusserian protocols, wherein a transitional mode of production is accorded the auto-dissolvent dynamic often attributed to (non-transitional) modes of production, but expressly denied them – and rightly so – by Balibar.

Balibar tentatively explores other routes. If the effects characteristic of a particular economic structure (for example, the tendency for the rate of profit to fall under capitalism) do not in and of themselves induce the dissolution

---

[195] Althusser and Balibar 1970, p. 303. Balibar's analysis is based upon Marx 1976a, p. 645 (quoted on p. 236).

[196] Althusser and Balibar 1970, p. 304.

[197] Althusser and Balibar 1970, p. 304. Balibar attributes it to Charles Bettelheim; see Bettelheim 1975, p. 47. For a critique of the Althusserian interpretation of the transition to capitalism, see Cohen 1978, p. 176ff.

[198] Vincent et al. 1974, p. 242.

of that structure, they may nevertheless furnish *'one of the conditions* (the "material basis") of a *different result,* outside the structure of production': the decisive intervention of political class struggle.[199] The period of primitive accumulation offers an example of such an intervention, 'whose result is to *transform* and *fix* the limits of the mode of production'. For its duration, there is a 'dislocation' between the different levels of the totality (in particular, between the juridico-political level and the economic structure) and dominance is displaced onto the political. This leads Balibar to conclude that

> In a transitional period, there is a 'non-correspondence' because the mode
> of intervention of political practice, instead of conserving the limits [of the
> mode of production] and producing its effects within their determination,
> displaces them and transforms them.[200]

The overdetermination peculiar to transitional social formations thus confirms the validity of what, in *For Marx,* Althusser had characterised as a 'basic Marxist proposition': *'the class struggle is the motor of history'.*[201] Nominally Marxist, certainly Maoist, this thesis was to feature as a basic Althusserian proposition after 1965. In *Reading 'Capital',* it is akin to a *deus ex machina* which supervenes in the implacable logic of structural causality to effect historical transformation.

What Balibar himself conceded to be 'very schematic suggestions' concluded on a positive note. Periods of transition, he conjectured, are 'characterized by the *coexistence* of several modes of production'. The non-correspondence between the two connections of the economic structure, and between the different social levels during them, 'merely reflects *the coexistence of two* (or more) *modes of production in a single "simultaneity", and the dominance of one of them over the other'.* The contours of this particular major region of the continent of history, Balibar remarks, await their cartographer.[202] If Marx opened up this region, it was Althusser and Balibar among others who re-opened it, following the Stalinist closure.[203] Of greatest salience here was the distinction made by them between *mode of production* and *social formation.* In his meticulous

---

[199] Althusser and Balibar 1970, pp. 292–3.
[200] Althusser and Balibar 1970, pp. 306–7.
[201] Althusser 1969a, p. 215.
[202] Althusser and Balibar 1970, pp. 307–8.
[203] See the excellent discussion in Benton 1984, pp. 115–40.

reading, Benton has identified three different conceptual contrasts in the single terminological pair mode of production/social formation: (i) between the concept of the economic instance and the concept of the social totality; (ii) between the concept of the social totality and the concept of the articulation of two or more such totalities within one society; and (iii) between social totalities as 'objects of knowledge' and social totalities as 'real objects'. As he points out, the first two concern varying degrees of intra-theoretical abstraction, while the third involves a distinction between the conceptual and the real-historical.[204] The problem with the first is that Althusser and Balibar engage in a 'logical' deduction of the superstructural instances from the definition of each mode of production as a variable combination of invariants. Strictly speaking, the third is inconsistent with Althusserian epistemology ('empiricist'). The second – quite distinct from the standard Soviet distinction between mode of production and socio-economic formation – has, to cite Benton again, been 'remarkably fruitful' for Marxist historiography and theoretical research.

In fact, the second connotation of the mode of production/social formation distinction – in its application to all societies (not just those in transition) – first appeared unequivocally in the second edition of Reading 'Capital'. In a footnote added to the introduction to his paper, Balibar reflected:

> Capital, which expounds the abstract theory of the capitalist mode of production, does not undertake to analyze concrete social formations which generally contain several different modes of production, whose laws of coexistence and hierarchy must therefore be studied.

At the same time, he noted that the

> insufficient elaboration, in the first draft, of the concepts which designate the articulation of the instances of the social formation, is in itself the (negative) cause of constant confusion in Marxist literature between the social formation and its economic infrastructure (which is itself often related to one mode of production).[205]

---

[204] Benton 1984, pp. 74–5.
[205] Althusser and Balibar 1970, p. 207, n. 5; see also p. 300, n. 24 – another addition to the second edition. Lenin is credited with having commenced theoretical treatment of this problem in his post-revolutionary texts (e.g. 'The Tax in Kind' [1921]) and in The Development of Capitalism in Russia (1899).

Although not present in the first edition, these distinctions and clarifications were made shortly after the publication of *Reading 'Capital'*.[206] Their cumulative effect is to differentiate between the Marxist concepts (themselves of different degrees of abstraction) employed in the analysis of any given historical/social reality and the particular realities (for example, Russia in 1917) under analysis. Rather than 'return[ing] us to the conceptual prison (mode of production = social formation)', as Thompson has it, Althusser and Balibar helped release us from it (to put it no higher) by emphasising the structural complexity of the social formation per se and the combination and articulation of at least two modes of production in any social formation. Appropriately enough, a fellow historian of Thompson's has signalled 'the *historiographic* advance' Althusser's reconceptualisation of Marx's topography facilitates.[207]

This positive evaluation needs to be tempered by recognition that Althusser's propositions were problematic. With the exception of classless societies, any mode of production in the global sense invariably comprises three instances with invariant structures. This implies that there is a transhistorical 'essence' of each practice (economic, political, ideological) prior to its articulation with the others in different modes of production, thus portraying the modes as concatenations/permutations of pre-formed elements. Similarly with modes of production in the restricted (economic) sense. The invariant elements (three terms and two connections) might be taken to define an essence of the economic which is then variously instantiated in the different modes of production. Deflection of the charge of structuralism or functionalism with the argument that the different combinations, and their particular articulation, determine the nature of the invariant practices and elements – Balibar's tactic – leads only to a vicious circularity which, moreover, subverts the project of a theory of modes of production as the transhistorical science of history, applicable to Stone and Space Age alike.[208]

---

[206] See, e.g., Linhart 1966; Althusser 1990, pp. 46–52; and Rey 1978.

[207] See Thompson 1978, p. 355 and cf. Anderson 1980, pp. 67–8. See also Stedman Jones 1979, p. 199.

[208] See Althusser and Balibar 1970, pp. 216, 223; and cf. Callinicos 1982, pp. 75–6.

The immortality of ideology

Something of the scale of Althusser and his comrades' project in *Reading 'Capital'* will now be apparent. In Chapter 2, we saw that he elaborated what he considered a novel epistemology and ontology. Thus far in Chapter 3, we have inventoried a distinctive representation of the canon and corpus of Marxism; an original version of the dialectic; a reconceptualisation of the social formation, its levels and their 'histories', and of the causality governing both global and regional structures; and a theory of modes of production, including a theory of transition. A final prominent component of the Althusserian system – perhaps the one that has aroused the greatest animosity – must be set in place before offering an assessment of the whole: Althusser's account of ideology.

The definition of political practice as the transformation of social relations into new social relations proposed in 'On the Materialist Dialectic' was left undeveloped. Althusser's characterisation of ideological practice as that which transforms 'men's "consciousness"', on the other hand, was taken up in 'Marxism and Humanism' and in an important text never published in France, but widely circulated in mimeographed form – 'Theory, Theoretical Practice and Theoretical Formation. Ideology and Ideological Struggle'. In the earlier essay, Althusser defined ideology as a 'system of representations' distinct from science 'in that in it the practico-social function is more important than the theoretical function'. As a functional ensemble of representations, ideology is *'an organic part of every social totality'* because indispensable to the existence of social formations. This holds good for class and classless societies alike. There will be no cessation of ideology under communism:

> It is as if human societies could not survive without these *specific formations . . .,* their ideologies. Human societies secrete ideology as the very element and atmosphere indispensable to their historical respiration and life. Only an ideological world outlook could have imagined societies without *ideology* and accepted the utopian idea of a world in which ideology (not just one of its historical forms) would disappear without trace, to be replaced by science . . . *historical materialism cannot conceive that even a communist society could ever do without ideology. . . .*[209]

---

[209] Althusser 1969a, pp. 231–2. The attribution of an ideological superstructure to communist societies is repeated in Althusser and Balibar 1970, p. 177.

Advertised as consonant with historical materialism, Althusser's assertion of the transhistorical character of ideology-in-general (as opposed to particular ideologies) is dissonant with the Marxist tradition and contrary to Marx (who did envision communist societies operating without ideology in the pejorative sense). Yet it may be that Althusser is right, Marx and other Marxists wrong. What was the rationale for his idiosyncracy?

The target of Althusser's theory of ideology was the supposed messianism involved in the postulate of a disalienation with the advent of communism, a society whose deepest 'laws of motion' would be transparent to the consciousness of its members in an 'end of ideology'. For Althusser, this was a chimera. He impugned any theory of ideology as 'false consciousness' as itself ideological, on two grounds. First, it implied the possibility of a true consciousness, whereas, epistemologically, consciousness was non-veridical by definition. Secondly, it circumscribed the social space and underestimated the objective power of ideology. For Althusser, ideology is an 'objective reality . . . independent of the subjectivity of the individuals who are subject to it', a system of representations dominated by a *'false conception* of the world'.[210] Men are 'ideological animals'. They need representations of the world and their relations to it in order to function as social agents. Ideology provides the requisite representation (which can be more or less conscious/ unconscious, untheorised/theorised). Analytically a relative autonomous superstructural level of society, in reality ideology is a *'cement* . . . sliding into all the parts of the [social] edifice'. It 'permeates' all human activities and practices, governing the 'lived' relations of individuals to the ensemble of their 'conditions of existence'. Indeed, '[i]deology is so much present in all their acts and deeds that it is *indistinguishable from their "lived "experience"'*.[211]

A correlate of the ubiquity of ideology is its permanence. Inherent in – coterminous with – 'lived experience', and diffused throughout the social formation, it is a dimension of any and every society. Its function as a factor of general social cohesion is a transhistorical necessity. Assuming the future creation of communist societies, on the other hand, its function as a cement of class exploitation and domination is a historical necessity. The termination of the latter will not cancel the former, since, in any form of society, the

[210] Althusser 1990, pp. 23–4.
[211] Althusser 1990, p. 25.

function of ideology is to ensure 'the *bond* among people in the totality of the forms of their existence, the *relation* of individuals to their tasks assigned by the social structure'. For ideology is *'indispensable . . . if men are to be formed, transformed and equipped to respond to the demands of their conditions of existence'.*[212] In class societies, this pan-historical function of social adaptation – hence reproduction – is overdetermined by another: the maintenance of a class order, fulfilled via the provision of justifications of the existing state of affairs to the exploited and rationalisations of it to the exploiters. (If ideologies are opiates, the rulers are equally addicted.) The role of ideological subjection in the reproduction of economic exploitation and political domination explains the falsity of ideology's representations in class societies, yet poses the problem of their perdurable 'deforming' presence under communism:

> In class societies, ideology is a representation of the real, but necessarily distorted, because necessarily biased and tendentious – tendentious because its aim is not to provide men with *objective knowledge* of the social system in which they live but, on the contrary, to give them a mystified representation of this social system in order to keep them in their 'place' in the system of class exploitation. Of course, it would also be necessary to pose the problem of the function of ideology in classless society – and it would be resolved by showing that the deformation of ideology is socially necessary as a function of the nature of the social whole itself, as a function (to be more precise) of *its determination by its structure*, which renders it – as a social whole – opaque to the individuals who occupy a place in society determined by this structure. The opacity of the social structure necessarily renders *mythic* that representation of the world which is indispensable for social cohesion.[213]

Whereas the tendentiousness of ideology attendant upon the exigencies of class rule is a potentially transitory phenomenon, the opacity of the social whole consequent upon its determination by a structure (which renders it impenetrable to its agents at the experiential level) is immutable. The system of coherent and 'obvious' ideological representations will therefore remain ideological in the negative sense – namely, *'deforming and mystifying'*. The

---

[212] Althusser 1990, p. 28; Althusser 1969a, p. 235.
[213] Althusser 1990, pp. 28–9.

bourgeoisie can be overthrown; the ascendancy of structural causality is without term.

In the conclusion to 'Freud and Lacan', Althusser counter-signed the Lacanian theme of the decentring of the human subject, conjecturing its construction by a structure which 'has no "centre" either, except in the imaginary misrecognition of the "ego", i.e. in the ideological formations in which it "recognizes" itself'.[214] In 'Marxism and Humanism', he attempted to articulate the Marxist theory of ideology and the Lacanian theory of the imaginary. 'Ideology,' he writes,

> is a matter of the *lived* relation between men and their world. . . . In ideology men . . . express not the relation between them and their conditions of existence, but *the way* they live the relation between them and their conditions of existence: this presupposes both a real relation and an 'imaginary', 'lived' relation. . . . In ideology the real relation is inevitably invested in the imaginary relation. . . .[215]

Anticipating a thesis he would only elaborate five years later (in 'Ideology and Ideological State Apparatuses'), Althusser is suggesting that human subjects are constituted in ideology – endowed with self-identity and the illusion of autonomy via (mis)recognition of themselves in the idealised images it offers for their inspection. This construction of subjectivity – of the subject of consciousness and experience – in ideology was the secret of its social efficacy.

Everything that has been said about the *social function* of ideology implies Althusser's second major thesis concerning it: although irreducible to cognition, ideology is the *antithesis of science*. Ideology is an ensemble of 'allusions-illusions' and '(mis)representations' from which there is no deliverance for the human subjects who are, in reality, the 'supports' of social structures; only theoretical practice can break the ideological mirror in which social consciousness is transfixed and furnish objective knowledge of those structures.[216] Althusser allows that the nature of ideology will change under

---

[214] Althusser 1971, p. 201. See also 'Cremonini, Painter of the Abstract' (1966), in Althusser 1971, pp. 216–17.
[215] Althusser 1969a, pp. 233–4. For Lacan's theory of the 'mirror stage', see his 1982, pp. 1–7.
[216] Althusser employs the metaphor of breaking the mirror in 'The "Piccolo Teatro":

communism.[217] And he stresses that there are not only ideological regions but also ideological tendencies in non-communist societies – the antagonistic ideologies of the different social classes. But ideology, be it that of a communist state or a proletariat, is ideology. Indeed, oppositional proletarian ideology is 'imprisoned' in the dominant bourgeois ideology, operating within its terms of reference and reproducing its forms in the very act of protesting against the rule of capital. The key to the cell is not to be found in some more concrete economic or political practice. On the contrary, liberation of the 'spontaneous' ideology of the proletariat from the grip of its antagonist can only come with the intervention of outside help – from counter-veiling Marxist *science*. The Leninist thesis of 'importation' is predicated on the crushing weight of ideology in general and the particular inadequacies of proletarian ideology.[218]

The power of ideology dictates in response the necessity of theory and the indispensability of ideological struggle. The ideology of the working class must be transformed. The science founded and developed by intellectuals can furnish knowledge of ideological formations; but it cannot dissipate them.[219] And it can be employed to produce 'a *new* form of ideology in the masses', one subject not to bourgeois influence but to 'the *Marxist science of society*'.[220] In order for this to be possible, the priority of 'theoretical training' must be acknowledged. Without it in the past, the workers' movement would never have been won to Marx's scientific theory. Without it in the present,

---

Bertolazzi and Brecht' (see Althusser 1969a, p. 144), where he examines the critical relationship of Brechtian dramaturgy to 'the spontaneous ideology in which men live'. In his 'Letter on Art' (1966), this argument was generalised (see especially Althusser 1971, p. 204), rendering Althusser's quadripartite schedule of social practices problematic. The attempt therein to define the *differentia specifica* of artistic practice vis-à-vis ideology and science was systematically developed in Macherey 1978.

Two points might be briefly noted about Althusserian aesthetics. First, in their modernism, they effected a radical and original break with both the threadbare 'socialist realism' that was Communist orthodoxy (and whose most vitriolic partisans had been Stalin's dauphin, Zhdanov, and his French under-study, Garaudy) and with the much more sophisticated realist aesthetic of Lukács. But secondly, however suggestive, they were marred in much the same way as Althusser's epistemology, according Literature (or Art), *qua* (non-scientific) critique of the ideological, some of Theory's privileges as a lonely refuge from, or counter-weight to, the tyranny of an otherwise all-pervasive ideology.

[217] Althusser 1969a, pp. 235–6.
[218] Althusser 1990, pp. 30–1; see also pp. 32–3.
[219] See, e.g., Althusser 1969a, p. 230; Althusser 1990, p. 22.
[220] Althusser and Balibar 1970, p. 131; Althusser 1990, p. 38.

the masses still ensnared in bourgeois ideology would remain trapped and the Communist Party would not progress in developing historical materialism and applying its principles. Accordingly, the training of militants to become 'men of science' represented the 'decisive intermediary link'.[221]

Marxist criticism of Althusser's account of ideology has focused on three complementary aspects of it: (i) the proposition that historical materialism cannot conceive an 'end of ideology'; (ii) the equation of 'lived experience' with the ideological and the correlative restriction of objective knowledge to the subject-less discourse of conceptual science; and (iii) the daunting implications of the above for the classical-Marxist project of working-class revolutionary self-emancipation and post-revolutionary self-determination. If, as Althusser maintained, the assimilation of science to the superstructure is the 'symptomatic point' at which historicism reveals its reductionism, then his privileging of Theory in the first and last instance is the symptomatic point at which the Althusserian problematic betrays its conjoint idealism of the intelligence and pessimism of the will.

A most unusual structuralism

In his critique of Althusser's theory of ideology as necessary illusion, Rancière argued that it superimposed 'a Comtean or Durkheimian type of sociology', concerned with the maintenance of a cohesive social order, upon historical materialism, theory of the class struggle.[222] Therewith, scientific practice had effectively been identified as the highest form of class struggle, the only genuinely subversive principle, the motor of history – on condition that it was autonomous of the social formation cemented by ideology. Put crudely, Althusser's account amounted to the proposition, *contra* Mao, that '*false ideas*

---

[221] See Althusser 1990, pp. 39–40. In his book on Montesquieu, Althusser had already written of the '*correction of errant consciousness by well-founded science*, of the unconscious consciousness by the scientific consciousness', arguing that '[w]ithout a *critique* of the immediate concepts in which every epoch thinks the history it lives, we shall remain on the threshold of a true knowledge of history and a prisoner of the illusions it produces in the men who live it': Althusser 1972, pp. 38, 99.

[222] Rancière 1985, pp. 104–5. As Steven B. Smith points out, however, 'if Althusser has given his Marxism a Durkheimian twist, he has also given his Durkheim a Freudian turn': Smith 1984, p. 134.

come from social practice'[223] – an inference deduced by Rancière from Althusser's and his own treatment of fetishism in *Reading 'Capital'*.

Capital, Althusser had suggested in his introductory paper,

> exactly measures a distance and an internal dislocation in the real, inscribed
> in its *structure*, a distance and a dislocation such as to make their own effects
> themselves illegible, and the illusion of an immediate reading of them the
> ultimate apex of their effects: fetishism.[224]

Rancière argued an analogous case at greater length in his own contribution. Whereas ideology is the conscious expression of the 'apparent motion' of capital, science 'deciphers the *hieroglyphic*', grasping the 'real motion' and accounting for its inverted (but objective) appearance to human subjects. The agents of production – workers and capitalists alike – are captives of ideology; 'mystification' is 'constitutive' of their being.[225] As Callinicos points out, the Althusserian reading of *Capital* 'reduces the structure of capitalism to a structure of *representation*'.[226] Althusser identified the concept of *Darstellung* – an index of structural causality – as 'the key epistemological concept of the whole Marxist theory of value', designating the *'authorless theatre'* of capitalism.[227] 'Commodity fetishism' was but one (capitalist) instance of an invariant feature of social formations: their opacity as a function of structural causality and, in consequence, the permanence of ideology. Thus, whereas it would disappear with the capitalist mode of production, ideology and its illusions would endure: the 'truth of history' – its deepest springs – would never be read in its 'manifest discourse'; effects and structures ('appearances' and 'essence') would never coincide; 'lived experience' would ever delude. Hence the necessity of science, the theoretical practice capable of deciphering the objective appearances of reality determined by a 'structure of structures'.

Althusser's Spinozist concept of structural causality has other deleterious consequences besides condemning subjects to the eternal tyranny of ideological delusion. As employed to theorise the nature of the social whole, it serves either (i) to provide a fragile solution to the issue of economic determination

---

[223] Rancière 1974, p. 96.
[224] Althusser and Balibar 1970, p. 17.
[225] See Rancière 1965, pp. 168–9.
[226] Callinicos 1982, p. 122.
[227] Althusser and Balibar 1970, pp. 188, 193; see also p. 29.

in the last instance, which cannot ward off a functionalist pluralism; or (ii) to endow social formations with such consistency (modes of production generate their own 'conditions of existence') that their reproduction as unities is ensured, their transformation *theoretically* unthinkable – the severest of structuralisms (or Spinozisms). (Indicative of both, perhaps, was that the Russian Revolution as analysed by Althusser verged on being the product of a fortuitous conjunction of a multiplicity of felicitous circumstances.) The concomitant demotion of human subjects as the makers of history in the name of science was accompanied by their location as 'supports' of the levels of the global structure. The 'role of the individual in history' was a false problem, to be displaced by a genuine one: 'the concept of *the historical forms of existence of individuality*'. The capitalist mode of production, for example, requires and therefore produces 'different forms of individuality', so moulding and endowing individuals that they can function as 'supports' of its processes: an extreme form of holism.[228]

Althusser urged the fidelity of his theoretical anti-humanism to historical materialism, observing of the artist Leonardo Cremonini that he had pursued

> the path which was opened up to men by the great revolutionary thinkers, theoreticians and politicians, the great materialist thinkers who understood that the freedom of men is not achieved by the complacency of its ideological *recognition*, but by *knowledge* of the laws of their slavery, and that the 'realization' of their concrete individuality is achieved by the analysis and mastery of the abstract relations which govern them.[229]

Here and elsewhere, Althusser's argument is to the effect that the emancipatory project of communism obliged Marx – and compels his successors – to disavow the *theoretical* pretensions of humanism in order to understand the practical modalities and mechanisms of class servitude – in order to found 'the *science* of liberation'.[230] For it is capitalism that reduces people to the status of 'supports' of its relations of production, he explained in his defence in 1975. In order to explain capitalism's 'terrible practical "reduction"' of men and women, it is

---

[228] See Althusser and Balibar, pp. 111–12. On differential individuality, see Balibar's remarks in Althusser and Balibar 1970, pp. 207–8, 252–3. Cf. Levine, Sober and Olin Wright 1987, especially pp. 73–5.

[229] Althusser 1971, p. 219.

[230] The phrase of Althusserian Jean-Paul Dollé in his 1966, p. 1917.

necessary to effect an analogous *theoretical* reduction, dispensing with the concept of man for explanatory purposes.[231] Whilst these propositions have something to be said for them, they do not answer the wider objections to Althusser's original theses. For, inverting humanism, these equated 'lived experience' with the ideological, depicting subjectivity as functional for class subjection; and posited, Spinoza-style, the persistence of mystificatory ideology – an unconscious system governing individuals – after the abolition of the other 'abstract relations' of capitalist society.[232] For all Althusser's apparent insouciance, the dilemma is acute: where, within the cohesive, self-reproducing social whole, is the principle of its subversion and transformation to be found? What meaning can be given to the project of working-class self-emancipation from capitalism, and to the associated producers' self-determination under communism, within the machinery of structural causality? If Althusser was proposing that all *non-communist* human societies are subjects of the 'kingdom of necessity', that would be one thing. Although drastically curtailing the claims of modern socialism, such a proposition has some historical plausibility.[233] But his texts make it clear that he envisaged human beings in communist society as falling under the inexorable sway of structural causality. Given Althusser's denegation of human agency in the affirmation of structural necessity, how can we speak of communism as the 'realm of freedom' ushered in by 'the conscious reconstruction of human society'?[234]

Althusserian austerity ruled such talk out of scientific order – Althusser characterising communism as the installation of a new mode of production. His relinquishment of any 'normative totality'[235] (even of any indictment of capitalism's inhumanity and injustice) may be partially explicable in terms

---

[231] See Althusser 1976a, pp. 200–6; see also p. 53.

[232] Cf. Spinoza 1955, pp. 108–9: 'men are mistaken in thinking themselves free; their opinion is made up of consciousness of their own actions, and ignorance of the causes by which they are conditioned. Their idea of freedom, therefore, is simply their ignorance of any cause for their actions'. For Spinoza's view in the *Political Treatise* that men could never be induced to live by reason alone, see Spinoza 1951, p. 289.

[233] See the historicisation of the dispute over human agency in Anderson 1980, Chapter 2.

[234] Marx 1981, p. 182.

[235] See Jay 1984, p. 411. An ex-student of Althusser's, Pierre Victor, relates that on one occasion, 'I said to him that if people were communists, it was for the sake of happiness. In substance, his reply was: you mustn't say that. It is order to bring about a change of mode of production': Gavi, Sartre and Victor 1974, p. 197.

of organisational constraints (the PCF's identification of the USSR as the norm) or conjunctural considerations (there was a lot of normativity about in 1965). Yet it is surely also symptomatic of that disenchantment and latent pessimism in Althusser's thought which has led Martin Jay to describe his and Adorno's philosophies as representing 'the Marxism of a more sober and disillusioned time'.[236]

Nowhere is that sobriety more apparent than in the Althusserian conception of history. Counteracting the evolutionism and historicism supposedly regnant in Marxism hitherto, Althusser and Balibar sought to redress the balance by propounding what, in the first edition of Reading 'Capital', the latter termed 'a most unusual structuralism'.[237] As Dews has noted, the Althusserians campaigned 'on two fronts: against the phenomenological assumption that history possesses a distinctive dialectical form of intelligibility, and against the Lévi-Straussian assumption that structural intelligibility is not characteristic of history'.[238] Althusser argued that in the Lévi-Straussian scheme of things,

Diachrony is reduced to the sequence of events . . ., and to the effects of this sequence of events on the structure of the synchronic: the historical then becomes the unexpected, the accidental, the factually unique, arising or falling in time for purely contingent reasons.[239]

Simultaneously, he suggested that Lévi-Strauss's concept of the synchronic was a variation on the Hegelian conception of historical time.[240] Althusser sought to elaborate a theory which avoided the reductionism of historicism and the contingency of structuralism, without slipping into an eclectic interactionism or the 'empiricist ideology' supposedly dominating historiography.[241] The duty of a scientific theory of history – in no wise recalcitrant to rigorous knowledge – was to produce the concepts that could explain the complexities of the historical process and of concrete societies, and not to take refuge in the alibi of the richness of life, the poverty of

---

[236] Quoted in Callinicos 1982, p. 83.
[237] See Balibar 1965, p. 205.
[238] Dews 1994, p. 111.
[239] Althusser and Balibar 1970, p. 108.
[240] See Althusser and Balibar 1970, p. 96.
[241] See Althusser and Balibar 1970, pp. 98–9. And, for some condescending and counter-productive remarks directed at historians and their practice, see Althusser and Balibar, pp. 109–10.

theory.[242] Yet Althusser's own propositions meet the structuralists more than half way, insisting that, for Marx and Marxism,

> the understanding of [contemporary bourgeois] society, far from being obtained from the theory of the genesis of this [historical] result, is, on the contrary, obtained exclusively from the theory of the 'body', i.e., of the *contemporary structure of society*, without its genesis intervening in any way whatsoever.[243]

Perhaps unbeknownst to him, on this occasion at least, Althusser possessed irreproachable pedigree for his formulation, which reproduced Marx's sometime conversion of the distinction between the *genesis* and the *structure* of the capitalist mode of production into the hermetically sealed partition between its pre-history and contemporary history.[244]

'If we were never structuralists,' Althusser confided in 1974, 'we can now explain why. . . . We were guilty of an equally powerful and compromising passion: *we were Spinozists.*'[245] Admission of Spinozism does not automatically compel acquittal on the count of structuralism; and it had been apparent some time before Althusser's confession (already anticipated, of course, not only in *Reading 'Capital'*, but in front of the Société française de philosophie). In any event, given that it *was* 'equally powerful and compromising', the consequence of Althusser's affiliation was to undermine his project for a Marxist theory of history. The claim that 'there is no history in general, but specific structures of historicity, based in the last resort on the specific structures of the different modes of production',[246] was simultaneously aimed at Althusser's Marxist antagonists and his (unholy) structuralist allies. Balibar's attempt to develop it, however, reproduced some of the shortcomings of both. On the one hand, transitional modes of production are teleological constructs, thus restoring an illicit Marxism. On the other, they lead to an infinite regress, therewith repeating the Lévi-Straussian 'division between a synchronic necessity

---

[242] See Althusser and Balibar 1970, p. 117, where Althusser, although noting its salutary aspects, rejects this dichotomy – whose second term had a prosperous career ahead of it.

[243] Althusser and Balibar 1970, p. 65 (see pp. 64–5). Cf. Dews 1994, p. 115.

[244] See Marx 1973, pp. 459–60.

[245] Althusser 1976a, p. 132.

[246] Althusser and Balibar 1970, p. 108.

and an untheorizable contingency'.[247] As to non-transitional modes of production, for Balibar both their 'statics' and their 'dynamics' were synchronic. The historicity of structures was denied in the assertion of their structuredness, history salvaged only at the cost of structurality. The total discontinuity between modes of production that resulted was intended as a counter-blast to the facile economic evolutionism into which Marx's theory had petrified. Retrospectively, it is probably more accurate to conclude with Andrew Levine that, insofar as Althusserianism converted Marxism into a materialist sociology, it was part of 'a revolt against historical materialism'[248] – the historical materialism not only of Stalin, Bukharin and Plekhanov, but of Marx and Engels as well. In order to rescue its founders from the distortion they had suffered at the hands of their successors, Althusser and Balibar so amended past bias as to introduce their own, despite their disclaimers fundamentally revising Marx when they professed to be returning to him. As French Communists writing in the early 1960s, they had no choice but to represent themselves as faithful disciples, rectifying archaic theoretical *forms* the better to reveal their revolutionary theoretical *content*.[249] Moreover, revision is no crime when its outcome is superior to the original. But the substitution of 'Spinozism' for 'Hegelianism' generated as many theoretical problems as it resolved, stripping Marx's theory – an integrated theory of history and capitalist society[250] – of central tenets (a vision of the general, progressive course of history; an internal principle of historical change; an explanation of how capitalism creates the potential for socialism and communism, and so forth) – and putting little in their place. For better or worse, Marx did belong to the nineteenth century – 'the century of history of history and of evolution': to make him acceptable to the twentieth (or rather the Paris of its sixth decade), by recasting historical materialism as a 'most unusual structuralism', is, in the last instance, perhaps to kill with kindness.

In the years following the publication of *For Marx* and *Reading 'Capital'*, many of the problems touched on here were to be acknowledged by their authors. Yet whatever the flaws in Althusser's reconstruction of historical materialism, and however tenuous its title to orthodoxy, it represented – and

---

[247] Dews 1994, p. 116.
[248] See Levine 1984, pp. 262–3.
[249] See Althusser 1990, pp. 60–1.
[250] See, e.g., Levine 1984, Chapter 5; Levine 1987, Chapter 5; and Wright 1983.

was widely experienced as – a liberation. If Althusser's constructions were problematic, the majority of his criticisms were pertinent and powerful. They released Marxists from more than one conceptual prison, re-establishing historical materialism as a research programme – one whose potential had been negated rather than exhausted in the enumeration of iron stages and laws, the incantation of derisory formulae, the reiteration of 'famous quotations'. If there is one sense in which Althusser's re-theorisation of Marxism did not represent a recommencement of historical materialism as such, there is another in which it did. And the 'extremism' which disfigured it was vital to the efficacy of his intervention. The danger in 'bending the stick' was that it might snap. But by so doing, Althusser reminded Marxists that there was a continent waiting to be explored.

What, finally, were the political implications of Althusserianism? Rancière's retrospective is persuasive: Reading 'Capital' logically entailed a left-wing critique of the PCF's political perspectives.[251] In the event, the apex of Althusser's radicalism – in public at least – was the assertion of the necessity and autonomy of theory, enclave of freedom in a world of ideological servitude. If it was important to avoid 'idealism' (the divorce of theory from practice), it was equally if not more crucial to escape 'pragmatism' (the treatment of theory as a 'servant of politics'). The former was ultimately less noxious than the latter. Thus, '[a]t the end of our analysis, . . . we rejoin the cardinal principle with which we began: the distinction between science and ideology.'[252]

In La Leçon d'Althusser, Rancière suggests that the national political conjuncture after 1962 – a quasi-'absence' of history – helps to explain Althusser's theoreticism (what Althusser might have called a 'flight forward' in theory).[253] Subsequently, the time of theory and the time of politics were to meet – and miss.

---

[251] See Rancière 1974, p. 95.
[252] Althusser 1990, p. 42.
[253] See Ranicère 1974, pp. 68–9.

Chapter Four
The Time of Theory, The Time of Politics

As Mao says: '*Never* forget the class struggle.'
Louis Althusser, 'Marxism and Class Struggle'

In a review of *For Marx* and *Reading 'Capital'* dating from 1966, Eric Hobsbawm noted:

> Their success has been startling. It is no reflection on the very considerable gifts of the author . . . to observe that he has been lucky in the moment of his emergence. The atmosphere of the Althusserian Latin Quarter is the one in which every self-respecting secondary schoolboy is a Maoist or at least a Castroite, in which Sartre and Henri Lefebvre are ancient monuments and the self-lacerations of the intellectual ex-communists of 1956 as incomprehensible as the 'opportunism' of Waldeck Rochet and Roger Garaudy. A new generation of rebels requires a new version of revolutionary ideology, and M. Althusser is essentially an ideological hard-liner, challenging the political and intellectual softening around him.[1]

The Althusserian challenge rapidly brought its protagonist into conflict both with the leadership of the PCF, anxious to curb its turbulent high-priest of theory, and the young pro-Chinese rebels, impatient to push their mentor further along the oppositional road than he was prepared to go. Trapped, as it were,

---

[1] Hobsbawm 1982, p. 145.

between the hammer and anvil, Althusser temporised. 'It will be necessary to be *fortiter in re, suaviter in modo'*, Marx informed Engels regarding the International Working Men's Association in 1864.[2] To oversimplify somewhat, Althusser's career between 1965 and 1975 can be characterised as proceeding *fortiter in modo, suaviter in re*. For on the one hand, he effected a leftist radicalisation of his theoretical positions, implying continued opposition to the 'opportunism' of the PCF; while, on the other, he submitted to the political authority of his party, rendering him an irritant rather than a threat. That the Maoist word, moreover, was no more compelling than the conformist deed is a conclusion which regrettably imposes itself.

The purpose of this chapter is to illuminate the relation between what, in 1974, Althusser called the 'internal' (intra-theoretical) and 'external' (extra-theoretical/political) logics of his ongoing labour of auto-critique and rectification from 1967 to 1974.[3] Our first task will be to return to the mid-1960s in order to examine Althusser's solidarity with certain pro-Chinese tendencies in the PCF and to recount the course of the events leading up to his refusal to break with the Party, despite strong – and increasing – Maoist sympathies. Next, the new definition of Marxist philosophy and conception of historical materialism propounded in these years will be surveyed. Thirdly, the major contribution made by Althusser to Marxism after 1965 – his theory of ideology and ideological state apparatuses – will be discussed. And finally – again departing from chronological order – Althusser's reaction to the May 'events' and the part played in them by the PCF will be detailed and interrogated.

The China syndrome

As was briefly noted in Chapter 1, Althusser's pro-Chinese inclinations did not escape the leadership of the PCF. In the opening paragraph of 'On the Materialist Dialectic', he himself allowed that Communist critics of 'Contradiction and Overdetermination' considered it 'theoretically and politically dangerous'.[4] Althusser proceeded to compound the peril, making

[2] See Marx and Engels 1975, p. 140.
[3] See the foreword to *Elements of Self-Criticism* in Althusser 1976a, pp. 102–3.
[4] Althusser 1969a, p. 163.

Mao a theoretically respectable figure. If the published information is correct, at his 'trial' on 30 November 1963, Althusser finessed his critics by adopting the tactic of distinguishing between the 'theoretical value' of Mao's concepts in *On Contradiction* and their utilisation by the CPC in the current conjuncture to sanction false political positions. His accusers, he retorted, were guilty of a 'theoretical pragmatism' inverse but akin to that of the Chinese, impugning genuine theory as a result of its conjunctural exploitation. Althusser upheld the authentically Marxist nature of Mao's theses on contradiction, but abjured their deformation at the CPC's hands, affirming the correctness of the PCF's own international line.[5] This did the trick – for the time being at least.

Suspicion of Althusser was not misplaced. Not only did his writings influence the PCF's intellectual constituency; they provided theoretical backing – a basis even – for the oppositional role played by his own students (and many of their peers) in the Party's strife-torn student organisation, the Union des étudiants communistes (UEC). Very schematically, in the late 1950s and early 1960s, under the impact of de-Stalinisation and the Algerian War, the official line faced challenges in two directions. On the Right, a substantial body of opinion, strongly influenced by the PCI's positions and by Casanovan *humanisme nouveau*, pressed for further measures of 'liberalisation' and 'modernisation'. On the Left, Maoist and proto-Trotskyist factions waged a covert struggle against the PCF's 'opening to the Right'. The loyalist Centre failed to hold. By the early 1960s, the 'Italians' were in the majority. It was then that the Maoist Left entered into a de facto alliance with the Centre to combat the perceived rightist threat. For pro-Chinese Althusserian militants, this involved campaigning against the 'revisionism' sponsored in the UEC's journal *Clarté*. The reverse side of the coin was public compliance with the PCF leadership on directly political matters.

Althusser's 'Problèmes étudiants', written one month after the confrontation with the *La Pensée* committee, is a product of this moment in the history of French Communism and a significant text for the evolution of his students. An intervention in the controversy that had arisen between the PCF and the

---

[5] For an extract from what is claimed to be Althusser's written defence, see Kessel 1972, pp. 64–6. Althusser's views on the negation of the negation might be usefully related to contemporary ideological debates in China; see Robin Munro's Introduction to Chen Erjin 1984, pp. 23–4.

Union national des étudiants français (UNEF) regarding their divergent perspectives on higher education, Althusser's article sought to establish the priorities of Communist students. Their first duty was 'to develop their knowledge of Marxism-Leninism' and conduct the scientific analysis that would yield objective knowledge of the university.[6] Against the position adopted by the UNEF, Althusser argued that what mattered to Marxists was less the 'form' in which knowledge was disseminated (the paedagogical relationship) than 'the *quality of the knowledge itself*'. For the vocation of Marxist intellectuals was 'to discover new scientific knowledge capable of illuminating and criticizing the overwhelming ideological illusions in which *everyone is imprisoned*'.[7] The real locus of class division in the university was not inequitable relations between teachers and students, but the content of the teaching – the division of the knowledge taught into science and ideology. This was the '*true fortress of class influence in the university*': 'it is by the very nature of the knowledge it imparts to students that the bourgeoisie exerts . . . the *profoundest influence* over them'.[8] Since the '*revolutionary cause*' is founded on science, Communist students should prioritise the demarcation of science from ideology – the defence and promotion of the former against the latter.[9] As regards Marxist science, they were under two obligations: its 'assimilation' and its 'dissemination, defence and illustration'.[10] Antipathetic to the slogan of *contestation globale*, Althusser concluded by underlining the Leninist distinction between a trade-union and a communist organisation, and reminding Communist students of their responsibility to 'aid the party' in its struggles.[11]

In his highly critical discussion of Althusser's text, Rancière remarks that Althusser's project of defending the autonomy of theory against the political encroachments of the PCF dictated this particular tactical intervention on its behalf.[12] In any case, at the time Rancière and his comrades of the UEC cell

---

[6] Althusser 1964a, p. 80.
[7] Althusser 1964a, pp. 86–7.
[8] Althusser 1964a, pp. 88–9.
[9] Althusser 1964a, p. 94, 98–9.
[10] Althusser 1964a, p. 103.
[11] Althusser 1964a, pp. 108–11. Earlier (p. 101), Althusser had provided a catalogue of political slogans (e.g. peaceful coexistence and renovated democracy) unobjectionable from the PCF's point of view.
[12] Rancière 1974, pp. 84–5; see also Rancière 1985, pp. 110–19.

at the École normale supérieure (the Cercle d'Ulm) took their cue from Althusser and made the defence of Marxist theory against any contamination by the humanist ideology of the UEC's leaders their battle-cry, somewhat to their surprise finding themselves temporarily aligned with the Politbureau. Following Althusser, top priority was assigned to 'theoretical training'. To this end, in January 1964 the *normaliens* had commenced a re-reading of the Marxist classics guided by Althusser's own protocols at what was called the École parisienne de formation théorique. In February of the following year, the first issue of *Cahiers marxistes-léninistes* (devoted to science and ideology) appeared, emblazoned with its Althusserian watchword: 'Marxism is all-powerful because it is true.'

At the Eighth Congress of the UEC in March 1965, the right-wing leadership was unseated and a new *bureau national* loyal to the PCF installed. Accounts were now settled with the 'Trotskyist' Left; open opposition to Communist support for Mitterrand's Atlanticist presidential candidacy led to the disciplining of the *Lettres* section. The Althusserians, preoccupied with the seminar that produced *Reading 'Capital'*, declined to adopt a public position on the Mitterrand issue. The diverse pro-Chinese currents in the PCF were divided between those who believed the eventual foundation of a new 'Marxist-Leninist' party openly affiliated to Peking to be necessary, and those who deemed *lutte interne* (internal struggle) for the reformation of the Party the most appropriate course of action. Among the latter were Althusser's students and disciples, who proposed to combat the PCF's current orientation by defending and disseminating Marxist theory.

With the PCF's Argenteuil Central Committee meeting in March 1966, some of them were to cross their Rubicon. Hitherto, political caution had been the order of the day. A double issue of *Cahiers marxistes-léninistes* in February 1966 entitled 'Vive le léninisme!' bore little obvious relation to the celebrated Chinese polemic of the same name, whatever contemporary conclusions its powerful theoretical reconstruction of Lenin's break with Menshevism implied. The next number was devoted to Althusser's own 'Historical Materialism and Dialectical Materialism' (an extract from a projected popular manual of Marxist theory intended to replace stereotyped Soviet and French products).[13]

---

[13] As with so many of Althusser's projects, it was never completed. Also of interest

Argenteuil, product of and response to the theoretical and ideological ferment within the PCF's ranks, spelt the doom of the autonomy of theory. A succession of writers has alleged that at Argenteuil Althusser was summoned to order and that, as a result of the criticisms addressed to him there, he arrived at a compromise with his party whereby he would be allowed to pursue his research in return for recanting the claim to autonomy and recognising the PCF's political authority. The truth is rather more complicated.

The Althusserian initiative had already provoked an extremely hostile response from its opponents at an assembly of Communist philosophers at Choisy-le-Roi in January 1966. The proceedings, never published, took place in the presence of the Politbureau and Central Committee and were marked by a long and virulent attack on theoretical anti-humanism from Garaudy, supported by Mury, and a counter-blast from Macherey (the only direct culprit in attendance). 'To say the least,' Robert Geerlandt has written, 'the debates at Choisy were *impassioned*.'[14]

The leitmotif of the contributions to the Central Committee debate three months later was the inadmissibility of the theory of theoretical practice. Although Althusser's critics affected to be concerned about its hyper-Leninism and dogmatism, the true reason for their antagonism was the confiscation of a leadership prerogative by a philosopher: the adjudication of theoretical positions. Not everyone was as indignant as Garaudy, who roundly denounced Althusser on behalf of 'the authentic humanism of our time' (namely, Marxism), one corresponding to 'men's most beautiful dream'. Sève, occupying the (semi-official) middle ground between Althusser's theoretical humanism and *garaudysme*, criticised the former's stance on the Marx/Hegel relationship, complained about his valorisation of non-Marxist French philosophy at the expense of the French Marxist tradition, and referred pointedly to 'the fraternal critique of the Party'. Michel Simon voiced his fears over the 'doctrinaire' effects an 'uneducated reading' of *Reading 'Capital'* might induce, bemoaning

---

in this connection is a 41-page synopsis of Althusser's perspectives, entitled 'The Historical Task of Marxist Philosophy', dating from 1967. Written for the fiftieth anniversary of the October Revolution and the centenary of Volume One of *Capital*, it was destined for publication in *Voprosy filosofi*. Predictably declined by the Soviets, it was published in a Hungarian collection of Althusser's writings the following year. See Althusser 2003, pp. 155–220.

[14] Geerlandt 1978, p. 38.

the absence of any reference to party literature (such as Thorez) in Althusserian texts and the implication that, minus Mao, nothing worthwhile had been produced by the international workers' movement since Lenin. The long resolution adopted by the Central Committee stated that 'there is a Marxist humanism', 'the humanism of our time'; rehearsed the application of the theory of state monopoly capitalism to the French social formation; and affirmed the PCF's affiliation to the pro-Moscow orthodoxy of the international Communist movement. At the same time, the freedom of intellectuals to pursue their research was acknowledged. In his summing-up – 'Le marxisme et les chemins de l'avenir' – Waldeck Rochet firmly repudiated the anti-humanism of the CPC and cautioned French Communists against the slightest complicity with it, announcing that 'communism without humanism would not be communism'. The PCF's policy of *la main tendue* was confirmed.[15]

The only references in Althusser's written work to the deliberations at Argenteuil are positive. In the French version of an interview conducted by the Italian Communist Maria-Antonietta Macciocchi in November 1967 (and published in *La Pensée* in April 1968) – 'Philosophy as a Revolutionary Weapon' – Althusser informed her that he set great store by the criticisms made by 'militants of the revolutionary class struggle'. As an example, he alluded to some made in March 1966, though without instancing any of them, which had been 'a great help'.[16] Several years later, in *Reply to John Lewis*, he noted that at Argenteuil 'the right of party members to carry out and publish their philosophical research' had been recognised.[17] At the time, Althusser maintained a public silence. In contrast, the response of the Cercle d'Ulm was immediate – and dramatic. A meeting three days after the Central Committee's (16 March) adopted a text entitled 'Le marxisme n'est pas un humanisme', which argued that, in 'liquidating' Marxist theory, the Central Committee had forfeited the allegiance of militants, concluding: 'against the Central Committee resolution, defence of Marxist-Leninist theory'.[18] This was followed in April by the dissemination of the impeccably Althusserian pamphlet, *Faut-il réviser la théorie marxiste-léniniste?*.[19] A clandestine meeting

---

[15] See *Cahiers du communisme* 1966, pp. 38, 104–7, 122–3, 272–80, 293–309.
[16] Althusser 1976b, pp. 47–8.
[17] Althusser 1976a, p. 75.
[18] Quoted in Kessel 1972, p. 148.
[19] Reprinted in Kessel 1972, pp. 149–61.

of 'Marxist-Leninist' cells of the UEC was held in July 1966 at Andresy to discuss the situation.[20] It was resolved not to affiliate to the Mouvement communiste français (the forerunner of the Parti communiste marxiste-léniniste de France, taxed with anti-intellectualism, hyper-Stalinism and revisionism), but to remain in the PCF, waging an open internal struggle and attending to 'theoretical training' in preparation for secession and the creation of a new party. In the interim, the PCF's Eighteenth Congress was greeted as a 'congress to terminate communism!'. The dissolution of the Cercle d'Ulm by the PCF, and expulsion of many of its members, prompted the foundation in December of the Union des jeunesses communistes marxistes-léninistes (UJCML), which counted among its number Robert Linhart, Jacques Rancière, Pierre Victor, and Dominique Lecourt. Balibar and others, by contrast, followed Althusser, persevering in the PCF.

By the time of the split, the Cultural Revolution had exploded in China. From its fourteenth number onwards (November/December 1966), *Cahiers marxistes-léninistes* became the UJC's theoretical and political organ. The first of three issues devoted to the 'Great Proletarian Cultural Revolution', among the (unsigned) articles it contained was one entitled 'On the Cultural Revolution' – singled out by the PCF's Claude Prévost as a dire warning of the extremes to which Althusser's Marxism could lead in youthful hands. The article was in fact by Althusser.[21]

'On the Cultural Revolution' confirms that, contrary to his own de-politicised account in *Elements of Self-Criticism*, Althusser's most serious 'flirtation' was neither with structuralism, nor Spinozism, but Maoism. Its sentiments are unequivocal, its enthusiasm unqualified. The Cultural Revolution was 'a historical fact *without precedent*' of 'enormous theoretical interest'. In the form of a rhetorical question, Althusser endorsed a thesis tirelessly repeated in Chinese polemics:

> is the future of socialism in a country one hundred per cent guaranteed –
> definitively, with no going back – by the simple fact that it has accomplished

---

[20] According to Kessel 1972, p. 196, although Althusser did not attend, a letter from him was read (of whose contents no indication is given). This has been denied by Robert Linhart (interview, Paris, April 1986).

[21] See Rancière 1974, p. 110, n. 1 for Prévost and p. 108 for Althusser's article. Rancière's attribution has been confirmed by Étienne Balibar (interview, Paris, June 1985).

a dual revolution, *political* and *economic*? Is it impossible for it to regress to capitalism?

Do we not already possess an example of this phenomenon: Yugoslavia?

Can a socialist country, then, not retain – even for a considerable period of time – *the*, or at least *some*, external forms of socialism (economic, political), whilst imparting to them a quite different economic, political, and ideological content (the mechanism of capitalist restoration), and allowing itself to be progressively neutralised and utilised politically, then dominated economically, by imperialism?

At a certain stage in their history, the argument runs, socialist states find themselves confronted by a choice between 'two roads': the 'revolutionary road' and the 'road of regression'. China is at this crossroads. In order to progress on the road to communism, it has elected to undertake a 'third revolution': the 'mass ideological revolution' which will furnish it with an ideological superstructure corresponding to its socialist infrastructure and state. Once equipped with this superstructure, the threat of capitalist restoration will recede.[22]

Taking up the perspectives on revolutionary transition and the durability of ideologies outlined at the end of 'Contradiction and Overdetermination', Althusser offered the thesis of potential 'regression' as congruent with Marxism by virtue of the non-evolutionist and non-economistic character of historical materialism. Going further, he argued that social classes are not defined *solely* by the objective location of social agents in the relations of production, but also by their members' positions in political and ideological relations, which remain *class* relations long after the installation of a socialist (economic) mode of production. Political and ideological class struggle persist in a socialist country and social classes are 'essentially' defined according to the part they play in them. Having indicated that the economy retains a determinant role as a result of the survival of, for example, petty commodity production and the existence of large inequalities of income, Althusser comes to his 'essential point':

---

[22] See Althusser 1966b, pp. 5, 7–8. (The identification of Yugoslavia as a lapsed socialist state is repeated on p. 11.) Although Yugoslavia was used as a cipher for the USSR in early Chinese polemics, Althusser never publicly declared the latter to be 'state-capitalist'. For the CPC's explanation of the Cultural Revolution, see Communist Party of China 1966, p. 10.

the thesis of 'regression' presupposes that in a certain conjuncture of the history of socialist countries, the *ideological* can be the *strategic point* where everything is decided. Hence the crossroads is situated in the ideological and the future depends on it. The fate of a socialist country (progress or regression) is played out in the ideological class struggle.[23]

This thesis was justified by reference to the theory of overdetermination (both the Althusserian distinction between determination and dominance and Mao's categories of contradiction). A socialist economic and political revolution does not automatically transform the bourgeois ideological superstructure, Althusser contended; the bourgeois adversary remains in place and must be dislodged. No novelty of Mao's, this necessity had been recognised by Marx and, above all, Lenin. What was new was the practical implementation of a 'classical' tenet of Marxism – something which would in turn yield theoretical fruits. Althusser's suggestion that the Cultural Revolution represented the application of 'Marxist principles regarding the nature of the ideological' might be amended to read 'Althusserian principles'. As read by him, the Chinese experience verified the theory he had advanced in 1965. Ideology comprised 'systems [of] ideas-representations' (theoretical ideologies) and 'attitudes-behaviour' (practical ideologies). An ideological revolution concerned both – for example, 'styles' of leadership (technocratic, bureaucratic, and so on) as well as theoretical humanism.[24]

The non-bureaucratic organisational means employed in the People's Republic were also of the greatest significance. The creation of non-party, mass organisations of ideological struggle was a decisive and commendable innovation in Communist strategy. After a revolutionary seizure of power, the Communist party (or its equivalent) would assume responsibility for running the state for the duration of the dictatorship of the proletariat. Therewith a 'partial but inevitable fusion' of party and state apparatus would occur, which posed the serious problem with which Lenin had wrestled just before his death: *'how to regulate the relations between Party and State in such a way as to avoid the faults of bureaucracy and technocracy, and their grave political effects?'*. The CPC was responding to this dilemma with the Cultural

---

[23] Althusser 1966b, pp. 11–12.
[24] Althusser 1966b, pp. 13–15.

Revolution – with the mass movements mobilised in it, whose main task was to challenge such retrogressive tendencies within state and party. The non-party organisations undertaking the third, ideological revolution were – and must be – '*distinct*' from the Communist Party, so as to compel it to '*distinguish itself*' from the state.[25]

Althusser concluded by affirming the relevance of the 'great lessons' of the Cultural Revolution, not only to the other 'socialist' countries, but to the whole international Communist movement and every Communist. Perhaps the most noteworthy implication drawn from them was that

> great revolutions can only be the work of the masses, and the role of revolutionary leaders, while providing them with the means to find their bearings and organise themselves, and imparting Marxism-Leninism as a compass and a law, is to go to school with the masses in order to be able to help them express their will and resolve their problems.[26]

According to Balibar, Althusser perceived in the Chinese experiment the first example of a socialist revolution criticising and rectifying itself. His illusions on this score – and some of their consequences – will be discussed in Chapters 5 and 6. For now, it is enough to register three facts. First – as Rancière points out – Althusser's views on China were well-nigh indistinguishable from those of the UJC in whose journal he expressed them; he drew identical political conclusions from his theoretical principles. Secondly, however, in contrast to some of his students, Althusser did not break with the PCF, judging it inopportune to do so. Yet, prior to May '68, this did not mean an irrevocable theoretical and political rupture with them. Balibar has suggested that Althusser 'never *seriously* envisaged' leaving the Party himself, but that his position at this stage was still 'ambiguous'.[27] The publication of a positive evaluation of the Cultural Revolution in a Maoist journal exemplifies that ambiguity. Thirdly, Althusser's partiality for the 'uninterrupted revolution' in China was to persist for another seven years or more, profoundly influencing his work – to such

---

[25] Althusser 1966b, pp. 15–16. It should be noted that Althusser had previously endorsed the non-violent 'means and methods' of ideological struggle supposedly characteristic of the Cultural Revolution: see Althusser 1966b, p. 8. For Lenin's 'last struggle', see Lewin 1975 (note pp. 113–14 for Lenin's decidedly non-Maoist concept of 'cultural revolution').

[26] Althusser 1966b, p. 16.

[27] Interview, Paris, June 1985. For Rancière's analysis, see his 1974, pp. 108–9.

an extent that it constituted a theoretico-political paradigm. In consequence, it became increasingly discrepant with the national and international perspectives of the party to which he paid his dues. Althusser's text of 1966 reveals a sympathy for the Maoist experience quite irreconcilable with the post-Stalin orientation of the PCF (as Garaudy's contemporaneous *Le Problème chinois* reveals). May '68 was the moment of this truth. But it was a turning-point at which Althusser failed to turn, even as workers and students declined the role allotted them in the authorless theatre of contemporary French capitalism. Thereafter, Althusser's career affords the curious spectacle of the China syndrome in uneasy coexistence with Communist observance.

The class struggle in theory

In his laudatory 1966 review of *For Marx* and *Reading 'Capital'*, Nicos Poulantzas noted that Althusser's attempt to resume Marxist philosophy was only the latest in a long line: the question of dialectical materialism had 'haunted Marxist thought'.[28] Althusser's writings from 1967 to 1974 are largely taken up with producing a new definition of Marxist philosophy and a revised account of the relations between it and historical materialism. Under conflicting pressure from party and left-wing critics alike over the theory of theoretical practice, Althusser retracted it, acknowledging an erstwhile 'theoreticism' – the failure to treat 'the union of theory and practice within *political practice*' – and 'positivism' – the failure to differentiate between philosophy and science, to appreciate the 'organic relationship' between philosophy and politics.[29] Althusser's attempt to correct his error essentially consisted in conceiving (and practising) philosophy as a *political intervention in theory* and a *theoretical intervention in politics*. The novelty of 'dialectical materialism' was no longer thought to reside in its scientificity as a theory of science (and its history), but in its 'partisan', 'materialist' practice of philosophy. Marxist philosophy, Althusser will argue from 1967 onwards, no more produces knowledge than any other philosophy. Rather, it states and defends theses, intervening conjuncturally in theory on behalf of revolutionary politics to protect the

---

[28] Poulantzas 1966, p. 1952.
[29] See 'To My English Readers' (October 1967), in Althusser 1969, pp. 14–15.

sciences against the intrusions of ideology; and in politics on behalf of a science – historical materialism – to defend 'correct' political positions from 'deviations'. Although deprived of its erstwhile scientific prestige, dialectical materialism was recompensed with very considerable prerogatives – and did not cease to haunt Althusser's thought.[30]

Rancière has condemned Althusser's redefinition of philosophy as a *prise de parti* for the Party: the PCF. To borrow a Maoist dictum, it was 'left in form, right in essence' – an inflection to the left whose function was the neutralisation of the student/leftist threat to the PCF's political, and Althusser's philosophical, authority.[31] (Althusser was a latter-day Kautsky or Plekhanov, ostensibly defending Maoist theoretical orthodoxy, but in reality a revisionist recuperating Maoism and underwriting reformism: for Mao, read Marchais.) Rancière's complaint is that Althusser was not enough of a Maoist. In contrast, this chapter will argue that if Althusser's revisions are to be faulted, it is more properly for their Maoism. The 'new' Althusser must be criticised not for his patrician aloofness from Maoist politics, but for straying too far in the direction of the oriental Zhdanovism propagated from Peking in reparation for his aristocratism of theory. The political significance of this development will be examined in the next chapter. Here, we shall chart Althusser's *over-reaction* to the criticisms made of him: his renunciation of the autonomy of theory and substitution of 'politicism' for 'theoreticism' – a shift which not only produced serious internal inconsistencies, but also resulted in a noticeable overall decline in the power and originality of Althusser's work.

In the foreword to the 1968 Italian edition of *Reading 'Capital'*, Althusser signalled the 'unilateralism' of his first definition of philosophy and promised a forthcoming 'rectification'.[32] The assimilation of philosophy to science and construction of dialectical materialism as a rationalist epistemology had constituted a derogation from Marxism. The rectification came in two instalments: 1967–8 and 1972. The first stage of Althusser's revision thus post-dated the Cultural Revolution, but preceded the May events. Without taking the form of an explicit self-criticism, the Introduction to the 'Philosophy Course for Scientists' held at the École normale supérieure between November

---

[30] See, e.g., Althusser 1971, p. 20 and Althusser 1976a, p. 149.
[31] Rancière 1974, pp. 49, 53–4, 110.
[32] Althusser and Balibar 1970, p. 8.

1967 and May 1968 revoked earlier positions, offering a new view of 'the relations that philosophy *should* maintain with the sciences if it is to serve them rather than enslave them'.[33] Only published in 1974 as *Philosophy and the Spontaneous Philosophy of Scientists*, this text was circulated in mimeographed form.[34] What became known as the 'second definition of philosophy' was made available to a wider audience in 'Philosophy as a Revolutionary Weapon', which introduced virtually all the themes (as well as the characteristic idiom) of Althusser's later work in this field – among them, the following thesis: 'Philosophy represents the class struggle in theory.'[35] In a lecture on 'Lenin and Philosophy' delivered to the Société française de philosophie in February 1968, this 'non-philosophical theory of philosophy' was developed via an analysis of Lenin's 'great "philosophical" work', *Materialism and Empirio-Criticism*.[36] In his address to a conference on Hegel held in April of the following year ('Lenin before Hegel'), Althusser summarised the essentials of his new conception, asserting that all its basic components were to be found – 'explicitly' or 'implicitly' – in Lenin's intervention of 1908 and indicating that all he had done was to 'to make them more explicit'.[37]

The terminus of Althusser's meditations on the subject of philosophy was reached with its definition – of Maoist provenance – as '*in the last instance, class struggle in the field of theory*' in *Reply to John Lewis* (1972–3).[38] In *Elements of Self-Criticism*, written at the same time but published two years later, Althusser explained that, if his original reduction of philosophy to science had represented a conjoint *theoretical* overestimation and *political* underestimation of it, the propositions advanced in 1967–8 had represented an 'improvised solution', a 'semi-compromise' which still failed to do justice to the last instance: class struggle.[39] The (theoreticist) unilateralism of the first definition had only been palliated by a bilateralism in which philosophy was

---

[33] Althusser 1990, p. 73.
[34] It was revised for publication. Unfortunately, it has not been possible to consult the original.
[35] Althusser 1971, p. 21.
[36] Althusser 1971, pp. 32, 49. The sentiments on philosophy and philosophers expressed by Althusser in front of his professional colleagues provoked considerable irritation on their part, necessitating the intervention of the chairman Jean Wahl: see Althusser 1968b, p. 132.
[37] Althusser 1971, p. 106; see pp. 105–6 for Althusser's summary.
[38] Althusser 1976a, p. 37.
[39] Althusser 1976a, p. 150.

doubly determined, by science and politics, both of which it represented equally.

To turn now to the first group of texts. The earlier identification of philosophy with science was repudiated.[40] Philosophy was not a 'theoretical practice' as defined in 'On the Materialist Dialectic'. It had no object and produced no concepts. Its theses and categories did not yield knowledge. Nevertheless, it retained a 'privileged link' with the sciences and its relation to them was 'constitutive' of its specificity.[41] What Althusser called the 'materialist thesis of objectivity' forged the link between the two. This comprised two propositions, formulated by his pupil Dominique Lecourt as (i) 'the primacy of being over thought' and (ii) 'the objectivity of knowledge'.[42] The stances adopted by various philosophies towards it provided a principle for the classification of philosophical discourse. The 'history' of philosophy could be reduced to a 'struggle between two tendencies': the idealist and the materialist.[43] Philosophies of the first tendency rejected the materialist thesis or ordered its components incorrectly. Philosophies of the second both subscribed to, and observed the priority of, (i). The struggle between these tendencies was endless, because the issues at stake could not be scientifically decided. Philosophical theses were amenable to rational justification, but unsusceptible of scientific proof. Philosophy, accordingly, was a *Kampfplatz* over which the guns would never fall silent. Indeed, unlike the sciences, philosophy had *'no real history'*, being an interminable discourse – a succession of variations on two basic themes which were really only one.[44] This did not mean that it was inconsequential. Quite the reverse.

The privileged link to which Althusser referred was, in reality, the relation between a modern affiliate to the materialist tendency – Marxist philosophy – and the sciences. Grounded in the materialist thesis, 'dialectical materialism' was the philosophy which *'represents . . . the "spontaneous"* convictions of scientists about the existence of the objects of their sciences, and the objectivity of their knowledge'.[45] The unprecedented novelty of Marxist philosophy was

---

[40] See, e.g., Althusser 1971, p. 50.
[41] Althusser 1971, p. 53; Althusser 1990, p. 108.
[42] Lecourt 1973, p. 36. See Althusser 1971, pp. 53–5 and Althusser 1990, pp. 132–3.
[43] Althusser 1971, p. 55.
[44] Althusser 1971, p. 56. See also Althusser 1990, pp. 121–2.
[45] Althusser 1971, p. 55.

that, apprised of its determinants, it put its 'practical functions' to good use. On the side of the sciences, it opposed all extra-scientific forms of idealism and further protected scientific practice by displacing the idealist element (residual yet resurgent) in scientists' own 'spontaneous philosophy'.[46] The vocation of Marxist philosophy was to remove the 'epistemological obstacles' or inhibitions to scientific progress constituted by the (idealist) 'philosophies of the philosophers' and the (contradictory) philosophies of the scientists. Its function was 'to trace a line of demarcation' within the theoretical domain between the ideological and the scientific, in order to 'free scientific practice from ... ideological domination'.[47] At stake was the defence of the sciences against deformation/exploitation and the sustenance of their progress.[48] Marxist philosophy was not a normative epistemology dispensing judgements on criteria of scientific validity; it was a philosophical practice geared to the 'materialist *defence* of the sciences' – a task for which it was qualified by its link with historical materialism:

> Now you will understand why we insist on the *novel* character of the materialist philosophy from which scientific practice may expect this service. For if it is to be able to serve scientific practice, this materialist philosophy must be prepared to combat all the forms of the idealist exploitation of the sciences; and if it is to be able to wage this combat *en connaissance de cause*, this philosophy must be capable of *mastering through knowledge and criticism* the organic link that binds it to the practical ideologies on which it, like any other philosophy, depends. We have seen under what conditions this critical control is possible: *only* in the case of a materialist philosophy connected to the discoveries through which Marx opened up the way to knowledge of the mechanisms of 'ideological social relations' (Lenin), and therefore a knowledge of the function of practical ideologies and their class antagonisms.[49]

Lenin's *Materialism and Empirio-Criticism* heralded this 'new *practice of philosophy*'.[50] In the course of his assault on the 'Machists', he had espoused the thesis of 'partisanship in philosophy' which Althusser now wished to

---

[46] See Althusser 1990, p. 131ff.
[47] Althusser 1990, pp. 83, 88, 99.
[48] Althusser 1990, p. 125.
[49] Althusser 1999, pp. 130, 142.
[50] Althusser 1971, p. 61.

resuscitate. All philosophies, so it is suggested, are partisan in the sense that they pertain to one basic tendency (materialist or idealist) and oppose the other. This is not the end of the matter, however. The 'practical' nature of all philosophy is constantly denied by its idealist practitioners even as they practise it. The reality thus denegated is the relationship of the two tendencies to social classes and the struggle between them. As Lenin had indicated, philosophy '*represents* the class struggle, i.e. politics':

> philosophy is a certain continuation of politics, in a certain domain, *vis-à-vis* a certain reality. Philosophy represents politics in the domain of theory or to be more precise: *with the sciences* – and, *vice versa*, philosophy represents scientificity in politics, with the classes engaged in class struggle.

Rather than denying its partisanship – its 'representation' in theory of the proletariat's materialist world-view – Lenin's philosophical practice proclaims it, '*acting according to what it is*'.[51]

Some pages into 'Lenin and Philosophy', Althusser enumerated a series of recurrent 'disputes' concerning the character and content of Marxism.[52] In *For Marx* and *Reading 'Capital'*, he had offered firm answers to them. That he considered his previous responses on the subject of Marxist philosophy to have remained in hock to the 'traditional terms', and his second attempt to have hit on the requisite 'new terms' by developing Lenin's own, is clear. The philosophical revolution induced by Marx's opening up of the 'continent of History' to scientific knowledge had registered its first exceptional effects with the leader of the Bolshevik Party. Marxism-Leninism still lacked its great philosophical work. But, by returning to Lenin, Marxist philosophers could overcome the 'necessary lag' of philosophy behind the sciences and accomplish 'the task . . . which history has assigned and entrusted to them': the elaboration and development of Marxist philosophy.[53]

In the auto-critique he drew up in 1972, Althusser conceded the justice of the common accusation that the class struggle had been absent from his early work. The texts of 1967–8, where it had finally made its entry, had begun to repair matters. Yet they represented a half-way house – an ultimately

---

[51] Althusser 1971, pp. 64–6.
[52] See Althusser 1971, pp. 38–9.
[53] See Althusser 1971, pp. 44–8.

unsatisfactory compromise. With increasingly violent accusations of revisionism ringing in his ears post-May, Althusser now confided his own discontent and proposed a further injection of class struggle.

The necessity of theory was a constant of *For Marx* and *Reading 'Capital'*. The indispensability of philosophy remains to the fore in the second phase of Althusser's career.[54] The reason, he explained in *Reply to John Lewis*, is that philosophy is – in the last instance – class struggle in theory. The philosophical positions adopted by philosophers ultimately reflect their class positions. Dialectical materialism represents the revolutionary working class. The materialist positions it adopts, like the idealist positions to which its opponents adhere, are ultimately determined by, and reflect, class interests. Contrary to received wisdom, philosophy is not 'pure *disinterested* speculation'; it impinges on what is extrinsic to it. All philosophical positions 'produce *effects* in the social practices' (including politics and the sciences) – progressive effects if they are 'correct' (Marxist-Leninist), retrogressive if not.[55] Althusser illustrates part of his argument by examining the theoretical and political effects of one of his antagonist's philosophical positions. The gravamen of his critique is that John Lewis's humanist thesis – 'It is man who makes history' – represents an epistemological obstacle to the progress of historical materialism, retarding its development (its production of new knowledge vital to political practice). Theoretically retrograde, the political consequences of Lewis's position are equally injurious. For to pronounce 'men' the makers of history is to help 'disorient or disarm' the workers, deflecting them from the class struggle and its organisations. In short, Lewis's philosophical thesis is one which 'directly or indirectly serves the political interests of the bourgeoisie'. The 'Marxist-Leninist' theses counterposed to him by Althusser, in contrast, supposedly have 'theoretically progressive' effects within historical materialism and are politically beneficial to the revolutionary cause of the proletariat.[56]

We will take a look at Althusser's Marxist-Leninist alternatives later. Meantime, the comprehensiveness of his retreat from the theory of theoretical practice must be highlighted. Affirming the 'primacy of politics over philosophy', Althusser repudiated his prior definition of philosophy as the

---

[54] See, e.g., Althusser 1976a, p. 37.
[55] See Althusser 1976a, pp. 57–8.
[56] See Althusser 1976a, pp. 59–64.

'Science of Sciences [and] Practices'.[57] In a long footnote in *Elements of Self-Criticism*, he characterised the classical project of epistemology as intrinsically idealist. His own *'speculative-rationalism'*, crystallised in a general theory of science (truth) and ideology (error), partook of its incorrigibly normative project. Alternatively, epistemology could be understood in materialist fashion as a theory of the 'conditions and forms of scientific practice and of its history in the different concrete sciences'. In this case, however, it would constitute that regional theory of *historical* materialism whose object was 'already existing knowledge'.[58]

In terms of the 'internal logic' of Althusser's work, the conjoint redefinition of philosophy and reconceptualisation of historical epistemology were intended to resolve a central problem in *For Marx* and *Reading 'Capital'*: the general relationship between theoretical discourses and the other social 'practices', and the particular relationship between Marxist theory and the working-class movement, disarticulated by Althusser. The theory of theoretical practice, in any case incapable of performing the task allocated it, had been accorded such pre-eminence that relative autonomy took the form of absolute autonomy and omnipotence. Philosophy, having abdicated in favour of science, was restored to its throne by the addition of the epithet 'scientific'. In the new definition, Marxist philosophy was neither an ontology (Althusser's 'materialist thesis' is epistemological and more properly described as a *realist* one – and thus scarcely peculiar to revolutionaries), nor an epistemology (although it defends realist theses). It was a practice: the continuation of revolutionary politics by theoretical means. For all the complexity of its location in the science/ideology/politics/philosophy quartet, the continuing prestige attached to Marxist philosophy is obvious.

Indeed, there is considerable continuity in Althusser's project, insofar as both the first and second definitions of philosophy were designed to 'serve', rather than 'enslave', the sciences (first among them, historical materialism). Althusser's *practice* of philosophy was always, so to speak, 'Anabaptist' – concerned, in Bachelardian fashion, to wrest Marx's scientific theory from the 'epistemological obstacles' which had accreted around it during his posterity, impairing the epistemological break constitutive of it. In the first instance,

---

[57] Althusser 1976a, p. 58, n. 18.
[58] See Althusser 1976a, p. 124, n. 19 and see also p. 117, n. 12.

however, the *theory* of that practice – the theory of theoretical practice – had taken a form inimical to Althusser's goal, as an epistemology which (in the words of Andrew Collier) was 'a little too much like the queen of the sciences, too little like their under-labourer'.[59] Thereafter, the epistemological enterprise was identified as part of the problem, while the solution lay in an anti-epistemology – a philosophy *for*, rather than *of*, science – which developed what had already been identified as the eminently worthwhile aspects of the Leninist practice of philosophy; and merged them with a Bacherlardian account of the anti-scientific tendencies of the philosophy not only of philosophers, but of scientists as well.[60]

Now, it should be acknowledged at the outset, first, that Althusser's new definition was a serious attempt to amend the earlier version; and secondly that, ably developed by Lecourt and others,[61] it has its merits. For it does amount to a Marxist version of the Lockean view of philosophy as an under-labourer to the sciences – a *philosophie du non* whose polemical practice respects and defends the objective knowledge (*index sui et falsi*) imparted by them. This said, however, it is difficult to avoid the conclusion that the first definition might have been rectified in such a way as to preserve its virtues without introducing the vices – or hostages to fortune – characteristic of the second. What were these?

The first criticism to be made is well-rehearsed. Althusser's simultaneous dismissal of epistemology as an inherently normative or juridical doctrine, on the one hand, and retention by fiat of the distinction between sciences and theoretical ideologies within a regional theory of historical materialism, on the other, is problematic. Granted, the search for a priori, external guarantees

---

[59] Collier 1979, p. 65.

[60] See Althusser and Balibar 1970, pp. 89–90 n. for Althusser's comments on *Materialism and Empirico-Criticism*; and, among other works by Bachelard, see his 1980 and 1964. At the same time, of course, the second definition of philosophy can been seen as an attempt to impart greater substance to the positions advance in the 'Note on Dialectical Materialism' (see Chapter 1 above, pp. 14–15).

[61] See Lecourt 1974, 1975, and 1977; Raymond 1973; Fichant and Pêcheux 1969; Macherey 1976 and 1983. The most sustained discussion by Althusser himself is to be found in *Philosophy and the Spontaneous Philosophy of the Scientists*. As Timothy O'Hagan has remarked in his excellent account of Althusser's untranslated transitional text, 'this gap in the corpus of Althusser translation means that the full novelty, subtlety and fragility of the new position has not been widely appreciated': O'Hagan 1982, p. 244, n. 2.

of the objectivity of scientific knowledge is both doomed and detrimental. But, just as criteria are needed in order to judge whether 'actually existing socialism' is socialism, so too some sort of criterion is required to determine whether 'actually existing knowledge' is knowledge. For is it what it claims to be? And how can philosophy perform its function if it does not possess the means to distinguish science from theoretical ideology? The denomination of a theoretical discourse as scientific (that is, as providing objective knowledge of a real object) implies and necessitates evaluative principles. In their absence, there are two possibilities: either no epistemological distinction can be drawn between, say, historical materialism and moral majoritarianism as social theories; alternatively, politico-ideological *parti pris* usurps the role denied juridical philosophy. The Althusserian substitution of 'materialist' history based upon the science of social formations (and its scientific theory of ideology) for 'speculative' epistemology tributary to bourgeois legal theory, far from correcting the relativist bent of the earlier work, exacerbates it. The scientificity of historical materialism is taken for granted – hence imponderable. Historical materialism, then, is not immune from these relativist – or dogmatist – implications. Althusser abandons the idea of philosophy providing it with an epistemological foundation and further rejects any submission of it to epistemological interrogation. Simultaneously, page after page claims the status of science for historical materialism – or at least Althusser's version of it. Speculative rationalism is denounced, one of relativism or dogmatism effectively embraced.

Paraphrasing Kant, Imre Lakatos once suggested that '[p]hilosophy of science without history of science is empty; history of science without philosophy of science is blind'.[62] Althusser's history is blind. What of his philosophy? Its problem is that it is at once too full and virtually empty, 'nothing in its own right, and, at the same time, practically everything'.[63] Regarding its role vis-à-vis the sciences, there are numerous objections. To begin with the most obvious. The reduction, after Engels and Lenin, of the history of philosophy to a secular struggle between two tendencies courts predictable caricature. Moreover, Althusser's (under)development of this 'historical thesis' detracts from the merit in his retraction of the previous

---

[62] Lakatos 1978, p. 102.
[63] Geras 1986b, p. 89. See also Kelly 1982, pp. 185–7.

equation between philosophy and science. (The imputation of a spontaneous materialism to the proletariat integral to the 'representative' function of Marxist philosophy is at best implausible.) More damaging, perhaps, is the effective recantation of the independence of science involved in assigning the defence of the sciences – including historical materialism – to a discursive practice which represents class struggle in theory. For, despite Althusser's restriction of its role to propagation of the 'materialist thesis' (as opposed to adjudication of scientific theories, and so forth); and although he denied any dogmatism or pragmatism, insisting that the class struggle in theory amounted to a struggle for or against the sciences, not to their politicisation (subordination to ideology), the second definition offers a point of entry for less benign forces. It is difficult to see how a Zhdanovist outcome can be forestalled. With *Reply to John Lewis*, the new definition bends the stick as far in the politicist direction as had the old in the theoreticist. Reductionism, rather than idealism, is the spectre it cannot exorcise.

As regards the role of philosophy in politics, what remain temptations or perils vis-à-vis the sciences materialise. The task of philosophy is to relay the scientific results of historical materialism (revolutionary theory) to the revolutionary movement. Relatedly, it must defend 'correct' political positions and prosecute 'deviations'. This supposes a finished doctrine – a dogma – which can supply the definitions of (in)correctness and absolutises the role of science in politics. Indicative of the former is Althusser's tactic against Lewis. In defiance of his own recognition of the heterogeneity of Marx and Lenin's writings, and the existence of competing Marxist orthodoxies (the PCF's, the CPSU's, the CPC's, to name but three), and invoking the authority of the great and the good from Marx to Mao, Althusser employs a certain 'Marxism-Leninism' to convict Lewis of revisionism. Here, the 'class struggle in theory' – a motley of Bachelard and Mao – assumes a shape, and takes on accents of the Communist *langue de bois*, which the earlier Althusser might have recognised as foes. Pursued to its conclusion, the road taken in *Reply to John Lewis* terminates in the quasi-Zhdanovite tutelage over the intellectuals – in the name of Marxism-Leninism – against which Althusser had once so eloquently intervened.

Arguably, the outstanding characteristic of the second definition is its ultimate lack of originality. Althusser acknowledges his indebtedness to *Materialism and Empirio-Criticism*, a work which had previously been credited with considerable polemical qualities, but found wanting as a satisfactory basis for Marxist philosophy. Its theses on 'partisanship' have been a talisman of Soviet (and Chinese) philosophy from Stalin onwards.[64] The 'materialist' mode of reading, adopted by the later Althusser in place of the symptomatic,[65] operates arbitrarily, extracting the supposedly materialist elements of a discourse and disposing of the rest. This was Althusser's procedure with Lenin, at any rate. Recourse to Lenin's work is one thing, the growing frequency of references to Mao and occasional superfluous affidavits for Stalin quite another. Althusser's *chinoiseries* on the class struggle in theory reveal both the profundity of the influence of the Cultural Revolution on him and the fact that it was an influence for the worse. In a text attacking the UJC in 1967, Mury (who had recently joined the Mouvement communiste français) upbraided Althusser for his apparent aversion to Mao's *On Practice* and for failing to 'breathe a word' on Lenin's *Materialism and Empirio-Criticism* and Stalin's *Dialectical and Historical Materialism*.[66] Mury was right to pinpoint this silence of Althusser's as symptomatic, wrong in his estimate of it: it is an index of the originality of Althusser's philosophical project within Communism. Althusser was no more an orthodox Stalinist or Maoist after 1968 than before it. But, with the renunciation of the first, and promulgation of the second, definition of philosophy in the precise form it took, Althusser sought salvation where none was to be found, mistaking a familiar and discredited refrain for a theoretical innovation. The words he 'breathed' on Lenin and (as we shall see) Stalin after 1965 did not need the author of *For Marx* and *Reading 'Capital'* to give vent to them.

Finally, the Maoist inflation of the place and role of the ideological could serve as a useful self-justification for Marxist intellectuals and academics. The very emphasis given to ideological struggle (and its philosophical sub-set) in the Maoist and Althusserian scheme of things, in addition to its idealist and voluntarist bent, could easily be turned to apologetic ends, providing a mystique for inaction. From his Bolivian prison-cell, Althusser's pupil Régis

---

[64] Lenin's work is accorded supreme significance in the *Short Course* (see Communist Party of the Soviet Union 1939, pp. 103–5) and held up by Zhdanov (in his 1950, pp. 87–8) as the model for Marxist philosophical practice.

[65] See Althusser 1971, pp. 110–12.

[66] See Kessel 1972, pp. 262–3.

Debray meditated on Althusser's original philosophy: it could be – and had been – exploited to indicate that 'all we had to do to become good theoreticians was to be lazy bastards'.[67] The second definition is open to equivalent exploitation. If philosophy is the class struggle in theory, then for a Marxist philosopher to philosophise is to fight the good fight; philosophy, to borrow the title of Althusser's interview, is a revolutionary weapon. Marxist philosophers may no longer be quite the *illuminati* they once were. But they can now flatter themselves that their desks have been turned into barricades (Brecht), the seminar room into a *place d'armes*.

If, then, Althusser was right to renounce the theory of theoretical practice in its original form, the conception (and practice) of philosophy he put in its place under the exigencies of an 'external' logic is not, ultimately, an advance over its shortcomings, but a partial retreat – one that is not redeemed by its positive aspects.

Proletarian positions, or the motor of history

Possessing particular allure as a result of its combination of a re-theorisation of Marxism (and Leninism) in contemporary terms, and an implied political radicalism (sympathetic at least to Maoism), Althusserianism rapidly acquired, if not hegemony, then certainly pre-eminence among young left-wing French intellectuals after 1965 – a prestige that endured until at least May '68. For many, Althusserianism was the highest stage of Marxism. Accordingly, the heroes of yesteryear – Sartre, Lefebvre, Goldmann and so on – were unceremoniously dispatched, along with the young Marx, to the outer limits of the Latin Quarter.[68] The controversy generated by Althusser's intervention was in direct proportion to its radicalism – and influence. The criticisms attracted by 'Contradiction and Overdetermination' have already been cited. 'Marxism and Humanism' provoked a debate in the Communist Party journal *La Nouvelle Critique* which lasted for close on a year (March 1965 – March 1966). The PCF's Central Committee met at Argenteuil in March 1966 to rule on the subject of Marxist humanism – and found against the Althusserian

---

[67] Debray 1973, p. 187.
[68] But they did not go quietly: see the ripostes cited in the Foreword on p. xv, n. 7 above.

line. Whereas a young Marxist intellectual like Poulantzas exchanged Sartrean for Althusserian loyalties, to the veteran Garaudy, theoretical anti-humanism was 'the specifically French variant of neo-dogmatism'.[69] Althusser did not recant his theoretical anti-humanism. What he did do after 1968, responding to 'internal' and 'external' logics, was to redraft his history of Marxism and to reconceptualise historical materialism. If it was necessary to select one passage from his work which encapsulates Althusser's message in the years 1967–75, it would be the following from 'Marxism and Class Struggle' (1971):

> the centre and core of the whole of Marx's theory . . . is *the class struggle*. The class struggle is therefore the 'decisive link', not only in the practice of the Marxist-Leninist workers' movement, *but also in theory*, in Marxist science and philosophy.[70]

Whether, in making the class struggle the centre and core of his own Marxism out of indulgence to Maoism, and in a forlorn attempt to appease critics of his theoreticism, Althusser improved on his earlier efforts, is doubtful.

In March 1969, Althusser wrote a 'Preface to *Capital* Volume One'. Returning to the question of the rupture between Marx and Hegel, he declared himself unrepentant except insofar as he had

> given a much too abrupt idea of [it] in advancing the idea that it was possible to locate this rupture in 1845. . . . Something decisively really does begin in 1845, but Marx needed a very long period of revolutionary *work*, before he managed to register the rupture he had made with Hegel's thought in really new concepts. The famous *Preface* of 1859 . . . is still profoundly Hegelian-evolutionist. The *'Grundrisse'* . . . are themselves profoundly marked by Hegel's thought. . . .
>
> When *Capital* Volume One appeared . . ., traces of the Hegelian influence still remained. Only later did they disappear *completely*: the *Critique of the Gotha Programme* . . . as well as the *Marginal Notes on Wagner* . . . are *totally and definitively exempt* from *any* trace of Hegelian influence.[71]

[69] See Poulantzas 1966, e.g. p. 1982; Garaudy 1970, p. 205.
[70] Althusser 1976b, p. 61.
[71] Althusser 1971, p. 90. Among the Hegelian motifs present in *Capital*, Volume One, Althusser cites the negation of the negation in Chapter 32. The theory of fetishism is now said to be 'a flagrant and extremely harmful . . . trace of Hegelian influence'

That only two short texts by Marx should have passed the Althusserian audition probably says more about Althusser's criteria than Marx. Althusser wished to retain the proposition of a break with Hegel in Marx's work, while at the same time indicating Marx's failure to party company with him until 1875. The suspicion must be that the real operation involved here is Althusser's calibration of Marx's œuvre against his own view of what constitutes a scientific theory of history, endorsing such works as conform to, discarding those that deviate from, the standard. Althusser's acknowledgement of the survival of Hegelianism results not in a revision of his own specification of the corpus of historical materialism to bring it into line with the canon, but a restriction of the canon to what is congruent with his preferences regarding the corpus.

Althusser's modification of his previous periodisation of Marxism was subsequently complemented by repudiation of the theoreticist fashion in which the advent of historical materialism had been understood. Deploying the new definition of philosophy and conception of the history of the sciences, in *Reply to John Lewis* and *Elements of Self-Criticism* Althusser admitted that he had substituted an epistemological history of Marxism for a 'materialist' history of Marx's break with 'bourgeois ideology' – a Marxism of Marxism:

> instead of explaining this *historical* fact in all its dimensions – social, political, ideological and theoretical – I reduced it to a simple *theoretical* fact: to the epistemological 'break' which can be observed in Marx's work from 1845 onwards. As a consequence I was led to give a *rationalist* explanation of the 'break', contrasting *truth* and *error* in the form of the speculative distinction between *science* and *ideology*, in the singular and in general. The contrast between Marxism and bourgeois ideology thus became simply a special case of this distinction . . . from this rationalist-speculative drama, the class struggle was practically absent.[72]

Simultaneously and relatedly, Althusser criticised his reduction of Marx's 'philosophical revolution' to the 'epistemological break'. In reality, the former

---

(pp. 91–2). Althusser's attack on the 1859 Preface continues on p. 92, where it is described as 'very ambiguous and (alas!) famous' and Stalin's use of it as '*his reference text*' noted. For more negative remarks on the *Grundrisse*, see pp. 97–8 (presumably Althusser had been obliged finally to confront it as a result of its appearance in French translation in 1967).

[72] Althusser 1976a, p. 106; see also pp. 123–4, 148–9, 156.

was prior to, and a precondition of, the latter.[73] This involved repudiation of the notion – retained in 'Lenin and Philosophy' – that philosophy invariably arrives *post festum*. How did the genesis of historical materialism look now? What were the conditions and determinants of Marx's scientific discovery?

The short answer is that they were both theoretical and extra-theoretical. Althusser's initial reconsideration of the relationship between Marxist science and the complex conjuncture in which it was engendered dates from June 1970. In an essay entitled 'On the Evolution of the Young Marx', he proposed that Marx's *scientific* revolution was based upon his *philosophical* conversion to proletarian class positions in theory; and that this philosophical development was in turn based upon his *political* evolution. Thus, between 1841 and 1845, Marx had progressed politically from a position of 'radical bourgeois liberalism to petty-bourgeois humanism, then to communism'. Philosophically, he had made the transition from Hegel to Feuerbach and thence to 'revolutionary materialism'. During these years, the object of his intellectual labours had changed from law to the state to political economy. Marx's political position, Althusser argued, was 'determinant' at each stage of his evolution, but his philosophical position was 'central', since it 'guarantee[d] the theoretical relation between the political position and the object of Marx's thought'.[74] Marx's shifting philosophical position represented 'the *class theoretical conditions* of his thought'. His philosophical revolution in 1845 had resolved the contradiction – evident in the 1844 *Manuscripts* – between communist political, and Hegelian-Feuerbachian philosophical, stances. The 'revolutionary materialism' heralded in the rupture with Feuerbach gave philosophical expression to his class politics. Politics – Marx's 'ever deeper engagement in the political struggles of the proletariat' – remained determinant. But philosophy assumed centrality, enabling Marx to make his break with bourgeois-ideological conceptions of history, economy and society, and to fashion historical materialism – science of the class struggle which was its condition of possibility:

> For the mechanisms [of class exploitation and domination] to become visible, it is necessary to *leave* these ideologies, that is, to 'settle' account with the philosophical consciousness which is the basic theoretical expression of these

---

[73] Althusser 1976a, p. 68.
[74] Althusser 1976a, p. 158.

ideologies. It is therefore necessary to abandon the theoretical position of the ruling classes, and take up a position from which these mechanisms can become visible: the proletarian standpoint. It is not enough to adopt a proletarian *political* position. This political position must be worked out into a theoretical (philosophical) position so that the causes and mechanisms of what is visible from the proletarian standpoint may be grasped and understood. Without this *displacement*, the science of History is unthinkable and impossible.[75]

It would appear that, if the early Althusser had reduced Marx's philosophical revolution to the epistemological break, the new schema performs the opposite reduction: of the epistemological break to the philosophical revolution. Marxist philosophy is the theoretical representative of the 'proletarian standpoint' from which the 'mechanisms of class exploitation and domination' are *already visible*. The *prise de position* in philosophy acts as a relay between the proletariat's experience (and concomitant spontaneous ideology) and Marxist science. The incipient reduction of science to philosophy and of philosophy to ideology shatters theoreticism and restores historicism. Historical materialism is the theorisation of proletarian vision: of the economic and political class struggle waged against the working class, of the class struggle it wages in return. In sum, the original Althusserian project of endowing historical materialism with an epistemological foundation independent of class consciousness/ experience has been abandoned. In its stead, we have the inconsistent propositions of the necessity and priority of science (a 'process without a subject') and the veracity of proletarian vision. Where once Althusser had effectively denied the sociological genesis of Marxism in order to defend its epistemological status, he now compromised its status in the course of accounting for its genesis.

With *Capital*, it was argued elsewhere, Marx returned to the working-class movement 'in a theoretical form what he took from it in a political and ideological form'. Historical materialism was 'the theoretical effect of a determinant cause': contemporary class struggles. Although *the* science of history (one providing objective knowledge of its object), it was *not* a science among others and could not be 'recognised by everyone' – only by the

---

[75] Althusser 1976a, pp. 159–61; see also pp. 67–70, 107–18.

proletariat and its allies. Workers, indeed, were better equipped to 'read *Capital*' than intellectuals, since it spoke in scientific terms of something they experienced daily: capitalist exploitation.[76]

Althusser's insistence that Marx's rupture with bourgeois ideology was unthinkable without the 'inspiration' of proletarian ideology, and the class struggle in which it was embodied,[77] also offered an explanatory framework for the 'survival' or 'restoration' of ideological elements in work post-dating the foundation of historical materialism. The latter was a '*revolutionary science*' and, as such, could no more instantly abolish its (ideological) pre-history than could a political revolution. Indeed, the theoretical class struggle over the science of history – for and against it – was interminable, a precondition of the progress of Marx's theory, but also a condition for its distortion or regression.[78]

Although, for the most part, Althusser maintained his initial hostility to the Hegelian heritage, he now conceded the implausibility of his earlier account by attempting to specify the positive input of Hegel's philosophy into Marx's doctrine. His first and most detailed reflection on the issue occurs in 'Marx's Relation to Hegel' (January 1968). Restating his conviction that the subject was a theoretico-political question of decisive importance, Althusser returned to *Reading 'Capital'*. Faithful to the contention that Marx's 'inversion' of the Hegelian dialectic was in reality a 'transformation', he reaffirmed the presence in Marx's œuvre of non-Hegelian conceptions of history, social structure and dialectic. Left in the shade, however, had been Marx's positive debt to Hegel: '*the idea of the dialectic*'. The Hegelian dialectic did, after all, contain a 'rational kernel'. Absent from Feuerbach's philosophy, but present in Hegel's, was a theory of history as '*a dialectical process of production of forms*'. If Hegel's conception of history and the dialectic intrinsic to it were inherently teleological, paradoxically Marx was nevertheless indebted to him for the indispensable concept of a 'process *without a subject*'. The conception of history as a process (of alienation) with a subject – Man – was foreign to Hegel, the provenance of left-Hegelian anthropological interpretations of his work, ancient and modern. Abstracting from the teleology inscribed in the negation of the

---

[76] See Althusser 1971, pp. 7–9, 72–4.
[77] Althusser 1976a, p. 121.
[78] Althusser 1976a, pp. 69–72.

negation, it was possible to extract from Hegel the category of 'a process without a subject'. This is what Marx had inherited; and it had permitted a scientific (and philosophical) revolution wherein history was understood (to borrow the title of a note dating from May 1973) as 'a process without a subject or goal(s)'.[79]

Having thus rehabilitated Hegel for theoretical anti-humanism, in 'Lenin before Hegel', Althusser sought to recruit Lenin for his new interpretation of the Marx-Hegel relationship.[80] His manœuvre is, to say the least, audacious: the enlistment of Hegel as a 'proto-Marxist'[81] – and a proto-Althusserian one at that. Commentators have been divided in their reaction to the re-admission of Hegel into the Marxist genealogy. Lucio Colletti and Sebastiano Timpanaro, for example, have construed this departure as a reconciliation with diamat and Hegelianism.[82] Althusser was certainly playing a dangerous philosophical game when, in 1969, he asserted that the 'Marxist tradition was quite correct to return to the thesis of the Dialectics of Nature, which has the polemical meaning (among others) that history is a *process without a subject*'.[83] But the 'rational kernel' he uncovered in Hegel scarcely warrants the remonstrations of Colletti and Timpanaro. The category of 'process without a subject', which had made a brief appearance in *Reading 'Capital'*, represented not a regression to diamat, but an addition to the arsenal of theoretical anti-humanism. Its prominence after 1967 is further evidence of Althusser's opposition to the left-Hegelianism which restricted an all too Hegelian dialectic to history conceived as a process with a subject. Althusser is possibly to be faulted for his reading of Hegel (Colletti considers it 'absurd', whereas Callinicos has defended it).[84] And his analysis of Lenin is certainly tendentious (he effectively proposed a 'Society of Marxist Friends of Lenin's Critique of the Hegelian Dialectic', ignoring the fact that Lenin's proposed 'Society of Materialist Friends of Hegelian Dialectics' had non-Althusserian terms of membership).[85] In contrast to the Italian Marxists, Callinicos has offered a positive evaluation

---

[79] See Althusser 1972, pp. 173–6, 181–6 and Althusser 1976a, pp. 94–9.
[80] See Althusser 1971, pp. 116–19.
[81] Levine 1981, p. 244.
[82] See Colletti 1977, p. 333 and Timpanaro 1980, p. 193.
[83] Althusser 1971, p. 117.
[84] Compare Colletti 1977, p. 333 with Callinicos 1983, p. 52.
[85] See Lenin 1966b, p. 234.

of the domestication of the category within Marxism. For him, it stands between historical materialism and any return to conceiving history as the creation of a collective subject, thus encapsulating Althusser's rupture with orthodox and Western Marxism.[86] As he points out, Althusser's concern to reinstate the class struggle at the centre of Marxism is also involved here. And, with this, we pass from the emendation of his history of Marxism to the amendments he made to his reconstruction of historical materialism.

As early as 1967, Althusser declared the 'two great principles of Marxism' to be: (i) 'it is the masses that make history'; and (ii) 'it is the class struggle that is the motor of history'.[87] His Maoist revision of the 'science of history' c. 1965 consisted essentially in retaining a strict theoretical anti-humanism whilst according an ever increasing role to the class struggle. The outcome was disappointing – a *gauchiste* antidote that was possibly more injurious to historical materialism than the Spinozist/structuralist virus.

At first, the theoreticist 'deviation' was believed not seriously to have affected the exposition of historical materialism.[88] In 1972, Althusser retracted this exemption: 'Very unfortunate consequences resulted as far as the presentation of the *modality* of Marxist science . . . was concerned.'[89] Absent from *Reading 'Capital'* was the 'class struggle and its effects in theory'. Its 'exceptional importance' had neither been appreciated nor registered; it had 'not figure[d] *in its own right'*.[90] Historical materialism had been treated as a science 'among others', whereas, in truth, it was a 'revolutionary *science'* – the science, as Althusser put it elsewhere, of 'the conditions, the mechanisms and the forms of the class struggle'.[91] Althusser confessed a 'flirtation' with 'structuralist terminology', though denying that it had gone any further, and admitted to his (heretical) Spinozism.[92] By harping on structuralism, he counter-attacked, critics had for the most part overlooked his dependence on Spinoza and mistaken quasi-Spinozist propositions for instances of the French ideology

---

[86] See Callinicos 1976, pp. 66–71; Callinicos 1982, p. 141; and Callinicos 1983, p. 93. See also Benton 1984, p. 18.

[87] Althusser 1990, p. 163. See also, e.g., Althusser 1971, pp. 23–4, 67, and 120.

[88] Althusser and Balibar 1970, p. 8.

[89] Althusser 1976a, p. 125.

[90] Althusser 1976a, pp. 130, 146, 148.

[91] Althusser 1976a, p. 115; see also pp. 67, 130–1.

[92] See Althusser 1976a, pp. 126–41.

(an example: 'structural causality', of which Althusser now offered no more than a partial defence).[93] Structuralism was a 'secondary deviation'; and the theory of modes of production had been expressly – and accurately – demarcated from it.[94]

Before charting Althusser's rectifications, mention should be made of an important auto-critique of his own constructions made by Balibar in 1972. This went much further than Althusser was prepared to. Stating that their 'main objective' had been to demonstrate the impossibility of explaining transition ('speaking plainly, social revolution') in evolutionist fashion, Balibar conceded that, in the process of portraying the passage from one mode of production to another as 'a "history" in the strongest sense (*unforeseeable* in the reality of its concrete forms)', he had converted 'non-transition' into a non-history.[95] Balibar now repudiated 'a *general theory* of modes of production' – 'a theory of *the* mode of production in *general* and of its *possible* "variations" ' – as being of 'typologistic or structuralist inspiration'. In addition, he rejected his treatment of historical transition, concluding that there could be no 'general theory' of it.[96]

In contrast to Balibar, Althusser gives the impression that he believed it possible to make amends without being obliged fundamentally to modify his system. The remedy for theoreticism and Spinozism was an injection of the class struggle. (Saül Karsz perhaps captured the later Althusser's position well when he wrote: 'If Marx without Mao is revisionism, Mao without Lenin is leftism.'[97]) The new orthodoxy, presented as the epitome of Marxist-Leninist rectitude, was set out at greatest length in the short *Reply to John Lewis*, via a juxtaposition of the respective theses of Lewis and his critic. To Lewis's proposition that 'it is man who makes history', Althusser counterposes the dictum: 'It is the *masses* who make history.' Against the British Communist's notion that 'Man makes history by "transcending" history' is set the scientific

---

[93] See Althusser 1976a, pp. 126–7 n.

[94] Althusser 1976a, p. 129.

[95] Balibar 1973, pp. 64–5. Balibar remarks: 'It is easy to understand what practical, political reasons (reasons that are more actual than ever) drove us to work in this direction' (p. 64). Althusser had precisely defined 'the *historical fact*' as '*a fact which causes a mutation in the existing structural relations*': Althusser and Balibar 1970, p. 102. See also Althusser 1969a, p. 126 and cf. Anderson 1980, p. 14.

[96] See Balibar 1973, p. 60ff.

[97] Karsz 1974, p. 131, n. 6.

precept: 'The class struggle is the motor of history.' These Marxist-Leninist axioms do not enjoy equal weight, however. For the second displaces the (idealist) question of the subject of history, replacing it with the question of the motor of history and identifying that motor. The second thesis is crucial, because '*it puts the class struggle in the front rank*'. As a consequence, it effects a demarcation between 'revolutionaries' and 'reformists'. Unlike the latter, the former do not disconnect classes and class struggle, appreciating that 'exploitation is already class struggle' and that the class struggle accordingly takes precedence. Thus the first thesis regarding 'the masses' must be subordinated to the second concerning 'the motor of history'.[98]

If reformism must be eschewed, so too must idealism:

> The class struggle does not go in the air, or on something like a football pitch. It is rooted in the mode of production and exploitation in a given class society. You therefore have to consider the *material* basis of the class struggle, that is, the material *existence* of the class struggle. This, in the last instance, is the unity of the relations of production and the productive forces *under* the relations of production in a given mode of production, in a concrete historical social formation. This materiality, in the last instance, is at the same time the 'base' . . . of the class struggle, and its material existence; because exploitation takes place in production, and it is exploitation which is at the root of the antagonism between classes and the class struggle . . . *all the forms of the class struggle are rooted in economic class struggle*. It is on this condition that the revolutionary thesis of the primacy of the class struggle is a materialist one.
>
> When that is clear, the question of the 'subject' of history disappears. History is an immense *natural-human* system in movement, and the motor of history is class struggle. History is a process, and *a process without a subject*.[99]

Idealism is to be guarded against by anchorage of the 'primacy of the class struggle' in the economic base, voluntarism by bringing Maoist axioms under the sway of theoretical anti-humanism. The following interesting situation has emerged. Post-1966, Althusser allowed that the 'masses' – but not 'man' –

---

[98] See Althusser 1976a, pp. 46–50.
[99] Althusser 1976a, pp. 50–1.

made history.[100] (At the same time, he never invoked the slogan of the Cultural Revolution: 'It is the popular masses who create history' – doubtless because of its humanist connotations.) Having made a concession on the fabrication of history, however, Althusser immediately qualified it: the very question of a maker is idealist. On the alert against hydra-headed theoretical humanism, Althusser prioritised the question of the 'motor' of history, reiterating the argument that society is constituted by 'the system of its social relations in which *its* individuals live, work and struggle',[101] thus subordinating the role accorded the masses to the primacy of objective social structures enveloping them. If, in the early work, via structural causality, social formations made and unmade themselves, in the later, the motor of history is also its maker.

Althusser's attack on Lewis's anthropocentric epistemology is instructive in this regard. Associating it with Vico's *verum-factum* principle, in which the identity of maker (man) and made (history) supplies an epistemological guarantee, Althusser insists that history is that much more intractable to apprehension than nature because 'the "masses" are always *separated* from history by the *illusion that they understand it*'.[102] Little or no retreat from the strictures of *Reading 'Capital'* is evident here, Althusser proceeding to advise Lewis of the impropriety of informing the workers that men make history.

How should these developments be judged? Jay suggests that the later Althusser's stress on the centrality of the class struggle – at the economic, political, ideological and theoretical levels – effected a clandestine reinstatement of an expressive concept of totality.[103] All history – and every history – became a history of class struggles; its 'core' and 'centre' was the class struggle. Further, the simultaneous allocation of a constructive role to the masses in history and maintenance of an unqualified theoretical anti-humanism resulted, as Anderson remarks, in 'incoherence', yielding 'no new synthesis' comparable to *Reading 'Capital'*.[104] The 'motor of history' has all the signs of an ad hoc importation designed to disrupt the eternal reproduction inscribed in the

---

[100] See Althusser 1971, pp. 23–4.
[101] Althusser 1976a, p. 53.
[102] Althusser 1976a, pp. 41, 55; see also p. 56.
[103] Jay 1984, p. 419.
[104] Anderson 1983, p. 39.

initial concept of mode of production. In order to conceive 'real history' as 'the process of the reproduction of social formations *and their revolutionary transformation*',[105] Althusser retreated to voluntarism. Paradoxical as it may sound to those accustomed to hear Althusserianism characterised as a 'structural super-determinism',[106] it needs emphasising. In the first Althusserian schema, history was determined but not predetermined. So remorseless was this determination, however, that the twin *bêtes noires* of indeterminacy and predetermination threatened it. This was the problem faced by Balibar and, by his own admission, he failed to resolve it: reproduction became a process without a history, historical transition a process with a goal. The adjustments introduced with a shift to the 'primacy of the class struggle' thus had an 'internal' as well as an 'external' logic. But the remission of 'determinism' was secured at the cost of an equally obstructive voluntarism.

It is only fair to Althusser to point out that this problem is not peculiar to him and that his unsatisfactory solution has numerous precedents. Absent from Marx's 1859 Preface is any discussion of class struggle. Its importance to Marxism, theoretically and politically, is not in doubt; the real question concerns its precise explanatory role. In his own accounts of social change, Marx propounded, without integrating, two general explanatory theses: (i) a 'structural' hypothesis according to which the systemic contradiction between the forces and relations of production is the 'motor of history' (the 1859 Preface provides a succinct presentation of it); and (ii) an 'agential' thesis according to which the class struggle is the 'motor of history' (the *Communist Manifesto* is invoked here). For some Marxists, it is a question of either/or. For others, the problem is to integrate the two axioms in such a way that the inverse perils of economistic and voluntaristic reductionism are avoided. The later Althusser opts exclusively for the second hypothesis. There is a certain irony to this in that the majority of those who adhere to it do so in protest against the (economic) fatalism entailed, so they believe, by the first. Thus, for example, in an article on feudalism in Europe, Rodney Hilton explains his subscription to (ii) by reference both to the demonstrable historical role of the class struggle and to his desire to 'emphasise the positive and creative

---

[105] Althusser 1976a, p. 97 (my emphasis).
[106] Miliband 1984, p. 32.

role of the exploited'.[107] By contrast, Althusser assents to the 'Marxist-Leninist' thesis supposedly enunciated in the *Communist Manifesto* as the basis of theoretical anti-humanism.[108] Despite this, Althusser did not escape voluntarism. Although he 'rooted' political and ideological class struggle in the economic class struggle, he veered from denying the primacy of the productive forces to affirming the primacy of the relations of production, which he further treated as relations of exploitation between social classes (in defiance of the rebuke delivered to Hegelian Marxism in *Reading 'Capital'* for ignoring the prior distribution of the means of production). The effect (and doubtless the absent cause) of the inversion of the primacy thesis was the Maoist discounting of the level of the development of the productive forces in the construction of socialism. In the name of anti-economism and anti-evolutionism, Althusser abandoned a classical tenet of historical materialism, substituting such theses as the dominance of the ideological level and the class struggle waged therein in socialist social formations. On the credit of the Cultural Revolution, elevated into an exemplum, the later Althusser aggravated the voluntarist tendencies already evident in his 1966 essay on China. As Debray once remarked, in the Paris of the late 1960s and early 1970s Maoism was theorised as 'the highest stage of historical rationality'.[109] The theoretical and political consequences of this involution were, as we shall see in the next two chapters, serious. The effect of the circumscription of the relations of production is equally grave. Althusser's conviction was that both the *reproduction* and the *transformation* of social formations are explicable by the ubiquitous class struggle. Yet the explanatory power of the class struggle is limited since, as Callinicos reminds Althusser, it stands in need of explanation itself – precisely one of historical materialism's tasks.[110]

If the 'primacy of class struggle' in reproduction and revolution alike leads to voluntarism, history as a 'process without a subject' is believed by Colletti (anticipating Thompson) to signify that 'history is not the site of any human emancipation' and to betoken Althusser's 'organic sympathy with Stalinism'.[111]

---

[107] Hilton 1984, p. 93.
[108] See Althusser 1976a, pp. 47–9.
[109] Debray 1983, p. 8.
[110] See Callinicos 1982, pp. 158–9.
[111] Colletti 1977, p. 334.

Althusser's propinquity to Stalinism is the subject of Chapter 5. What is the justice of Colletti's first charge? Insofar as Althuser's category precludes any pre-ordained end to history (and, in particular, the 'realisation' or emancipation of a collective or singular subject as its goal), Colletti's view can be endorsed – as a statement of fact. In other words, Althusser is quite right to deny the proposition that history *is* the site of human emancipation. Yet he would also appear to deny that it *might be*, that is, that there *can be* any self-emancipation in history – a proscription which not only covers the past, but extends to the present and future as well. Thus, socialist revolution is not exempt from Althusser's scrutiny of conscious and voluntary human agency – for him (as for Spinoza) the 'asylum of ignorance'. Voluntarist when it comes to class struggle, Althusser courts the charge of structural necessitarianism when it comes to agency.[112] History – social reproduction and transformation – is inexplicable according to either.

It would seem, then, that Althusser opted for the worst of both worlds in retaining strict anti-humanist theoretical protocols while relaxing structural causality to accord an exorbitant role to class struggle. That these two propositions are, moreover, inconsistent only highlights his failure to rectify *For Marx* and *Reading 'Capital'*. Just as his new conception of history fared little better in accounting for its own history than had the theory of theoretical practice, so too it reproduced the aporiae of the earlier conception. Emblematic, perhaps, of the deadlock was the most significant theoretical piece written after 1965, 'Ideology and Ideological State Apparatuses' (1969–70). In 1974, Althusser confessed that in his early work, and under Spinoza's influence, he had made ideology 'the universal element of historical existence'.[113] Despite his efforts at emendation, he was to repeat the error in 1969.

The universal element of historical existence

That Althusser's renewed attention to ideology was in some sense a response to May '68 has been a commonplace of commentary on his work. In March 1969, he remarked of an analysis of the events that it had the merit of posing

---

[112] See Anderson 1980, pp. 21, 58 and Benton 1984, pp. 209–14.
[113] Althusser 1976a, p. 141.

'the problem of the constitution of a *Marxist theory of the mechanisms of ideology*'.[114] The following June, 'Ideology and Ideological State Apparatuses' appeared. Its primary significance resided not in its attempt to constitute a new Marxist theory of ideology (texts in 1964 and 1965 anticipated that); nor in the importance assigned ideology (ditto); nor again, in the theme of ideological class struggle (it was central to 'On the Cultural Revolution'), but, rather, in Althusser's attempt to produced a renovated theory of ideology as part of a new theoretical synthesis. The text published in *La Pensée* in 1970 was composed of two extracts (dated January-April 1969) from a more substantial manuscript entitled *On the Superstructure (Law-State-Ideology)*. This was itself part of an ambitious project, subsequently abandoned, which might be seen as Althusser's attempt to integrate the lessons of 1968 in order to resolve the problems in his original system, and whose confident foreword asserted that 'we are entering an era which will witness the triumph of socialism throughout the world . . . *the revolution is already on the agenda*'.[115] The abandonment of the full-scale work, the publication of extracts from it which took up 'the point of view of reproduction', and the addition of a postscript (dated April 1970) urging adoption of 'the point of view of the class struggle', dramatise the disjunction between Althusser's focus on the maintenance of the capitalist order and his insistence on the possibility of its revolutionary subversion through ideological and political class struggle. For Althusser's study is marked by an unresolved tension between functionalism – an automaticity of social *reproduction* via state apparatuses – and voluntarism – a contingency of social *transformation* via the *deus ex machina* of class struggle.

---

[114] Althusser 1969b, p. 3.

[115] Althusser 1995a, p. 24. The text of *De la superstructure* contains twelve sections: Foreword; What is Philosophy?; What is a Mode of Production?; On the Reproduction of the Conditions of Production; Infrastructure and Superstructure; Law; The State; The Political and Trade Union State Apparatuses; On the Reproduction of the Relations of Production; Reproduction of the Relations of Production and Revolution; The Juridical Ideological State Apparatus; On Ideology. At the end of it, a second volume is promised dealing with: social classes; class struggle; ideologies; the sciences; philosophy; the proletarian class standpoint in philosophy; revolutionary philosophical intervention in scientific practice and in the practice of proletarian class struggle. The aim of the whole work was, as Althusser put it in the foreword, to 'to take stock of Marxist philosophy' that it might fulfil its allotted role as a '*revolutionary weapon*': dusk had fallen and Marxist philosophy was about to take wing (cf. Althusser 1971, pp. 44–6). (I am grateful to Louis Althusser for his permission to consult this text and to Étienne Balibar for making a copy available to me.)

It opened by glossing Marx's famous dictum in his letter to Kugelmann of 11 July 1868.[116] The problem posed is that of social reproduction and, relatedly, social order. The continued existence of any social formation necessitates reproduction of the dominant mode of production therein (its forces and relations of production), which confers unity on it. The productive forces comprise the means of production and labour-power. Reproduction of the former involves reproduction of the material conditions of production (instruments of production and raw materials) – the task of what Marx called Department I. Reproduction of labour-power – to which Althusser rapidly passes – involves more than payment of subsistence wages to workers. For a start, the minimum wage required by workers is historically variable (greater in 1970 than 1870) and their historical needs (for example, for paid holidays) are recognised only as an outcome of class struggle. But, in addition, labour-power must constantly be reproduced in the necessary quantity and equipped with the requisite variety of 'technical skills' and ideological propensities. In capitalist social formations, these are furnished outside the sphere of production – above all, in the education system, but also within the family. A precondition of the reproduction of labour-power, then, is 'the reproduction of its subjection to the ruling ideology': '*it is in and under the forms of ideological subjection that provision is made for the reproduction of the skills of labour power*'.[117]

Thus, Althusser argues, under capitalism the superstructure intervenes decisively in the reproduction of labour-power, hence of the productive forces. What of the relations of production? Since the superstructure likewise plays a role here, Althusser is obliged to revert to his 'old question: what is a society?'. The response is as follows: according to Marx's 'spatial metaphor', every society comprises an infrastructure (the economic base) and a superstructure (the political-legal and ideological levels). The infrastructure is 'determinant' in the last instance; the levels of the superstructure have their own 'indices of effectivity' ('relative autonomy' and 'reciprocal action'). There is, Althusser believes, a positive and a negative aspect to this topography. Positive: it simultaneously nominates the ultimately determinant level and assigns 'effectivity' to the others. Negative: it is 'metaphorical' – hence '*descriptive*'. The remedy is to be sought not in renunciation of the classical

---

[116] Althusser 1971, 123. See Marx and Engels 1975, p. 196.
[117] Althusser 1971a, pp. 123–7.

metaphor, but in theorisation of its (descriptive) content – an operation which must be conducted from the vantage point of *reproduction*.[118]

Althusser's own attempt commences with the political level: the state. According to the Marxist tradition, it is a 'repressive apparatus' and a 'machine' of class domination – a proposition to which Althusser assents. Yet the 'Marxist-Leninist "theory" of the State' is also descriptive and must be supplemented by distinctions (i) between state *power* (the objective of political class struggle) and state *apparatus* (the 'machinery' of class rule – police, army, courts, prison, and so forth – which may partially or wholly survive seizure of state power); and (ii) between the 'Repressive State Apparatus' (RSA) and the 'Ideological State Apparatuses' (ISAs).[119] Althusser supplies a provisional list of the ISAs: churches, schools, the family, legal institutions, the political system and parties, trade unions, the media, cultural forms.[120] The majority of these are '*private* institutions', but this does not disqualify designation of them as pertaining to the state, it is argued, since the private/public distinction is 'internal' to bourgeois law and the state is 'above the law'; functionally, they are state apparatuses.[121] It is their modality that distinguishes them from the RSA. Whereas it operates largely (though not exclusively) by *repression*, they function primarily by *ideology*, and only secondarily by repression.[122] The common purpose of the diverse superstructural institutions labelled ISAs confers 'unity' on them, for 'the ideology by which they function is always in fact unified, despite its diversity and contradictions, *beneath the ruling ideology*' – that of the ruling class. In order to retain state power for an extended period, a class must achieve and preserve '*hegemony over and in*' the ISAs, which can be both the '*stake*' and the '*site*' of class struggle.[123]

Having set out these hypotheses, Althusser returns to the question of the reproduction of the relations of production, proposing that it is largely 'secured by the exercise of State power in the State Apparatuses'. The RSA and ISAs do not have equal weight in the process, however. Operating under the

[118] Althusser 1971a, pp. 128–31.
[119] Althusser 1971, pp. 131–4.
[120] Althusser 1971, p. 136. In a note, Gramsci is credited by Althusser with being the 'only one who went any distance in the road I am taking'.
[121] See Althusser 1971, pp. 137–8.
[122] Althusser 1971, p. 138.
[123] Althusser 1971, pp. 139–40.

'commanding unity' of the policies implemented by the political representatives of the ruling class, the RSA ensures its 'political conditions' by force. Protected by the RSA, the ISAs play the predominant role, preponderant among them, in capitalist societies, being the education system. (Althusser conjectures that, in the capitalist era, the 'School-Family couple' has replaced the 'Church-Family couple' of feudalism.) At school, a captive audience is endowed with the appropriate skills and dispositions for the various class 'roles' its members will perform thereafter, via the transmission/inculcation of the dominant ideology. The 'vital result' – for capitalism – of the reproduction of the exploitative relations of production is primarily obtained in the education system.[124]

The article proceeds to a discussion of ideology. Rejecting the theory offered by Marx in *The German Ideology* as non-Marxist, and signalling his intention to initiate a theory of 'ideology *in general*', Althusser adopts a formulation from the 'work of the break' – 'ideology has no history' – but imparts novel content to it:

> the peculiarity of ideology is that it is endowed with a structure and a
> functioning such as to make it a non-historical reality, i.e., an omni-historical
> reality, in the sense in which that structure and functioning are immutable,
> present in the same form throughout what we can call history. . . .

Electing discretion over valour, Althusser confines his discussion to history as defined in the *Communist Manifesto*. The admission of an 'organic link' between his perspectives on ideology and Freud's on the perdurability of the unconscious (which leads Althusser to amend his proposition to '*ideology is eternal*') reinstates the permanence.[125] By way of introduction to his main contention, Althusser presents two preliminary theses. First, 'ideology represents the imaginary relationship of individuals to their real conditions of existence'. Already familiar from 'Marxism and Humanism', this asserts that ideology does not represent the real relations regulating people's existence, but their imaginary relationship to them. The necessity of this 'imaginary' relation is

---

[124] Althusser 1971, pp. 141–9. In *De la superstructure*, Althusser refers to a forthcoming book – presumably by himself – entitled *Écoles* (Althusser 1995a, p. 114, n. 57). It never materialised. Baudelot and Establet 1971 sought to substantiate and develop Althusser's theses.

[125] Althusser 1971, pp. 151–2.

postponed to later discussion. Meanwhile, a second thesis is proposed: 'the materiality of ideology'. The imaginary relation has a 'material existence', contrary to what Althusser calls the 'ideology of ideology'. In the latter, an individual is a subject endowed with a consciousness wherein the ideas in which he believes are formed and preserved – whence derives (or at least should) action in conformity with those beliefs. Thus, a 'good Catholic' not only believes in God, but attends church on specified days, goes to confession and communion, contributes to the collection plate, and used to eat fish on Fridays. Althusser proposes to invert the order of this 'idealist scheme', turning humanism's master-categories against it:

> where only a single subject . . . is concerned, the existence of the ideas of his belief is material in that *his ideas are his material actions inserted into the material practices governed by material rituals which are themselves defined by the material ideological apparatus from which derive the ideas of that subject.*

The subject is, as it were, more acted than acting. By participating of his 'own free will' in the practical rituals of, say, the Catholic Church, he subjects himself to the ideology subscribed in them. The pivot of this schema is the category of the subject – from which Althusser infers two conclusions: 'there is no practice except by and in ideology' and 'there is no ideology except by the subject and for subjects'.[126]

The stage is now set for the third and 'central' thesis: 'the category of the subject is constitutive of all ideology *but . . . the category of the subject is only constitutive of ideology insofar as all ideology has the function (which defines it) of "constituting" concrete individuals as subjects'.* The basic function of ideology is to transform individuals into subjects, inverting, via 'interpellation', the real relations between individuals and social formation into an imaginary relation wherein they live the relation with their real conditions of existence as if they were determinant of them – as if they were *constitutive*, rather than *constituted*, subjects. In other words, ideology constitutes individuals as conscious subjects of society ('free subjectivities, centres of initiatives') so as to enforce their *subjection* to the social order and its demands on them. Employing Lacan's concept of the 'mirror-phase', Althusser suggests that the (self-)recognition inherent in the constitution of subjects, and the illusions of

---

[126] Althusser 1971, pp. 153–9.

autonomy and uniqueness characteristic of subject-status, pertain to the realm of the 'imaginary'.[127]

Christian theology is taken as paradigmatic of the invariant structure of ideology (the secret of anthropology is theology):

> The duplicate mirror-structure of ideology ensures simultaneously:
> 1. the interpellation of 'individuals' as subjects;
> 2. their subjection to the Subject;
> 3. the mutual recognition of subjects and Subject, the subjects' recognition of each other, and finally the subject's recognition of himself;
> 4. the absolute guarantee that everything really is so, and that on condition that the subjects recognise what they are and behave accordingly, everything will be all right: Amen – 'So be it'.
>
> Result: caught in this quadruple system of interpellation as subjects, of subjection to the Subject, of universal recognition and of absolute guarantee, the subjects 'work', they 'work by themselves' in the vast majority of cases, with the exception of the 'bad subjects' who on occasion provoke the intervention of one of the detachments of the (repressive) State apparatus. But the vast majority of (good) subjects work all right 'by themselves', i.e. by ideology (whose concrete forms are realised in the Ideological State Apparatuses).

Via the mechanism of interpellation, the 'subjected beings' who are social agents (mis-)recognise themselves as free, constitutive subjects at the 'centre' of their world. The reality occluded from and by this drama of recognition is the reproduction of exploitative relations of production and the oppressive relations dependent on them. Ideology, embodied in and transmitted by ISAs, involves 'misrecognition/ignorance' of the real relations which shape and dominate the lives of concrete men and women. By means of ideology, which binds individuals to the socials structure, and one of whose typical effects is its own denegation, an exploitative and oppressive social order is reproduced, without having to declare itself for what it is.[128]

In the postscript appended for publication, Althusser signals the 'abstractness' of his propositions. First, reproduction of the relations of reproduction is a

---

[127] Althusser 1971, pp. 160–5.
[128] Althusser 1971, pp. 168–70; see also Althusser 1976a, p. 95.

matter of class struggle. Given that it can only be 'realised' through class struggle, the effects of the ideological mechanism advanced to explain it depend on concrete conditions; they are not pre-given. The 'point of view of reproduction' is ultimately inseparable from the 'point of view of the class struggle'. Secondly, focus on the mechanism of 'ideology in general' leaves unanswered the question of *class ideologies*: 'Whoever says class struggle of the ruling class says resistance, revolt and class struggle of the ruled class.' The ISAs are neither the 'realisation' of ideology in general, nor the unimpeded realisation of the dominant ideology. A 'very bitter and continuous class struggle' is required in order to install and preserve the ISAs and, therewith, hegemony. Moreover, the matrix of class ideologies and ideological class struggles lies not in the ISAs, but in 'the social classes at grips in the class struggle: . . . their conditions of existence, their practices, their experience of the struggle, etc.'[129]

Does Althusser's essay – always suggestive and often brilliant – fundamentally rectify the problems associated with his earlier texts on ideology? The answer, surely, is no. One result of Althusser's original elective affinity with Spinoza had been a theory of ideology in which its 'practico-social' function in class society was dependent upon its provision of false conceptions of the world. The unremittingly mystifying effects of ideology meant that it constituted a 'social cement' ensuring cohesion and reproduction. Ideology was both an invariable component of any society and invariant in its structure. Only in the subject-less discourse of science could its illusions be shattered and 'real conditions of existence' known. If this is correct, then a marked feature of the new theory is its replication, in certain essentials, of the old one. The importance of the ideological superstructure (hence the extra-economic) in social reproduction had been highlighted by the Cultural Revolution in the East and May '68 in the West. Rather than acknowledge its pertinence in ad hoc fashion, Althusser essayed a new theoretical synthesis. The upshot of his adoption of the 'point of view of reproduction' was a reworked theory of ideology still dependent on Lacan and Spinoza,[130] and whose functionalism

---

[129] Althusser 1971, pp. 170–3.
[130] See Althusser 1971, p. 164 for Althusser's election of Spinoza as the precursor of the properly Marxist conception of ideology. It should be noted that Althusser makes it quite clear that he is not exempting scientists or Marxist theoreticians from 'being in ideology'; all men and women are 'ideological animals' (pp. 162, 164).

undermined its likely *maoisant* ambition theoretically to found the paramountcy of ideological class struggle. A conjoint theoretical and political intervention, Althusser's text was theoretically flawed and, doubtless inadvertently, politically pessimistic, ideology proving as resilient as ever. In *Reading 'Capital'*, the economic structure reproduced itself and its superstructural conditions of existence to eternity. At the same time, in the form of 'fetishism', ideology became well-nigh coextensive with social relations. In the new account, reproduction of the relations of production, and therewith of the social formation, is effected by the ideology materialised in the ISAs and inculcated in social agents by them. The actual institutions discharging this function are of limited relevance, since ideology is an omni-historical reality with an invariant structure and function, generating the 'useful illusion' (Nietzsche) of subject-hood through which subjection is accomplished. Theoretical humanism is incorporated as the paradigm of ideology-in-general, the subject-form as the ideological effect par excellence: *'There are no subjects except for and by their subjection.'*[131] Thus Althusser's theory peremptorily inverts humanism, equating subjectification/subjectivity with subjection and ascribing to the structural-systemic level the agency denied at that of the subject/individual.

The theoretical consequences of the form taken by this particular emphasis on 'consent', rather than 'coercion', in the maintenance of capitalist exploitation were two-fold. First, as Callinicos following Hirst remarks, Althusser slides into 'ideologism', reducing the relations of production to inter-subjective relations.[132] Secondly, the 'point of view of reproduction' trumps the 'point of view of the class struggle'. Or, rather, in the class struggle in ideology the cards are always stacked in favour of the ruling class, because its particular interests coincide with the universal functional requirements of social reproduction. No space is left for oppositional ideology; little efficacy can be assigned the oppositional ideologies Althusser nonetheless posits. His attempt to ameliorate 'ideologism' (and incipient voluntarism) by reference back to 'the *total process* of the realization of the reproduction of the relations of production' (including the 'processes of production and circulation') remained

---

[131] Althusser 1971, p. 169.
[132] See Callinicos 1982, p. 76.

unelaborated; while his causal prioritisation of class struggle was perhaps part of the problem rather than a solution.[133]

In his 'Self-Criticism' Balibar suggested that the properly Marxist theory of ideology had become possible with 'Mao Tse-Tung and his period (on the practical basis of the "cultural revolution")'.[134] We have already seen Althusser in his text of 1966 greeting events in China as the implementation of Marxist principles regarding ideology – an application which would give impetus to theoretical research. His essay of 1969 can in part be taken as an attempt to provide rigorous theorisation of the inchoate principles officially underpinning the Great Proletarian Cultural Revolution – a reconstruction of historical materialism attuned to the characteristic concerns and emphases of Maoism. The ascription of dominance to the ideological superstructure in socialist social formations is controversial enough. The voluntarist wager was that ideological class struggle was the crucible in which the future took shape – impelling progress towards communism or, alternatively, impeding it and facilitating regression to 'state capitalism'. The transfer of this schema from East to West – its projection onto capitalist states – produces analogous aberrations, with some surprising political consequences.

Althusser's inflation of the strategic role of the ideological was accompanied by an expansion of the state – in the form of the ISAs – to cover everything from play-schools to political parties. Therewith the state was emptied of existence as an objective structure and diffused into *any* institution or social form, public or private, which contributes to social cohesion and reproduction. The political superstructure (the state and its apparatuses), like the ideological, ceases to be a superstructure and becomes ubiquitous, coterminous with social relations. The result, as Anderson points out, of this attenuation of the state proper is the erasure of the distinction between state and 'civil society', thereby 'undermin[ing] any scientific attempt to define the specificity of bourgeois democracy in the West'.[135] The potential for ultra-leftist political deductions

---

[133] Althusser 1971, pp. 170–2; see also pp. 140, n. 11; 141, n. 12. Cf. Anderson 1980, pp. 54–6. The criticism of Althusser's essay attempted here is to be distinguished from those that adjudge its author *politically* complicit with its *theoretical* results (whether out of affiliation to Stalinism, or membership of the academy, or both); see the pertinent remarks in Pêcheux 1982, p. 214.

[134] Balibar 1973, p. 57.

[135] Anderson 1977, p. 34.

from the ISAs scheme is clear. For it obscures (or can) important distinctions between various forms of capitalist state – most crucially, between bourgeois democracy and fascism. What, to say the least, are pertinent differences are rendered indifferent. Althusser stopped short of any such dementia, naturally. But that his fusion of state and the totality of ideological and political institutions in conformity with Maoism could licence it, is incontrovertible. Paradoxically, however, an antipodal political conclusion – one that was anathema to Althusser – could be derived from his theses – and was. Designed to account for 'that subtle everyday domination beneath which can be glimpsed, in the forms of political democracy . . . what Lenin, following Marx, called the dictatorship of the bourgeoisie', Althusser's theory can offer theoretical sustenance to a political strategy which declines his own impeccably Leninist conclusions: Eurocommunism.[136] As we shall see in Chapter 6, the leader of the Spanish Communist Party, Santiago Carrillo, was to exploit its theses in support of a gradualist strategy of 'democratisation' of the capitalist state. Thus, an unintended consequence of Althusser's dissolution of the state is to evacuate 'revolution' of its Leninist meaning, transforming it into a process of 'revolutionisation' which can be construed in either Maoist or Eurocommunist fashion.

Although enormously influential in French and British Marxism, Althusser's paper has been criticised from all sides. Under the banner of Maoism, ex-Althusserian Rancière accused it of theorising the 'necessary domination of bourgeois ideology' and constituting an '*ultra-left Platonism*'; while, under that of revisionism, post-Althusserian Hirst, despite paying tribute to its originality, detected 'economism', 'class essentialism', 'functionalism', and a pre-Freudian notion of the subject.[137] Somewhat surprisingly, it has been left to an unabashedly Hegelian Marxist – Fredric Jameson – to characterise Althusser's initiative as 'the first new and as yet insufficiently developed

---

[136] See Althusser 1971, pp. 133, 135 and cf. Anderson 1977, pp. 36–9. In *De la superstructure*, Althusser had gone out of his way to insist that '[a]t at time when everyone is asking themselves abut the "transition" to socialism, it is necessary to recall *that there is no parliamentary road to socialism*. It is the masses who make revolutions and not deputies – even if the Communists and their allies fleetingly and miraculously achieve a parliamentary majority' (Althusser 1995a, p. 137).
[137] See Rancière 1974, pp. 143, 146; Hirst 1979, pp. 40–73. An excellent summary of these and other criticisms can be found in Benton 1984, pp. 96–107.

conception of the nature of ideology since Marx and Nietzsche'.[138] At about the same time Jameson was writing these words, Althusser was penning a 'Note on the ISAs' in which he rejected the charge of functionalism, arguing that insufficient attention had been paid to his postscript, wherein the '*primacy of the class struggle*' had been categorically affirmed.[139] By 1979, however, he was apparently no longer committed to the concept of ISAs.[140] The 'ISAs decade', as it has been dubbed by Michael Gane,[141] was over. But this is anticipating. Our next concern is not the career of Althusser's concept, but the time and place of its conception.

Paris in Spring

'Like everyone else in France, we were caught unawares by the events of May '68', Sartre reminisced with de Beauvoir in 1974.[142] The contrast between the modesty with which he, for example, entered into fraternal colloquy with the insurgent students and the silence of Althusser has plagued the latter's reputation ever since. Two of the less spectacular graffiti to appear on the walls of the Latin Quarter said it all: *À quoi sert Althusser? Althusser, Plekhanov, même combat!* That his absence was in fact due to illness is somewhat beside the point. For, in March 1969, he wrote two analyses of May – a letter to Macciocchi and a reply to an article by Michel Verret of the PCF – whose propositions have generated considerable antagonism. When, in 1976, Callinicos concluded that, over the Paris Spring, Althusser had 'returned meekly to the

---

[138] Jameson 1977, pp. 393–4.

[139] See Althusser 1983, pp. 455–6. Althusser also took the opportunity to reject the criticism that he had identified political parties (including revolutionary ones) as ISAs, thus assimilating them to the state. In *De la superstructure* (Althusser 1995a, p. 137), apparently with one eye across the Channel, he had already observed that on his account the PCF was not 'reduced to the role of executor of the will of the bourgeois state, or to the role of Her Majesty's Opposition'. In 1983, p. 457, Althusser writes: '*I have never written that a political party is an ideological state apparatus. I have even said something quite different* (if only briefly, I admit), namely that the political parties are only "components" of a specific ideological state apparatus: of the *political* ideological state apparatus, which realises the political ideology of the ruling class, so to speak, in its "constitutional regime" (. . . the parliamentary-representative régime under the bourgeoisie in its "liberal" phases).' For his discussion of the political ideological state apparatus, see Althusser 1983, pp. 457–60.

[140] See Therborn 1980, p. 85.

[141] See Gane 1983.

[142] See de Beauvoir 1984, p. 371.

fold',[143] he probably spoke for the majority of revolutionary socialists. When the time of politics intersected with – indeed, outstripped – the time of theory, Althusser's disconcertment is evident. 'In political, ideological and philosophical struggle, the words are also weapons, explosives or tranquillisers and poisons', he had told an interlocutor in November 1967.[144] To categorise Althusser's words of 1969 as tranquillisers or poisons would be to mimic the rather melodramatic scenario of Althusser's second definition of philosophy. But whatever else they were, they were certainly not incendiary.

No rehearsal of the course of the 'revenge of history'[145] that was May is possible here. The explosion detonated by de Gaulle's attempt to 'make France marry her century' has been documented countless times. One fact is agreed on: 'Paris was not Petrograd; May did not reach October.'[146] Whether it could have been, and might have done, are questions that have been debated with more or less vehemence ever since. Rather than enter into the debate, we shall simply note that the PCF, engaged prior to May in electoral negotiations with Mitterrand's Federation of Left Democratic Socialists, did not simply refuse its revolutionary vocation: it utterly failed as a reformist organisation.[147]

What – so far as we can gauge – was Althusser's position on the eve of May? In her autobiography, Macciocchi quotes him as remarking some time in 1967: 'there is a contradiction between what I write and the political situation – between the theory which I seek to advance and the strategy of the Communist parties.'[148] This conforms to the analysis presented here. Althusser's position was well to the left of his party's official line. Enthusiastic about the Cultural Revolution, and initially far from hostile to those of his followers who had broken with the 'revisionist' PCF, he elected to remain within the Party, conducting a radicalisation of his own positions at once incompatible with its gradualist horizons and congruent with

---

[143] Callinicos 1976, p. 95.
[144] Althusser 1971, p. 24.
[145] Sève 1984, p. 145: a somewhat incongruous remark, of course, coming from the PCF's official philosopher.
[146] Anonymous 1968, p. 1. For other contemporary treatments, see Seale and McConville's informative narrative in their 1968 and Quattrocchi and Nairn's evocative 1968.
[147] See Hobsbawm 1982, pp. 240–1. On the day Althusser read his 'Lenin and Philosophy' at the Sorbonne (24 February 1968), the PCF and the FGDS had made their 'common declaration'.
[148] Macciocchi 1983, p. 30.

the ascendant Maoism of its opponents. That he retained revolutionary hopes
of the contemporary situation is evident from the first letter in his published
correspondence with Macciocchi. Dated 3 February 1968, it advised here that
'the present period holds out infinite possibilities and resources':

> We have been so conditioned to underestimate things that both our bodies
> and our spirits are wrapped in a Nessus's shirt. Even when we think we
> are overestimating, we still underestimate. The masses are potentially
> (potentially: in fact – but no one gives them the means) far *ahead* of 'us'.[149]

In the second week of May 1968, the French 'masses' confirmed Althusser's
conjecture. When, that August, he was well enough to resume his
correspondence, he naturally turned his attention to the events. Perceiving
in them 'the first stage of a process that is going to take a long time to play
itself out', Althusser pondered the 'big question': 'which parts of the working
class really wanted, politically, to go beyond the material benefits which were
won?'; and stated his conviction that the 'younger workers . . . were ready to
go very far indeed' and that 'next time' the older ones 'will probably be
willing to go further'. As for the June election results (the Communists and
Socialists were decisively beaten), they were 'fragile' and formed 'a part of
the "lesson of reality" concerning the parliamentary road'.[150] A few months
later, Althusser reminded his correspondent that:

> A Communist Party must have a 'mass' revolutionary political line . . .
> [which] unite[s], in the closest possible fashion, 'theory and practice': in
> other words, concrete analysis of the concrete situation (carried out by
> applying Marxist science in concrete political investigation) and 'the masses',
> who are, in the final analysis, the only ones who can make history.[151]

Put simply, this letter reveals its author as an Althusserian Maoist. What did
Althusser, partisan of 'concrete analysis' and the 'mass line', make of May
'68 when he come to meditate on it the following March?

Althusser's long letter commenced with the observation that:

> something of great importance happened in May, something of the greatest
> importance for revolutionary prospects in the 'capitalist countries of the

---

[149] Macciocchi 1973b, p. 4.
[150] Macciocchi 1973b, pp. 295–6.
[151] Macciocchi 1973b, p. 300.

West', something which *must* have repercussions on our policies, or else our policies risk being 'dragged along' by events. And I do not mean by the events of May, which are now a part of the past, but by present and future events which, one day, are going to go far beyond those of May.[152]

This promising opening is rapidly disappointed by what follows. In effect, Althusser disavows the militant temper of his previous letters and utilises his own concepts in such a way as to narrow, though by no means totally bridge, the political gulf between him and his party. First, via a distinction between chronological and historical order, he insists – as though it were a novelty – on the predominance of the general strike (which saw ten million workers on strike by 22 May); praises the PCF for its insight in appreciating this fact; and criticises the students for 'erasing' it from the record.[153] Secondly, May constituted a 'historic *encounter*' – not a 'fusion' – between working-class revolt and student insurgency. For the requisite fusion to transpire in the future, the students would have '*to come a very long way* from where they presently are, and the Workers' Movement (yes, it too) will also have to move a certain distance'. Whereas the students had launched leftist slogans, the workers had chanted 'defensive political slogans' and voiced their immediate economic demands, thereby revealing a 'discrepancy' between the two which had nothing to do with the leaderships of the PCF and CGT, but which, on the contrary, dramatised the distance between the entire working class and their 'utopian' petty-bourgeois juniors. The dénouement is virtually construed as a victory:

> *above all*, the working class now had etched on its memory (and this is a *definitive* inscription) the knowledge that the bosses, the Government and the state apparatus had been thrown into stark fear overnight by the action of the masses, that action was therefore possible, and that such action, one day, could lead to something that the working class had heard spoken of – since the Paris Commune, since 1917 in Russia and 1949 in China: the *Proletarian Revolution*.[154]

Having posited the determinant role of the general strike and the distance between workers and students, Althusser proposed a third thesis. The

---

[152] Macciocchi 1973b, p. 302.
[153] Macciocchi 1973b, pp. 302–3.
[154] Macciocchi 1973b, pp. 306–10.

so-called student movement was, in reality, a heterogeneous phenomenon, composed of diverse 'middle strata' and dominated by *'petty-bourgeois ideology'*.[155] Noting the impetus given to this 'international movement' by contemporary anti-imperialist struggles (Algeria, Cuba, Vietnam), and the global 'defeat' of bourgeois ideology, Althusser identified it as an *'ideological revolt'* mainly directed against what he would shortly nominate the educational ISA. As such, it was 'objectively *progressive'*, playing a *'positive role'* in the anti-imperialist struggle. This, however, raised the central problem facing it: the conditions and time-scale of its merger with the workers' movement.[156]

At this stage, Althusser registered the loss of 'contact' between the Communist parties and students/young intellectuals – a state of affairs which pre-existed May. By way of causes, he cited the impact of the Algerian War and the Cultural Revolution (including the CPC's 'scissionist slogans'), recommending further investigation. His main concern was that as a result the young had been tempted into *'petty-bourgeois* leftism'. Invoking Lenin, he urged a corrective strategy combining detailed analysis of the events and patient education of the students that they might see the errors of their utopian ways. Thus enlightened, they would be ready 'to unite with the working class, to recognise the principle . . . of the latter's *leadership* of the revolutionary struggle'.[157] Althusser's letter closed with a description of May as 'the *most significant event in Western History* since the Resistance and the victory over Nazism'.[158]

Before commenting on Althusser's analysis, a few words must be said about 'On Michel Verret's Article on the "Student May"' (published in *La Pensée* in June 1969). In the course of his assault on Althusser, Rancière justly remarks the difference in tone between the two pieces (both dated 15 March).[159]

---

[155] Macciocchi 1973b, p. 311. The following variants are listed: 'the *dominant* libertarian anarchism, but also Trotskyism, anarcho-syndicalism, Guevarism, and the ideology of the Chinese Cultural Revolution'.

[156] Macciocchi 1973b, pp. 312–15.

[157] Macciocchi 1973b, pp. 316–19.

[158] Macciocchi 1973b, p. 320.

[159] See Rancière 1974, p. 136. Rancière explains it by the fact that one text was intended for external consumption, the other for internal. Things may not be so straightforward. In her 1983, p. 368, Macciocchi claims that Althusser, pressurised by the PCI via the intermediary of the PCF, withdrew his letters at the last moment from the French edition of her book, having failed to persuade her to renounce publication of it in France.

For, although the article reiterates the point that May was primarily the *Mai des prolétaires*, Althusser here undertook a defence of 'our student comrades' against his fellow-Communist's swingeing criticism of them, insisting on the importance and progressiveness of their revolt, emphasising the need for 'unity in action' with them, reminding his readers that Lenin considered 'leftism' appreciably less dangerous than 'rightism', and advising Verret of the suspicion in which the PCF was held by many students for historical reasons.[160] Their actions, he writes, were 'sometimes adventurist, but courageous and even heroic'.[161] If they were to be criticised for their 'errors', for its part the PCF should thoroughly analyse the causes of its 'loss of contact' with them, not hesitating to admit and rectify its own errors where necessary.[162]

Notwithstanding the implicit qualifications made to the Italian letter by the French article, judgement on Althusser's written analysis of May '68 must be negative. To be sure, his recognition of the positive importance of May is commendable in comparison with the PCF's desire to put the crisis (and concomitant challenge to its political authority) behind it as soon as possible and return to popular frontist business as usual. Yet herein lies the 'discrepancy'. Althusser's own reflections are hardly commensurate with an event characterised as 'the most significant ... in Western history since the Resistance and the victory over Nazism'. They cannot be described as a 'concrete analysis', since they abstract from the role of the PCF. In fixing on the action of the student movement to the exclusion of any discussion of either the record of his own party or the course of the general strike, Althusser's analysis has the paradoxical effect of reinstating the primacy of the 'student May' it appropriately commenced by denying. In 'Student Problems', he had followed Lenin in insisting that a Communist party 'must not be at the *same level* ... as [a] trade union, but *in advance of it*'.[163] In May, the PCF was on a par with the CGT; and both lagged behind sections of the working class – even at the level of immediate economic demands. When Althusser invoked the discrepancy between the students' 'dreams' and the workers' 'demands', implicitly exonerating the role of the Communist organisations by reference

---

[160] See Althusser 1969b, pp. 4; 6–7; 10, n. 3; 12–13.
[161] Althusser 1969b, p. 11.
[162] Althusser 1969b, pp. 12–13.
[163] Althusser 1964a, p. 110.

to the latter, it is he who is inverting the historical order. The PCF and CGT did everything they could to keep the general strike, which lasted for a month, on an economistic track, jumping at the Grenelle Agreements of 27 May – only to be spurned by the rank and file. The real discrepancy, as one of Althusser's earlier letters hints, was between the horizons of both students *and* a significant proportion of the working class, on the one hand, and those of the PCF and CGT on the other. Even were Althusser's point correct, the spectacle of a proponent of the 'mass line' accepting that a revolutionary political party satisfy itself with returning ten million workers to work forthwith is arresting. What is the raison d'être of a revolutionary party armed with Marxist theory but to know when an objectively favourable situation obtains – and act accordingly?

The naïveté of Althusser's analysis lies here: in the assumption – against all the evidence – that the PCF was still such a party. For, if some of the students were deluded ultra-leftists, then the PCF was sub-Kautskyist until forced out of its immobility by manifestly more advanced sections of the working class and Kautskyist thereafter. 'Fusion', it is true, did not occur. Yet Althusser might have noticed that the PCF, competing with bourgeois parties in vilification of the students ('agents of bourgeois adventurism', and so forth), worked overtime to sabotage any possibility of it. Whether May was or was not a revolutionary or pre-revolutionary situation is debatable. That the PCF interposed itself between the French social order and the mass movements contesting it from below, thereby inhibiting further development of the challenge, is not.[164] Such vanguardist illusions as the students entertained had their source precisely in the PCF's abstention from the avant-garde role Althusser bizarrely continued to accord it. It may once have spoken of revolution. Wherever else it heard revolution 'spoken of' in 1968, the French working class did not hear it from the lips of PCF spokesmen. Had Althusser returned to the Resistance – the penultimate 'most significant event in Western history' – he might have discovered the founding moment of the political orientation more or less sustained by the PCF up to, and during, May '68. To maintain that May was the not the right time, but 'one day . . .' (revolution *sine die*); to harbour the slightest illusion that MM Waldeck Rochet, Marchais

---

[164] See the observations in Debray 1978a, pp. 142–3.

and Séguy were constrained by the economism of the workers; to put the onus on rectifying student 'errors' – these are propositions which say little for the virtues of 'theory', since they prohibit comprehension of the 'concrete situation' during (and after) May. The PCF *was* 'dragged along by events' – and responded by trying to drag them down to its level.

To blame theory would of course be to do it an injustice. Whilst signalling a measure of dissent on certain issues, Althusser utilised – and deformed – his own repertoire of concepts to produce an analysis, proximate to the PCF's own, of a social dynamic in which it participated only to frustrate. 'We didn't lose our heads', Waldeck Rochet congratulated his Central Committee in July 1968, in a report that should have disabused Althusser about the PCF the (non-existent) 'next time'. Althusser, Macciocchi writes, 'fell ill in the very midst of May, caught between the revolt he had invoked and the reality of its configuration'.[165] Possibly hyperbolical, this comment nevertheless captures the contradictions of his position, exacerbated thereafter. Althusser's Marxism and May '68: *un rendez-vous manqué.*

For Rancière, in 1968 Althusserianism revealed itself to be a 'philosophy of order' and perished *la nuit des barricades.* Before 1968 Althusser had concealed his 'heterodoxy' behind 'orthodoxy'; after May, vice versa.[166] That this was not how all Maoists saw it is sufficiently attested by Ranicère's book, written to disillusion those who still claimed Althusser for their own.[167] Nevertheless, to his ex-disciples and many others, Althusser was the lost leader. Emerging from May profoundly transformed ideologically, and soon to amalgamate with other leftist currents to form the Gauche prolétarienne, leading lights of the UJC would henceforth abandon their attempt to detach him from the PCF and seek an informal alliance with other Parisian *maîtres à penser* (Sartre, Foucault, and so on). As we shall see in Chapter 6, the *gauchiste* harvest of May '68 was eventually to prove detrimental to the whole French Left. Ten years on, Althusser would condemn the PCF for its behaviour in 1968: 'the party deliberately cut itself off from the student and petty-bourgeois masses,

---

[165] Macciocchi 1983, p. 359.
[166] Rancière 1974, pp. 9–10, 136–7.
[167] Interestingly, it was to be described by Althusser himself in 1978 as 'very honest and, on many points, judicious': Althusser 1978b, p. 8.

because it did not have control over them, and pressurised the working class to restrict its activity to material demands'.[168] But it was too little too late.

The '*ruptural unity*' theorised in 'Contradiction and Overdetermination' nearly came to pass in France in 1968 – only to be passed up by its theoretician. The 'most important event in Western history' since 1945 found Althusser politically wanting. Thereafter, publicly loyal to his party's domestic horizons, Althusser preserved his revolutionary credentials by executing a rectification of *For Marx* and *Reading 'Capital'* conformable to Maoism, investing his political hopes in the evolution of the People's Republic. Subjected to identical criticisms from the Maoist Left after May '68 as he had faced from the Communist Right before it, Althusser reneged on central aspects of his system. In place of a new system, he offered what were essentially *pièces de circonstance* notable for their simultaneous fidelity to questionable components of the earlier work and to desultory Chinese verities. Employing an increasingly hortatory rhetoric of the class struggle, he retreated from the highly sophisticated and original versions of Marxist philosophy and historical materialism of 1962–5 into the schematic Marxism-Leninism of 1968–74. The reconceptualisation of dialectical materialism as a 'new practice of philosophy', and of historical materialism as the 'revolutionary science' of history, combined with the abandonment of epistemology and the retention of theoretical anti-humanism, resulted not only in impoverishment but in an incoherence fatal to the subsequent fortunes of Althusser's Marxism. To compare the pamphlet enclosed with *Réponse à John Lewis* – 'Qu'est-ce que la collection Théorie?' – with the original programme of the *Théorie* series is to measure the distance travelled in eight years. 'On progresse!', it proclaims. Fourteen years on, this phase of Althusser's career might be better summed up: one step forward, two steps back.

Two months after de Gaulle's electoral triumph in June 1968, one of the most significant events in 'Eastern' history since 1945 occurred. On 20/21 August, the USSR and other Warsaw Pact countries invaded Czechoslovakia to terminate 'socialism with a human face' and, in the process, de-Stalinisation in Eastern Europe. In contrast to Garaudy, whose indiscreet protests occasioned his

---

[168] Althusser 1978c, p. 112.

expulsion from the PCF, Althusser remained silent. Only after an interval of almost four years would he advise his readers that '[t]he national mass movement of the Czech people . . . merits the respect and support of all Communists'.[169] Althusser's contemporary tactiturnity on May and August has engendered its full share of suspicions. Was he the new Kautsky or Plekhanov? Or a Mao? – Or Stalin?

[169] Althusser 1976a, p. 77.

Chapter Five
Questions of Stalinism

> My aim was . . . to make a start on the first *left-wing* critique
> of Stalinism. . . .
>
> > Louis Althusser, 1975

In *Reply to John Lewis*, Althusser finally put his
cards on the table. Admirers have been few and
far between. Initially received with acclaim among
some French Maoists, the *Reply* found little favour
elsewhere and its reputation has further declined
over the years.[1]

In contrast, in his 1976 introduction to the English
edition Althusser's pupil, Grahame Lock, suggested
that, taken in conjunction with other works, it 'allows
us to constitute a genuinely new theory of the Stalin
period'.[2] That Althusser's writings, at different levels
and often obliquely, are concerned with the problems
put on the agenda by the Twentieth Congress and
its Khrushchevite and Maoist sequels is clear. And
that one of Althusser's ambitions was to contribute
to an explanation and critique of the 'Stalin period'
is attested not only by the comment that serves
as an epigraph to this chapter, but by recurrent

---

[1] See, *inter alia*, Colletti 1977, p. 334; Timpanaro 1980, p. 244 n. 40; Callinicos 1976,
pp. 92–4 and 1982, p. 78; Gerratana 1977; and Thompson 1978, p. 111. Even Maoists
were divided in their reaction – Rancière's book being provoked by Althusser's text
and Philippe Sollers, editor of the influential (and then puerilely Sinophiliac) *Tel Quel*
characterising it as a 'little pink book' (Sollers 1974, pp. 140–1 n.).
[2] Althusser 1976a, p. 6.

references to such a project from 'Contradiction and Overdetermination' onwards. Yet no extended discussion by Althusser himself ever materialised. His longest published reflection on the subject is the 'Note on "The Critique of the Personality Cult"' (sixteen pages) written in 1972 and appended to the French edition of *Reply to John Lewis*. It is in this text that the contours of Althusser's critique must be sought. Here, to the *'right-wing critique'* fashionable in bourgeois – and Trotskyist – circles, Althusser counter-poses a *'left-wing critique'* which will account for Stalinism by 'undertak[ing] serious research into its basic historical causes: that is . . . into the Superstructure, relations of production, and therefore the state of class relations and the class struggle in the USSR'.[3] Whilst Althusser himself did not provide such an analysis, what he does offer leaves little room for optimism on the shape it would assume. The elements of a critical analysis furnished by him amount to an ambiguous perspective on the 'unfinished history' of Stalinism. Substantiation and explanation of this assertion are the purpose of the present chapter.

A new theory of Stalinism?

The theses proposed in *Reply to John Lewis* cannot, strictly speaking, be said to constitute a novel theory of *Stalinism* for the simple reason that Althusser eschews the very term as non-Marxist. Like 'the cult of personality', it is theoretically vacuous; it 'designates a *reality'*, but *'explains* nothing'. As an alternative he offers the properly Leninist concept: *'the "Stalinian" deviation'*.[4]

Before proceeding, we should note that Althusser's disdain for the categories advanced by Khrushchev in 1956 (in particular, the 'pseudo-concept' of the 'cult'),[5] and adopted by the majority of Communist parties thereafter, is not as original as he would appear to think. In one of his last major political essays – 'Czechoslovakia: The Socialism that Came in from the Cold' (1970) – Sartre remarked of Khrushchev's 'tragi-comic speech' that it contained 'not an idea, not an analysis, not even an attempt at an interpretation'.[6] Already in 1956, Sartre was writing that the leaders of the CPSU had merely 'replaced

---

[3] Althusser 1976a, p. 82.
[4] Althusser 1976a, p. 81 and n.
[5] Althusser 1976a, p. 80.
[6] Sartre 1983, pp. 101–2.

white Masses by black Masses, and had not got away from the cult of personality'.[7] So one does not have to wait until the 1970s for a call from within French Marxism for a materialist analysis of Soviet history – nor for an attempt (on a scale as massive as Althusser's is miniature) to begin the task: the ultimately abandoned second volume of Sartre's *Critique of Dialectical Reason*.[8] Sartre was not alone, of course. Broadly speaking, within Marxist culture four lines of analysis challenging the CPSU's position were available after 1956. Three were Communist and contemporary with the Twentieth Congress: (1) Togliatti's reflections in the famous 'Interview with *Nuovi Argomenti*' of 1956;[9] (2) the CPC's *The Historical Experience of the Dictatorship of the Proletariat* (1956) and *On the Question of Stalin* (1963); and (3) the socialist-humanist critique that echoed throughout Europe (and which in Britain is associated, above all, with E.P. Thompson). The fourth, coeval with Stalinism itself, but heresy within the international Communist movement until the apogee of Eurocommunism in the 1970s, was that developed by Trotsky and his followers in political opposition to the dictator and his heirs.

Althusser does not mention, like alone discuss, the proto-Eurocommunist and Maoist analyses – a reticence in contrast to his open antagonism to the humanist and Trotskyist traditions. Althusser's seigneurial dismissal of humanism has been discussed in Chapter 1. A hall-mark of *Reply to John Lewis* is the conflation of 'anti-Communist bourgeois theory and . . . the "anti-Stalinist" theory of Trotskyism'. Indeed, the latter is assimilated to the category of 'right-wing' critiques and 'denunciations'. The absence of a left-wing critique, the substitution for the requisite analysis of Khrushchev's indictment, is said to provide 'the most violent bourgeois anti-Communism and Trotskyist anti-Stalinism . . . with a historical argument: it gives them a justification, a second wind, a second life.'[10] Since this sentiment would go largely unchallenged among the French Communists and Maoists who formed his natural audience, Althusser presumably felt under no obligation to justify

---

[7] Sartre 1969, p. 84.

[8] See Sartre 1985. A section has been published in English as Sartre 1977.

[9] Believing, like Althusser, that with the 'cult of personality', 'we are outside the criterion of judgement which is proper to Marxism', Togliatti likewise invoked the 'difficult task of a comprehensive political and historical analysis': Togliatti 1979, pp. 139, 141.

[10] Althusser 1976a, pp. 82–3.

what amounts to a tactic of guilt-by-association redolent of the phenomenon that was the object of his critique. Noting that Althusser either ignores or reproves previous Marxist analyses, Communist and non-Communist, we can now explore what he offers as an alternative to Orwell, Khrushchev and Trotsky.

In *For Marx*, Althusser's reconceptualisation of the structure of social formations had enabled him to characterise the USSR under Stalin in terms of a dislocation between a 'socialist infrastructure' and a deformed superstructure.[11] In 1972 he ventured the following hypothesis:

1. The International Communist Movement has been affected since the 1930s, to different degrees and in very different ways in different countries and organizations, by the effects of a *single* deviation, which can provisionally be called the 'Stalinian deviation'.

2. Keeping things *well in proportion*, that is to say, respecting essential distinctions, but nevertheless going beyond the most obvious phenomena – which are, in spite of their extremely serious character, historically secondary: I mean those which are generally grouped together in Communist Parties under the heading of 'personality cult' and 'dogmatism' – the Stalinian deviation can be considered as *a form* (a *special form*, converted by the state of the world class struggle, the existence of a single socialist State, and the State power held by the Bolshevik Party) of the *posthumous revenge of the Second International*: as a revival of its main tendency.

3. This main tendency was . . . basically an economistic one.[12]

Hedged round with qualifications, this hypothesis contains three clear propositions: (i) the relation of the history of the international Communist movement to a 'deviation' dating from the 1930s; (ii) the identification of that 'deviation' as an inheritance from the Second International; and (3) the specification of it as 'economism'. These are proffered as laying the foundations of a left-wing critique of Stalinism. Stalinism, it is suggested, was characterised

---

[11] See Althusser 1969a, p. 240. Interestingly, this essay made no reference to the debate in the PCF sparked off by the publication in *La Nouvelle Critique* of Michel Verret's 'Remarques sur le culte de la personnalité' in December 1963, and which included contributions from Besse, Cohen, Prévost, Sève and Simon – but no Althusserian intervention.

[12] Althusser 1976a, p. 89.

by the substitution of *'economism-humanism'* (roughly, the primacy of the productive forces as the 'motor' of the transition to communism and the abrogation of the dictatorship of the proletariat in favour of a 'state of the whole people') for *'Marxism-Leninism'* (roughly, the primacy of the relations of production and class struggle, under the dictatorship of the proletariat, as the 'motor' of the transition to communism). It was connected to Stalin and the Bolshevik Party's defection from Leninist orthodoxy, which had conceived socialism as a transitional social formation comprising a contradictory combination of capitalist and communist modes of production; and their introjection of the Menshevik tradition, wherein socialism was a 'stable' mode of production whose advent was guaranteed and whose development would generate its own corresponding superstructure. As a return to Menshevism, Stalinism represented a *re-Hegelianisation* of Marxism – the Ruse of Reason 'inverted'.[13]

This social-democratic theoretico-political ensemble had, moreover, been imposed on the Third International. And, by implication, if Stalinism represented the 'posthumous revenge of the Second International', then Khrushchevism, Brezhnevism and post-Stalinist Communism represented the posthumous retribution of *Stalinism* – its persistence in transformed forms, and hence the enduring penetration of Marxism by bourgeois ideology.[14] Althusser's initial conclusion is grave:

> As astonishing as this may seem, the whole history of the Labour Movement and Lenin's theses are witness to it: Marxism itself can, in certain circumstances, be considered and treated as, *even practised as a bourgeois point of view*. Not only by 'armchair Marxists', who reduce it to academic bourgeois sociology, and who are never anything but 'functionaries of the dominant ideology' – but also by sections of the Labour Movement and their leaders.[15]

---

[13] See Althusser 1969a, pp. 107–8. The source for Althusser's view of socialism is Lenin 1919, especially pp. 107–8, 115. It is spelt out in greater detail and compellingly argued in Balibar 1977. According to Balibar, his book was originally planned as a joint venture with Althusser. Due to the latter's illness, he undertook it alone (interview, Paris, June 1985). The original title for *Reply to John Lewis* proposed to New Left Books was Mao's *Never Forget the Class Struggle!*. *New Left Review*'s own flirtation with Maoism having recently been terminated, the suggestion was declined.

[14] See Althusser 1976a, p. 83ff.

[15] Althusser 1976a, p. 87.

However, if the Marxism of the Second and Third Internationals and the 'line' of the Stalin period were characterised by the *'elimination of the relations of production and of the class struggle'*,[16] neither Stalin nor, a fortiori, the Third International could be reduced to this 'deviation'. Stalin had 'other historical merits' – namely, abandoning the 'miraculous idea of an imminent "world revolution"' and embarking on the "construction of socialism" in one country'. As a consequence, Communists were indebted to him for Stalingrad and for the knowledge that 'principles of Leninism' existed.[17]

For the time being, let us ignore the oft-remarked fact that Stalin honoured these 'principles' more in the breach than in the observance. Two aspects of this account – one political, the other theoretical – stand out. First, as Gerratana has observed, by means of a 'left-wing critique' Althusser succeeds in attributing to Stalin some of the merits he claimed for himself.[18] Secondly, Althusser's essay at a Marxist explanation falls somewhere short of that. Contra Lock, this analytical framework does not facilitate a theoretical great leap forward. What it does offer is a reduction of complex history to simplex theory: Stalinism, as Rancière has observed, is converted into 'a predicate of *economism*, a historical form of appearance of the ideological couple economism/humanism'.[19] Althusser would doubtless respond that his censure of a 'deviation' (whose theoretical conditions of possibility he has identified) was simultaneously aimed at the politics and practices it encompassed.[20] But this will not do. Insofar as Althusser discusses such realities, his account tends to the evasive, sometimes to the apologetic. Moreover, a Marxist who disputes the worth of all existing critiques and confides his ambition to better them, making the capacity so to do so a *point d'honneur* of his own Marxism, is surely under some obligation to tackle the subject without pleading lack of time or space. All we have to go on is what Althusser gives us; his readers cannot be blamed for overlooking what he neglected to include.

A question suggests itself: how could Althusser – in 1972 – have offered this as his analysis of Stalinism and as the long-awaited, genuinely Marxist

---

[16] Althusser 1976a, p. 88.
[17] See Althusser 1976a, p. 91.
[18] See Gerratana 1977, pp. 116–17.
[19] Rancière 1974, p. 183.
[20] In an article reprinted in his 1982, Lecourt has; see pp. 125–6 n.

left-wing critique? It so happens that a possible answer is close to hand – in the hypothesis advanced at the end of his 'Note':

> If we look back over our whole history of the last forty years or more, it seems to me that . . . the only *historically existing* (left) 'critique' of the fundamentals of the 'Stalinian deviation' to be found . . . is a concrete critique, one which exists in the facts, in the struggle, in the line, in the practices, their principles and their forms, of the Chinese Revolution. A silent critique, which speaks through its actions, the result of the political and ideological struggles of the Revolution, from the Long March to the Cultural Revolution and its results. A critique *from afar*. A critique from 'behind the scenes'. To be looked at more closely, to be interpreted. A *contradictory* critique, moreover – if only because of the disproportion between acts and texts. Whatever you like: but a critique from which one can learn, which can help us to test our hypotheses, that is, help us to see our own history more clearly. . . .

And Althusser concludes:

> If I have been able . . . even very feebly to echo these historic struggles and to indicate, behind their ideological effects, the existence of some real problems: this, for a Communist philosopher, is no more than his duty.[21]

This passage indicates that the key to understanding the relationship of Althusser's work to *Stalinism* lies in its relationship to *Maoism*. Chapter 1, tracing some of the events and controversies leading to the CPC's secession from the Soviet-dominated international Communist movement in the early 1960s, noted Althusser's covert sympathy for the Chinese line in opposition to the CPSU and PCF – a political filiation which influenced the theoretical content of his Marxism. And, in the last chapter, it was argued that Althusser's auto-critiques of 1967–72 drew much of their inspiration from Maoist themes issuing from the Cultural Revolution – an event to which he devoted an enthusiastic theoretical and political analysis. The origin of the ambiguities of Althusser's politics is to be found here: in the belief that the Chinese revolution – from the Long March to the Cultural Revolution – afforded a manifestly superior model of socialist 'development' and democracy to, and hence an immanent critique of, the Stalinist and post-Stalinist régimes in the

---

[21] Althusser 1976a, pp. 92–3.

USSR – was, indeed, the embodiment of Leninist rectitude. Not only was the historical record upon which Althusser proposed to base a theoretical critique of the Soviet experience far less positive than he supposed; his credulity prevented him (and many others) from 'seeing [their] own history more clearly'. For all that he distanced himself from the CPC's official verdict on Stalin ('the disproportion between acts and texts'), Althusser's *Reply to John Lewis* bears the scars of its Maoist genesis. Affiliated to the CPC as the contemporary standard-bearer of Leninism, Althusser misjudged the Chinese experience; produced an evasive account of Stalinism; erected a Marxist-Leninist orthodoxy which reconnected his intellectual project to earlier episodes in Communist history; and condemned himself to an incongruous position in the PCF.

The left critique of Stalinism

To characterise the CPC's verdict on Stalin as 'ambiguous'[22] would be something of an understatement. By 1963, posing as the champions of Leninist orthodoxy, the Chinese were engaged in a neo-Stalinist defence of Stalin and critique of his successors. As anyone who reads *On the Question of Stalin* can see for themselves, they maintained that Khrushchevite revisionism was 'inseparably connected with [Khrushchev's] complete negation of Stalin'. With the Twentieth Congress the CPSU had 'embarked on a revisionist course', whose terminus was the overthrow of socialism and restoration of capitalism in the USSR. The exclamation with which *On the Question of Stalin* concluded expressed an attachment which would survive Khrushchev and Mao alike: 'Long live the great revolutionary teachings of Marx, Engels, Lenin and Stalin!'.[23] Prior to this, it is true, explicit or implicit criticisms had been made of Stalin by the Chinese.[24] But thereafter, what pro-Chinese Marxists regarded as a discrepancy between meritorious non-Stalinist deeds and pro-Stalinist words became the norm.

---

[22] As does Rancière 1974, p. 109.
[23] Communist Party of China 1965, pp. 131, 59–60, 138. For a summary of the verdict, see pp. 118–23.
[24] See, e.g., Communist Party of China 1960, pp. 94–5 for an attack on 'a kind of theory' about socialism which is Stalin's kind.

Althusser's own discussion certainly avoided any such clamant apologia. For he saw the Chinese revolution as a 'concrete critique' of Stalinism and sought to theorise it as such. This project dates back at least to the end of the 1960s; 'On the Cultural Revolution' is the clearest anticipation of it. Macciocchi relates a conversation with Althusser in the 1960s in which, having noted the lack of democracy and the state-party fusion in the USSR, he remarked: 'China re-raises the problems of the USSR and exposes its limits'. She claims that the idea of a joint book on China was floated, whose guiding thread would have been the idea that China's course represented a 'left critique of Stalinism'.[25] Macciocchi's own *Daily Life in Revolutionary China* (1971), the eulogistic product of an extended visit to the People's Republic in 1970–1, concludes with a section on the 'left critique' and refers to an unpublished text by Althusser on the same subject.[26] Judging from Macciocchi's description, this featured the hypothesis advanced in *Reply to John Lewis* a few years later, but was firmer in asserting a continuity between Stalinism and Khrushchevism in their common negation of proletarian democracy, and a discontinuity between Stalinist and Chinese models in precisely this respect. For Althusser, Mao's China was the incarnation of the democratic communism negated in the USSR.

It is therefore not surprising to find him keeping his distance from Chinese adjudications on Stalin and his successors. He admitted – and took seriously – the dictator's 'crimes' and 'dogmatism'. Notwithstanding his endorsement of the thesis that Yugoslavia was 'state-capitalist', he never publicly maintained the same of the USSR post-Stalin. Still less did he assent to the line unveiled at the CPC's Ninth Congress when, following the clashes on the Ussuri, the USSR was denounced as 'fascist' and 'social-imperialist'.[27] It would appear, then, that Althusser did not believe a 'bureaucratic-monopoly capitalist class' had been conjured up by the spells cast by Khrushchev one February day in

---

[25] See Macciocchi 1983, pp. 330, 383, 400. As so often, illness seems to have been a factor in the non-fruition of the project; see the desperate remarks attributed to Althusser on p. 383.

[26] See Macciocchi 1973a, pp. 487–91. In her 1983, p. 403, Macciocchi cites Althusser's help in finding a French publisher for *Daily Life*. The PCF, by contrast, banned it from the Fête de l'Humanité in 1971.

[27] The only reference to the Ninth Congress in Althusser's work occurs in 1971, p. 106, where he briefly compares the contemporary divisions in the international Communist movement with the crisis of the Second International in 1914.

234 • Chapter Five

1956. On the other hand – and at the same time – his view of the effects of the 'secret speech' on international Communism was *analogous* to that of the CPC. In *For Marx*, he had given Khrushchev some credit for making serious theoretical work possible once again; this point was to be repeated in *Reply to John Lewis*.[28] Now, as then, however, the positive side of the Twentieth Congress was at least counter-balanced by the negative side: its sponsorship of '*bourgeois* ideological and political themes within the Communist Parties'.[29] Where the CPC posited a total discontinuity between the Stalin and post-Stalin periods in the USSR and the Communist movement – and one which redounded to the credit of the former – Althusser's position was more complicated. As already indicated, he discerned a negative continuity from Stalin to Khrushchev, simultaneously belied and betokened by Khrushchev's trivial discussion. Yet he was tempted by the CPC's apportionment of blame between the two leaders.

If Althusser was sufficiently independent-minded to reject the absurd proposition that all was basically well with the USSR and Communism until Stalin's death; and if he refused the shallowness of the official Soviet critique and the resultant inadequate rectifications, in the name of a more substantial enquiry and a much more radical rupture with the Stalinist legacy – then this did not save him from illusions about the residual 'merits' of Stalin. The naïveté sprang from two sources: the gathering speed of the rightwards evolution apparent among Western Communist parties under Khrushchev and Brezhnev; and the verdict delivered by the leaders of the country which represented a – *the* – radical rupture. In other words, under the influence of the CPC, Althusser too seems to have made *some* connection between the CPSU's new 'revisionist' course and Khrushchev's '*complete* negation of Stalin'. That similar suppositions had currency in the Althusserian milieu early on is evident from *Cahiers marxistes-léninistes*. The 'political resolution' adopted by the UJC in December 1966, for example, condemned the PCF's 'anti-Stalinism' as a means of avoiding the requisite concrete analysis which would illuminate both Stalin's 'great merits [and] his errors'.[30]

---

[28] Althusser 1976a, pp. 74–5.
[29] Althusser 1976a, p. 75; see also p. 83.
[30] See *Cahiers marxistes-léninistes* 1967, p. 74.

The PCF's inability – for political reasons – to undertake a Marxist analysis and evaluation of Stalinism was, however, to be duplicated by the Althusserians. And, here, they were in good (or bad) company. For the CPC itself has, of course, proved singularly incapable of a serious reflection either on its own history, or on that of the international Communist movement. Officially loyal to Stalin throughout its career, the CPC has thereby condemned itself (among other things) to misunderstanding even the victorious revolution it led – despite him. Deutscher once observed that 'Clio, the Muse of History, has failed to obtain admittance to the Kremlin'.[31] She has been no more welcome in the Great Hall of the People. Those who have apotheosised its occupants have been condemned to suffering, to a greater or lesser extent, a similar myopia.

The CPC's own balance-sheet of the 'historical experience of the dictatorship of the proletariat' did inform one epic piece of historical research which owed something to Althusser's philosophical theses – and received his imprimatur in return: Charles Bettelheim's *Class Struggles in the USSR*, nominated by him in 1976 as one of only two exceptions to the dearth of bona fide Marxist histories of the USSR and the international Communist movement.[32] Lock's introduction to *Reply to John Lewis* reveals reservations about central aspects of Bettelheim's account. Rejecting the category of 'state bourgeoisie' which issues from Bettelheim's serious underestimation of property in the means of production, Lock entered strong objections to the thesis of capitalist restoration in the USSR. Nevertheless, the superiority of Maoism to Trotskyism was intimated on the grounds that the latter shared Stalin's economism. The CPC, in contrast, had effected a 'practical break' with the 'Stalinian deviation'; its policies had been 'consciously anti-humanist and anti-economist'.[33]

Does Bettelheim's work – by far the most serious attempt to utilise the 'lessons' of the Cultural Revolution in accounting for the history of the Soviet Union – deserve Althusserian plaudits? Theoretically, as Callinicos has argued, in order to explain Stalinism and justify the thesis of capitalist restoration in the Khrushchevite aftermath, it effects 'a series of reductions – productive

---

[31] Deutscher 1982, p. 17.
[32] See Althusser 1977b, p. 8, n. 2. In his 1976, p. 48, n. 2, Bettelheim acknowledges the impetus given to the 'revival' of Marxism in France by Althusser's anti-economistic recasting of historical materialism.
[33] See Althusser 1976a, pp. 23–7.

forces to production relations, production relations to superstructure, superstructure to ideology' – which underpins the conclusion that the failure to initiate a cultural revolution consequent upon 'economism' led to the restoration of capitalism.[34] Politically, as Ralph Miliband has emphasised, Bettelheim's effective apologia for Stalin and commination of Khrushchev serve only to restore a continuity between Lenin and Stalin that is historically false and politically disarming.[35] *Class Struggles in the USSR* is something of a test case for the left-critique, insofar as it seeks both to carry out the programme of 'serious research' invoked by Althusser and to legitimise the Cultural Revolution. Lauding the beneficent influence of the latter, Bettelheim decries the 'congealed Marxism' inherited by the Bolsheviks from the Second International – a Marxism common to Stalin and Trotsky, from whose grip only Lenin was free.[36] As a result of their belief that nationalisation was equivalent to socialisation, their concomitant failure to appreciate the continuation of class struggle under the dictatorship of the proletariat, and their unilateral emphasis, instead, on the development of the productive forces, the leaders of the Bolshevik Party had failed to prevent the ascendancy of a bureaucracy which 'represent[ed] the embryo of a new bourgeoisie in the apparatus of the state and of the ruling party'.[37] Only a cultural revolution as in China could have delivered revolutionisation of the relations of production; alas, it was unforthcoming. As to Stalin, his 'inflexible rigour' in pursuit of the 'construction of socialism in one country' was indeed contaminated by economism. Nevertheless, the resolute strategy of industrialisation 'kept alight the beacon of the October Revolution [and] sustained the people's confidence in the victorious outcome of their struggles'. The 'mistakes' accompanying Stalin's implementation of Lenin's thesis of 'socialism in one country' were 'doubtless historically inevitable'.[38] It is not clear whether, in attempting a vindication of the possibility of socialist transformation regardless of 'material foundations',[39] Bettelheim has ultimately achieved anything more than exculpation of Stalinism.

---

[34] Callinicos 1982, p. 78.
[35] See Miliband 1984, pp. 189–201.
[36] See Bettelheim 1976, pp. 16, 47–8, 20ff. For a more detailed account of the 'Bolshevik ideological formation', see Bettelheim 1978, pp. 500–87.
[37] Bettelheim 1976, p. 314.
[38] Bettelheim 1976, pp. 40–1.
[39] See, e.g., Bettelheim 1976, p. 42.

Althusser did not go as far as Bettelheim. But he shared his colleague's identification of 'economism' with a central and ineliminable tenet of classical Marxism: material abundance as a necessary, if insufficient, condition of socialism and communism. Like Bettelheim, he proceeded from the quite proper rejection of any simple equation between nationalisation (public ownership) and socialisation (post-capitalist relations of production), and of the Stalinist view that the development of the productive forces spontaneously generates socialist relations of production, towards voluntarism. The paradoxical outcome in both cases – though less pronounced in Althusser's than Bettelheim's – was to salvage Stalin's historical 'merits' from his economistic 'deviation'. More serious than Althusser's residual illusions concerning Stalin's régime – for which he never displayed any enthusiasm – was the wholesale transfer of the delusion once entertained by Communists about Stalin's Russia to Mao's China. Nevertheless, Althusser's remarks on Stalin's 'merits' are utterly inappropriate. A few, albeit unoriginal, comments on them are therefore in order.

To begin with, they risk restoring continuity between Stalin and Lenin. Although governed by a deviation founded on the primacy of the productive forces, the 'great change' of 1929 to enforced collectivisation and break-neck industrialisation would be the continuation in adverse circumstances of Leninist strategy (the 'construction of socialism in one country'). What Althusser curiously neglects in his denunciation of economistic interpretations of Soviet history is something his former pupil Linhart has graphically recalled: 'the double constraint of war and famine at once forged and deformed the Soviet Republic from the outset'.[40] A plausible hypothesis is that the very project of 'socialism in one country' was a product of the isolation of a post-revolutionary state which, crippled by backwardness, devastated by war and ravaged by scarcity, was the epitome of the kingdom of necessity; that it contributed to the reinforcement of the isolation until the changed correlation of forces at the end of World War II; and that after 1945 'socialism in one zone' (Eastern Europe) was established by Stalin at the price of the salvation of Western Europe from communism.[41] By simply caricaturing the Left Opposition's

---

[40] Linhart 1976, p. 127. The work of an Althusserian Maoist, Linhart's book, narrower in scope and smaller in scale than Bettelheim's, is vastly superior. The date and place of its composition, rife with defections and conversions, make it a singular achievement.

[41] For an indication that Althusser by no means possessed a conformist mind-set

alternative, Althusser imbues Stalin's course – the 'revolution from above' supposedly 'supported from below' – with a redemptive historical inevitability. The price of that fateful substitution of autarchy for internationalism – a substitution which occurred before the 1930s – is still being paid. Its domestic harvest, from the catastrophe in the countryside to the carnage of the *Yezhovschina*, needs no recounting.

As to Stalingrad, it would be the height of irresponsibility in the Cold-War conjuncture of the 1980s to discount it. For it was there that the Red Army halted the Wehrmacht and turned the tide of the Second World War, thus creating a symbol as potent for Althusser's generation as Petrograd had been for an earlier one. To assign the credit to Generalissimo Stalin, however, is to relapse into the staple diet of Cominform agitprop – as if 'errors' (and far worse) on *Stalin*'s part, which littered the road to Stalingrad, had not helped to bring the Soviet Union and, with it, the cause of socialism, to the brink of disaster.

If a 'deviation' is required to explain the Stalin period, then a likely candidate is the doctrine of 'socialism in one country', a notion foreign to classical Marxism and Bolshevism alike – an 'ideological monster', in Sartre's words.[42] Perhaps a necessity, it was one of which Bukharin and Stalin made a virtue. Premised upon the improbability of revolution outside Russian borders after 1923, and the possibility of durable 'peaceful coexistence' between the Soviet state and the imperialist powers, it dominated the CPSU and the Comintern's strategy from the mid-1920s. Its logic, as Trotsky divined, was that '[m]essianic nationalism [was] supplemented by bureaucratically abstract internationalism', in which the Communist parties 'play[ed] the role of frontier patrols'.[43] Its contribution to the roll-call of tragedies that have befallen socialism in this century – from the degeneration of the Russian Revolution itself, via the defeat of the German Communist Party, to the wars between post-capitalist states in Asia in the 1970s – might bear some investigation. It is a legacy of Stalin's to international Communism which Left, Right and Centre of the movement have not repudiated. As it happens, the pseudo-theory of 'revolution

---

on the subject of the immediate postwar strategies of the French and Italian Communist parties, see Macciocchi 1983, pp. 378–9.

[42] Sartre 1985, p. 109.

[43] Trotsky 1969, pp. 149, 151. See also E.H. Carr's remarks on the 'victory of Narkomindel over Comintern' in his 1982, pp. 151–2.

by stages' which accompanied it, and which was designed to legitimate the prevention of revolutions transgressing limits acceptable to Stalinist *Realpolitik*, was accurately identified some time ago as a 'revenge by Menshevism for the affronts which Bolshevism heaped upon it in 1917'.[44] In detecting in Stalinism, then, a 'posthumous revenge of the Second International' decades later, Althusser was on to something – but not the right thing.

What is required, however, is not the identification of theoretical deviations, but – as Althusser also recognised – historical explanation and evaluation of the social system christened with Stalin's name and which, albeit in substantially modified form, has survived its first minister; of the transplantation, in all of its enormous complexity, of variants of that system to four continents – from Eastern Europe in the 1940s to Southern Africa and South-East Asia in the 1970s; and of the political organisations modelled, tightly or loosely, on the monolithic CPSU. Set against this programme – or even one-third of it – the distinguishing characteristic of Althusser's contribution is its inadequacy. Designed to help us understand what he once called 'the reasons for this unreason',[45] instead it supplies an involuntary affidavit for the theoretical and historical poverty of Maoism.

Contrary to Althusser's peremptory judgement, it is just not the case that Marxist research of the highest calibre into this 'unfinished history' was lacking. Two years before he penned his *Reply to John Lewis*, Fernando Claudin's magnificent *Communist Movement* appeared. Written by a former leader of the Spanish Communist Party, it represented an attempt (in its author's words) 'to use Marxism . . . to make a critical analysis of the political theory and practice of Marxism since the October revolution'.[46] In its conclusions, it acknowledged the influence and echoed some of the theses of a left critique contemporary with Stalinism: Trotsky's. Had Althusser turned to his writings, he would have discovered an analysis which, whatever its many imperfections, did illuminate 'our history'. In the writings of such independent followers as Deutscher, he would have found an outstanding body of work which extended that critique to developments after 1940 – and without making the slightest concession to 'the most violent bourgeois anti-Communism'. In 1976,

---

[44] Trotsky 1969, p. 259.
[45] Althusser and Balibar 1970, p. 34.
[46] Claudin 1975, p. 9.

Althusser was to cite Claudin's work alongside Bettelheim's as 'exceptional'.[47] By then, ten years of affiliation to the 'concrete critique' underway in China had elapsed – and taken their theoretical, historical and political toll.

Red star over China

Althusser commenced *Reply to John Lewis* by noting that time had not stood still since the composition of 'On the Young Marx':

> A good deal of water has flowed under the bridge of history since 1960. The Workers' Movement has lived through many important events: the heroic and victorious resistance of the Vietnamese people against the most powerful imperialism in the world; the Proletarian Cultural Revolution in China (1966–69); the greatest workers' strike in world history . . . in May 1968 in France – a strike which was 'preceded' and 'accompanied' by a deep ideological revolt among French students and petty-bourgeois intellectuals; the occupation of Czechoslovakia by armies of the other countries of the Warsaw Pact; the war in Ireland, etc. The Cultural Revolution, May 1968 and the occupation of Czechoslovakia have had political and ideological repercussions in the whole of the capitalist world.[48]

These were indeed dramatic years, witness to an acceleration of history. While the West-European Communist parties explored national roads to socialism in fraught symbiosis with Moscow, the anti-imperialist movements of the Third World went over to the offensive, encouraged by the militant message from Lin Piao in Peking and Che Guevara in Havana. The radicalising influence of the Cuban Revolution, Algerian independence, and the Vietnamese liberation struggle in the West is well-known. In the event, Algerian independence in July 1962 was virtually the last revolutionary success for twelve years. With the exception of South Yemen (1967), it was a decade of defeat. When Guevara went down fighting in Bolivia in October 1967, the Cuban guerrilla road ended in a cul-de-sac. In the absence of the 'many Vietnams' for which he had called, one Vietnam was condemned to solitary defiance of imperialist

---

[47] Althusser 1977b, p. 8, n. 2.
[48] Althusser 1976a, pp. 35–6.

onslaught. The 'revolution in the counter-revolution' detected by Debray in 1965 reinforced imperialism's weak links.[49]

Within the 'socialist camp' the USSR's vacillation between reform and consolidation at home, adventurism and negotiation abroad, further discredited it in the eyes of many socialists. The advent of the Cultural Revolution in China in 1966, combined with Peking's internationalist rhetoric, seemed to many to promise *the* alternative to the post-Khrushchevite settlement in the USSR. And among those who believed that the red star had re-risen in the East was Althusser, who remarked to Debray in 1967 that 'in the cases of Vietnam and China . . . we are dealing with historical successes'.[50] In their polemic with the CPSU, the CPC had coined the caustic slogan: 'the satellites went up to the sky while the red flag fell to the ground'. Perhaps echoing the Chinese, in 1968 Althusser avowed that '[t]o change the world is not to explore the moon. It is to make revolution and build socialism without regressing to capitalism. The rest, including the moon, will be given to us in addition'.[51] In thus looking to China for a communism that criticised and surpassed the Soviet version, Althusser took the CPC's texts for its acts.

It must be said that the attractions for left-wing Communists of the CPC's position in the two- and then three-way split which rent the international Communist movement from the late 1950s onwards were considerable. The 'general line' proposed by the CPSU consisted of 'the battle for peace, democracy, national independence and socialism'.[52] Arguing that the position of socialism in this list reflected the low priority assigned it by the Kremlin, and assailing the CPSU for treating 'fraternal parties as pawns on their diplomatic chessboard', the Chinese advertised the alternative of robust proletarian internationalism and 'people's war'.[53] This militant international line aimed at the 'colluding and contending super-powers' was complemented by domestic radicalism. The construction of socialism required not

---

[49] See Debray 1970, p. 150. For this period, see Fred Halliday's outstanding 1983, pp. 82–6.

[50] Althusser 1977a, pp. 259–60.

[51] Althusser 1972, p. 186.

[52] See the CPSU's 'Open Letter' of 14 July 1963, in Communist Party of China 1965, p. 575.

[53] Communist Party of China 1965, p. 321. 'People's war' and the 'encirclement' of the world's 'cities' (the USA and Western Europe) by its 'countryside' (Asia, Africa and Latin America) were the subject of Marshal Lin Piao's epochal 1965.

Khrushchevite humanist velleities, but uninterrupted revolution – political and ideological revolution to consolidate socialist economic revolution.[54] The CPC defended what it called the 'basic teachings' of Marxism-Leninism on socialist revolution and the dictatorship of the proletariat, taking as its canonical text Lenin's most libertarian work *The State and Revolution*.[55] Proffering the 'mass line' ('from the masses, to the masses') as the model union of theory and practice, the CPC made its bid for the loyalties of Communists disaffected with the USSR. These themes, in conjunction with the apparent egalitarianism of the Chinese social order, influenced a significant minority of Communists to transfer their allegiances from Moscow to Peking. With the unleashing of the Cultural Revolution, the CPC, proclaiming 'politics in command', could be perceived as translating words into deeds as Mao enjoined the Red Guards to 'bombard the headquarters of the bourgeoisie' and 'storm the strongholds of revisionism'.

Althusser's contemporary reaction to what was – on the face of it – a massive, popular anti-bureaucratic mobilisation has already been surveyed. The Cultural Revolution was not merely congruent with Marxist and Leninist orthodoxy. It constituted a decisive *practical* advance over Lenin's, let alone Stalin's, strategy in Russia – a practical vindication of Althusser's own (anti-economistic and anti-evolutionist) theoretical positions which would make possible a left-wing critique of Stalinism *and* reanimate the revolutionary project in the West. The reports brought back to Paris by such sources as Jean Daubier, Macciocchi and Bettelheim can only have confirmed Althusser in his beliefs.[56] In his indulgence, Althusser was not alone. Excepting loyal Communists, it would have been difficult in France in the 1960s to find a left-wing intellectual prepared to go public with dissenting opinions. One respected foreign voice raised against the Chinese leadership was Deutscher's. In a premonitory analysis written in 1966, he compared the upheaval and its political significance to the *Zhdanovschina* and hyper-nationalism of Stalin's

---

[54] Communist Party of China 1965, p. 471.

[55] See Communist Party of China 1965, pp. 366–7.

[56] In her 1973a, p. 2, Macciocchi cautioned against wholesale transfer of faith from Moscow to Peking: advice which is ignored in the pages that follow (see, e.g., p. 104). In Macciocchi 1973b, pp. 220–1, she recalled Althusser suggesting that while 'a "guiding star" like the USSR' was no longer necessary, 'what is not possible is to do away altogether with international examples of revolution to offer to the masses.'

last years.[57] His views went unheeded. As a 'dogmatist night' descended, the *maoisant* Western intelligentsia celebrated an unprecedented revolutionary initiative against bureaucracy, technocracy, the social division of labour, the division between town and country, and so on. Rather than 'sweeping away all ghosts and monsters', the Cultural Revolution summoned up the ghosts of Stalinism past and gave birth to monsters, pursuing a sanguinary course of repression against millions – from disgraced leaders to materialistic workers, from 'capitalist roaders' to the 'stinking ninth category' (namely, intellectuals).[58] *En route*, an obscurantism and voluntarism were promulgated – and enacted – which only the leaders of Democratic Kampuchea – recipients of Chinese patronage – would exceed. Terminated in 1976 with the arrest of the Gang of Four, the Cultural Revolution was officially disowned by the CPC thereafter.[59] Repudiating the ideology of the previous decade, the new leadership henceforward dedicated itself to a 'central task': 'economic construction'.[60] To the dismay of China's foreign admirers, the slogan of the 'four modernisations' supplanted revolutionary rhetoric and theoretical orthodoxy was suitably redefined.[61]

The one legacy of Maoism to emerge intact was China's foreign policy.[62] In this sphere, Maoism without Mao was the order of the day. If it was difficult for Althusser and others to read the domestic situation with any degree of accuracy, there is less justification for their credulity in China's version of proletarian internationalism. Its limitations might have been apparent to a French Marxist from the praise lavished on de Gaulle for his intransigence with NATO over France's independent nuclear deterrent. Quite the reverse of a concrete critique of Stalinist *Realpolitik*, Chinese foreign policy was a replication of it. Ominous in this regard was the fate of the Indonesian Communist Party (KPI) in 1965. Counselled by a Peking eager for diplomatic compacts with its neighbours to adopt a 'stagist' strategy, the third largest Communist party in the world, three and a half million strong, was literally

---

[57] See Deutscher 1970, pp. 333–9. See Maitan 1976, pp. 262–3 for confirmation of Deutscher's worst fears.

[58] See, e.g., Halliday 1983, pp. 163–4.

[59] The official verdict of the new leadership was given in Communist Party of China 1981; see, e.g., pp. 17, 32.

[60] Communist Party of China 1981, p. 77.

[61] See Robin Munro's introduction to Chen Erjin 1984. Cf. Bettelheim 1978.

[62] See Communist Party of China 1981, pp. 41–4.

annihilated. Disingenuously attributing the blame to KPI leader Aidit's Khrushchevism, the CPC overlooked both its own sponsorship of his positions and their similarity to the strategy imposed on it by the Comintern at Stalin's behest – with analogous consequences – in 1927.[63]

It was from the late 1960s onwards that China's foreign policy assumed its definitive shape. Largely isolated in the Communist world (minus, that is, the mixed blessing of solidarity from Enver Hoxha's Albanian Workers' Party), the CPC pursued a strategy whose anti-Soviet extremism and accommodation with imperialism completely contradicted its image as a left-wing critic of the USSR. In search of state alliances and recognition as a regional power, China's leaders colluded with reaction the world over.[64] The year Althusser wrote his encomium of the Chinese Revolution witnessed the Sino-US rapprochement. Even as the Shanghai communiqué of 28 February celebrating 'peaceful coexistence' was released, the B-52s were continuing their efforts to bomb Vietnam back to the Stone Age. The second French edition of Althusser's opuscule was published in August 1973. The following month, Allende's Popular Unity government succumbed to a military coup; the régime of his murderers was speedily recognised by Peking.[65] Thereafter, things went from bad to worse, culminating in the invasion of Vietnam at the end of the decade to the ill-concealed delight of a State Department alert to the potential of the 'China card'. Something approaching the 'Holy Alliance' into which the Russians had been accused of entering in 1963 became a reality in the 1970s – with China occupying the seat its propaganda had assigned to the USSR.

That it would end thus was neither foreseeable nor inevitable. But a little more circumspection over the Chinese polemics of the 1960s would have been in order. For the conversion of the CPC into a conscientious objector to Soviet *raison d'état* was, to say the least, belated. In retrospect, it is clear that its left-turn in the Khrushchev era was dictated by China's contemporary diplomatic isolation and its ensuing anxiety that Soviet-American détente was being conducted at its expense. Similarly, the right-turn at the end of the 1960s was a response to the failure of the earlier strategy of splitting the 'socialist camp'

---

[63] See, e.g., Westoby 1981, p. 191.
[64] See Halliday 1977, p. 167 and 1983, p. 162; Maitan 1976, p. 337ff.
[65] This seems to have a turning-point for Balibar in his attitude to China (personal communication from Perry Anderson).

and the international Communist movement to its own advantage. Whatever, in the 'new' foreign policy 'messianic nationalism' was not even to be accompanied by 'bureaucratically abstract internationalism'.

It would be inaccurate to characterise Althusser as a Maoist of strict observance. His correspondence with Debray in 1967 over his pupil's theorisation of Guevarism (*Revolution in the Revolution?*), for example, evinces considerable sympathy for an enterprise that was anathema in Moscow and Peking equally. The present leader of the PCI – Alessandro Natta – was, however, right to detect a Maoist strain in the correspondence between Althusser and Macciocchi in 1968 (something he bitterly resented, insofar as the PCI found itself the target of a left-wing critique by one of its own parliamentary candidates). Yet he also displayed insight when he suggested that Althusser – held responsible for Macciocchi's 'flirtation with extremism' – 'himself offers the best rebuttal of his position when he analyses the "events" in France in 1968'.[66] Over May, Althusser's ultimate loyalty to his party, right or wrong, is self-evident – as is the retreat form the practical implications of his theoretical and political positions. 'Don't give an inch to the revisionists', Macciocchi quotes Althusser as counselling her in connection with her epistolary critique of the PCI.[67] Macciocchi may not have; Althusser did. His habitual caution about anything which challenged the authority of the PCF typically issued in a withdrawal to theory and political *attentisme*.[68] Althusser's abiding commitment was to a unified 'international workers' movement' which no longer existed, to an imaginary International.[69] The resulting political and theoretical syncretism and centrism could not, of course, transcend the very real divisions in the Communist movement.

---

[66] See Macciocchi 1973b, p. 334.

[67] Macciocchi 1983, p. 359.

[68] Evidence of Althusser's oscillation between militancy and caution occurs in his letters to Macciocchi. Thus, on 2 April 1968 he advised her: 'Politics is a protracted war. Do not be in a hurry. Try to see things far in advance and know how to wait, today. Don't live in terms of subjective urgency' (Macciocchi 1973b, p. 23). A clear example of Althusser's reflex retreat to theory can be found in his letter to Debray of 1 March 1967. In the passage already quoted on p. 52, n. 157, having reminded his correspondent of the 'political urgency' of theoretical work – something recognised by Marx and Lenin – Althusser speculates that Guevara might currently be imitating them. Guevara – and Debray – were of course doing the exact opposite.

[69] In *De la superstructure*, Althusser looks forward to the reunification of the international Communist movement, commenting 'Pazienza' (Althusser 1995a, p. 234, n. 124).

With the Soviet invasion of Czechoslovakia and termination of 'reform Communism', a latent Western schism became manifest in international Communism. Destroying any remaining illusions about liberalisation in the Soviet bloc, what Ernst Fischer called *Panzerkommunismus* gave birth to Eurocommunism. By 1969, the bifurcation of the Communist world had been superseded. The 'polycentrism' anticipated by Togliatti in his 'Yalta Memorandum'[70] duly came to pass: one now divided into at least three. However willing most Communist parties were to join in the assault on Maoism at the international conference of June 1969, a substantial number of them firmly resisted attempts to reassert Soviet paramountcy.[71] While the PCF retreated from its initially forthright stand against the occupation of Prague, its rapprochement with French social democracy continued. Although no improvement of inner-party democracy resulted, the PCF did allow a celebrity like Althusser to pursue his own course – on condition that it did not transgress the Party's jurisdiction. By the early 1970s, the discrepancy between the PCF's ideological and political positions and Althusser's was enormous. June 1972: a month in which Georges Marchais signed the *Common Programme* on behalf of the Communist Party and Louis Althusser was composing a *Reply to John Lewis* in defence of Marxism-Leninism.

After Stalin, Mao

In the last chapter, it was suggested that Althusser's auto-critique and rectification chimed with Maoism. The result – the 'orthodoxy' unveiled in *Reply to John Lewis* – objectively represents a notable retreat in Althusser's opposition to theoretical Stalinism, constituting a regression to the tone and style of an earlier era.

In his first essays, Althusser had been prepared occasionally to include Stalin in his list of authorities. Thus, in the Introduction to *For Marx*, he had approvingly cited Stalin's intervention against Marr. Now, as the Althusserian Jean-Marc Gayman has pointed out, Stalin's *Marxism and Linguistics* (1950) and *Economic Problems of Socialism in the USSR* (1952) were welcomed by PCF ideologues at the time as a rectification of (theoretical) Lysenkoism, since they

---

[70] See Togliatti 1979.
[71] See Marcou 1980, p. 77ff.

substituted the opposition between science and ideology for that between bourgeois and proletarian science.[72] The real determinants of Stalin's pseudo-rectification escaped Althusser a decade after the event as much as they had party philosophers at the time. The implication that the 'Greatest Philologist in the World' proposed his amendments for reasons of theoretical principle is inept. Stalin's real concern, as Gayman has shown, was to endow state and party with the technocratic authority of neutral science; it was this consideration that dictated replacement of voluntarism by scientism.[73] Similarly, Stalin's *Foundations of Leninism*, a series of lectures delivered at Sverdlov University in April 1924 intended to codify Lenin's theoretical legacy, were adjudged 'excellent' by Althusser in 1962.[74] That few other Marxists post-Khrushchev have found Stalin's usurpation so is of less immediate importance than the fact that this was the text amended later the same year to feature as a cardinal Leninist principle the 'victory of socialism in one country'.[75] In any event, a regrettable feature of Althusser's later writings is intermittent obeisance to Stalin's theoretical merits. The commendation in *For Marx* of his expulsion of the negation of the negation from the laws of the dialectic was repeated in 1968 and 1969.[76] In 1967, for the first and only time in Althusser's published work, *Dialectical and Historical Materialism* – *parvum opus* of theoretical Stalinism – received a tribute, for all Althusser's reservations about its expository rigour.[77]

---

[72] See Althusser 1969a, p. 22 (a point repeated in Althusser and Balibar 1970, p. 133); and cf. Gayman 1979, p. 176ff. Gayman cites texts by Desanti and others from *La Nouvelle Critique*, no. 45, 1953. Althusser's point was taken up by the young Balibar in his 1966, which served as an introduction to Stalin's *Marxism and Linguistics*.

[73] See Gayman 1979, pp. 190–1.

[74] Althusser 1962a, p. 97, n. 16.

[75] See Stalin 1973, pp. 118–19.

[76] See Althusser 1972, p. 181 and Althusser 1971, p. 91. Neither is a ringing endorsement. In the second, Althusser comments: 'Stalin was right, for once, to suppress "the negation of the negation" . . ., it must be said to the advantage of other, even more serious errors'.

[77] See 'On Theoretical Work', in Althusser 1990, p. 53. This is the more surprising given that in the exactly contemporaneous 'The Historical Task of Marxist Philosophy', Althusser was writing the following about the *'evolutionist* interpretation of Marxism': 'Basically, it consists in applying to Marx the finalist, teleological schemas of the Hegelian dialectic, Darwinian biology, Spenserian "philosophy", and so on. We have an example of it in Plekhanov's interpretation of Marxist philosophy, and in the mechanistic, economistic, fatalistic interpretation of historical materialism defended by certain theoreticians and leaders of the Second International. "Marxist" evolutionism holds, for example, that the modes of production follow one another in an inevitable, immutable order: we find a trace of this in Stalin's famous list, contained in his short

Stalin's authority for the distinction between historical and dialectical materialism was also invoked in 1966 and 1968.[78] His insistence on the working class's requirement of '*philosophy* in the class struggle' was noted, probably with irony, in *Reply to John Lewis*.[79]

Thus, in the course of his complementary critiques of theoretical Stalinism and theoretical humanism, Althusser occasionally employed the former against the latter. That he was a critic of the former is plain, though perhaps at its plainest in a text unpublished in French ('Theory, Theoretical Practice and Theoretical Formation'). By 1969, he was sketching the explicit critique of *Dialectical and Historical Materialism* which was to feature in *Reply to John Lewis* and become a familiar item in his own work and that of his collaborators thereafter.[80] The Althusserian version of Stalin's treatise – 'Historical Materialism and Dialectical Materialism' (1966) – had little in common with the views of the 'coryphaeus of science'. And Althusser's general emphasis throughout the 1960s was on the non-existence of Marxist philosophy and the under-development of historical materialism. Yet over and above their status as gratuitous provocations (*pour épater les humanistes?*), and tokens of a refusal to 'disappear' Stalin, these references are symptomatic of the ambiguities of Althusserianism, traceable, once again, to Maoism.

Althusser conceived the historical and dialectical materialism fashioned in *For Marx* and *Reading 'Capital'* as a return to Marx and reconstruction of Lenin, thus as a rupture with the theoretical Stalinism that exploited and deformed

---

book *Dialectical and Historical Materialism*. Evolutionism also holds, like Hegelian idealism and all the philosophies of history (which, in this respect, are religious), that there is a "meaning" to history, conceived as a *finality* governing it: we can find traces of this in the formulas that effectively identify historical necessity with fatality, speak of the *inevitable* triumph of socialism, and so on. "Marxist" evolutionism is incapable of accounting theoretically for the possibility and necessity of the political activity of the Communist parties, for the possibility of the failures of the workers' movement, and even for some of its successes, whenever they are unexpected and paradoxical in the sense that they fail to conform to its mechanistic schemas or the immutable order of the modes of production (the Cuban revolution, the possibilities of revolution in the "backward" countries, etc.). Evolutionism breeds technicist and economistic illusions and political passivity; it systematically underestimates the adversary's capacity to react; it underestimates the role of class struggle, politics, ideology and philosophy in the class struggle' (Althusser 2003, p. 188). Later, Althusser criticises Stalin's 'technicist' definition of the productive forces (p. 197).

[78] See Althusser 1966a, p. 90; Althusser 1972, p. 165.
[79] Althusser 1976a, p. 37.
[80] See Althusser 1971, p. 92.

Marxism and Leninism. By the same token, the orthodoxy articulated in *Reply to John Lewis* was the rectification and consummation of this rupture. The reality was somewhat different. With his auto-critique and revision Althusser regressed, via Maoism, to a schematic Marxism-Leninism which, in the *Reply*, is unhappily redolent of Cominform Marxism. In other words, on the most favourable reading, Althusserianism mark two was no substantive alternative either to theoretical Stalinism – or to Althusserianism mark one; on the least, it could not constitute a left-wing alternative to the Stalinisation of Marxist theory since its elected model maintained links with the apogee of that process (the Cominform period).[81] Seduced by Maoism, Althusser turned aside from what, despite remaining areas of ambiguity, was the far more original and fruitful course of 1960–5.

The Chinese defence of Marxist-Leninist orthodoxy against the renegade Khrushchev was largely based on casuistry. Who but Stalin, for example, had set the precedent of considering the USSR a 'state of the whole people'? Again, who – if not Stalin – had first exhorted the Communist parties to raise the 'banners' of 'bourgeois-democratic freedoms and national sovereignty' surrendered by the bourgeoisie, and to prioritise the struggle for the 'preservation of peace'?[82] Loyal to Stalin's name, in these instances the CPC was disloyal to his writ. In other respects, however, the Chinese proved star pupils – especially of the *style* of Cominform ideological campaigns (for

---

[81] Nevertheless, in Althusser 1976a, p. 79, n. 1, Althusser listed a set of 'formulae and slogans which were claimed to be "scientific" but were no more than "ideological", and which concealed very strange practices' – *viz*.: 'the economist evolutionism of Stalin's *Dialectical and Historical Materialism*; the conjuring away of the historical role of Trotsky and others in the Bolshevik Revolution (*Short History of the CPSU(B)*); the thesis of the sharpening of the class struggle under socialism; the formula "everything depends on the cadres", etc. Among ourselves: the thesis of "bourgeois science/ proletarian science", the thesis of "absolute pauperisation", etc.' Unlike the CPC, Althusser also rejected Stalin's notion of a socialist mode of production – central to the new orthodoxy elaborated in *Economic Problems of Socialism in the USSR* (see Gayman 1979, pp. 195–6).
[82] The first 'deviation' was enshrined in the 1936 Constitution; see Stalin 1973, pp. 347, 367–8 for declarations on the disappearance of 'antagonistic classes' from the USSR. The continuity between Stalin and Khrushchev on this issue was noted by Althusser and his colleagues, who drew the anti-Stalinist conclusion. The second 'deviation' was promulgated in Stalin's swan-song at the Nineteenth Congress of the CPSU in 1952 (see Stalin 1973, pp. 508–11) – a speech criticised by Althusser in *De la superstructure* (Althusser 1995a, p. 143).

example, against Yugoslavia).[83] Moreover, Althusser's reservations about *Dialectical and Historical Materialism* were not shared by the CPC leadership. In 1941, Mao had advanced proposals for 'reforming the method and the system of study throughout our Party' – among them, employment of the *Short Course* as 'the principal material'.[84] Following Khrushchev's speech, the CPSU ceased to reprint Stalin's text and the mendacious compendium in which it featured. The CPC, by contrast, continued to distribute Stalin's works; in the company of Zhdanov, they remained standard items in Maoist bibliographies the world over. The ossified Marxism bequeathed by Stalin to the international Communist movement found its doughtiest defender in Chinese Communism. The CPC referred to this system by its traditional designation: Marxism-Leninism. More accurately, it can be termed theoretical Stalinism.

Having fabricated 'Leninism' as part of the campaign against Trotsky, Stalin and his supporters proceeded to the concoction of a state doctrine. As Georges Labica has recalled, Stalin's catechism of 1938 is inseparable from the *Short Course* in which it appeared. Placed in Chapter 4 immediately after the section on Lenin's *Materialism and Empirio-Criticism*, it was presented as the systematisation of classical Bolshevism. Thus 'Marxism-Leninism' was, in Labica's words, '*the theoretical consecration of Stalinist politics*'.[85] At the Twentieth Congress, Stalin was criticised in the name of the doctrine forged by him as the guarantor of his infallibility. In himself attempting to turn the weapon of 'Marxism-Leninism' against 'dogmatism', Althusser, accordingly, was playing with theoretical fire. Here, at least, the CPC was right: there was an organic connection between Marxist-Leninist orthodoxy and the career of the 'great revolutionary'. Given this, the surprising thing is just how far *For Marx* and *Reading 'Capital'* (where Marxism-Leninism as such is rarely mentioned) did break with the Gensek's Marxism. As Labica has indicated and Althusser himself intimated, 'Marxist philosophy' – dialectical materialism – was the 'blind-spot' of the original Althusserian project.[86] The point is that the rectification made by Althusser, rather than distancing him from the Stalinist legacy, brought him nearer to it. The second definition of philosophy as 'class

---

[83] See Marcou 1979, p. 159.
[84] See Mao Tse-Tung 1967, pp. 162, 169.
[85] Labica 1984, pp. 23–4; see also p. 58.
[86] Labica 1984, p. 109.

struggle in theory' could not contribute to the deconstruction of theoretical Stalinism, and aid a de-Stalinisation of Marxist theory, since it is at the opposite end of the same spectrum as its putative antagonist.

In turning to the CPC's version of Marxism-Leninism – 'Marxism-Leninism-Mao Zedong Thought' – as 'Marxism-Leninism applied to the experience of the Chinese Revolution and Chinese socialism, Marxism-Leninism enriched by this experience and expressed in a form directly accessible to the masses',[87] Althusser substituted a faith in China's state philosophy for faith in the USSR's. While the official doctrine of the Cultural Revolution did not restrict class struggle to the ideological sphere, it did pronounce it of paramount importance in a socialist society, identifying ideology as the Archimedean point from which the fate of the revolution would be decided. What Lecourt in his excellent study of Lysenkoism has fittingly termed the 'imaginary class struggle'[88] conducted under the *Zhdanovschina* against 'bourgeois science', aesthetic 'cosmopolitanism' and 'decadence', and so on, was reproduced, indeed exceeded, in the decade of the Cultural Revolution. The class struggle in theory naturally extended to Marxism and licensed the treatment of defeated leaders – Liu, Deng, Lin – as agents of the bourgeoisie, in an Oriental re-run of the Stalinist witch-hunts. The rubric of 'criticism and self-criticism' canonised by Zhdanov in 1947[89] provided a spurious Marxist cover for ideological and psychological blackmail. The texts were stereotyped, the acts Stalinist. Fidelity to the Chairman's *obiter dicta* and pietism for the *Little Red Book* became the epitome of 'party spirit' – the Maoist equivalent of adhesion to the dogmas of proletarian science. The delirious cult of Mao ('great teacher, great leader, great supreme commander, great helmsman') symbolised this repetition of history as tragedy. This was no concrete critique of Stalinism. The sole disparity between deeds and words was between the reality in China and its textual transfiguration in Paris (but not only there).

It would be as misleading to imply the slightest assent on Althusser's part to the practices of the Maoist radicals between 1966 and 1976 as it would to cast him as a born-again Zhdanovist. Yet, although he always rejected the thesis of proletarian science, and displayed no inclination to follow Jiang

---

[87] Althusser 1966b, p. 10.
[88] Lecourt 1977, p. 128.
[89] See Zhdanov 1950, pp. 107–8.

Quing in reading musical notes as indices of class position, his politicised second definition of philosophy inhabits the same ideological universe of imaginary class struggle that was waged, all too materially, in the People's Republic. It would be an exaggeration to say that *Reply to John Lewis* re- rather than *de*-Stalinises Marxism. But, at the same time – and whatever Althusser's intentions – it represents not a settling of accounts with the residual Stalinist conscience of *Reading 'Capital'*, but, in its 'Maoisation' of Marxism, a rapprochement with the modern representatives of that conscience. Rather the theoreticist deviation than the theorisation of deviations?

Perhaps the best way to conclude this fifth chapter is to return to the remarks made by Althusser in 1975 which head the first. Althusser was right to consider Khrushchev's initiative a 'right-wing destalinisation'; correct, too, in regarding the consequent humanist renaissance *within* the Communist parties as theoretically and politically inadequate – but quite wrong to tar all Marxist humanisms and historicisms with a bourgeois brush. The refusal to surrender the later Marx and Lenin to the Stalinist parody of them; the belief that a Marxist explanation and critique of Stalinism demanded more than ethical judgements; the implication that a non-Stalinist Communist political strategy required a 'renewal' of Marxist theory – these also were commendable, even if Althusser sometimes gave the impression that he was unique in appreciating their necessity. On the other hand, Althusser never did 'reflect' on Khrushchev, Prague and Lin Piao. And his reflections on Stalin did not amount to the concrete analysis theoretical humanism had been taxed with a constitutional incapacity to generate, but to an essay in theoretical reductionism (even if it was accurate in identifying economism as a central plank of Stalinism). When, moreover, Althusser's 'left-wing' critique was finally issued, it contained the major surprise of a defence of Stalin against critiques from the Left. However disappointing the outcome, the point is not to lament or execrate, but to understand, it. And the explanation, this chapter has tried to argue, must be sought where Althusser sought inspiration for the 'revolutionary project in the West': Maoist China.

For over a decade, Althusser was caught up in the Parisian illusion of the epoch, which in turn engendered illusions about past epochs. The debacle in China in the 1970s was to have a dismaying impact on sections of the Marxist intelligentsia in France. In retrospect, Althusser's inconsistency in adhering to the PCF while fixing his colours to the Chinese mast is something to be grateful for; it probably saved him from the kind of widespread renegacy which will be illustrated in Chapter 6. Nevertheless, the collapse of Althusser's elected alternative had an influence on him as strong as its emergence. Formerly, he had taken refuge from Stalinist practice in Marxist theory, while reading in the Maoist Cultural Revolution a Leninist 'letter from afar' (one always stamped 'return to sender' by the PCF). Henceforth his confidence in that theory was profoundly shaken and his thinking infected with a pessimism that was perhaps scarcely less inclement to Marxism than the Stalinism he now criticised much more forthrightly.

Chapter Six
The Eclipse of Althusserianism

At last the crisis of Marxism has exploded!

Louis Althusser, 'The Crisis of Marxism'

In Chapters 4 and 5, the theoretico-political positions arrived at by the later Althusser were examined. The bulk of Anglophone commentary on his work posits one main caesura in it: the break between the Althusser of 1960–7 and the Althusser of 1967–; between the exponent of the theory of theoretical practice and the militant of the class struggle in theory; between the self-declared defender of Marxism and the professed partisan of Marxism-Leninism. And it is not wrong to do so. Yet this discrimination can be made at the price of overlooking or obscuring a more profound mutation in Althusser's career: the distance which separates the self-confident champion of the scientificity of Marxism from the herald and interrogator of the 'crisis of Marxism'. And, where attention has been paid to that complex phenomenon – the crisis of Marxism – there has been no comparable focus on the crisis of Althusserianism by which it was accompanied.

The crisis announced by Althusser in Venice in November 1977 in fact concerned three overlapping and interlocking crises which, taken individually or collectively, were somewhat narrower in scope than a crisis of Marxism as such: (i) a crisis of Marxism-Leninism which weighed with particular gravity on the *maoisant* French Left; (ii) a crisis of Communism, induced by the vicissitudes of Eurocommunism as a 'third way' between Stalinism and social democracy, and implicating the PCF; and (iii) a crisis of Althusser's Marxism, infected with theoretical and political scepticism as Maoism collapsed, Eurocommunism stalled, and 'actually existing socialism' stagnated in the second half of the 1970s. The paradox of this last crisis was that whilst it involved renunciation of many of the theoretical leitmotifs of Althusserianism, it simultaneously permitted a significant political reorientation – *from Maoism to 'centrism' or left Eurocommunism*. Where many of his peers and ex-students abandoned any kind of allegiance to Marxism, Althusser himself emerged as a Communist militant critical of his party and its history, but equally unaccommodating to its enemies on the Right.

Marxism yesterday and today

In June 1975, a jury of the University of Picardy heard Althusser's defence of his 'doctoral thesis' (comprising his work between 1959 and 1965). In what *Le Monde* described as 'an astonishing performance', he explained how his 'philosophical intervention was the work of a member of the Communist Party, acting . . . within the Labour Movement and for it'; how, in order to influence the real Prince (the leadership of the PCF), he had spoken in the name of an imaginary Prince; how, emulating Lenin's *What Is to Be Done?*, he had 'bent the stick' in the direction of theoretical anti-humanism to combat *garaudysme* and so on; and how he had practised the class struggle in theory so as to challenge '*the ideological hegemony of the ruling class*'.[1] In his *Soutenance*

---

[1] See Anonymous 1975 and Althusser 1976a, pp. 165–75. 'The politics which constitute philosophy,' writes Althusser, 'bear on and turn around . . . *the ideological hegemony of the ruling class*, whether it is a question of organising it, strengthening it, defending it or fighting against it' (Althusser 1976a, p. 167). This theme was taken up in Althusser 1975 and in *La Transformación de la filosofía* – a lecture given at the University of Granada in March 1976. In the latter, Althusser argued that, contra Stalin's 'terroristic practices', just as the post-revolutionary state should be a 'non-state' preparing its own disappearance, so Marxist philosophy must be a 'non-philosophy' – a 'new practice of philosophy serv[ing] the proletarian class struggle without imposing upon it an oppressive ideological unity . . ., but rather creating for it the ideological conditions for the liberation and free development of social practices': Althusser 1990, pp. 264–5. Althusser's brief invocation of Machiavelli to explain his '*extremism*' (Althusser 1976a, pp. 170–1) is illuminated in the conclusion to a lecture dating from 1977, 'Machiavelli's Solitude'; see Althusser 1999, pp. 115–30.

(published in revised form in October of the same year in *La Pensée*), Althusser did not speculate on the fate of his theoretical intervention or on its political fruits. But he did make – or rather repeat – a remark of some importance for his future evolution. As a theoretical discourse with scientific pretensions, historical materialism was under an obligation to progress – to provide 'new knowledge, about imperialism *and* the State *and* ideologies *and* socialism *and* the Labour Movement itself': 'Marxist theory can fall behind history and even behind itself, if it ever believes that it has arrived'.[2] So, in June 1975, Althusser was defending – albeit in qualified form – his theoretical project in the early 1960s, ascribing to it an unambiguously anti-Stalinist political significance, and claiming that his writings from 1967 onwards had made some of the necessary amendments to the original theses. More generally, he was characteristically postulating the existence of a scientific theory – historical materialism – which could be defended philosophically and which, as a research programme, was open to, indeed required, development. The continent of history discovered by Marx remained to be explored. Among the territories to be charted were the histories of socialism and Marxism.

In the last chapter, some doubt was cast on Althusser's political self-evaluation. On this occasion, however, his promises were partially fulfilled. In 1976, Lecourt published a major study of Lysenkoism in the *Théorie* series (*Proletarian Science?*), to which Althusser contributed a short but remarkable introduction: 'Unfinished History'. In strong contrast to the silences of *For Marx* and *Reading 'Capital'* and the ambiguities of *Reply to John Lewis*, Althusser explicitly returned to the formative years of his own Marxism: the Cold War in theory. Deploring the silence of the CPSU and fraternal parties alike, he noted that:

> An extraordinary paradox . . . asserts itself here, just as it does in the case of the terrible reality later baptised with the derisory name of 'personality cult', and in many other episodes in the history of the labour movement: the Communist Parties, provided by Marx for the first time in history with scientific means of understanding history . . . *seem to be powerless to account as Marxists for their own history* – especially when they have made a mistake.[3]

[2] Althusser 1976a, p. 195.
[3] Althusser 1977b, pp. 7–8.

Althusser disparaged the pseudo-rectifications made by the CPSU and PCF and invoked the authority of Lenin for the claim that 'the labour movement must analyse and understand its past . . . so that it will not be fighting in the dark'. The *'primacy of Marxist politics'* dictated a historical-materialist account of the USSR and the Communist movement bearing on the profound causes of errors, not merely the visible effects of an unanalysed and uncriticised cause.[4] The root cause of Lysenkoism had been left unexamined and unrectified, not because the means were lacking but for political reasons – a consideration which led Althusser to what was easily his most outspoken reflection on Stalinism past and present. It was time to 'stop telling (ourselves) stories', he concluded, and to pose the 'simple but serious problem': *'what social relations today constitute the Soviet social formation?'*[5] Althusser offered no response to his question here, though he did take the opportunity to rectify *Reply to John Lewis* by now characterising the 'political line' of the Stalin period as one of 'economism and voluntarism'. Instead, he turned to the Lysenko episode, remarking the PCF's 'vanguard' role in it and the fact that the Stalinist *'ontological* version' of dialectical materialism guaranteeing Lysenko's theories had been treated to a superficial rectification, which preserved its substance and its 'apologetic function' as a practical ideology 'glorifying the existing state of affairs'.[6] *Histoire terminée, histoire interminable?*

What prompted Althusser's most forthright condemnation of the Stalin period, his first written indictment of continuing repression in the USSR and 'elsewhere' (China as well as Eastern Europe?), and his criticism of the PCF's evasion of the issues involved is not known. But it can be surmised. Althusser's question was on the agenda. If one man could be said to have put it there, it was Alexander Solzhenitsyn, the first volume of whose *Gulag Archipelago* appeared in 1974 (the year its author was exiled). In the mid-1970s, freelance French Marxists suddenly discovered the Gulag – and it came as a revelation of Damascene proportions. In a move diametrically opposed to Althusser's call for a Marxist analysis of the history made in Marxism's name, many followed the Russian novelist in assigning responsibility for that history to

---

[4] Althusser 1977b, pp. 9–10.
[5] Althusser 1977b, p. 13; see pp. 11–13.
[6] Althusser 1977b, pp. 13–16. In addition to Lecourt 1977, see Lecourt 1982, pp. 133–45 and Balibar 1977 on Stalinist ideology. Althusser was publicly rebuked for the 'obvious excesses' of his text in *L'Humanité*, 14 May 1976.

Marxism. First off the mark was the former leader of Gauche prolétarienne and sometime Clausewitz of French Marxism, André Glucksmann, with *La Cuisinière et le mangeur d'hommes* (1975) – an ideological extravaganza hailed by fellow theoretical anti-humanist and leftist Michel Foucault, who now declared Stalinism to be 'the truth' of Marxism.[7] Glucksmann followed this up two years later with *The Master Thinkers*, a Parisian-irrationalist version of Popper's *Open Society and its Enemies*, which also had some stern words for Althusser.[8] The *nouveaux philosophes* proper were introduced to the French public by their most assiduous and sententious (self-)publicist, Bernard-Henri Lévy, in June 1976. 'Solzhenitsyn,' Lévy informed readers of *Les Nouvelles Littéraires*, 'plays the same role for these people as Althusser played ten years ago'.[9] Precisely: once, Marxism had been all-powerful because it was true – and engendered such marvels as the Cultural Revolution; now Marxism was all-powerful because it was scientific – and gave birth to monsters. By a simple reversal of moral signs, an angelic was converted into a diabolical scientism. Marxism, totalitarian science and science of totalitarianism, remained the demiurge of history. 'If we have any objection against Marxism,' Foucault confided in 1976, 'it lies in the fact that it could effectively be a science'.[10] *Qua* scientific discourse, Marxism secreted a will-to-power whose truth was the Gulag. Or, as Lévy put it in his popularisation of the self-styled 'New Philosophy', *La Barbarie à visage humain* (1977): 'The Soviet camps are Marxist, as Marxist as Auschwitz was Nazi'.[11] The coincidence of Solzhenitsyn's epic and the debacle in China thus unleashed a concerted ideological campaign, which recycled the themes of the Cold War: not 'socialism or barbarism', but 'socialism = barbarism'; 'Communism = Nazism'. In September 1977 *Time* magazine, exultant at the intellectual *renversement des alliances* on the Left Bank, splashed its front cover: 'Marx Is Dead'. And, indeed, by the end of the year, what has been termed 'a new "Parisian consensus"' – an anti-Marxist one – had crystallised.[12]

As Dews and others have argued, the political and theoretical perspectives of post-'68 *gauchisme* prepared the ground for the *nouvelle philosophie*. In his

---

[7] Quoted in Callinicos 1982, p. 108.
[8] See Glucksmann 1981, pp. 120–2.
[9] *Les Nouvelles Littéraires*, 10 June 1976.
[10] Foucault 1980, p. 84.
[11] Lévy 1977, p. 167.
[12] Dews 1979, p. 129. For another excellent account, see Dews 1985.

text on May 1968 – *Strategy and Revolution in France in 1968* – Glucksmann had opined that '[b]eneath the ballot papers survives the revolutionary situation disclosed in May' and concluded: 'the horizon is revolution, or counter-revolution'.[13] This was the immediate horizon of Gauche prolétarienne, a Maoist organisation formed from a fusion of elements of the UJC and the Mouvement du 22 mars. In an issue of *Les Temps Modernes* devoted to 'New Fascism, New Democracy' in 1972, Glucksmann expounded its ultra-leftist political perspectives: that reaction (the Pompidou régime) took the form of a 'fascism from on high'; that it was buttressed by a social fascism beneath – the PCF, which had saved the day for capitalism in 1968; and that the revolutionary movement must organise a 'new popular resistance' against it, imitating the exemplary actions which would stimulate the masses to rebellion and thence to a people's war. In the event, it was in Italy and West Germany that analogous phantasms were acted out – by the Red Brigades and the Red Army Faction. For the most part, the ultra-leftists of the Latin Quarter gratified their image as 'new partisans' with rhetorical terrorism against the Gaullists and their Communist *collabos*; only in their heads did the critique of arms replace the weapon of criticism. Important for our purposes is that the anti-Sovietism the Maoists had learned from the CPC, and the anti-Communism they promulgated in a Gallic re-run of the 'third period', could easily slide into an outright anti-Marxism. And this was exactly what happened in the mid-1970s when, having foundered on its own fantasies, the ultra-leftist, anti-Leninist spontaneism and populism preached (if not exactly practised) by the 'servants of the people' metamorphosed into a romantic philosophy of power and ethic of resistance; a critique of Communism into a critique of Marxism per se. In the subsequent revaluation of values, May '68 and its *gauchiste* aftermath were perceived, in Foucault's words, as 'something profoundly anti-Marxist'.[14] Marxism was now identified with a technocratic, authoritarian practice of politics whose terminus was *l'enfer concentrationnaire* (capitalism had once equalled fascism; now it was socialism's turn). The PCF's behaviour in May and June had not been an aberration, but an exemplary instance of Marxism's complicity with *raison d'état*. Marxism was incapable of explaining the USSR because it was responsible for it. In

---

[13] Glucksmann 1968, pp. 83, 120.
[14] Foucault 1980, p. 57.

the shape of the PCF, it had been hostile to May '68 because the Paris Spring was inimical to its totalitarian project.

Few recantations have been as abject as this collective desertion. The utterly unoriginal critique of Marxism fashionable in France in the second half of the 1970s went through the motions of distancing itself from the Right. Yet its popularity with *Time*, Giscard d'Estaing et al. was scarcely fortuitous, but rooted in its recuperation of May '68 and the dominant anarcho-libertarian ideology of May for the Free World. The regrettable truth, however, is that the born-again anti-Marxists would never have succeeded in palming off such a mélange of Camus, Popper, Solzhenitsyn and Foucault as anything but rehashed Cold-War ideology had it not been for the PCF's derelictions on the subject of Stalinism. In Paris, as elsewhere, it takes two to tango. If the threat posed to the French social order by the Union of the Left made the expiations of the *enragés* 'expeditions of some timely men' (Nietzsche), the occasional superficial criticisms of the Brezhnev régime ventured by PCF leaders from October 1975 onwards were seen for the opportunistic adjustments to the exigencies of electoral opinion they were. The PCF's posthumous loyalty to Stalinism, and concomitant elusion of serious research and debate on the Soviet experience, returned to plague it even as its post-1956 strategy apparently neared success. Where anarchism had constituted a punishment for the sins of opportunism, anti-Communism was the nemesis of residual Stalinism.

The questions posed by Althusser in 1976, then, were already being answered with stock replies from the Cold-War repertoire. The Parisian consensus was (in Foucault's words) that '[t]hose who hope to save themselves by opposing Marx's real beard to Stalin's false nose are wasting their time'.[15] Any Marxist account of the 'unfinished history' would receive a not so polite refusal in the best salons. Even as Althusser announced an end to story-telling, another kind of story became a bestseller. Historical materialism found itself ruled out of court by the confluence of two currents: the new philosophy and poststructuralism. The alliance Althusser had sought in the early 1960s unravelled after 1968 as the philosophers of desire and power tributary to May drove high structuralism from the seminar room. Althusserianism was thus doubly compromised – as a Marxism and as a structuralism. Althusser's

---

[15] Quoted in Callinicos 1982, p. 108. Naturally, there were dissenters – and eloquent ones: see, e.g., Debray 1978b; Lecourt 2001; and Linhart 1979.

Soutenance betrays an insouciance oblivious to the major, if largely, implicit challenge that had been mounted to historical materialism in such works as Deleuze and Guattari's *Anti-Oedipus* (1972) and Foucault's *Discipline and Punish* (1975). No response from the Althusserians was forthcoming as poststructuralism swept all before it. With Glucksmann, the 'transition from classicism to romanticism'[16] effected in French philosophy post-May took an explicitly anti-Marxist turn. And what the 'deconstructionist' philosophical challenge to Marxism had been unable to accomplish was achieved on the ideological *Kampfplatz* in record time. By 1977, historical materialism was generally regarded as theoretically and politically discredited in France. A fight-back was long overdue. If one senior French Marxist philosopher could have been expected to shoulder the task, the obvious candidate was Althusser.

In the event, he revealed himself incapable of it. He came less to defeat his antagonists in a head-on confrontation than to underwrite – albeit unwittingly, by demission and default – some of their pronouncements. In the early 1960s, Althusser had hitched Marxism to structuralism's rising star. In the second half of the 1970s, he proved powerless to meet the challenge of the poststructuralism that emerged from its forebear. And it was precisely the Marxism-Leninism with which Althusser had aligned himself in a retreat from 'structuralism' after 1965 that was most immediately put in question by his fellow countrymen. When Althusser came to deliver his paper on 'The Crisis of Marxism' to a conference organised by the Italian group, *Il Manifesto*, on the subject of post-revolutionary societies in November 1977, the theoretical confidence and combativeness of former years had evaporated. Previously, for Althusser the significant crisis of Marxism had been that which commenced with the Twentieth Congress of the CPSU. Now, in contrast, he postulated a crisis of much longer duration and graver dimensions whose contemporary acuity paradoxically offered an opportunity for Marxism. As Althusser explained at the beginning of his text, the challenge to Marxism was to be met by accepting the reality, but attempting to transform the meaning, of the 'crisis of Marxism'.

---

[16] Dews 1979, p. 129. For far and away the best overall discussion, Marxist or non-Marxist, of poststructuralism, see Dews 1987.

First of all, what was this crisis?

> A phenomenon which must be grasped at the historical world level, and which concerns the difficulties, contradictions and dilemmas in which the revolutionary organizations of struggle based on the Marxist tradition are now involved. Not only is the unity of the International Communist Movement affected, and its old forms of organization destroyed, but its own history is put in question, together with its traditional strategies and practices.[17]

Bereft of 'any really living reference for socialism' and haunted by Stalinism, Marxists were on the defensive. This state of affairs could not be ameliorated by provision of the requisite analysis of Soviet history. For, behind the failure hitherto to supply it, there lay 'the extreme difficulty . . . and perhaps even, in the present state of our theoretical knowledge, almost the impossibility of providing a really satisfactory Marxist explanation of a history which . . . was made in the name of Marxism'. If Marxist theory was not responsible for the history made in its name, it was implicated in and 'compromised' by it.[18]

The conjoint political and theoretical crisis of Marxism could be met by ignoring it or weathering it in expectation of better times to come. A third possibility – one endorsed by Althusser – was

> to view the matter with sufficient historical, theoretical and political perspective, in order to try to discover . . . the character, meaning and implications of the crisis. If we succeed in this, we can then start talking in a different way, and, emerging from our long history, instead of stating that 'Marxism is in crisis', we can say: 'At last the crisis of Marxism has exploded! At last it is in full view! At last something vital and alive can be liberated by this crisis and in this crisis.'[19]

Far from being a 'recent phenomenon', the crisis dated back to the 1930s. It was then that

> Marxism – which had been alive, living from its own contradictions – became blocked, entrenched in 'theoretical' formulae, within a line and practices, imposed by the historical control of Stalinism. . . . In doing violence to what

---

[17] Althusser 1979b, p. 226.
[18] Althusser 1979b, pp. 227–8.
[19] Althusser 1979b, p. 229.

Marxism had been, with its openness as well as its difficulties, Stalin in effect provoked a serious crisis within it, but in the same act he blocked it and prevented it from exploding.[20]

The current eruption did not simply visit destruction, but, in liaison with the popular struggles of the 1960s and 1970s, held out the promise of a 'possible liberation and renewal'.

Yet there was no longer any question of a return to Marx à la Althusser:

We cannot consider our historical, political and even theoretical tradition as a *pure* heritage, which was distorted by an individual called Stalin, or by the historical period which he dominated. There is no original 'purity' of Marxism that only has to be rediscovered. During the whole testing period of the 1960s when we, in our different ways, went 'back to the classics', when we read or re-read Marx, Lenin and Gramsci, trying to find in them a living Marxism, something which was being snuffed out by Stalin-type formulae and practices, we were all forced, each in our own way, even within our differences, to admit the obvious – namely, that our theoretical tradition is not 'pure'; that, contrary to Lenin's over-hasty phrase, Marxism is not a 'block of steel' but contains difficulties, contradictions and gaps, which have also played, at their own level, their role in the crisis, as they already did at the time of the Second International, and even at the beginning of the Third (Communist) International, while Lenin was still alive.[21]

Marxism was not a seamless scientific web. Marx had laid the foundations of what Althusser now defined as 'a theory of the conditions and forms of the class struggle in capitalist societies'. But that theory was incomplete and bore the imprint of the dominant bourgeois ideology of its time, by which it had been penetrated throughout its history. The classics themselves were flawed. By way of illustration, Althusser pointed to what he termed the 'fictitious' unity of *Capital* and the purely quantitative theory of exploitation derivative from it. He alluded to the 'enigma' of Marxist philosophy – the dialectic announced by Marx, fashioned in positivist and evolutionist form by his successors, and catechised by Stalin. Moreover, he perceived 'two theoretical gaps of great importance' in Marx and Lenin's contributions: the

---

[20] Althusser 1979b, p. 230.
[21] Althusser 1979b, p. 231.

theory of the state and of revolutionary organisations. As to the first, Marxism did not possess a theory as such, only injunctions to avoid what Lenin called 'constitutional illusions' – a crippling political lacuna. As for the second, again, Marxism lacked a genuine theory of the 'functioning' of political parties and trade unions, leading to the dual danger of a reproduction of bourgeois forms in the process of their contestation and a 'fusion' of state and party/ unions in any post-revolutionary social order.[22]

The issues of state and party had been dramatised by the powerful mass movements that had arisen in Italy, Spain and France (and, we might add, by the Cultural Revolution). They were *'burning* political questions', the answers to which would help determine the fate of the social and labour movements alike. At the same time, mass practice furnished a condition of possibility for the resolution of the crisis – which itself represented a 'historical opportunity of liberation'. Marxism, Althusser concluded,

> has in its history passed through a long series of crises and transformations. . . .
> We are *now*, in the present crisis, faced with a similar transformation [to
> that which occurred after the collapse of the Second International – GE]
> which is already finding its roots in the struggle of the masses. It can bring
> about the renewal of Marxism, give new force to its theory, modify its

---

[22] See Althusser 1979b, pp. 232–5. In an interview with Rossana Rossanda for *Il Manifesto* in December 1977, Althusser elaborated on these points, arguing that Marx, as if *'paralysed* by the bourgeois representation of the state, politics, etc.', had never proceeded to the 'critique of politics' which must accompany his 'critique of political economy' – and nor had his successors (Althusser 1978d, pp. 6–7). But this was a vital requirement: 'Above all, it is a question of not reducing [politics] to the forms officially sanctioned as political by bourgeois ideology: the state, popular representation, political struggle over the possession of state power, political parties, etc. If one enters into this logic and remains in it, one risks falling not only into "parliamentary cretinism", but above all into the juridical illusion of politics: for politics is defined by political law, and this law consecrates (and only consecrates) the forms of politics defined by bourgeois ideology' (p. 8). The 'totally unforeseen political initiatives' of the ecological and feminist movements, for example, constituted a potentially fruitful new departure, which both challenged 'classical bourgeois forms of politics' and put in question the Marxist conception of politics and the party (pp. 8–9). 'Profound[ly] contaminat[ed] by bourgeois ideology', the organisational form of the Communist parties was modelled on the bourgeois political apparatus and characterised by the separation of leaders from ordinary militants and of the party from the masses. Theoretical rectification and practical transformation were urgent, since the Communist parties must preserve their 'exteriority' and 'autonomy' vis-à-vis the state if they were to act as one of the instruments of the 'withering away' of the post-revolutionary state – and hence of communism (p. 9).

ideology, its organisation and its practices, opening up a real future of social, political and cultural revolution for the working class and for all working people.[23]

Among the first to demur at Althusser's diagnosis was Ursula Schmiederer, who protested in her contribution to the same conference that it was not Marxism which was in crisis but Marxism-Leninism.[24] As we shall see later, Althusser was not alone among the leading lights of West-European Marxism in detecting symptoms of a general crisis of Marxism in the 1970s. Nevertheless, it is the case that the crisis began as a crisis of Maoism before spreading to the ranks of Communist parties disorientated by the misadventures of Eurocommunism. The omission from a text eloquent on the subject of Stalinism of the slightest allusion to the experience of Maoist China – Althusser's lately deceased 'really living reference for socialism' – is surely the crucial index here. Deprived of this 'reference', Althusser's long-standing disenchantment with the USSR found unequivocal expression. When the red star over China fell, Althusser's Marxism was precipitated into crisis alongside that of his leftist critics, impelling him to his Venetian ruminations.

Althusser is to be faulted not so much for the perception of a crisis as for his delineation and treatment of it – for the focus and tenor of his remarks. The crisis of Stalinism and the Communist alternatives to it was amplified to implicate Marxism *tout court*. Althusser's intervention was thus hardly calculated to arrest the advance of anti-Marxism. Belated recognition of the fact that Stalin, rather than Khrushchevism and theoretical humanism, represented the veritable crisis is to be welcomed. Having recently joined them, however, Althusser erred in conceding the territory that independent Marxists had fought to hold. Indicative of this syndrome was his pessimism as to the capacity of historical materialism to provide a convincing account of the Soviet social formation. It combined belated distance from Maoist simplicities with dejected assertions about the obstacles to any materialist explanation of Russian history: a proposition dear to the hearts of the new philosophers. Apparently unaware of the disarming implications of such a conclusion, Althusser compounded it by proceeding to query the independence of Marxism from Stalinism. Again, insofar as this constituted an admission

---

[23] Althusser 1979b, p. 237.
[24] Schmiederer 1979, p. 162.

of his own lingering illusions about Marxism-Leninism, it can be applauded. But, to the extent that it implied a contamination of Marxism *in toto*, it is unbalanced and, to say the least, does an injustice to those who learned their Marxism elsewhere than in the *Short Course* and the *Little Red Book*.

It can be objected to Althusser's periodisation that locating the emergence of the crisis – 'for us' – in the 1930s is a revealing imprecision, suggesting a residual myopia. Yet this would be somewhat beside the point. For the significant thing was that Althusser now foreswore any return to a pristine historical experience or to the Marxist-Leninist classics, announcing problems of a politico-theoretical nature in Marx and Lenin themselves. Naturally, there was nothing pernicious as such in this appreciation (what Marxist outside Tirana would gainsay it?) – only in the extravagance of its enunciation. It was as if, having discovered that the return to Marx of the 1960s had been accompanied by presuppositions from Marxist-Leninist orthodoxy, and that the rectifications of his own Marxism had been mortgaged to Maoism, Althusser was projecting these specific shortcomings onto Marx and Lenin – just as he had once precariously projected Marxism and Leninism onto the Cultural Revolution. The immediate consequences of the new theoretical scepticism emerged in his declaration that Marxism lacked a theory of state and politics – a judgement which confused prevalent schematism, theoretical underdevelopment, and a dearth of strategic thinking with sheer absence. Moreover, the Marxist philosopher who had been second to none in the vehemence and fastidiousness with which he asserted the gulf separating historical materialism from all species of bourgeois ideology, cavilling at the complaisance of his contemporaries, was now to be heard regretting its contamination by nineteenth-century ideological motifs. Therewith the herald of Marx's revolutionary singularity endorsed the claim made by Foucault in 1966 and cancelled the epistemological break. From being the science of history, historical materialism now dwindled into the problematic commencement of a theory of capitalist society. What must change in Marxism was left unspecified. But on this account – anti-dogmatism with a vengeance – it was little short of everything.

To be sure, the tone of Althusser's address was incongruously optimistic. It ended on an almost exultant note. Althusser's reflections on Marxism did not, however, warrant any such optimism. Reacting against his own former theoreticism and Marxism-Leninism, Althusser settled a personal account. In the process, he lent his prestigious voice to a refrain hardly conducive to dispelling mere melancholy and encouraging the collective effort required for an alleviation, let alone resolution, of the crisis. Indeed, his pronouncement could be interpreted as handing over much of the Marxist legacy to its detractors – a counter-signature rather than a counter-statement. What was in effect an autobiographical balance-sheet assumed the airs of an official court of inquiry which neglected to call other witnesses and hear other evidence. Judge and jury, Althusser proclaimed a crisis of Marxism and looked to its salvation in popular practice. The hopes invested in the advance of Eurocommunism which sustained his affirmative conclusion were to receive their quietus at the hands of the PCF leadership and French electorate the following spring. And then a crisis of French Communism – and Althusserianism – exploded.

The crisis of Communism

We have seen that, in the mid-1970s, historical materialism came under fire in France from the batteries of the poststructuralists and new philosophers. By the end of the decade, a paradigm pre-eminent in French intellectual culture since the Liberation had been routed. Such fire as was returned by Althusser at least was insufficient to hold up the enemy advance. Yet, if Marxist theory and, with it, the reputation of 'actually existing socialism' suffered a dramatic reverse in these years, the mass Communist parties of Western Europe were on the offensive for the first time since the Resistance. With the end of the postwar boom, a spectre was haunting Western Europe (and the State Department): Eurocommunism.

May '68 and the Italian 'hot autumn' the following year were a turning-point. For, although the reunification of revolutionary theory and practice considered imminent by some in an era of dual crisis – of capitalism and Stalinism – failed to materialise, the Communist parties of Italy, France and Spain were the main beneficiaries on the Marxist Left of the upsurge in working-class and popular militancy in Europe at the turn of the decade. The repressed – class politics – returned. With the onset of capitalist crisis, what Carrillo termed the 'Eurocommunist road to power' was the order of the day. The novelty of the Eurocommunist manifesto consisted in its *explicit* divergence from Comintern canons in an attempt to adapt socialist strategy to the conditions of bourgeois democracy under advanced capitalism. It comprised acceptance of a gradualist and constitutional conception of, and strategy for, socialism, envisaging an eventual rupture with capitalist polity and economy. This involved, to a greater or lesser degree, public distanciation from the Russian model; as distinct from Soviet-style socialism, the Western article would be democratic in means and ends. National and constitutional roads to power had a respectable pedigree in Khrushchevism. What converted this latter-day variant into a Western schism in the Communist movement was the autonomy from Moscow it claimed as a prerequisite of its project. Impelled by the Brezhnevite consolidation in Eastern Europe which had disappointed the promise of Khrushchevism, the Communist parties of Western Europe drew further away from the socialist mother country and closer to their own national traditions. In Italy the PCI made its 'historical compromise'; in Spain the PCE entered a 'pact of freedom'; and in France the PCF signed a Common Programme with the Socialists and Left Radicals, sealing a Union of the Left which was widely expected to triumph at the polls in March 1978.

Eurocommunism, then, entailed at least de facto renunciation of the 'Leninism' that had been official orthodoxy (however pro forma) for decades. In the PCF's case, de facto reorientation away from the Comintern heritage became de jure abrogation, when it was proposed in February 1976 at the Party's Twenty-Second Congress that the 'dictatorship of the proletariat' should be excised from its statutes. The nuanced response this elicited from Althusser – 'On the Twenty-Second Congress of the French Communist Party' – signposted his own evolution away from quasi-Maoist political positions. In a contribution to the discussion leading up to the Twenty-First Congress in October 1974, Althusser had entered various caveats about the PCF's strategic formulations, without by any means dissociating himself from them.[25] He now effectively demarcated his own position both from the official PCF orientation and from Comintern orthodoxy, giving the Twenty-Second Congress a guarded welcome and seeking to disengage what he regarded as its many positive features from the negative ones.

It was, he wrote, 'a *decisive event*, a crucial "turning-point" in the history of the Communist Party and the French Workers' Movement'.[26] Convened

---

[25] See Althusser 1976a, pp. 208–15.
[26] Althusser 1977c, p. 3.

amidst a double crisis – of imperialism and the Communist movement – the Congress represented an attempt to break out of the 'historical impasse' constituted by the crisis of the latter and forge a new strategy, which could bring the 'new forms of struggle' invented by popular movements in the era of détente to fruition. '*Never*', Althusser believed, had they been 'so powerful' – victorious in the Third World, advancing in the First.[27] Having warned that it would nevertheless be perilous to underestimate the capacity of imperialism to respond to these challenges directly or by proxy, Althusser moved on to discuss what he delineated as the six initiatives of the Twenty-Second Congress.

First, despite strong reservations on the theory of state monopoly capitalism underpinning PCF strategy, Althusser endorsed the perspective of 'democratic socialism'.[28] Secondly, he registered his agreement with the PCF's programme on the unprecedented possibility of a 'peaceful' and 'democratic' transition to socialism given the changed global balance of forces.[29] Thirdly, as regards abandonment of the dictatorship of the proletariat, Althusser argued that the deliberations had been notable for the absence of their real referent: Stalin. Since the policy document asserted the 'leading role' of the working class in a 'broad popular alliance', Althusser had no quarrel with it, considering it congruent with Marx and Lenin's theses on the indispensability of alliances. What was unsatisfactory was the ceremonial abrogation of the dictatorship of the proletariat without any discussion of the historical balance-sheet of the Soviet experience and the international Communist movement. The Congress had ignored Stalinism, domestic and foreign, decreeing the abandonment of the dictatorship of the proletariat on the grounds of its potential confusion with fascist dictatorship. This would not do: the reality of Soviet socialism under Stalin must be openly addressed:

> The list of examples provided to show that the word 'dictatorship' is intolerable . . . forgets to mention Stalin: not just the individual Stalin as such, but the structure and confusion of the Soviet Party and state; the line, 'theory' and practices imposed by Stalin for forty years, not just in the USSR but on the Communist Parties the world over.

---

[27] Althusser 1977c, pp. 4–5.
[28] Althusser 1977c, pp. 7–8.
[29] Althusser 1977c, pp. 8–9.

I am not pretending that this is a simple matter, and not for a moment can one reduce the social reality of the USSR to Stalinist practices. But fascism is fascism: the workers rapidly realised what they could expect form it. On the contrary, they expected from Soviet socialism, in which they placed all their hopes for emancipation and liberation, something quite different from the regime of mass terror and extermination which held sway beneath Stalin after the 1930s, and the practices that persist in the USSR sixty years after the Revolution and twenty-two years after Stalin's death. Yes, there were the Red Army, the Partisans and Stalingrad, unforgettable. But there were also the trials, the confessions, the massacres and the camps. And there is what still survives.[30]

In revoking the Marxist and Leninist category, the Congress had performed a 'symbolic act', simultaneously adopting a *'different'* socialism from the Soviet variety – democratic socialism – and taking an implicitly critical position on the USSR. The 'theoretical meaning' of this 'scientific concept' had not been broached – a consideration which led Althusser to the sanguine conclusion that it would reappear on the agenda.[31]

After a brief discussion of the slogan 'Union of the People of France',[32] Althusser came to the crucial issues raised by the concept of the dictatorship of the proletariat: the transition to socialism, the conception of socialism, the theory of the state and so on – questions which the Congress had tabled in determining the concept's redundancy. He began by insisting that the reality of the 'class dictatorship' or 'rule' of the bourgeoisie in capitalist social formations (contemporary France included) explained the formula 'dictatorship of the proletariat'. It referred to a type of state, signifying the 'class rule' of the proletariat and its allies in economic production, politics and ideology – a rule whose 'political form' was a 'mass democracy' genuinely superior to capitalist democracy, and whose rationale was the counteraction of bourgeois class rule: the transformation of its institutional forms via 'destruction' or 'revolutionisation' of the bourgeois state apparatus; the prevention of capitalist resurgence; and development towards communism. If this point was grasped, Althusser believed, a way could be found out of what he labelled 'the absurd

---

[30] Althusser 1977c, pp. 9–10.
[31] Althusser 1977c, p. 10.
[32] See Althusser 1977c, pp. 11–12.

dilemma: either pure theory or pure historical relativism'.[33] The notion of the dictatorship of the proletariat did not exclude allied classes from power. It did not prescribe mandatory forms of transition (violence) or post-revolutionary régime (dictatorship – quite the reverse). It indicated, and was a response to, the ultimate reality (the content) of any form of bourgeois state, dictatorial or democratic – a reality the working class and its allies would have to confront both before and after the attainment of state power, if communism was to be realised. It thus did not rule out peaceful transition given a favourable correlation of forces; it directed the attention of socialist strategy to the existing balance of forces. To Althusser's mind, the current configuration in France was auspicious – as it had not been in Russia in 1917. The abandonment of the dictatorship of the proletariat had focused minds on this potentiality and the necessity of 'the broadest possible alliance around the working class' – desiderata which Stalinist 'workerism' had occluded. But, in treating Stalinist dogma as the *'truth'* of the Marxist and Leninist tradition on the state, the Congress had inhibited itself from understanding that its own formulations were compatible with the latter.[34]

An accurate appreciation of the classical precept was also crucial to a realistic conception of socialism, itself a precondition of a viable strategy for communism. Socialism had been presented in Stalinist fashion as a *'stable mode of production'*, rather than as Marx and Lenin had conceived it: a *'contradictory period of transition between capitalism and communism'*. There was no socialist mode of production. Socialism – the dictatorship of the proletariat – was itself the 'transition period' from capitalism to communism.[35] Several different historical outcomes were conceivable: regression to capitalism, retardation in socialism, progress towards communism. If this was the case, then the strategy of the workers' movement had to be one of communism. From the standpoint of a transition to communism, the Congress's vision of socialism was utopian, conjuring away problems and fostering illusions.[36] As was its handling of the problem of the state under socialism – another area where the failure to think through the concept of

---

[33] Althusser 1977c, p. 13.
[34] Althusser 1977c, pp. 14–15.
[35] Althusser 1977c, p. 15.
[36] Althusser 1977c, p. 16.

the dictatorship of the proletariat left its mark. A basic thesis of Marxism and Leninism was that *'it is not just the bourgeois state that is oppressive, but any state'* – including the revolutionary state. Marx and Lenin had treated the 'destruction' of the bourgeois state and the 'withering away' of the socialist state – a temporary expedient – *conjointly*. The former was a quite specific operation: 'revolutionisation' of the existing state apparatuses (suppression of some, creation of new ones, transformation of all), in preparation for the '"withering away of the state", i.e. its replacement by mass organisations'.[37] Althusser pronounced this requirement to be 'part of the Marxist theory of the state'. The 'destruction' of the bourgeois state was the necessary precondition for the eventual 'withering away' of the state per se and the attainment of a classless future: communism. The 'socialist countries' offered a grim warning of the consequences that would ensue from the failure to anticipate and embark on this task.[38] In the very act of unwittingly posing this question, the Twenty-Second Congress had deprived itself of the means with which to answer it.[39]

Sixthly, and finally, Althusser turned to the area of inner-party democracy and, in particular, to the vexed question of 'democratic centralism', noting the disparity between the abundance of freedoms the PCF promised France and its parsimony towards its own membership. The Comintern principle was upheld by Althusser as a response to the 'vital political necessity of ensuring the *best possible* unity . . . of thought and action in the Party'. But it derived its urgency from an even greater imperative – namely, that the Party's 'existence is vital . . . *for the struggle of the working class*: to provide it with a vanguard organisation'. It was according to this criterion that actually existing democratic centralism in the PCF should be judged. For organisational forms could effectively contradict the Party's raison d'être. The modus operandi of democratic centralism in the PCF was indeed dysfunctional, eliminating opposition and fabricating unanimity. The Party's apparatus controlled its inner life. For Althusser, this was not a result inherent in Leninist principles of organisation. On the contrary. At the same time, however, the PCF's shortcomings were not remediable by the restoration of organised tendencies

---

[37] Althusser 1977c, p. 17.
[38] Althusser 1977c, pp. 17–18.
[39] Althusser 1977c, p. 18.

(the norm in the Bolshevik Party until the Tenth Congress in 1921). Such groupings were apparently 'out of the question in the French Party' – a threat to its unity and a diversion from the real issues. What was required, if the PCF was to perform its proper function, was 'more freedom' – an end to 'bureaucratic centralism'. In optimistic vein, Althusser conjectured that the time was propitious for a discussion about democratic centralism – its substantial modification – so that the Party could fulfil its raison d'être and, in so doing, become *'the Party of the Twenty-Second Congress'*.[40]

Althusser's text did not go down well with the leadership of the PCF. Finally delivered to a meeting of the UEC in December 1976, its publication in the party press was apparently vetoed.[41] It is not hard to see why. For, although Althusser's address marked a change of political direction away from Maoism, it by no means represented an accommodation with the official line. Althusser's serious reorientation towards Eurocommunism stopped well short of endorsing the particular variant adopted by the PCF in 1970s. On stamocap, the dictatorship of the proletariat, the programme of national, democratic socialism, the inner-party régime, and so on, Althusser adopted positions more critical of his party than he himself either understood or – for tactical reasons – elected publicly to admit. Herein lay the irony. Althusser's generally positive appreciation of the initiatives of the Twenty-Second Congress was based upon his identification of an evolutionary logic which would, he believed, propel the PCF beyond the half-way house it had thus far attained. But this assessment of what was involved in the PCF becoming the party of the Twenty-Second Congress was contradicted by the very different evolutionary process at work. *Pace* Althusser, the PCF was not in transit to internal democracy and a strategy for a revolutionary rupture with French capitalism. In becoming the party of the Twenty-Second Congress, the PCF was furthering the process of social-democratisation of the Western-Communist parties evident since the 1950s. The surprising feature of Althusser's text is the spectacle of the former champion of the 'Marxist-Leninist theory of the

---

[40] Althusser 1977c, pp. 18–22.
[41] Althusser himself claimed in 1977 that Catala, general-secretary of the UEC, initially cancelled the talk, which had been drafted in response to an invitation from the UEC's Cercle de philosophie (personal communication from Perry Anderson). In his 1981, p. 14, Douglas Johnson makes no mention of this, but does suggest that Althusser was summoned before Marchais and Chambaz to discuss his text.

state' recording the abandonment of one of its main planks with a certain serenity, as a result of his confidence in the PCF's trajectory.

Althusser's starting-point is less controversial: the proposition that the cumulative impact of popular struggles in the metropolitan heartlands and of revolutionary movements in the Third World had created a considerable potential for anti-capitalist and anti-imperialist advance in these years. Indeed, that advance was already being made. The counter-revolutionary offensive in the periphery of 1962–73 was checked, and then reversed, in the mid-1970s, as the liberation struggles in South-East Asia and Southern Africa – the Vietnamese at their head – were crowned with success. In Southern Europe, the Greek, Spanish and Portuguese dictatorships lurched from crisis to collapse – in the last case opening up the prospect of a transition to socialism in the West more tangibly than at any time since the onset of the Cold War. In Italy and France itself, the Communist Parties were poised to assume a major role in governments committed to radical social change. Despite the signal set-back in Portugal, a new 'springtime of peoples' was expected in many left-wing quarters. Whether the Union of the Left was a plausible vehicle for any such socialist renaissance in France is open to question. Here, Althusser's endorsement of the PCF's version of democratic socialism must give us pause. For a start, this socialism could not be divorced – as he appears to imply – from the theory of stamocap which underwrote it. The PCF's strategic orientation was towards an 'advanced democracy' as the necessary precondition of any transition to socialism – a constant of its politics for at least twenty years and the perspective from which Althusser had dissented in the 1960s. According to the official doctrine of stamocap, the contemporary phase of monopoly capitalism witnessed a 'fusion' of bourgeois polity and the monopoly fraction of capital, thereby creating the objective basis for an alliance of the 'French people' against this fraction and its undemocratic state. The PCF thus posited a contradiction between democracy per se and the dominance of a fraction of the capitalist class, which an 'anti-monopoly alliance' would resolve in favour of the former. This struggle was held to constitute a transitional phase prior to the transition to socialism – a phase which Claudin, himself an eloquent exponent of left-Eurocommunism, termed 'the transition to the transition'.[42]

---

[42] Claudin 1978, p. 101.

Althusser did not go as far as his former pupil Poulantzas in relinquishment of Leninism and diminution of the objectives of socialism. But nor did he *publicly* line up with his colleague Balibar to defend that orthodoxy and confront the PCF's alternative strategy head-on as a continuation of Stalinism, not its rectification.[43] Althusser occupied a position somewhere between the two: he impeached the PCF's theories, but not really its politics. Or, rather, to the extent that he challenged the latter, it was in the form of a theoretical critique. Thus, arguing the congruence of the Party's popular frontism with the Leninist tradition, he asserted the inadequacy of its theory to its new – and largely positive – strategic orientation, an inadequacy which accounted for the negative political features.

How should this distinctive position of critical support for the PCF be characterised? Callinicos has suggested that Althusser's politics in this period are best classed as 'centrist' and should be compared with the perspectives of Austro-Marxism (a prior attempt to steer a course between the social democracy of the Second International and the Bolshevism of the Third).[44] Althusser counter-posed to the PCF's *socialisme aux couleurs de la France* not a strategy of dual power and frontal assault on the bourgeois state, but a combination of popular unity at the base and electoral alliance at the summit with 'revolutionisation' of the state apparatus. Althusser's 'third way' was one between revolutionary socialism on the one hand and Eurocommunism on the other. As such, it is open to a number of queries.

On the face of it, there is a world of difference between Althusser's horizons and those, for example, of Carrillo as set out in *'Eurocommunism' and the State* (1977) – a work which proudly claimed the popular-front strategy of the 1930s as the antecedent and vindication of Eurocommunism.[45] From a stamocap perspective, Carrillo argued for adopting the objective of 'democratising the capitalist State apparatus' and appropriated Althusser's ISAs essay in his support.[46] Against this strategy of 'democratisation' must be set Althusser's alternative: 'revolutionisation'. But are they ultimately that different? Althusser's

---

[43] See especially Balibar 1977 and cf. Poulantzas 1978. See also the helpful résumé of Althusserian political theory in Lock 1981, Chapter 4.
[44] See Callinicos 1982, p. 79.
[45] See Carrillo 1977, p. 110ff.
[46] Carrillo 1977, p. 13; see p. 54ff.

1970 essay, as we saw in Chapter 4, was amenable to both Maoist (ultra-leftist) and Eurocommunist (reformist) readings. His text of 1977 is ambiguous, but *tends* in the direction of a distinctive variety of the latter. For although he denied the equivalence of 'democratisation' and 'destruction', categorising the former operation as (potentially) reformist, his characterisation of the second fell short of its conventional content. It involved 'revolutionisation' – a definition which, for good or ill, is at some distance from Lenin's and goes part of the way towards the Eurocommunist thesis of the divisibility of the bourgeois state.

The strategy of a democratic and peaceful transition via a war of position in which a new hegemonic historical bloc is gradually forged, and so on, is predicated on the bourgeois state lacking the basic political unity ascribed to it by classical Marxism – an integrity the rupture of which requires a revolution. If classical Marxism is right, then Eurocommunist strategy is fraught with dangers for the working class, its party/government, and allies. And the lessons to be drawn from the Chilean experience may be rather different from those derived by Enrico Berlinguer on behalf of the PCI. *Pace* Carrillo, the issue is not so much the 'democratic' potential of the ideological or representative (parliamentary) state apparatuses as the adamantine presence of the repressive state apparatus. A government of the Left unbuttressed by organs of popular power could end either by capitulating – adapting to the order of capital, rather than transforming it – or by succumbing to the 'special bodies of armed men' (Lenin) – and dragging down its dis-/unarmed supporters with it. At the very least, it may be wagered that the 'last fight' to which the workers' anthem refers would, at some stage, be engaged – if not as a result of the 'resort to force' envisaged by Marx for the establishment of socialism, then in the form of the 'slave-owners' war' predicted by him in response to the prospect of its democratic advent.[47] And, in that confrontation, the revolutionary forces would face a rather more considerable opponent, domestic and possibly foreign, than the monopoly bourgeoisie. Revolutionary violence is neither inevitable, nor merely optional. All that can be said with some certainty is that an arithmetical majority for the Left at the ballot-box and, with it, constitutional legitimacy is no guarantee of either the power or the 'right' to govern – as the murder of Chile yesterday, the agony of Nicaragua

---

[47] See Marx 1977, pp. 324, 400.

today, bear witness. Eurocommunism, the reversion of the West-European Communist parties (and others) to the strategic horizons of the Second International, would appear to be a defiance of the historical record. Born on 21 August 1968 (date of the invasion of Czechoslovakia), was not its obituary written on 11 September 1973 (date of the overthrow of Allende)?[48]

The self-emancipation of the oppressed from economic exploitation, political domination and ideological subjection is unlikely to be achieved by any such strategy – one whose themes, and the objections to them, are, of course, nothing new.[49] And here it is worth registering the absence from Althusser's reaction to the PCF's programme of any reference to the history of strategic thinking on the Marxist Left – from the Second International to the Bolshevik tradition, from popular frontism to Eurocommunism; or to the history of the PCF and its *grands tournants* – from the Third Period to the Popular Front to the Moscow-Berlin axis, from the Resistance and coalition government to Cold War, from ghettoisation to de-Stalinisation and the Union of the Left. Inattentive to the historical sources and precedents of the Union of the Left in, for example, Kautsky's 'attrition strategy', Stalin's conception of 'socialism in one country', and the theory and practice of the Popular Fronts in the 1930s, Althusser over-indulged the illusions of Eurocommunism in its French version – a social-democratic conception of transition joined to an unreformed Stalinist apparatus. Having finally rallied to the position of a popular front at base and summit and veritable inner-party de-Stalinisation, Althusser failed to strike a balance, leaving himself vulnerable to the massive disappointment that failure – amid so many hopes – could be expected to provoke.[50]

---

[48] See Debray 1978a, p. 66, 151–2. In a letter of 10 October 1975 to the Portuguese socialist Luiz Francisco Rebello, Althusser underlined the point that no revolution would ever have occurred but for the disintegration of the standing army. In Portugal, as elsewhere, this institution was the 'pillar of the bourgeois state apparatus'; Chile was the counter-proof. See Althusser and Rebello 1976, pp. 33–6 and see also Althusser 1977c, p. 5: 'The horror of Vietnam and Chile should not be forgotten. Nor should Portugal.'

[49] See Anderson 1977 and 1980, Chapter 7; Mandel 1978; and Salvadori 1979.

[50] This is the more surprising given that Althusser's comments on the policy of the Western Communist parties in the 'Note on the ISAs' (contemporaneous with his intervention on the Twenty-Second Congress, but unpublished in French) amounted to a repudiation of the PCF's whole orientation: 'most Western European Communist Parties describe themselves today as "parties of government". *Even if they do occasionally participate in government* (and it can be correct to do this under certain conditions) *a Communist Party can under no circumstances be defined as a "party of government"* – whether one is dealing with a government under the dominant control of the bourgeois

Failures there were. The Eurocommunism to which Althusser had turned in refuge from Maoism itself rapidly came to grief as a plausible alternative to Soviet socialism. In Italy, the PCI elected to become a 'party of government' rather than a 'party of struggle'; the *via Italiana* terminated in an entente with Christian Democracy from 1976 onwards which was all to the advantage of the latter, 'the Christian Democrats [making] the history, the Communists . . . the compromise'.[51] But it was in France in 1978 that the greatest reverse was suffered. For it was there that the parties of the Left, jubilant after their triumphs in the cantonal (1976) and municipal (1977) elections, were predicted to win an outright majority at the legislative elections. The PCF had grown dramatically after entering the Union of the Left. Through a vigorous recruitment campaign, its membership rose by almost 250,000 – to 632,000 – between 1972 and 1978. But, as early as June 1972 (prior to signature of the Common Programme), in a report which did not become public knowledge until 1975, Marchais shared with his Politbureau colleagues his anxiety that the Socialists would be the prime electoral beneficiary of the envisaged alliance. They were. And, in the end, inter-party competition on the Left counted for more than the hopes of PCF militants and supporters. Exploiting manifesto disagreements as a pretext, the PCF ruptured the Union in September 1977, spent the new few months – the run-up to the elections – vilifying its social-democratic partner, and patched up the coalition the day after the first round (13 March), just in time for the second. The result was a momentous defeat. If the Politbureau expected the dismay of its activists to be discharged in rage against the leaders of the Socialist Party (PS), it must have been disagreeably surprised by the sequel.

The rank-and-file revolt was widespread, encompassing a broad range of party opinion, left and right. Althusser's own written response came in two stages. On 6 April, *Le Monde* published a long letter signed by him, Balibar,

---

class or with a government under the dominant control of the proletarian class ("dictatorship of the proletariat"). This point is of decisive importance. . . . A Communist Party can . . . under no circumstances behave as an ordinary "party of government", since being a party of government would mean being a State party, which either means that one serves the bourgeois state, or that one perpetuates the State of the dictatorship of the proletariat, when the whole point is to contribute to its destruction' (Althusser 1983, pp. 460–1). Note that the PCF had been declared a 'party of government at every level' by Marchais in March 1974 – a formula which dated from the late 1940s.
[51] Abse 1985, p. 28.

the historians Guy Bois and Maurice Moissonier, the philosopher Georges Labica, and the Germanist Jean-Pierre Lefebvre. 'In once again losing the elections,' they wrote,

> the Left has not only lost a battle. An immense fund of hope has, it is to be feared, been dashed for a long time to come. A great popular force is in need of reconstruction. It would be a tragic response to try to conceal . . . the extent of the defeat and of the problems it poses. In the space of a few months, hasn't the Left starkly revealed its own political weaknesses and internal contradictions: the division, never surmounted, between the parties; the discrepancy between the language, the objectives, and a political practice that is often routine and electoralist? The Communist Party knew how to take the initiative, to propose the Union and its programme. But was it able to foresee the real nature of the difficulties and obstacles it would encounter, to find the means to overcome them by mobilising the masses for the defence and extension of the Union? Did it know how to transform itself in order to become the instrument of the popular movement? Why wasn't it able to avoid the constant see-saw movement which by turns revives the dangers of 'right opportunism' and 'sectarianism', and the succession of volte-faces which cast doubt on its strategy and the correctness of its methods of political work?[52]

These were the questions being raised and discussed throughout the Party. In contrast to party militants, apprised of the gravity of the situation in which the PCF now found itself, the leadership was alarmingly complacent on its root causes. Further, it was refusing to open the party press to members who dissented from Charles Fiterman's report of 29 March and the Politbureau declaration of 20 March: 'The French Communist Party bears no responsibility for this situation'. Althusser and co. made it clear that they at least could not assent to the Politbureau's 'authoritarian' assertion of the rectitude of the PCF's line throughout. Nor would they accept that the post-mortem should be conducted within its terms of reference. What was now needed was a genuine, in-depth discussion and critique of the Party's recent political history unprejudiced by a fixed agenda and rigged verdict. Such an inquest required full and accurate information, complete freedom of debate and circulation of

---

[52] Althusser et al. 1978.

ideas, and the elaboration of initiatives from the base of the Party. There could be no serious objection to demands for complete information, an open press and an 'extraordinary' (that is, democratic) congress, since these were in perfect accord with PCF statutes. Every Communist knew them to be 'indispensable' to an authentic collective analysis and discussion – and to any future recovery.

As it turned out, all Communists but the members of the Politbureau knew these things. For his part, Althusser now moved over to the attack. To coincide with the Central Committee meeting of 26–8 April, he published a four-part intervention in *Le Monde* (25–8 April) entitled 'Ce qui ne peut plus durer dans le Parti communiste'. A revised version, including a preface that dealt with Marchais's report to that meeting, was published in the *Théorie* series in May 1978. In his rejoinder to the Central Committee deliberations, Althusser sharply criticised the secrecy surrounding their debates, after which Marchais's apologetic report was unanimously endorsed.[53] In 'Avancer sur la voie du 22è Congrès', the PCF's general-secretary had ridiculed 'desk-bound' intellectuals engaging in a 'monologue'; decreed that '[t]he Socialist Party is responsible for the disunity and the defeat'; warned critics that '[w]e are a democratic party . . . not a debating society'; and concluded on a triumphalist note: 'The Communist Party is now, and will increasingly be, the party which the workers and France need'.[54]

To Althusser's mind, his superior's discourse represented a 'system of ideological and political *intimidation*' of all those who had legitimate doubts about the Party's behaviour.[55] The attempt to dragoon the rank and file and prevent debate was, however, nothing new. The very 'vertical' structure of the PCF partitioned ordinary members from one another and reproduced the leadership's omnipotence. Lyrical on the subject of the collective discussion underway, Marchais was predictably taciturn on its stage-management in accordance with tradition.[56] Althusser proceeded to savage what he labelled the 'religious conception of the Truth' entertained by the Politbureau, wherein it was the possessor and guardian of a truth with which the masses were to

---

[53] See Althusser 1978c, p. 6ff.
[54] Marchais 1979. For Althusser's caustic response to the first reproach, see 1978c, p. 11.
[55] Althusser 1978c, p. 14.
[56] See Althusser 1978c, pp. 17–18.

be 'impregnated'. Marchais's exclusive concentration on the competition between PCF and PS, his treatment of the class struggle by 'preterition', and his assumption of the leadership's infallibility bore witness to a total renunciation of historical materialism.[57] Althusser's preface closed on a severe note. The real 'lag' in consciousness was the leadership's; it was insufficiently conscious of the 'exigencies of the class struggle'. This state of affairs had two inter-related causes: the wholesale abandonment of concrete analysis and the deforming influence – on the Party's theory and practice – of bourgeois ideology. Given the Party's subjection to this ideology, and the isomorphism between its internal organisation and the bourgeois state, the real question concerned its fitness to perform its revolutionary role.[58]

These themes were developed in the main body of the text. In the first part, 'Strategy: The Disguised Turn', Althusser rejected any Manichean evaluation of the respective merits of the PCF and the PS. In contrast to the leadership, PCF militants had entertained few illusions about the PS. But to assign total responsibility to the latter was 'to confuse dialectics with paranoia'. In any case, who, if not the Politbureau, had facilitated the PS's strategy of out-manoeuvring the PCF? A more compelling analysis, one rooted in the facts, was arising from the base 'spontaneously' – an occurrence which *could really mark an epoch in the political history of the French Party*.[59] Contrary to the declarations of Fiterman and co., the PCF's strategy had not been altogether 'consistent'. The leadership was dissimulating the difference – the contradiction – between the (official) line of 1972–7 (collaboration with the PS) and that of September onwards (sectarian struggle against the PS) – an adjustment which had led to the March debacle. In autumn 1977, the PCF's leaders had abruptly made the Party's defence of its position against what was perceived as the threat from its partner the primary objective. To this they had been prepared to sacrifice the *dynamique unitaire* of the Union of the Left and the popular hopes invested in it.[60] Fearful of any examination of its vacillation, the Politbureau denied the turn of 1977 and took refuge in its own (inherited) infallibility.

---

[57] Althusser 1978c, pp. 25–6.
[58] Althusser 1978c, pp. 29–30.
[59] Althusser 1978a, pp. 21, 23.
[60] Althusser 1978a, p. 24.

Unlike them, Althusser did not believe that the leaders were always right. It was not simply the errors of the past that stood in need of rectification, he argued, echoing previous sentiments; their causes must be investigated and tackled as well.[61] The Party's organisation was an obstacle to these tasks – as the title of the second article put it, 'a machine for dominating'. Indicative of the PCF's command-structure was that the Common Programme had been a deal struck by Politbureau, and the Union of the Left an alliance between two political parties under the firm control of their leaderships. The 'promises' of the Twenty-Second Congress had been reneged on. In the approach to the elections, '*nothing was moving any longer from the base to the summit: everything came from above*'.[62] The policies thus imposed did not even have the merit of consistency. In a series of 'unexplained turns', what had been anathema one day (for example, the *force de frappe* and *autogestion*) became articles of faith the next.[63] The militants had had to endure and explain these somersaults. Despite them, they could

> testify to the deep and moving trust which the workers placed . . . *in the existence of the Union of the Left*. This trust had deep roots in historical memory which encompasses not only the fraternity of the Popular Front, but all the crushed working-class revolts in the history of France, going right back to 1848 and the Paris Commune; the great historical struggles that followed the First World War; and the immense social hopes that accompanied the Resistance.
>
> This time, after a century and a half of defeats and painful advances, bringing no genuine liberation, the hope was there and victory was at last assured, at arm's reach. Is it really understood what this means: *the possibility or near-certainty that, for the first time in history, an age-old tradition would be broken and victory secured?*[64]

The hopes and energies that had tenaciously survived the dissensions of September 1977 might not outlive the defeat of March 1978. A precondition of the PCF's recovery was that the leadership's traditional secrecy, part and parcel of the Stalinist legacy, should be terminated.[65]

---

[61] Althusser 1978a, p. 25.
[62] Althusser 1978a, pp. 26–7.
[63] Althusser 1978a, p. 27.
[64] Althusser 1978a, p. 28.
[65] Althusser 1978a, p. 29.

Indeed, the whole party 'machine' must finally be transformed. This was the demand emanating from the rank and file – not just for their own sakes, but for the sake of French workers 'who cannot be victorious . . . without the CP, but who cannot win with *this* Communist Party *as it is today'*. The requisite Communist party was a 'revolutionary party' governed by a fundamentally modified democratic centralism. At present, in its 'structure and mode of functioning' the PCF resembled more the representative and military apparatuses of the bourgeois state.[66] Two related features of the PCF's structures were highlighted by Althusser: substitutionism and the 'basic and absolute principle of *vertical partitioning'*. The latter mechanism served to ensure the dominance of the higher echelons over the lower and to prevent militants entering into independent contact with each other. Organisational forms arguably appropriate to a previous era were now without the slightest justification. For the combination of the military and parliamentary models 'cannot but reproduce and strengthen the *bourgeois mode of politics'*. The self-reproducing leadership corps was bound by a 'pact of unanimity' whereby differences of opinion within it were concealed from party members. The party machine was a veritable 'machine for dominating, controlling and manipulating the Party militants'.[67]

If the PCF's organisation was authoritarian, its ideology was a 'caricature'. The confidence of militants in the leaders was exploited by the latter through an internal ideology which identified the Party with its omniscient leadership. Althusser believed this to be a crucial issue. Repeating the arguments of his intervention on the Twenty-Second Congress, he insisted that party unity was not an intrinsic good. The raison d'être of a Communist party was to serve as an organisation of/for working-class struggle; party unity must be subordinated to that primary obligation. Party ideology should therefore not be considered exclusively from the viewpoint of its efficacy as a 'cement' of unity.[68] At a theoretical level, the PCF's recent history had been one of 'official platitudes'. Marxist theory in the PCF had not emerged unscathed from the ravages of Stalinism; it was in a 'lamentable state', had 'reached zero-point', 'disappeared'.[69] The leadership was indifferent both to the global crisis of

---

[66] Althusser 1978a, p. 30.
[67] See Althusser 1978a, pp. 31–3.
[68] Althusser 1978a, p. 34.
[69] Althusser 1978a, p. 35.

Marxism and to its national form: the erosion of historical materialism in the Party. In place of Marxist theory, the Politbureau served up stamocap – a doctrine which Althusser now scathingly attacked as a French version of Soviet orthodoxy. Stamocap was a theory 'made to order', predicated upon an idealist concept of 'objective interest' (of the French people in ridding themselves of monopolists), and resulting in a voluntarist notion of class struggle as consciousness-raising (of retarded social strata).[70] The PCF had abandoned the concrete analysis of concrete situations with which Althusser equated genuine Marxist theory. The costs of this neglect were heavy, for such analysis facilitated both the '*discovery* of the real' and the 'determination' of an appropriate political line. Averse to any such thinking, the PCF leadership clung to its concoctions, superimposing its ideology on reality, 'apply[ing] it from above to anything that moves' – a theoretical practice in conformity with the Stalinist tradition. In Marchais and Fiterman's reactions to the election results there was '*no concrete reality and no concrete analysis*'.[71]

Marchais's resort to backward consciousness to explain the PCF's electoral stasis neatly side-stepped a contributory factor rather closer to home: the Party's image and reputation. 'The leadership,' Althusser reflected,

> may imagine that the Twenty-Second Congress was a Fountain of Youth that washed away the bad memories of the past. But people have a long memory, and blackmailing talk about anti-communism no longer cuts any ice at all! . . . Talk away! It is all very well to be heir to the October Revolution, and to preserve the memory of Stalingrad. But what of the massacre and deportation of recalcitrant peasants baptised as kulaks? What of the crushing of the middle classes, the Gulag Archipelago, the repression that still goes on twenty-five years after Stalin's death? When the only guarantees offered are words that are *immediately contradicted* in the only possible field of verification, namely, the internal practices of the Party, then it is clear that the [electoral] 'buffer' also lies within the Party itself.[72]

There had, after all, been 'real "Moscow trials" right here in France' between 1948 and 1965 – 'abominations' for which no reparation had been made.[73]

---

[70] See Althusser 1978a, pp. 35–6.
[71] Althusser 1978a, p. 37.
[72] Althusser 1978a, p. 38.
[73] Althusser 1978a, p. 39.

The history of Stalinism in the PCF was an unfinished one. It could be ignored; it would not go away.

In his final article – 'The Solution: Leave the Fortress' – Althusser recalled the Marxist tradition's emphasis on working-class *self*-emancipation and contrasted with this the PCF's typical treatment of its members and of workers as '*others*' – instruments of a line determined outside their ranks. Having abandoned the 'principles of class independence', the Party had 'reproduc[ed] bourgeois political practice within itself'. Stalinism-with-a-human-face it might be; Stalinism it remained. Manipulative of its members, the leadership was equally suspicious of those the Party was supposed to represent: the workers and their potential allies. If a political organisation was to be judged by its ability to attend and respond to its natural constituency, the PCF currently stood condemned. Confronted with anything outside the control of the party apparatus, the leadership invariably repudiated it – as in May 1968.[74] Its habitual authoritarianism was particularly evident in its conception and practice of alliances. Rather than forging an alliance characterised by a '*primacy of combat*', the Politbureau had opted for an electoral compact marked by a '*primacy of contract*'. Worse, under cover of an agreement which Althusser considered a 'unitary electoralism' witnessing to a 'right opportunism', the leadership had conducted a sectarian campaign of electoral competition against the PS, representing PCF domination of its partner as the hegemony of the working class. It had ruled out 'popular union' and 'unity' from the very beginning as a result of its 'deep-rooted, tenacious and inveterate distrust of the masses'.[75] The PCF, Althusser observed, 'exists in French society like a garrison in a fortress'. This may once have had a rationale. But not any longer. The defeat of the Union of the Left represented a clear repudiation of the Party's political and organisational practices. It was the dénouement of a long drama:

> We must look things straight in the face: the March 1978 defeat is the defeat of a political line and practice which are one with the Party's fortress-like functioning and its refusal to go out and 'lose itself' (i.e. find itself again) in the masses.

---

[74] See Althusser 1978a, pp. 40–1.
[75] Althusser 1978a, pp. 42–3.

Vacation of the fortress did not – and should not – entail the PCF's transformation into a bourgeois liberal party 'like the rest'. It meant 'resolutely involving the Party in the mass movement'. The Party must draw on the strengths of its working-class and popular base 'to change "what can last no longer"' – and in such a way as to preserve, or rather restore, the PCF's autonomy as a working-class political organisation. In particular, contrary to the advice of the bourgeois leader-writers, it was not democratic centralism per se that was at fault.[76]

Althusser concluded his intervention by identifying four 'conditions of change'. First, Marxist theory must be rejuvenated: 'lucid, critical and rigorous theory' was the precondition of the PCF's regeneration. Secondly, a critique, preparatory to a reform, of the Party's structure and modus operandi was urgently required. Thirdly, a concrete analysis of the class situation in France must be made forthwith. Fourthly, a new kind of alliance should be forged between the working class and 'popular forces', one which articulated compacts at the summit and unity at the base, with priority accorded to the latter; this line of *popular union* must eschew reformism and sectarianism alike.[77] In response to the title of Marchais's report, in the *Théorie* edition Althusser added that the course he was proposing could draw inspiration from the Twenty-Second Congress, on condition that its contradictions were recognised and its tendencies to 'democratic adventurism' checked.[78] On the basis of the four principles he had outlined, the PCF could change: 'It will be able to leave behind all the equivocations and constrictions inherited from the past; to redeem its errors and failures; and to assist the rallying of the popular masses for their long-awaited victory.'[79]

In March 1978, both the PCF's most eminent philosopher and his party reached turning-points: the former turned; the latter failed to. Far and away the most directly political piece he had ever published, *What Must Change in the Communist Party* is also Althusser's single most powerful text. Thompson complains that Althusser's 'exposure' merely rehearsed long-familiar criticisms of the PCF – by Trotskyists, Socialisme ou Barbarie, the rebels of 1956, Sartre,

---

[76] Althusser 1978a, pp. 43–5.
[77] See Althusser 1978a, p. 45.
[78] Althusser 1978c, p. 124.
[79] Althusser 1978a, p. 45.

288 · Chapter Six

the students of 1968, and so forth.[80] Notwithstanding the partial justice of this claim, Anderson's judgement that Althusser's critique is 'the most violent oppositional charter ever published within a party in the post-war history of Western Communism'[81] better captures the status of Althusser's intervention. *Pace* Thompson, the point is that it was *Althusser* speaking from *within* the PCF – and not Sartre from without. The novelty of the crisis of 1978 was that there were as many voices raised inside as outside the Party – far too many for the leadership to be able to resort to traditional disciplinary sanctions. Doubtless, it would have been preferable for Althusser publicly to have adopted these positions much earlier (May '68 is the indicated occasion). Had he done so, however, he would have faced expulsion – as the fate of Balibar, in very different circumstances three years later, demonstrates. Althusser had chosen to be – and to remain – a member of the largest working-class party in France. During his thirty years of party membership, he had missed the moments of 1956 and 1968; he did not miss the moment of 1978. That April he made the transition from private to public opposition, breaking his silence to issue a left-wing manifesto on 'what must change' in the most authoritarian Communist party in Western Europe. It would be too easy to argue 'better late than never'. But what would Althusser's French and British critics have said had he once again judged it inopportune? The moment come, Althusser acquitted himself as well as any of those named by his critic.

That said, Althusser's text was not without its serious faults. In the *Théorie* version he noted that for political reasons the PCF, like the CPSU, had proved '*incapable* of writing its own history'. And, earlier, he had reflected that '*once the book of errors is opened, the end is by no means as clear as the beginning*'.[82] Indeed. This is precisely where Althusser's admonitions themselves require interrogation. The main political motif and historical model of Althusser's critique is the Popular Front of the 1930s. Insofar as he gestured uncritically towards that experience as the necessary corrective to the present imbroglio, his text was in part a symptom of what it sought to cure. (The references to the prewar Thorez are only the most obvious 'slips' of Althusser's pen: if anyone is to be credited with responsibility for the Stalinisation of the PCF,

---

Thompson 1978, p. 403.
[81] Anderson 1980, p. 113.
[82] Althusser 1978c, pp. 71–2; Althusser 1978a, p. 25.

it is surely the self-styled *fils du peuple*.) In his nostalgia for 1936, Althusser shared a certain historical 'amnesia' with the targets of his critique. The 'popular front of labour, liberty and peace', launched to 'bar the road to reaction', was hardly an unqualified success for the French (not to mention Spanish) masses.[83]

If Althusser was critical towards what another rebel – Ellenstein – termed 'Gallocommunism' (summed up in the PCF's slogan: *Ni Washingon, ni Rome, ni Moscou*), he was evasive about the Eurocommunism by which Ellenstein and others wanted it replaced. Politically, Althusser sided neither with the pro-Italian current, nor with Marchais and the centre, nor with the Leroy group (let alone Thorez's widow and Stalin's ghost: Jeanette Vermeersch). Indeed, the level of generality at which political strategy is treated in Althusser's text makes precise judgement of his personal orientation difficult. His position was too idiosyncratic to be assimilated to any current in the Politbureau. He did not want the Party to take the Italian or Russian roads; he was no happier with national communism. Like Ellenstein, he wanted much greater freedom in the Party – but not the abolition of democratic centralism (and not the lifting of the ban on organised tendencies). In common with the hard-liners, he was concerned about the abrogation of the dictatorship of the proletariat – but for different reasons. Unlike Leroy et al., he was not demanding a reversion to the quasi-'third period' or post-1947 relations with the Socialists. No more was he calling for a return to unconditional electoral alliance with them. On the contrary, in opposition to both 'democratic adventurism' and 'sectarianism', he set his sights on a genuine popular front.

---

[83] Althusser was not, however, uncritical of the Popular-Front experience; see Althusser 1983, p. 459. As to Thorez's 'pas de "mannequins"' (the title of an article in *L'Humanité*, 14 August 1931), its worthiness is somewhat qualified by the particular circumstances of its enunciation in the midst of the factional struggle against the Barbé-Célor group in the PCF; see Carr 1982, pp. 169–74. An instructive comparison with Althusser's text here is what is perhaps its immediate precedent in French Communism – Jean Baby's *Critique de base* (1960). Baby, a significant Communist intellectual, went on to become a Maoist close to the UJC, writing *La grande controverse sino-soviétique (1956–1966)*, in which he paid tribute to Althusser's 'remarkable studies' (Baby 1966, p. 428). Baby's *Critique* anticipated most of Althusser's points. But although it too featured 'pas de mannequins' (Baby 1960, p. 130), Baby strongly criticised the PCF's leader for his contribution to the reigning 'authoritarian centralism' (p. 137). For another powerful internal critique, see the *Unir* group's *Histoire du Parti communiste français* (1961–6).

Althusser's history, then, was cursory and deficient. His proposals for reform of bureaucratic centralism were inadequate in the light of his own systematic indictment of it. His politics, however elusive and independent, remained within the strategic framework he criticised. And, last but not least, for all that his intervention amounted to a mordant critique of the PCF's tactics, organisation and ideology, it ultimately registered little advance over previous initiatives. In other words, the major problem with it is not its belatedness relative to Sartre's *Spectre of Stalin* or Baby's *Critique de base* (even if *le retard de 1956* was not only the PCF's), but the fact that Althusserian Marxism largely reproduced, rather than really improving on, their analyses of the iron law of oligarchy in the Communist Party.

What was the fate of his text – and of the wider rebellion convulsing the PCF? As in the past, its leadership weathered the storm. Althusser's belief that 'blackmailing talk about anti-communism' would not wash this time proved false. The Politbureau's appeals to party members to hold the line against the 'new wave of anti-communism' – a palpable reality – worked their magic. Equally effective was a strategy of divide and rule whereby the intellectuals, in any case at odds with each other, were marginalised.[84] If the first reflex of the rank and file after March was rebellion, its second – and one much more ingrained – was loyalty. At a high price, order was restored without resort to expulsions. By mid-June, every federation had passed Marchais's report. At the Twenty-Third Congress the following May, Marchais beat both 'Right' and 'Left'. Its leadership entrenched, the PCF failed to change as so many had hoped and urged, ushering in, in consequence, the 'French political winter'[85] during which the Party would experience the most serious crisis in its history, entering the second half of the 1980s fighting for its political life.

In May 1978 Althusser gave a short interview to *Paese Sera* in which he further castigated Marchais's 'non-reply'; advised that resignations from the

---

[84] The leadership could rely here upon an inveterate distrust of intellectual celebrities with access to the 'bourgeois press' (to criticise the party in whose pages was traditionally held *porter de l'eau au moulin de l'adversaire*). Althusser had himself reproved 'recourse to the bourgeois press and its blackmail of the party' at the Fête de l'Humanité in 1973, when commenting on the 'Daix affair' (see *La France Nouvelle*, 18 September 1973, p. 11).

[85] The words of Althusserian Michel Pêcheux – one of its victims (Pêcheux 1982, p. 211).

PCF would be 'the best present one could give the leadership and Marchais . . . exactly what they want'; and asserted that '[i]t is absolutely vital to stay in the party and fight for its transformation'. The situation in which the PCF found itself, he contended, was inherent in the signature of the Common Programme.[86] The following month, Althusser informed *Les Nouvelles Littéraires* that his intervention, like those of a growing number of Communist intellectuals, was founded upon a 'wish for more democracy'. 'If I did not believe,' he was quoted as saying,

> that the positions which I defend have a future, I would not defend them. As to whether this hope will be disappointed, that's another matter. Anything can happen. . . . I'm excommunicated today but I have no desire to be a martyr. I'm a philosopher. I'm not caught up by the effects of everyday public politics, which is what is condemning me for the time being. But once again, I don't work in the immediate present.

'Unless the Party disappears', Althusser insisted, he would remain a member of it because

> the fact of having joined the Party – in 1948 – is not a biographical accident for me: it was the absolute precondition for being able to be a political activist. . . . The fact of being in the Party has given my philosophical writings a political significance. If I left it, that would be *finished*.[87]

Althusser was to make no further written contribution to the campaign to change the PCF (though his colleagues did).[88] And although he remained a party member, there were to be no more published philosophical writings. For what did happen was . . . 'biographical accident'.

Adieu to Althusserianism

Vincent Descombes has suggested that with the institution of the primacy of 'lived experience' in his 'Preface to *Capital* Volume One', 'Althusser did away

---

[86] See Althusser 1978e. Althusser accepted a suggestion from his interviewer that his criticisms of the PCF's structure and methods equally applied to the other Western Communist parties: a statement for which he was accused by the PCF's Paul Laurent of having 'declared war' on them.
[87] See Althusser 1978f.
[88] See Balibar et al. 1979.

with Althusserianism'.[89] Certainly, as has been illustrated in Chapter 4, Althusser retreated from the most original – but also some of the more questionable – aspects of his initial project within Marxism; and offered no alternative of comparable novelty and power. But to speak, as Descombes proceeds to, of the Althusserian enterprise being brought to an 'official close' is an exaggeration. Although its prestige had been dented, in 1969 Althusser's Marxism was still in the ascendant in France and elsewhere. And where there was a de facto retraction of high Althusserianism, there was no intimation on Althusser's part at least that he and his colleagues believed they had nothing new to offer. (One indication of this, perhaps, is that the majority of volumes in the *Théorie* series were published *after* 1969.) It was not at the end of the 1960s, but in the second half of the 1970s, that Althusser's Marxism entered into crisis. 'The Crisis of Marxism' repudiated the strategy underlying *For Marx* and *Reading 'Capital'* and cast a sceptical glance over the theories of Marx and Lenin themselves that would have been unthinkable as late as 1975. It was in Venice in 1977 that Althusser heralded the end of an era.

In his survey of historical materialism since the mid-1970s, Anderson has argued that the term 'crisis of Marxism' is a misnomer, since what was actually involved was a crisis of Latin Marxism – a phenomenon which had taken two main forms: reunciation (for example, Glucksmann, Colletti and Semprun) or 'dilution or diminution' (such as Althusser and Poulantzas).[90] The perception of a crisis of Marxism among its Southern-European partisans in the 1970s was certainly no idiosyncrasy of Althusser's. Claudin, for example, had anticipated him by seven years (and was to be praised for having done so), Colletti by three.[91] In 1979, subsequent to the apostasies of Colletti and Claudin, Sebastiano Timpanaro would announce a similar conclusion, but recommend a different reaction.[92] The peculiarity of Althusser's evolution within this wider history was that, unlike Colletti, he remained a Marxist, while, unlike Timpanaro, he questioned the validity of the Marxist legacy – and relinquished Althusserianism. Striking evidence of this is to be found in a text never published in France, dating from late 1977/early 1978: 'Marxism Today' – a

[89] Descombes 1981, pp. 134–5.
[90] See Anderson 1983, pp. 29–30.
[91] See Claudin 1975, e.g., pp. 8, 662 (cf. Althusser 1979b, p. 228); Colletti 1977, pp. 340, 350.
[92] See Timpanaro 1980, pp. 255, 261.

document gleefully described by Colletti (no mean butcher himself) as a 'wholesale slaughter' of historical materialism.[93]

Measured against the balance-sheet he had drawn up in 1965 – 'Theory, Theoretical Practice and Theoretical Formation' – Althusser's considerations on the state and status of Marxism in 'Marxism Today' are remarkable for their simultaneous, indivisible attenuation of historical materialism and abnegation of Althusserianism. He began by suggesting that in once denying he was a Marxist, Marx himself had cautioned against interpretation of his thought as a 'system' – a philosophy of history or science of political economy. The sub-title of *Capital* signified Marx's disclaimer of any pretension to 'science'. He had transformed the very meaning of the term 'critique', his 'critique of political economy' representing not an epistemological enterprise, but a theoretico-political *prise de position* for the working class. The thought of Marx and Engels had become 'critical and revolutionary' inside the workers' movement, through their participation in its practice. Kautsky and Lenin had, it transpired, been wrong – and dangerously so:

> Behind this view of a scientific theory produced by bourgeois intellectuals, and 'introduced . . . from without' into the working-class movement lies a whole conception of the relations between theory and practice, between the Party and the mass movement, and between party leaders and simple militants, which reproduces bourgeois forms of knowledge and power in their separation.[94]

Against the Kautskyist and Leninist genealogy of historical materialism was to be set the primacy of the 'direct and practical experience' its founders had had of exploitation, and workers' resistance to it, in England and France; Marx 'became "the organic intellectual of the proletariat"'. Moreover, the experiential dimension had been determinant throughout Marx's career. His theory had been fashioned, tested and developed in the crucible of class struggle. And what was true of his lifetime held good thereafter:

---

[93] Colletti 1984, p. 71.

[94] Althusser 1990, p. 270. See also Althusser 1983, pp. 463–4 and 'On Marx and Freud' (1976), in Althusser 1996, pp. 112–13. Thus, Althusser unequivocally assented to views – from which he previously dissented – entertained by Marx himself on the relationship between historical materialism and the workers' movement: see, e.g., Marx 1976a, p. 98 and Marx 1976b, p. 177.

> We can respond to Kautksy's formula as follows: Marx's thought was formed
> and developed *inside the working-class movement*, on the basis of that movement
> and its positions. It was from within the working-class movement, paying
> its way through struggles and contradictions, that Marx's thought was
> diffused from the first Marxist circles to the great mass parties.[95]

If Lenin was wrong to take up Kautsky's formula of importation, he had also
erred in developing Engels's thesis of the 'three sources' of Marxism. For he
had thereby fallen into 'the platitude of a history of ideas' quite incapable of
accounting for the intimate relation between Marx's discovery of a social
reality occluded in and by the problematic of German idealism and his
adoption of proletarian theoretical positions. To write the history of Marxism
under the sign of the history of ideas was to traduce Marx's revolution in
thought, reducing it to a series of 'inversions': of English political economy
into economic science; of German philosophy into dialectical materialism;
and of French utopian socialism into a 'materialist' philosophy of history
and – 'practical version' of this same 'messianism' – scientific socialism.[96] The
problem, however, was that if this presentation of Marxism – orthodoxy from
the Second International onwards – was not explicitly licensed by Marx, no
more was it a mere invention. Marx had alluded to an 'inversion' of Hegel;
had, despite adopting an increasingly critical stance towards it, remained
attached to the idea of a philosophy of history; and had speculated on a
'transparent' social formation beyond capitalism – communism – that would
usher in an Edenic 'kingdom of freedom'. Marx's writings were thus shot
through with 'latent or manifest idealism' – from the 'materialist' philosophy
of history profiled in *The German Ideology*, via the 'evolutionism' of the 1859
Preface, to the 'fictive unity' of *Capital* itself.[97] Indeed, in its conception of
science *Capital* was all too indebted to Hegel.[98] The effect of a more than

---

[95] Althusser 1990, pp. 270–1.

[96] Althusser 1990, p. 271.

[97] Althusser 1990, pp. 271–2. In his interview with Rossana Rossanda, Althusser
had argued that Marxist theory was '"finite", limited . . . to the analysis of the capitalist
mode of production, and of its contradictory tendency, which opens up the possibility
of the transition to the abolition of capitalism': Althusser 1978d, p. 6.

[98] See Althusser 1990, pp. 272–3. Althusser first broached this issue in his 1977
foreword to Gérard Duménil's *Le Concept de loi économique dans 'Le Capital'* (1978).
Written in what he described as a conjuncture of 'historical and theoretical retreat'
(Althusser 1998a, p. 248), its theses on the Marx/Hegel relationship should be compared
with their polar opposites in *Reading 'Capital'*.

residual allegiance could be located at precise points in Marx's *magnum opus* – for example, a tendency to an 'economistic interpretation of exploitation' which abstracted from its 'concrete conditions'. So, although Kautsky and Lenin had misrepresented Marx's thought, unwittingly subverting its revolutionary status, Marx had facilitated their (mis)interpretations through his failure wholly to settle accounts with his former philosophical conscience.

Unlike Lenin, however, whom Althusser now rebuked for his imprudent dictum, Marx himself had never harboured illusions about the omnipotence of his theory. He had presented his ideas in two different fashions and forms: first, as 'principles of comprehensive analysis' (for example, of the structure of social formations) and in 'theoretical form'; and, secondly, as part of the reality they were advanced to explain – among the 'ideological forms' of which the 1859 Preface speaks. In the latter, 'Marx no longer considers [his ideas] as principles of explanation of the given whole, but solely in terms of their possible effect in the ideological struggle. Therewith the ideas change their form; they pass from "theoretical form" to "ideological form"'.[99]

Here was to be found the genuinely 'materialist' side of Marx's work. Yet, despite his acute consciousness of ideological struggle, Marx was oblivious to the possibility that his own thought might be deformed and exploited – a blindness related to the paucity of his reflections on the superstructure (law, state and ideology). The Marxist tradition had added 'nothing' to what it had inherited from him:

> it is a surprising paradox that from a theoretical point of view Marxism is still at the stage of Marx, or rather somewhere short of him. His thought has given rise to commentaries and illustrations (sometimes brilliant, most often dull) and to some applications. . . . Yet for the most part Marxism has been repeated, and distorted or ossified in the process. This is an astonishing phenomenon, given that Marxism presented itself not as utopian but as scientific, and that no science in the world lives without progressing – progress which involves critically questioning its first forms of expression, its 'beginning'. Nothing of the sort occurred in the case of Marxism. . . . Up until recent years, when a movement of critical research finally seems to be taking shape, Marxist theory has never been recommenced or developed.

---

[99] Althusser 1990, pp. 274–5.

> Now, this paradox refers us not only to the incontestable effects of the class
> struggle and the domination of bourgeois ideology, which have kept Marxism
> on the defensive, theoretically; it also refers us to lacunae in Marx. . . .[100]

Among the most serious lacunae, Althusser reiterated, was Marx's failure to
pose the problem of the organisations of class struggle in and through which
his ideas would become a material force. He had not foreseen that any such
institution would require an apparatus and that the consequent 'division
between apparatus and militants could reproduce the bourgeois division of
power and cause problems so serious as to end in tragedy'. Rosa Luxemburg
has sensed the danger, but had failed to tackle the problem theoretically. For
the most part satisfied to repeat what Marx said, his successors had 'blindly
plunged into the darkness of night: in the dark on the State, in the dark on
ideology, in the dark on the Party, in the dark on politics – at the extreme,
toppling Marx's thought into something utterly alien to him'.[101]

Marxism, then, had not simply not progressed beyond Marx: it had regressed.
With Kautsky and Plekhanov, it was converted into an evolutionist philosophy
of history. *Capital* was habitually construed as a treatise of scientific political
economy. And, on the authority of Engels's 'unfortunate' late works, dialectical
materialism was proffered as the Marxist philosophy, one supplying an
'absolute guarantee' of historical materialism (one of its regions) and of
scientific socialism (its application). Finally, under Stalin, Hegel had prevailed
over Marx and travesty became tragedy:

> In Marx's name, for years and years Stalin fixed the formulae of this poor
> man's Hegelianism, this Absolute Knowledge without exterior, from which
> any topography had disappeared – and for good reason. Since 'the cadres
> decide everything', the definition of the True was the prerogative of the
> leaders, the bourgeois ideology of the omnipotence of ideas triumphed in
> the monstrous unity of State-Party-State ideology, the masses had only to
> submit in the very name of their liberation.[102]

To account for this catastrophe, it was insufficient to invoke the influence of
bourgeois ideology: the reproduction of its forms in the working-class

---

[100] Althusser 1990, pp. 275–6.
[101] Althusser 1990, p. 276.
[102] Althusser 1990, p. 277.

movement required explanation – something only a comprehensive theory of ideology, which Marxism precisely lacked, could facilitate. Marxist leaders had related problems and 'deviations' in their organisations to the intrusion of the dominant ideology. Inattentive to the fact that revolutionary organisations 'secrete' an ideology for the purposes of internal unity, they had not been alert to the potential contradiction between Marxist ideology and this organisational ideology. Bereft of a theory of the party, they had not foreseen that the latter 'could end up reproducing in the Party itself . . . the structure of the bourgeois state'.[103] Lenin, Gramsci and Mao had, in their different ways, grappled with the formidable difficulties involved, but had proved unable to fashion the requisite theory of state, ideology and party.

Althusser was not, he insisted, implying that its absence was responsible for the history made in Marxism's name. Such a fantasy of 'historical mastery' rested on another idealist postulate – namely, that Marxist theory was exempt from the vicissitudes of the history of class struggle from which it stemmed, and in whose 'deformations and tragedies' it was implicated. As to these, Althusser echoed Spinoza's celebrated rejection of moralism and voluntarism:

> Marxism will not rid itself of the tragedies of its history by condemning or deploring them; that way lie moralism and theoretical and political abdication. It is vital for Marxism to recognise these tragedies, to take responsibility for them, put them on the agenda, and forge the theoretical means required to understand them at their roots. Nor does this have anything to do with the intellectual curiosity of illuminating an irreversible past. At stake in such a radical reflection is *Marxism today*: let it finally begin to know itself as it is, and it will change.[104]

Repeating the opinions he had expressed in Venice, Althusser argued that change had been rendered both possible and necessary by the contemporary pattern of class struggle, which had detonated the *'general crisis of Marxism'* – a political, ideological and theoretical phenomenon. It was now vital 'to see clearly into the State, ideology, the Party, and politics'. Marxism, he concluded, had always been in a *'critical* position' – at once locked in combat with the dominant ideology and itself under siege – because its own fate was tied to

---

[103] Althusser 1990, pp. 277–8.
[104] Althusser 1990, p. 279.

the unpredictable course of the class struggle. Today, more than ever, the masses were 'on the move' and Marxism, for so long in abeyance, 'on the verge of profound changes'. Marxists must follow the precedent set by Marx and settle their accounts – an operation which would extend far beyond intellectuals and parties, since '[i]n the last resort it is the business of the popular masses in the ordeal of their struggle'.[105]

By way of response to Althusser's reflections, there is little to add to what has already been remarked of 'The Crisis of Marxism'. The two texts combine theoretical pessimism and political optimism in equal proportions. Both are injudicious. Viewed in the light of the disappointment of the optimism in March 1978, it is the pessimism that is thrown into relief and which endures. And, in taking his scalpel to Marx, Engels, Lenin, Gramsci and Mao, Althusser's autopsy was inflicting deep wounds on his own contribution, now located somewhere within the virtual theoretical nullity that was the recorded history of Marxism. In 1965, making his own the axioms of Lenin he now criticised as tokens of idealism, Althusser had also cited Engels on *Capital*: without it, and the scientific theory it offered, we would still be 'groping in the dark'. Even with Marx, it transpired in 1978, Marxists had been doing little else vis-à-vis the state, politics, party and ideology for over one hundred years; no Spinozist light had illuminated itself and the darkness.[106] Seriatim, the theses of *For Marx* and *Reading 'Capital'* were erased, together with the epistemological break – long-time first article of Althusserianism. Flawed from the outset, undeveloped since Marx, deformed under Stalin, compromised by a tragic history, replete with idealism, historical materialism was now a very different creature from the omnipotent because true doctrine of high Althusserianism.

As was that other avant-garde science of yesteryear – psychoanalysis. In an essay written in 1976 but only published (against Althusser's will) eight years later – 'The Discovery of Dr. Freud' – Althusser queried its status as radically as he retracted claims previously advanced on behalf of Marxism. Rescinding the theses of 'Freud and Lacan', he argued that Freud had not produced a scientific theory of the unconscious and that Lacan's efforts to impart scientific 'form' to the content of Freud's work had resulted only in

---

[105] Althusser 1990, pp. 279–80.
[106] See Althusser 1990, p. 5 and Marx and Engels 1977, p. 162.

'a fantastic philosophy of psychoanalysis that has fascinated intellectuals for decades throughout the world'.[107] Lacan had remained within philosophy. So too, 'Marxism Today' implied, had Althusser – in search of a non-existent object.

Lacan was still credited with having repulsed noxious interpretations of Freud; Althusser did not even go that far in his own case. He urged no claims on behalf of his return to, and reading of, Marx. *For Marx* and *Reading 'Capital'* were relegated to the theoretical void of Marxism after Marx. Amid ideological adversity, Althusser revoked the omnipotence of theory and, in blatantly voluntarist fashion, apotheosised the practice of the masses. 'Marxism Today' is Althusser's real auto-critique – one whose imbalance does its author and his subject less than justice. If a date must be chosen, it was in 1977–8 that Althusser did away with Althusserianism. At any rate, with 'Marxism Today' the Althusserian undertaking proper came to a melancholy close.

The starting-point of this chapter can now be rejoined. With the dissipation of Maoism, Althusser's own complementary theoretical and political stance was no longer viable. Theoretically, he descended into pessimism and scepticism. Politically, he displayed a new-found willingness publicly to adopt oppositional positions. For the first time, questions of contemporary socialist strategy were addressed in his increasingly fragmentary writings, however imperfectly. Simultaneously with the retraction of his aggrandisement of historical materialism in *For Marx* and *Reading 'Capital'*, the erstwhile 'pope of theory'[108] hoped for a renewal of a Marxism now bereft of concrete models in popular practice: the masses who made history could also redeem theory. Some of the song at least remains the same. In the spring of 1978, Althusser witnessed the dashing of such hopes as he had invested in the Union of the Left. Paradoxically, theoretical dejection and political frustration gave rise to an uncompromising assault on the Stalinist legacy within the PCF; *What Must*

---

[107] See Althusser 1996, pp. 85–104. For the history of this text, see Roudinesco 1986, pp. 645–7. For Althusser's letter to *Le Monde* of 11 May 1984 protesting against the unauthorised publication, see Althusser 1996, pp. 82–3. And on his intervention against Lacan in the controversies surrounding the dissolution of the latter's École freudienne, see Althusser 1996, pp. 125–43 and Roudinesco 1986, pp. 650–60.

[108] The title of James 1984, the phrase was coined by E. Altvater and O. Kallscheuer in 1979.

Change in the Communist Party was a left-wing critique of Stalinism – even if it was not the first.

In a remarkably up-beat interview dated July 1978 with his German colleague Peter Schöttler, Althusser confided that he affiliated 'to the tradition of Marx and Lenin without any hesitation':

> I do not particularly like the expression 'Marxism-Leninism', which is too 'crude' to correspond to reality. I prefer to speak of the Marxist and Leninist tradition, which does not stop at Lenin. . . . I think that some of the formulations of Marx, Lenin and their successors (I am not talking about Stalin . . .) contain approximations, even errors. But essentially they are 'correct' politically, even if it is necessary to go back over some of their theoretical formulations and improve them. Comrades who declare themselves against 'Leninism' are justified if, by this, they mean the *Foundations of Leninism* fixed and glossed in an utterly tendentious manner by Stalin. If, on the other hand, they mean Lenin's thought, which contains its share of problems and even contradictions . . ., I believe they are wrong.[109]

Complacent (in public at least) about the impact of the new philosophers,[110] in this, his last published statement on the subject, Althusser revealed himself curiously unaware of the gravity of the crisis afflicting the intellectual and political enterprise he had defended for thirty years – a crisis which did not spare a master of Marxism and some of his pupils.

---

[109] Althusser 1978b, p. 10. Althusser proceeds (pp. 11–13) to a very sharp attack on Eurocommunism.

[110] See Althusser 1978b, p. 11.

Conclusion: Unfinished History

> All knowledge at the moment of its construction is a
> polemical knowledge; it must first destroy to clear a space
> for its own constructions.
>
> Gaston Bachelard, *La Dialectique de la durée*

The argument of this book can now be briefly
resumed. Having joined the PCF immediately after
the postwar 'left'-turn in the international Communist
movement, Althusser took almost no part in the
controversies of the political and intellectual Cold
War. Only four years after Khrushchev's 'secret
speech' to the Twentieth Congress of the CPSU
in 1956 did he enter the fray. By the time of his
return to Marx, a new division had supervened
in the Communist world: the Chinese schism.
Althusser's project was the renovation of Communist
political practice by a renewal of Marxist theory.
Philosophically hostile to the humanist Marxism
stimulated within the Communist parties by
de-Stalinisation (and then recuperated by their
leaderships), the rejuvenation of Marxism essayed
in *For Marx* and *Reading 'Capital'* was politically
consonant with Maoism. Such sympathies were,
however, firmly subordinated to the theoretical
orthodoxy Althusser attempted to re-articulate in his
major works.

Repelled by the subjectivism of Zhdanov's
intendancy, Althusser expounded a novel version of
dialectical materialism as the theory of theoretical

practice – a highly sophisticated anti-empiricist epistemology which posited abrupt discontinuities between science and ideology (expansively defined) and within the history of science. In effect at once epistemology and ontology, Marxist philosophy in its Althusserian rendering was immunised against the dictates of the class struggle. But what it lacked in political militancy it sought to make up for in the services it performed on behalf of historical materialism, whose claim to be the science of history it upheld. If Althusser's ambition was to constitute Marxist philosophy, his project vis-à-vis historical materialism was no less radical: to reconstruct it in non-economistic, non-humanist and non-historicist form, preliminary to the comprehensive development it required after its sojourn in the 'dogmatist night'. The upshot was a new conception of the dialectic which, unlike any 'inversion' of Hegel's, stripped it of abstraction and fatalism via the category of overdetermination; a reconceptualisation of the structure of social formations which respected their constitutive complexity through the assignment of relative autonomy to irreducible political and ideological regions, the totality being governed by a structural causality wherein determination in the last instance, but not dominance, was the preserve of the economic; an anti-teleological theory of modes of production as articulated combinations of relations and forces of production, whose account of historical transition proscribed evolutionism; and a distinctive conception of ideology as representations of people's imaginary relations to their real conditions of existence which, denying any end of it under communism, impugned historical messianism.

An enterprise of great scope and originality, executed with enormous determination, this recasting of Marxism, founded upon a forced re-reading of Marx, was seriously vitiated – by a 'theoreticism' that toppled over into idealism and conventionalism; by an astringent theoretical anti-humanism which occluded human agency in its prioritisation of structural necessity; by an ultimately anti-historical anti-historicism productive of its own fair share of difficulties in understanding historical change as a consequence of its emphasis on social reproduction, and yielding an ahistorical structurality or, alternatively, an unstructured history. These and other problems eventually became apparent to Althusser, who would seek to resolve them.

Meantime, the unleashing of a Cultural Revolution in China, and Althusser's election of it as a cynosure of democratic communism, drew him into a 'flirtation' with Maoist opposition to the PCF's leadership which did not cease when he to declined to follow his students out of the Party in 1966. The ultimate ambivalence over Stalinism inherent in Althusser's political affiliations was, if anything, henceforth exacerbated. The conflicting demands of conformity to the Politbureau and indulgence towards Maoist China marked his career for roughly a decade, resulting in a combination of public adherence to the party line and theoretical *gauchisme*. The auto-critique and rectification undertaken by him from *Philosophy and the Spontaneous Philosophy of Scientists* (1967) onwards, in an effort to satisfy his critics, effected a radicalisation of his theoretical positions – redefining philosophy as, in the last instance, the class struggle in theory, proposing that the masses made history, and foregrounding the thesis that its motor was the class struggle. But these adjustments to Althusser's Marxism did not add up to a coherent or plausible alternative to his initial versions of historical and dialectical materialism, being characterised by an unresolved tension between functionalism – an automaticity of social reproduction via state apparatuses – and voluntarism – a contingency of social transformation via the *deus ex machina* of class struggle. Moreover, rather than settling accounts with theoretical Stalinism, they substituted a schematic Marxism-Leninism for the original theoretical system of *For Marx* and *Reading 'Capital'*. The nadir of this declension was reached with *Reply to John Lewis*, a pamphlet which conjoined a militant rhetoric of class struggle with an evasive account of Stalinism. Althusserian affinity for the Chinese experiment and its ideology also marred the most substantial contribution made by Althusser to historical materialism after 1965 – the ambitious theory of ideology expounded in 'Ideology and Ideological State Apparatuses' (1970).

Then, in the mid-1970s, a dramatic change of direction occurred. Under the impact of the termination of a discredited Cultural Revolution and the anti-Marxist turn among French intellectuals, Althusser re-opened the question of Stalin, abandoned quasi-Maoist responses to it, and posed some questions of his own (which he did not, however, attempt to answer). The shattering of illusions about China did not issue in renegacy, but it did infect Althusser's thinking with a certain pessimism. Politically, from 1976 onwards a reorientation – towards centrism or left Eurocommunism – was evident which, whilst it facilitated a more forthright indictment of Stalinism, produced no real alternative political strategy to Gallocommunist horizions. Theoretically, Althusser betrayed an increasing scepticism as to the explanatory merits of historical materialism, of whose contributions to theories of politics and ideology he now despaired. Where the misadventures of Maoism had impelled him to serious engagement with the political strategy of the PCF, the vicissitudes of Eurocommunism in its local form (the Union of the Left) provoked him to the frontal assault on the Stalinist legacy in his party with which his public career to all intents and purposes closed. Amid the crisis of Marxism he had announced in 1977, Althusser also queried the Marxist and Leninist legacies and relinquished Althusserianism, effectively effacing the epistemological break whose vindication had been the object of the Althusserian exercise. If, despite its limitations and belatedness, *What Must Change in the Communist Party* appeared to herald a new era for Althusser the Communist militant, 'Marxism Today' unwittingly wrote the obituary of Althusser the Marxist philosopher.

Such was the fate of Althusser's enterprise at its author's hands. With 'Marxism Today', he bowed, inadvertently or otherwise, to the anti-Althusserian consensus that had already crystallised in France – and which has since been consolidated. Elsewhere too, as noted in the Foreword, the explicit critical judgements have for the most part being going one way: against Althusser. For some – apolitical literary deconstructionists – he is too faithful to Marxism and, consequently, unworthy of a place in the theoretical adventure playground that is poststructuralism at its worst. For others – the post-Althusserians – he is to be praised for having prepared the way for their own 'post-Marxist' paradigms. If, for the Nietzschean avant-garde, he is the Marxist same, for humanist Marxism, he is the Stalinist other. As far as some Anglophone Marxists are concerned, on the other hand, he is simply all-too-French. Thus, in Althusser's case, we cannot report that the magnitude of his achievement has been obscured only to the extent that we have grown accustomed to it.[1]

I should like to propose an alternative verdict on Louis Althusser's detour of theory – a reckoning which stops well short of espousing high Althusserianism, but which does not anathematise, repress, disappear or patronise it either. Althusser once remarked that he had never ceased to be disconcerted by other people's construction and utilisation of his work; writing

---

[1] Cf. the remarks on Montesquieu in Althusser 1972, p. 14.

books, he reflected, was like casting a message in a bottle onto the open seas.[2] Twenty years after that message was launched in the shape of *For Marx* and *Reading 'Capital'* – years in which its recipients have themselves been disconcerted or unruffled, outraged or enthused, provoked or encouraged – what is there to be said in its favour?

First, Althusser's re-reading of Marx, however tendentious textually and contentious theoretically, had the great virtue of reorienting Marxists away from the uncritical cult of Marx's early works to serious scrutiny of his later writings, restoring *Capital* to its rightful paramountcy. To be sure, the Althusserian symptomatic reading substituted one unilateralism (Marx versus the young Marx) for another (the 1844 *Manuscripts* versus *Capital*). Yet the privilege accorded to Marx post-1844 was *not* the mirror-image of its antagonist, but a salutary counter-reaction against it, since 'historical materialism' – the research programme initiated in 1845 and developed thereafter – is theoretically superior to, and politically more significant than, what preceded it.[3] By 'bending the stick' so far in the direction of the mature Marx, Althusser not only disrupted contemporary vogues, established certainties and official platitudes; he also put on the agenda a genuinely satisfactory account of Marx's career – one that presents a picture neither of seamless continuity nor of outright discontinuity (be it to the credit of Marx in Paris or Marx in the British Museum). Whether as provocation or stimulus, Althusser's periodisation unquestionably incited debate on, and research into, historical materialism its genesis and development – at a virtually unsurpassed level. Gareth Stedman Jones's forthcoming *Return of the Repressed?*, a synthesis of the best modern scholarship and an original contribution in its own right, constitutes – whatever its non-Althusserian conclusions – sufficient testimony to its positive impact; while scholarly translations of Marx by the Althusserian Germanist, Jean-Pierre Lefebvre, and the indispensable *Dictionnaire critique du marxisme* (1982) featuring articles by Balibar, Macherey and many others, confute insinuations of charlatantry.

Althusser's rationalist epistemology, and the modes of reading and critique associated with it, are untenable – condemned, by an 'internalism' which

---

[2] Personal communication from Perry Anderson.
[3] For analogous judgements, see Geras 1983 p. 78 (note the rider on p. 79) and Anderson 1980, pp. 107–8.

insulates theoretical discourse from empirical evidence and severs it from its real referent, to the relativism inherent in any conventionalism. Even so – and this is the second point – his theory of the cognitive process as a process of production of knowledge has a lot to be said for it as a philosophy *for* science. Rejecting the positivist misrepresentation of science, Althusser countered both the jejune materialism of orthodox Marxism's reflection theory and the sophisticated idealisms of its Western-Marxist opponents. *Contra* scientism and historicism alike, the theory of theoretical practice posited the historicity and scientificity of science. Although the development of it subverted realism, the distinction it featured between the 'object of knowledge' and the 'real object' encapsulated this simultaneous commitment to the specificity of scientific practice – the historical production and transformation of intra-scientific objects – and epistemological materialism – the independent, extra-scientific existence of the objects of which knowledge is produced. Thus, for all that the concepts of problematic and epistemological break in practice set up the conundrum of commensurability (hence the reconciliation of scientific change with scientific progress), and ultimately obstructed theorisation of a science's conditions of existence, incidentally functioning as pretexts to read Marx's œuvre through patently non-Marxist optics, they did focus attention on crucial 'intrinsic' aspects of scientific research programmes. Moreover, they served to highlight the counter-intuitive nature of science, the peculiarity of its systematic discourse, the *sui generis* nature of its discontinuous history. Above all, the first version of Althusserian philosophy had the considerable merit of insisting on the cognitive autonomy of scientific theory (albeit by granting it independence from the non-theoretical): a timely correction. For by so doing, Althusser struck a fierce blow against Stalinist pragmatism *without signing science over to it* – reminding a new generation of Marxists (and some older ones) that Marx's ambition was to found a new *science*. Characteristically, Althusser overstated his case, thinking, as Poulantzas had occasion to remark of him (and as he more or less admitted), 'in extremes'.[4] The fact that historical materialism is not straightforwardly a science among others, however, does not mean that it does not aspire to be a science – one whose results amount to objective knowledge which can be employed to further the project of changing the world.

---

[4] See Poulantzas 1980, p. 167 and cf. Althusser 1976a, pp. 170–2.

Thus, if the final shape assumed by Althusser's anti-empiricist epistemology aligns it with the idealism and relativism it commenced by eschewing, it nevertheless represented a decisive advance in Marxist reflection on the philosophy of science, approximated only by Della Volpe's works. (In certain respects, a regression, even the second definition of philosophy has something going for it as a Marxist variant of the Lockean conception of philosophy as an under-labourer to, rather than the queen of, the sciences.) Important philosophical work by such British Marxists as Ted Benton, Alex Callinicos, Andrew Collier and especially Roy Bhaskar, author of the most substantial contemporary philosophy of science by an Anglophone Marxist, all owe different acknowledged debts to Althusser's initiative and indicate its legitimacy.[5] In their search for a realist approach to the natural and social sciences, these writers have pursued the path opened within Marxism by it. Given their ambitions, it has not been the last word, naturally. But, in conjunction with non-Marxist philosophies of science, it has been a starting-point or staging post – a position Marxism must progress beyond, not regress behind.

Althusser's periodisation of Marx and his epistemology have, it has been suggested, much to commend them. What of the reconstruction of the basic concepts of historical materialism propounded by Althusser and Balibar in opposition to the evolutionism of Second International and Stalinist Marxism, and the alternative schemas of their antagonists in the Western-Marxist tradition? Our third conclusion can be that what Fredric Jameson considers 'the Althusserian revolution'[6] in the conceptualisation of social formations has aided Marxist researchers in the most diverse fields to explore some of the *terra incognita* of the 'continent' whose discovery Althusser attributed to Marx: the continent of history. If, as Jürgen Habermas has argued, '[t]heories, especially of Marxist inspiration, ultimately prove their worth by making a contribution to the explanation of concrete historical processes',[7] Althusser's

---

[5] See Benton 1977 and 1984; Callinicos 1982 and 1983; Collier 1988; Bhaskar 1978 and 1986 – a prologue to his forthcoming *Dialectic*. It should be noted that Benton and Collier are likewise indebted to Bhaskar. The latter has recently confirmed that Althusser was 'the foremost *Marxist* influence' on his *Realist Theory of Science*, characterising him as 'the best and most advanced Marxist for philosophy of science' (interview with Roy Bhaskar, London, February 1987).

[6] Jameson 1981, p. 37; for Jameson's discussion of it, see pp. 23–58.

[7] Habermas 1985, p. 89.

has more than proved its worth. The single most important achievement of *For Marx* and *Reading 'Capital'* was to help renew Marxism – often in spite of Althusser's epistemological protocols and in directions unforeseen by him. The effect of this particular return to Marx, in France and beyond, was to impart a new vigour and greater sophistication to Marxist inquiry – Communist and non-Communist, under Althusser's immediate auspices or not – in a multiplicity of domains. From philosophy to political science, from historiography to literary criticism, linguistics and cultural studies, from economics to anthropology, from social theory to legal studies, the harvest of Althusserianism in 'abstract' and 'concrete' investigations, and in syntheses of the two, has been abundant and rich.

No cursory list can do justice to the continuing productivity and vitality of the Althusserian research programme. But a few pointers can be offered. Thus, among historical works significantly indebted to the meta-historical labours of Althusser and Balibar, one could cite Guy Bois's extraordinary study of Norman feudalism, building into an analysis of the laws of motion of the feudal mode of production; Robert Linhart's challenging re-examination of Leninist theory and Bolshevik practice on the peasant question and the organisation of industrial labour in the fledgling, embattled Soviet state; Peter Schöttler's rewarding exploration of the contradictory nature and chequered history of the *bourses de travail* in Third-Republic France, which attests to the fertile aspects of later Althusserian propositions on ideology and class struggle; or, outside France and Althusser's immediate orbit, Perry Anderson's marvellous syntheses of European historical development from antiquity to Absolutism and Gareth Stedman Jones's signal contributions to English working-class history.[8] Althusserianism, then, has influenced concrete analyses and explanations of the past that are as empirically controlled as they are conceptually engaged. Add to this its part in a renaissance of Marxist anthropology – whether via Emmanuel Terray's defence of the applicability of historical materialism to 'primitive' social formations or Pierre-Philippe

---

[8] See Bois 1984; Linhart 1976; Schöttler 1985; Anderson 1974a and 1974b; Stedman Jones 1983 and 1984. The balance-sheet thus vindicates the verdict not of Thompson, but of his colleague Pierre Vilar. In a long essay originally published in *Annales* in 1973, the latter signalled 'the constructive and useful elements in Althusser's powerful contribution to a Marxist science': Vilar 1973, p. 65.

Rey's profound survey of the effects of colonialism in the Congo[9] – and its capacity for engagement with the real world should not be in doubt.

So much for the influence, direct or indirect, exclusive or combined, of Althusser's Marxism on historiography and anthropology. What, briefly, of its impact on politics, economics and sociology? In the first category there are the contributions of the Greek Marxist Nicos Poulantzas, whose fundamental work on different forms of the capitalist state deservedly made him the single most influential Marxist political theorist of the postwar period; of the Swede Göran Therborn, whose studies of successive state structures and the theory of ideology, like the comparative history of classical sociology and Marxism that preceded them, represented impressive advances; of the Argentinian Ernesto Laclau, whose essays on fascism and populism sponsored a controversial new approach to old and intractable problems; of Balibar himself, whose excavation of the original significance of the dictatorship of the proletariat reclaimed the Marxist and Leninist concept from its subsequent debasement.[10] In economics, what is probably the most informative Marxist work on contemporary capitalism derives from a French current part descended from the Althusserian tradition – the 'regulation school'. Outstanding here have been Michel Aglietta's ambitious theory of the development of capitalism in the USA from the 1860s to the 1970s; and the enquiries of Alain Lipietz into the role of money and credit in the current recession and into the vicissitudes of global Fordism, for example. Across the Channel, on the other hand, the vigorous critique of modernisation and underdevelopment theory developed by John Taylor is perhaps the central contribution by an English Althusserian.[11] Finally, Althusserian impetus to sociological research can be gauged from the trio of comprehensive analyses by Christian Baudelot, Roger Establet and their colleagues of France's education network, petty bourgeoisie

---

[9] See Terray 1972 and Rey 1971. Maurice Bloch has paid tribute to Althusser's contribution to 'what has really been a revolution in Marxist anthropology': Bloch 1983, p. 170. Equally weighty here, of course, has been the commanding œuvre – related but nevertheless distinct – of Maurice Godelier.

[10] See Poulantzas 1973, 1974, 1976, 1978, and the posthumous collection 1980; Therborn 1976, 1978, and 1980; Laclau 1977; Balibar 1977. On Poulantzas and Laclau, see the important work by the former's leading British pupil, Bob Jessop (especially Jessop 1982 and 1985).

[11] See Aglietta 1979; Lipietz 1985 and 1987; and Taylor 1979. For a fruitful employment of regulation-school categories, see Davis's excellent 1986.

and class system; from Poulantzas's delineation of the class structure of advanced capitalism; from the American Marxist Erik Olin Wright's contrasting map of modern classes and his dissection of economic inequality in the US; and from Manuel Castell's research in urban sociology.[12]

Elsewhere, too, Althusser's recasting has proved its worth and versatility – in the innovative initiatives of Pierre Macherey in literary theory (taken up in British most notably by Terry Eagleton);[13] of Michel Pêcheux and his colleagues in linguistics and discourse theory;[14] of Bernard Edelman in the Marxist theory of law.[15] These are only the most salient examples of attempts at a creative development and application of Althusser's work, especially his theory of ideology, often conjugated with post-Saussurean linguistics and Lacanian psychoanalysis – the tip of a partially Althusserian iceberg in aesthetics, cultural studies, literary criticism, media and film studies, and so on.[16] Moreover, this culpably *pre-feminist* Marxism has been utilised by feminist theoreticians to explore problems of crucial significance to the oppression of women, but whose analysis had been obstructed by its predecessors – the sexual division of labour, for example, or the socio-cultural (re)production of

---

[12] See Baudelot and Establet 1971; Baudelot, Establet and Malemort 1974; Baudelot, Establet and Toiser 1979; Poulantzas 1975; Wright 1978 and 1979; Castells 1977.

[13] See Macherey 1978 and Eagleton 1976. See also, for example, Balibar and Macherey 1981; Balibar 1974; Balibar and Laporte 1974; and for impressive recent essays grounded in an Althusserian problematic, Sprinker 1987. Eagleton's retrospective estimation of the Althusserian moment can be found in the preface to his 1986, pp. 2–4. A major essay in cultural and literary history facilitated by Althusserian analytical notions is Mulhern 1979.

[14] See Pêcheux 1982; Pêcheux et al. 1975; Gadet and Pêcheux 1981. See also, example, Robin 1973; Henry 1977; Gadet 1987; Gadet et al. 1979. Élisabeth Roudinesco is the author of some valuable studies of the theory, history and politics of psychoanalysis; see especially Roudinesco 1977 and 1986.

[15] See Edelman 1979.

[16] The publication of 'Freud and Lacan' in 1969 (in *New Left Review*, no. 55) and of 'Ideology and Ideological State Apparatuses' two years later had a profound impact in Britain. For examples of research informed by Althusser's theory of ideology, and conducted under the sign of the 'Triple Alliance', see the work of writers associated with the film journal *Screen* – among others Heath 1972 and 1981; and MacCabe 1978 and 1985 (note the comments on Althusser in the interesting introductory text, 'Class of '68: Elements of Intellectual Autobiography 1967–81'). The highly original and illuminating work of the Centre for Cultural Studies, under the direction of Stuart Hall, also displays an Althusserian input – but one much subordinate to that of Gramsci and not to the exclusion of the British Marxist historiographical tradition. See, e.g., Hall et al. 1978 and Clarke, Critcher and Johnson (eds.) 1978 – especially Johnson's own contributions.

gender.[17] In philosophy, meanwhile, the Althusserian contribution has likewise been notable – especially in aiding a better appreciation of the oeuvre of Althusser's 'real companion in heresy', Baruch Spinoza.[18]

None of this work is unproblematic or above reproach, naturally. And Althusserianism has also given birth to its fair share of aberrations. Nevertheless, if Paul Hirst exaggerated somewhat when, contesting Thompson's verdict, he claimed that the Althusserian current 'remains the most original and productive in modern Marxist theory and research', he erred on the side of accuracy.[19] In any event, the diverse literature generated in an Althusserian matrix to date contradicts a familiar image of Althusser and the Althusserians (mere reproductions of Their Master's Voice) as pseudo-Marxological, metaphilosophical, supra-historical, anti-empirical, hyper-theoretical and apolitical[20] – or crypto-Stalinist.

That last epithet leads into a fourth point. If, quite the reverse of being analytically barren – a sterile repetition – Althusser's conceptual clarifications and constructions effected a certain recommencement of historical materialism, did they by the same token contribute to the de-Stalinisation of Marxist theory? Here, again, taking Althusser not at his word but at his work and its effects, the historical record dictates an affirmative response. Althusserianism was not an avatar of Stalinism. On the contrary, it was Althusser's iconoclasm *within the PCF* which initiated a genuine theoretical de-Stalinisation. With the inception of his enterprise, the 'intellectual ice-age'[21] through which the Party had passed, and for whose duration the talents of such as Lefebvre or Desanti had been squandered, came to an end. Althusser was not quite a lonely pioneer. Khrushchevite liberalisation had emboldened other Communist

---

[17] See the discussion of the substantial literature in Michèle Barrett's excellent overview in her 1980; and see also Benton 1984, pp. 134–40. Thus Juliet Mitchell's pioneering 'Women: The Longest Revolution' of 1966 (reprinted in modified form in her 1971) drew upon elements of Althusser's break with economistic Marxism – as did her remarkable 1974.

[18] See, e.g., Moreau 1975; Macherey 1979; and Balibar 1998. The quotation is from Pêcheux 1982, p. 214.

[19] Hirst 1985, p. 87, n. 2. Cf. Anderson's observation two years earlier that of the Western-Marxist schools 'the Althusserian current has probably persisted most strongly': Anderson 1983, p. 23.

[20] See, *inter alia*, Aron 1969, e.g., pp. 73, 78–9, 252: a verdict repeated in Aron 1983, p. 584, where allusion is nevertheless made to the testimony of others regarding Althusser's liberating impact.

[21] Hobsbawm 1982, p. 119.

intellectuals to independent, fruitful exploration. But his endeavour was qualitatively distinct, insofar as it amounted to the articulation of a *whole theoretical system*. Its significance was three-fold. To begin with, the very pronouncement that Marx's philosophy remained to be constituted meant that, despite Stalin and Zhdanov, everything was still to play for here; while Althusser's own initiative in this newly-opened space represented a substantial break with Stalinist orthodoxy – one whose inconsistencies ultimately (and mercifully) discredited the very idea of resuming dialectical materialism in anything like the received, superintending sense. Next, insistence on the imperfection of historical materialism *both* as a historical consequence of its ossification in the international Communist movement from the mid-1920s, *and* as a normal theoretical correlate of its status as a scientific paradigm, liberated Marxism from a dogmatic conception of science in general, and of historical materialism in particular, as a fixed and finished doctrine. With their installation of recasting, development and progress as criteria of scientificity, rather than indices of revisionism, Althusser's epistemological propositions licensed the research required to make good the deficit of decades. 'It would be very rash to believe that everything has been said': a characteristically laconic statement of the utmost significance.[22] For therewith Althusser helped to emancipate younger Communist intellectuals from the Stalinisation of Marxism, not only re-reading *Capital* himself, but enjoining others to read Marx as opposed to Thorez or Suslov. Finally – and critically – Althusser's reclamation of Marx's 'immense theoretical revolution' was conducted, in arresting and commendable contrast to other leading representatives of Western Marxism, without surrendering historical materialism to the Stalinist misrepresentation of it: histomat. Refusing the Western-Marxist anti-naturalism wherein Stalinist positivism enjoyed its posthumous revenge, Althusser retrieved the 'materialist conception of history' from its parody. In other words, this was a theoretical de-Stalinisation which declined to write off the classical-Marxist tradition as inherently vulgar.

Althusser's treatment of other members of the Western-Marxist tradition was crude and cavalier, his typology of Marxisms undiscriminating, and his own reconstruction of historical materialism defective. Moreover, he accepted elements of the Stalinist codification of Marxism – its division into dialectical

---

[22] See Althusser 1969a, p. 63, n. 27.

and historical materialism, for example, or the travesty of Trotskyism. Only in the third phase of his career did he overcome his reticence, resolve some ambiguities and arraign diamat as forcefully as he had interrogated humanist alternatives to, and rectifications of, it. In this sense – and late in the day – 'Unfinished History' opened the book of errors, Althusser's included. But, if Althusserianism was a consequence of Stalinism, it was scarcely its continuance.[23] For when all is said and done, Althusser's critiques of evolutionism and economism, of historicism and humanism; his renovation of historical materialism as the non-teleological theory of the history of social formations; and his commencement of the elaboration of its undeveloped regional theories – these exploded the Garaudyist dispensation, put an enormous research programme on the agenda, and reconnected French Marxism with its classical antecedents and with contemporary philosophy. Aware of what 'dogmatism' really meant, Alasdair MacIntyre has signalled 'the profound debt of gratitude that we all owe to Althusser for having brought French Marxism back into dialogue with the rest of French philosophy', concluding: 'So far as French philosophy was concerned, he de-Stalinised Marxism more thoroughly than any other Marxist did'.[24] Althusser's erection of new and problematic orthodoxies may partially qualify, but does not cancel, the breach he made in official Marxism. The testimony of his students and others to his liberating intellectual influence – and generosity – is there for those who want to read it.[25] To those, on the other hand, who still wish to insist that in the first or last instance Althusser was a Stalinist, it might be replied à la Sartre: Louis Althusser may have been a Stalinist; but not every Stalinist is Louis Althusser.

What one far from uncritical commentator has described as 'an intellectual *tour de force* which is overwhelming in its scope and pretensions'[26] thus incontestably had immediate and long-term effects on the development of historical materialism that were positive for Marxist culture as a whole. Its intellectual contribution to the inter-continental renaissance of Marxist theory

---

[23] Cf. Thompson 1978, p. 404.
[24] MacIntyre 1981, p. 16.
[25] See, e.g., Buci-Glucksmann 1976, p. 28; Debray 1973, pp. 197–8 and Debray 1975, p. 100; Lecourt 1982, p. 132; Lindenberg 1975, pp. 20–1; Raymond 1976, p. 137; Robin and Guilhaumou 1976, p. 36.
[26] Hirsh 1982, p. 163.

314 of Conclusion: Unfinished History

in the 1960s and 1970s was second to none. The ultimate and obvious limitations of Althusser's accomplishment, especially when measured against its initial promise and ambitions, render it no less remarkable and leave its beneficiaries, past and present, no less indebted. As messages in bottles go, *For Marx* and *Reading 'Capital'* fared well.

Althusser's Marxism also contained and encouraged some bad habits and they must be entered in the balance-sheet. First, there was an intellectual exclusivity about it, betrayed by intimations of a 'theory degree zero' prior to its own emergence and occasional depiction of the history of Marxism (minus Marx, Lenin and Mao) as a night in which in all pre-Althusserians were humanist-historicists, that had negative consequences for its own development. Disinclined to make the thorough acquaintance of other post-classical currents or to engage in dialogue and debate with interlocutors, adopting a tone of authority with critics or simply ignoring them, Althusser elected to pursue his project in splendid isolation: it was he who ended up being marginalised. Secondly, Althusserianism was characterised by an overweening confidence in, a fundamental immodesty about, the powers of Marxism – an assertion of its supremacy that contained its own nemesis. Thirdly, although Aron's reproach that Althusserianism was Marxism for *agrégés*[27] is quite unjust, it is the case that neither Althusser nor his followers furnished the concrete analysis of the French situation his reconstruction was supposed to facilitate and which he continually invoked – a dereliction whose grave repercussions on the political reputation of Althusser's Marxism need no underlining. Fourthly – and finally – if Althusser made an enormous contribution to the de-Stalinisation of French Marxism, he then proceeded after his own fashion to 'Maoise' it – an involution which was theoretically retrogressive and politically perilous, the illusion of the Parisian epoch rapidly giving way to a disillusionment from which French Marxism has never recovered.

That Althusser was always constrained, politically and theoretically, by the twin horizons of the PCF and Maoist China; and that almost all of his work after 1965 is ultimately (and for whatever reason) footnotes to *For Marx* and *Reading 'Capital'* – these too are facts to which attention has been drawn.

---

[27] See Aron 1969.

Although they represented a genuine attempt to rectify the demerits of classical Althusserianism, Althusser's revisions – the second definition of philosophy and the Marxist-Leninist theses of *Reply to John Lewis* – were a cul-de-sac, their outcome in inverse proportion to the effort expended on them. In the absence of a concrete analysis of contemporary France, no credible theoretico-political project materialised in the quite new conjuncture ushered in by the May events of 1968. It will have been noticed that a considerably less positive evaluation has been offered here of the second phase of Althusser's career than of its first and third. The Althusser who demands continuing, though critical, admiration is the innovative philosopher of 1960–5 – one whose self-confessed polemical extremism, destroying in order to create space for his own constructions, was vital to the establishment and productivity of his research programme (and is not without distinguished – for example, Engelsian – precedent). The Althusser who deserves respect is the independent militant of *What Must Change in the Communist Party*. His career between 1968 and 1975, on the other hand, retains its importance largely because it is his and forms an episode of a depressing history perhaps still too close for comprehension as opposed to lamentation or ridicule: the fate of a generation of French Marxisms – not only Althusser's, but Sartre's, *Tel Quel*'s, Glucksmann and co.'s – which, transfixed by the rhetoric of Maoism, took a fast boat to China.

Étienne Balibar has recently suggested, first, that after May '68 Althusser more and more found himself in the position which, like Lenin, he had always censured – reacting to events and being 'dragged along' by them, rather than anticipating developments and taking initiatives; and secondly that, under political fire, he *unduly* criticised his original positions.[28] There is no reason to quarrel with Balibar's first statement: a transition from *attentisme* to *suivisme* is discernible post-May. And I would like to register my agreement with the second. In the course of Althusser's attempt to repay the imaginary debt he had contracted by not being *gauchiste*, much that might have been patiently

---

[28] Interview with Étienne Balibar, Paris, June 1985. See also Balibar and Macherey 1982 – an interview in which the former describes Althusser's 'later corrections' as 'regressions in relation to the earlier work'. 'Althusser,' he goes on to remark (p. 48), 'read his own texts with the eyes of certain of his critics' – inadvisedly, in Balibar's view.

emended or developed was abandoned – in favour of a theoretical and political orientation which failed to propitiate his leftist critics. There is no point in speculating on what might have been. History did not pass that way. Instead, it passed by the Cultural Revolution, May '68, the Union of the Left, the crisis of French Marxism . . .

At the end of 'Unfinished History', Althusser reflected that, whilst Lysenko's history was concluded, that of Lysenkoism was seemingly endless.[29] If the signs are reversed, a similar relationship might be posited between Althusser and Althusserianism: *histoire terminée, histoire interminable*. Althusser's career would appear to be over. Yet this partisan and artisan of Marxism is among the Marxist philosophers. Inscribed in history, his detour of theory can be judged better. Accordingly, if Althusser lacks the political record and literary qualities of a Sartre; if his œuvre is dwarfed by the encyclopaedism of Lukács's, Adorno's or Habermas's; if his contribution must count as much less extraordinary than Gramsci's in his *Prison Notebooks* (composed at *that* time and in *those* conditions), nonetheless his achievement is very considerable. The history of Althusserianism, on the other hand, now shorn not only of its original *élan* but of many of its pretensions and vices, continues – to the undoubted benefit of Marxist and socialist culture. It has ended only to the extent that much of what is best in it – its 'rational kernel' – has been assimilated into the culture, becoming part of the theoretical consciousness – or, often, unconscious – of left-wing intellectuals. In that sense, something of the moment of Louis Althusser has passed into a wider history – which is not to say that we are all Althusserians now.

---

[29] See Althusser 1977b, p. 16. Althusser's actual reference is to the causes of Lysenkoism.

Postscript: The Necessity of Contingency

In Memory of Michael Sprinker, 1950–99

We do not publish our own drafts, that is, our own mistakes.
But we do sometimes publish other people's.

Louis Althusser (1963)

1. Althusser after Althusserianism

Intellectually quasi-non-existent either side of
the Channel following the murder of his wife in
November 1980, Louis Althusser was physically
interred a decade later. Commenting in 1994, however,
David Macey could report that '[t]he death of the
philosopher has led to a resurrection of his writings'.[1]
The 1990s were indeed marked by a quite unexpected
revival of interest in Althusser. The main spur to this
raising of the dead was the simultaneous appearance
in France in 1992 of his autobiography and the first
instalment of a biography. These revealed the
existence of a hitherto unknown Althusser, something
of whose complexity is disclosed by the subsequent
volumes in a posthumous edition of his work,
completed in 1998. And this is to omit from the
reckoning the philosopher's extensive archives,
containing some book-length manuscripts, which
researchers have begun to delve into, but which have
doubtless yet to deliver up all their secrets.

---

[1] Macey 1994, p. 45.

What does the posthumous edition comprise? In sum, nine volumes, drawn from the archives deposited at the Institut mémoires de l'édition contemporaine after Althusser's death, mostly published by Éditions Stock in conjunction with IMEC, and individually or jointly edited by Olivier Corpet, Yann Moulier Boutang, and François Matheron. They may be classified as follows:

(i) Two volumes of autobiographical writings issued in 1992 – the two memoirs (1985/1976) presented in *L'avenir dure longtemps, suivi de Les Faits*, and the prison-camp notebooks and correspondence (1940–5) assembled in *Journal de captivité*. An expanded version of *L'avenir*, featuring other autobiographical texts as well as three chapters removed by Althusser from his 'confessions', was put together in 1994. An English translation of the first edition had been marketed in the UK by Chatto & Windus the year before. (Unaccountably, its US counterpart renders the Gaullist *obiter dictum* of Althusser's title *The Future Lasts Forever*.)

(ii) Two volumes of psychoanalytical writings – *Écrits sur la psychanalyse*, from correspondence with Jacques Lacan (1963–6) through to Althusser's interventions in the controversy over the dissolution of the École freudienne de Paris (1980), published in 1993; and *Psychanalyse et sciences humaines*, the edited transcripts of two seminar presentations from 1963–4, released in 1996. An abridged English edition of the *Écrits* came out from Columbia the same year as the seminars.

(iii) Four volumes of philosophical and political texts. The first, *Écrits philosophiques et politiques I* (1994), retrieved the bulk of Althusser's 'early writings' (1946–50), translated by Verso in 1997 as *The Spectre of Hegel*; an unfinished manuscript on 'Marx in his Limits' (1978), due to appear in English in 2006 in a Verso edition of the later writings, *Philosophy of the Encounter*; and extracts from late Althusserian speculations as to an 'Underground Current of the Materialism of the Encounter' (1982), likewise scheduled for inclusion in that volume. The second, entitled *Sur la philosophie* (1994), collects written 'interviews' and correspondence with Fernanda Navarro (1984–7), ruminating on the 'aleatory materialism' mooted in 1982, which will figure in the upcoming Verso collection. A third volume – *Sur la reproduction* (1995) – is composed of the unpublished 1969 book on 'The Reproduction of the Relations of Production' from which the ISAs essay was extracted the following year, together with that article and a retrospective 'Note' of 1976. A further offering of *Écrits philosophiques et politiques* (1995), arranged thematically, selects diverse material from 1962–7: in particular, unfinished works on Feuerbach and 'The Humanist Controversy' (1967); texts related to the 'Philosophy Course for Scientists' (1967–8); and an opuscule on Machiavelli derived from a lecture course given in 1972. *Machiavel et nous* was issued as a separate volume in English by Verso in 1999; while the texts from the 1960s, together with a programmatic piece on 'The Historic Task of Marxist Philosophy' (1967) hitherto available only in Hungarian, and the 'Three Notes on the Theory of Discourses' (1966) excluded from *Writings on Psychoanalysis*, were translated by Verso in 2003 in *The Humanist Controversy and Other Writings*.

(iv) An 800-page collection of Althusser's correspondence with his sometime Italian lover and translator, Franca Madonia, *Lettres à Franca (1961–1973)*, which ranges far beyond an epistolary romance, published in 1998. At time of writing, there would appear to be no plans to translate any of this material.

So much by way of rudimentary inventory of French publication and English translation. It is also worth mentioning that, under the stimulus of this ambitious programme, there were several reissues in France. In 1996, Presses Universitaires de France published a variorum edition of *Lire 'le Capital'*, regrouping the four instalments of the second edition (1968–73) in the order of the two-volume original (1965). Later the same year, Éditions la Découverte reprinted *Pour Marx* with a preface and biographical note by Étienne Balibar. Finally, in 1998, Yves Sintomer's collection of out-of-print material from 1955–77, virtually all of it translated into English at some stage, appeared from Presses Universitaires de France.

As for the secondary literature, by the early 1990s, the existing syntheses of Althusser's thought, whether in French (Karsz and Cotten) or English (Callinicos, Benton, Smith, etc.), were out of print. Apart from the occasional contribution (especially by Antonio Negri), the four collections published in English in the course of the decade – by E. Ann Kaplan and Michael Sprinker, by myself, by Jacques Lezra, and by Antonio Callari and David Ruccio – either effectively predated the posthumous edition or focused their attention elsewhere.[2] The same was true of two full-length studies by Robert Paul Resch and Margaret Majumdar; and of two earlier French texts – one grouping Balibar's various writings on Althusser, the other the proceedings of a conference held in Paris shortly after the philosopher's death, edited by Sylvain Lazarus.[3] Writing about Althusser gathered new impetus with the publication of *L'avenir dure longtemps* and Volume One of Moulier Boutang's *Louis Althusser*.[4] In addition to special issues of *Magazine littéraire* and *Futur antérieur* in 1992 and 1993 respectively, two substantial volumes of conference papers edited by François Matheron and Pierre Raymond appeared in French in 1997.[5] In 1999, in response to the flurry of Althusseriana, an expanded edition of the 1974 Trotskyist anthology *Contre Althusser* was put out, featuring at least one markedly less hostile new text by Daniel Bensaïd.[6] The same year two ex-pupils – Pierre Macherey and Dominique Lecourt – supplied intriguing insights into the collective adventure of Althusserianism.[7] From 2000 onwards, an important literature on the late Althusser began to emerge, especially with articles by André Tosel in French, Wal Suchting in English, and Vittorio Morfino in Italian – the last of these only one instance of a flourishing culture of publications on and by Althusser in Italy sponsored by the Associazione Louis Althusser directed by Maria Turchetto.[8] In the Anglophone world, meanwhile, although Andrew Levine's *A Future for Marxism? Althusser, the Analytical Turn and the Revival of Socialist Theory* did not redeem the promise of its title, Warren Montag's concise and illuminating *Louis Althusser* the previous year was the first account in English to register the full impact of the posthumous edition in Althusser studies.[9] A forthcoming translation of Mikko Lahtinen's Finnish book in the same series as these pages is set to be

---

[2] See Kaplan and Sprinker 1993; Elliott 1994; Lezra 1995; Callari and Ruccio 1996; and Negri 1996.

[3] See Resch 1992; Majumdar 1995; Balibar 1991; Lazarus 1993. The last of these contains a key text by the Italian Marxist Costanzo Preve: see Preve 1993. For Preve's latest balance-sheet of Althusserianism, which has significantly influenced my own thinking on the subject, see his 2003.

[4] See Moulier Boutang 1992.

[5] See Matheron 1997 and Raymond 1997.

[6] See Avenas et al. 1999.

[7] See Macherey 1999 and Lecourt 1999.

[8] See Tosel 2001; Suchting 2004; and Morfino 2002.

[9] See Levine 2003, whose material on Althusser is largely a reworking of his 1981 article, and Montag 2002.

the first to take its full measure.[10] Geoffrey Goshgarian's introductions to *The Humanist Controversy* and *Philosophy of the Encounter* are the initial, impressive fruits of intensive research in the archives.[11]

Before engaging with the unknown Althusser, some 'directions for use' are in order. Although, on occasion, Althusser himself seems to have envisaged a 'posthumous works and correspondence',[12] at other times he expressed misgivings over the phenomenon. Thus, at two points separated by an interval of fifteen years, he regretted that Marx's consignment of such drafts as *The German Ideology* to his bottom drawer (plus resident mice) had not been accorded due respect by editors and commentators.[13] Since the bulk of Marx's writings remained unpublished at his death, the paradoxical effect of any consistent application of the implied editorial etiquette would, of course, have been to deprive posterity of precisely those works of Marxian maturity that Althusser counterposed to Marx's early writings. In Althusser's own case, while it would have drawn a veil over the 'autobiographical hallucination' of *L'avenir dure longtemps* – that 'plea-indictment-confession . . . composed for an imaginary tribunal'[14] – it would not have exempted another draft, manifestly destined for posthumous publication, which was unquestionably no mistake or out-take: *Machiavelli and Us*. Accordingly, if we would do well to heed Gramsci's cautions about the status of 'posthumous works';[15] handle Althusser's with a care conspicuous by its absence in the shanghaiing of his 'self-analysis' by disobliging critics to depict the philosophico-political history in which he was a subject as a deranged process with a murderous *telos*; and bear in mind that these materials discover the philosopher-general mostly in his laboratory (sometimes in his labyrinth) – nevertheless, extrusion of them as unauthorised is neither feasible, nor desirable.

In the remainder of this Postscript, I propose to do no more than successively skim Althusser's autobiographies, his early works, texts from the Althusserian moment, and the late writings, before proceeding to a schematic periodisation

---

[10] See Lahtinen 2007.
[11] See Goshgarian 2003 and 2006.
[12] In a letter of 18 November 1963 to Franca Madonia: see Althusser 1998c, p. 486.
[13] See Althusser 1995b, pp. 385–7 (from which my epigraph is taken) and Althusser 1994a, p. 381.
[14] The apt characterisations of Albiac 1998, p. 82 and Balibar 1996, p. v.
[15] See Gramsci 1971, pp. 382–6 (esp. p. 384).

and tentative evaluation of the published œuvre that seek to fix Althusser in his approximate limits.

2. Partial recall

Within months of its release in April 1992, *L'avenir dure longtemps, suivi de Les Faits* had sold 40,000 copies, attracting sustained attention in the French press.[16] The longest book written by Althusser became the best-selling; the thinker who had endured a living death for the last decade of his life suddenly enjoyed a posthumous existence of sorts among an audience much of which had probably never heard of, let alone read, *For Marx* and *Reading 'Capital'*.

Across the Channel, coverage of the French original and its rapid translation focused predominantly on the sensational dimension of *l'affaire Althusser*. The ritual monotony of the titles prefacing reviews – 'A Marxist Murderer', 'Sex, Murder and Philosophy', 'Marx and Murder', 'The Paris Strangler' – explains the space devoted by the mainstream press to the deceased adherent of an iniquitous doctrine. Where, doubtless inadvertently, French commentators had sometimes given the impression that Althusser's murder of his wife weighed less heavily with them than his failure to abjure the God that failed,[17] their Anglo-American counterparts were readier to insinuate the equation: *fait divers* = *fait philosophico-politique*; or Marxism = Madness = Murder.

'I am one thing, my writings are another', proclaimed Nietzsche in his putative autobiography.[18] The point applies to Althusser, as to any other thinker: the genesis, the structure, the validity, and the effectivity of a body are thought are analytically distinct issues for any inquiry that aims at something other than *ad hominem* incrimination or exculpation of ideas. At any rate, the secrets of Althusserian Marxism will not exposed by inspection of its artisan's adolescent bedclothes; 'as a general rule,' he once objected to Plekhanov's imprudent speculations on the causes of the French Revolution, 'concepts are not hidden in beds'.[19] By way of variation on a Sartrean theme, it might simply be remarked: Louis Althusser became a manic-depressive

---

[16] See, for example, Contat 1992.
[17] A point made to me by David Macey (personal communication).
[18] Nietzsche 1975, p. 69.
[19] Althusser and Balibar 1970, p. 112.

murderer, no doubt about it. But not every manic-depressive murderer is Louis Althusser. The heuristic inadequacy of literary supplement psychobabble is contained in these two sentences.

The first thing to note about the occasion for Althusser's renewed notoriety is that the status of both his texts is no less complex than their character. *Les Faits*, begun in 1976 but not completed, was scheduled for inclusion in a journal that never saw the light of day. *L'avenir dure longtemps*, almost four times the length and characteristically drafted in feverish haste in the spring of 1985 between bouts of hospitalisation, was initially intended for publication, but then simply laid aside. No will having been left by Althusser, his closest surviving relative – a nephew – became his executor and decided to authorise their release.

Althusser's unavailing struggle against the psychological torment that preceded and punctuated his public career – the 'war without memoirs or memorials' evoked in 'Freud and Lacan'[20] – was thus granted a memorial and yielded memoirs of a kind. But can the autobiographer's tale of how he became what he was be trusted any more than Nietzsche's *Ecce Homo*? That there are reasonable grounds for doubt is suggested, if by nothing else, by the marked discrepancies between *The Facts* and *The Future Lasts a Long Time*. The former, under a typically laconic (and ironic) title, is composed in a comic register (it contains, for example, fictional encounters with Pope John XXIII and General de Gaulle).[21] The latter pertains to the converse mode – its tragic score unrelieved by the falsely optimistic notes it strikes towards its conclusion. Essentially covering the same terrain, they do so quite differently, offering not so much a mutual corrective as alternative perspectives on Althusser's destiny. The effect of their appearance between the same covers is – or should be – to remind readers that autobiography is as much rhetoric as record; and hence, art (or artlessness) hiding art, a compromise formation between biographical 'facts' and literary conventions.

Where readings have not been flagrantly culpable, they have too often been ingenuous, in pre-Freudian fashion taking Althusser at his word and therewith subscribing to 'an idea of reading which makes a written discourse

---

[20] Althusser 1971, p. 190.
[21] See Althusser 1993, pp. 346–7.

the immediate transparency of the true, the real discourse of a voice'.[22] As the author of *Reading 'Capital'* insisted at the outset, there is no such thing as an innocent reading. Althusser's own strategy vis-à-vis Marx – the 'symptomatic reading' that sought to reconstruct the latent structural matrix generating the manifest discourse of his texts – was modelled on the Freudian interpretation of dreams. His analysis of the Althusser case and the reasons for his unreason – the tangled causal skein that issued in an act of destruction and self-destruction – requires an analogous operation. The occasionally oneiric discourse of *The Future Lasts a Long Time* cries out for a symptomatic reading.

It is immeasurably aided by Moulier Boutang's meticulous reconstruction of Althusser's life up to 1956, which permits critical scrutiny of his own tendentious rendition. For there were many Althussers, of whom Althusser's is only one – one who must be approached *en connaissance de cause*. Yet the problem, baldly stated, is that, despite his biographer's endeavours, such knowledge is not at our disposal and is unlikely to be even when – if – his second volume on the years 1956–90 finally materialises. The bare facts of what Althusser once dubbed his 'auto-heterobiographical circumstances'[23] are in the process of being established; the implacable logic of his unconscious remains recalcitrant to elucidation. 'Nothing,' he justly remarked in one version of those 'facts' from another scene, 'could be more simple than the unconscious elements which analysis deals with, yet the combinations they assume in individual cases could not be more complex'.[24]

Because they appear under his signature, Althusser's own disconcerting simplicities were received as the disclosure of that individual combination in all its complexity – as if, *contra* Pascal's *Pensées* but in accordance with Descartes's *Discourse on Method*, the Althusserian heart had its reasons and they were transparent to Althusser's head. Furthermore, his projection of the shadow of 'Althusser' onto the young Althusser – the construction of his own history in the 'future anterior'[25] – has been accepted as the authoritative (because authorised) version.

---

[22] Althusser and Balibar 1970, p. 16.
[23] Althusser 1995a, p. 229.
[24] Althusser 1993, p. 362.
[25] See Althusser 1969a, p. 54.

The Future Lasts a Long Time advertises itself as the public explanation which Althusser was at once excused and denied by the *non-lieu* ('no grounds') decreed after the murder of his wife.[26] Reminding us that there was an Althusser before and after – as well as during – Althusserianism, the author stipulates that *The Future* constitutes 'not a diary, not my memoirs, not an autobiography',[27] but rather what he once described to his biographer as a 'traumabiography'. He claims to be 'stick[ing] closely to the facts', but immediately adds a rider: 'hallucinations are also facts'.[28] We are dealing not with the tranquil recollection of a life lived, but the anguished retrospection of a death foretold – one which amply confirms Malraux's observation that what is tragic about death is its transformation of life into destiny. In the words of its editors, *The Future* is 'an inextricable tangle of "facts" and "phantasies"'.[29]

Althusser seeks to situate his text by allusion to Foucault's edition of Pierre Rivière's testament and Rousseau's *Confessions*. Other autobiographical writings that come to mind are Sartre's *Words* and Schreber's *Memoirs of My Nervous Illness*. In effect, this is a fragmentary 'wild (self-)analysis': something akin to the testimony of a Nietzsche in the language of a Freud. Just as, in a typical assertion of the singularity of the autobiographer, Althusser can lay claim to Rousseau's privilege and bane – 'I am like no one in the whole world'[30] – so his confessions are exceptional, for better and worse alike.

Much of their poignancy, as well as their ambivalence, derives from a fact so blinding as to risk invisibility: *The Future Lasts a Long Time* is a symptom of the manic-depressive syndrome that it hopes to exorcise through a public talking- and writing-cure. Its overture, replete with literary melodrama, is the crime scene; following seeming self-detection, its *envoi* takes the form of the explanatory commentary of an 'old doctor friend',[31] therewith in some measure reinstating the *non-lieu* whose deleterious effects it hoped to conjure. The first half of the book is given over to the aetiology of its subject's mental illness in a 'family romance', played out in interwar Algeria and southern

---

[26] See Althusser 1993, pp. 27–8.
[27] Althusser 1993, p. 29.
[28] Althusser 1993, p. 81.
[29] Althusser 1993, p. 9.
[30] Rousseau 1953, p. 17.
[31] See Althusser 1993, pp. 280–6.

France, which soon acquires the contours of a familial horror-story. From his maternal aunt Althusser learnt the family secret: that his mother's fiancé had been killed during the First World War; that she had subsequently accepted the marriage-proposal of his brother; and that she had named her only son after the love of her youth – and life. Once again, this is a paradigmatic instance of a standard feature of autobiography: minor antecedents entailing major consequences. At all events, thus informed, Althusser claims to have drawn a devastating conclusion: he had, so to speak, been born, not made. For inscribed in the infant Louis's first name was the true – and other – object of his mother's affections:

> Above all, it contained the sound of the third person pronoun (*lui*), which deprived me of any personality of my own, summoning as it did an anonymous other. It referred to my uncle, the man who stood behind me: '*Lui*' *was Louis*. It was him my mother loved, not me.[32]

As depicted by him, Althusser's mother is a *mater dolorosa* straight out of the pages of de Beauvoir's *Second Sex*.[33] Remembered as a violated wife – 'a martyred mother bleeding like a wound'[34] – Lucienne Althusser, neé Berger (the maiden name to which she reverted after her husband's death, just as her son assumed it after 1980), is portrayed as a castrating mother, impelled by her phobias to enforce a strict régime of social and sexual 'hygiene' on Althusser and his sister Georgette. From the domestic milieu in which her writ ran, his father was literally or metaphorically absent, inspiring in his son the sense that he had no father. The consequence, so Althusser claims, was a feeling of fathomless solitude, relieved only by his relationship with his maternal grandparents ('my true family, my only family') in the 'infant paradise' of the Bois de Boulogne overlooking Algiers, or of Larochemillay in the Morvan, to which they retired.[35]

As Althusser notes, the related themes of the 'fatherless child' and 'solitude' would recur in his philosophical writings.[36] *Cherchez la femme* is the leitmotif of his case history:

---

[32] Althusser 1993, p. 39.
[33] See de Beauvoir 1972, pp. 529–30.
[34] Althusser 1993, p. 38.
[35] See Althusser 1993, p. 61ff.
[36] See Althusser 1993, pp. 171–4.

I fulfilled [my mother's] wishes and expectations of the other Louis ... – *and I did it in order to seduce her*. I strove for goodness, purity, virtue, a pure intellect, a disembodied state, academic success, and to crown it all a 'literary' career. ... To accomplish all this, I was to go to the École normale supérieure, not at Saint-Cloud where uncle Louis was to have gone, but the one in the rue d'Ulm. Then I became the well-known intellectual who fiercely refused to 'dirty his hands' in the media ... and got my name on the cover of a few books which my mother proudly read.[37]

Thus to win his mother's love by fulfilling her desire was for Althusser simultaneously to realise his own being, by fashioning an ego. The paradoxical effect of his project – as with its repetition in his relationship with his teachers – was to exacerbate the perceived original ex-centricity: seduction of others meant Althusser's seduction into his own betrayal. For, 'I always had the impression I was not myself, that I didn't really exist, that my existence depended solely *on pretence*, indeed was a pretence'.[38]

In revelations onto which critics have latched, Althusser maintains that such 'deception' extended to his philosophical culture (or, more precisely, the lack of it).[39] What is unquestionably true is that his formal education was interrupted, after he had come sixth in the national examinations for admission to the rue d'Ulm, by the advent of war in September 1939. The political option current in the Catholic and monarchist circles in which he had moved at the Lycée du Parc in Lyon materialised with the collapse of the Third Republic. Among those sacrificed in the 'strange defeat' of June 1940 was Althusser. That the experience of captivity was a formative influence is clear. Notwithstanding the manifold privations it records, his account stresses the redeeming features: while Sartre had never felt freer than under the Occupation, Althusser enjoyed a sense of security in his prisoner-of-war camp.[40] Accordingly, liberation in 1945 induced not elation but disorientation, betokening reversion to the solitude which enhanced that 'nostalgic desire for "union"' motivating subsequent attachments.[41]

---

[37] Althusser 1993, p. 57.
[38] Althusser 1993, p. 58.
[39] See Althusser 1993, pp. 165–6.
[40] See Althusser 1993, p. 107.
[41] Althusser 1993, p. 96.

Postwar, these attachments essentially reduced to three: the École normale supérieure – 'a maternal ambiance, . . . like an *amniotic* fluid'[42] – where Althusser resumed his education and secured an academic post after being received second at the philosophy *agrégation* in 1948; Hélène Rytman – Jewess, *résistante*, ex-Communist fallen on hard times – whom he met in 1946; and the French Communist Party, which he joined in November 1948.

Hélène's gift to Althusser, as he recalls it, was 'a world of solidarity and struggle, a world of reasoned action, . . . a world of courage'.[43] Yet the prospect of redemption so miraculously opened up soon gave way to the threat of perdition. The relationship with Hélène, eight years his senior, was traumatic from the outset, so Althusser claims, plunging him into a deep depression which necessitated the first of a score of hospitalisations, following a diagnosis of schizophrenia. According to Althusser, he and Hélène nevertheless performed an indispensable maternal and paternal function for one another. She was everything for which he had yearned:

> She loved me as a mother loves a child . . . and at the same time like a good father in that she introduced me . . . to the real world, that vast arena I had never been able to enter. . . . Through her desire for me she also initiated me . . . into my role as a man, into my masculinity. She loved me as a woman loves a man![44]

Indissolubly linked to these rites of passage was Althusser's induction into the world of French Communism, which he embraced, so he narrates, after the loss of his Roman Catholic faith.[45] As the hopes borne by the Resistance succumbed to the Cold War, and the 'united front' of 1944–7 fractured into the 'two camps' of 1948, Althusser chose his camp: outside the Party, no political salvation. Even without aggravating circumstances, the conjuncture would have proved inclement for the new academic recruit. Aggravating circumstances there were, however, in the form of Hélène's exclusion from the Party and Althusser's assumption of the mission to secure her readmission. So explosive an issue was this that if no salvation was to be had outside the Party, damnation beckoned within it.

---

[42] Althusser 1993, p. 163.
[43] Althusser 1993, p. 131.
[44] Althusser 1993, p. 132.
[45] See Althusser 1993, p. 205.

Althusser basically reiterates the standard account of the affair, attributing his wife's misfortunes to the malevolence of Elsa Triolet; and confirms the details supplied by one of the participants in it.[46] Althusser sought to clear her name of having been a double agent. Of no benefit to her, his zeal served only to expose him to the censure of the PCF cell at the École for his dangerous liaison. Althusser maintains that the experience induced a realistic appreciation of the PCF and its methods. Thanks to Moulier Boutang, we know that the comparative equanimity with which he affects to have greeted the sanction of his comrades is belied by the historical record.

In *The Facts*, reflecting on his imprisonment in Germany, Althusser recounts a plan which consisted in giving the camp guards to think that an escape had been effected and then, some weeks later, when they had failed to recapture the escapees, making the genuine attempt. For him it exemplified 'the nub of all philosophical (as well as political and military) problems: how to escape the circle while remaining within it'.[47] Having identified his attachments, *The Future* turns into a tale of a 'circle of circles' – the family, the École, the relationship, the Party, the clinic – and their mutual implication and overdetermination to produce a singular fate. Applying his own formula, it might be said that his narrative enacts his inability to find an exit from circles whose arc was inflected but not designed by him, and which degenerated from the seemingly virtuous to the intermittently vicious to the ultimately infernal. Thus, on his account, he and Hélène formed a couple who by the end could live neither with, nor without, each other. What crystallised, in Althusser's final harrowing image of November 1980, amounted to a 'private Hell', terminated only by a murder in which 'self-destruction was symbolically achieved through the destruction of others'.[48]

As if in uncanny echo of Nietzsche's exaltation – 'My time has not yet come, some are born posthumously'[49] – the closing pages of *The Future* are leavened with a desperate optimism of the will:

---

[46] See Roudinesco 1986, p. 384 and Le Roy Ladurie 1982, pp. 76–7.
[47] Althusser 1993, p. 319.
[48] Althusser 1993, pp. 252, 276.
[49] Nietzsche 1975, p. 69.

> So, despite its dramas, life can still be beautiful. I am sixty-seven, and though
> it will soon all be over, I feel younger now than I have ever done, never
> having had any youth since no one loved me for myself.
>
> Yes, the future lasts a long time.[50]

Perhaps – but not for the author of these lines. With ultimate pathos, what
the text cannot know is that, rather than registering the conquest of Althusser's
illness, its conclusion betrays the manic phase of his manic-depressive cycle.
Within weeks of its completion, hounded by the gutter-press, he was back
in hospital. Louis Althusser's time had come and gone. Most are not (re)born
posthumously.

The overwhelming impression conveyed by *The Future* is of Althusser's
indivisible destructiveness and self-destructiveness. Moulier Boutang's
exhaustive research confirms that this propensity is mimed by the text itself,
in a consistent self-defamation which conceals a fact: Althusser was a man
with qualities. His own express wish was that his testament would resolve
his enigma to public satisfaction, thus putting an end to demands for its
explanation and releasing him into an emancipatory anonymity.[51] In the event,
its publication generated a further massive burst of the kind of voyeurism
attendant upon the events of 1980–1. For if not the 'tissue of lies and half-
truths' bemoaned by one of his closest associates,[52] it is, as Moulier Boutang
conclusively demonstrates, a re-writing of a life through the prism of its
wreckage.

Althusser's biographer has laid bare the profundity of his revisions in six
main respects. First – and crucially – the inversion of the Althusserian family
romance can be firmly dated – to July 1964 – and confidently attributed – to
none other than Hélène Rytman. She it was, in a letter of 26 July 1964, who
ventured the 'wild analysis' of the familial dynamic as a fatality from the
outset faithfully reproduced by her companion.[53] Having, like Althusser's
closest male friend of the 1950s – the suicide Jacques Martin – endured a
wretched childhood, Hélène abetted Althusser in the projection of the manic-
depressive shadow of maturity onto his infancy. Secondly, a central relationship

---

50 Althusser 1993, p. 279.
51 See Althusser 1993, pp. 210–11.
52 Pierre Macherey, quoted in Fox 1992.
53 See Moulier Boutang 1992, pp. 74–5.

in the young Althusser's existence is underplayed and left largely unexamined in his emplotment of his life story: his intense bond with his sister Georgette, whose own history of 'nervous illness' tracked his own. Suffice it to indicate that, some two weeks after receiving Hélène's letter in the summer of 1964, Althusser had a dream about her that anticipates the murderous scenario of November 1980.[54] Thirdly, Althusser postdates the onset of his recurrent depression to the postwar period, passing over in silence the trials he experienced both during his schooldays and then in captivity. The latter have, however, left their trace in the desolate record he kept in Schleswig of what he called *une vie sans histoire*.[55]

Two further contributions by Moulier Boutang concern Althusser's relationship with Roman Catholicism and the controversy over Hélène Rytman's Resistance record. Regarding the former, it would appear that the prewar activist in Jeunesse chrétienne was politically considerably further to the right than he is prepared to concede in *The Future*. More importantly, his gravitation to the left after the War involved no abrupt break with the faith of the Church into which he was born. If the organisation to which Althusser transferred his allegiances proved so recalcitrant to the rehabilitation of his companion, Moulier Boutang gives us to understand, it was because there was no smoke without fire. Postponing illumination of this obscure episode to his sequel, Moulier Boutang meanwhile suggests that Althusser's claim in *The Facts* to have voted for Hélène's exclusion from the Peace Movement amounts to a screen-memory for the catastrophic breakdown he suffered after bowing to the will of his comrades at the École normale.[56]

Finally, Moulier Boutang's research in and of itself allows us definitively to reject Althusser's affectation, *à la* Wittgenstein, of ignorance of the history of philosophy in general and of Marxism in particular. This gesture of ingratiating self-depreciation (or propitiation), foregrounding the unlettered genius capable of creation *ex nihilo*, rebounded on its author, being widely (and gleefully) construed by reviewers as exposing (in the words of one of them) 'the philosopher emperor who had no clothes'.[57]

---

[54] See Moulier Boutang 1992, p. 75.
[55] Althusser 1992, p. 245; see especially ibid., p. 88.
[56] See Moulier Boutang 1992, p. 423ff.
[57] See Papineau 1993.

In the course of a disappointing discussion of his 'road to Marx' and his relationship to Marxism, which admits the charge of 'imaginary Marxism' pressed by Raymond Aron, Althusser fixes upon *ne pas se raconter d'histoires* – not to tell stories and not to tell ourselves stories – as 'the one and only definition of materialism'.[58] Here, at any rate, honouring his Machiavellian maxim more in the breach than the observance, self-imprisoned in what Sartre referred to as the 'retrospective illusion' of the autobiographical genre, Althusser tells himself and his readers more than one story, some of them tall. Rather than paving the way for subsequent volumes in the posthumous edition of Althusser's œuvre, and enabling an informed assessment of it, such stories were apt to queer their pitch. In turning to those volumes, we would do better to take Althusser not at his fabular, partial, retrospective word – but at his work.

3. Fateful rendezvous

The same year as *L'avenir dure longtemps* was published, Althusser's *Journal de captivité* appeared. In a kind of testament of lost youth, or to the pitiless demarcation of generation, the 'terrible education of deeds'[59] undergone by the prewar royalist Roman Catholic found its muffled echo. The intrusion of 'historical problems' in 'a life without history'; the vacillation of faith, rescued by resort to the wager of Althusser's constant companion Pascal; the volatilisation of his politics, reorientated towards Communism by the counter-example of Vichy, that 'parade of counter-revolutionary France in which Nazi Germany took the salute'[60] – these helped induce the postwar 'intellectual in arms' summoned up in the preface to *For Marx*.[61]

Whatever his final destination, with the release in 1994 of a first volume of philosophical and political writings containing texts from 1946–51, it became possible to identify Althusser's postwar point of departure with some certainty. In short, it transpired that the intellectual 'biography' of Marx outlined in *For Marx* and *Reading 'Capital'* was something in the nature of an intellectual 'autobiography'. The work of the mature Althusser conducted a tacit settlement

---

[58] Althusser 1993, p. 221.
[59] Althusser 1969a, p. 21.
[60] Kedward 1969, p. 163.
[61] See Althusser 1992, pp. 70, 245, 159–60, 349–52.

of accounts with his own erstwhile philosophical consciousness: the critique of Hegelian Marxism conducted therein was, at the same time, a critique of the young Althusser. One result, as we read the early writings, is an intermittent sense of *déjà lu*. Not for nothing did Althusser remark in a review of Marx's newly translated Paris *Manuscripts* in 1962: 'even our own experience should remind us that it is possible to be "Communist" without being "Marxist"'.[62]

The philosophico-political adventure recorded in them involves an intricately overlapping and cross-cutting transition – from Catholicism to Communism, and from a variant of Hegelianism to a variety of Marxism. In their centre-piece – the 1947 Master's thesis 'On Content in the Thought of G.W.F. Hegel' – Althusser wrote:

> Germany's political disarray made, perhaps, as deep an impression on the young Hegel as did the formalism of its religious life; interestingly, it is only with difficulty that we can distinguish his political from his religious thought amongst the concerns of his early years.[63]

With due alteration of detail, the observation applies to its author. Indeed, formal adhesion to the PCF in 1948 at the age of thirty coincided with maximum engagement in the activities of the Catholic group Jeunesse de l'Église, as if Althusser became a Communist precisely because he was a Catholic. When, a year later, no longer lapsing but lapsed, Althusser remonstrated with his ex-teacher Jean Lacroix's 'personalist' philosophy, he was keen to confide 'something I have experienced along with a number of your former students':

> Namely, that in *actively* rallying to the working class, we have not only not repudiated what had been our reasons for living, but have liberated them by fully realising them. . . . The Christian I once was has in no way abjured his Christian 'values', but now I live them . . ., whereas earlier I aspired to live them.[64]

'Actively rallying to the working class': it is scarcely fortuitous if the diction of Althusser's apologia was straight out of the lexicon of Gallic Stalinism.[65]

---

[62] Althusser 1969a, p. 160.
[63] Althusser 1997, p. 45.
[64] Althusser 1997, p. 221.
[65] In particular, the exhortations of the Politbureau member responsible for intellectuals, Laurent Casanova: see Casanova 1949, e.g., pp. 19, 80.

Like the young Marx under the German Confederation a century earlier, the young Althusser of the French Fourth Republic was immersed in the ideas of the age. Some of these were spawned by the 'return to Hegel' most prominently associated with Alexandre Kojève, prompting Jacques Derrida to react to Francis Fukuyama's re-edition of the 'end of history' in the early 1990s by recalling that 'eschatalogical themes . . . were, in the 50s, . . . our daily bread'.[66] Althusser's postwar native philosophical language was that of French Hegelianism; his ideological orientation akin to what the ex-Communist Edgar Morin once dubbed 'Hegelo-Stalinism'.[67] It is also apparent, however, that at the height of the Cold War Althusser shared the crude anti-Hegelian turn of Stalinist Marxism. While it would seem to be the case that he never fully endorsed the impostures of Lysenkoism (the 'two sciences', bourgeois and proletarian); and did not succumb to the ferruginous romance of 'socialist realism' (Soviet boy and girl meet Machine Tractor Station), he certainly did subscribe to Zhdanovism – party partisanship in philosophy – against which later claims for the autonomy of theory were staked. To borrow the terms of his letter to Lacroix,[68] the 'philosopher's rendezvous with the railwaymen' proceeded under the sign of the Cold War in culture – a period when the PCF was ranged against the *Coca-colonisation* of Fourth-Republic France. Whatever their intrinsic worth, Althusser's early writings are redolent of a conjuncture of combatant philosophy, in which the shade of Hegel is barely distinguishable from the spectre of Stalin.

Repatriated after five years of imprisonment, his religious faith intact but his political orientation upended by the infernal surprise of 1940, Althusser resumed his education at a moment memorably described by Ernest Gellner: 'End-of-war and post-war France was like the human condition, but a damn sight *more so*. If ever there was a situation when men could not find reassurance for their identity, dignity or conviction, this was it.'[69] As indicated by the earliest of the prewar texts – 'The International of Decent Feelings' (1946) – Althusser found reassurance in *not* heeding the ideology of the 'human

---

[66] Derrida 1994, p. 14.

[67] Morin 1970, p. 60; see pp. 27–62 on 'La Vulgate ou l'heure de Stalingrad'.

[68] See Althusser 1997, p. 226: 'I enclose . . . a picture of the Dijon railwaymen which appeared in *L'Humanité*. . . . I hope that people, observing the calm strength and dignity of these men, will not one day say of us that "the philosopher missed his rendezvous with the railwaymen"'.

[69] Quoted in Rustin 1996, p. 55.

condition' propagated by 'novelists turned prophets' – Malraux, Camus, Koestler and co. '[A]nguish,' he wrote, 'is not the proletariat's lot: *there is no emancipating oneself from the human condition, but it is possible to emancipate oneself from the workers' [condition]'.*[70] Unlike 'the false prophets of history', 'Marxists and their Christian or non-Christian allies' possessed the sense of a redemptive ending:

> The road to man's reconciliation with his destiny is essentially that of the appropriation of the products of his labour, of what he creates in general, and of history as his creation. This reconciliation presupposes a transition from capitalism to socialism by way of the emancipation of the labouring proletariat, which can, through this act, rid not only itself, but also all humanity of contradiction. . . .[71]

The echo of Marx's early works – the proletariat as 'universal class' – is resonant; and the Paris *Manuscripts* positively invoked. However, in repudiating 'a "Western" socialism without class struggle' as a 'system of protection against Communism', Althusser was swayed by a certain Hegelianism, foregrounding a master-slave dialectic. That he not only undertook an intensive study of Hegel, alongside Marx, in these years, but was a Hegelian, is evident from his Master's thesis. If 'The International of Decent Feelings' was turned down by the journal for which it was intended on account of its virulent polemic, Althusser seemingly never sought to publish this remarkable document. Suggesting that post-Hegelian philosophy had not superseded Hegel, Althusser's text extravagantly displayed the historicist vices he would subsequently reprove in those who conflated the Marxist and Hegelian dialectics:

> By way of history, Hegel's thought escapes the prison of a dawning age and the confines of a civil servant's mentality, offering itself to our gaze in the freedom of its realisation and its objective development. In a sense that is not un-Marxist, our world has become philosophy, or, more precisely, Hegel come to maturity now stands before us – is, indeed, our world: the world has become Hegelian to the extent that Hegel was a truth capable of becoming

---

[70] Althusser 1997, p. 26.
[71] Althusser 1997, p. 31.

a world. We need only read: fortunately, the letters are there before our eyes, writ large in the text of history – letters become men.[72]

Contemporary readers would have had no difficulty spelling out those letters: not the Emperor at Jena, but the Generalissimo of Stalingrad. Hegel was indeed 'the last of the philosophers'. Yet it was 'in the new slave of modern times' – the proletariat – that the freedom prematurely announced by the *Phenomenology of Spirit* was in the process of being realised. Marx's immanent critique of the *Philosophy of Right* had demonstrated the contradictory nature of Hegel's perversely consistent benediction of the Prussian state in 1821, when actuality did not embody rationality. For all that, however, Marx had not surpassed Hegel, who represented his 'silent rigour':

> Having denounced the alienation of the bourgeois world he lived in, and having merely predicted the end of alienation in the coming revolution, [Marx] was no more able than Hegel to leap over his time, and his own truths were recaptured by what they denounced. As philosopher, Marx was thus a prisoner of his times and hence of Hegel, who had foreseen this captivity.[73]

The Marxist conception of history – a materialist humanism irreducible to any natural or economic determinism – was 'thoroughly informed by Hegelian truth':

> For Marx, there is a *positive* side to capitalism. . . . Without capitalism – without, that is, alienation in its extreme form – man would have succeeded neither in transforming his material powers into something universal, nor, above all, in reappropriating, through the brotherhood of man, the universality of his essential being. . . . Capitalist alienation is the birth of humanity. We need not force the terms unduly in order to identify the fecundity of this division with the Passion of Hegelian Spirit, which does not go forth from itself by chance, but in order to appropriate its true nature, and which, in this fall, attains the revelation of a depth realised by the totality. The proletarian discovers the truth of humanity in the depths of human misery.[74]

---

[72] Althusser 1997, p. 36.
[73] Althusser 1997, p. 133.
[74] Althusser 1997, p. 138.

Peppered with references to Kojève's *Introduction to the Reading of Hegel*, published as Althusser was preparing his thesis in autumn 1947, 'On Content' is not a Kojèvian work. In a review of that volume written concurrently, Althusser reproached it for its unilaterally anthropological interpretation of Hegelianism, which valorised subject at the expense of substance. The upshot was an 'existentialist Marx' – 'a travesty in which Marxists will not recognise their own'. Even so, Kojève was to be applauded for 'restor[ing] part of Hegel's veritable grandeur'.[75]

Even as Althusser's notice was appearing, Andrei Zhdanov was laying down the line of 'two camps' – bellicose imperialism/irenic socialism – at the inaugural meeting of the Cominform and intimidating a conference of 'Soviet philosophical workers': 'The question of Hegel was settled long ago. There is no reason whatsoever to pose it anew.'[76] In 1950, an anonymous article, in fact penned by Althusser, was published in *La Nouvelle Critique* – a new PCF journal significantly sub-titled 'Revue du marxisme militant'. With Zhdanov's admonition as one of its epigraphs, 'The Return to Hegel: The Latest Word in Academic Revisionism' noted the vogue for Hegel in France since the 1930s:

> The consecration followed: Hyppolite instated at the Sorbonne; Hegel recognised, via his commentator, as one of the masters of bourgeois thought; commentaries in the windows of all the book shops; the 'labour of the negative' in every term paper; master and slave in every academic talk; the struggle of one consciousness against another in Jean Lacroix; our theologians discoursing on the 'lesser *Logic*'; and all the to-do connected with the academic and religious jubilation over a reviving corpse.[77]

Althusser, who had been compiling what he termed *hégéliâneries* ('Hegelian inanities') – the 'Hegelian "Robinsonade" of master and slave' included[78] – decried the pervasive recourse to Hegel's philosophy of history or the state. It served the needs of the 'moribund bourgeoisie', which had renounced liberalism in this, the crisis-ridden imperialist stage of capitalism. In particular,

---

[75] Althusser 1997, p. 172.
[76] Zhdanov 1950, p. 102.
[77] Althusser 1997, p. 174.
[78] Althusser 1997, p. 181.

it validated 'the projects of reaction in France'.[79] Moreover, the Hegel revival
tailored the revisions of Marx require to impugn Communism:

> The working class has recognised in the founder of the thought of scientific
> socialism the theoretical weapon it needs for its liberation. Marxism is today
> the mode of thought of millions of human beings organised in Communist
> parties throughout the world, a mode of thought that is triumphing in the
> socialist countries, the Peoples' Democracies, and the daily struggles of the
> working class and colonised peoples still subject to capitalist exploitation.
> In this mode of thought, it is the 'rational' aspect of the dialectic that
> has been developed, together with authentic knowledge of the material
> content of history; this knowledge points – both in science and in the
> events inseparable from it – to the inevitable collapse of the bourgeoisie and
> the victory of the working class, which will emancipate the whole human
> race. . . . The time has come *in which the overriding preoccupation of bourgeois
> philosophers and littérateurs is the following question:* . . . *'What does Marx have
> to be for the Communists to be wrong?'*[80]

The question of Hegel had long since been resolved for the proletariat by the
'masters of scientific socialism', who had rescued a revolutionary method
from a reactionary system. By contrast, the bourgeois return to him amounted
to *'a revisionism of a fascist type'*.[81]

Althusser's excoriation of modern 'irrationalism' occasionally reads like a
cruder, miniature version of the monument to this ideological moment in the
history of international Communism: Lukács's *Destruction of Reason* (1953).
An isolated incident, mercifully it did not entail the destruction of his own.
By now, all roads were perceived to lead either to Washington or to Moscow.
On 1 July 1949, Pope Pius XII, whose record on fascism had been lamentable,
issued a decreed proscribing Catholics from association with Communists,
and menacing recusants with sanctions.[82] That February, Althusser's 'A Matter
of Fact' had featured in *Cahiers de Jeunesse de l'Église*, one of the main French
groups targeted. There, he reprehended the social doctrine of the Church –
propounded in the papal encyclicals *Rerum novarum* (1891) and *Quadragesimo*

---

[79] Althusser 1997, p. 180.
[80] Althusser 1997, pp. 181–2.
[81] Althusser 1997, p. 183.
[82] See Calvez 1956, pp. 582–602 (esp. pp. 590–1).

anno (1931) – as 'a form of reactionary reformism'.[83] As to its present political stance,

> If we consider its policies on a global scale, we must admit that, apart from a few active but isolated small groups, the Church comprises . . . an objective . . . force that maintains a deep . . . commitment to world-wide reaction, and is struggling alongside international capitalism against the forces of the working class and the advent of socialism.[84]

Contrariwise, its future depended on

> the number and courage of those Christians who . . . are developing an awareness of the necessity of the struggle and joining the ranks of the world proletariat. . . . The Church will live thanks to those who . . . are once again discovering that the Word was born among men and dwelt among them – and who are already preparing a humane place for it amongst men.[85]

The July anathemas of the Holy Office resolved Althusser's 'matter of fact' for him. Henceforth, it was not equally to Roman Catholicism, but exclusively to Soviet-style Communism, that he looked for salvation. The 'Youth of the Church' having been suppressed, the 'youth of the world' – Vaillant-Couturier's characterisation of Communism – absorbed Althusser's energies. In an extraordinary seventy-page letter to Lacroix, completed in January 1950, Althusser cited this phrase with the ardour of the convert. Part airing of grievances, part confession of faith, this epistle affords privileged access to the convictions and motivations of its author in his high-Stalinist years. For a start, the later partisan of a 'left critique of Stalinism' entertained not the least doubt as to the legitimacy of the Rajk show-trial in Hungary in September 1949. Second, the former Hegelian dismissed 'the good old problem of the end of history and alienation', claiming that in Marx's residual use of the category '[a]lienation is an economic concept, in the broad sense'.[86] Third, a version of Vico's *verum-factum* principle, held up to ridicule in the *Reply to John Lewis* in 1973, was advocated: the proletariat knew the truth of history

---

[83] Althusser 1997, p. 191. One aspect of this reformism – the new theology of marriage, generating 'the illusion of emancipation' for women – is mordantly analysed in 'On Conjugal Obscenity' in Althusser 1997, pp. 231–40.

[84] Althusser 1997, p. 191.

[85] Althusser 1997, p. 195.

[86] Althusser 1997, pp. 206, 209.

because it made history; *proprio sensu*, historical materialism was a proletarian science. Finally, lauding Zhdanov's 'On Philosophy' as 'a text admirable in every respect', Althusser extolled the 'extraordinary freedom' vouchsafed Communist intellectuals in and through their conformity to the 'partisan positions' defined by the Party.[87] The respective conditions of party and intellectuals were marked by a fundamental asymmetry:

> I would like you to understand that the truth . . . is the iron law and condition of the Party, and that we intellectuals, perhaps, do not always live in the same condition. The 'condition' that is ours does not require us, *materially, as a question of life and death, to possess the truth, to put it to the test of struggle, to share it with other men. . . . We are not condemned to the truth.*[88]

Hence the duty to 'show ourselves worthy of our admirable brothers, who are suffering and struggling for their freedom, for our freedom'.[89] Hence the imperative of a 'rendezvous with the railwaymen' – those heroes of a Resistance mythology, not devoid of all reality, impressed upon Althusser and his like, who were incessantly reminded of the railwayman's rendezvous with the firing squad.[90]

Reflecting on the immediate postwar period in *For Marx*, Althusser observed that 'the intellectuals of petty-bourgeois origin' recruited by the PCF 'felt that they had to pay . . . the imaginary Debt they thought they had contracted *by not being proletarians*'.[91] Even those, unlike Althusser, who had participated in the Resistance were unquestionably *made* to feel it by an organisation which, substituting itself for the class in whose name it spoke, impelled its intellectuals to self-abasement before *la force tranquille* of the proletariat – that is, itself. If for no other reason, Althusser necessarily missed his rendezvous.

The preface to *For Marx* suggests that '[i]n his own way, Sartre provides us with an honest witness to this baptism of history', adding: 'we were of his race as well'. Yet the vocation of the 'partisan philosopher' differed significantly from that of the 'committed intellectual'. No ambivalence towards

---

[87] Althusser 1997, pp. 210, 221.

[88] Althusser 1997, p. 224.

[89] Althusser 1997, p. 226.

[90] The fate, for example, of Pierre Sémard, Communist leader and secretary of the railway workers' union, shot by the Nazis on 7 March 1942.

[91] Althusser 1969a, p. 27. Cf. Morin 1970, p. 107ff. and Le Roy Ladurie 1982, p. 75 for a similar sense of 'original sin' attendant upon non-proletarian origins.

politics and power attached to those who, seeking to escape the 'intellectual condition' and contribute to the cause of human emancipation, submitted to the voluntary servitude of Communist party discipline in the West after the Second World War. As regards that baptism of history, Althusser's early writings provide us with an honest witness. It is the less surprising that, when he reappeared on the public stage, forewarned and forearmed, Althusser advanced masked.

4. Selective affinities

'I have,' Althusser wrote to Lacan on 26 November 1963,

> been pursuing obscure works on Marx for some fifteen years. I have finally, slowly, laboriously emerged from the night. Things are clear to me now. That austere inquiry, that long and harsh gestation, was needed.[92]

By now, the inquiry went beyond Marx and had assumed a collective shape. Prior to the 'Reading *Capital*' seminar of 1965 which consolidated and deployed their results, a sequence of seminars had been staged at the École normale supérieure.[93] In the wake of Althusser's opening salvo on the subject, that of 1961–2 was devoted to 'The Young Marx'. The following academic year, coinciding with publication of Lévi-Strauss's *Savage Mind* and Foucault's *Birth of the Clinic*, attention switched to 'The Origins of Structuralism', with Althusser himself speaking on 'Foucault and the Problematic of Origins' and 'Lévi-Strauss in Search of his Alleged Ancestors'. At the time of the first exchange of letters with Lacan, Althusser and his pupils were engaged in a seminar on 'Lacan and Psychoanalysis', during which Althusser wrote the article on 'Freud and Lacan' carried by *La Nouvelle Critique* – the very PCF publication in which psychoanalysis had been anathematised as a 'reactionary ideology' fifteen years before.

'Freud and Lacan' has hitherto represented the sole published evidence of Althusser's own input into the joint enterprise of 1963–4, which saw contributions from (among others) Balibar, Michel Tort, Jacques-Alain Miller, and Yves Duroux. In *Psychanalyse et sciences humaines* (1996), we now have

---

[92] Althusser 1996a, p. 148.
[93] See the presentation of Althusser et al. 1996, p. vi and the introduction to Althusser 1996a, pp. 1–2.

edited transcripts of the papers he presented – the first on 'The Place of Psychoanalysis in the Human Sciences', the second on 'Psychoanalysis and Psychology'. Surveying the Gallic encounter with Freud, in the former Althusser was concerned to demarcate Freudian theory from the 'philosophy of inter-subjectivity', and hence from the Sartrean 'existential analysis' that took its 'concrete' bearings from Georges Politzer's *Critique of the Foundations of Psychology* (1928). At the same time he declined an anthropologisation of Freudian concepts that effectively construed the super-ego as a latter-day 'pineal gland' joining biological individual and social collective. (This equally applied to the identification of psychoanalyst and shaman by Lévi-Strauss, said to be 'becoming a specialist in the generalisation of the pineal gland'.[94]) Lacan's 'methods of intellectual terrorism', on the other hand, were justified in so far as they were motivated by a 'radical refusal' of 'mechanistic' or 'inter-subjectivist' distortions of psychoanalysis, serving a 'return to Freud and a theoretical interpretation of [his] texts'.[95] They thus facilitated specification of the '*de jure* relationship . . . between psychoanalysis and the world of the human sciences':

> To penetrate this world, we need the point which Archimedes demanded in order to be able to see further . . . in my opinion there are two anchorage points. One is the theoretical results of the problematic inaugurated by Marx. . . . And the other . . . is the possibility of a consistent, rigorous and valid definition of psychoanalysis: this is what Lacan gives us.[96]

Althusser's second paper, full of allusions to Anna Freud and Melanie Klein, evinced antipathy to the discipline seemingly most proximate to psychoanalysis – psychology – whose credentials had been submitted to withering inspection in Georges Canguilhem's celebrated 1956 lecture 'What Is Psychology?'.[97] Psychoanalysis had effected an 'epistemological break'; it represented the 'irruption of a radically new discipline' with the 'potential to disrupt the field in which it irrupts'.[98] Successive attempts at recuperation of it by psychology rested upon an identification of 'individual',

---

94 Althusser 1996b, p. 56.
95 Althusser 1996b, pp. 69–70.
96 Althusser 1996b, pp. 71–2.
97 See Canguilhem 1968, pp. 364–81.
98 Althusser 1996b, pp. 78–9.

'subject', and 'ego' typical of that discipline, which occluded the imaginary structure of the ego and irreducible alterity of the unconscious.[99] Freud's revolution, 'which you have restored' (so Althusser flattered Lacan), entailed 'rejection of any *homo psychologicus*'.[100] Meanwhile, against any absorption of psychoanalysis by biology, Althusser maintained that Freud's discovery revolved around the 'transition from the biological to the cultural', or the infant's entry into the 'symbolic order' via 'the defiles of the signifier'.[101]

The leitmotivs sounded in the seminar papers of 1963–4 resound in the 'culturalist' interpretation advanced in 'Freud and Lacan' (later acknowledged to be such by Althusser),[102] with which *Writings on Psychoanalysis* opens. The remainder of the volume records the rise and fall of the alliance between Althusserian Marxism and Lacanian psychoanalysis institutionalised with Lacan's relocation of his own seminar to the École normale in 1964 through Althusser's intermediation. Two themes are of especial interest. The first is Althusser's counterposition of a 'logic of irruption' to the problematic of 'origins', in conceptualising the beginnings of a historical process.[103] The term habitually employed by Althusser to describe the advent of both Marxism and Freudianism is *surgissement*, with its sense of 'sudden appearance' or 'springing up'. Ben Brewster's otherwise excellent translations of the 1960s and 70s tend to conceal this, since they invariably render the French by 'emergence' with its more genetic-evolutionary connotations. In correspondence with his analyst René Diatkine dating from 1966, in which Althusser sought to impress upon him Lacan's 'unique originality',[104] the idiom of *surgissement* – felicitously translated as 'irruption' by Jeffrey Mehlman – is frequent. Contrary to the 'necessarily teleological . . . structure of any genesis', both Freud's theory and its object – the unconscious – were to be conceived as the 'irruption of a new reality' – something Althusser sought to clarify by reference to the 'irruption mechanism of a determinate mode of production', as analysed by Balibar in *Reading 'Capital'*.[105] In the

---

[99] See Althusser 1996b, pp. 104–6.
[100] Althusser 1996a, p. 149.
[101] Althusser 1996b, pp. 81–2.
[102] See Althusser 1996a, p. 32.
[103] See Althusser 1996a, p. 61.
[104] Althusser 1996a, pp. 48–9.
[105] See Althusser 1996a, pp. 57–64.

instance of the unconscious, Lacan's 'hypothesis that the structures of language (say, of the symbolic) play a determining role in the mechanism issuing in [its] irruption' was upheld; the Lacanian simile – 'the unconscious is structured *like* a language' – meant that there could be 'no question of reducing the theory of the unconscious to a chapter or a subchapter of general linguistics'.[106]

This brings us to a second intriguing aspect of the Althusserian rapprochement with Lacan: the determination – vain, as it happened – to obviate his assimilation to what Althusser disdained as 'the idealist aberrations of the "structuralists"' in a letter to Lacan of 11 July 1966, a few months before his addressee's *Écrits* were collected.[107] This is plainly apparent from 'Three Notes on the Theory of Discourses' composed in the second half of 1966. These initiated a sequence of lengthy exchanges over the next eighteen months among a group comprising Althusser, Balibar, Duroux, Tort, Pierre Macherey and Alain Badiou, which Althusser hoped would lead to a collective 'Elements of Dialectical Materialism' – a 'true work of philosophy that can stand as our *Ethics*', as he put it in a letter to Balibar of 14 October 1966.[108]

In the 'Notes' to hand, much taken up with the articulation of the unconscious and ideology, the structuralist pretension to unify the 'human sciences' via the linguistic model was met with a *fin de non recevoir* by an Althusser insistent upon the differential singularity of the sciences. Lacanian reference to Saussure and Jakobson, fertile in itself, nevertheless indulged the illicit hegemonising ambitions of structural linguistics as relayed by Lévi-Strauss.[109] The 'regional' discipline of linguistics, whose object was the particular discourse known as *langue*, could function as an 'epistemological guide' for the missing 'general theory of discourses' to which psychoanalysis, whose object was the discourse of the unconscious, likewise pertained.[110] Contrary to any linguistic 'formalism', however, it did not constitute that general theory and psychoanalysis was misconceived as a sub-set of it, with a consequent de-materialisation of Freudian theory:

---

[106] Althusser 1996a, pp. 64, 73.

[107] Althusser 1996a, p. 171.

[108] Althusser 2003, p. 34. An unpublished circular dated 11 July 1966 indicates that a seminar on Spinoza was scheduled for the academic year 1966–7, which Althusser was slotted to introduce with a paper on 'Spinoza's anti-Cartesianism', and in which Badiou and Macherey were due to participate.

[109] See Althusser 2003, pp. 45–6.

[110] See Althusser 2003, pp. 80–1.

What really does expose us to the risk of 'losing the libido' is a mistaken conception of the object, and thus of the claims of linguistics. If we interpret the phrase 'the unconscious is structured like a language' as one which presupposes *the deductive application* of linguistics to an object called the unconscious, then we are indeed dealing with a formulation that is *reductive* of its specific object, and with the loss of the libido.[111]

'So many questions. . . . How can one answer them in the present state of affairs?,' Althusser inquired of his interlocutors at the end of his third note.[112] But if, according to a letter of 1977, '[e]very question does not necessarily imply an answer', a decade earlier Althusser was confident that he had at least tabled some of the relevant questions; and, as he informed the Société française de philosophie in February 1968, 'humanity only finds an answer to the problems which it *can* pose'.[113] Indeed, in his November 1963 letter to Lacan, Althusser had struck an evangelical note:

> I am prophesying, but we have entered, in large measure thanks to you, into an era in which one can finally be a prophet in one's own country. I have no merit in running the risk of this prophecy; henceforth we have a right to it, since we possess the means for it, in this country at last become *ours*.[114]

The intervening years have more nearly vindicated St. Mathew. At time of writing, however, Althusser had published the majority of the articles whose collection in *Pour Marx* in September 1965 propelled him into the Parisian limelight – but not before they had aroused the political suspicion of his party. Days after communicating with Lacan, the text he enclosed with his letter – 'On the Materialist Dialectic' – was the subject of a session of the management commitment of *La Penseée*, presided over by Georges Cogniot, co-founder of the journal and secretary to Communist leader Maurice Thorez. At a PCF Central Committee meeting the previous month on the Sino-Soviet split, Althusser's work had been criticised by Lucien Sève for Maoist inclinations;

---

[111] Althusser 2003, p. 73.
[112] Althusser 2003, p. 82.
[113] Althusser 1996a, p. 5; Althusser 1968b, p. 173. The critical allusion on both occasions is to Marx's claim in the 1859 Preface, dear to Gramsci, that '[m]ankind . . . inevitably only sets itself such tasks as it is able to solve': Marx 1975, p. 426.
[114] Althusser 1996a, pp. 149–50.

and rejoinders to 'Contradiction and Overdetermination' (1962) by party philosophers had taken Althusser to task on a variety of scores, from the Marx-Hegel relationship to the primacy of the economic. In a bravura 'Reply to a Critique', formulated in advance of the *La Pensée* confrontation on 30 November 1963, Althusser anticipated – and repudiated – his critics' objections. Although tactically distancing himself from the political line of the Chinese Communist Party, he upheld the 'theoretical value' of the categories introduced in Mao's *On Contradiction*.[115] As to the complaint of 'dualism' lodged by those who registered a culpable silence on the 'dialectics of nature', Althusser responded that since he lacked 'competence' on the 'structures peculiar to natural processes', he had held his tongue on the subject. 'A scientist who has made a foolish remark . . . keeps quite, often for some years, for fear of making another. This is not generally the case in our philosophical domain', Althusser tartly rebuked his comrades.[116]

'Althusserianism's paradox,' Jacques Derrida reflected in 1989, 'was that it claimed hardening and transformation simultaneously. . . . But in both traits . . . it was playing to lose – more and faster.'[117] If 'Maoism' affords convenient shorthand for the political terms of that paradox, 'structuralism' is the *appellation mal contrôlée* for its theoretical terms, Sève's diagnosis of a structuralist 'contamination' giving moderate expression to a critical consensus overdue for revision.[118] An astringent text of 1966, 'On Lévi-Strauss', penned shortly after Maurice Godelier's sketch of a Marxist-structuralist synthesis in *Aletheia*, and circulated to Emmanuel Terray and others, reproved the 'functionalism' of the Lévi-Straussian social unconscious, the 'formalism' of the structuralist combinatory, and the homologisation of words, women and goods consequent upon an abusive extrapolation of Saussureanism to non-linguistic objects. Albeit that they were 'too hasty', Althusser reckoned that his criticisms had located 'the precise point that distinguishes us from Lévi-Strauss himself and, *a fortiori*, from all the "structuralists"'.[119]

That demarcation had been publicly signalled in a lecture, 'The Philosophical Conjuncture and Marxist Theoretical Research', before a packed auditorium

[115] See Althusser 1995b, p. 381.
[116] Althusser 1995b, p. 379.
[117] Kaplan and Sprinker 1993, p. 210.
[118] See Sève 1978, p. 481.
[119] Althusser 2003, p. 31.

at the École normale in June 1966. The grandiose research programme mapped by Althusser looked for domestic allies to the tradition of historical epistemology (Cavaillès, Bachelard, Koyré and Canguilhem), and to Lacanian psychoanalysis, rather than Lévi-Strauss, let alone 'fashionable Parisian ideological by-products'[120] – the structuralist fashion raised to fever pitch by two products of that year, Foucault's *Les Mots et les choses* in April and Lacan's *Écrits* in November.

'Imaginary Marxisms': such was Aron's verdict on the Sartrean and Althusserian enterprises of the 1960s. Conceded, as we have seen, by Althusser in *The Future Lasts a Long Time* and elsewhere, it – or rather Althusser's instrumentalist construal of it as a mere *ruse de guerre* – is disavowed by Balibar in the preface to the re-edition of *Pour Marx*.[121] What he calls 'the quarrel of the "real" and "imaginary" Marxisms' triggered by *For Marx* was intensified that November by *Lire 'le Capital'*, where, to underscore Marx's putative rupture with the 'German ideology', Balibar himself ventured to describe historical materialism as 'a most unusual *structuralism*'[122] – most unusual because Althusserian affinities actually lay elsewhere: with Spinozism.[123]

For Marx may be regarded as an anti-*History and Class Consciousness* (translated into French in 1960); *Reading 'Capital'* was more than an anti-*Critique of Dialectical Reason* (published the same year). If the classification of their results as an 'imaginary Marxism' designed to turn the flank of the PCF leadership is misleading, the 'return to Marx' of their self-conception is unilluminating. The motto in which the Royal Society spurned the authority of the past – *Nullius in verba* (in the words of no-one else) – was not an option for Althusser, obliged by organisational allegiances to invoke the founder. Yet, in so doing, he not only mounted a critique of 'historical' Marxism and Communism,[124] but also deployed Marx against himself. Hence, perhaps, another paradox, encapsulated by Sève: 'One of the most powerful Marxist thinkers of this century . . . was doubtless never exactly a Marxian'.[125]

---

[120] Althusser 2003, p. 9.
[121] Compare Althusser 1993, pp. 148, 221 and Althusser 1994b, pp. 37, 88 with Balibar 1996, pp. xiii–xiv.
[122] Althusser et al. 1996, p. 650.
[123] The most detailed discussion of Althusser's Spinozism to date is Thomas 2002.
[124] See Preve 1993.
[125] Raymond 1997, p. 135 n. 99; see pp. 135–6.

However that might be, as the introduction to the 1996 reissue of *Lire 'le Capital'* makes clear, the twelve seminar sessions on *Capital* held in the Salle des Actes from January to April 1965 conjugated several different projects, whose intertwinement accounts for the richness of the published record: a 'critical re-reading of Marx's scientific œuvre'; a 'recasting of the categories and figures of the dialectic', steered by the notion of 'structural causality' and intimately related to a reinterpretation of the basic concepts of Freudian psychoanalysis; an endeavour to substitute a problematic of 'theoretical practice' for the 'theory of knowledge'; and a 'final project which, subjectively at least, governed all the others' – 'the search for a communist politics, Spinozist in inspiration ("theoretical anti-humanism"), which would conceive [communism] as the becoming-necessary of freedom, rather than as the "exit from the kingdom of necessity"'.[126] In other words, the Althusserians' whole-hearted conviction was that only *theoretical* anti-humanism in the present could orientate a *practical* humanism of the future. For as Althusser remarked around the same time of the painter Cremonini, in a text fittingly reprinted in Volume Two of *Écrits philosophiques et politiques*,

> Cremonini . . . follows the path which was opened up to men by the great revolutionary thinkers, theoreticians and politicians, the great materialist thinkers, who understood that the freedom of men is not achieved by the complacency of its ideological *recognition*, but by *knowledge* of the laws of their slavery, and that the 'realisation' of their concrete individuality is achieved by the analysis and mastery of the abstract relations which govern them.[127]

Several implications of Althusser and his colleagues' re-reading of *Capital*, presenting their reconstruction of 'historical and dialectical materialism' as Marx's explicit or implicit construction of it, should be noted. First, Marx's opening up of the 'continent of history' to scientific exploration in *Capital* constituted an 'immense theoretical revolution' strictly analogous to the achievements of Galileo in physics or Lavoisier in chemistry. However, it had only been begun by him: he had founded a research programme that remained to be developed, rather than promulgating a doctrine that need only be quoted,

---

[126] See Althusser et al. 1996, pp. v–vi.
[127] Althusser 1971, p. 219.

by his successors. The second, inherent in Althusser's delimitation of historical materialism as an autonomous science with its own object, method and theory, was renunciation of the 'materialist' metaphysic inherited from the Second International by the Third, wherein Marxism was an autarchic cosmology or 'world-view', subsuming the totality of natural and social phenomena, of which historical materialism was merely a sub-set. The third, in conjunction with Althusser's reassertion of the scientificity of Marxist theory, was an insistence upon its incompletion – not only as a result of the inevitable limitations of Marx's own contribution, but as a normal correlate of its scientific status. If it was to make good its claim to be a 'science among others', then, by definition, it must be capable of progression and self-rectification, producing the new knowledge characteristic of the 'adventure of science in development'.[128] Finally – an inference from the Galilean analogy – to this end the problematic within which Marx had worked was open to recastings of the type being proposed by Althusser, in response to the misadventures of a science in stagnation. Just as the science of physics, as opposed to phases in its history, was not designated by a proper noun, so too the science of history – 'historical materialism' – was not the property in perpetuity of a founding father. The 'theoretical contributions necessary for the present period' would, as Althusser tactfully but pointedly observed with reference to 'Leninism', 'later be called by a name which does not exist as yet'.[129] Whether or not the that name spelt 'Althusserianism', the import was clear. In so far as they merely reiterated the Marxism of Marx, Marxists negated its scientificity, therewith abdicating their intellectual responsibility.

Althusser's belief that that scientificity inhered in the non-humanist, as well as non-economistic and non-historicist, bases of Marx's mature writings caused consternation within and without PCF ranks. At an assembly of Communist philosophers in January 1966, which the main culprit could not attend because of illness, Roger Garaudy led the assault on the Althusserian reversal of alliances against theoretical humanism, sanctioned by the belief that nothing *in* human was alien to it;[130] and was repaid in kind by Macherey.

---

[128] Althusser 1969a, p. 245.
[129] Althusser 1969a, p. 176.
[130] See François Regnault's remarks in Lazarus 1993, p. 175 and cf. Althusser 1993, pp. 185–6.

Two months later, the PCF Central Committee, while conceding freedom of research, resolved that 'Marxism is the humanism of our time'.[131] Althusser was undeterred by the ubiquitous accusations of *lèse-humanité*. Immediately after *For Marx* and *Reading 'Capital'*, he had set to work on an alternative manual of Marxism-Leninism to those available from Progress Publishers and/or Éditions Sociales, from which extracts were published in the *maoisant* organ of the Communist students of the rue d'Ulm the month after the Central Committee meeting at Argenteuil. In 1967 he delivered a lecture course on *The German Ideology* which started with an examination of Feuerbach, whose 'philosophical manifestoes' of 1838–45 Althusser had translated in 1960 and whose *Essence of Christianity* he would publish in the *Théorie* series in 1968.[132] In turn, he envisaged incorporating this material, in which the secret of Feuerbachian anthropology resided in theology, into a work on 'The Break', proposing to assume responsibility for the chapters on Feuerbach, the 1844 *Manuscripts* and the 'Theses on Feuerbach', while Balibar took charge of *The German Ideology*.

An unfinished counter-polemic on 'The Humanist Controversy', in which Althusser demurred at his leaders' pronouncements,[133] traversed much of the relevant terrain. A scherzando preface evoked Erich Fromm's commission, and then rejection, of a text for an international symposium on humanism.[134] The ensuing article – 'Marxism and Humanism' – had elicited numerous critical responses in Communist periodicals. Whereas it had 'settled the question of the early Marx's intellectual development with no ifs, ands and buts . . . in two lines',[135] Althusser now scanned his evolution at some length, offering his most extensive discussion of the 'works of the break' and emphasising the centrality for Marx and Engels of Stirner's *The Ego and its Own*.[136] The '*notion* of man' was an 'epistemological obstacle' to the science of history. In his mature works,

> Marx *starts out from the abstract*, and says so. This does not mean that, for
> Marx, men, individuals, and their subjectivity have been expunged from

---

[131] See Althusser 2003, pp. 299–300, nn. 13–14 and Verdès-Leroux 1987, pp. 113–27.
[132] See Althusser 2003, pp. 85–154.
[133] See Althusser 2003, p. 225.
[134] The symposium was published as Fromm 1967.
[135] Althusser 2003, p. 223.
[136] See Althusser 2003, p. 258.

real history. It means that the *notions* of Man, etc., have been expunged *from theory*, for, in theory, no-one has yet, to my knowledge, met a flesh-and-blood man, only the *notion* of man. Far from being able to found and serve theory, these ideological notions have only one effect: they *foreclose* theory. These notions of Theoretical Humanism have been eliminated from Marx's scientific theory, and we have every right to eliminate them, root and branch – for the simple reason that they act only as *'epistemological obstacles'* there.[137]

Reaffirming Marx's theoretical anti-humanism, Althusser likewise asserted 'the anti-historicism, anti-evolutionism, and anti-structuralism of Marxist theory'. But if he was manifestly playing to win, Althusser was advised that it would be a long game: 'We are not labouring under any illusions: theoretical humanism has a long and very "bright future" ahead of it. We shall not have settled accounts with it by next spring'[138] – especially since next spring was May '68.

The Paris Spring derailed the last major collective venture by the Althusserians, the 'Philosophy Course for Scientists' staged in 1967–8. Althusser's own fifth lecture, anatomising the 'invariant' structure of the classical theory of knowledge, was published in 1995, thus completing *Philosophy and the Spontaneous Philosophy of Scientists* (1974).[139] While the course was underway, complementary private exchanges with Badiou, Balibar and co. pondered the nature of philosophy, endeavouring to stabilise a 'politicist' definition of it.[140] In the midst of them, Althusser queried one of the central results of the symptomatic reading of *Capital* advanced in 1965:

> I . . . wonder if it might not be the case that what we regarded as irrational residues in *Capital* (a discrepancy between the old categories and the those that would be required by the new scientific problematic) – that is, a certain anthropological Hegelianism . . . does not 'represent' in *Capital* the 'philosophy' heralded by Marx in the *Theses on Feuerbach*.[141]

---

[137] Althusser 2003, pp. 264–5.
[138] Althusser 2003, pp. 232–3.
[139] See Althusser 1995b, pp. 257–98.
[140] See Badiou's paper in Lazarus 1993, pp. 29–45.
[141] Althusser 1995b, p. 321.

This consideration would weigh heavily with the later Althusser, who might have subscribed to Derrida's detection of the *'coup de force* of an artificial strategy . . . an interpretative violence' committed, but not admitted, in *Reading 'Capital'*.[142]

The aftershocks of May were soon the order of the day. In 1965, Balibar had sought to infer 'elements for a theory of transition' from an analysis of the concept of reproduction. Post-May, Althusser embarked on a conjoint theory of reproduction and revolution. Significantly, however, only the first volume, treating the former, was substantially completed in March–April 1969; a second, given over to 'class struggle in capitalist socialist formations', was seemingly never started. 'The Reproduction of the Relations of Production', presented by Jacques Bidet, was finally published in 1995. It prompts three immediate observations. The first is that Althusser, aware that it can be a short step from fluency to facility, proved to be his own best editor in singling out the sections on the ISAs and ideology in general for *La Pensée* in 1970. These represent his main contribution to historical materialism after 1965, albeit that in his 1966 critique of Lévi-Straussian functionalism he had drafted the script of his critics, who would argue that the attributes denied to human agency were transferred to social structures in Althusser's account of ISAs. If the rest of the text adds nothing of enduring value to them, it is largely because – second observation – echoes of the Cultural Revolution in China pervade this didactic exposition of the fundamentals of Althusserian Marxism-Leninism. Notwithstanding seriatim criticisms of then actually existing socialism, Althusser's political optimism was seemingly unbounded: 'We are entering an age which will witness the triumph of socialism the world over'.[143] Contrariwise, and thirdly, anarcho-libertarianism, with its prioritisation of 'repression' and denigration of knowledge as authoritarian, was accurately identified as the proximate ideological beneficiary of the student revolt.[144]

In this respect at least, May was (as Foucault surmised) 'profoundly anti-Marxist'. Of more immediate significance here, it was explicitly or implicitly anti-Communist, with decisive consequences for an Althusser trapped between the anvil of Communist discipline and the hammer of ultra-leftist contestation.

---

[142] See Kaplan and Sprinker 1993, pp. 223–4.
[143] Althusser 1995a, p. 21.
[144] See Althusser 1995a, pp. 213–15.

The intricacies of Althusser's transactions with the parties to the dispute cannot detain us here. (Suffice it to say that they have invariably been discussed with a confidence in inverse proportion to competence.) But that the contradictory pressures of the conjuncture post-May primed a series of 'auto-critiques', injecting ever greater doses of class struggle – *deus ex machina* redirecting structural causality – and debouching into a doctrine of philosophical correctness whose concessions to critics issued in a 'bad returned of the repressed',[145] is evident enough.

Esprit de système, esprit de contradiction: even as Althusser composed the most dogmatic of his 'rectifications' – *Reply to John Lewis* (1972) – he was privately parodying the 'laws of the dialectic' and his own promulgation of the 'Theses of Marxist-Leninist philosophy'.[146] Matters took a more serious turn in the mid-1970s with the anti-Marxist operation 'new philosophy' in the wake of Solzhenitsyn's enormously influential *Gulag Archipelago*. And, soon enough, it was French Marxism in general and Althusserianism in particular that were experiencing a crisis.

In an undelivered conference paper of 1976 published without his permission in 1983, Althusser had retracted his ratification of Lacan.[147] The following year he proclaimed the 'crisis of Marxism' at a conference organised by *Il Manifesto* in Venice. 'The day of reckoning' had arrived, so a dejected letter of January 1978, to which Althusser attached his Venetian talk, confided to a Georgian friend.

> I see clear as day that what I did fifteen years ago was to fabricate a little, typically French justification, in a neat little rationalism bolstered with a few references (Cavaillès, Bachelard, Canguilhem, and, behind them, a bit of the Spinoza-Hegel tradition), for Marxism's (historical materialism's) pretension to being a science. . . . I only half believed in it, like anyone of 'sound mind', but the doubtful half had to be there so that the other half could write. . . . Not everything about this adventure was vain or worthless. . . . But the question is how to 'manage' this presumed or presumptive past in a situation like the one we're saddled with today. The only answer that I can find for the moment is silence. . . . A silence that can become permanent,

---

[145] Regnault's phrase in Lazarus 1993, p. 172.
[146] See Althusser 1994a, pp. 346–56.
[147] See Althusser 1996a, pp. 85–104.

why not? Or a step back in order to publish a few little things after all, on Machiavelli, Gramsci and company, or a few impudent remarks on philosophy, an old idea that I've been carrying around with me for some time . . . or, who knows, something on the Epicurean tradition. It's not much in a day and age in which one ought to be armed with enough concrete knowledge to be able to discuss matters such as the state, the economic crisis, organisations, the 'socialist' countries, and so on. But I don't have that knowledge. Like Marx in 1852, I would have to 'begin again from the very beginning'; but it's very late, given my age, fatigue, lassitude and, also, my isolation. Of course, there's also the possibility of returning to *Capital*, now that we can pretty well see what doesn't work in its reasoning, something that has to do with, not the Idea of the undertaking, but its arguments. Still, there too, if we want to be logical, it wouldn't be enough to take the mechanism apart; one would have to 'put it back together again'. But that requires having other parts and something altogether different from the limited philosophical culture that I possess.[148]

In an abortive manuscript from Summer 1978 – 'Marx dans ses limites' – whose essential thrust is conveyed in 'Marxism Today', Althusser did address, even if he failed to resolve, the 'crisis of Marxism'.[149] Lashing out at Glucksmann, Lévy and the like, he nevertheless called for a 'labour of correction and revision' of the Marxism of Marx, Lenin, and Gramsci.[150] By then, the electoral ides of March 1978 had tolled the knell of the phase of French politics opened by May '68, provoking the frontal assault on the PCF leadership in *Le Monde* with which Althusser's public career came to an effective end. As we now know, however, Althusser did not cease to think and write in the interval between the murder of his wife and his own death ten years later. Stepping back, as he had anticipated in his letter to Merab Mamardashvili, he did indeed return to the – an – 'Epicurean tradition' and Machiavelli.

---

[148] Althusser 1994a, pp. 527–8 (I am grateful to Geoffrey Goshgarian for supplying me with his draft translation of Althusser's late texts, which I use in what follows). See also the letter to Mauricio Malamud of 8 March 1984, in Althusser 1994b, pp. 85–92.

[149] Cf. Anderson 1982, p. 30.

[150] See Althusser 1994a, pp. 357–524.

5. Brief encounters

The extremely uneven, often fragmentary materials associated with the late Althusser can be divided into two groups:

(i) The late writings proper: 'The Underground Current of the Materialism of the Encounter', drafted in 1982; 'Philosophy and Marxism', constructed between 1984 and 1987 but also drawing on Althusser's 1976 Spanish talk on 'The Transformation of Philosophy';[151] *The Future Lasts a Long Time*, contrived in 1985; and three chapters – on Spinoza, Machiavelli, and the 'political situation' – originally intended for *The Future*, but ultimately omitted from it.

(ii) *Machiavelli and Us* – a set of lectures given in 1972, revised on and off in accordance with the idiom of the late Althusser up until 1986 or thereabouts, and carefully polished for posthumous publication.

The first group of texts, with their freight of generic references and (mis)quotations, revolves around the postulate of what Althusser calls an 'aleatory materialism', or 'materialism of the encounter'. Supposedly originating with Epicurus, and variously continued by Machiavelli, Hobbes, Pascal, Spinoza, Rousseau, Marx, Heidegger, Wittgenstein and Derrida, this '"authentic" materialism' is positively contrasted with an incorrigible 'dialectical materialism', derided as a 'yellow logarithm'.[152] 'My principal thesis,' Althusser writes in 'The Underground Current',

> [is] *the existence of an almost completely unknown materialist tradition in the history of philosophy:* . . . *a materialism of the encounter*, and therefore of the aleatory and of contingency. This materialism is opposed, as a wholly different mode of thought, to the various materialisms on record, including that widely ascribed to Marx, Engels and Lenin, which, like every other materialism in the rationalist tradition, is a materialism of necessity and teleology, i.e., a transformed, disguised form of idealism.[153]

---

[151] Published in French alongside 'Philosophy and Marxism' in Althusser 1994b, pp. 143–78, it appeared in English translated from the Spanish in Althusser 1990, pp. 241–65.
[152] Althusser 1994b, pp. 35, 32.
[153] Althusser 1994a, pp. 539–40.

356 • Postscript: The Necessity of Contingency

'Philosophy and Marxism' affords a fuller version of the same capsule definition:

> My intention, here, is to insist on the existence of a materialist tradition that
> has not been recognised by the history of philosophy. That of Democritus,
> Epicurus, Machiavelli, Hobbes, Rousseau (the Rousseau of the second
> *Discourse*), Marx and Heidegger, together with the categories that they
> defended: the void, the limit, the margin, the absence of a centre, the
> displacement of the centre to the margin (and vice versa), and freedom. A
> materialism of the encounter, of contingency, in sum, of *the aleatory*, which
> is opposed even to the materialisms that have been recognised as such,
> including that commonly attributed to Marx, Engels and Lenin, which, like
> every other materialism of the rationalist tradition, is a materialism of
> necessity and teleology, i.e., a disguised form of idealism.[154]

In thus isolating anti-finalism as the defining characteristic of any consequent
'materialism', the late Althusser was resuming the Spinozist critique of Hegelian
teleology encapsulated in the category of 'a process without a subject or
goal(s)'.[155]

Acknowledged not to be 'a Marxist philosophy', 'aleatory materialism'
is proposed as a potential 'philosophy *for Marxism*' – one to which Marx
himself was only ambiguously affiliated, for 'constrained to think within a
horizon torn between the aleatory of the Encounter and the necessity of the
Revolution'.[156] As André Tosel has written in a fine essay, Althusser no longer

> looks exclusively to Marx for the philosophy supposedly contained 'in the
> practical state' in *Capital* in his theory of the capitalist mode of production
> and its structural causality, and which allegedly refutes reference to Hegel's
> teleological logic. This theory is itself now subject to critique as the product
> of a persistent metaphysical rationalism and purged of what bound it to
> the principle of reason. The critique is conducted via the themes of the
> materialism of the underground current of the encounter, by a new philosophy
> developed independently of Marx by Epicurus, Machiavelli, Spinoza,
> Rousseau and Heidegger, which has become the norm of the critique of
> Marx's idealist rationalism.[157]

---

[154] Althusser 1994b, p. 42.
[155] As Callinicos 1995, p. 43 rightly notes.
[156] Althusser 1994b, pp. 37–8; Althusser 1994a, p. 560.
[157] Tosel 2001, p. 32.

Pierre Raymond's severe estimate of the 'very approximate' character of what Althusser himself called the 'intuitions' of 'The Underground Current'[158] and 'Philosophy and Marxism' are difficult to gainsay: 'Althusser . . . accumulates some very different philosophical sources . . . and heterogeneous themes which he never analyses distinctly or precisely'[159] – as it were, Epicurus, Machiavelli, Spinoza, Marx (and a host of others), *même combat*! In a heroic exercise in fine-grained exegesis of these convoluted texts, to which readers are referred, Wal Suchting, while pinpointing numerous inconsistencies and obscurities, plausibly distils a methodological 'anti-necessitarianism', rather than a traditional philosophical indeterminism, from them.[160]

Less perplexing is Althusser's sustained analysis of Machiavelli, which confirms the soundness of Emmanuel Terray's judgement prior to the publication of *Machiavelli and Us* that there was little or nothing fortuitous about the encounter between the secretaries to the Florentine *signoria* and the Parisian *grande école*.[161]

In *The Future Lasts a Long Time* Althusser characterises Spinoza as a 'nominalist', commenting: 'Marx taught me that nominalism was the royal road to materialism'.[162] And, in response to Navarro, invoking Wittgenstein's 'the world is what the case is', he isolates the 'fundamental thesis' of nominalism as the existence exclusively of singular 'cases, situations, things . . . totally distinct from one another'.[163] Althusser's Machiavelli is a nominalist in the stipulated sense. Frequently admired as a secular theoretician of politics, as commonly belaboured as *the* cynical technician of power, Machiavelli – so Althusser argues in 'The Underground Current' – had a quite different order of achievement to his credit: 'a philosophical theory of the encounter between fortune and *virtù*'.[164] Althusser indicated his intention to elaborate on these 'brief notes'. Nothing with Althusser ever being simple, however, in fact he already had – as early as 1972, in *Machiavelli and Us*.

---

[158] Althusser 1994b, p. 123.
[159] Raymond 1997, p. 174. Raymond points to his own 1982 as the source of many of Althusser's formulations.
[160] See Suchting 2004, p. 66.
[161] See his fine essay in Callari and Ruccio 1996, pp. 257–77.
[162] Althusser 1993, p. 217.
[163] Althusser 1994b, p. 46.
[164] Althusser 1994a, p. 545.

Althusser's text started life as a course for candidates of the philosophy *agrégation* at the École normale in January-February 1972. Around 1975–6, he significantly revised it – especially the introduction – gave it its present title, and wrote a preface. Having summarised its conclusions in a lecture on 'Machiavelli's Solitude' in 1977, Althusser then returned to *Machiavelli and Us* in his final decade, systematically replacing references to the 'dialectic' and 'dialectical materialism' by the discourse of 'aleatory materialism'.[165]

In his intellectual biography of Machiavelli, Quentin Skinner maintains that 'in order to understand Machiavelli's doctrines, we need to begin by recovering the problems he evidently saw himself confronting'.[166] Althusser too was intent upon a recovery of Machiavelli's problems, the better to displace perennial controversies over the Florentine diplomat (for example, whether he was the founder of positive 'political science'), and reveal him instead as what (transposing Negri's characterisation of Spinoza) we might name 'the savage anomaly'. For Althusser, Machiavelli does not merely criticise the Renaissance humanism rooted in classical antiquity. In pursuit of *la verità effettuale della cosa*, he unequivocally repudiates it, together with 'the entire tradition of Christian theology and all the political theories of antiquity'.[167] The upshot is 'Machiavelli's solitude', stranded as he is between classical and Christian traditions, on the one hand, and the modern tradition of natural law theory, on the other.

As Timothy O'Hagan has remarked, 'if Althusser's Machiavelli is solitary, his reading of Machiavelli is not'.[168] Foreshadowed by Hegel in 1802, elaborated by De Sanctis in 1870, and adopted by Gramsci in the 1930s, according to it the overriding 'problem' posed to and by Machiavelli is 'the constitution of Italian national unity'.[169] Althusser shares this sense of the Machiavellian problematic and the correlative conception of *The Prince* as a 'revolutionary manifesto'. The real novelty of Althusser's interpretation lies elsewhere. It hones in on Machiavelli's *dispositif théorique*, and its effects on 'the modality of [his] object', as the key to his philosophical importance. The peculiarity of

---

[165] See the 'editorial note' in Althusser 1999, pp. vii–viii and Negri's remarks in Matheron 1997, p. 144ff.
[166] Skinner 1980, pp. 1–2.
[167] Althusser 1999, pp. 7–8.
[168] O'Hagan 1988, p. 462.
[169] Althusser 1999, p. 53.

this *dispositif* is that it states a series of general theses on history which are literally contradictory, yet organised in such a way as to generate concepts not deducible from them, for the purposes of theorising an *'"object" which is in fact a determinate objective'*.[170] Machiavelli's object is not some theory of the 'laws' of history or politics, but the conjunctural conditions for the foundation of a new principality. Machiavelli's 'endeavour to think the conditions of possibility of an impossible task, to think the unthinkable' induces 'a strange *vacillation* in the traditional philosophical status of [his] theoretical propositions: as if they were undermined by a different instance from the one that produces them – the instance of political practice'.[171] Inscribing in itself the place of the political practice that can alone determine the identity of 'a New Prince in a New Principality', Machiavelli's theory of the conjuncture inhabits the space of the putatively universal – the abstract-theoretical – to think the irreducibly singular – the concrete-historical case of sixteenth-century Italy. If 'the first theorist of the conjuncture'[172] can specify the conditions for a fruitful encounter between *virtù* (or the political agency of the Prince) and *Fortuna* (or the contingency of the real), his grasp of the necessity of contingency precludes any prediction of what is, by definition, aleatory. Consequently,

> Machiavelli is not in the least utopian: he simply thinks the conjunctural *case* of the thing, and goes *dietro alla verità effettuale della cosa*. He asserts it in concepts which are philosophical and no doubt make him, in his temerity, solitude, and scorn for the philosophies of the tradition, the greatest materialist philosopher in history – the equal of Spinoza, who declared him *'acutissimus'*.[173]

Where the 'early writings' shed light on the pre-Althusserian *terminus a quo* – in short, Catholicism and Hegelianism – the late texts table the question of the post-Althusserian *terminus ad quem*: is Antonio Negri right to posit what, alluding to Heidegger's 'turn', he has dubbed 'Althusser's *Kehre*'?[174] Is the last Althusser radically distinct from his earlier philosophical selves? Or are there discernible and demonstrable elements of continuity, as well as discontinuity, between them – elements that might in turn necessitate a

---

170 Althusser 1999, p. 42.
171 Althusser 1999, pp. 20, 52.
172 Althusser 1999, p. 18.
173 Althusser 1999, p. 103.
174 Negri 1996, p. 58.

re-reading of the overly familiar Althusser of the 1960s and 1970s and a more nuanced delineation of him at the zenith of his celebrity? As the original date of composition of *Machiavelli and Us* might predispose us to think, an answer in the affirmative to the second question is indicated. Althusser unrehearsed contains references to themes and authors already present in the mature Althusserian discourse on method, before taking centre-stage in the closing meditations on a philosophy for Marxism. It might even be argued that the principal merit of the 'The Underground Current' and related texts is that they facilitate a litmus test on the Althusser of the 1960s and 1970s, indicating underlying themes across his œuvre.[175]

In his valuable lexicon of the late Althusser, Vittorio Morfino detects 'the presence of various themes that indicate a strong continuity with the works of the 1960s':

(1) the concept of process without a subject and hence the negation of any form, whether internal or external, of teleology;
(2) the primacy of relations over related elements;
(3) theoretical anti-humanism;
(4) the claim that philosophy has no object;
(5) the definition of the structure of metaphysics according to the schema Origin – Subject – Object – Truth – End – Foundation.[176]

These constitute the rational core of 'aleatory materialism' and yet, terminological discontinuities harbouring conceptual continuities, are invariably couched in a sometimes confusing 'new constellation of terms':

(1) void/nothing
(2) encounter
(3) fact/*Faktum*/factual/facticity
(4) conjuncture/conjunction
(5) necessity/contingency[177]

---

[175] Cf. Morfino 2002, p. 147.
[176] Morfino 2002, p. 146.
[177] Morfino 2002, p. 147–8.

Indeed, if one theme, explicitly formulated as such, runs like a red thread through Althusser's œuvre, then it is the 'necessity of contingency', aimed at surmounting what *Reading 'Capital'* identified as the 'classical opposition . . . necessity/contingency'.[178] 'Corner-stone', as Morfino notes, 'not only of the late Althusser but also of the earlier one',[179] it postulates that 'instead of thinking contingency as a modality of necessity, or an exception to it, we must think necessity as the becoming-necessary of the encounter of contingents'.[180] Mentioned only in passing in 'The Underground Current',[181] it is probably to Antoine Augustin Cournot's definition of chance events as the unpredictable but intelligible consequence of the encounter of independent causal series that we owe the category of 'necessary contingency'.[182] Introduced to Cournot by Jean Guitton at the Lycée du Parc from 1936,[183] Althusser invoked him sparingly but approvingly in the 1960s, most strikingly in an unpublished working note from 1966 that reads like an outline for 'The Underground Current':

> 1. Theory of the encounter or *conjunction* (= genesis ...) (cf. Epicurus, clinamen, Cournot), chance, etc., precipitation, coagulation. 2. Theory of the *conjuncture* (= structure) . . . philosophy as general theory of the *conjuncture* (= *conjunction*).[184]

As François Matheron has argued, the category of the 'encounter' is not some

> belated discovery of Althusser's. It constitutes one of the fundamental tendencies of the articles collected in *For Marx*. It is posited in all the texts

---

[178] Althusser and Balibar 1970, p. 110.
[179] Morfino 2002, p. 167.
[180] Althusser 1994b, p. 42.
[181] See Althusser 1994a, p. 566.
[182] See Anderson 1992, pp. 295–6: 'In a famous definition, [Cournot] declared chance events to be those that were produced by the encounter of two independent causal series. Since the universe was not the outcome of a single natural law, but was plainly governed by a variety of different mechanisms, there were both processes governed by more or less linear causal sequences, and occurrences set off by intersections between them. This was the difference between what was regular and what was random, each equally intelligible – the contrast, for example, between the movement of planets and meteors, or of tides and glaciers. . . . The innovation of his philosophy of history was to be what he called an *aetiology*: a systematic enquiry into the weave of causes that composed the fabric of history. The task of such an enquiry was to trace out the complicated patterns of chance and necessity that had shaped human development, by distinguishing between threads of "independence" and "solidarity" within its causal continuum.'
[183] See Moulier Boutang 1992, p. 141.
[184] Quoted in Althusser 1997, p. 10.

whose object is the conjuncture, and which seek to show what it means to think theoretically from the standpoint of a task to be accomplished, rather than from the angle of the *fait accompli*.[185]

Shortly after referring to Cournot ('ce grand méconnu'), 'The Underground Current' itself peters out with a contrast between two conceptions of mode of production in Marx – one 'historico-aleatory', the other 'teleological' – referring back to Balibar's genealogy of the capitalist mode of production in *Reading 'Capital'*, while regretting that Marx himself succumbed to the second.[186] Minus the critical note, however, the project of an alternative logic of the constitution and transformation of modes of production – characterised as a 'theory of the encounter' or 'conjunction', in an unpublished letter of 1966[187] – recurs in Althusser's work. In 'The Humanist Controversy', for example, we read:

> capitalism is the result *of a process that does not take the form of a genesis*. The result of what? Marx tells us several times: of the process of an *encounter* of several distinct, definite, indispensable elements, engendered in the previous historical process by different *genealogies* that are independent of each other and can, moreover, be traced back to several possible 'origins'. . . . To put it plainly, capitalism is not the result of a *genesis* that can be traced back to the feudal mode of production as if to its origin . . .; it is the result of a complex process that produces, at a given moment, the encounter of a number of elements susceptible of . . . constituting it in their very encounter.[188]

As intimated by Terray in a remarkable text predating publication of the late writings,[189] what else, in retrospect, was Althusser's philosophical manifesto of 1962 – 'Contradiction and Overdetermination' – but the adumbration of something like a theory of the necessary contingency of history, prioritising conjuncture and conjunction over structure? Neither a transcription of historical necessity, nor a ratification of historical accident, on Althusserian premises revolution is the explicable exception that proves the implacable rule, because

[185] Matheron 1997, pp. 39–40.
[186] See Althusser 1994a, pp. 569–76.
[187] Althusser 1966c: an item in the exchanges between Althusser et al. of 1966–8, which refers to Althusser's second letter to René Diatkine in Althusser 1996a, pp. 54–77.
[188] Althusser 2003, p. 296.
[189] See Terray 1993, pp. 63–8.

the exception *is* the rule. This 'materialism of singularity',[190] imputed to the trio of Machiavelli, Spinoza and Marx but perfected in the work of the first, underwent magnification in the mirror of Machiavelli after 1980. In a letter sent to Franca Madonia while at work on *Reading 'Capital'*, Althusser critically adjudged Gramsci 'the Machiavelli of modern times', remarking that 'he reads Lenin through Machiavelli, just as he reads Machiavelli through Lenin'.[191] *Mutatis mutandis*, does the last Althusser invite an altogether dissimilar verdict?

Rather than essay an answer, I shall table some further questions and proposals for research prompted by late Althusser. The first is this: is Balibar right to perceive a recurrent tension in Althusser between the Leninist/Machiavellian analyst of the *singularity of conjunctures* and the structuralist-Marxist theorist of *invariant structures* – between, one might say, 'Contradiction and Overdetermination' and 'On the Materialist Dialectic', or even between *For Marx* and *Reading 'Capital'*?[192] And, if this is the case, does the option for 'aleatory materialism' not so much resolve as dissolve it?

Second, is there a precedent of sorts for his position in non-Marxist, Anglophone philosophy of history? More particularly, in the work of J.T. Bury, who seems to have drawn upon Cournot for his conception of history as a 'chapter of accidents' – for example, in the essay 'Cleopatra's Nose', whose starting-point is Pascal's famous observation that 'if *it* had been shorter, the whole face of the world would have been different'.[193] If so, is Althusserian aleatorism altogether distinct from a certain commonsense empiricism among British historians, captured in H.A.L. Fisher's oft-quoted view of history as 'the interplay of the contingent and the unforeseen'? Or, alternatively, is it closer to Georges Sorel's concern with the 'logic of contingency', rendering a French Marxist thinker brusquely dismissed in *For Marx* a possible native 'precursor'?

Finally, with Althusser's late thinking on necessity and contingency, are we not present at the strangest of encounters, however brief? 'Our whole age,' Foucault once pronounced,

---

[190] See Matheron 1997, p. 140.
[191] Althusser 1998c, p. 624.
[192] See Callari and Ruccio 1996, pp. 109–19.
[193] Pascal 1966, p. 162. I am grateful to Alex Callinicos for drawing my attention to Bury (personal communication).

> is trying to escape Hegel. But any real escape . . . presupposes . . . that we
> know what is still Hegelian in that which allows us to think against Hegel,
> and that we can assess the extent to which our appeal against him is perhaps
> one more of the ruses he employs against us.[194]

Insofar as the internal link between necessity and contingency is an Hegelian postulate,[195] was 'aleatory materialism' the ultimate ruse of Hegelian reason? And what are we to make of the irony of intellectual history that the last Althusser, erstwhile author of a dissertation on Hegel, had staged a return to the youngest Marx, sometime author of a doctorate on Democritus and Epicurus?

6. The day of reckoning: Althusser in his limits

Any future intellectual biographer of Althusser will have to bear in mind his strictures in 'On the Young Marx' as to 'the necessity and contingency of [Marx's] beginning'; or in the introduction to *Reading 'Capital'*, where he renounces 'every teleology of reason', urging a reconceptualisation of

> the historical relation between a [theoretical] result and its conditions of
> existence as a relation of production . . . and therefore as what, in a phrase
> that clashes with the classical system of categories, . . . we can call the *necessity
> of its contingency.*

Or, again, in *Elements of Self-Criticism*, when, revisiting Marx's 'epistemological break', he asserts that every science is

> born out of the unpredictable, incredibly complex and paradoxical – but, in
> its contingency, necessary – *conjunction* of ideological, political, scientific . . .
> philosophical and other *'elements'.*[196]

In short, she or he will have to be guided by the maxim that contingency is the mother of invention and make a virtue of it, permitting readers 'to witness in an emerging life, once the Gods of Origins and Goals have been dethroned, the birth of necessity'.[197]

---

[194] Foucault 1971, pp. 74–5.
[195] See, e.g., Burbridge 1980.
[196] See Althusser 1969a, p. 64; Althusser and Balibar 1970, p. 45; and Althusser 1976a, p. 112.
[197] Althusser 1969a, p. 71.

Pending such a venture, having completed our rapid tour of the posthumous edition of Althusser's writings, we are now in a position to mimic the operation he performed on Marx – with this crucial difference: that the object of the exercise is not to locate an *epistemological* discontinuity, whether between the young Althusser and the mature Althusser, or middle Althusser and late Althusser, but to indicate *conceptual* discontinuities and therewith bring out any conceptual *continuity* or continuities. Accordingly, employing Althusser's own idiom and risking the wrath of adepts of the 'narcissism of small differences', we can suggest the following approximate periodisation of his published œuvre:

(i)   1945–50: the Early Works
(ii) 1950–9: the Works of the Break
(iii) 1960–75: the Mature Works
(iv) 1976–8: the Transitional Works
(v)   1979–86: the Late Works

(i)   The period of the early works is the pre-Althusserian phase of the writings collected in English as *The Spectre of Hegel* (though *Spectres of Hegel and Stalin* might have been a more apt, if less palatable, title). As we have seen, they trace a dual, non-linear transition from Catholicism to Communism and from left Hegelianism to what Althusser himself would later characterise as the 'poor man's Hegelianism' of Stalinist Marxism.

(ii) 'Works of the break' can serve as a catch-all for Althusser's exiguous, heterogeneous output of the 1950s, ranging from the two decidedly anti-Hegelian texts 'On Marxism' (1953) to the splendid short book on *Montesquieu* (1959) – a decade in which Althusser abandons the ideological formation of his youth without explicitly settling accounts with it.

(iii) The mature works of 1960–75 must be sub-divided into two moments:

(a)   the 'rationalist' moment of 1960–6, or the articles and seminar papers assembled in *For Marx* and *Reading 'Capital'*. This moment – of the elaboration of 'structural Marxism' under the auspices of the 'Theory of theoretical practice' – is the one in which for hostile critics Althusser's stance resembles that of the Wilhelmine bureaucracy, whose mind-set could allegedly be summed up thus: that's all very well in *practice*, but does it work in *theory*? Insofar as Althusser came to confess to 'theoreticism' as the mortal sin of these years, he read his work through the eyes of those critics. This catalysed a second moment of the mature works:

(b)   the 'politicist' moment of 1967–75, represented in texts from *Philosophy and the Spontaneous Philosophy of the Scientists* (1967) through to *Essays in Self-Criticism* (1973–5). This moment – of the unavailing auto-critique and rectification of Althusserianism – involves a new definition of philosophy as 'class struggle in theory'. Whatever the revisions of structural Marxism, it pertains to the same period – the mature works – because of the ongoing, unqualified insistence on the *scientificity* of Marxism (indeed, of 'Marxism-Leninism'); and the conviction that it inheres in the non-economistic, non-historicist, non-humanist, and so forth, bases of Marx's own mature works.

(iv)   Around 1976, a new period begins, which is one not of the auto-critique, but of the auto-*deconstruction* – even self-*destruction* – of Althusserianism and the radical problematisation of the scientificity of Marxism itself. It is most dramatically attested to in the 1977 talk 'The Crisis of Marxism' and the 1978 encyclopaedia article 'Marxism Today' – texts whose content overlaps with that of the abandoned manuscript on 'Marx in His Limits'. Writings of *a break*, they can also be regarded as in some sense *transitional* works, paving the way for a final period of Althusserian production.

(v)   The fragmentary late works of the 1980s – soon to be available in English as *Philosophy of the Encounter* – open a new, intentionally reconstructive phase, in which various Althusserian constants are cashed in the non-Marxian and non-Marxist currency of 'aleatory materialism'. Less a radical change of direction than an inflection, the key innovation of this period is a retraction: the non-attribution of Althusser's own constructions to Marx himself – indeed, quite the reverse, their deployment against him and his successors.

In other words, 'aleatory materialism' may be regarded as the continuation by other means of Althusser abiding project from the 1960s onwards: the deconstruction of historical Marxism – or the ideological orthodoxy of Communism – and the reconstruction of historical materialism. And, in its anti-finalist Althusserian rendition, historical materialism was all along (to extend his own category) be a theory of history as a *process without an origin, a subject, a centre, or goal(s)*.

The tentative assessment promised at the outset of this Postscript can take its bearings from the privative character of that formula – process *without* an origin, a subject, and so on – and the negative character of the corresponding polemical slogans: anti-historicism, anti-humanism, anti-essentialism, and so forth. In sum, Althusser's achievement – still substantial enough, in all conscience – was a primarily *negative* one, successively deconstructing historical Marxism in the 1960s and then his own full-scale alternative to it in the 70s, but failing to replace them – whether in the 60s, 70s or 80s – with a positive alternative. Hence, not only do the late writings not represent as radical a departure from *For Marx* and *Reading 'Capital'* as superficial acquaintance might suggest, but they do not mark a genuine advance over them, *a fortiori* since their rational kernel ('materialism of the encounter' for short) – the hub without the hubbub, so to speak – is extractable from the mystical shell ('structuralism' for convenience sake) in those great works.

Therein, to recapitulate, Althusser launched an assault on aspects of the Stalinist legacy in the context of an attack on forms of intentionally *anti-* Stalinist Marxism, deemed incapable of furnishing the requisite theoretical resources with which to sustain a consistent political opposition to Stalinism from the Left and put history back on the tracks of human emancipation from economic exploitation, political oppression and ideological domination. Indeed, Althusser subjected virtually the whole of formerly existing Marxism to swingeing criticism on the grounds that, notwithstanding the obvious differences between its representatives, they all performed variations on Hegelian themes. For what were habitually construed as the mutually antipathetic traditions of orthodox and Western Marxism exhibited the common vice of 'historicism': the 'economism' typical of the Kautskyist Second International and the Stalinist Third International; and the 'humanism' characteristic of recurrent reactions against it (such as Lukács in the 1920s or Schaff in the 1960s). Both these broad tendencies amounted to secularised versions of an Hegelian theodicy, depicting human history as an expressive-normative totality possessed of an origin, a centre, a subject, and a goal.

Economism – a 'poor man's Hegelianism'[198] – constituted a technological determinism, plotting a meta-narrative of the inexorable progression of the

---

[198] Althusser 1971, p. 78.

productive forces in a fixed, linear sequence of modes of production, from primitive communism, via antiquity, feudalism and capitalism, to advanced communism. Its ineluctable advent, in a 'negation of the negation' executed by the proletariat, would mark humanity's leap from the 'kingdom of necessity' to the 'realm of freedom'. In seductive yet deceptive contrast, humanism – a 'rich man's evolutionism'[199] – secreted a teleological philosophical anthropology, projecting an odyssey of the human essence, divided against itself in the forms of class society that culminated in the capitalist present, only to be re-appropriated under the classless community of the communist future. Its realisation by the revolutionary *praxis* of the universal class would consummate humanity's rites of passage, from the condition of alienation to the 'end of history'.

The scandal of the Althusserian anatomy of these seemingly antithetical interpretations of Marxism consisted in his identification of them, and their political correlates ('mechanism' and 'voluntarism'), as mirror-images – not in their diverse inspiration or aspiration, but in their theoretical schematism and historical messianism. This homology, traceable to a common Hegelian ancestry, allowed for a degree of amalgamation of the two (as in Althusser's own early writings). Both the humanist inversion of Hegel, conducted by Feuerbach and adopted by the young Marx, and the economistic inversion of Hegel, perpetrated by the Second International and bequeathed to the Third, preserved an historicist philosophical *structure* even as they re-conjugated its *elements*. Thus, despite the hostility of Cold-War Stalinism to Hegel, inscribed in it, Althusser argued, was an Hegelianisation of Marxism whereby the phenomenal forms of ideology and politics function as the ruses of Economic Reason. Consequently, historical materialism assumed the shape of what Marx had dismissed in 1877 as 'a general historico-philosophical theory, the supreme virtue of which consists in being supra-historical'.[200]

Althusser's objections to any such theoretical 'reductionism' were simultaneously analytical and political. In so far as it abstracted from the constitutive complexity and specificity of historical conjunctures, it was explanatorily impotent before the 'implacable test of the facts' of modern

---

[199] Althusser 1990, p. 56.
[200] Marx and Engels 1975, pp. 293–4.

history,[201] whose revolutionary events (Russia in 1917) and *non*-events (Germany in 1918–19) had obstinately declined to comply with its predictions. It thereby precluded a precondition of rational political practice – a defining characteristic of 'scientific', as opposed to 'utopian', socialism: the 'concrete analysis' indispensable to the real comprehension, and hence potential transformation, of 'concrete situations'.

Geared to a reformation of Communism via a renovation of historical materialism, the veritable intellectual *épuration* launched in a plenum by a self-professed 'political agitator in philosophy' who aspired to be the Luther of the one and the Newton of the other, was obliged to proceed as if it were restoring the authentic tradition. Of more – non-Marxological – moment than its textually tendentious character, however, is the discrepancy between the cogency of Althusser's critiques of classical and post-classical Marxism and the vulnerability of his counter-constructions. This has invariably been explained by his complicity with the 1960s Parisian cult of impersonality, or 'structuralism'. As demonstrated above, however, Althusser was at pains to dissociate himself from the French ideology; and it is primarily to Spinoza that we should look for the key to the originality – and fragility – of Althusserianism in its re-conceptualisation of the dialectic, reconfiguration of the structure of social formations, and re-theorisation of ideology.

Whatever the 'sources' of Althusserianism, its 'component parts' proved on inspection to be flawed in ways that permitted their deconstruction at Althusser's own hands or those of others:

(i)   its 'anti-empiricism', for example, by an unstable compromise between rationalism and conventionalism, seeding perspectivist or realist rejections;

(ii) its 'anti-humanism' by a paradoxically historicist dissolution of human nature and repetition of the structure/agency dichotomy, tilting the theorisation of ideology in a functionalist direction;

(iii) its 'anti-historicism' by its institution of a theory/history antinomy, emphasising social reproduction while rendering social transformation inscrutable;

(iv) and its 'anti-economism' by an elliptical resolution of the base/ superstructure conundrum via the volatile category of 'relative autonomy'.

---

[201] Althusser 1976a, p. 187.

Above all, while Althusser's treatises on the emendation of the Marxist intellect took deadly aim at such articles of faith as the end of history and the end of ideology, or the inevitability, transparency and ultimate harmony of communism, they left others – of science, class, party, and state – substantially intact. Moreover, in pairing Lenin and Mao as the antidote to the young Marx, Stalin and Khrushchev, they erected an imaginary Leninism and Maoism which, when put to the question, did not survive the ordeal of what Trotsky once called 'the merciless laboratory of history'.

The decline in Althusser's public powers after 1968 was, of course, overdetermined by another – case – history. Even so, there is no mistaking his loss of direction amid the series of defeats suffered by the European Left in the 1970s, from Portugal to France, which put the seal on hopes for an alternative to Soviet or Chinese 'real socialism', and led to a general decline in the reputation of Marxism among Western intellectuals. The net effect was to impart to Althusser a highly paradoxical historical significance, such that he may be regarded not only as the focus of the last truly international, impassioned debate in Marxist philosophy, but as one of the leading protagonists in two decisive episodes in postwar French thought. The first was the anti-existentialist and, more broadly, anti-phenomenological turn of the 1960s, concerted under the umbrella term of 'structuralism'. Althusser's distinctiveness within it was to advocate a re-articulation of Marxist philosophy and Communist politics as the basis for answers to the burning questions of the politico-philosophical conjuncture. In so doing, he repudiated the available models of the compliant party ideologue and the independent committed intellectual. As to his answers, Alasdair MacIntyre's aforecited verdict may stand: 'So far as French philosophy was concerned, he de-Stalinised Marxism more thoroughly than any other Marxist did'.[202] Yet, to the extent that he did, but failed to establish a viable substitute, a common deduction was that Althusser had proved the unsustainability of any version of Marxism. Thus it was that the self-declared partisan of a 'return to Marx' became the inadvertent artisan of the turn from Marx associated with 'poststructuralism'. For by virtue of the contradictory complexity of his Marxism, that transfer of allegiances could proceed via an anti-Marxist radicalisation of certain of his theses.

---

[202] MacIntyre 1981, p. 16.

* * *

To conclude: thus to fix Althusser in his limits is to recognise the limitations of the 'imaginary Marxism' with which he sought to supplant the 'Hegelo-Stalinism' he had subscribed to at the beginning of his career; to register its essentially destructive charge, in spirit and substance alike; to record the self-evident failure of its ambition, which subjectively and objectively governed everything else, to renew communist politics; and thereby, just this once giving him the last word, stifle any inclination to tell (ourselves) stories – even (or especially) about Louis Althusser.

References

Abse, Tobias 1985, 'Judging the PCI', *New Left Review*, I, 154: 5–40.

Aglietta, Michel 1979 [1976], *A Theory of Capitalist Regulation: The US Experience*, translated by David Fernbach, London: New Left Books.

Albiac, Gabriel 1998 [1997], 'Althusser, Reader of Althusser: Autobiography as Fictional Genre', translated by Christine Campbell, *Rethinking Marxism*, 10, 3: 80–9.

Althusser, Louis 1963, 'Annexe: monisme et "acte social total"', *La Pensée*, 110: 43–6.

Althusser, Louis 1964a, 'Problèmes étudiants', *La Nouvelle Critique*, 152: 80–111.

Althusser, Louis 1964b, 'Teoria e metodo', *Rinascita*, 25 January: 27–8.

Althusser, Louis 1964c, 'Gli strumenti del marxismo', *Rinascita*, 1 February: 28–9.

Althusser, Louis 1965, *Pour Marx*, Paris: Maspero.

Althusser, Louis 1966a, 'Matérialisme historique et matérialisme dialectique', *Cahiers marxistes-léninistes*, 11: 90–122.

Althusser, Louis 1966b, 'Sur la révolution culturelle', *Cahiers marxistes-léninistes*, 14: 5–16.

Althusser, Louis 1966c, 'Sur la genèse', unpublished letter, 22 September 1966.

Althusser, Louis 1968a, 'La filosofia, la politica e la scienza', *Rinascita*, 15 March: 23.

Althusser, Louis 1968b, 'Lénine et la philosophie', *Bulletin de la Société française de philosophie*, 4: 127–81.

Althusser, Louis 1969a [1965], *For Marx*, translated by Ben Brewster, London: Allen Lane.

Althusser, Louis 1969b, 'A propos de l'article de Michel Verret sur "Mai étudiant"', *La Pensée*, 145: 3–14.

Althusser, Louis 1971, *Lenin and Philosophy & Other Essays*, translated by Ben Brewster, London: New Left Books.

Althusser, Louis 1972, *Politics and History: Montesquieu, Rousseau, Hegel and Marx*, translated by Ben Brewster, London: New Left Books.

Althusser, Louis 1975, 'Les communistes et la philosophie', *L'Humanité*, 5 July.

Althusser, Louis 1976a [1972–5], *Essays in Self-Criticism*, translated by Grahame Lock, London: New Left Books.

Althusser, Louis 1976b, *Positions (1964–1975)*, Paris: Éditions Sociales.

Althusser, Louis 1977a [1974], 'Letter to Régis Debray', 7 March 1967, in Régis Debray, *A Critique of Arms*, translated by Rosemary Sheed, Harmondsworth: Penguin.

Althusser, Louis 1977b [1976], 'Unfinished History', translated by Grahame Lock, in Dominique Lecourt, *Proletarian Science? The Case of Lysenko*, London: New Left Books.

Althusser, Louis 1977c, 'On the Twenty-Second Congress of the French Communist Party', translated by Ben Brewster, *New Left Review*, I, 104: 3–22.

Althusser, Louis 1978a, 'What Must Change in the Party', translated by Patrick Camiller, *New Left Review*, I, 109: 19–45.

Althusser, Louis 1978b, 'Statt eines Vorworts: vier Fragen an Louis Althusser', in *Die Krise des Marxismus*, Hamburg: VSA.

Althusser, Louis 1978c, *Ce qui ne peut plus durer dans le Parti communiste*, Paris: Maspero.

Althusser, Louis 1978d, 'Entretien', *Dialectiques*, 23: 5–12.

Althusser, Louis 1978e, 'Al "punto zero" della teoria', *Paese Sera*, 6 May.

Althusser, Louis 1978f, 'Je ne veux pas être un martyr', *Les Nouvelles Littéraires*, 15 June.

Althusser, Louis 1979a, Letter to Perry Anderson, 28 March 1979, unpublished.
Althusser, Louis 1979b [1977], 'The Crisis of Marxism', translated by Grahame Lock, in *Power and Opposition in Post-Revolutionary Societies*, edited by *Il Manifesto*, London: Ink Links.
Althusser, Louis 1983 [1977], 'Note on the ISAs', translated by Jeremy Leaman, *Economy and Society*, 12, 4: 455–65.
Althusser, Louis 1990, *Philosophy and the Spontaneous Philosophy of Scientists and Other Essays*, edited by Gregory Elliott and translated by Ben Brewster et al., London: Verso.
Althusser, Louis 1992, *Journal de captivité: Stalag XA – 1940–1945*, edited by Olivier Corpet and Yann Moulier Boutang, Paris: Stock/IMEC.
Althusser, Louis 1993 [1992], *The Future Lasts a Long Time and The Facts*, translated by Richard Veasey, London: Chatto & Windus.
Althusser, Louis 1994a, *Écrits philosophiques et politiques I*, edited by François Matheron, Paris: Stock/IMEC.
Althusser, Louis 1994b, *Sur la philosophie*, edited by Olivier Corpet, Paris: Gallimard.
Althusser, Louis 1994c [1992], *L'avenir dure longtemps, suivi de Les Faits*, edited by Olivier Corpet and Yann Moulier Boutang, Paris: Le Livre de Poche.
Althusser, Louis 1995a, *Sur la reproduction*, Paris: Presses Universitaires de France.
Althusser, Louis 1995b, *Écrits philosophiques et politiques II*, edited by François Matheron, Paris: Stock/IMEC.
Althusser, Louis 1996a [1993], *Writings on Psychoanalysis: Freud and Lacan*, edited by Olivier Corpet and François Matheron and translated by Jeffrey Mehlman, New York: Columbia University Press.
Althusser, Louis 1996b, *Psychanalyse et sciences humaines. Deux conférences [1963–1964]*, edited by Oliver Corpet and François Matheron, Paris: Le Livre de Poche.
Althusser, Louis 1997, *The Spectre of Hegel: Early Writings*, edited by François Matheron and translated by G.M. Goshgarian, London: Verso.
Althusser, Louis 1998a, *Solitude de Machiavel et autres textes*, edited by Yves Sintomer, Paris: Presses Universitaires de France.
Althusser, Louis 1998b [1964], Presentation of Pierre Macherey, 'George Canguilhem's Philosophy of Science', in Pierre Macherey, *In a Materialist Way: Selected Essays*, edited by Warren Montag and translated by Ted Stolze, London: Verso.
Althusser, Louis 1998c, *Lettres à Franca (1961–1973)*, Paris: Stock/IMEC.
Althusser, Louis 1999 [1995], *Machiavelli and Us*, edited by François Matheron and translated by Gregory Elliott, London: Verso.
Althusser, Louis 2003, *The Humanist Controversy and Other Writings*, edited by François Matheron and translated by G.M. Goshgarian, London: Verso.
Althusser, Louis 2006, *Philosophy of the Encounter: Late Writings*, edited by François Matheron and translated by G.M. Goshgarian, London: Verso.
Althusser, Louis and Étienne Balibar 1970 [1965], *Reading 'Capital'*, translated by Ben Brewster, London: New Left Books.
Althusser, Louis and Luiz Francesco Rebello 1976, *Cartas sobre a Revolução Portuguesa*, Lisbon: Seara Nova.
Althusser, Louis et al. 1965, *Lire 'le Capital'*, two vols, Paris: Maspero.
Althusser, Louis et al. 1978, Letter to *Le Monde*, 6 April.
Althusser, Louis et al. 1996 [1965], *Lire 'le Capital'*, edited by Étienne Balibar et al., Paris: Presses Universitaires de France.
Anderson, Perry 1965, 'Problems of Socialist Strategy', in *Towards Socialism*, edited by Perry Anderson and Robin Blackburn, London: Fontana.
Anderson, Perry 1974a, *Passages from Antiquity to Feudalism*, London: New Left Books.
Anderson, Perry 1974b, *Lineages of the Absolutist State*, London: New Left Books.
Anderson, Perry 1976, *Considerations on Western Marxism*, London: New Left Books.
Anderson, Perry 1977, 'The Antinomies of Antonio Gramsci', *New Left Review*, I, 100: 5–78.
Anderson, Perry 1979a, Letter to Louis Althusser, 27 January 1979, unpublished.
Anderson, Perry 1979b, Letter to Louis Althusser, 3 February 1979, unpublished.

Anderson, Perry 1980, *Arguments within English Marxism*, London: New Left Books.
Anderson, Perry 1983, *In the Tracks of Historical Materialism*, London: New Left Books.
Anderson, Perry 1992, *A Zone of Engagement*, London: Verso.
Anonymous 1968, 'Themes', *New Left Review*, I, 52: 1–8.
Anonymous 1975, 'Dr. Althusser', *Radical Philosophy*, 12: 44.
Aron, Raymond 1969, *D'une sainte famille à l'autre. Essai sur les marxismes imaginaires*, Paris: Gallimard.
Aron, Raymond 1983, *Mémoires*, Paris: Julliard.
Avenas, Denise et al. 1999, *Contre Althusser, pour Marx*, Paris: Éditions de la Passion.
Bachelard, Gaston 1951, *L'activité rationaliste de la physique contemporaine*, Paris: Presses Universitaires de France.
Bachelard, Gaston 1964 [1938], *The Psychoanalysis of Fire*, translated by Alan C. M. Ross, Boston: Beacon Press.
Bachelard, Gaston 1975 [1940], *La Philosophie du non*, Paris: Presses Universitaires de France.
Bachelard, Gaston 1980 [1938], *La Formation de l'esprit scientifique*, Paris: J. Vrin.
Baby, Jean 1960, *Critique de base. Le Parti communiste français entre le passé et l'avenir*, Paris: Maspero.
Baby, Jean 1966, *Le grande controverse sino-soviétique (1956–1966)*, Paris: Grasset.
Badiou, Alain 1967, 'Le (re)commencement du matérialisme dialectique', *Critique*, 240: 438–67.
Balibar, Étienne 1965, 'Sur les concepts fondamentaux du matérialisme historique', in Althusser et al. 1965.
Balibar, Étienne 1966, 'Marxisme et linguistique', *Cahiers marxistes-léninistes*, 12/13: 19–25.
Balibar, Étienne 1970 [1965], 'On the Basic Concepts of Historical Materialism', in Althusser and Balibar 1970.
Balibar, Étienne 1973, 'Self-Criticism: An Answer to Questions from *Theoretical Practice*', *Theoretical Practice*, 7/8: 56–72.
Balibar, Étienne 1974, *Cinq études du matérialisme historique*, Paris: Maspero.
Balibar, Étienne 1977 [1976], *On the Dictatorship of the Proletariat*, translated by Grahame Lock, London: New Left Books.
Balibar, Étienne 1991, *Écrits pour Althusser*, Paris: La Découverte.
Balibar, Étienne 1996, 'Avant-Propos', in Althusser et al. 1996.
Balibar, Étienne 1998 [1985], *Spinoza and Politics*, translated by Peter Snowdon, London: Verso.
Balibar, Étienne and Pierre Macherey 1981 [1974], 'On Literature as an Ideological Form', in *Untying the Text*, edited by Robert Young, London: Routledge & Kegan Paul.
Balibar, Étienne and Pierre Macherey 1982, 'Interview', *Diacritics*, 12: 46–52.
Balibar, Étienne et al. 1979, *Ouvrons la fenêtre, camarades!*, Paris: Maspero.
Balibar, Renée 1974, *Les Français fictifs*, Paris: Hachette.
Balibar, Renée and Dominique Laporte 1974, *Le Français national*, Paris: Hachette.
Barrett, Michèle 1980, *Women's Oppression Today*, London: Verso.
Barthes, Roland 1978 [1964], *Elements of Semiology*, translated by Annette Lavers and Colin Smith, New York: Hill and Wang.
Baudelot, Christian and Roger Establet 1971, *L'école capitaliste en France*, Paris: Maspero.
Baudelot, Christian, Roger Establet, and Jacques Malemort 1974, *La petite bourgeoisie en France*, Paris: Maspero.
Baudelot, Christian, Roger Establet, and Jacques Toiser 1979, *Qui travaille pour qui?*, Paris: Maspero.
Beauvoir, Simone de 1972 [1949], *The Second Sex*, translated by H.M. Parshley, Harmondsworth: Penguin.
Beauvoir, Simone de 1984 [1981], *Adieu – A Farewell to Sartre*, translated by Patrick O'Brian, London: André Deutsch and Weidenfeld and Nicholson.
Bensaïd, Daniel 1999, '"Un univers de pensée aboli"', in Avenas et al. 1999.
Benton, Ted 1977, *Philosophical Foundations of the Three Sociologies*, London: Routledge & Kegan Paul.

Benton, Ted 1984, *The Rise and Fall of Structural Marxism*, Basingstoke: Macmillan.
Besse, Guy 1963, 'Deux questions sur un article de Louis Althusser', *La Pensée*, 107: 52–62.
Bettelheim, Charles 1975 [1968], *The Transition to Socialist Economy*, translated by Brian Pearce, Brighton: Harvester Press.
Bettelheim, Charles 1976 [1974], *Class Struggles in the USSR – First Period: 1917–1923*, translated by Brian Pearce, Hassocks: Harvester Press.
Bettelheim, Charles 1978 [1977], *Class Struggles in the USSR – Second Period: 1923–1930*, translated by Brian Pearce, Hassocks: Harvester Press.
Bettelheim, Charles 1978, 'The Great Leap Backward', in Neil G. Burton and Charles Bettelheim, *China since Mao*, New York and London: Monthly Review Press.
Bhaskar, Roy 1978 [1975], *A Realist Theory of Science*, Brighton: Harvester Press.
Bhaskar, Roy 1986, *Scientific Realism and Human Emancipation*, London: Verso.
Bloch, Maurice 1983, *Marxism and Anthropology*, Oxford: Oxford University Press.
Boguslavsky, B.M. et al. 1976, *ABC of Dialectical and Historical Materialism*, Moscow: Progress Publishers.
Bois, Guy 1984 [1976], *The Crisis of Feudalism: Economy and Society in Eastern Normandy c. 1300–1550*, Cambridge and Paris: Cambridge University Press/Éditions de la Maison des Sciences de l'Homme.
Buci-Glucksmann, Christine 1976, 'Sur la critique de gauche du stalinisme', *Dialectiques*, 15/16: 25–36.
Bukharin, N.I. 1969 [1921], *Historical Materialism: A System of Sociology*, Ann Arbor: University of Michigan Press.
Burbridge, J. 1980, 'The Necessity of Contingency: An Analysis of Hegel's Chapter on Actuality in the *Science of Logic*', in *Art and Logic in Hegel's Philosophy*, edited by W.E. Steinkrauss and K.L. Schmitz, Atlantic Highlands: Humanities Press.
Cahiers du communisme 1966, 5–6, 'Débats sur les problèmes idéologiques et culturels'.
Cahiers marxistes-léninistes 1967, 15.
Callari, Antonio and David Ruccio (eds.) 1996, *Postmodern Materialism and the Future of Marxist Theory: Essays in the Althusserian Tradition*, Hanover: Wesleyan University Press.
Callinicos, Alex 1976, *Althusser's Marxism*, London: Pluto Press.
Callinicos, Alex 1982, *Is There a Future for Marxism?*, Basingstoke: Macmillan.
Callinicos, Alex 1983, *Marxism and Philosophy*, Oxford: Oxford University Press.
Callinicos, Alex 1995, 'Lost Illusions', *Radical Philosophy*, 74: 42–4.
Calvez, Jean-Yves 1956, *La Pensée de Karl Marx*, Paris: Éditions du Seuil.
Canguilhem, Georges 1979 [1968], *Études d'histoire et de philosophie des sciences*, Paris: J. Vrin.
Canguilhem, Georges 1981 [1977], *Idéologie et rationalité dans l'histoire des sciences de la vie*, Paris: J. Vrin.
Carr, E.H. 1982, *Twilight of the Comintern, 1930–1935*, New York: Pantheon.
Carrillo, Santiago 1977, *'Eurocommunism' and the State*, translated by Nan Green and A.M. Elliott, London: Lawrence and Wishart.
Casanova, Laurent 1949, *Le Parti communiste, les intellectuels et la nation*, Paris: Éditions Sociales.
Castells, Manuel 1977 [1972], *The Urban Question: A Marxist Approach*, translated by Alan Sheridan, London: Edward Arnold.
Caute, David 1964, *Communism and the French Intellectuals, 1914–60*, London: André Deutsch.
Cavaillès, Jean 1960 [1947], *Sur la logique et la théorie de la science*, Paris: J. Vrin.
Clarke, John, Chas Critcher, and Richard Johnson (eds.) 1978, *Working-Class Culture*, London: Hutchinson.
Clarke, Simon 1980, 'Althusserian Marxism', in Clarke et al., *One Dimensional Marxism*, London: Alison & Busby.
Claudin, Fernando 1975 [1970], *The Communist Movement – From Comintern to Cominform*, translated by Brian Pearce and Francis MacDonagh, two vols, New York: Monthly Review Press.

Claudin, Fernando 1978 [1977], *Eurocommunism and Socialism*, translated by John Wakeham, London: New Left Books.

Cohen, G.A. 1978, *Karl Marx's Theory of History: A Defence*, Oxford: Clarendon Press.

Cohen-Solal, Annie 1985, *Sartre*, Paris: Gallimard.

Colletti, Lucio 1977 [1974], 'A Political and Philosophical Interview', in *New Left Review* (ed.) 1977.

Colletti, Lucio 1984 [1980], *Le Déclin du marxisme*, Paris: Presses Universitaires de France.

Collier, Andrew 1979, 'In Defence of Epistemology', in *Issues in Marxist Philosophy*, Volume 3, edited by J. Mepham and D.H. Ruben, Brighton: Harvester Press.

Collier, Andrew 1988, *Scientific Realism and Socialist Thought*, Brighton: Harvester Press.

Communist Party of China 1960, *Long Live Leninism*, Peking: Foreign Languages Press.

Communist Party of China 1963, 'Whence the Differences? – A Reply to Thorez and Other Comrades', in *Whence the Differences?*, Peking: Foreign Languages Press.

Communist Party of China 1965, *The Polemic on the General Line of the International Communist Movement*, Peking: Foreign Languages Press.

Communist Party of China 1966, 'Decision of the Chinese Communist Party Concerning the Great Proletarian Cultural Revolution', in *The Great Proletarian Cultural Revolution*, Peking: Foreign Languages Press.

Communist Party of China 1981, *Resolution on CPC History (1949–81)*, Peking: Foreign Languages Press.

Communist Party of the Soviet Union 1939, *History of the Communist Party of the Soviet Union (Bolsheviks)*, Moscow: Foreign Languages Publishing House.

Communist Party of the Soviet Union 1961, *The Road to Communism: Documents of the 22nd Congress of the Communist Party of the Soviet Union*, Moscow: Foreign Languages Publishing House.

Contat, Michel 1992, 'Review of *L'avenir dure longtemps*', *Le Mondes des livres*, 24 April.

Cornu, Auguste 1955–70, *Karl Marx et Friedrich Engels. Leur vie et leur oeuvre*, four vols., Paris: Presses Universitaires de France.

Cotten, Jean-Pierre 1979, *La Pensée de Louis Althusser*, Toulouse: Privat.

Cutler, Anthony et al. 1977–8, *Marx's 'Capital' and Capitalism Today*, two vols., London: Routledge & Kegan Paul.

Davis, Mike 1986, *Prisoners of the American Dream: Politics and Economy in the History of the US Working Class*, London: Verso.

Debray, Régis 1970, *Strategy for Revolution*, edited by Robin Blackburn, London: Jonathan Cape.

Debray, Régis 1973, *Prison Writings*, translated by Rosemary Sheed, London: Allen Lane.

Debray, Régis 1975, *Les Rendez-vous manqués*, Paris: Éditions du Seuil.

Debray, Régis 1978a, *Lettre ouverte aux communistes français et à quelques autres*, Paris: Éditions du Seuil.

Debray, Régis 1978b, *Modeste contribution aux discours et cérémonies officielles du dixième anniversaire*, Paris: Maspero.

Debray, Régis 1983 [1981], *Critique of Political Reason*, translated by David Macey, London: Verso.

Della Volpe, Galvano 1980 [1950], *Logic as a Positive Science*, translated by Jon Rothschild, London: New Left Books.

Derrida, Jacques 1994 [1993], *Specters of Marx: The State of the Debt, the Work of Mourning, and the New International*, translated by Peggy Kamuf, London: Routledge.

Desanti, Dominique 1985 [1975], *Les Staliniens. Une expérience politique, 1944–1956*, Paris: Marabout.

Descombes, Vincent 1980, *Modern French Philosophy*, translated by L. Scott-Fox and J.M. Harding, Cambridge: Cambridge University Press.

Deutscher, Isaac 1970, *Russia, China, and the West: A Contemporary Chronicle, 1953–1966*, edited by Fred Halliday, London: Oxford University Press.

Deutscher, Isaac 1982 [1949], *Stalin: A Political Biography*, Harmondsworth: Penguin.

Dews, Peter 1979, 'The "Nouvelle Philosophie" and Foucault', *Economy and Society*, 8, 2: 121–71.

Dews, Peter 1985 [1980], 'The "New Philosophers" and the End of Leftism', in *Radical Philosophy Reader*, edited by R. Edgley and R. Osborne, London: Verso.

Dews, Peter 1987, *Logics of Disintegration – Post-Structuralist Thought and the Claims of Critical Theory*, London: Verso.

Dews, Peter 1994, 'Althusser, Structuralism and the French Epistemological Tradition', in Elliott (ed.) 1994.

Dollé, Jean-Paul 1966, 'Du gauchisme à "l'humanisme socialiste"', *Les Temps Modernes*, 239: 1890–917.

Eagleton, Terry 1976, *Criticism and Ideology: A Study in Marxist Literary Theory*, London: New Left Books.

Eagleton, Terry 1986, *Against the Grain: Essays 1975–1985*, London: Verso.

Edelman, Bernard 1979 [1973], *Ownership of the Image: Elements for a Marxist Theory of Law*, translated by Elizabeth Kingdom, London: Routledge & Kegan Paul.

Elliott, Gregory (ed.) 1994, *Althusser: A Critical Reader*, Oxford: Blackwell.

Engels, Frederick 1976 [1925], *Dialectics of Nature*, translated by Clemens Dutt, Moscow: Progress Publishers.

Engels, Frederick 1977 [1878], *Anti-Dühring: Herr Eugen Dühring's Revolution in Science*, translated by Emile Burns, Moscow: Progress Publishers.

Elster, Jon 1985, *Making Sense of Marx*, Cambridge: Cambridge University Press.

Elster, Jon 1986, *An Introduction to Karl Marx*, Cambridge: Cambridge University Press.

Erjin, Chen 1984, *China: Crossroads Socialism*, translated by Robin Munro, London: Verso.

Establet, Roger 1965, 'Présentation du plan du *Capital*', in Althusser et al. 1965.

Feather, Howard 1986, 'Reconstructing Structural Marxism', *Radical Philosophy*, 43: 32–6.

Ferry, Luc and Renaut, Alain 1985, *La Pensée 68. Essai sur l'anti-humanisme contemporaine*, Paris: Gallimard.

Feuerbach, Ludwig 1960, *Manifestes philosophiques. Textes choisis (1839–1845)*, edited and translated by Louis Althusser, Paris: Presses Universitaires de France.

Fichant, Michel and Michel Pêcheux 1969, *Sur l'histoire des sciences*, Paris: Maspero.

Foucault, Michel 1971, *L'ordre du discours*, Paris: Gallimard.

Foucault, Michel 1974 [1969], *The Archaeology of Knowledge*, translated by A.M. Sheridan Smith, London: Tavistock.

Foucault, Michel 1977 [1966], *The Order of Things*, London: Tavistock.

Foucault, Michel 1980, *Power/Knowledge – Selected Interviews and Other Writings 1972–1977*, edited by Colin Gordon, Brighton: Harvester Press.

Fougeyrollas, Pierre 1976, *Contre Lévi-Strauss, Lacan et Althusser. Trois essais sur l'obscurantisme contemporaine*, Paris: Éditions de la Jouquère.

Fox, Edward 1992, 'A Marxist Murderer', *Independent Magazine*, 11 July 1992.

Futur antérieur 1993, *Passages. Sur Althusser*.

Fromm, Erich (ed.) 1967 [1965], *Socialist Humanism: An International Symposium*, London: Allen Lane.

Gadet, Françoise 1989 [1986], *Saussure and Contemporary Culture*, translated by Gregory Elliott, London: Hutchinson Radius.

Gadet, Françoise and Michel Pêcheux 1981, *La Langue introuvable*, Paris: Maspero.

Gadet, Françoise et al. 1979, *Les Maîtres de la langue*, Paris: Maspero.

Gane, Michael 1983, 'On the ISAs Episode', *Economy and Society*, 12, 4: 431–55.

Garaudy, Roger 1962, 'Rapport', *Cahiers du communisme*, 7–8: 75–106.

Garaudy, Roger 1963, 'À propos des "Manuscrits de 1844" de Marx et quelques essais philosophiques', *Cahiers du communisme*, 3: 107–26.

Garaudy, Roger 1969 [1959], *Perspectives de l'homme*, Paris: Presses Universitaires de France.

Garaudy, Roger 1970 [1966], *Marxism in the Twentieth Century*, translated by René Hague, London: Collins.

Gavi, Philippe, Jean-Paul Sartre, and Pierre Victor 1974, *On a raison de se révolter*, Paris: Gallimard.

Gayman, Jean-Marc 1979, 'Lutte de classes et guerre des langues en URSS', in Gadet et al. 1979.

Geerlandt, Robert 1978, *Garaudy et Althusser. Le débat sur l'humanisme dans le Parti communiste français et son enjeu*, Paris: Presses Universitaires de France.

Geras, Norman 1983, *Marx and Human Nature – Refutation of a Legend*, London: Verso.

Geras, Norman 1986a [1972], 'Althusser's Marxism: An Account and Assessment', in *Literature of Revolution*, London: Verso.

Geras, Norman 1986b [1983], 'Louis Althusser', in *Literature of Revolution*, London: Verso.

Gerratana, Valentino 1977, 'Althusser and Stalinism', *New Left Review*, I, 101/102: 110–21.

Glucksmann, André 1968, 'Strategy and Revolution in France in 1968', *New Left Review*, I, 52: 67–121.

Glucksmann, André 1977 [1967], 'A Ventriloquist Structuralism', in *New Left Review* (ed.) 1977.

Glucksmann, André 1981 [1977], *The Master Thinkers*, translated by Brian Pearce, Brighton: Harvester Press.

Godelier, Maurice 1972 [1966], *Rationality and Irrationality in Economics*, translated by Brian Pearce, London: New Left Books.

Goldmann, Lucien 1969 [1952], *The Human Sciences and Philosophy*, translated by Hayden V. White and Robert Anchor, London: Jonathan Cape.

Goldmann, Lucien 1970, *Marxisme et sciences humaines*, Paris: Gallimard.

Goshgarian, G.M. 2003, 'Introduction' to Althusser 2003.

Goshgarian, G.M. 2006, 'Introduction' to Althusser 2006.

Gramsci, Antonio 1971 [1948–51], *Selections from the Prison Notebooks*, edited and translated by Quintin Hoare and Geoffrey Nowell Smith, London: Lawrence and Wishart.

Gramsci, Antonio 1977, *Selections from the Political Writings (1910–1920)*, edited by Quintin Hoare and translated by John Mathews, London: Lawrence and Wishart.

Habermas, Jürgen 1985, 'A Philosophico-Political Profile', *New Left Review*, I, 151: 75–105.

Hall, Stuart 1981, 'In Defence of Theory', in *People's History and Socialist Theory*, edited by Raphael Samuel, London: Routledge & Kegan Paul.

Hall, Stuart et al. 1978, *Policing the Crisis: Mugging, the State, and Law and Order*, Basingstoke: Macmillan.

Halliday, Fred 1977, 'Marxist Analysis and Post-Revolutionary China', *New Left Review*, I, 100: 165–92.

Halliday, Fred 1983, *The Making of the Second Cold War*, London: Verso.

Heath, Stephen 1972, *The Nouveau Roman: A Study in the Practice of Writing*, London: Elek.

Heath, Stephen 1981, *Questions of Cinema*, Basingstoke: Macmillan.

Hegel, G.W.F. 1956, *The Philosophy of History*, translated by J. Sibree, New York: Dover.

Henry, Paul 1977, *Le mauvais outil. Langue, sujet et discours*, Paris: Klincksieck.

Hilton, Rodney 1984, 'Feudalism in Europe: Problems for Historical Materialists', *New Left Review*, I, 147: 84–93.

Hindess, Barry and Paul Q. Hirst 1975, *Pre-Capitalist Modes of Production*, London: Routledge & Kegan Paul.

Hindess, Barry and Paul Hirst 1977, *Mode of Production and Social Formation: An Auto-Critique of 'Pre-Capitalist Modes of Production'*, Basingstoke: Macmillan.

Hirsh, Arthur 1982, *The French New Left*, Montreal: Black Rose Books.

Hirst, Paul 1979, *On Law and Ideology*, Basingstoke: Macmillan.

Hirst, Paul Q. 1985, *Marxism and Historical Writing*, London: Routledge & Kegan Paul.

Hobsbawm, Eric J. 1982 [1973], *Revolutionaries: Contemporary Essays*, London: Quartet.

Hyppolite, Jean 1971 [1968], 'Le "scientifique" et l'"idéologique" dans une perspective marxiste', in *Figures de la pensée philosophique I*, Paris: Presses Universitaires de France.

James, Susan 1984, 'The Pope of Theory', *The Listener*, 17 May.

Jameson, Fredric 1974, *Marxism and Form: Twentieth-Century Dialectical Theories of Literature*, Princeton: Princeton University Press.

Jameson, Fredric 1977, 'Imaginary and Symbolic in Lacan: Marxism, Psychoanalytic Criticism and the Problem of the Subject', *Yale French Studies*, 55/56: 338–95.

Jameson, Fredric 1981, *The Political Unconscious: Narrative as a Socially Symbolic Act*, London: Methuen.

Jay, Martin 1984, *Marxism and Totality: The Adventures of a Concept from Lukács to Habermas*, Cambridge: Polity Press.

Jessop, Bob 1982, *The Capitalist State: Marxist Theories and Methods*, Oxford: Martin Robertson.

Jessop, Bob 1985, *Nicos Poulantzas: Marxist Theory and Political Strategy*, Basingstoke: Macmillan.

Johnson, Douglas 1981, 'Althusser's Fate', *London Review of Books*, 16 April–6 May: 13–15.

Johnson, Richard 1981, 'Against Absolutism', in Samuel (ed.) 1981.

Kaplan, E. Ann and Michael Sprinker (eds.) 1993, *The Althusserian Legacy*, London: Verso.

Karol, K.S. 1980, 'The Tragedy of the Althussers', *New Left Review*, I, 124: 93–5.

Karsz, Saül 1974, *Théorie et politique: Louis Althusser*, Paris: Fayard.

Kedward, H.R. 1969, *Fascism in Western Europe 1900–45*, London and Glasgow: Blackie.

Kelly, Michael 1982, *Modern French Marxism*, Oxford: Basil Blackwell.

Kessel, Patrick 1972, *Le Mouvement 'maoiste' en France 1*, Paris: Union Générale d'Éditions.

Khrushchev, Nikita S. 1984 [1956], 'Secret Report to the 20ᵗʰ Party Congress of the CPSU', in *The Stalinist Legacy: Its Impact on 20ᵗʰ-Century World Politics*, edited by Tariq Ali, Harmondsworth: Penguin.

Korsch, Karl 1970 [1923], *Marxism and Philosophy*, translated by Fred Halliday, New York: Monthly Review Press.

Labica, Georges 1980 [1976], *Marxism and the Status of Philosophy*, translated by Kate Soper and Martin Ryle, Brighton: Harvester Press.

Labica, Georges 1984, *Le Marxisme-Léninisme (éléments pour une critique)*, Paris: Bruno Huisman.

Labica, Georges and Gérard Bensussan (eds.) 1985 [1982], *Dictionnaire critique du marxisme*, Paris: Presses Universitaires de France.

Lacan, Jacques 1982 [1966], *Écrits: A Selection*, translated by Alan Sheridan, London: Tavistock.

Laclau, Ernesto 1977, *Politics and Ideology in Marxist Theory: Capitalism – Fascism – Populism*, London: New Left Books.

Laclau, Ernesto and Mouffe, Chantal 1985, *Hegemony and Socialist Strategy: Towards a Radical Democratic Politics*, London: Verso.

Lahtinen, Mikko forthcoming, *Niccolò Machiavelli and Aleatory Matearialism. Louis Althusser and the Machiavellian Conjuncture*, HM Book Series, Leiden: Brill Academic Press.

Lakatos, Imre 1978, *The Methodology of Scientific Research Programmes*, Cambridge: Cambridge University Press.

Lazarus, Sylvain (ed.) 1993, *Politique et philosophie dans l'oeuvre de Louis Althusser*, Paris: Presses Universitaires de France.

Lecourt, Dominique 1973, *Une Crise et son enjeu. Essai sur la position de Lénine en philosophie*, Paris: Maspero.

Lecourt, Dominique 1974, *Bachelard, ou le jour et la nuit*, Paris: Grasset.

Lecourt, Dominique 1975 [1969–72], *Marxism and Epistemology: Bachelard, Canguilhem, Foucault*, translated by Ben Brewster, London: New Left Books.

Lecourt, Dominique 1977 [1976], *Proletarian Science? The Case of Lysenko*, translated by Ben Brewster, London: New Left Books.

Lecourt, Dominique 1982, *La Philosophie sans feinte*, Paris: Hallier / Albin Michel.

Lecourt, Dominique 2001 [1978–99] *The Mediocracy: French Philosophy since the Mid–1970s*, translated by Gregory Elliott, London: Verso.

Lefebvre, Henri 1970 [1940], *Dialectical Materialism*, translated by John Sturrock, London: Jonathan Cape.

Lefebvre, Henri 1975 [1971], *L'idéologie structuraliste*, Paris: Éditions du Seuil.

Lenin, V.I. 1960 [1899], 'Our Programme', in *Collected Works*, Volume 4, Moscow: Progress Publishers.

Lenin, V.I. 1961a [1902], 'What Is to Be Done?', in *Collected Works*, Volume 5, Moscow: Progress Publishers.
Lenin, V.I. 1961b [1929], 'Philosophical Notebooks', in *Collected Works*, Volume 38, Moscow: Progress Publishers.
Lenin, V.I. 1963 [1894], 'What the "Friends of the People" Are and How They Fight the Social-Democrats', in *Collected Works*, Volume 1, Moscow: Progress Publishers.
Lenin, V.I. 1964, *Collected Works*, Volume 24, Moscow: Progress Publishers.
Lenin, V.I. 1965 [1919], 'Economic and Politics in the Era of the Dictatorship of the Proletariat', in *Collected Works*, Volume 30, Moscow: Progress Publishers.
Lenin, V.I. 1966a, *Collected Works*, Volume 31, Moscow: Progress Publishers.
Lenin, V.I. 1966b, *Collected Works*, Volume 33, Moscow: Progress Publishers.
Lenin, V.I., 1968 [1913], 'The Three Sources and Three Component Parts of Marxism', in *Collected Works*, Volume 19, Moscow: Progress Publishers.
Le Roy Ladurie, Emmanuel 1982, *Paris – Montpellier. P.C. – P.S.U., 1945–1963*, Paris: Gallimard.
Levine, Andrew 1981, 'Althusser's Marxism', *Economy and Society*, 10, 3: 243–83.
Levine, Andrew 1984, *Arguing for Socialism – Theoretical Considerations*, London: Routledge & Kegan Paul.
Levine, Andrew 1987, *The End of the State*, London: Verso.
Levine, Andrew 2003, *A Future for Marxism? Althusser, the Analytical Turn and the Revival of Socialist Theory*, London: Pluto Press.
Levine, Andrew, Elliott, Sober, and Erik Olin Wright, 1987, 'Marxism and Methodological Individualism', *New Left Review*, I, 162: 67–84.
Lévi-Strauss, Claude 1977 [1958], *Structural Anthropology*, translated by Claire Jacobson and Brooke Grundfest Schoepf, Harmondsworth: Penguin.
Lévi-Strauss, Claude 1981 [1962], *The Savage Mind*, London: Weidenfeld and Nicolson.
Lévi-Strauss, Claude 1986 [1964], *The Raw and the Cooked*, translated by John and Doreen Weightman, Harmondsworth: Penguin.
Lévy, Bernard-Henri 1977, *La Barbarie à visage humain*, Paris: Grasset.
Lewin, Moshe 1975 [1968], *Lenin's Last Struggle*, translated by A.M. Sheridan-Smith, London: Pluto Press.
Lezra, Jacques (ed.) 1995, *Depositions: Althusser, Balibar, Macherey, and the Labor of Reading*, Yale French Studies, 88, New Haven: Yale University Press.
Lindenberg, Daniel 1975, *Le Marxisme introuvable*, Paris: Calmann-Lévy.
Linhart, Robert 1966, 'La NEP: analyse de quelques caractéristiques de la phase de transition soviétique', *Études de planification socialiste*, 3: 156–97.
Linhart, Robert 1976, *Lénine, les paysans, Taylor. Essai d'analyse matérialiste historique de la naissance du système productif soviétique*, Paris: Éditions du Seuil.
Linhart, Robert 1979 [1978], 'Western "Dissidence" Ideology and the Protection of Bourgeois Order', in *Power and Opposition in Post-Revolutionary Societies*, edited by Il Manifesto, London: Ink Links.
Lin Piao 1965, *Long Live the Victory of People's War*, Peking: Foreign Languages Press.
Lipietz, Alain 1985 [1983], *The Enchanted World: Inflation, Credit and the World Crisis*, translated by Ian Patterson, London: Verso.
Lipietz, Alain 1987 [1985], *Miracles and Mirages: The Crises of Global Fordism*, translated by David Macey, London: Verso.
Lisbonne, Bernard 1981 [1978], *Philosophie marxiste ou philosophie althussérienne*, Paris: Anthropos.
Lock, Grahame 1981, *The State and I: Hypotheses on Juridical and Technocratic Humanism*, The Hague: Leiden University Press.
Lock, Grahame 1988 [1981], 'Louis Althusser and G.A. Cohen: A Confrontation', *Economy and Society*, 17, 4: 499–517.
Lovell, Terry 1980, *Pictures of Reality: Aesthetics, Politics and Pleasure*, London: BFI.
Löwy, Michael 1973, *Dialectique et révolution. Essais de sociologie et d'histoire du marxisme*, Paris: Anthropos.
Löwy, Michael 1984, 'Stalinist Ideology and Science', in *The Stalinist Legacy*, edited by Tariq Ali, Harmondsworth: Penguin.

Lukács, Georg 1971 [1923], *History and Class Consciousness: Studies in Marxist Dialectics*, translated by Rodney Livingstone, London: Merlin Press.

Lukács, Georg 1972, *Political Writings, 1919–1929 – The Question of Parliamentarism and Other Essays*, edited by Rodney Livingstone and translated by Michael McColgan, London: New Left Books.

MacCabe, Colin 1978, *James Joyce and the Revolution of the Word*, Basingstoke: Macmillan.

MacCabe, Colin 1985, *Theoretical Essays: Film, Linguistics, Literature*, Manchester: Manchester University Press.

McCarney, Joseph 1989, 'For and Against Althusser', *New Left Review*, I, 176: 85–98.

MacIntyre, Alasdair 1981, 'Strangers', *London Review of Books*, 16 April – 6 May: 15–16.

Macciocchi, Maria Antonietta 1973a [1971], *Daily Life in Revolutionary China*, translated by Kathy Brown et al., New York: Monthly Review Press.

Macciocchi, Maria-Antonietta 1973b [1969], *Letters from inside the Italian Communist Party to Louis Althusser*, translated by Stephen M. Hellman, London: New Left Books.

Macciocchi, Maria-Antonietta 1983, *Deux mille ans de bonheur*, Paris: Grasset.

Macey, David 1994, 'The Lonely Hour of the Final Analysis', *Radical Philosophy*, 67: 45–7.

Macherey, Pierre 1965, 'A propos du processus d'exposition du "Capital"', in Althusser et al. 1965.

Macherey, Pierre 1976, 'L'histoire de la philosophie considerée comme une lutte de tendances', *La Pensée*, 185: 3–25.

Macherey, Pierre 1978 [1966], *A Theory of Literary Production*, translated by Geoffrey Wall, London: Routledge & Kegan Paul.

Macherey, Pierre 1979, *Hegel ou Spinoza*, Paris: Maspero.

Macherey, Pierre 1983, 'In a Materialist Way', in *Philosophy in France Today*, edited by Alan Montefiore, Cambridge: Cambridge University Press.

Macherey, Pierre 1999, *Histoires de dinosaure. Faire de la philosophie, 1965–1997*, Paris: Presses Universitaires de France.

Magazine littéraire 1992, no. 304 [special issue on Althusser].

Maitan, Livio 1976 [1969], *Party, Army and Masses in China: A Marxist Interpretation of the Cultural Revolution and its Aftermath*, translated by Gregor Benton and Marie Collitti, London: New Left Books.

Majumdar, Margaret 1995, *Althusser and the End of Leninism?*, London: Pluto Press.

Mandel, Ernest 1978, *From Stalinism to Eurocommunism: The Bitter Fruits of 'Socialism in One Country'*, translated by Jon Rothschild, London: New Left Books.

Mao Tse-Tung 1967, *Selected Readings from the Works of Mao Tse-Tung*, Peking: Foreign Languages Press.

Marchais, Georges 1978, *Avancer sur la voie du 22è Congrès*, Paris: Parti Communiste Français.

Marcou, Lilly 1979, *L'Internationale après Staline*, Paris: Grasset.

Marcou, Lilly 1980, *Le Mouvement communiste international depuis 1945*, Paris: Presses Universitaires de France.

Marcuse, Herbert 1964, *One-Dimensional Man: Studies in the Ideology of Advanced Industrial Society*, Boston: Beacon Press.

Marx, Karl 1972, 'Marginal Notes on Adolph Wagner's *Lehrbuch der politischen Ökonomie*', *Theoretical Practice*, 5: 40–65.

Marx, Karl 1973 [1939–41], *Grundrisse*, translated by Martin Nicolaus, Harmondsworth: Penguin/*New Left Review*.

Marx, Karl 1974, *The First International and After*, edited by David Fernbach, Harmondsworth: Penguin/*New Left Review*.

Marx, Karl 1975, *Early Writings*, edited by Lucio Colletti and translated by Gregor Benton and Rodney Livingstone, Harmondsworth: Penguin/*New Left Review*.

Marx, Karl 1976a [1867], *Capital: A Critique of Political Economy*, Volume 1, translated by Ben Fowkes, Harmondsworth: Penguin/*New Left Review*.

Marx, Karl 1976b [1847], 'The Poverty of Philosophy', in Karl Marx and Frederick Engels, *Collected Works*, Volume 6, London: Lawrence and Wishart.

Marx, Karl 1977, *Surveys from Exile*, edited by David Fernbach, Harmondsworth: Penguin/*New Left Review*.

Marx, Karl 1978 [1885], *Capital: A Critique of Political Economy*, Volume 2, translated by David Fernbach, Harmondsworth: Penguin/*New Left Review*.

Marx, Karl 1981 [1894], *Capital: A Critique of Political Economy*, Volume 3, translated by David Fernbach, Harmondsworth: Penguin/*New Left Review*.

Marx, Karl and Frederick Engels 1975, *Selected Correspondence*, Moscow: Progress Publishers.

Marx, Karl and Frederick Engels 1976 [1932], 'The German Ideology', in *Collected Works*, Volume 5, London: Lawrence and Wishart.

Marx, Karl and Frederick Engels 1977, *Selected Works*, Volume 3, Moscow: Progress Publishers.

Matheron, François (ed.) 1997, *Lire Althusser aujourd'hui*, Paris: *Futur antérieur*/ L'Harmattan.

Matheron, François 2001, 'Louis Althusser ou l'impure pureté du concept', in *Dictionnaire Marx contemporain*, edited by Jacques Bidet and Eustache Kouvélakis, Paris: Presses Universitaires de France.

Medvedev, Roy and Zhores Medvedev 1977, *Khrushchev: The Years in Power*, Oxford: Oxford University Press.

Merleau-Ponty, Maurice 1969 [1947], *Humanism and Terror*, translated by John O'Neill, Boston: Beacon Press.

Merleau-Ponty, Maurice 1973 [1955], *Adventures of the Dialectic*, translated by Joseph Bien, Evanston: Northwestern University Press.

Miliband, Ralph 1984, *Class Power and State Power: Political Essays*, London: Verso.

Mitchell, Juliet 1971, *Woman's Estate*, Harmondsworth: Penguin.

Mitchell, Juliet 1974, *Psychoanalysis and Feminism*, Harmondsworth: Allen Lane.

Montag, Warren 2002, *Louis Althusser*, Basingstoke: Palgrave.

Moreau, Pierre-François 1975, *Spinoza*, Paris: Éditions du Seuil.

Morfino, Vittorio 2002, 'Il materialismo della pioggia di Louis Althusser. Un lessico', in *Incursioni Spinoziste*, Milan: Mimesis.

Morin, Edgar 1970 [1959], *Autocritique*, Paris: Éditions du Seuil.

Moulier Boutang, Yann 1992, *Louis Althusser. Une biographie – Tome I: La formation du mythe (1918–1956)*, Paris: Grasset.

Mulhern, Francis 1979, *The Moment of 'Scrutiny'*, London: New Left Books.

Mury, Gilbert 1963, 'Matérialisme et hyperempirisme', *La Pensée*, 108: 38–51.

Negri, Antonio 1996 [1993], 'Notes on the Evolution of the Thought of the Later Althusser', translated by Olga Vasile, in Callari and Ruccio (eds.) 1996.

Nemeth, Thomas 1980, 'Althusser's Anti-Humanism and Soviet Philosophy', *Studies in Soviet Thought*, 21, 4: 363–85.

New Left Review (ed.) 1977, *Western Marxism: A Critical Reader*, London: New Left Books.

Nietzsche, Friedrich 1975 [1908], *Ecce Homo: How One Becomes What One Is*, translated by R.J. Hollingdale, Harmondsworth: Penguin.

O'Hagan, Timothy 1982, 'Althusser: How to be a Marxist in Philosophy', in *Marx and Marxisms*, edited by G.H.R. Parkinson, Cambridge: Cambridge University Press.

O'Hagan, Timothy 1988, 'Introduction to Althusser, "Machiavelli's Solitude"', *Economy and Society*, 17, 4: 468–79.

Osborne, Peter 1989, 'Anti-Anti-Althusserianism', *Radical Philosophy*, 51: 42–4.

Papineau, David 1993, 'The Philosopher Emperor Who Had No Clothes', *Independent on Sunday*, 14 November 1993.

Pascal, Blaise 1966, *Pensées*, translated by A.J. Krailsheimer, Harmondsworth: Penguin.

Patton, Paul 1978, 'Althusser's Epistemology', *Radical Philosophy*, 19: 8–18.

Pêcheux, Michel 1982 [1975], *Language, Semantics and Ideology*, translated by Harbans Nagpal, Basingstoke: Macmillan.

Pêcheux, Michel et al. 1975, 'Analyse du discours, langue et idéologies', *Langages*, 37.

Plekhanov, G.V. n.d. [1908], *Fundamental Problems of Marxism*, translated by Julius Katzer, London: Lawrence and Wishart.

Poulantzas, Nicos 1966, 'Vers une théorie marxiste', *Les Temps Modernes*, 240: 1952–82.
Poulantzas, Nicos 1973 [1968], *Political Power and Social Classes*, translated by Timothy O'Hagan et al., London: New Left Books/Sheed & Ward.
Poulantzas, Nicos 1974 [1970], *Fascism and Dictatorship: The Third International and the Problem of Fascism*, translated by Judith White, London: New Left Books.
Poulantzas, Nicos 1975 [1974], *Classes in Contemporary Capitalism*, translated by David Fernbach, London: New Left Books.
Poulantzas, Nicos 1976 [1975], *The Crisis of the Dictatorships: Portugal, Greece, Spain*, translated by David Fernbach, London: New Left Books.
Poulantzas, Nicos 1978, *State, Power, Socialism*, translated by Patrick Camiller, London: New Left Books.
Poulantzas, Nicos 1980, *Repères*, Paris: Maspero.
Preve, Costanzo 1993, 'Louis Althusser: la lutte contre le sens commun dans le mouvement communiste "historique" au XXᵉ siècle', in Lazarus (ed.) 1993.
Preve, Costanzo 2003, 'L'eredità intelletuale di Louis Althusser (1918–1990) e le contraddizioni teoriche e politiche dell'althusserismo', in *Un secolo di marxismo. Idee e ideologie*, Pistoia: CRT.
Quattrocchi, Angelo and Tom Nairn 1968, *The Beginning of the End: France, May 1968*, London: Panther.
Rancière, Jacques 1965, 'Le concept de critique et la critique de l'économie politique des "Manuscrits de 1844" au "Capital"', in Althusser et al. 1965.
Rancière, Jacques 1974, *La Leçon d'Althusser*, Paris: Gallimard.
Rancière, Jacques 1985 [1970], 'On the Theory of Ideology – Althusser's Politics', in *Radical Philosophy Reader*, edited by Roy Edgley and Richard Osborne, London: Verso.
Raymond, Pierre 1973, *Le Passage au matérialisme*, Paris: Maspero.
Raymond, Pierre 1976, '. . . et la théorie dans la lutte des classes', *Dialectiques*, 15/16: 137–48.
Raymond, Pierre 1982, *La Résistible fatalité de l'histoire*, Paris: Albin Michel.
Raymond, Pierre (ed.) 1997, *Althusser philosophe*, Paris: Presses Universitaires de France.
Rée, Jonathan 1982, 'The Anti-Althusser Band-Wagon', *Radical Science Journal*, 12: 81–100.
Resch, Robert Paul 1992, *Althusser and the Renewal of Marxist Social Theory*, Berkeley: University of California Press.
Rethinking Marxism 1998, 10, 3, 'Rereading Althusser'.
Rey, Pierre-Philippe 1971, *Colonialisme, néo-colonialisme et transition au capitalisme*, Paris: Maspero.
Rey, Pierre-Philippe 1978 [1968], 'Sur l'articulation des modes de production', in *Les Alliances de classes*, Paris: Maspero.
Robin, Régine 1973, *Histoire et linguistique*, Paris: Armand Colin.
Robin, Régine and Jacques Guilhaumou 1976, 'L'identité retrouvée', *Dialectiques*, 15/16: 37–41.
Roemer, John (ed.) 1986, *Analytical Marxism*, Cambridge: Cambridge University Press.
Roudinesco, Élisabeth 1977, *Pour une politique de la psychanalyse*, Paris: Maspero.
Roudinesco, Élisabeth 1986, *La Bataille de cent ans. Histoire de la psychanalyse en France: 2 – 1925–1985*, Paris: Éditions du Seuil.
Rousseau, Jean-Jacques 1953 [1781], *The Confessions*, translated by J.M. Cohen, Penguin: Harmondsworth.
Rustin, Michael 1996, 'Ernest Gellner, 1925–1995', *Radical Philosophy*, 76: 55–6.
Salvadori, Massimo 1979 [1976], *Karl Kautsky and the Socialist Revolution 1880–1938*, translated by Jon Rothschild, London: New Left Books.
Samuel, Raphael 1980, 'British Marxist Historians, 1880–1980: Part One', *New Left Review*, I, 120: 21–96.
Sartre, Jean-Paul 1964a, *Situations IV. Portraits*, Paris: Gallimard.
Sartre, Jean-Paul 1964b, *Situations VI. Problèmes du marxisme 1*, Paris: Gallimard.
Sartre, Jean-Paul 1965, *Situations VII. Problèmes du marxisme 2*, Paris: Gallimard.
Sartre, Jean-Paul 1966, 'Jean-Paul Sartre répond', *L'Arc*, 30: 87–96.

Sartre, Jean-Paul 1968 [1960], *Search for a Method*, translated by Hazel E. Barnes, New York: Vintage.

Sartre, Jean-Paul 1969 [1956], *The Spectre of Stalin*, translated by Irene Clephane, London: Hamish Hamilton.

Sartre, Jean-Paul 1976 [1960], *Critique of Dialectical Reason I: Theory of Practical Ensembles*, translated by Alan Sheridan-Smith and edited by Jonathan Rée, London: New Left Books.

Sartre, Jean-Paul 1977, 'Socialism in One Country', *New Left Review*, I, 100: 141–63.

Sartre, Jean-Paul 1983 [1972], *Between Existentialism and Marxism*, translated by John Mathews, London: Verso.

Sartre, Jean-Paul 1985, *Critique de la raison dialectique II. L'intelligibilité de l'Histoire*, Paris: Gallimard.

Saussure, Ferdinand de 1981 [1916], *Course in General Linguistics*, translated by Wade Baskin, Glasgow: Fontana.

Schaff, Adam 1978 [1974], *Structuralism and Marxism*, Oxford: Pergamon.

Schmidt, Alfred 1981 [1971], *History and Structure: An Essay on Hegelian-Marxist and Structuralist Theories of History*, translated by Jeffrey Herf, Cambridge, MA.: M.I.T. Press.

Schmiederer, Ursula 1979 [1978], 'Politics and Economics in Capitalism and in "Actually Existing Socialism"', in *Power and Opposition in Post-Revolutionary Societies*, edited by *Il Manifesto*, London: Ink Links.

Schöttler, Peter 1985 [1982], *Naissance des bourses du travail. Un appareil idéologique d'État à la fin du XIXe siècle*, translated by Jean-Pierre Lefebvre and Peter Schöttler, Paris: Presses Universitaires de France.

Scruton, Roger 1984, 'Grand Theories for Little Minds', *The Times*, 17 July.

Seale, Patrick and Maureen McConville 1968, *French Revolution 1968*, Harmondsworth: Penguin.

Sève, Lucien 1978 [1974], *Man in Marxist Theory and the Psychology of Personality*, translated by John McGreal, Brighton: Harvester Press.

Sève, Lucien 1984, *Structuralisme et dialectique*, Paris: Éditions Sociales.

Skinner, Quentin 1981, *Machiavelli*, Oxford: Oxford University Press.

Smith, Steven B. 1984, *Reading Althusser: An Essay on Structural Marxism*, Ithaca: Cornell University Press.

Sollers, Philippe 1974, *Sur le matérialisme*, Paris: Éditions du Seuil.

Soper, Kate 1986, *Humanism and Anti-Humanism*, London: Hutchinson.

Spinoza, Benedict de 1951, *A Theological-Political Treatise & A Political Treatise*, translated by R.H.M. Elwes, New York: Dover.

Spinoza, Benedict de 1955, *On the Improvement of the Understanding, The Ethics, & The Correspondence*, translated by R.H.M. Elwes, New York: Dover.

Spriano, Paolo 1985 [1983], *Stalin and the European Communists*, translated by Jon Rothschild, London: Verso.

Sprinker, Michael 1987, *Imaginary Relations – Aesthetics and Ideology in the Theory of Historical Materialism*, London: Verso.

Stalin, Joseph 1973, *The Essential Stalin – Major Theoretical Writings 1905–52*, edited by Bruce Franklin, London: Croom Helm.

Stedman Jones, Gareth 1977 [1971], 'The Marxism of the Early Lukács', in *New Left Review* (ed.) 1977.

Stedman Jones, Gareth 1979, 'History and Theory', *History Workshop Journal*, 8: 198–202.

Stedman Jones, Gareth 1983, *Languages of Class – Studies in English Working Class History 1832–1982*, Cambridge: Cambridge University Press.

Stedman Jones, Gareth 1984 [1971], *Outcast London: A Study in the Relationship between Classes in Victorian Society*, Harmondsworth: Penguin.

Stedman Jones, Gareth 1988, *Return of the Repressed?*, unpublished manuscript.

Sucting, Wal 2004, 'Althusser's Late Thinking about Materialism', *Historical Materialism*, 12, 1: 3–70.

Taylor, John G. 1979, *From Modernization to Modes of Production: A Critique of the Sociologies of Development and Underdevelopment*, Basingstoke: Macmillan.

Terray, Emmanuel 1972 [1969], *Marxism and 'Primitive' Societies*, translated by Mary Klopper, New York: Monthly Review Press.

Terray, Emmanuel 1993, *Le troisième jour du communisme*, Arles: Actes Sud.

Therborn, Göran 1976, *Science, Class and Society: On the Formation of Sociology and Historical Materialism*, London: New Left Books.

Therborn, Göran 1978, *What Does the Ruling Class Do When it Rules? State Apparatuses and State Power under Feudalism, Capitalism and Socialism*, London: New Left Books.

Therborn, Göran 1980, *The Ideology of Power and the Power of Ideology*, London: Verso.

Thomas, Peter 2002, 'Philosophical Strategies: Althusser and Spinoza', *Historical Materialism*, 10, 3: 71–113.

Thompson, E.P. 1978, *The Poverty of Theory and Other Essays*, London: Merlin Press.

Thompson, E.P. 1981, 'The Politics of Theory', in Samuel (ed.) 1981.

Timpanaro, Sebastiano 1980 [1970], *On Materialism*, translated by Lawrence Garner, London: Verso.

Togliatti, Palmiro 1979, *On Gramsci and Other Writings*, edited by and translated by Donald Sassoon, London: Lawrence and Wishart.

Tosel, André 2000, 'Les aléas du matérialisme aléatoire dans la dernière philosophie de Louis Althusser', *Cahiers philosophiques*, 84: 7–39.

Trotsky, Leon 1969 [1931], *The Permanent Revolution & Results and Prospects*, New York: Pathfinder Press.

Verdès-Leroux, Jeanine 1987, *Le Réveil des somnambules. Le Parti communiste, les intellectuels et la culture (1956–1985)*, Paris: Éditions de Minuit.

Vilar, Pierre 1973, 'Marxist History, A History in the Making: Towards a Dialogue with Althusser', *New Left Review*, I, 80: 65–106.

Vincent, Jean-Marie et al. 1974, *Contre Althusser*, Paris: Union Générale d'Éditions.

Waldeck Rochet, Robert 1962, 'Problèmes philosophiques', *Cahiers du communisme*, 2: 98–125.

Westoby, Adam 1981, *Communism since World War II*, Brighton: Harvester Press.

Wood, Allan 1981, *Karl Marx*, London: Routledge & Kegan Paul.

Wright, Erik Olin 1978, *Class, Crisis and the State*, London: New Left Books.

Wright, Erik Olin 1979, *Class Structure and Income Determination*, New York: Academic Press.

Wright, Erik Olin 1983, 'Giddens's Critique of Marxism', *New Left Review*, I, 138: 11–35.

Zhdanov, A.A. 1950, *On Literature, Music and Philosophy*, London: Lawrence and Wishart.

Bibliography of the Published Writings of Louis Althusser

1936
1. 'Journal de khâgne' (October 1936–June 1937).
   Extracts published in *Magazine littéraire*, no. 304, November 1992, pp. 23–7.

1938
2. Letter to Jean Guitton of 11 July 1938.
   Extracts published in *Lire*, 1987, pp. 83–4.
   Reprinted in Jean Guitton, *Un siècle, une vie*, Robert Laffont, Paris, 1988.

1941
3. 'Journal de captivité' (21 January 1941–12 March 1945).
   Published in Louis Althusser, *Journal de captivité: Stalag XA/1940–1945. Carnets-correspondences-textes*, edited and introduced by Oliver Corpet and Yann Moulier Boutang, Édition Stock/IMEC, Paris, 1992, pp. 15–230.
4. 'Chronique d'un prisonnier' (June 1941).
   Extracts published in *Journal de captivité*, pp. 13–14.
5. Letters to family and friends, 10 September 1941–13 February 1945.
   Published in *Journal de captivité*, pp. 233–333.

1943
6. 'Testament pour la vie future'.
   Published in *Le Lien* (journal of Stalag XA), no. 12, March–April 1943.
   Reprinted in *Journal de captivité*, pp. 337–40.
7. 'Français râleur'.
   Published in *Le Lien*, no. 14, July 1943.
   Reprinted in *Journal de captivité*, pp. 341–2.
8. 'Pudeur du prisonnier de guerre'.
   Published in *Le Lien*, no. 15, August 1943.
   Reprinted in *Journal de captivité*, pp. 343–4.
9. 'L' espérance'.
   Published in *Le Lien*, no. 17, Christmas 1943.
   Reprinted in *Journal de captivité*, pp. 345–52.
10. 'Leur espérance'.
    Published in *Le Lien*, no. 17, Christmas 1943.
    Reprinted in *Journal de captivité*, pp. 553–4.

1945
11. Review of Georges Izard, *L'homme est révolutionnaire*.
    Published in *Dieu vivant*, no. 6, 1946, pp. 149–52.

1946
12. 'En attendant le blé américain, Rome sommeille'.
    Published (under the pseudonym of Robert Leclos) in two parts in *Témoignage chrétien*, 10 May 1946 and 17 May 1946.

13. 'L'internationale des bons sentiments'.
    Published in Louis Althusser, *Écrits philosophiques et politiques. Tome I*, edited and introduced by François Matheron, Éditions Stock/IMEC, Paris, 1994, pp. 35–57.
    Translated as 'The International of Decent Feelings' by G.M. Goshgarian, in Louis Althusser, *The Spectre of Hegel: Early Writings*, edited and introduced by François Matheron, Verso, London, 1997, pp. 21–35.

1947
14. 'Du contenu dans la pensée de G.W.F. Hegel'.
    Extracts published as 'L'ésprit d'Iéna contre la Prusse', in *Magazine littéraire*, no. 293, November 1991, pp. 43–5.
    Published in full in *Écrits philosophiques et politiques. Tome I*, pp. 59–238.
    Translated as 'On Content in the Thought of G.W.F Hegel' by G.M. Goshgarian, in *The Spectre of Hegel*, pp. 36–139.
15. 'L'homme, cette nuit'.
    Review of Alexandre Kojève, *Introduction à la lecture de Hegel*, published in *Cahiers du sud*, no. 286, 1947, pp. 1057–9.
    Reprinted in *Écrits philosophiques et politiques. Tome I*, pp. 239–42.
    Translated as 'Man, That Night' by G.M. Goshgarian, in *The Spectre of Hegel*, pp. 170–2.

1948
16. 'Une question des faits'.
    Published in *Jeunesse de l'Église*, Cahier X, *L'Évangile captif*, Paris, February 1949, pp. 13–24.
    Reprinted in *Écrits philosophiques et politiques. Tome I*, pp. 261–75.
    Translated as 'A Matter of Fact' by G.M. Goshgarian, in *The Spectre of Hegel*, pp. 185–96.

1949
17. Letter to Jean Lacroix of 25 December 1949–21 January 1950.
    Published in *Écrits philosophiques et politiques. Tome I*, pp. 277–325.
    Translated as 'Letter to Jean Lacroix' by G.M. Goshgarian, in *The Spectre of Hegel*, pp. 197–230.

1950
18. 'Le retour à Hegel. Dernier mot du révisionnisme universitaire'.
    Published (under the signature of 'La commission de critique du cercle des philosophes communistes) in *La Nouvelle Critique*, no. 20, November 1950.
    Reprinted in *Écrits philosophiques et politiques. Tome I*, pp. 243–60.
    Translated as 'The Return to Hegel: The Latest Word in Academic Revisionism' by G.M. Goshgarian, in *The Spectre of Hegel*, pp. 173–84.
19. Contribution to the discussion, 'Journées nationales d' études pédagogiques des professeurs de philosophie'.
    Published in *Revue de l'enseignement philosophique*, vol. 1, nos. 1–2, 1951, p. 12.

1951
20. 'Sur l'obscenité conjugale'.
    Published in *Écrits philosophiques et politiques. Tome 1*, pp. 327–39.
    Translated as 'On Conjugal Obscenity' by G.M. Goshgarian, in *The Spectre of Hegel*, pp. 231–40.

1953
21. 'À propos du marxisme'.
    Published in *Revue de l'enseignement philosophique*, vol. 3, no. 4, August–September 1953, pp. 15–19.
    Translated as 'On Marxism' by G.M. Goshgarian, in *The Spectre of Hegel*, pp. 241–7.

22. 'Note sur le matérialisme dialectique'.
Published in *Revue de l'enseignement philosophique*, vol. 3, no. 5, October–November 1953, pp. 11–17.
Translated as 'Note on Dialectical Materialism' by G.M. Goshgarian, in *The Spectre of Hegel*, pp. 247–57.

1954
23. 'L'enseignement de la philosophie'.
Published in *Esprit*, vol. 22, no. 6, June 1954, pp. 858–64.

1955
24. 'Sur l'objectivité de l'histoire (Lettre à Paul Ricoeur)'.
Published in *Revue de l'enseignement philosophique*, vol. 5, no. 4, April–May 1955, pp. 3–15.
Reprinted in Louis Althusser, *Solitude de Machiavel et autres textes*, edited and introduced by Yves Sintomer, Presses Universitaires de France, Paris, 1998, pp. 17–31.

1958
25. 'Montesquieu: la politique et l'histoire'.
Extracts published as 'Despôte et monarque chez Montesquieu' in *Esprit*, vol. 26, no. 11, November 1958, pp. 595–614.
Published in full as *Montesquieu. La politique et l'histoire*, coll. 'Le Philosophe', Presses Universitaires de France, Paris 1959, 126 pp.
Translated as 'Montesquieu: Politics and History' by Ben Brewster, in Louis Althusser, *Politics and History: Montesquieu, Rousseau, Hegel and Marx*, New Left Books, London, 1972, pp. 9–109.
26. 'Note du traducteur'.
Published in Ludwig Feuerbach, *Manifestes philosophiques. Textes choisis (1839–1845)*, edited and translated by Louis Althusser, coll. 'Épiméthée', Presses Universitaires de France, Paris, 1960, pp.1–9.

1960
27. 'Les "Manifestes philosophiques" de Feuerbach'.
Published in *La Nouvelle Critique*, no. 121, December 1960, pp. 32–8.
Reprinted in Louis Althusser, *Pour Marx*, François Maspero, Paris, 1965, pp. 35–43.
Translated as 'Feuerbach's "Philosophical Manifestoes"' by Ben Brewster, in Louis Althusser, *For Marx*, Allen Lane, London, 1969, pp. 41–8.

1961
28. 'Sur le jeune Marx (Questions de théorie)'.
Published in *La Pensée*, no. 96, April 1961, pp. 3–26.
Reprinted in *Pour Marx*, pp. 45–83.
Translated as 'On the Young Marx: Theoretical Questions' by Ben Brewster, in *For Marx*, pp. 49–86.

1962
29. Review of Raymond Polin, *La Politique morale de John Locke*.
Published in *Revue d'histoire moderne et contemporaine*, no. 36, April–June 1962, pp. 150–5.
Reprinted in *Solitude de Machiavel et autres textes*, pp. 33–42.
30. 'Contradiction et surdétermination (Notes pour une recherche)'.
Published (minus an appendix) in *La Pensée*, no. 106, December 1962, pp. 3–22.
Reprinted (with the appendix) in *Pour Marx*, pp. 85–128.
Translated as 'Contradiction and Overdetermination: Notes for an Investigation' by Ben Brewster, in *New Left Review*, I, no. 41, January–February 1967, pp. 15–35; reprinted in *For Marx*, pp. 87–128.

31. 'Le "Piccolo", Bertolazzi et Brecht (Notes sur un théâtre matérialiste)'.
    Published in *Esprit*, vol. 30, no. 12, December 1962, pp. 946–65.
    Reprinted in *Pour Marx*, pp. 129–52.
    Translated as 'The "Piccolo Teatro": Bertolazzi and Brecht – Notes on a Materialist Theatre' by Ben Brewster, in *For Marx*, pp. 129–51.
32. 'Devant le surréalisme: Alvarez–Rios'.
    Published in *Les Lettres françaises*, 29 November–6 December 1962.
    Reprinted in *Écrits philosophiques et politiques. Tome II*, edited and introduced by François Matheron, Éditions Stock/IMEC, Paris, 1995, pp. 569–72.

1963
33. 'Les "Manuscrits de 1844" (Économie politique et philosophie)'.
    Published in *La Pensée*, no. 107, February 1963, pp. 106–09.
    Reprinted in *Pour Marx*, pp. 153–60.
    Translated as 'The "1844 Manuscripts of Karl Marx": Political Economy and Philosophy' by Ben Brewster, in *For Marx*, pp. 153–9.
34. 'Philosophie et sciences humaines'.
    Published in *Revue de l'enseignement philosophique*, vol. 13, no. 5, June–July 1963, pp. 1–12.
    Reprinted in *Solitude de Machiavel et autres textes*, pp. 43–58.
35. 'Sur la dialectique matérialiste (De l'inégalité des origines)'.
    Published in *La Pensée*, no. 110, August 1963, pp. 5–46.
    Reprinted (minus an appendix) in *Pour Marx*, pp. 161–224.
    Translated as 'On the Materialist Dialectic: On the Unevenness of Origins' by Ben Brewster, in *For Marx*, pp. 161–218.
36. 'Marxisme et humanisme'.
    Published in *Cahiers de l'Institut de science économique appliquée*, no. 20, June 1964, pp. 109–33.
    Reprinted in *Pour Marx*, pp. 225–49.
    Translated as 'Marxism and Humanism' by Ben Brewster, in *For Marx*, pp. 219–41.
37. Letters to Jacques Lacan, 26 November 1963–11 July 1966.
    Letter of 26 November 1963 published in *Magazine littéraire*, no. 304, November 1992, pp. 49–50.
    Published in full in Louis Althusser, *Écrits sur la psychanalyse: Freud et Lacan*, edited and introduced by Olivier Corpet and François Matheron, Éditions Stock/IMEC, Paris, 1993, pp. 272–304.
    Translated by Jeffrey Mehlman in Louis Althusser, *Writings on Psychoanalysis: Freud and Lacan*, edited by Olivier Corpet and François Matheron, Columbia University Press, New York, 1996, pp. 147–73.
38. 'Réponse à une critique'.
    Extracts published in Patrick Kessel, *Le Mouvement 'maoiste' en France – Textes et documents. Tome 1: 1963–1968*, Union générale d'éditions, Paris, 1972, pp. 64–6.
    Published in full in *Écrits philosophiques et politiques. Tome II*, pp. 353–91.
39. 'La place de la psychanalyse dans les sciences humaines'.
    Published in Louis Althusser, *Psychanalyse et sciences humaines. Deux conférences (1963–1964)*, edited and introduced by Olivier Corpet and François Matheron, Le Livre de Poche, Paris, 1996, pp. 17–72.

1964
40. 'Problèmes étudiants'.
    Published in *La Nouvelle Critique*, no. 152, January 1964, pp. 80–111.
    Partially translated as 'Student Problems' by Dick Bateman, in *Sublation* (University of Leicester), May 1967, pp. 14–22.
41. 'Conferenza dibattito del Professore Louis Althusser'.
    Published in Italian in *La Provincia di Forli*, 8 January 1964, pp. 5–10.
    Unpublished in French.

42. 'Teoria e metodo' and 'Gli strumenti del marxismo'.
    Published in Italian in *Rinascita*, 25 January 1964 and 1 February 1964.
    Unpublished in French.
43. Presentation of Pierre Macherey, 'La philosophie de la science de Georges
    Canguilhem'.
    Published in *La Pensée*, no. 113, February 1964, pp. 50–4.
    Translated by Ted Stolze in Pierre Macherey, *In a Materialist Way: Selected Essays*,
    Verso, London, 1998, pp. 161–5.
44. 'Psychanalyse et psychologie'.
    Published in *Psychanalyse et sciences humaines*, pp. 73–122.
45. 'Freud et Lacan'.
    Published in *La Nouvelle Critique*, nos. 161–2, December 1964–January 1965, pp.
    88–108.
    Reprinted in Louis Althusser, *Positions*, Éditions Sociales, Paris, 1976, pp. 9–34;
    and in *Écrits sur la psychanalyse*, pp. 23–52.
    Translated as 'Freud and Lacan' by Ben Brewster, in *New Left Review*, I, no. 55,
    May–June 1969, pp. 49–65; reprinted in Louis Althusser, *Lenin and Philosophy
    and Other Essays*, New Left Books, London, 1971, pp. 172–202 and subsequently
    in Louis Althusser, *Essays on Ideology*, Verso, London, 1984, pp. 141–71; retranslated
    by Jeffrey Mehlman in *Writings on Psychoanalysis*, pp. 13–32.
46. Letters to Hélène Rytman of 27 and 30 July 1964.
    Published in Louis Althusser, *L'avenir dure longtemps, suivi de Les Faits*, second
    edition, edited and introduced by Olivier Corpet and Yann Moulier Boutang,
    Le Livre de Poche, Paris, 1994, pp. 421–8.
47. Transcripts of dreams, 10–12 August 1964.
    Extracts published in Spanish in *La Jordana semanal*, no. 73, November 1990.
    Published in French as 'Rêves prémonitoires' in *L'avenir dure longtemps*, second
    edition, pp. 429–32.
48. 'Cremonini, peintre de l'abstrait'.
    Published in German in *Tendenzen*, no. 3, 1965.
    Revised and expanded version published in *Démocratie nouvelle*, no. 11, November
    1966, pp. 105–20.
    Reprinted in *Écrits philosophiques et politiques. Tome II*, pp. 574–89.
    Translated from the 1966 version as 'Cremonini, Painter of the Abstract' by Ben
    Brewster, in *Lenin and Philosophy and Other Essays*, pp. 209–20.

1965
49. 'Note complémentaire sur l'"humanisme réel"'.
    Published in *La Nouvelle Critique*, no. 164, March 1965, pp. 32–7.
    Reprinted in *Pour Marx*, pp. 251–8.
    Translated as 'A Complementary Note on "Real Humanism"' by Ben Brewster,
    in *For Marx*, pp. 242–7.
50. 'Préface: Aujourd'hui'.
    Published in *Pour Marx*, pp. 9–32.
    Translated as 'Introduction: Today' by Ben Brewster, in *For Marx*, pp. 19–39.
51. 'Théorie, pratique théorique et formation théorique. Idéologie et lutte idéologique'.
    Published in Spanish in *Casa de las Americas* (Havana), no. 34, 1966, pp. 5–31.
    Translated from the French typescript as 'Theory, Theoretical Practice and Theoretical
    Formation. Ideology and Ideological Struggle' by James H. Kavanagh, in Louis
    Althusser, *Philosophy and the Spontaneous Philosophy of the Scientists & Other
    Essays*, edited and introduced by Gregory Elliott, Verso, London, 1990, pp. 1–42.
    Unpublished in French.
52. 'L'objet du *Capital*'.
    Extracts published as 'Esquisse du concept d'histoire' in *La Pensée*, no. 121, August
    1965, pp. 2–21.
    Published in full in Louis Althusser, Étienne Balibar and Roger Establet, *Lire 'le
    Capital'. Tome II*, François Maspero, Paris, 1965, pp. 7–185.

Reprinted in revised form in Louis Althusser and Étienne Balibar, *Lire 'le Capital'*, second edition, two volumes, François Maspero, Paris, 1968, vol. I, pp. 87–184 and vol. II, pp. 5–78; and in Louis Althusser, Étienne Balibar, Roger Establet, Pierre Macherey and Jacques Rancière, *Lire 'le Capital'*, third edition, Presses Universitaires de France, Paris, 1996, pp. 245–418.

Translated from the second edition as 'Part II: The Object of *Capital*' by Ben Brewster, in Louis Althusser and Étienne Balibar, *Reading 'Capital'*, New Left Books, London, 1970, pp. 71–198.

53. 'Préface : Du *Capital* à la philosophie de Marx'.
Published in Louis Althusser, Jacques Rancierè and Pierre Macherey, *Lire 'le Capital'*. *Tome I*, François Maspero, Paris, 1965, pp. 9–89.
Reprinted in *Lire 'le Capital'*, second edition, vol. I, pp. 9–85 and in *Lire 'le Capital'*, third edition, pp. 1–79.
Translated from the second edition as 'Part 1: From *Capital* to Marx's Philosophy' by Ben Brewster, in *Reading 'Capital'*, pp. 11–69.

54. *Pour Marx*, coll. 'Théorie', François Maspero, Paris, September 1965, 261 pp.
Translated as *For Marx* by Ben Brewster, Allen Lane, London, 1969 (subsequently reissued by New Left Books and Verso, London).
Contains 27, 28, 30, 31, 33, 35, 36, 49, 50.

55. *Lire 'le Capital'*, two volumes, coll. 'Théorie', François Maspero, Paris, November 1965, 663 pp. (with É. Balibar, R. Establet, P. Macherey and J. Rancière).
Reissued in four volumes, 'Petite Collection Maspero', François Maspero, Paris, 1968–73; and in one volume, coll. 'Quadrige', Presses Universitaires de France, Paris, 1996.
Volumes I and II of the second edition translated as *Reading 'Capital'* by Ben Brewster, New Left Books, London, 1970.
Contains 52, 53.

56. 'Sur le "Contrat Social" (Les décalages)'.
Published in *Cahiers pour l'analyse*, no. 8, *L'impensé de Jean-Jacques Rousseau*, Paris, 1967, pp. 5–42.
Reprinted in *Solitude de Machiavel et autres textes*, pp. 59–102.
Translated as 'Rousseau: The Social Contract (The Discrepencies)' by Ben Brewster, in *Politics and History*, pp. 111–60.

1966
57. 'Matérialisme historique et matérialisme dialectique'.
Published in *Cahiers marxistes-léninistes*, no. 11, April 1966, pp. 90–122.

58. 'Réponse à André Daspre'.
Published in 'Deux lettres sur la connaissance de l'art', in *La Nouvelle Critique*, no. 175, April 1966, pp. 141–6.
Reprinted in *Écrits philosophiques et politiques*. *Tome II*, pp. 560–8.
Translated as 'A Letter on Art in Reply to André Daspre' by Ben Brewster, in *Lenin and Philosophy and Other Essays*, pp. 203–8; reprinted in *Essays on Ideology*, pp. 173–9.

59. Cover presentation of Pierre Macherey, *Pour une théorie de la production littéraire*, François Maspero, Paris, 1966.

60. 'Conjuncture philosophique et recherche marxiste théorique'.
Published in *Écrits philosophiques et politiques*. *Tome II*, pp. 394–415.
Translated as 'The Theoretical Conjuncture and Marxist Theoretical Research' by G.M. Goshgarian, in Louis Althusser, *The Humanist Controversy and Other Writings*, edited by François Matheron, Verso, London, 2003, pp. 1–18.

61. Letters to René Diatkine of 18 July and 22 August 1966.
Published in *Écrits sur la psychanalyse*, pp. 57–110.
Translated by Jeffrey Mehlman, in *Writings on Psychoanalysis*, pp. 35–77.

62. 'Sur Lévi-Strauss'.
Published in *Écrits philosophiques et politiques*. *Tome I*, pp. 418–32.
Translated as 'On Lévi-Strauss' by G.M. Goshgarian, in *The Humanist Controversy and Other Writings*, pp. 19–32.

63. 'Trois notes sur la théorie des discours' (September–October 1966).
Published in *Écrits sur la psychanalyse*, pp. 117–70.
Translated as 'Three Notes on the Theory of Discourses' by G.M. Goshgarian, in *The Humanist Controversy and Other Writings*, pp. 33–84.
64. 'Sur la révolution culturelle'.
Published anonymously in *Cahiers marxistes-léninistes*, no. 14, November–December 1966, pp. 5–16.

1967
65. 'Sur le travail théorique. Difficultés et ressources'.
Published in *La Pensée*, no. 132, April 1967, pp. 3–22.
Translated as 'On Theoretical Work: Difficulties and Resources' by James H. Kavanagh, in *Philosophy and the Spontaneous Philosophy of Scientists & Other Essays*, pp. 43–67.
66. 'Principes de la philosophie de Feuerbach'.
Published as 'Sur Feuerbach' in *Écrits philosopiques et politique. Tome II*, pp. 172–251.
Translated as 'On Feuerbach' by G.M. Goshgarian, in *The Humanist Controversy and Other Writings*, pp. 85–154.
67. Letter to Régis Debray of 1 March 1967.
Published in Régis Debray, *La Critique des armes*, Éditions du Seuil, Paris, 1974, pp. 262–9.
Translated by Rosemay Sheed in Régis Debray, *A Critique of Arms*, Penguin, Harmondsworth, 1977, pp. 258–67.
68. 'Prefazione'.
Published in Spanish in Louis Althusser, *La révolucion teorica de Marx*, Siglo XXI, Mexico/Buenos Aires, 1967, pp. ii–xvi.
Unpublished in French.
69. Letters to R. Domergue.
Published in Portuguese in Louis Althusser and R. Domergue, *Marxismo segundo Althusser: Polemica Althusser-Garaudy*, Signal, San Paolo, 1967.
Unpublished in French.
70. Obituary of Jacques Martin.
Published in *Association Amicale des anciens élèves de l'École normale supérieure (1967)*, Paris, 1967, p. 54.
71. 'La tâche historique de la philosophie marxiste'.
Published in revised form in Hungarian as 'A Marxista Filózofia Történelmi Feladata', in Louis Althusser, *Marx–Elmélet Forradalma*, Kossuth, Budapest, 1968, pp. 272–306.
Translated from the French typescript as 'The Historical Task of Marxist Philosophy' by G.M. Goshgarian, in *The Humanist Controversy and Other Writings*, pp. 155–220.
Unpublished in French
72. 'La querelle de l'humanisme'.
Extract published in 'Sur le rapport de Marx à Hegel' in Jacques d'Hondt (ed.), *Hegel et la pensée moderne*, Presses Universitaires de France, Paris, 1970, pp. 85–111.
Published in full in *Écrits philosophiques et politiques. Tome II*, pp. 435–532.
Translated as 'The Humanist Controversy' by G.M. Goshgarian, in *The Humanist Controversy and Other Writings*, pp. 221–305.
73. 'Aux Lecteurs'.
Published in *Pour Marx*, La Découverte/Poche, Éditions la Découverte, Paris, 1996, pp. 259–65.
Translated as 'To My English Readers' by Ben Brewster, in *For Marx*, pp. 9–15.
74. 'Notes sur la philosophie' (19 October 1967–8 February 1968).
Published in *Écrits philosophiques et politiques. Tome II*, pp. 301–48.
75. 'La philosophie comme arme de la révolution (Réponse à huit questions)'.
Interview with Maria Antonietta Macciocchi published in Italian in abridged form as 'La filosofia coma arma della rivoluzione', in *L'Unità*, 1 February 1968.
Published in French in *La Pénsée*, no. 138, April 1968, pp. 26–34.

Reprinted in *Positions*, pp. 35–48 and in *Solitude de Machiavel et autre textes*, pp. 145–58.

Translated as 'Philosophy as a Revolutionary Weapon' by Ben Brewster, in *New Left Review*, I, no. 64, November–December 1970, pp. 3–11; reprinted in *Lenin and Philosophy and Other Essays*, pp. 13–25.

76. 'Cours de philosophie pour scientifiques: Introduction' (20 November–18 December 1967).

Extract from revised version of second lecture published as 'Justesse et philosophie', in *La Pensée*, no. 176, August 1974, pp. 3–8.

Revised version of first four lectures published as *Philosophie et philosophie spontanée des savants (1967)*, coll. 'Théorie', François Maspero, Paris, September 1974, 157 pp.

Translated as 'Philosophy and the Spontaneous Philosophy of the Scientists (1967)' by Warren Montag, in *Philosophy and the Spontaneous Philosophy of the Scientists & Other Essays*, pp. 69–165.

Fifth lecture ('Du côté de la philosophie') published in *Écrits philosopiques et politiques. Tome II*, pp. 257–98.

77. 'Avertissement'.

Published in *Lire 'le Capital'*, second edition, vol. I, pp. 5–6.

Translated as 'Foreword to the Italian Edition' by Ben Brewster, in *Reading 'Capital'*, pp. 7–8.

1968

78. 'Sur le rapport de Marx à Hegel'.

Published in Jacques d'Hondt (ed.), *Hegel et la pensée moderne*, Presses Universitaires de France, Paris, 1970, pp. 85–111.

Reprinted in Louis Althusser, *Lénine et la philosophie, suivi de Marx et Lénine devant Hegel*, François Maspero, Paris, 1972, pp. 49–71.

Translated as 'Marx's Relation to Hegel' by Ben Brewster, in *Politics and History*, pp. 161–86.

79. 'Lénine et la philosophie'.

Published (with the ensuing discussion) in *Bulletin de la Société française de philosophie*, no. 4, October–December 1968, pp. 127–81.

Reprinted (minus the discussion) as Louis Althusser, *Lénine et la philosophie*, coll. 'Théorie', François Maspero, Paris, January 1969, 58 pp. and in *Lénine et la philosophie, suivi de Marx et Lénine devant Hegel*, pp. 5–47; reprinted with the discussion in *Solitude de Machiavel et autres textes*, pp. 103–44.

Translated as 'Lenin and Philosophy' by Ben Brewster, in *Lenin and Philosophy and Other Essays*, pp. 27–68; reprinted in *Philosophy and the Spontaneous Philosophy of the Scientists & Other Essays*, pp. 167–202.

80. Letters to Maria Antonietta Macciocchi, 3 February 1968–15 March 1969.

Published in Italian in Maria Antonietta Macciocchi, *Lettere dall'interno del P.C.I.*, Giangiacomo Feltrinelli, Milan, 1969, pp. 3–6, 23–6, 53–64, 126–7, 331–61.

Translated by Stephen M. Hellman in Maria Antonietta Macciocchi, *Letters from inside the Italian Communist Party to Louis Althusser*, New Left Books, London, 1973, pp. 3–5, 21–3, 48–57, 112–13, 295–320.

Unpublished in French.

81. 'A Magyar Olvasohoz' ('To My Hungarian Readers').

Published in Hungarian in *Marx–Az Elmélet Forradalma*, pp. 9–15.

Published in French in Saül Karsz, *Théorie et politique: Louis Althusser*, Fayard, Paris, 1974, pp. 315–20.

82. 'La filosofia, la politica e la scienza (Una lettera di Louis Althusser sul pensiero di Gramsci)'.

Published in *Rinascita*, 15 March 1968.

Unpublished in French.

83. Letter to Paolo Grassi of 6 March 1968.

Published in *Écrits philosophiques et politiques. Tome II*, pp. 535–9.

84. 'Sur Brecht et Marx'.
Published in *Écrits philosophiques et politiques. Tome II*, pp. 541–8.
Translated as 'On Brecht and Marx' by Max Statkiewicz, in Warren Montag, *Louis Althusser*, Palgrave Macmillan, Basingstoke and New York, 2003, pp. 136–49.
85. Cover presentation of Jean-Pierre Osier (ed. and trans.), Ludwig Feuerbach, *L'essence du christianisme*, François Maspero, Paris, 1968.
86. 'Avertissement'.
Published in Alain Badiou, *Le Concept de modèle*, François Maspero, Paris, 1969, pp. 7–8.
87. Introduction.
Published in Spanish as 'Introducción', in Louis Althusser *et al.*, *Polemica sobre Marxismo y Humanismo*, Siglo XXI, Mexico and Buenos Aires, 1968, pp. 1–2.
Unpublished in French.
88. Replies by Louis Althusser.
Published in Spanish as 'Respuestas de Louis Althusser', in Althusser *et al.*, *Polemica sobre Marxismo y Humanismo*, pp. 172–201.
Unpublished in French.

1969
89. 'Présentation'.
Published in Emmanuel Terray, *Le Marxisme devant les sociétés 'primitives'*, François Maspero, Paris 1969, pp. 7–9.
Translated as 'Publisher's Introduction to the French Edition' by Mary Klopper, in Emmanuel Terray, *Marxism and 'Primitive' Societies*, Monthly Review Press, New York and London, 1972, pp. 1–3.
90. 'A Letter to Translator'.
Published in *For Marx*, pp. 257–8; reprinted in *Reading 'Capital'*, pp. 323–4.
Unpublished in French.
91. Letter to the translator (on 'Freud and Lacan'), 21 February 1969.
Extracts published in *New Left Review*, I, no. 55, May–June 1969, p. 48; reprinted in *Lenin and Philosophy and Other Essays*, pp. 177–8, *Essays on Ideology*, pp. 141–2, and *Writings on Psychoanalysis*, pp. 31–2.
Published in French in *Écrits sur la psychanalyse*, pp. 53–4.
92 'Avertissement aux lecteurs de Livre 1 du "Capital"'.
Published in Karl Marx, *Le Capital. Livre I*, Garnier–Flammarion, Paris, 1969, pp. 5–30.
Translated as 'Preface to *Capital* Volume I' by Ben Brewster, in *Lenin and Philosophy and Other Essays*, pp. 69–101.
93. 'À propos de l'article de Michel Verret sur "Mai étudiant"'.
Published in *La Pensée*, no. 145, June 1969, pp. 3–14.
94. 'Comment lire "Le Capital"?'
Published in *L'Humanité*, 21 March 1969.
Reprinted in *Positions*, pp. 49–60.
Translated as 'How to Read Marx's "Capital"', in *Marxism Today*, October 1969, pp. 302–5.
95. 'De la superstructure (Droit-État-Idéologie)'.
Revised extracts published as 'Idéologie et appareils idéologiques d'État (Notes pour une recherche)', in *La Pensée*, no. 151, June 1970, pp. 3–38.
Reprinted in *Positions*, pp. 67–125 and in Louis Althusser, *Sur la reproduction*, edited and introduced by Jacques Bidet, Presses Universitaires de France, Paris, 1995, pp. 269–314.
Extracts translated as 'Ideology and Ideological State Apparatuses: Notes towards an Investigation' by Ben Brewster, in *Lenin and Philosophy and Other Essays*, pp. 121–73; reprinted in *Essays on Ideology*, pp. 1–60.
Original manuscript published in revised and expanded form as 'La Reproduction des rapports de production' in *Sur la reproduction*, pp. 19–252.

96. 'Lénine devant Hegel'.
   Published in W.R. Beyer (ed.), *Hegel-Jahrbuch 1968/69*, Meissenheim a. Glan, 1970, pp. 45–58.
   Reprinted in *Lénine et la philosophie, suivi de Marx et Lénine devant Hegel*, pp. 73–90.
   Translated as 'Lenin before Hegel' by Ben Brewster, in *Lenin and Philosophy and Other Essays*, pp. 103–20.
97. 'Crise de l'homme et de la société'.
   Published in 'L'Église aujourd'hui', *Lumière et vie* (Lyon), no. 93, May–June 1969, pp. 26–9.
98. Letter of 1969 to Pesenti.
   Published in Italian as 'Lettera a Pesenti', in *Rinascita*, no. 32, 1969.
   Unpublished in French.

1970
99. Postscript to 'Idéologie et appareils ideologiques d'État'.
   Published in *La Pensée*, no. 150, June 1970, p. 38.
   Reprinted in *Positions*, pp. 122–5 and *Sur la reproduction*, pp. 312–14.
   Translated by Ben Brewster in *Lenin and Philosophy and Other Essays*, pp. 170–73; reprinted in *Essays on Ideology*, pp. 57–60.
100. Untitled typescript.
   Published in Saül Karsz, *Théorie et politique*, pp. 321–3.
101. 'Note to the English Edition'.
   Published in *Reading 'Capital'*, p. 8.
   Unpublished in French.
102. 'Foreword'.
   Published in *Lenin and Philosophy and Other Essays*, pp. 7–9.
   Published in French in Saül Karsz, *Théorie et politique*, pp. 324–6.
103. 'Sur l'évolution du jeune Marx'.
   Published in Louis Althusser, *Éléments d'autocritique*, Hachette, Paris, 1974, pp. 103–26.
   Translated as 'The Conditions of Marx's Scientific Discovery' by Ben Brewster, in *Theoretical Practice*, nos. 7–8 January 1973, pp. 4–11; and as 'On the Evolution of the Young Marx' by Grahame Lock, in Louis Althusser, *Essays in Self-Criticism*, New Left Books, London, 1976, pp. 151–61.

1971
104. 'Prefazione'.
   Published in Spanish in Marta Harnecker, *Los Conceptos elementales del materialismo histórico*, second edition, Siglo XXI, Mexico/Buenos Aires, 1971, pp. xi–xvi.
   Published untitled in French in Saül Karsz, *Théorie et politique*, pp. 327–32; reprinted as 'Marxisme et lutte de classe', in *Positions*, pp. 61–6.
   Translated as 'Marxism and Class Struggle' by Patrick Lyons, in *Radical* (Oxford), no. 1, November 1985, pp. 12–13.
105. 'Machiavel et nous'.
   Published (with subsequent revisions) in *Écrits philosophiques et politiques. Tome II*, pp. 42–168.
   Translated as *Machiavelli and Us* by Gregory Elliott, Verso, London, 1999.

1972
106. *Lénine et la philosophie, suivi de Marx et Lénine devant Hegel*, 'Petite Collection Maspero', François Maspero, Paris, 1972, 93 pp.
   Contains 78, 79, 96.
107. 'Une question posée par Louis Althusser'.
   Published in *Écrits philosopiques et politiques. Tome I*, pp. 345–56.
108. 'Éléments d'autocritique'.
   Published in Louis Althusser, *Éléments d'autocritique*, Hachette, Paris, 1974, pp. 9–101.

Reprinted in *Solitude de Machiavel et autres textes*, pp. 159–98.
Translated as 'Elements of Self-Criticism' by Grahame Lock, in *Essays in Self-Criticism*, pp. 101–61.

109. 'Sur une erreur politique. Les maîtres auxiliaires, les étudiants travailleurs et l'agrégation de philosophie'.
Published in two parts in *France nouvelle*, 25 July 1972, pp. 9–12 and 1 August 1972, pp. 10–13.

110. 'Note sur "la critique du culte de la personnalité"'.
Published in Louis Althusser, *Réponse à John Lewis*, François Maspero, Paris, 1973, pp. 69–90.
Translated as 'Note on "The Critique of the Personality Cult"' by Grahame Lock, in *Essays in Self-Criticism*, pp. 78–93; reprinted in *Essays on Ideology*, pp. 115–32.

111. 'Réponse à John Lewis'.
Published in revised form in *Réponse à John Lewis*, pp. 9–68.
Translated as 'Reply to John Lewis (Self-Criticism)' by Grahame Lock, in *Marxism Today*, October 1972, pp. 310–18 and November 1972, pp. 343–9; reprinted (with revisions) in *Essays in Self-Criticism*, pp. 35–77 and *Essays on Ideology*, pp. 65–114.

112. Letters to Jean Guitton of July and August 1972.
Published in *Lire*, 1987, pp. 84–6.
Reprinted in Jean Guitton, *Un siècle, une vie*, Robert Laffont, Paris, 1988.

1973

113. Cover presentation of Dominique Lecourt, *Une Crise et son enjeu (Essai sur la position de Lénine en philosophie)*, François Maspero, Paris, 1973.

114. Cover Presentation of Bernard Edelman, *Le Droit saisi par la photographie (Éléments pour une théorie marxiste du droit)*, François Maspero, Paris, 1973.

115. 'Remarque sur une catégorie: "procès sans Sujet ni Fin(s)"'.
Published in *Réponse à John Lewis*, pp. 91–8.
Translated as 'Remark on the Category: "Process without a Subject or Goal(s)"' by Grahame Lock, in *Essays in Self-Criticism*, pp. 94–9; reprinted in *Essays on Ideology*, pp. 133–9.

116. 'Qu'est que la collection *Théorie*?'.
Leaflet enclosed with *Réponse à John Lewis*.

117. *Réponse à John Lewis*, coll. 'Théorie', François Maspero, Paris, June 1973, 101 pp.
Translated by Grahame Lock, in *Essays in Self-Criticism*, New Left Books, London, 1976, pp. 33–99; reprinted in *Essays on Ideology*, pp. 61–139.
Contains 110, 111, 115.

118. 'Sur le transfert et le contre-transfert (Petites incongruités portatives)'.
Published in *Écrits sur la psychanalyse*, pp. 171–86.

119. Intervention on 'Les communistes, les intellectuels et la culture'.
Published in *France Nouvelle*, 18 September 1973.

120. Cover presentation of Pierre Raymond, *Le Passage au matérialisme*, François Maspero, Paris, 1973.

1974

121. Letter to Jean Guitton of 1974.
Extracts published in *Lire*, pp. 86–7.
Reprinted in Jean Guitton, *Un siècle, une vie*, Robert Laffont, Paris, 1988.

122. *Éléments d'autocritique*, coll. 'Analyse', Librairie Hachette, 1974, 127 pp.
Translated as 'Elements of Self-Criticism' by Grahame Lock, in *Essays in Self-Criticism*, pp. 101–61.
Also contains 103.

123. 'Avertissement'.
Published in Louis Althusser, *Philosophie et philosophie spontanée des savants (1967)*, pp. 7–8.
Translated as 'Preface' by Warren Montag, in *Philosophy and the Spontaneous Philosophy of the Scientists and Other Essays*, pp. 71–2.

124. *Philosophie et philosophie spontanée des savants (1967)*, coll. 'Théorie', François Maspero, September 1974, 157 pp.
Translated as 'Philosophy and the Spontaneous Philosophy of the Scientists (1967)' by Warren Montag, in *Philosophy and the Spontaneous Philosophy of the Scientists and Other Essays*, pp. 69–165.
125. 'Quelque chose de nouveau'.
Published in *L'Humanité*, 12 October 1974.
Translated as 'Something New' by Grahame Lock, in *Essays in Self-Criticism*, pp. 208–15.

1975
126. Cover presentation of Jean-Pierre Lefebvre (ed. and trans.), G.W.F. Hegel, *La Société civile bourgeoise*, François Maspero, Paris, 1975.
127. 'Est-il simple d'être marxiste en philosophie? (Soutenance d'Amiens)'.
Published in *La Penseé*, no. 183, October 1975, pp. 3–31.
Reprinted as 'Soutenance d'Amiens' in *Positions*, pp. 127–72 and in *Solitude de Machiavel et autre textes*, pp. 199–236.
Translated as 'Is it Simple to Be a Marxist in Philosophy?' by Grahame Lock, in *Essays in Self-Criticism*, pp. 161–207; reprinted in *Philosophy and the Spontaneous Philosophy of the Scientists & Other Essays*, pp. 203–40.
128. 'Les communistes et la philosophie'.
Published in *L'Humanité*, 5 July 1975.
129. Letters to Luis Francisco Rebello, 17 August 1975–9 December 1975.
Published in Portuguese in Louis Althusser and Luis Francisco Rebello, *Cartas sobre a revoluçao portuguesa*, Seara Nova, Lisbon, 1976, pp. 15–25, 33–6, 41–2.
Unpublished in French.

1976
130. *Positions (1964–1975)*, Éditions Sociales, Paris, March 1976, 173 pp.
Contains 45, 75, 94, 104, 127.
131. 'La transformation de la philosophie'.
Published in Spanish as *La transformción de la filosofia*, Universida de Granada, Granada, 1976.
Published in French in Louis Althusser, *Sur la philosophie*, Éditions Gallimard, Paris, 1994, pp. 139–78.
Translated from the Spanish as 'The Transformation of Philosophy' by Thomas E. Lewis, in *Philosophy and the Spontaneous Philosophy of the Scientists & Other Essays*, pp. 241–65.
132. 'La découverte du Dr. Freud'.
Published in *Revue de médicine psychosomatique et de psychologie médicale*, vol. 25, no. 2, 1983, pp. 81–97.
Reprinted in Léon Chertok (ed.), *Dialogue franco-soviétique sur la psychanalyse*, Éditions Privat, Toulouse, 1984, pp. 81–97; and in *Écrits sur la psychanalyse*, pp. 195–219.
Translated as 'The Discovery of Dr. Freud' by Jeffrey Mehlman, in *Writings on Psychoanalysis*, pp. 85–104.
133. 'Être marxiste en philosophie'.
Extract published as 'Une conversation philosophique', in *Diagraphe*, no. 66, December 1993, pp. 55–62.
134. [Some Questions on the Crisis of Marxist Theory and the International Communist Movement].
Published in Spanish as 'Algunas cuestiones de la crisis de la teória marxista y del movimiento comunista internacional', in Louis Althusser, *Nuevos Escritos*, Editorial Laia, Barcelona, 1978, pp. 9–54.
Unpublished in French.

135. Letter to Élisabeth Roudinesco of 12 August 1976.
Published in *Écrits sur la psychanalyse*, pp. 220–21.
Translated by Jeffrey Mehlman, in *Writings on Psychoanalysis*, pp. 104–5.
136. 'Avant-propos: Histoire terminée, histoire interminable'.
Published in Dominique Lecourt, *Lyssenko. Histoire réelle d'une 'science prolétarienne'*, François Maspero, Paris, 1976, pp. 7–19.
Reprinted in *Solitude de Machiavel et autre textes*, pp. 237–46.
Translated as 'Introduction: Unfinished History' by Grahame Lock, in Dominique Lecourt, *Proletarian Science? The Case of Lysenko*, New Left Books, London, 1977, pp. 7–16.
137. Cover presentation of Étienne Balibar, *Sur la dictature du prolétariat*, François Maspero, Paris, 1976.
138. 'Les faits'.
Published in Louis Althusser, *L'avenir dure longtemps, suivi de Les Faits*, edited and introduced by Oliver Corpet and Yann Moulier Boutang, Éditions Stock/ IMEC, Paris, 1992, pp. 281–356; reprinted in second, expanded edition, Le Livre de Poche, Paris, 1994, pp. 317–400.
Translated as 'The Facts' by Richard Veasey, in Louis Althusser, *The Future Last A Long Time*, Chatto & Windus, London, 1993, pp. 287–364.
139. 'D'une nuit l'aube'.
Published in *L'avenir dure longtemps, suivi de Les Faits*, second edition, pp. 436–43.
140. Letter to M.B. of October 1976.
Published in Spanish as '¿Existe en Marx una teoria de la religion?', in Louis Althusser, *Nuevos Escritos*, Editorial Laia, Barcelona 1978, pp. 166–8.
Unpublished in French.
141. 'Sur Marx et Freud'.
Published in German as 'Über Marx and Freud', in Louis Althusser, *Ideologie und ideologische Staatsapparate*, VSA, Hamburg, 1977, pp. 89–107.
Published in French in abridged form as 'La Découverte du Dr. Freud dans ses rapports avec la théorie marxiste', in *The Unconscious: Nature – Function – Methods of Study*, Vol. I, Metsniebera, Tbilisi, 1978, pp. 239–53.
Published in full under the original title in *Écrits sur la psychanalyse*, pp. 222–45.
Translated from the French typescript as 'On Marx and Freud' by Warren Montag, in *Rethinking Marxism*, vol. 4, no. 1, Spring 1991, pp. 17–30; retranslated from the full version by Jeffrey Mehlman in *Writings on Psychoanalysis*, pp. 105–24.
142. 'Note sur les appareils idéologiques d'État (AIEs)'.
Published in German as 'Anmerkung über die ideologischen Staatsapparate', in *Ideologie und Ideologische Staatapparate*, pp. 154–68.
Published in French in *Sur la reproduction*, pp. 253–67.
Translated in abridged form from the German as 'Extracts from Althusser's "Note on the ISAs"' by Jeremy Leaman, in *Economy and Society*, vol. 12, no. 4, November 1983, pp. 455–65.
143. 'The Historic Significance of the 22nd Congress'.
Published in Étienne Balibar, *On the Dictatorship of the Proletariat*, trans. Grahame Lock, New Left Books, London, 1977, pp. 193–211.
Published in French in revised form as *22ème Congrès*, coll. 'Théorie', François Maspero, Paris, May 1977, 71 pp.
Revised version translated as 'On the Twenty-Second Congress of the French Communist Party' by Ben Brewster, in *New Left Review*, I, no. 104, July–August 1977, pp. 3–22.

1977
144. 'Avant–propos'.
Published in Gérard Duménil, *Le Concept de loi économique dans 'Le Capital'*, François Maspero, Paris, 1977, pp. 7–26.
Reprinted in *Solitude de Machiavel et autres textes*, pp. 247–66.

145. 'Sur Lucio Fanti'.
Published in the catalogue of the Lucio Fanti exhibition, Krief-Raymond gallery, Paris, 21 April–21 May 1977.
Reprinted in *Écrits philosophiques et politiques. Tome II*, pp. 591–5.

146. 'Alcune parole grosse'.
Published in Italian in *Paese Sera*, 16 April 1977.
Unpublished in French.

147. Cover presentation of Michelle Loi (ed. and trans.), *Luxun: pamphlets et libelles (1925–1936)*, François Maspero, Paris, 1977.

148. 'Solitude de Machiavel'.
Published in German as 'Die Einsamkeit Machiavellis', in Louis Althusser, *Schriften. Band 2: Machiavelli, Montesquieu, Rousseau – Zur politischen Philosophie der Neuzeit*, Argument Verlag, West Berlin, 1987, pp. 11–29.
Published in French in *Futur antérieur*, no. 1, Spring 1990, pp. 26–40; reprinted in *Solitude de Machiavel et autres textes*, pp. 311–24.
Translated from the French typescript as 'Machiavelli's Solitude' by Ben Brewster, in *Economy and Society*, vol. 17, no. 4, November 1988, pp. 468–79; reprinted in *Machiavelli and Us*, pp. 115–30.

149. 'Lam'.
Published in Spanish in *Exposicion antalogica 'Hammaje a Wilfredo Lam, 1902–1982'*, Madrid, 1982, pp. 141–2.
Published in French in *Wilfredo Lam: 1902–1982*, catalogue of the Wilfredo Lam exhibition at the Musée d'Art moderne de la ville de Paris, 23 March–22 May 1983; reprinted in *Écrits philosophiques et politiques. Tome II*, pp. 598–9.

150. 'Finalmente qualcosa di vitale si libera dalla crisi e nella crisi del marxismo'.
Published in Italian in *Il Manifesto*, 16 November 1977.
Published in French as 'Enfin le crise du marxisme!', in *Il Manifesto* (ed.), *Pouvoir et opposition dans les sociétés postrévolutionnaires*, Éditions du Seuil, Pairs, 1978, pp. 242–53; reprinted in *Solitude de Machiavel et autres textes*, pp. 267–80.
Translated from the French as 'The Crisis of Marxism' by Grahame Lock, in *Marxism Today*, July 1978, pp. 215–20, 227; reprinted in *Il Manifesto* (ed.), *Power and Opposition in Post-Revolutionary Societies*, Ink Links, London, 1979, pp. 225–37.

151. 'Éléments d'autobiographie – seulement ce qui peut intéresser la théorie'.
Published in *L'avenir dure longtemps, suivi de Les Faits*, second edition, pp. 446–50.

1978
152. Letter to Merab Mamardashvili of 16 January 1978.
Published in *Écrits philosophiques et politiques. Tome I*, pp. 525–9.
Translated by G.M. Goshgarian, in *Philosophy of the Encounter: Late Writings*, Verso, London, 2006.

153. 'Le marxisme aujourd' hui'.
Published in Italian as 'Il marxismo oggi', in *Enciclopedia Europea*, Vol. VII, Garzanti, Milan, 1978, pp. 280–2; reprinted in Louis Althusser, *Quel che deve cambiare nel partito comunista*, Garzanti, Milan, 1978, pp. 107–26.
Published in French in *Revue M*, no. 43, January 1991, pp. 7–11; reprinted in *Solitude de Machiavel et autres textes*, pp. 292–310.
Translated from the French typescript as 'Marxism Today' by James H. Kavanagh, in *Philosophy and the Spontaneous Philosophy of the Scientists & Other Essays*, pp. 267–80.

154. 'La questione dello stato, oggi e nella transizione'.
Interview with Rossana Rossanda published in Italian *Il Manifesto*, 4 April 1978; reprinted as 'Il marxismo como teoria "finita"', in Louis Althusser et al., *Discutere lo stato*, De Donato, Bari, 1978, pp. 7–21.
Published in French as 'Entretien' in *Dialectiques*, no. 23, Spring 1978, pp. 5–12; reprinted as 'Le Marxisme comme théorie "finie"' in *Solitude de Machiavel et autres textes*, pp. 281–96.

155. Letter (with Étienne Balibar, Guy Bois, Georges Labica, Jean-Pierre Lefebvre and Maurice Moissonier) of April 1978.
     Published as 'Des intellectuels communistes signent une lettre collective pour réclamer "une véritable discussion politique" dans leur parti', in *Le Monde*, 6 April 1978.
156. 'Ce qui ne peut plus durer dans le parti communiste'.
     Published in four instalments in *Le Monde*, 25–8 April 1978.
     Reprinted in expanded form as *Ce qui ne peut plus durer dans le parti communiste*, coll. 'Théorie', François Maspero, Paris, May 1978, 125 pp.
     Le Monde articles translated as 'What Must Change in the Party' by Patrick Camiller, in *New Left Review*, I, no. 109, May–June 1978, pp. 19–45.
157. 'Al "punto zero" della teoria'.
     Interview with Giorgio Fanti published in Italian in *Paese Sera*, 6 May 1978.
     Unpublished in French.
158. 'Louis Althusser: "Je ne veux pas être un martyr"'.
     Interview published in *Les Nouvelles littéraires*, 15 June 1978.
159. 'Marx dans ses limites'.
     Published in *Écrits philosophiques et politiques. Tome I*, pp. 357–524.
     Translated as 'Marx in his Limits' by G.M. Goshgarian, in Louis Althusser, *Philosophy of the Encounter*.
160. Interview with Peter Schöttler.
     Published in German as 'Staat eines Vorworts: vier Fragen an Louis Althusser', in Louis Althusser, *Die Krise des Marxismus*, VSA, Hamburg, 1978, pp. 7–17.
     Unpublished in French.

1980
161. 'Lettre ouverte aux analysants et analystes se réclamant de Jacques Lacan'.
     Published in *Écrits sur la psychanalyse*, pp. 249–57.
     Translated as 'Open Letter to Analysands and Analysts in Solidarity with Jacques Lacan' by Jeffrey Mehlman, in *Writings on Psychoanalysis*, pp. 127–34.
162. 'Remarques complémentaires sur la réunion du PLM – Saint-Jacques du 15 mars 1980'.
     Published in *Écrits sur la psychanalyse*, pp. 258–66.
     Translated as 'Complementary Remarks on the Meeting of March 15, 1980, at the Hotel PLM Saint-Jacques' by Jeffrey Mehlman, in *Writings on Psychoanalysis*, pp. 135–43.
163. Tribute to Jean-Paul Sartre.
     Published in *Le Monde*, 17 April 1980.
     Translated in *Telos*, no. 44, 1980, p. 197.

1982
164. Untitled manuscript.
     Extract published as 'Sur la pensée marxiste', in *Futur antérieur, Sur Althusser. Passages*, L'Harmattan, Paris, 1993, pp. 11–29.
     Further extracts published as 'Le courant souterrain du matérialisme de la rencontre', in *Écrits philosophiques et politiques. Tome I*, pp. 531–79.
     Further extract published as 'Note sur les Thèses sur Feuerbach', *Magazine littéraire*, no. 324, September 1994, pp. 38–42.
     Partially translated as 'The Underground Current of the Materialism of the Encounter' by G.M. Goshgarian, in *Philosophy of the Encounter*.

1984
165. Letter to Mauricio Malamud of 8 March 1984.
     Published in *Sur la philosophie*, pp. 85–92.
     Translated by G.M. Goshgarian, in *Philosophy of the Encounter*.
166. Letter to Yves Suaudeau of 20 April 1984.

Extract published in *Écrits sur la psychanalyse*, p. 191.
Translated by Jeffrey Mehlman, in *Writings on Psychoanalysis*, p. 82.
167. Letter to François Bott of April 1984.
Extracts published in *Le Monde*, 11 May 1984.
Published in full in *Écrits sur la psychanalyse*, pp. 192–3.
Translated by Jeffrey Mehlman, in *Writings on Psychoanalysis*, pp. 82–3.
168. Letters to Fernanda Navarro, 11 June 1984–3 November 1987.
Published in *Sur la philosophie*, pp. 92–137.
Translated by G.M. Goshgarian, in *Philosophy of the Encounter*.
169. 'Philosophie et marxisme'.
Interviews with Fernanda Navarro published in Spanish as Louis Althusser, *Filosofía y marxismo*, Siglo XXI, Mexico, 1988.
Published in French in a revised version as 'Philosophie et marxisme: entretiens avec Fernanda Navarro (1984–1987)', in *Sur la philosophie*, pp. 13–79.
Translated as 'Philosophy and Marxism: Interviews with Fernanda Navarro (1984–1987)' by G.M. Goshgarian, in *Philosophy of the Encounter*.

1985
170. Summary of a discussion on liberation theology with Stanislas Breton.
Extracts published in Stanislas Breton, 'Althusser aujourd'hui ', in *Archives de philosophie*, no. 56, July–September 1993, pp. 417–30.
171. Letter to Dominique Lecourt of 19 March 1985.
Published in *L'avenir dure longtemps, suivi de Les Faits*, second edition, pp. 452–6.
172. 'L'avenir dure longtemps'.
Published in *L'avenir dure longtemps, suivi de Les Faits*, edited and introduced by Olivier Corpet and Yann Moulier Boutang, Éditions Stock/IMEC, Paris, 1992, pp. 7–279.
Reprinted in *L'avenir dure longtemps, suivi de Les Faits*, second edition, Le Livre de Poche, 1994, pp. 27–315.
Translated as 'The Future Lasts A Long Time' by Richard Veasey, in *The Future Lasts a Long Time and The Facts*, Chatto & Windus, London, 1993, pp. 11–286.
173. 'L'unique tradition matérialiste' (April–May 1985).
Chapters 1 and 2 ('Spinoza' and 'Machiavelli') published as 'Le véritable tradition matérialiste', in *Lignes*, no. 18, January 1993, pp. 75–119.
Reprinted, together with chapter 3 ('Situation pol[itique]: analyse concrète?'), in *L'avenir dure longtemps, suivi de Les Faits*, second edition, pp. 467–526.
Partially translated as 'The Only Materialist Tradition, Part 1: Spinoza' by Ted Stolze, in Warren Montag and Ted Stolze (eds.), *The New Spinoza*, University of Minnesota Press, Minneapolis, 1997, pp. 3–19.
174. 'Deux mots'.
Published in *Le Monde des livres*, 24 April 1992.
Reprinted in *L'avenir dure longtemps, suivi de Les Faits*, second edition, pp. 457–9.

1986
175. 'Préface'.
Published in *Sur la philosophie*, pp. 27–8.
Translated by G.M. Goshgarian, in *Philosophy of the Encounter*.
176. 'Portrait du philosophe matérialiste'.
Published in *Écrits philosophiques et politiques. Tome I*, pp. 581–2.
Translated as 'Portrait of the Materialist Philosopher' by G.M. Goshgarian, in *Philosophy of the Encounter*.

1992
177. *L'avenir dure longtemps, suivi de Les Faits. Autobiographies*, edited and introduced by Olivier Corpet and Yann Moulier Boutang, Éditions Stock/IMEC, Paris, April 1992, x + 357pp.

Second, expanded edition, Le Livre de Poche, March 1994, 573 pp.
Contains 46, 47, 138, 139, 151, 171, 172, 173, 174.
First edition translated as *The Future Lasts a Long Time and The Facts* by Richard
Veasey, Chatto & Windus, London, 1993.

178. *Journal de captivité: Stalag XA/1940–1945. Carnets – correspondences – textes*, edited
and introduced by Olivier Corpet and Yann Moulier Boutang, Éditions
Stock/IMEC, Paris, September 1992, xix + 356 pp.
Contains 3, 4, 5, 6, 7, 8, 9, 10.

1993
179. *Écrits sur la psychanalyse: Freud et Lacan*, edited and introduced by Olivier Corpet
and François Matheron, Éditions Stock/IMEC, Paris, September 1993, 310 pp.
Partially translated as *Writings on Psychoanalysis: Freud and Lacan* by Jeffrey
Mehlman, coll. 'European Perspectives', Columbia University Press, New York,
1996, ix + 194 pp.
Contains 37, 45, 61, 63, 91, 118, 132, 135, 141, 161, 162, 166, 167.

1994
180. *Sur la philosophie*, coll, 'L'Infini', Éditions Gallimard, Paris, April 1994, 179 pp.
Contains 131, 165, 168, 169, 175.
181. *Écrits philosophiques et politiques. Tome I*, edited and introduced by François
Matheron, Éditions Stock/IMEC, Paris, October 1994, 588 pp.
Contains 13, 14, 15, 16, 17, 18, 20, 107, 152, 159, 164, 176.

1995
182. *Écrits philosophiques et politiques. Tome II*, edited and introduced by François
Matheron, Éditions Stock/IMEC, Paris, October 1995, 606 pp.
Contains 32, 38, 48, 58, 60, 62, 66, 72, 74, 76, 83, 84, 105, 145, 149.
183. *Sur la reproduction*, edited and introduced by Jacques Bidet, coll. '*Actuel Marx*
Confrontation', Presses Universitaires de France, Paris, October 1995, 316 pp.
Contains 95, 142.

1996
184. *Psychanalyse et sciences humaines. Deux conférences (1963–1964)*, edited and introduced
by Olivier Corpet and Yann Moulier Boutang, coll. 'Biblio-essais', Le Livre de
Poche Paris, November 1996, 123 pp.
Contains 39, 44.

1998
185. *Solitude de Machiavel et autres textes*, edited and introduced by Yves Sintomer,
coll. '*Actuel Marx* Confrontation', Presses Universitaires de France, Paris, October
1998, 324 pp.
Contains 24, 29, 34, 56, 75, 79, 108, 127, 136, 144, 148, 150, 153, 154.
186. *Lettres à Franca (1961–1973)*, edited and introduced by François Matheron and
Yann Moulier Boutang, Éditions Stock/IMEC, Paris, November 1998, 832 pp.

Index

The name of Louis Althusser has been omitted from this Index.

www.ingramcontent.com/pod-product-compliance
Lightning Source LLC
Chambersburg PA
CBHW060019030426
42334CB00019B/2099